The Tourism System

Alastair M. Morrison
Xinran Y. Lehto
Jonathon G. Day

eighth edition

Kendall Hunt
publishing company

All interior images and graphs not credited are Courtesy of the authors.
Cover image ©Shutterstock, Inc.
Quick Trip image ©tele52/Shutterstock.com

Kendall Hunt
publishing company

www.kendallhunt.com
Send all inquiries to:
4050 Westmark Drive
Dubuque, IA 52004-1840

To Sheng Hua (Jing), Alick, and Andy

To my husband, Mark, for his love and endless support

To Jana, Samuel, and Thomas

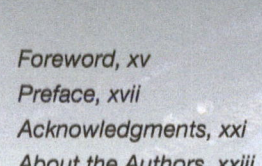

CONTENTS

PART ONE

DESTINATION: Planning, Developing, and Controlling Tourism, 1

The Tourism System began as a very large blank sheet of paper taped to a wall in my faculty office at Michigan State University. At that time, in the late 1970s, there were few tourism textbooks. Those that existed might contain a chapter on the geography of tourism or the anthropology of tourism but they were stand-alone chapters that did not show how the topics were inter-related. A pioneer tourism educator, Robert McIntosh, wrote in a 1975 memo to me his definition of tourism. "Tourism is the science, art, and business of attracting visitors, accommodating them and catering to their needs and wants."

We wanted to go beyond this definition. When I invited Alastair Morrison to join me in this venture I had no idea that the partnership would last for over thirty years. Together we added pieces to that sheet of paper, scouring books and articles until the system took shape.

We identified four parts to the system—the traveler both as an individual and as segments of the market as well as the process by which the travel decision is made; the travel itself—deciding where, when, and how to go; the destination consisting of the attractions and services used by the traveler in addition to the development of a tourism policy to guide the development of tourism within the confines of the regulatory framework; and marketing—the development of a marketing plan, the selection of an appropriate marketing mix, and the choice of distribution channels.

A primary goal was to demonstrate how the pieces came together as a whole—as a system. We wanted to help students and practitioners alike understand how tourism works and how to make it work for them, the businesses they ran, and the destinations they were part of. The idea was that if anyone involved in tourism—be it hotelier, tour operator, state director of tourism, and so forth—could see how the various aspects of tourism tied together, they could identify changes in potential travelers, destinations, transportation and channels of distribution, and anticipate how those changes would impact them. They would become proactive rather than reacting to changes.

Additionally, we stressed the links between four parts of the system. As David A. Pattinson, the then-Chief Executive of the Scottish Tourist Board, and author of the Foreword in the first edition noted ". . . it is essential to understand the component parts . . . but also the linkages and relationships between these components . . ." (*The Tourism System: An Introductory Text,* page xvi).

Subsequent editions saw changes, updates, and additional features. Quotes germane to the chapter topic were placed at the beginning of each chapter; "Quick Trips"—short, practical pieces designed to stimulate discussion—were added to illustrate each learning outcome and suggested student activities were placed at each chapter end.

A significant change in format occurred in the fourth edition in 2002. In the first three editions, we led with the section on the market followed by travel, destination, and marketing. The fourth edition began with the destination followed by marketing, the market, and travel. The reason for this was that most students reading the book would end up managing a facility at a destination—typically a hotel or restaurant. We wanted to show upfront that their business was part of a destination and that the success of the business was tied to the success of the tourism destination.

There has been significant growth in tourism since Alastair and I began this partnership. In 1985, when the first edition of *The Tourism System* was published, there were 320.1 million international tourism arrivals. In the first half of 2017 that number was 580 million and the forecast for the entire year was over 1.1 billion.

As I enjoy my retirement I am confident that *The Tourism System* is in the very good hands of Alastair Morrison, Xinran Lehto, and Jonathon Day and will continue to make a significant contribution to the tourism literature.

Robert Christie Mill
Professor Emeritus
University of Denver

The Tourism System has had seven editions since 1985, all co-authored by Robert Christie Mill and Alastair M. Morrison. A novel departure begins with this 8th edition, under the guidance of a new authorship team. The three authors of the new edition gratefully acknowledge the many years of hard work and dedication from Robert Christie Mill who decided to retire from the writing of this book.

The Tourism System continues to move from strength to strength. All the authors have practical experience in destination management and marketing, particularly in Australia, Canada, China, Indonesia, New Zealand, Singapore, United Kingdom, and the United States. They are teaching tourism and hospitality management at a university level in different countries, and training tourism practitioners around the world. With home backgrounds from the UK, China, and Australia, plus extensive travel experiences, the three authors have attempted to make *The Tourism System* more global in scope through examples, cases, and the approximately 120 Quick Trips.

As in all eight editions, the authors avoid the "laundry list" approach that is so common in describing tourism in introductory texts. Although sub-sectors of tourism and the destination product are recognized, the preference is to treat the phenomenon as a set of interrelated parts working together toward shared outcomes and goals.

The revisions have been made especially with learners in mind and the 8th edition is much more student-friendly in tone. Extensive "lists of things and numbers" have been eliminated as far as was possible. A significantly improved illustration program is incorporated that includes several new contributions from the authors themselves.

New **Quick Trips** are written and these have been more closely integrated with the contents of each chapter. Each Quick Trip illustrates important practical issues, applications of management concepts, or significant trends in tourism in a way intended to engage the reader and stimulate class discussion. The contents have a strong global flavor with examples coming from many different countries.

The **Activities** provide a means for students to get out of the classroom and learn through independent discovery. The **Glossary** has been expanded and updated for the 8th edition.

The following is a description of the four parts and seventeen chapters in this 8th edition of *The Tourism System*, highlighting many of the important changes from the previous edition.

DESTINATION

PART 1 of *The Tourism System* is dedicated to destinations as they are the supply-side fulcrum for tourism. Chapters 1–6 in the 8th edition are substantially revised and reorganized to better represent the new realities of destination management with, for example, a greater emphasis on sustainable tourism and visitor experiences.

Chapter 1 (The Tourism System and Destinations) is significantly revised in the new edition. For the first time, this chapter starts with an overview of the tourism system. An extended discussion on the destination product and a more balanced description of the five components follow. A new destination system model is introduced showing how the destination product components work together. Other players in tourism are described as well.

Chapter 2 (Tourism Impacts: The Need for Sustainable Tourism) is revised and provides an introduction to sustainability and the triple-bottom-line impacts of tourism. The chapter introduces the functions of corporate social responsibility (CSR) and social entrepreneurs as well as the role of the traveler in contributing to sustainability through responsible travel practices.

Chapter 3 (Government Involvement, Tourism Policy, and Organizations) starts by reviewing the roles of government in tourism. It then introduces a new tourism policy-setting process. Influential tourism organizations at different geographic levels are classified and profiled, including UNWTO, WTTC, WTCF, PATA, ETC, CTO, SPTO, Destinations International, and others.

Chapter 4 (Tourism Legislation and Regulation) is reorganized and updated. It explains the reasons for and categories of tourism laws and regulations. Specific forms of destination area legislation and regulation are described. Self-regulation within the tourism sector is also discussed.

Chapter 5 (Tourism Destination Planning) introduces for the first time the 5 Ps framework for tourism planning. This chapter retains the classic tourism destination planning process of *The Tourism System* that has been so popular in prior editions.

Chapter 6 (Sustainable Tourism Development) places a greater emphasis on sustainable tourism and the triple-bottom-line concept. A new section describing different forms of tourism development is another highlight.

MARKETING

PART 2 of *The Tourism System* focuses on tourism marketing. Part 2 has been significantly updated in the 8th edition. Chapters 7 and 8 have both been revised and updated and a new chapter, Chapter 9, focusing on product and experience development, has been added. These changes provide the 8th edition with a concise but comprehensive introduction to tourism marketing functions. Throughout this Part, the tourism planning process is applied as a foundational concept for marketing-related planning.

Chapter 7 (Tourism Marketing) has been revised to provide an overview of the marketing function. New concepts such as the use of big data and consumer profiling complement descriptions of more traditional segmentation and target marketing techniques. The branding section has also been enhanced to reflect the importance of this aspect of marketing.

Chapter 8 (Tourism Promotion) has been updated to reflect the changing nature of tourism promotion. The chapter addresses increasing barriers to promotion and permission marketing as well as providing an overview of the promotional "toolbox" available to tourism marketers today.

Chapter 9 (Tourism Products and Experience Development) is new to the 8th edition. It introduces important concepts of experiential travel and experience development. The chapter outlines the components of the product development toolbox and introduces the product life cycle and the importance of product renewal.

DEMAND

PART 3 of *The Tourism System* focuses on the demand side of tourism. Chapters 10–14 in the 8th edition are completely reorganized and revised to better reflect rapidly changing aspects of contemporary visitor behavior including, for example, the changing role and impact of technology such as use of mobile devices, websites, and virtual reality on traveler mobility, diaspora, and behavior. An entirely new chapter (Chapter 11) is dedicated to the understanding of the travel consumptive experience.

Chapter 10 (Tourism Motivation and Travel Benefits) is almost completely rewritten. This chapter presents numerous theories and propositions pertaining to visitor motivations from both historical and contemporary perspectives.

Added is a new section that focuses on how tourism can be integral to the wellness of the contemporary visitor and marketing and destination experience design implications are presented throughout the chapter.

Chapter 11 (Tourism Experience) is a new chapter added to the 8th edition. This chapter describes how visitors consume a destination product. It introduces component and procedural views of the tourism experience, and addresses topics such as place sense-making, the role of destination aesthetic qualities, and major experience design themes. It discusses how best to design and deliver satisfactory destination experiences for travelers.

Chapter 12 (Traveler Decision-Making and Travel Information) is updated and revised in several ways. The chapter now introduces several models of traveler decision-making and how they can be used in destination management. The role of travel information and the behavioral patterns of traveler information search and use are freshened to reflect the fast-evolving landscape of information technology and destination information management.

Chapter 13 (Forces Shaping Tourism) is comprehensively revised, with increased emphasis on the roles of national culture and psychographic factors influencing travel behavior. Nine Quick Trips are added to the chapter to provide better contextual understanding of the forces shaping tourism demand.

Chapter 14 (Traveler Segments) is revamped to provide a current view of the modern traveler. Much of the focus is placed on strengthening the sections focusing on business travelers. Thirteen Quick Trips are added to this chapter providing examples and discussions of current industry practices regarding the various traveler segments, including, for instance, travel expense management systems.

TRAVEL

PART 4 of *The Tourism System*, as with Part 3, has been completely overhauled and updated. This Part explores mobility and the organizations that facilitate travel through the tourism system. Chapters 15–17 in the 8th edition address travel flows, travel trade intermediaries, and transportation modes.

Chapter 15 (The Evolution of Travel and Travel Flows) is almost entirely new and now incorporates a section on the history of travel flows. It provides comprehensive data on current flows of tourism by world region and for individual countries. Forecasts for travel flows and key trends are reviewed.

Chapter 16 (Travel Trade Intermediaries) has been expanded and moved to Part 4. The chapter includes a greater emphasis on online travel agencies (OTAs) and has expanded to include meeting and convention sector intermediaries. The chapter introduces sharing economy companies as important new intermediaries in the tourism system. It also includes a discussion of the importance of travel-related media as information intermediaries.

Chapter 17 (Traveling—Transportation Modes and Carriers) has been completely revised and reorganized. The chapter includes major modes of transportation—both between destinations and around destinations. It incorporates the latest trends impacting transportation including airline trends and high-speed rail. The chapter also explores transportation that encapsulates the tourism experience including cruising, touring, and luxury rail experiences.

Having highlighted the changes and features of the 8th edition of *The Tourism System*, the authors acknowledge the inputs received from many adopters of previous editions. As adopters themselves, the authors had a good understanding of how to design and write an improved textbook. Above all, they strived to prepare a lively, interesting, and accessible book that was as up-to-date and international as possible. They recognized the importance of the **Quick Trips** to teachers and so these were expanded and enhanced. They also tried hard to make *The Tourism System* more visually appealing.

The authors share an affiliation with Purdue University and are thankful for all this great research university has done for them. We hope students, adopters, and other readers enjoy *The Tourism System* as much as we have done in preparing the 8th edition of this classic work in tourism.

Alastair M. Morrison, Xinran Y. Lehto, and Jonathon G. Day
Purdue University

ACKNOWLEDGMENT

The authors acknowledge the many contributions of Professor Robert C. Mill of the University of Denver to the seven previous editions of *The Tourism System* as well as his key role in initiating this text. Bob's outstanding efforts spanned more than twenty-seven years and many of the imprints of his work remain in this new 8th edition of *The Tourism System*.

ALASTAIR M. MORRISON, MBA, PHD, CDME, CTME

© Alastair Morrison

Alastair is the CEO of Belle Tourism International Consulting, Ltd. (BTI) and a Distinguished Professor Emeritus of the School of Hospitality and Tourism Management at Purdue University, West Lafayette, Indiana. He serves as a Visiting Professor at the University of Greenwich in London and is Co-Editor-in-Chief of the *International Journal of Tourism Cities*. Alastair is a consultant to the Bandung Institute of Tourism (Indonesia) and Hubei University of Economics (China) on postgraduate studies and research.

Alastair is the author of five books in tourism marketing and development, and hospitality and travel marketing—*The Tourism System, Marketing and Managing Tourism Destinations, Hospitality and Travel Marketing, Global Marketing of China Tourism*, and *Tourism: Bridges across Continents*. He has contributed more than 150 articles to tourism and hospitality academic research journals as well.

Alastair received several teaching awards and honors at Purdue University, including the university-wide Murphy Award for Outstanding Undergraduate Teaching. His name has been entered in Purdue's Book of Great Teachers. In 1998, the International Society of Travel & Tourism Educators (ISTTE) selected him as the recipient of the Lifetime Achievement Award for his contributions to tourism education. Alastair has been elected as a Fellow of the world's most elite organization of tourism scholars, the International Academy for the Study of Tourism (IAST), and to the Hospitality and Tourism Management Academy.

Alastair has had a wide variety of experience in global tourism. He has provided marketing and development advice in Australia, Bahrain, Cabo Verde, Cambodia, China, Ghana, Honduras, Hong Kong SAR, India, Indonesia, Italy, Jamaica, Macao SAR, Malaysia, Mexico, New Zealand, Poland, Russia, Scotland, Singapore, Slovenia, South Africa, Sri Lanka, Thailand, Trinidad and Tobago, and Vietnam. Recently, he designed a training program in destination management for Indonesia and has developed and facilitated training programs on behalf of the UN World Tourism Organization (UNWTO) for eight South Asian countries and the China-Tibet Tourism Bureau, European Union, the U.S. Agency for International Development, Swisscontact, and Destinations International.

Alastair is active in several major industry associations. He is a co-founder and has been the President and Past-President of the International Tourism Studies Association (ITSA). He has served as Chairman of the Travel & Tourism Research Association (TTRA)–Canada Chapter, Board member of the CenStates TTRA Chapter, Vice President of the International Society of Travel and Tourism Educators (ISTTE), and Chairman of Association of Travel Marketing Executives (ATME). He was awarded the distinction as one of the first recipients of the Certified Travel Marketing Executive (CTME) designation from ATME. He has designed and presented the *Destination Marketing Planning, Travel Information & Research, International Tourism & Convention Marketing*, and *Communications and Technology in Destination Management* courses for Destinations International as part of its Certified Destination Management Executive (CDME) Program.

Previously, Alastair was a Visiting Professor at Peking University and at the University of Strathclyde Business School, Scotland. He also served as the Queensland Tourist & Travel Corporation Visiting Lecturer at James Cook University in Queensland, Australia. He has taught tourism marketing and promotion at National Kaohsiung University of Hospitality and Tourism Management (Taiwan), University of Monterrey (Mexico), Hong Kong University, IULM (Milan, Italy) and AILUN (Sardinia, Italy).

Prior to joining the Purdue faculty, Alastair worked in Canada as a management consultant in hospitality and tourism, most recently as President of The Economic Planning Group of Canada (EPG).

XINRAN Y. LEHTO, PHD

© Xinran Lehto

Xinran Y. Lehto is a Professor at the School of Hospitality and Tourism Management, Purdue University. She is an Associate Editor of the *Journal of Hospitality and Tourism Research,* and serves on the Editorial Boards of five other international academic journals. She is currently the President of the International Tourism Studies Association. Prior to her academic appointments, Dr. Lehto worked in the travel and tourism industry as a marketing officer for China National Tourism Administration (CNTA) and a planning executive for Chan Brothers Travel, Singapore.

Dr. Lehto is well-published. She has over one hundred research publications in refereed international journals including the top-rated *Annals of Tourism Research, Tourism Management,* and *Journal of Travel Research.* Dr. Lehto is the recipient of multiple Best Paper awards from various international conferences and Article of the Year awards from two refereed journals.

Dr. Lehto's research expertise area is tourism marketing. Her research addresses how destinations can effectively market experience-based vacation products to unique segments such as family travelers. Much of her work is concerned with developing understanding of how visitors interact with a destination through leisure and hospitality experiences; what outcomes and benefits tourism provides; and how personal, interpersonal, and cultural factors influence destination experience design, marketing practices, and visitor satisfaction.

Dr. Lehto emphasizes the ramifications of her research to the travel and tourism sector. She disseminates her research in a wide variety of forums including international conferences and colloquia, refereed journal articles, technical reports, and public presentations. She has worked closely with community agencies to evaluate and develop programs and strategies related to tourism and leisure services.

JONATHON DAY, MBA, PHD

© Jonathon Day

Dr. Jonathon Day, an Associate Professor in Purdue's School of Hospitality and Tourism Management, has over twenty-five years' experience in tourism management. He is the founder and President of Placemark Solutions, Inc. An award-winning marketer, Dr. Day has worked with destination management organizations in Australia, New Zealand, and the Americas.

Dr. Day is committed to ensuring tourism is a force for good in the world. He is the author of "Introduction to Sustainable Tourism and Responsible Travel," as well as over twenty-five peer-reviewed articles in journals including *Tourism Analysis*, *Journal of Travel & Tourism Marketing*, *Annals of Tourism Research*, and *International Journal of Contemporary Hospitality Management*. He currently chairs the Travel Care Code (travel-carecode.org), a network of academic and marketing organizations promoting responsible travel.

Dr. Day is active in several industry organizations. He is Chair of Tourism Innovation Partnership for Social Entrepreneurship, Chair of the Global Sustainable Tourism Council's Communication and Membership Workgroup, and a member of the Executive of Tourism Education Futures Initiative. He is a past President of Travel & Tourism Marketing Association, past Board Member of the Hospitality Sales and Marketing Association International (HSMAI), and a past Trustee of the HSMAI Foundation.

Dr. Day speaks regularly on destination management and sustainable tourism. He has conducted training in Australia, Canada, Chile, China, Colombia, New Zealand, and the United States. He has developed and facilitated training programs for the United Nations World Tourism Organization, the Global Sustainable Tourism Council, and Destinations International's Certified Destination Management Executive (CDME) program.

Dr. Day's interests focus on sustainable tourism, responsible travel, and strategic destination governance within the tourism system. He is interested in the role of business in solving grand challenges through corporate social responsibility programs and social entrepreneurship.

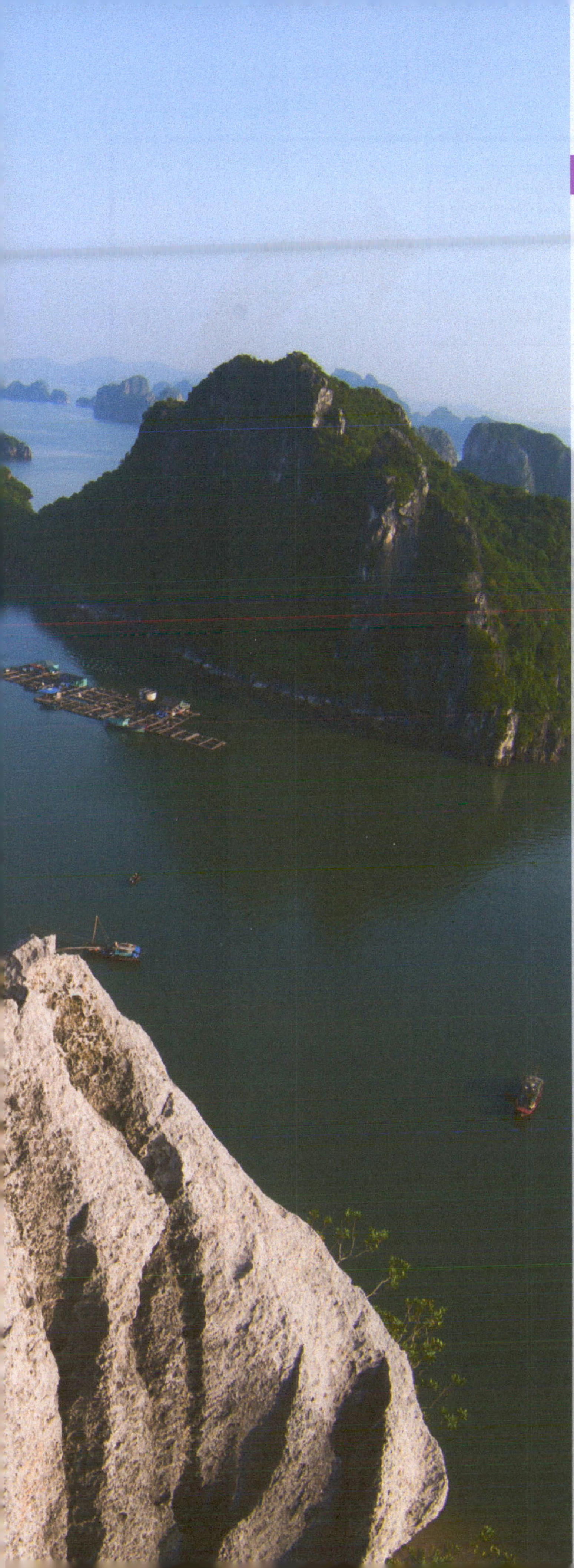

Destination

Planning, Developing, and Controlling Tourism

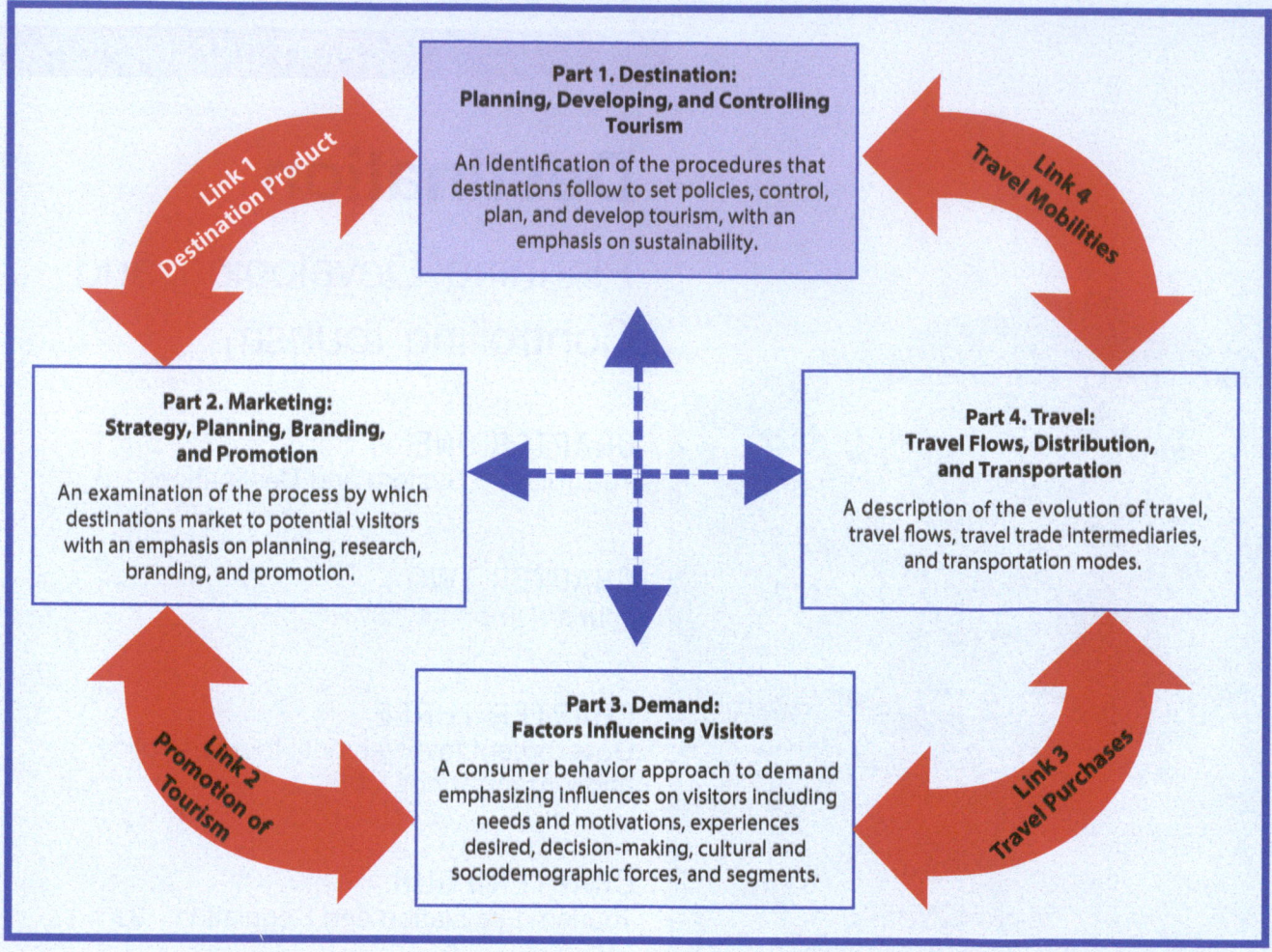

An identification of the procedures that destinations follow to set policies, control, plan, and develop tourism, with an emphasis on sustainability.

Every destination that chooses to encourage tourism must be prepared to handle the inflows of visitors, and to deal with the challenge that tourism has the potential of generating both positive and negative impacts. A *destination product* is assembled consisting of infrastructure, transportation, built facilities, attractions and events, and service quality and friendliness. *Tourism policies* and *destination plans* are developed. There are many different *tourism organizations* involved with destinations. A *legislative and regulatory framework* is required to ensure that the tourism policy and plan are implemented properly and that impacts are controlled. The application of *sustainable tourism principles* and the analysis of individual tourism project opportunities are essential to effective destination development.

LINK 1: THE DESTINATION PRODUCT

The linkage between Parts 1 and 2 (*Destination* and *Marketing*) is called the *destination product*. Again, a change in the destination may cause a change in marketing and vice versa. For example, the staging of a mega-event or the introduction of a new flagship attraction (*Destination*) may require a shift in the marketing of the destination (*Marketing*), as is the case with the Summer Olympics in Tokyo in 2020. If a travel intermediary begins to send larger groups (*Marketing*), this may require a change in the size of accommodations and other facilities and services (*Destination*).

CHAPTER ONE

The Tourism System and Destinations

Partnerships Unlimited

If you just focus on the smallest details, you never get the big picture right.

LEROY HOOD, U.S. scientist

YOUR LEARNING DESTINATION

You will be able to explain the tourism system, its main parts and links, and describe how the systems approach applies to the destination product.

WHAT YOU NEED TO KNOW

Having read this chapter, you will be able to:

- Define tourism.
- Identify the reasons for using a systems approach for tourism.
- Explain the four parts of the tourism system and the links between the parts.
- Define a destination and elaborate on the tourism destination system.
- Elaborate on the components of the destination product.
- Review the factors that make a destination successful.
- Describe the other major players in tourism.

BREAKING THE ICE

Ask most people about tourism and they are likely to say, "Isn't that something that travel agents do?" The simple answer to their question is "not hardly" as it's much more than that and destinations and visitors are at the core of tourism. So, strap on your seatbelts for the journey with the authors around The Tourism System. You will not get bored!

You might see your future being in hotels and resorts, event and meeting planning, or in food and beverage operations. There are many great and exciting career areas in tourism. Good luck to you with your professional plans and dreams. As you embark on your career journey, it will always be good for you to keep the "big picture" of tourism in mind.

KEY TAKEAWAY POINTS

- Tourism is not an industry; it is a phenomenon that requires a systems approach.

- The five components of the destination product are infrastructure, transportation, built facilities, attractions and events, and service quality and friendliness.

- Components in the destination product can play multiple roles.

- Built facilities, along with service quality and friendliness, are the core of the destination product.

- Tourism is a people business and host-guest relationships are critical to positive visitor experiences.

- There are no universally-accepted criteria for successful destinations.

LET'S EXPLORE THE TOURISM SYSTEM

Travel. It leaves you speechless, then turns you into a storyteller.

IBN BATTUTA

Shown below is the image that the authors chose for the cover of this book. It is a beautiful, "birds-eye" view over Ha Long Bay in Vietnam (Figure 1.1). As the quote above says, these kinds of moments can leave you speechless, but they remind us of why we travel. To produce unforgettable moments like this for visitors, there is a tourism system of "partnerships unlimited"; let's discover it together.

The tourism system as a term has two parts—tourism and system. Let's start first with a discussion of tourism and then you will be introduced to the system. There are different perspectives on tourism that you should know about, so let's begin with its definition.

What Is Tourism?

There are many definitions of tourism and to be honest it is bewildering if you are new to the topic. However, the "official" definitions are the best place to start.

• **Official definitions**

You should know that in writing this book, the authors set out to do two things: Describe how tourism works and indicate how people can use this knowledge to make tourism work for them, their destinations, or businesses. The first challenge was to put a label on the phenomenon—*tourism*—about which the authors wanted to write.

The most official definition of tourism comes from UNWTO (United Nations World Tourism Organization 2010). This specialized agency of the United Nations describes tourism as a "*phenomenon*":

> "Tourism is a social, cultural and economic phenomenon which entails the movement of people to countries or places outside their usual environment for personal or business/professional purposes. These people are called visitors (which may be either tourists or excursionists; residents or non-residents) and tourism has to do with their activities, some of which imply tourism expenditure."

UNWTO identifies three main branches of tourism: *inbound tourism*—visits to a country by non-residents of that country; *outbound tourism*—visits by the residents of a country to other countries; and **domestic**

© Jimmy Tran/Shutterstock.com

FIGURE 1.1   Visitor perched with a great perspective over Ha Long Bay, Vietnam.

tourism—visits by residents within their own country. Figure 1.2 shows that each of these three have four trip-purpose segments (vacation, VFR, personal, and MICE and business). The three can be grouped into **internal tourism**—visits by residents and non-residents within a country (domestic + inbound international); **national tourism**—visits by the residents of a country to other countries plus visits by residents within their own country (domestic + outbound international); and **international tourism**—the combination of inbound and outbound tourism for a specific country.

Figure 1.3 shows the most authoritative statistics, from UNWTO, on international tourism arrivals (inbound tourism) for 2016. You will see that about 75 percent of all international tourism arrivals were to two regions: Europe, and Asia and the Pacific.

While these statistics are impressive, domestic tourism is even greater in terms of numbers of trips. United States residents had 2.2 billion person trips in the United States in 2016 (79 percent of which were for leisure and 21 percent for business). Australian residents took 90.7 million domestic overnight trips in 2016 (Tourism

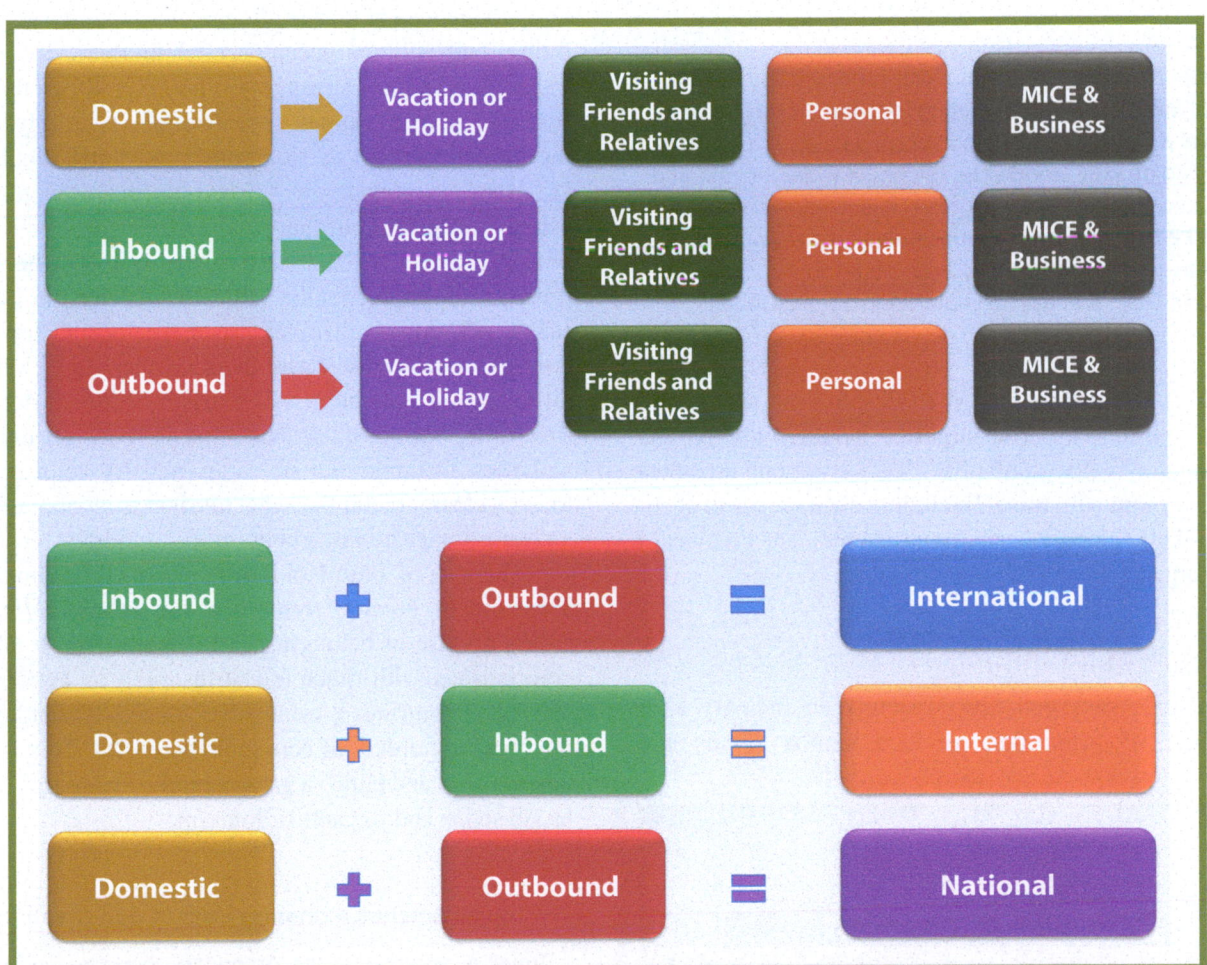

FIGURE 1.2   Branches of tourism.

UNWTO Regions	International Arrivals 2016	Percent of Total
Europe	615,200,000	49.8%
Asia and Pacific	308,700,000	25.0%
Americas	199,900,000	16.2%
Africa	57,800,000	4.7%
Middle East	53,600,000	4.3%
World	1,235,200,000	100%

FIGURE 1.3 International visitor arrivals by region in 2016. Source: UNWTO. 2017.

Research Australia 2017). The domestic travel figure for Canada was 115 million overnight person trips in 2016 (Statistics Canada 2017). Of course, all these domestic tourism statistics pale against those for the People's Republic of China, where there were 4.44 billion domestic trips for 2016 (State Council of the Peoples Republic of China, 2017) (Figure 1.4).

Another global authority, the World Travel & Tourism Council (WTTC), refers to tourism as the *travel and tourism sector*. WTTC (2017) does a great job of estimating and communicating the economic importance of this sector worldwide:

"Travel & Tourism is a key sector for economic development and job creation throughout the world. In 2016, Travel & Tourism directly contributed US$2.3 trillion and 109 million jobs worldwide. Taking its wider indirect and induced impacts into account, the sector contributed US$7.6 trillion to the global economy and supported 292 million jobs in 2016. This was equal to 10.2% of the world's GDP, and approximately 1 in 10 of all jobs."

It is interesting that WTTC splits the sector into *travel* and tourism. You might be wondering why. The explanation is that some of WTTC's corporate members identify more with travel, including airlines, travel agencies, GDSs (global distribution systems), and credit card companies.

Is Tourism an Industry?

Wells and Wensveen (2003) define an industry as a "number of firms that produce similar goods and

FIGURE 1.4 Many people visiting the Forbidden City in Beijing.

services and therefore are in competition with one another." In no sense of the word does this describe a tourism industry. Although there is intense competition in tourism, many businesses and other organizations offer complementary rather than competing products and services. Airlines, hotels, restaurants, travel agencies, and attractions do not compete with each other. They add value for each other and combine services and products to offer visitors satisfying travel and destination experiences. That is why the authors say tourism is "partnerships unlimited."

However, the idea of a tourism industry gives some unity to the idea of tourism. It enhances the image, credibility, and political acceptance of tourism. Tourism's image is *ambiguous* to many scholars and certainly to the "person on the street." For example, scholarly arguments are common as to whether the label should be "tourism" or "hospitality." Most ordinary people are astonished to find out that it is possible for a person to pursue a career in "tourism." There is a link between travel, tourism, recreation, and leisure, yet the link is fuzzy. All tourism involves travel, yet not all travel is tourism. All vacation travel involves recreation, yet not all tourism is recreation. All tourism occurs during leisure time, but not all leisure time is spent on tourism activities. Defining tourism as an industry helps people to get a clearer picture of what tourism is all about. With a clearer image comes a better understanding.

The idea of a tourism industry gives those involved a feeling of *greater credibility and respectability*. It builds a sense of belonging and camaraderie. It allows comparisons with other industries such as agriculture and manufacturing. It establishes tourism's standing in the "pecking order" of economic activities. This is certainly useful and builds a greater public awareness of the broad scope and impacts of tourism.

Travel: America's Unsung Hero of Job Creation

"Travel is essential to the American economy, and provides an indispensable source for job creation. The travel industry, America's seventh-largest employer, supports a total of 15.3 million domestic jobs, and directly employs 8.6 million workers in every corner of the country, from coastal cities through the heartland." (US Travel Association 2017)

The idea of a tourism industry is *politically attractive*. One of tourism's strengths is that its benefits are felt by many businesses, organizations, and people.

Visitor spending finds its way into many pockets and purses. At first glance, this might seem an ideal way to get political support for the planning, development, management, and marketing of tourism. However, this apparent strength has been a huge challenge for those interested in tourism. As tourism touches so many businesses and people in varying degrees, its overall impacts are difficult to measure. For example, there is no single industry code for tourism under the North American Industry Classification System (NAICS) (U.S. Census Bureau 2017).

The system of *Tourism Satellite Accounts (TSA)* was introduced to better reflect the impacts of visitor spending throughout the economies of destinations (Osborne and Markowitz 2017). Statistics New Zealand (2017) highlight why tourism is different from traditional industries:

> "Tourism, unlike 'conventional' industries, such as agriculture or manufacturing, that are classified according to the goods and services they produce, is defined by the characteristics of the customer demanding tourism products. Tourism products can cut across standard industry definitions, and therefore require a different approach."

Many people whose lives or businesses are touched by tourism are mainly engaged in other activities. Storekeepers sell to visitors and residents. Although they may know that tourism affects them, it is often difficult to evaluate how much it does. From a political standpoint, the idea of a tightly defined tourism industry allows organizations to advocate about tourism's impact and economic significance. This results in more effective lobbying with governments which brings greater political support and assistance for tourism.

Yet, tourism is not an industry. Tourism is *an activity or phenomenon*. The activities within tourism are intertwined with and influence several industries. Tourism takes place when, in international terms, people cross borders for leisure and business for less than one year. Tourism also occurs within each country, as people travel certain distances from their home environments for pleasure or business trips. The study of tourism is the study of this activity or phenomenon and its impacts. The business of tourism is the business of encouraging this type of activity and taking care of people while they are engaged in tourism.

WHY USE A SYSTEMS APPROACH FOR THE STUDY OF TOURISM?

Many people talk about the subject of this book as "the tourism industry." You have already heard that there are at least three good reasons for talking about tourism as an industry. However, the authors choose to characterize tourism as a *system*, rather than as an industry. This is done for several reasons. The first is to emphasize the *interdependency* in tourism; that it consists of several interrelated parts working together to achieve common purposes, which is called the *Tourism System*. The tourism system is like a spider's web—touch one part and reverberations are felt throughout the system.

The tourism system approach is based on *general systems theory*. The father of general systems theory was a biologist, Ludwig von Bertalanffy. He defined a system as "a set of elements standing in interrelation among themselves and with the environments." Von Bertalanffy (1973) also suggested that general systems theory was "a way of seeing things that were previously overlooked or bypassed."

The authors are not the first to talk about a tourism system. Two of the pioneers of the concept were Clare Gunn, Emeritus Professor of Texas A&M University, and Neil Leiper of Southern Cross University in Australia. Gunn (1994) describes the *functioning tourism system*, consisting of the supply side of attractions, services, promotion, information, and transportation, and states that:

> "No matter how it is labeled or described, tourism is not only made up of hotels, airlines, or the so-called tourist industry but rather a system of major components linked together in an intimate and interdependent relationship."

Leiper (1990) believes that a tourism system consists of five elements: a human element (tourist), three geographical regions (traveler-generating region, transit route, and tourist destination region), and an industrial element (the travel and tourism industry). Although Leiper acknowledges the term "industry" in his system, he firmly supports the need to more holistically view tourism as a system rather than as an industry:

"Unfortunately, many persons closely involved with the business of tourism hold a dogma that tourism is an industry. The dogma has been reiterated in academic literature. The origins of this belief are understandable, but that does not mitigate the flawed thinking."

Clearly, it is very easy to use a "laundry list" approach to describe tourism—describing the businesses that obviously are part of tourism one by one, such as airlines, hotels, and resorts. However, this approach fails to include local communities, and other businesses and organizations affected by tourism, that may or may not see themselves as part of the so-called "tourism industry." For example, many people working for hotels and restaurants do not feel they are part of tourism. Their business begins with customers walking in the front door; they fail to examine the question "Why are they walking in our front door?" This myopic view has meant that many organizations have ended up being reactive to changes that have occurred outside their front doors, rather than being proactive and anticipating future changes in tourism. For a student beginning to study tourism, it is important to get "the big picture" right away. The *Tourism System* model framework of the book provides a more comprehensive view of tourism: it captures "the big picture."

A second reason for using a systems approach is because of the *open system* nature of tourism. The tourism system is not a rigid form, rather it is dynamic and constantly changing. New concepts and phenomena such as space tourism are always arriving in tourism. Adventure travel, dynamic packaging, destination branding, destination management, ecotourism, strategic alliances, sustainable tourism development, tourism satellite accounting, and voluntourism are just a few of the relatively new concepts introduced to tourism. Tourism is greatly affected by external influences such as politics, demographics, technology, war, terrorism, crime, and disease. For example, changes are constantly sweeping through tourism as a result of many years of terrorism and political uncertainty, and due to technological innovations. The tragedy of 9/11 traumatized tourism in the United States and elsewhere, as did the many terrorist acts in European cities between 2015 and 2017. The Ebola outbreaks in West Africa in 2014–2016 had a catastrophic effect on African tourism; as did the MERS outbreak in 2015 in South Korea. The following quote about Turkey (Figure 1.5) underlines the susceptibility of tourism to outside influences:

© Seqoyah/Shutterstock.com

FIGURE 1.5   Istanbul is a fantastic tourism city in Turkey.

As each year passes, tourism is becoming more complex to describe. Therefore, a third reason for the system is the *complexity and variety* in all aspects of tourism. For example, there are thousands of specialized tours and packages available for travelers today; you can select from a menu that ranges from archaeology to zoology. There is an enormous variety of approaches to each type of tourism business and organization. For example, travel trade intermediaries seldom play just one role today; with the removal of airline commissions, many travel agents have become tour wholesalers and operators. Sharing economy providers such as Airbnb and Uber have introduced other options for visitors to the traditional offers. "Laundry list" approaches to tourism fail to reflect the great complexity present in tourism in the second decade of the twenty-first century. Above

all, you will learn that it is difficult to put each part of tourism into its own pigeonhole. It just does not work that way anymore.

Competition in today's tourism is both fierce and intense. Huge multinational companies are vying for business on a global scale. International brands such as McDonald's and Starbucks know no boundaries. Destinations are competing with others with marketing budgets unprecedented in size. The systems approach better displays the great level of *competitiveness* present in tourism today. Grasping the full implications of the tourism system has led many previously competitive organizations and destinations to acknowledge the similarity of their goals and form *partnerships*. For example, the BestCities Global Alliance is a long-term joint marketing effort described as follows:

"BestCities Global Alliance is a network of twelve premier meeting destinations." *The mission of the BestCities Global Alliance is to* "deliver exceptional standards in conference, event and association management, helping our clients achieve meaningful impact through a global network of industry experts" (BestCities Global Alliance 2017).

FIGURE 1.6   Cape Town is one of the members of BestCities Global Alliance.

Tourism involves an interaction of many organizations and people whose goals and interests are sometimes not compatible. The fifth reason for using the systems approach is to acknowledge a level of *friction and disharmony* in tourism in the early twenty-first century. A monumental struggle is taking place in how tourism services are distributed. Lured by the economics, convenience, and speed of new technologies such as the Internet and social media networking, many suppliers and transportation carriers are *bypassing* the traditional channels of distribution, especially retail travel agencies. Airlines have forsaken the restrictions of government agencies in teaming up with foreign airlines to form *global strategic alliances*. The government stranglehold on tourism marketing in many destinations is being challenged, as private sector businesses, associations, and nonprofits are demanding a greater say. Local residents are questioning the "development at all costs" paradigm as they see precious local environments and ecosystems and heritage cultural treasures being threatened.

The spider moves when its web shakes and another insect is trapped. Likewise a change in one part of the tourism system often causes a change in another part of the system. Therefore, the final reason for using the systems approach is because of the need for *responsiveness* in a specific system part to changes in another system part. Tourism is dynamic and ever-changing. The linkages in the system represent the feedback mechanisms between pairs of system parts that allow changes to be assimilated. Expanding the spider's web metaphor just once more might provide a good example of the feedback-response mechanism. An intelligent spider may recognize that the larger the web, the more insects that are caught. Feedback from travelers through research studies has shown that more visitors are tending to favor multi-destination over single-destination trips. Tourism destinations are responding by joining together in multi-destination partnerships and new *regional destination brands* to better accommodate this change in demand. By grasping "the big picture," former marketing foes are becoming friends, with each partner having the potential to get a larger share of the visitor market. For example, the provincial tourism agencies in New Brunswick (Figure 1.7) and Nova Scotia in Canada paired together to form the Bay of Fundy Tourism Partnership.

THE TOURISM SYSTEM MODEL

The *Tourism System model* described in this book consists of four parts: *Destination*, *Marketing*, *Demand*, and *Travel*. The authors started this book with Destination out of choice, but it could easily have begun with Travel, Demand, or Marketing.

FIGURE 1.7   The Hopewell Rocks in New Brunswick and Bay of Fundy.

The four system *Parts* and four *Links* combine in the Tourism System Model shown in Figure 1.8. The model is displayed in this way to emphasize the interactions and interdependency among the four Parts of the system. The four-way arrow in the middle of the model indicates that interactions happen between other pairs of system Parts (Demand and Destination, Travel and Marketing).

Part 1: Destination: Planning, Developing, and Controlling Tourism

An identification of the procedures that destinations follow to set policies, control, plan, and develop tourism, with an emphasis on sustainability.

Every destination that chooses to encourage tourism must be prepared to handle the inflows of visitors, and to deal with the challenge that tourism has the potential of generating both positive and negative impacts. A *destination product* is assembled consisting of infrastructure, transportation, built facilities, attractions and events, and service quality and friendliness. *Tourism policies* and *destination plans* are developed. The many different *tourism organizations* involved in these processes are described. A *legislative and regulatory framework* is required to ensure that tourism policies and destination plans are implemented properly, and that impacts are controlled. The process of *sustainable tourism* development and the analysis of individual tourism project development opportunities are explained.

Link 1: Destination Product.   The linkage between Parts 1 and 2 (Destination and Marketing) is called the *destination product*. Again, a change in the destination may cause a change in marketing and vice versa. For example, the staging of a mega-event or the introduction of a new flagship attraction (Destination) may result in a shift in the marketing of the destination (Marketing), as

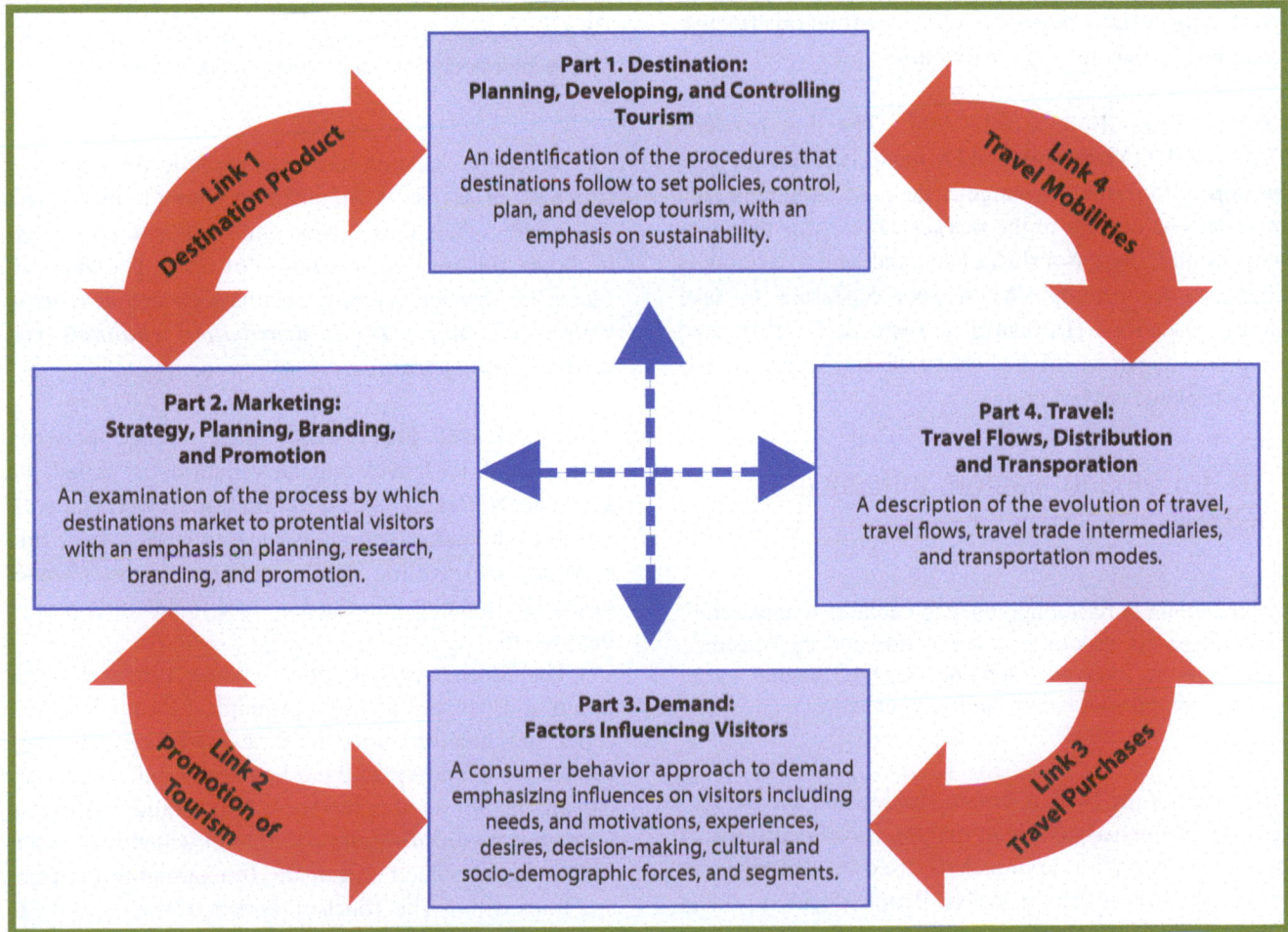

FIGURE 1.8   The Tourism System model.

is the case with the Tokyo Summer Olympics in Japan in 2020. If a travel intermediary begins to send larger groups (Marketing), this may require a change in the size of accommodations and other facilities and services (Destination).

Part 2: Marketing: Strategy, Planning, Branding, and Promotion

An examination of the process by which destinations market to potential visitors with an emphasis on planning, research, branding, and promotion.

Now in the second part of the system, destinations must reach people in the market and encourage them to travel by using marketing principles and techniques. The uniqueness of tourism marketing is explained. The processes of *market segmentation* and *positioning*, and the application of the *product life cycle*, are described. A step-by-step procedure for marketing is introduced. Destination *positioning* and *branding* are reviewed. Marketing success depends to a large extent on effective communications through *promotion*.

Link 2: Promotion of Tourism.   The link between Parts 2 and 3 (Marketing and Demand) is called the *promotion of tourism*. A change in the marketing approach may cause a change in the market. Often, it is the other way around, there is a shift in demand, and marketing is changed accordingly. When people started to take shorter vacations (Demand), tourism destinations and suppliers began to offer short-break and weekend getaway packages (Marketing).

Part 3: Demand: Factors Influencing Visitors

A consumer behavior approach to demand emphasizing influences on visitors including needs and motivations, experiences desired, decision-making, cultural and sociodemographic forces, and segments.

Part 3 of the book is devoted to demand and the factors that influence people in making travel decisions. A consumer behavior approach is used to describe the travel decision-making process. People decide to travel if they have learned that travel satisfies their *needs and motives*, if they can get the *experiences* they want, and if they can travel based on their external constraints

(culture and sociodemographics). Travelers' *buying decision processes* and market *segments* are described.

Link 3: Travel Purchase.   The linkage between Parts 3 and 4 (Demand and Travel) is called *travel purchase*. An arrow pointing in both directions, clockwise and counterclockwise, characterizes it. This means that each of the two parts (Demand and Travel) may influence the other part. For example, new segments in the market may emerge based on special interests or characteristics of groups of people (Demand). These people may decide to take advantage of exploring these special interests or mixing with other people of similar characteristics while traveling (Travel). A new travel mode may be introduced or become more popular (Travel). Space tourism is clearly an example of this, but as of now only the wealthiest of people (Demand) have been able to afford it.

Part 4: Travel Flows, Distribution, and Transportation

A description of the evolution of travel, travel flows, travel trade intermediaries, and transportation modes.

When the decision has been made to book a travel trip, a set of decisions are taken on whom to travel with and where, when, how to plan and book, and how to get to the destination. The evolution of travel is explained. Flows of travelers among destinations are described. Online and offline *travel distribution channels* and *modes of transportation* are reviewed.

Link 4: Travel Mobilities.   The linkage between Parts 4 and 1 (Travel and Destination) is called the *travel mobilities*. It is the combination of who is traveling (travel market segments) and where, when, and how they are traveling. Again, a change in either Travel or Destination may cause a response in the other part of the system.

The Tourism System goes beyond a mere description of tourism and its basic principles. Principles, concepts, and theories from disciplines such as psychology, economics, planning, and marketing that influence tourism are incorporated in the book. You should realize that tourism is a *multidisciplinary* field in which many contributions are valued and made. In examining the parts and links within The Tourism System, those involved in tourism can see where they fit, who is affected by their actions, and how they are affected by the actions of other system participants.

TERMINOLOGY

In this book, *travel* refers to the act of moving outside of one's usual environment for business or pleasure, but not for commuting or traveling to or from school. *Tourism* is the term given to the activity or phenomenon that occurs when people travel. This encompasses everything from the planning of the trip, the travel to the destination, the stay itself, the return, and the reminiscences about it afterward. It includes the activities the traveler undertakes as part of the trip, the purchases made, and the interactions that occur between *host* and *guest* in the destination. In sum, it is all of the activities and impacts that occur when a visitor travels.

The term *recreation* overlaps in many ways with tourism. Recreation is what happens during an individual's leisure time. *Leisure time* is the time people have discretion over. During leisure time people can do what they want. The activities that people engage in during leisure time are known as recreation. Some say that to be recreation, the activity should be constructive and pleasurable. This might involve either aspect to recreation. A game of tennis or golf two miles from home after work would constitute recreation. If one were to drive one hundred miles to a resort for the weekend, the game of tennis would be part of tourism and the golfer would be on a *trip*. A tourism trip does not have to include an overnight stay in the destination.

The traveler sees what he sees, the tourist sees what he has come to see.

G. K. CHESTERTON

To avoid the sometimes negative connotations associated with the word "tourist," the term *visitor* has been used throughout this book. The authors also use *traveler* when appropriate.

THE TOURISM DESTINATION SYSTEM

The rest of this chapter is devoted to destinations. Chapters 2–6 tell you about the planning, development, and control of tourism within destinations. Figure 1.9 gives you a "roadmap" for the discussion about destinations in Chapters 1–6. Just as tourism overall needs a systems approach, so do destinations and Figure 1.9 supplies a simple model of this.

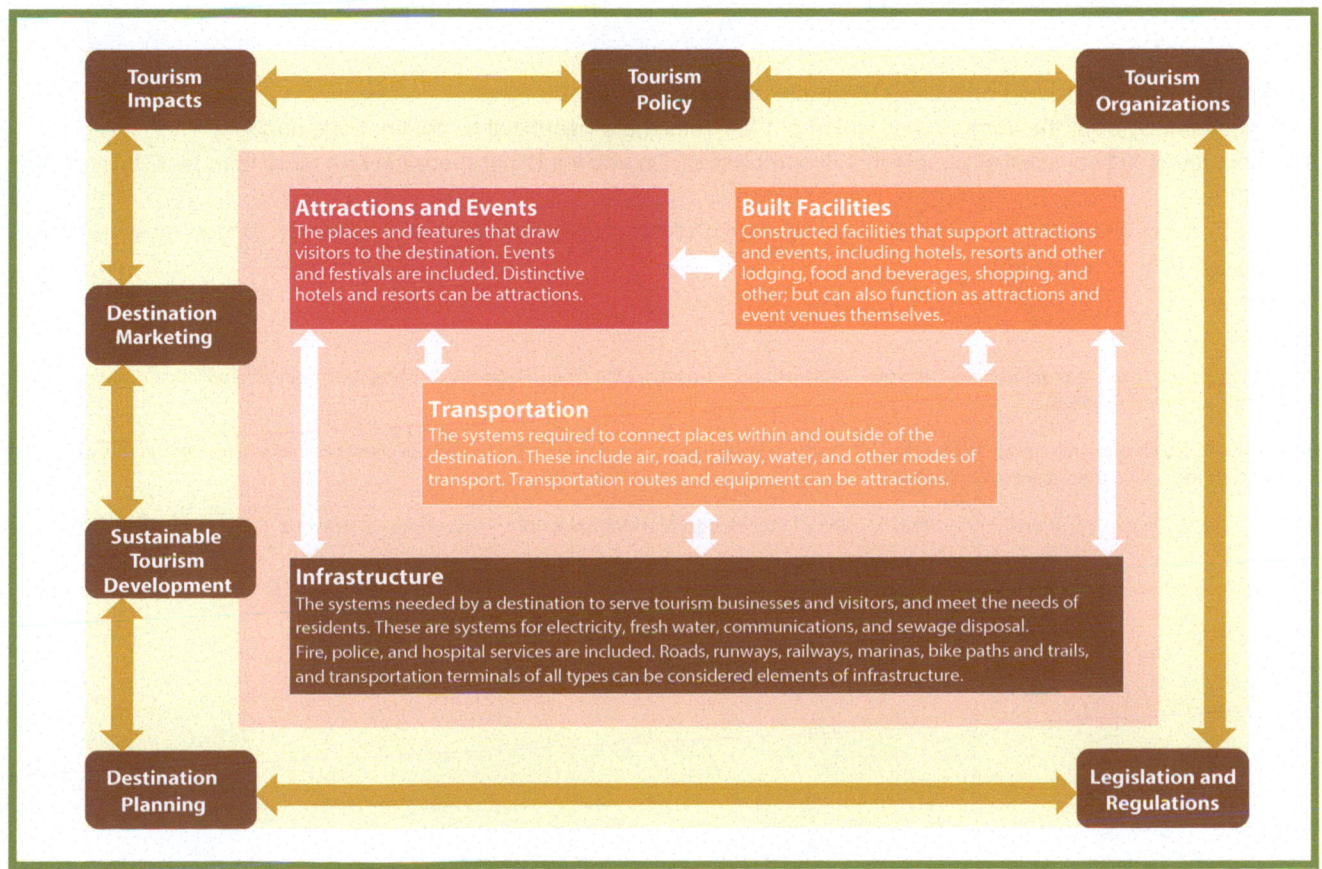

FIGURE 1.9   Overview of the tourism destination system.

QUICK TRIP 1.1

Tourists vs. Travelers

There was an interesting article in *Elite Daily* comparing tourists and travelers. The author argued there were seven differences between the two groups:

- Tourists squander; travelers wander.
- Tourists dream about home; travelers feel at home in foreign places.
- Tourists haul their baggage with them; travelers travel light.
- Tourists need maps; travelers are off the grid.
- Tourists buy Rosetta Stone; travelers get drunk.
- Tourists take pictures non-stop; travelers take it all in.
- Tourists live by the book; travelers write the book.

Other sources suggest that tourists observe when they are in destinations, while travelers experience them.

There are counter-arguments to this point of view. An article in *Business Insider,* for example, suggests that tourists do the following right:

- Tourists know how to maximize their time off.
- Tourists can be lazy *sans* (without) guilt.
- Tourists can easily unwind.
- Tourists can do what they *actually* want to do.
- Tourists can explore the beaten path.
- Tourists can get the best photos.
- Tourists can play off *faux pas* (insensitive mistakes).
- Tourists can share their experiences with others.
- Tourists can fend off muggers with massive guidebooks.

Think about This

1. Which of the two (tourist or traveler) best describes you when you travel?
2. If you accept what the authors say, which of the two is more beneficial to destinations and why?
3. There are only two types of people in this comparison. Do you think that there may be more than two? Why or why not?
4. The authors and UNWTO choose to use the term visitor, rather than tourist or traveler. Do you agree with this choice? Why or why not?

Sources

Cawley, K. 2016. The 7 real differences between a tourist and a traveler. *Elite Daily,* February 24. http://elitedaily.com/life/difference-tourist-and-traveler/1395939/

Hoeller, S.-C. 2015. Why it's better to be a tourist than a traveler. *Business Insider,* May 21. http://www.businessinsider.com/why-its-better-to-be-a-tourist-than-a-traveler-2015-5

Singer, T. 2013. Tourist vs. Traveler infographic. Land of Travel. http://landoftravel.com/?s=tourist+vs.+traveler

Before launching into a detailed description of Figure 1.9 and the tourism destination system, you need to have a clear idea of what a destination is.

Definition of a Destination

A destination is a geographic area that attracts visitors. Destinations range in size from the largest of countries to the smallest of villages (Morrison 2013). Usually, but not always, the destination is marketing and developing tourism, and has a destination management organization (DMO). The world has **mature destinations**, including many cities in Europe and North America, and **emerging destinations**, such as found in parts of Asia, Africa, and the Middle East. All destinations have a "product" and that's the next topic for a detailed discussion.

Destination Product

The destination product is a combination of interdependent components. The components are interdependent because in order to produce satisfying visitor experiences, all components must be present and work together as a system. From the central portion of Figure 1.9, you can see the five main components of the destination product: (1) infrastructure; (2) transportation; (3) built facilities; (4) attractions and events; and (5) service quality and friendliness. Infrastructure and transportation are required to help ensure the basic services and accessibility of the destination. Attractions and built facilities draw visitors to destinations and cater to their needs. Service quality and friendliness add the human dimension and provide the experiences that visitors are seeking.

The discussion of destination product components is arranged in a chronological order beginning with the infrastructure and transportation that must be present for a destination to develop.

* **Infrastructure**

Infrastructure provides the basic services for a destination to operate.

Definition. The dictionary meaning of infra is under (as in under or on the ground); however, this can be extended to also be supporting. Infrastructure development consists mainly of underground and surface preparation and construction. Infrastructure represents the systems needed by a destination to serve tourism businesses and visitors and meet the needs of residents. These are systems for electricity, fresh water, natural gas, telephone, and sewage disposal. Another common name for these is **utilities**. Fire, police, and medical services are another part of infrastructure provision. Roads, runways, railways, marinas, and transportation terminals of all types can be considered elements of transportation infrastructure. For recreation and tourism, **public amenities** such as parks and gardens, pathways and trails, and public toilets should also be included.

Broadband internet services are increasingly being included within the definition of utilities. The provision of comprehensive **Wi-Fi services** in destinations is becoming an important priority and is part of the infrastructure.

Roles. Built facilities, attractions, and events are not accessible for visitor use until the basic infrastructure is installed (see Figure 1.10). Utilities provide essential services to tourism businesses without which they cannot operate including energy and power, water, telephone, Internet, and sewage and solid waste disposal. Emergency, police, public health, and medical services are required to ensure the safety and security of visitors and residents. Transportation infrastructure provides the systems, terminals, facilities, and services required by transportation companies, visitors, and residents to reach and move around the destination. Public amenities support the lifestyles and leisure activities of locals and visitors, and add to the beautification of destinations.

Features and Characteristics. The provision and maintenance of infrastructure is almost always a government responsibility. You will see in Chapter 3 that infrastructure investment and construction is one of the potential government roles in tourism. The maintenance and operation of infrastructure is often done by local government departments with or without the assistance of public utility companies.

The infrastructure of a destination is shared by visitors and residents. Upgrading infrastructure to attract visitors may also improve the living standards of locals.

Classification. Figure 1.10 shows that infrastructure can be classified into utilities, services, transportation infrastructure, and amenities. Compared to attractions, events, and built facilities, infrastructure gets very little attention from tourism scholars. Perhaps, although essential, it is unglamorous to researchers, and hardly noticed by visitors until something goes wrong with the infrastructure.

Utilities	Services
• Communications (telephone, Internet, Wi-Fi, mail/post) • Electricity and natural gas • Water and sewerage	• Emergency (fire, water rescue, etc.) • Health and medical • Police • Waste disposal
Transportation Infrastructure	Other Amenities
• Roads and highways • Transport terminals (airports, marinas, rail stations, etc.)	• Path and bikeway systems • Public parks and gardens • Public toilets

FIGURE 1.10   Classification of infrastructure for destinations.

Free City-Wide Wi-Fi in Helsinki

"Many cities offer Wi-Fi hotspots for visitors. Very few local governments, however, offer free, unrestricted, high-speed Wi-Fi, fast enough for streaming video—the sort that makes your paid-for home Wi-Fi look sluggish. And even fewer provide upload speeds on par with download speeds.

Yet visit the Finnish capital of Helsinki, and there is a free hotspot almost everywhere you need one. It's fast enough to allow video calling and HD streaming. And it doesn't require a reading of lengthy terms and conditions, nor a password, nor the need to divulge your age, gender, or email address."

Source: Mirani, L. 2015. Quartz.

You can see there is a close connection between infrastructure and transportation. As defined, "transportation infrastructure" includes transport route systems and terminals.

• **Transportation**

Transportation is an essential component for all destinations. There is a detailed description of transportation in Chapter 17 (Traveling—Transportation Modes and Carriers), so you will just see a summary here.

Definition. The systems required to connect places within and outside of the destination. These include air, road, railway, water, and other modes of transport. Within destinations, *public transportation* represents shared passenger transport services available to the general public and typically coordinated by local governments.

Roles. Transportation provides access to and from destinations. Visitors also need transport to move around within destinations and certain attractions. In addition, transportation can function as an attraction, such as in sightseeing cruises, historic and scenic train journeys, funicular railways, cable car systems (Figure 1.11), hot-air ballooning, and so on.

A classic example of mixed-role transportation is the cruise ship. Cruise ships sail and take people from port to port; so they are a mode of transportation. Onboard, however, they are like floating resorts, with accommodation, food and beverage service, entertainment and recreation, activities, and so on. What's the

© Ingus Kruklitis/Shutterstock.com

FIGURE 1.11 Transportation and attraction combined. Cable car system over River Thames in Greenwich, England.

lesson for you here? The point is that the destination product components are not completely mutually exclusive, and they can overlap as in cruise ships.

Features and Characteristics. As you already know, transportation needs to be supported by infrastructure. Each transportation mode has its own distinctive features and characteristics, which are reviewed in detail in Chapter 17.

Classification. The most common approach is to classify by *transportation modes*, with the major ones being road, sea, air, and rail. The providers include airlines, shipping lines, ferry services, railways, bus and motor coach operators, car rental companies, taxi and limousine services, bicycle rental, and others. There are other ways to categorize transportation including short-, medium-, and long-haul, which means the time spent on the transportation journey. Definitions of "haul" vary by country, and for example in the UK long-haul is seven or more hours on a mode of transportation. Public transportation and privately-operated transportation is another means of categorization.

• **Built facilities**

Built facilities require infrastructure and transportation, but without them destinations cannot host and satisfy visitors. Along with service quality and friendliness, they are the core of the destination product.

Definition. Constructed facilities that support attractions and events, including hotels, resorts and other lodging, food and beverages, shopping, convention and exhibition centers, and others. They can also function as attractions and event venues. Figure 1.13 is a collage of built facility images.

Roles. Facilities are necessary to serve visitors as they are away from their homes. They can play a supporting role to a destination's attractions and events, or they can function as attractions and event venues themselves.

Features and Characteristics. Every different type of built facility has its own features and characteristics. It is becoming harder to differentiate the components of built facilities, since more "integrated" and "multi-use"

FIGURE 1.12 Luxury train journeys are popular attractions worldwide.

© Shutterstock, Inc. (The Ghan, Australia, STRINGER Image/Shutterstock.com; The Blue Train, South Africa, Peter Titmuss/Shutterstock.com; The Belmond Pullman, England, Peter Moulton/Shutterstock.com; The Deccan Odyssey, India, CRS PHOTO/Shutterstock.com)

When Is a Train Not Just a Train?

You are learning about the destination product and that it has five main components. However, the authors want you to have a flexible view on the roles of these components as they can "multi-task" for destinations. What is meant by multi-tasking? An example of luxury train journeys will help you grasp this.

A luxury train journey is both an attraction and a mode of transportation. Like a cruise ship, it also facilitates multi-destination travel. The following table shows the top-rated trains in the world for these experiences:

Ranks	Condé Nast Traveler, Best Trains in the World 2015
1.	Venice Simplon-Orient-Express
2.	Pride of Africa, Rovos Rail, South Africa
3.	Belmond Royal Scotsman, UK
4.	The Ghan, Great Southern Rail, Australia
5.	Palace on Wheels, India
6.	The Blue Train, South Africa
7.	Trans-Siberian Express, Golden Eagle Luxury Trains
8.	Belmond British Pullman, UK
9.	Belmond Hiram Bingham, Peru
10.	Rocky Mountaineer, Canada

Figure 1.12 has photos of the Ghan, Blue Train, Pullman, and the Deccan Odyssey (India). These trains have grandly appointed interiors and put an emphasis on first-class food and beverage services.

Think about This

1. What are the most attractive features and characteristics of these train journeys to visitors?
2. To whom do these train journeys most appeal and why?
3. What are the benefits that these train trips provide for destinations that are included along their routes?
4. What sorts of unique experiences are included in these journeys to increase the involvement and satisfaction of passengers?

Sources

The Luxury Train Club. 2017. *Condé Nast Traveler—Best Trains in the World 2015.* https://www.luxurytrainclub.com/news/cond%C3%A9-nast-traveller-best-trains-in-the-world-2015/

Malathronas, J. 2016. 11 of the world's most luxurious train journeys. *CNN Travel.* http://edition.cnn.com/travel/article/luxury-train-travel/index.html

Sessa, A. 2017. The best new luxury train trips. *Condé Nast Traveler,* March 9. https://www.cntraveler.com/gallery/the-best-new-luxury-overnight-train-trips

The Telegraph. 2017. The world's most luxurious train journeys. August 8. http://www.telegraph.co.uk/luxury/travel/worlds-most-luxurious-train-journeys/

FIGURE 1.13 Collage of built facilities.

© (Shopping, Dubai Mall, D_Zheleva; visitor centres GTS Productions/Shutterstock.com; convention and exhibition centers, Jakob J. Javits Convention Center, New York, Sam Aronov; hotels, resorts and other lodging, The Venetian Macau, Thitisan/Shutterstock.com; food and beverages, Rawpixel.com/Shutterstock.com)

projects are being constructed for tourism and leisure purposes. The integrated resorts in destinations such as Las Vegas, Macau, and Singapore are great examples of this trend. They include hotel rooms, convention and exhibition facilities, food and beverages, attractions and events, and other amenities.

Short descriptions of each type of built facility follow:

- *Hotels, Resorts, and Other Lodging.* Provide for visitor needs to eat and sleep. Lodging ranges from hotels of an international standard to recreational vehicle parks. Figure 1.14 provides a listing of accommodation types according to four categories (traditional lodging; specialist accommodations; recreational accommodations; and other accommodations) (Luxury Accommodations 2017; Mealey, 2017).

Often hotels and resorts are divided into chain-operated and independent properties. There are various rating and grading systems that divide them from the most luxurious five-star hotels and resorts to very basic one-star properties. Some of these systems are operated by government agencies based upon regular inspections.

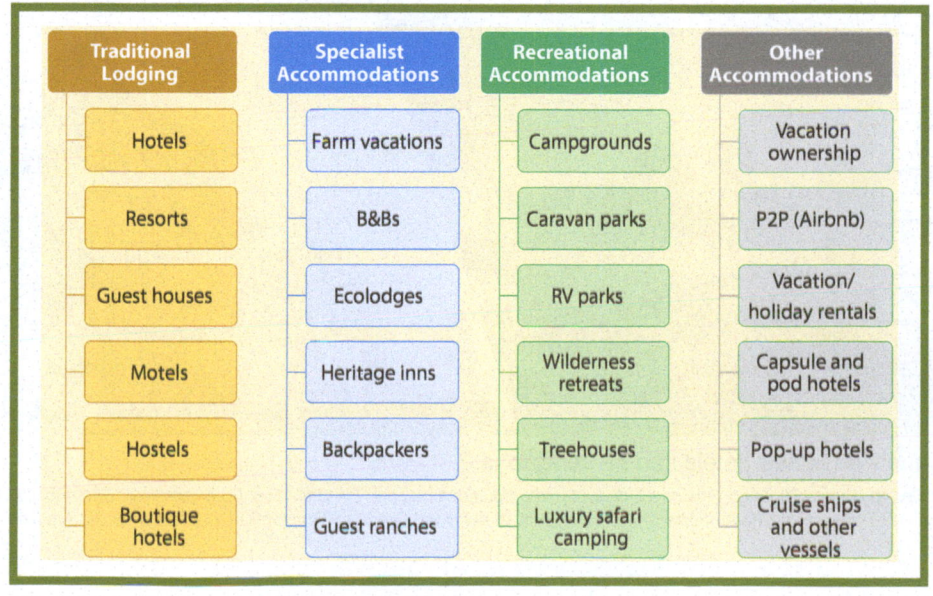

Traditional Lodging	Specialist Accommodations	Recreational Accommodations	Other Accommodations
Hotels	Farm vacations	Campgrounds	Vacation ownership
Resorts	B&Bs	Caravan parks	P2P (Airbnb)
Guest houses	Ecolodges	RV parks	Vacation/ holiday rentals
Motels	Heritage inns	Wilderness retreats	Capsule and pod hotels
Hostels	Backpackers	Treehouses	Pop-up hotels
Boutique hotels	Guest ranches	Luxury safari camping	Cruise ships and other vessels

FIGURE 1.14 Types of accommodations.

QUICK TRIP 1.3

A Hotel Does Not Need to Be a Box

Hotels are an essential component of the destination product; however, they have the potential to perform multiple roles. Almost all hotels provide accommodation, food and beverages, and entertainment. However, hotels and resorts can also perform the role of attractions.

Some complain that hotels are just rectangular "boxes" of rooms that are not eye-appealing or much different from each other. For example, big-box hotels are convention-oriented hotels located in city centers that have at least 50,000 square feet of meeting space, and they are often connected or next to a large convention center.

Who said all hotels must be rectangular boxes? In fact, recently many uniquely-designed hotels and resorts have entered the market, including boutique hotels each with their own distinctive styles. Architecture can also make hotels become attractions and not just places to eat and sleep. Figure 1.15 provides four examples of hotels that are designed to be different from boxes from the outside in.

- Sheraton Huzhou Hot Spring Resort, Zhejiang Province, China: On Taihu (Lake Tai) and quite close to Shanghai, this is a twenty-seven-story structure that resembles part of a donut. It has 321 rooms and a total floor area of around 95,000 square meters.

FIGURE 1.15 Uniquely designed hotels can be attractions.

© Sheraton Huzhou Hot Spring Resort, Zhejiang Province, China, 06photo/Shutterstock.com; Spitbank Fort Boutique Hotel, England, David Peter Robinson/ Shutterstock.com; Taj Palace Udaipur, India, PeteInPerth/Shutterstock.com; Inntel Hotel Zaandam, Amsterdam, The Netherlands, Sira Anamwong/Shutterstock. com)

- Spitbank Fort, Portsmouth, England: A five-star boutique hotel with eight suites in a renovated fort in the Solent River. It opened in 2012 in this nineteenth-century structure.
- The Lake Palace, Udaipur, India: Operated by Taj Hotels Resorts and Palaces, this scenic resort hotel sits on Lake Pichola and resembles a white-sailed ship. It was originally built in 1746 and contains sixty-six rooms and seventeen suites.
- Inntel Hotel, Zaandam, Netherlands: The façade of this hotel is made from seventy stacked Amsterdam-style houses and cottages. It is a four-star hotel with 160 rooms in a twelve-story structure.

Some of these four properties fall into the category of "design hotels" which are notable for their design (architecture, interior decoration, and/or furnishings).

Historic and heritage inns and hotels are another category that attracts visitors. The Lake Palace and Spitbank Port Boutique Hotel fit into this category. So do many of the properties in the Paradores chain in Spain. Some historic hotels are called "grand dames" including the Raffles in Singapore, the Peninsula in Hong Kong, the Plaza Hotel in New York, the Chateau Laurier in Ottawa, and the Dorchester in London.

Think about This

1. Many experts are saying that traditional hotels are losing their appeal, especially with the millennials. Do you agree with them? Why or why not?
2. One of the features of these four hotels is that they take advantage of the characteristics of the local areas in which they are situated. How important is it for hotels to "localize" to be unique and more attractive to visitors?
3. Can you gather more examples of hotels in your region that function as attractions, not just places to eat, drink, and sleep? What are they and why do they attract visitors?
4. These hotels are unique because of their physical characteristics. How can hotels and resorts use distinctive personal service to attract visitors?

Sources

Designboom. 2017. MAD Architects: Sheraton Huzhou Hot Spring Resort. https://www.designboom.com/architecture/mad-architects-sheraton-huzhou-hot-spring-resort/

Glancey, J. 2010. Much of a Dutchness: The Hotel Inntel in Zaandam. *The Guardian,* March 31. https://www.theguardian.com/artand-design/2010/mar/31/hotel-inntel-zaandam

Harrison, K. T. 2017. What is a design hotel? https://www.tripsavvy.com/what-is-a-design-hotel-2251174

Harrison, K. T. 2017. What is a grand hotel or grand dame hotel? https://www.tripsavvy.com/what-is-a-grande-dame-hotel-2251184

Inntel Hotels. 2017. Amsterdam Zaandam. https://www.inntelhotelsamsterdamzaandam.nl/en/

MAD. 2017. Sheraton Huzhou Hot Spring Resort. http://www.i-mad.com/work/sheraton-huzhou-hot-spring-resort/?cid=4

Main, L. 2015. Three ways traditional big box hotels can compete with boutiques. ehotelier, July 17. https://ehotelier.com/insights/2015/07/17/three-ways-traditional-big-box-hotels-can-compete-with-boutiques/

Paradores de Turismo de España. 2017. Paradores Hoteles & Restaurantes. http://www.parador.es/en

Spitbank Fort Boutique Hotel. 2017. https://solentforts.com/spitbank-fort/

Taj Hotels Resorts and Palaces. 2017. Taj Lake Palace, Udaipur. https://taj.tajhotels.com/en-in/taj-lake-palace-udaipur/

The Telegraph. 2017. 50 of the world's most unusual hotels. February 24. http://www.telegraph.co.uk/travel/hotels/articles/the-worlds-most-unusual-weird-hotels/

Watkins, E. 2013. Big box hotels aren't dead yet. Hotel News Now, October 22. http://hotelnewsnow.com/Articles/20691/Big-box-hotels-arent-dead-yet

- *Food and Beverages.* Every visitor needs to eat, but food and local cuisine are also elements of a destination's culture. Indeed, food and how it is presented can be an attraction for visitors. Figure 1.16 provides a unique example of this with the *Dinner in the Sky* concept (Cudny 2016). The popular night markets in Asian cities such as Taipei, Hong Kong, Bangkok, and Singapore are example of an attraction primarily based on food (Figure 1.17). You might hear the term **destination dining** used, this means a restaurant or other foodservice offer that people make a point of visiting.

As with hotels, one distinction is between chain-operated restaurants and independents. It is also important to differentiate places for eating and dining-out destinations. There are many types of offers "for just eating" as people seek to eat quickly and conveniently. In the latter group, national and ethnic restaurants and other international cuisines are becoming increasingly popular.

There are many types of restaurant and foodservice concepts ranging from fine-dining restaurants to streetside food stalls. Figure 1.18 identifies many of the available restaurant and foodservice concepts in destinations.

- *Shopping.* For destinations, shopping is an activity for visitors, but it can also be an attraction, and shopping centers can host events (International Council of Shopping Centers 2017). Figure 1.19 illustrates six of the types of shopping that visitors are likely to encounter on their trips. These include outlet malls, high-street shops or city center shopping, duty-free shops, shopping malls, souvenir shops, and convenience stores.

Figure 1.19 illustrates six major shopping styles that can be enjoyed in city destinations.

© CRM/Shutterstock.com

FIGURE 1.16 Dinner in the sky in Brussels, Belgium.

© LMspencer/Shutterstock.com

FIGURE 1.17 Eating and shopping combined at the night markets in Taiwan.

Traditional	Outdoor and Convenience	International
Buffets	Barbecues	Beer gardens
Cafes	Convenience stores	Bistros
Cafeterias	Fairs and festivals	Brasseries
Casual	Food trucks	Delicatessens
Catering	Night markets	Mongolian barbecue
Coffee and tea bars	Pop-up restaurants	National and ethnic
Fast casual	Service stations	Osteria
Fast food/QSV	Stadiums	Pizzeria
Fine dining	Street vendors	Smörgåsbord
Pubs, taverns, inns	Transport dining	Taqueria
Snack bars	Transport kiosks	Tavola
Steakhouses	Vending machines	Teppanyaki

FIGURE 1.18 Types of restaurants and foodservice.

FIGURE 1.19 A variety of shopping opportunities for visitors.

© *Outlet shopping, Richmond, British Columbia, Canada, Volodymyr Kyrylyuk/Shutterstock.com; high street shopping, London, Willy Barton/Shutterstock.com; duty free shopping, Malpensa Airport, Milan, Italy, Paolo Bona/Shutterstock.com; shopping mall, The Shoppes at Marina Bay Sands, Singapore, Chatchawat Prasertsom/Shutterstock.com; souvenir shop, Barcelona, Spain, Pamela Loreta Perez/Shutterstock.com; convenience store, Bangkok, Thailand, O n E studio/ Shutterstock.com)*

QUICK TRIP 1.4

The Best Cities to Shop until You Drop

What are the best shopping cities in the world? There are several different rankings available and here are the results from three of them:

Ranks	Condé Nast Traveler	CNN Travel	Travel Channel
1.	New York	New York	Tokyo
2.	Dubai	Tokyo	New York
3.	Chicago	London	Moscow
4.	Hong Kong	Kuala Lumpur	Milan
5.	Santa Fe	Paris	London
6.	Paris	Hong Kong	Dubai
7.	San Francisco	Buenos Aires	Los Angeles
8.	Florence	Vienna	Paris
9.	London	Dubai	Rome
10.	Tokyo	Madrid	Madrid
11.	Milan	Milan	Hong Kong
12.	Boston	Seoul	Austin
13.	Rome		
14.	Singapore		
15.	Aspen		

There are some variations in the three rankings; however, New York, Tokyo, Dubai, London, Paris, Hong Kong, and Milan are in all of them.

QUICK TRIP 1.4 CONTINUED

Think about This

1. How important is shopping to city tourism destinations?
2. Do you agree with these rankings or are there other cities that you think should have been included?
3. In your opinion and experience, what are the key characteristics of successful city shopping destinations?
4. Do you think that shopping tourism is a branch of tourism in which the shopping motivates people to travel? Why or why not?

Sources

Kim, V. 2014. 12 best shopping cities in the world. CNN Travel. http://edition.cnn.com/travel/article/worlds-best-shopping-cities/index.html

Morton, C. 2015. The best shopping cities in the world. *Condé Nast Traveler*. https://www.cntraveler.com/galleries/2015-01-03/best-shopping-cities-in-the-world-readers-choice-awards-2014

Travel Channel. 2017. World's best shopping cities. http://www.travelchannel.com/interests/shopping/photos/best-shopping-cities-around-the-world

When visitors are attracted to a destination specifically because of the shopping, this is called **shopping tourism**. UNWTO defines shopping tourism as "a contemporary form of tourism fostered by individuals for whom purchasing goods outside of their usual environment is a determining factor in their decision to travel" and says there are millions of shopping visitors:

> "Shopping for pleasure is no longer a purely incidental activity to dip into while travelling for leisure. Today, for millions of tourists it represents the principal—or one of the principal—motivations for travelling" (UNWTO 2014).

An important characteristic of visitor shopping is that it often represents a high percentage of the total spending in destinations. The proportion varies by country and whether it is inbound or domestic tourism. For example, in Japan in 2016 it was estimated that 38.1 percent of all the spending by Chinese visitors was for shopping (The Japan Times 2017). Barclays, in 2014, estimated that 37.7 percent of overseas visitor spending in the UK in 2013 was on shopping and that would rise to 38.5 percent in 2017.

- *Convention and Exhibition Centers.* There are different varieties of these based upon the types of MICE events they serve. They include convention centers, exhibition and trade show facilities, conference centers and resorts, and congress centers. These centers are critical to many cities that rely heavily on the MICE (meeting, incentive, convention, exhibition) markets and business events.

  Many convention and exhibition centers are run by local governments or by DMOs. There is a trend, however, to privatize the operation of centers. Some of these facilities are huge, such as the Messegelände Hannover (Hanover Fairground) in Germany with 496,000 square meters (5.3 million square feet) of covered space and McCormick Place in Chicago with 2.6 million square feet. Trade Show Executive (2015) defines North American convention centers into four tiers according to total available square feet of space; Tier 1—1 million and over; Tier II—350,000–999,999; Tier III—125,000–349,999; Tier IV—50,000–124,999).

- *Other Built Facilities.* These are structures that are needed by visitors and to support other built facilities. Visitor information centers (VICs) and welcome centers are a good example of facilities that serve people while they are visiting or on their way to visit destinations. New Zealand has a system of eighty official VICS known as i-SITEs, which perform the following roles: itinerary planning and information; bookings nationwide for accommodation, transport, activities, attractions; free maps, weather and mountain safety information; and local information on events, attractions, restaurants, and so on (Tourism New Zealand 2017).

Performing arts centers, theatres, auditoriums, fairgrounds, and festival areas are other built facilities that support attractions, events, and other built facilities (International Association of Amusement Parks and Attractions (IAAPA 2017). For example, state fairgrounds in the United States are the venues for annual state fairs; and in Europe, fairgrounds are used to host exhibitions. Municipal and university auditoriums are large, tiered seating venues often used for performances and speeches.

- **Attractions**

Every destination offers a unique mixture of attractions. They play a central role in bringing visitors to destinations.

Definition. The places and things that draw visitors to the destination. Some attractions are built, others are based on nature, culture, and history and heritage. Distinctive resorts and hotels, transportation routes and equipment, and cuisine also function as visitor attractions.

Roles. Attractions often are the main reasons why people visit specific destinations. They either act alone or in combination with other attractions in appealing to and serving visitors. The "holding power" of attractions influences the length of stay in destinations.

Features and Characteristics. Attractions are very varied in scope and "holding power." Primary attractions are those that tend to be the most recognized by visitors and may influence choices of destinations. Secondary attractions tend to be selected after visitors arrive in destinations, or they may be experienced en route.

Classification. Attractions can be grouped into man-made; natural; climate; history and heritage; arts, culture, and traditions; industrial; dark; and other categories. Figure 1.20 provides some examples of the attractions within each of these eight categories.

You will learn more about attractions and events in subsequent chapters. For example, in Chapter 6 there is a discussion about *flagship* attractions, which are major tourism attractions or resort areas that provide a primary reason for people to visit specific destinations. *Hallmark events* are the "flagships" among events, and these are major occasions that draw international audiences.

Chapter 6 also introduces you to the concepts of *hubs*, *clusters*, *circuits,* and *trails*, all of which involve combinations of attractions and events, built facilities, and service quality. Chapter 9 is about product

Man-made	Natural	Climate	History and Heritage
▪ Theme parks ▪ Water parks ▪ Family recreation centers ▪ Amusement parks ▪ Zoos and aquariums ▪ Science centers ▪ Museums ▪ Resorts and hotels ▪ Sport stadiums ▪ Themed dining ▪ Casinos ▪ Shopping	▪ National parks ▪ State and provincial parks ▪ Marine parks ▪ Botanical and other gardens ▪ Wildlife refuges ▪ Conservation areas ▪ Wetlands, lakes and rivers ▪ Caves, hot springs, volcanoes ▪ Landscape scenery	▪ Beaches, sun, sea and sand ▪ Snow and ice ▪ Natural phenomena (*Aurora Borealis*) ▪ Fall colors ▪ Sunrises and sunsets	▪ Castles, forts, and palaces ▪ Walls ▪ Bridges ▪ Historic homes ▪ Historic streets, villages and towns ▪ Literary writers
Arts, Culture, and Traditions	Industrial	Dark	Other
▪ Art galleries ▪ Cathedrals, churches, mosques ▪ Cultural centers ▪ Markets and bazaars ▪ Performances	▪ Agritourism ▪ Wineries and breweries ▪ Factory outlet stores ▪ Factory tours ▪ Mine tours ▪ Movie and TV series	▪ Battlefields and military cemeteries ▪ Concentration camps ▪ Locations of famous crimes ▪ Natural disaster sites ▪ Prisons and jails	▪ Accessible, en route attractions ▪ Themed circuits and routes ▪ Trail systems

FIGURE 1.20 **Classification of attractions.**

development from the destination marketing perspective, and there is more discussion of destination product components there.

• **Events**

Definition. Gatherings of groups of people for short periods of time for entertainment, celebration, family, and business reasons or purposes.

Roles. Events perform multiple roles including allowing destinations to create visitor demand in off-peak periods. They provide entertainment for visitors and local residents. Events enable destinations to celebrate and present their distinct local cultures and traditions. MICE events perform various roles for organizations including marketing, training and education, and networking.

Features and Characteristics. Events are short-term, lasting normally for a week or less. They are recurring or non-recurring. Many events, especially festivals, provide an opportunity for community involvement.

Classification. There are many different types of events that take place in destinations. However, there are at least six major categories of events including cultural and other festivals; entertainment events; sport events; MICE and business events; wedding and other family events; and other events (Getz 2008; Getz and Page 2016) (Figure 1.21).

• **Service quality and friendliness**

Definition. Service quality and friendliness represent the human factor in the destination product. All those involved in "hosting" visitors are involved, and include both tourism service staff and local communities. It is the way that visitor services are delivered by service providers, as well as the general feeling of friendliness and warmth radiated by the resident population of the destination.

Roles. For staff working in tourism, the role is to provide professional, competent, and courteous service that meets, and preferably exceeds, visitor expectations. For residents, the role is having friendly and empathetic attitudes toward the people visiting their communities.

Features and Characteristics. Host-guest relationships are at the heart of the destination product since tourism is very much a people-to-people business. These relationships require a dedicated and constant effort in destinations since the people involved are always changing.

Classification. Service quality and friendliness can be categorized into five main parts.

Service Quality. The service quality provided by staff in tourism businesses has a major influence on visitor satisfaction. As such, staff orientation, training, and assessment are critical to preparing skilled and empathetic employees in destinations. The training can be divided into two main categories, which are skills training and *hospitality training*. *SuperHost* is a great example of a customer service and hospitality training program and it was originally developed in British Columbia, Canada (go2HR Tourism Society 2017).

Experience and Interpretation Delivery. You will learn in Part 3 (Demand) about the growing importance of experiences to visitors. While unbelievable scenery, adrenalin-sapping action, and viewing ancient treasures are a major part of experiences, the human factor enhances and extends the memorability and enjoyment of these moments.

People are often involved in the delivery of interpretation within the destination and specific attractions. *Interpretation* is helping visitors to have a deeper understanding of and appreciation for what they are seeing and experiencing in the destination. It can be educational, but it also can be fun and inspiring.

Quality Assurance. In every destination, steps should be taken to assure the quality of the services and goods that visitors purchase. For example, being sold fake products at the same prices as the real brand items is a major danger that visitors experience in many

Cultural and Other Festivals

- Carnivals
- Cultural/ethnic
- Historic
- Holiday
- Parades
- Religious

Entertainment Events

- Concerts
- Music festivals
- Shows
- Theatre

Sport Events

- Amateur sports
- International and national games
- Marathons
- Professional sports
- Tournaments

MICE and Business Events

- Conferences and conventions
- Exhibitions and trade shows
- Congresses
- Incentives

Weddings and Other Family Events

- Anniversaries
- Family celebrations
- Family reunions
- Graduations
- Weddings

Other Events

- Celebrations
- National holidays
- Political rallies
- State and other fairs
- Viewing natural phenomena

FIGURE 1.21 Classifications of events.

© Shutterstock, Inc. (Cultural and other festivals, Oktoberfest, Munich, Germany, ESB Professional/Shutterstock.com; entertainment events, music festival, Monkey Business Images; sport event, stadium spectators, Eo naya/Shutterstock.com; MICE and business events, conference speaker, Matej Kastelic/Shutterstock.com; weddings and other family events, Dimitry Sheremeta/Shutterstock.com; other events, viewing solar eclipse in New York, James Kirkikis/Shutterstock.com)

destinations worldwide. Additionally, visitors are the targets on numerous scams by tour guides, transport providers, and even people in the street.

Numerous approaches are used to protect visitors including the licensing of vendors and providers, *quality assurance programs* such as Hong Kong's *Quality Tourism Services (QTS)*, and ultimately police protection.

Community Awareness. Although the visitor is most directly affected by the degree of hospitality shown by service providers, the overall feeling of welcome within a community enhances or detracts from the experience.

Residents of a destination area cannot be trained to act in a hospitable way toward visitors, but a community awareness program helps develop more positive attitudes toward visitors. The objectives of a training program are to build acceptance of tourism and to develop greater understanding and empathy for visitors.

Volunteering. Many destinations operate volunteer programs in which residents help serve visitors with information, suggestions, directions, and other problem-solving. Often, the volunteers work at visitor information centers (VICs), airports and other transport terminals, city centers, and near major attractions. These programs are beneficial to visitors and communities, and are a way of involving residents in tourism. They also add to the authenticity of experiences for visitors.

The Quality Assurance Scheme in Hong Kong Tourism

The Quality Tourism Services (QTS) Scheme makes it easy for you to find shops, restaurants, and budget visitor accommodation that you can trust. Under the scheme administered by the Hong Kong Tourism Board (HKTB), QTS-accredited establishments must pass stringent annual assessments showing that they meet high standards of product quality and service.

Source: Hong Kong Tourism Board. 2017.

Now you know more about the five major components of the destination product and realize that some of them can play multiple roles. You also probably can guess that some destinations are "brand names" themselves and draw visitors because of worldwide recognition and great reputations. Some might call these "**bucket list**" places to visit and they include destinations such as Paris, Venice, Bali, Rome, the Great Wall of China, the Taj Mahal, and others. Apart from being "household names," the destination product components in these famous places work interdependently as a system to allure visitors.

FIGURE 1.22 Scenes from some of the world's friendliest cities.

© (Perth, Australia, f11photo/Shutterstock.com; Thimphu, Bhutan, Pema Gyamtsho/Shutterstock.com; San Miguel de Allende, Mexico, Kobby Dagan/Shutterstock.com; Charleston, South Carolina, USA, f11photo/Shutterstock.com)

QUICK TRIP 1.5

What Are the Friendliest Cities in the World?

Many places say their residents are really friendly, but it is hard to judge whether they are or not. Other destinations have a reputation of having locals who are aloof and disinterested in visitors. It's been said that you cannot paint a smiley face on everyone, and surely this is true within destinations.

So, what are the friendliest cities in the world?

	Condé Nast Traveler	Travel & Leisure
1.	San Miguel de Allende, Mexico	Thimphu, Bhutan
2.	Perth, Australia	Charleston, South Carolina
3.	Gothenburg, Sweden	Chiang Mai, Thailand
4.	Evora, Portugal	San Miguel de Allende, Mexico
5.	Chiang Rai, Thailand	Queenstown, New Zealand
6.	Auckland, New Zealand	Galway, Ireland
7.	Siem Reap, Cambodia	Dublin, Ireland
8.	Oporto, Portugal	Savannah, Georgia
9.	Beirut, Lebanon	Luang Prabang, Laos
10.	Dublin, Ireland	Cork, Ireland
11.	Malmo, Sweden	Ubud, Indonesia
12.	Halifax, Canada	Edinburgh, Scotland
13.	Wellington, New Zealand	Sydney, Australia
14.	Luang Prabang, Laos	Christchurch, New Zealand
15.	Hobart, Australia	Hobart, Australia

Figure 1.22 shows some images of the friendly people in four of the top-ranked city destinations.

Think about This

1. Why are so many cities in Asia, Ireland, New Zealand, and Australia included in these rankings?
2. Do you think friendliness to others is something that can be trained? Why or why not?
3. How do the friendliness or unfriendliness of locals influence visitor experiences?
4. Would you now be more inclined to visit the cities ranked in the table above? Why or why not?

Sources

Condé Nast Traveler. 2017. The 2017 friendliest cities in the world. August 17. https://www.cntraveler.com/galleries/2015-08-14/the-2015-friendliest-and-unfriendliest-cities-in-the-world

Katz, B. P. 2017. The friendliest cities in the world. Travel & Leisure, March 1. http://www.travelandleisure.com/slideshows/worlds-friendliest-cities

Criteria for Destination Success

Then, what makes a destination successful in tourism? Unfortunately, you cannot have a template to answer this question as there is no universally-accepted set of success criteria. However, there are some approaches to determining "best destinations" of which you should be aware.

- **Media and guidebook rankings of best destinations**

There are several annual rankings of best destinations prepared by consumer travel magazines, guidebooks, and newspapers. The publishers include TripAdvisor, Lonely Planet, *The Telegraph*, *Travel + Leisure*, *National Geographic Traveler*, Fodor, *US News and World Report*, *Condé Nast Traveler*, Rough Guides, and others. The ranks are either based on reader surveys or done by panels of experts. You will find the results of some of these rankings in Quick Trip 1.6.

These best destination listings are popular with consumers and their sources are respected and credible. However, there are doubts about their objectivity since no specific and detailed criteria are given for the selections. Moreover, many of the lists change each year and this seems counterintuitive.

- **Visitor volume-based rankings**

Often you will hear of the world's top tourism destinations being introduced as those with the highest volumes of international visitors. This is often done by using the latest statistics from UNWTO as shown in Figure 1.23. It shows that the top three country destinations in the world in 2016 were France, United States, and Spain.

Rank	Countries	International Arrivals 2016
1.	France	82,600,000
2.	USA	75,600,000
3.	Spain	75,600,000
4.	China	59,300,000
5.	Italy	52,400,000
6.	UK	35,800,000
7.	Germany	35,600,000
8.	Mexico	35,000,000
9.	Thailand	32,600,000
10.	Turkey	n.a.

FIGURE 1.23 Top 10 countries by international arrivals in 2016. Source: UNWTO, 2017.

However, having the most visitors does not necessarily indicate that these ten countries are the "best" destinations. Having the most visitors is just one measure of success, and there are many others. In fact, some visitors may decide to avoid heavily visited places and go to more "off-the-beaten track" and smaller destinations. A larger set of criteria is needed to evaluate destinations. Also, these UNWTO figures are only for countries, not for cities, resort areas, and regions within countries.

- **Criteria-based evaluations of destinations**

These are evaluation procedures that are based on criteria developed by experts and organizations involved in destination planning, management, and marketing. The criteria are developed on a third-party basis, so they are objective and free of commercial bias.

A good example is the *GSTC Destination Criteria* prepared by the Global Sustainable Tourism Council based in Washington, DC. These criteria are specified in four sections: (A) demonstrate sustainable destination management; (B) maximize economic benefits to the host community and minimize negative impacts; (C) maximize benefits to communities, visitors, and culture; minimize negative impacts; and (D) maximize benefits to the environment and minimize negative impacts.

Another set of criteria, the 10 As, was developed by one of the authors and is discussed in Quick Trip 1.7 and illustrated in Figure 1.24.

Tourism and destinations are not just made up of the destination product components; there are other major "players" involved in tourism. The following section introduces you to these types of organizations.

Other Components of Tourism Destinations

You should recognize that the destination product does not cover all the players involved in tourism. In fact, there are many more as illustrated in Figure 1.25. They include destination management organizations (DMOs), travel trade intermediaries, associations, government agencies, parks and recreation organizations, and consumer service providers.

Preview of Other Destination Chapters

Figure 1.9 gives you a roadmap to the tourism destination system. Chapter 1 has introduced you to the tourism system and the destination product components. The following chapters explore more aspects of the tourism destination system beginning with the impacts of tourism in Chapter 2 and then moving on to tourism policy

QUICK TRIP 1.6

Best Destination Rankings

People are always curious about the best places to visit. Knowing this, publishers of magazines, newspapers, and guidebooks produce annual "best destination rankings" for countries and cities. The table below shows four of these ranking lists for 2016–2017. You will notice that all the lists are different. Also, you might spot that there are very famous destinations in some lists, but there are some places that are not very well-known.

Rank	TripAdvisor	Lonely Planet	The Telegraph	Travel + Leisure
1.	Bali, Indonesia	Bordeaux, France	Chile	San Miguel de Allende, Mexico
2.	London, UK	Cape Town, South Africa	Canada	Charleston
3.	Paris	Los Angeles	Chandigarh, India	Chiang Mai, Thailand
4.	Rome	Merida, Mexico	Granada, Spain	Kyoto, Japan
5.	New York City	Ohrid, Macedonia	Hadrian's Wall, England	Florence
6.	Crete, Greece	Pistoia, Italy	New Zealand	Oaxaca, Mexico
7.	Barcelona	Seoul	Copenhagen	Hoi An, Vietnam
8.	Siem Reap, Cambodia	Lisbon	New Orleans/Memphis	Cape Town, South Africa
9.	Prague	Moscow	Ulaan Baatar, Mongolia	Ubud, Indonesia
10.	Phuket, Thailand	Portland, Oregon	Peru	Luang Prabang, Laos
11.	Istanbul		Arras, France	Santa Fe
12.	Jamaica		Hossa National Park, Finland	Rome
13.	Hoi An, Vietnam		Russia	Siem Reap, Cambodia
14.	St. Petersburg, Russia		Pula, Croatia	Udaipur, India
15.	Roatan, Honduras		Bermuda	Barcelona
16.	Marrakech		Wittenberg, Germany	
17.	Ambergris Caye, Belize		San Francisco	
18.	Rio de Janeiro		Oman	
19.	St. Martin/St. Maarten		Lech, Austria	
20.	Playa del Carmen, Mexico		Liuwa, Zambia	

Think about This

1. Why do believe these lists are so different from one another?
2. Which of the lists do you think is the most accurate and why?
3. Would these types of rankings influence your choice of destinations? Why or why not?
4. Are there are other destinations that you feel should be on these lists and why?

Sources

Lonely Planet. 2017. Best in Travel 2017. Top Cities. https://www.lonelyplanet.com/best-in-travel/cities

The Telegraph. 2017. The 20 best destinations to visit in 2017. http://www.telegraph.co.uk/travel/lists/20-best-destinations-for-2017/

Travel + Leisure. 2017. The 2017 World's Best Awards. http://www.travelandleisure.com/worlds-best

TripAdvisor. 2017. Top 25 destinations—World. https://www.tripadvisor.com/TravelersChoice-Destinations-cTop-g1

(Chapter 3), legislation and regulation (Chapter 4), tourism destination planning (Chapter 5), sustainable tourism development (Chapter 6), and destination marketing (Chapters 7–9). You will learn more about government agencies and major tourism associations in Chapters 3 and 4; and DMOs are discussed in Chapters 5–9. Travel trade intermediaries and major transportation carriers are reviewed in Part 4 (Travel).

QUICK TRIP 1.7

The 10 A's of Successful Destinations

What are the criteria for a successful destination? There are no universally accepted rules for judging this; however, our lead author has come up with an approach known as the 10 As and here they are:

- *Awareness*: This attribute is related to visitors' level of knowledge about the destination and is influenced by the amount and nature of the information they receive. Is there a high level of awareness of the destination among potential visitors?
- *Attractiveness*: The number and geographic scope of appeal of the destination's attractions comprise this attribute. Does the destination offer a diversity of attractions that are appealing to visitors?
- *Availability*: This attribute is determined by the ease with which bookings and reservations can be made for the destination, and the number of booking and reservation channels available. Can bookings and reservations for the destination be made through a variety of distribution channels?
- *Access*: The convenience of getting to and from the destination, as well as moving around within the destination, constitutes this attribute. Is there convenient access to and from the destination by all modes of transportation? Is there convenient transportation within the destination?
- *Appearance*: This attribute measures the impressions that the destination makes on visitors, both when they first arrive and then throughout their stays in the destination. Does the destination make a good first impression? Does the destination make a positive and lasting impression?
- *Activities*: The extent of the array of activities and experiences available to visitors within the destination is the determinant of this attribute. Does the destination offer a wide range of activities and experiences in which visitors want to engage?
- *Assurance*: This attribute relates to the safety and security of the destination for visitors. Is the destination clean, safe, and secure?
- *Appreciation*: The feeling of the levels of welcome and hospitality contribute to this attribute. Do visitors feel welcome and receive good service in the destination?
- *Action*: The availability of a long-term tourism plan and a marketing plan for tourism are some of the required actions. Is the tourism development and marketing in the destination well-planned?
- *Accountability*: This attribute is about the evaluation of performance by the DMO. Is the DMO measuring the effectiveness of its performance?

You will notice that some of these As relate to the destination product, including access, appearance, attractiveness, activities, assurance, and appreciation. Others are related to destination planning, marketing, and management (awareness, availability, action, and accountability) (Figure 1.24).

Think about This

1. How important is it for a destination to make a positive first impression on visitors (appearance)?
2. What roles can local people play in demonstrating to visitors that they are appreciated?
3. What should destinations do to assure visitors of their safety and security?
4. Are there other success criteria for destinations that you feel should be added to the 10 As?

Source

Morrison, A. M. 2013. *Marketing and Managing Tourism Destinations*. London: Routledge.

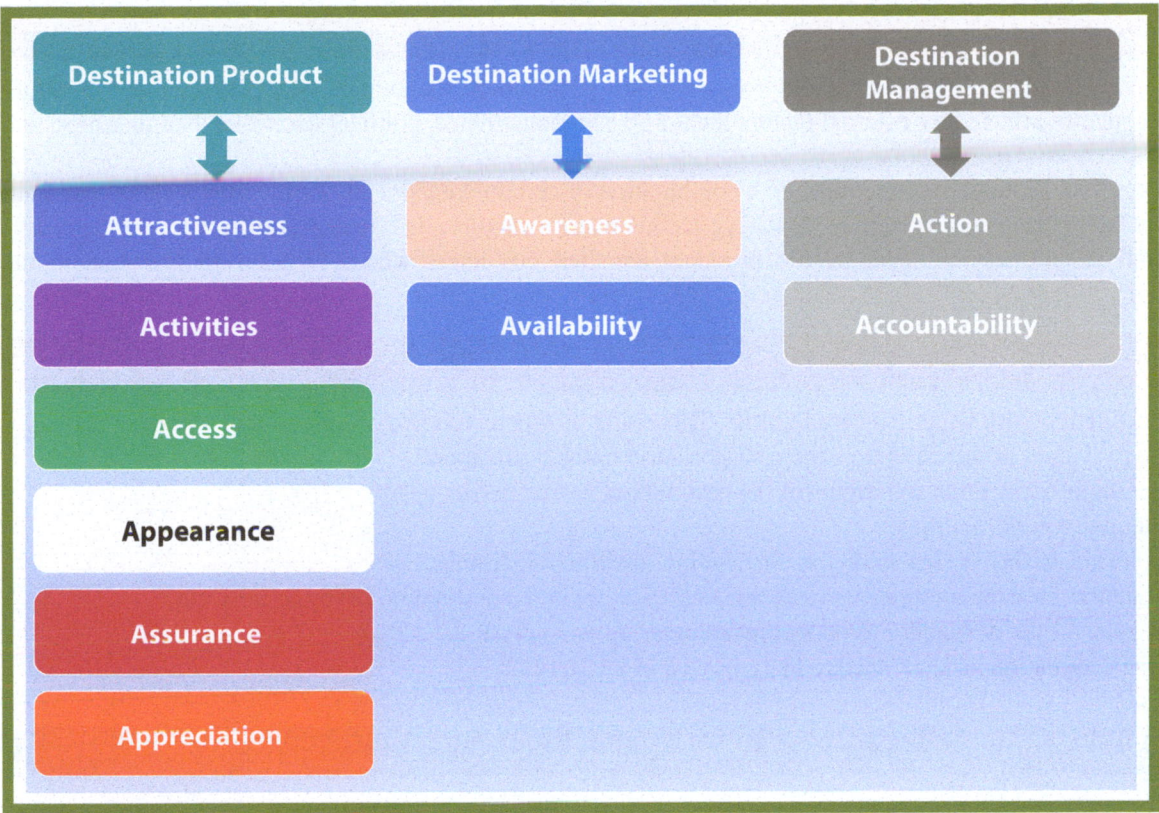

FIGURE 1.24 The 10 As of successful destinations.

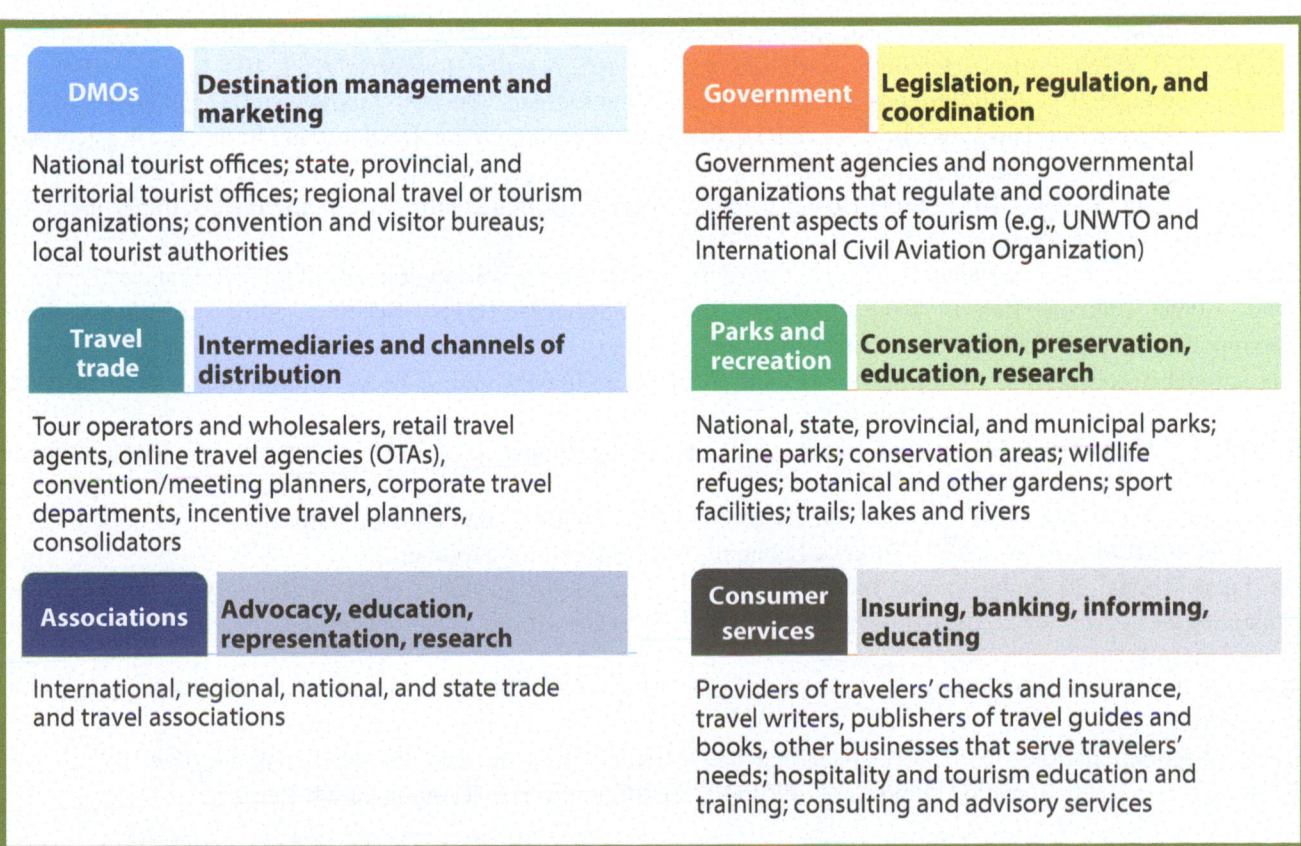

FIGURE 1.25 Other players involved in tourism.

SUMMARY

Tourism is a phenomenon that should be viewed from a systems perspective. The tourism system is open and therefore is easily and frequently affected by external factors including economic trends, political decisions, health scares, and natural disasters.

To be a successful destination there must be a combination of certain components. Attractions, events, and built facilities are needed to bring people in, they must have adequate infrastructure and transportation to support them. Service quality and friendliness of local people produces satisfied customers who will want to recommend the destination.

ACTIVITIES

1. Choose a destination with which you are familiar. This could be where you live or a place that you have visited.
2. Who are the providers of infrastructure and transportation in the destination?
3. What are the major attractions and events of the destination?
4. What are the major built facilities?
5. How do you evaluate the service quality and friendliness within the destination?
6. Do the destination product components integrate well together in the destination? Why or why not?
7. Are there aspects of the destination product that are missing and need to be added?
8. How does the destination product need to be improved in the future?

REFERENCES

Barclays. 2014. UK Tourism Dynamics. https://www.barclayscorporate.com/insight-and-research/uk-regional/uk-tourism-dynamics.html

BestCities Global Alliance. 2017. About us. http://www.bestcities.net/about-us/.

Cudny, W. 2016. *Festivalisation of Urban Spaces*. Switzerland: Springer Geography.

Getz, D. 2008. Event tourism: Definition, evolution, and research. *Tourism Management*, 29, 403-428.

Getz, D., and Page, S. J. 2016. Progress and prospects for event tourism. *Tourism Management*, 52, 593–631.

Global Sustainable Tourism Council. 2017. GSTC-Recognized Standards for Destinations. https://www.gstcouncil.org/gstc-criteria/gstc-destination-criteria/

go2HR Tourism Society. 2017. SuperHost Customer Service Training. https://www.go2hr.ca/training/superhost-customer-service-training

Gunn, C. A. 1994. *Tourism Planning: Basics, Concepts, Cases*, 3rd ed. Washington, DC: Taylor & Francis.

Hong Kong Tourism Board. 2017. Quality Tourism Services (QTS) Scheme. http://www.discoverhongkong.com/us/plan-your-trip/qts-scheme/index.jsp

International Association of Amusement Parks and Attractions (IAAPA). 2017. IAAPA Facts. http://www.iaapa.org/about-iaapa/history-facts/iaapa-facts

International Council of Shopping Centers. 2017. Shopping Center Definitions. https://www.icsc.org/research/references/c-shopping-center-definitions

International Monetary Fund. 2017. Turkey's economy hit by declining tourism. https://www.imf.org/en/News/Articles/2017/02/21/NA230217Turkeys-Economy-Hit-By-Declining-Tourism

The Japan Times. 2017. Japan saw record foreign visitors, tourist spending in 2016. January 17. https://www.japantimes.co.jp/news/2017/01/17/national/japan-saw-record-foreign-visitors-tourist-spending-2016/#.Wa_jJcgjHn1

Leiper, N. 1990. *Tourism Systems: An Interdisciplinary Perspective*. Palmerston North, New Zealand: Massey University.

Luxury Accommodations. 2017. Understanding the different types of accommodations in tourism. http://www.luxuryaccommodationsblog.com/post/114961446726/different-types-accommodation-tourism

Mealey, L. 2017. 10 things you should know about restaurant concepts. *The Balance*, May 29. https://www.thebalance.com/about-restaurant-concepts-2888685

Mirani, L. 2015. Helsinki's free, city-wide Wi-Fi network is faster than your home internet. Quartz. https://qz.com/414061/helsinkis-free-city-wide-wi-fi-network-is-faster-than-your-home-internet/

Morrison, A. M. 2013. *Marketing and Managing Tourism Destinations*. London: Routledge.

Osborne, S., and Markowitz, S. 2017. U.S. Travel and Tourism Satellite Accounts for 2013–2016. U.S. Bureau of Economic Analysis. https://www.bea.gov/scb/pdf/2017/06%20June/0617_travel_and_tourism_satellite_accounts.pdf

State Council of the Peoples Republic of China. 2017. China tourism revenue grows fast in 2016. http://english.gov.cn/archive/statistics/2017/01/09/content_281475537285546.htm

Statistics Canada. 2017. Statistics by Subject—Domestic Travel. http://www.statcan.gc.ca/eng/subjects/travel_and_tourism/domestic_travel

Statistics New Zealand. 2017. Tourism Satellite Account: 2016. The contribution made by tourism to the New Zealand Economy. http://m.stats.govt.nz/browse_for_stats/industry_sectors/Tourism/tourism-satellite-account-2016.aspx

Tourism New Zealand. 2017. Visitor Information Centres. http://www.newzealand.com/int/visitor-information-centre/

Tourism Research Australia, Austrade. 2017. National Visitor Survey Results. https://www.tra.gov.au/research/domestic-tourism-by-australians/domestic-tourism-statistics/domestic-tourism-statistics

TradeShowExective.com. 2015. North America's largest convention centers. http://www.tradeshowexecutive.com/pdf/convcenters/TSX-ConvCenters_2015-08.pdf

UNWTO. 2010. *Understanding Tourism: Basic Glossary*. Madrid, Spain: UN World Tourism Organization.

UNWTO. 2014. Global Report on Shopping Tourism. Madrid, Spain: UN World Tourism Organization.

UNWTO. 2017. UNWTO Tourism Highlights: 2017 Edition. http://www.e-unwto.org/doi/book/10.18111/9789284419029

UNWTO. 2017. UNWTO World Tourism Barometer. Volume 15. June 2017.

U.S. Census Bureau. 2017. North American Industry Classification System. https://www.census.gov/eos/www/naics/

U.S. Travel Association. 2017. Travel: America's Unsung Hero of Job Creation. https://www.ustravel.org/research/travel-americas-unsung-hero-job-creation

Vegter, O. 2016. How important are tourist attractions for a country's economy? *Quora*, March 12. https://www.quora.com/How-important-are-tourist-attractions-for-a-countrys-economy

Von Bertalanffy, L. 1973. *General Systems Theory: Foundations, Development, Applications*. New York: G. Braziller.

Wells, A. T., and J. G. Wensveen. 2003. *Air Transportation: A Management Perspective*. 5th ed. Pacific Grove, CA: Brooks/Cole Cengage Learning.

World Travel & Tourism Council. 2017. *Travel & Tourism Global Economic Impact & Issues 2017*. London: WTTC.

ADDITIONAL RESOURCES

Barcellona, N. 2016. 15 different types of restaurant concepts. Forketers. http://www.forketers.com/offline-marketing/types-restaurant-concepts/1544/

Bay of Fundy Tourism Partnership. 2017. About us. http://bayoffundytourism.com/about/

Dinner in the Sky. 2017. Dinner in the Sky. http://dinnerinthesky.com/

U.S. Travel Association. 2017. Travel Volume to and within the United States. https://www.ustravel.org/system/files/Media%20Root/Document/Research_Fact-Sheet_US-Travel-and-Tourism-Overview.pdf

CHAPTER TWO

Tourism Impacts
The Need for Sustainable Tourism

Take only memories, leave only footprints

CHIEF SEATTLE

YOUR LEARNING DESTINATION

You will be able to identify the impacts of tourism—positive and negative—and explain how tourism has the potential to help solve some of the challenges facing the world and to meet some of the sustainable development goals. You'll be able to describe the key principles of sustainable tourism development.

WHAT YOU NEED TO KNOW

Having read this chapter, you will be able to:

- ✓ Explain the principles of sustainability and sustainable tourism.
- ✓ Explain the three major economic impacts of tourism on destination areas and how these impacts are measured.
- ✓ Describe the strategies to maximize the economic impact of tourism and how tourism's role in economic development can be analyzed.
- ✓ Discuss the potentially positive and negative social and cultural impacts of tourism on destination areas.
- ✓ Describe the potentially positive and negative environmental impacts of tourism on destination areas.
- ✓ Examine tourism impacts from a systems perspective.
- ✓ Identify ways you can positively impact the world when you travel.

BREAKING THE ICE

Is tourism a good thing? Over one billion people traveled internationally each year since 2012, according to the United Nations World Tourism Organization (2017). Those travelers spent in excess of $US 1 trillion (yes—with a T). And international travelers are just the tip of the iceberg. In most destinations, domestic travel represents a far greater percentage of the overall travel undertaken than international travel. Some people estimate that each year there are more than 6 billion trips. All those people traveling make an impact! Is the impact of all those people traveling a positive? It depends.

Tourism can enrich destination communities, encourage preservation of natural places, and encourage the celebration of culture and heritage. But it can also lead to exploitation, degradation of the environment, and destruction of traditional ways of life. The big challenge for tourism is to ensure we maximize the benefits and minimize the negatives. Tourism can be a force for good in this world—helping to solve some of the grand challenges facing humanity—but that doesn't just happen. In this chapter we'll check out some of the ways tourism can have a negative impact and how it can be a force for good.

KEY TAKEAWAY POINTS

- Tourism has significant impacts. Ensuring the benefits of tourism are achieved and the potential negatives of tourism are minimized requires action by members throughout the tourism system.

- Tourism can generate economic activity, attract money from outside the destination, and generate jobs. It can generate tax revenues for governments—often reducing the tax burden on destination communities. Nevertheless, there are costs associated with tourism, and efforts must be made to reduce "leakage" to ensure that the greatest benefits are achieved.

- Tourism changes societies.

- Tourism can assist in the preservation of heritage and culture but may also lead to commodification of culture and reduced cultural authenticity.

- Tourism tends to use higher amounts of resources like energy and water than other activities do; it also produces waste.

- Tourism may place greater pressure on ecosystems or contribute to the preservation and conservation of natural places and biodiversity.

- Measuring the impacts of tourism requires understanding both the direct and indirect impacts.

- Travelers, including you, can make a real difference when they travel.

SUSTAINABILITY AND TOURISM

"Sustainability" is a concept that is often discussed but rarely defined, so confusion around the topic is common. For many people, sustainability is just about environmental issues, and there is no doubt that ensuring the quality of the environment is an important element of sustainability. But constraining the discussion to just the environment misses other important dimensions of sustainability.

Many definitions of sustainability are based on the definition of sustainable development proposed in the report "Our Common Future." It says sustainable development "meets the needs of the present without compromising the ability of future generations to meet their own needs" (WCED 1987). A second important concept commonly incorporated in definitions of sustainability is looking beyond only economic considerations and considering social and environmental impacts of tourism. Of course, impacts can be positive or negative, and one way to conceptualize the balancing of the potential impacts is to use a triple bottom line (TBL) approach. The "triple bottom line" borrows from the profit and loss statement in accounting. A profit and loss report looks at the positives (revenues) and negatives (expenses) and shows if the company is making a profit (more positives than negatives) or a loss (more negatives than positives). The triple bottom line looks at positives and negatives along three dimensions: economic, social or cultural,

FIGURE 2.1 Leaving only footprints is a challenge for even the most responsible travelers.

QUICK TRIP 2.1

The Global Impact of Tourism

Both the United Nations World Tourism Organization and the World Travel and Tourism Council recognize the global value of tourism. The United Nations World Tourism Organization is the United Nations agency responsible for promoting responsible, sustainable, and universally accessible tourism. The World Travel and Tourism Council is a group of CEOs from all sectors of tourism with the objective of promoting awareness of travel and tourism's economic contribution, expanding markets in harmony with the environment, and to reduce barriers to growth.

The UNWTO highlights the value of tourism in its infographic—*Why tourism matters.*

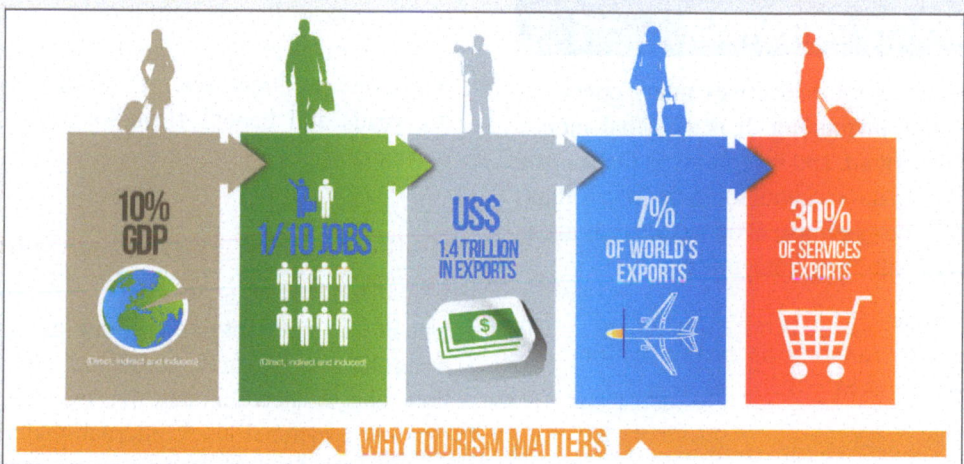

World Tourism Organization (2016), "Why Tourism Matters", infographic (online) available at: www.unwto.org.
© UNWTO, 92844/49/17.

In 2012 WTTC released a report highlighting the economic advantages of travel and tourism. Important findings from the study included:

- Tourism outperforms many other sectors of the economy. It contributes more to global GDP than the automotive manufacturers, mining, communications, or financial sector
- Drives foreign trade
- Encourages investment
- Encourages infrastructure development
- Spurs broader economic growth

The WTTC projects that in the ten years to 2027 tourism will grow to 11.4 percent of global GDP and employ (directly or indirectly) 11 percent of the world's workers.

Think about This

1. What are the potential benefits to tourism that result from the publication of these UNWTO or WTTC statistics?
2. Because the WTTC figures are published by an organization that represents tourism companies and organizations, there is some level of skepticism about the magnitude of some of the estimates. What can the WTTC do to enhance the credibility of these results?
3. Which of the above results do you feel are the most impressive and why?
4. Many tourism experts have argued that tourism does not get enough recognition and respect as a serious economic activity. How would you use the UNWTO or WTTC figures to argue the case that tourism deserves great recognition and respect from governments and other elements of society?

Sources

United Nations World Tourism Organization. 2017. http://media.unwto.org/content/infographics

World Travel and Tourism Corporation. 2012. Comparative Economic Impact of Travel and Tourism.

World Travel and Tourism Corporation. 2017. Travel and Tourism Economic Impact 2017 World.

and environmental. These three dimensions are sometimes described simply as profit, people, and planet. These three dimensions are not discrete or separate—they overlap—but the triple bottom line approach provides a good way to conceptualize the many trade-offs in considering the impacts of tourism.

In the next section, you will learn how tourism impacts the economy, society and culture, particularly in destination communities, and the environment.

ECONOMIC IMPACTS OF TOURISM

The economic value of tourism drives many conversations about the value of tourism. It is said that money makes the world go 'round, and it certainly is the starting point for many conversations about tourism. Tourism has several potential economic impacts on destination areas. Generally, these fall into three categories:

1. Increasing income
2. Increasing money from outside the destination
3. Increasing employment

Increasing Income

Most tourism businesses operate "for profit," and tourism generates revenues or income within the destination. In fact, the benefits of tourism expenditures go beyond the money visitors spend directly with members of the tourism system. The tourism businesses themselves create economic activity to serve the visitors. Consider this scenario: Visitors make an initial round of expenditures in the destination area. These expenditures may be for lodging, food, beverages, entertainment, clothing, gifts and souvenirs, personal care, medicines, cosmetics, photography, recreation, tours, sightseeing, guides, local transportation, and miscellaneous other items. These expenditures are received as income by local tour operators, handicraft sellers, hotel operators, restaurants, and other tourism businesses. In the second round of expenditures, the tourism businesses use some of the money to purchase goods, pay wages and salaries, and for other expenses. The income in the next (third) round may be spent or saved. For example, employees who have received wages or salaries may spend some of that on rent or food, and they may put some into their savings. The money paid for goods in the third round may be spent on the producer's raw materials such as seed, fertilizer, and other imported materials.

- **Government revenues from tourism income**

Governments can benefit from tourism through both the direct and indirect expenditures of tourism. Anyone who as paid a tax on their airline ticket or when they checked out of a hotel knows that tourism is taxed directly. These funds may go back to general funds that pay for public services like schools and police, or they may be allocated to tourism promotion. Indirect government revenues are generated by the taxes paid on goods and services provided to visitors. Many destinations highlight the tax that their local constituents don't have to pay because of the tax paid by visitors. Of course, tourism and travelers have costs for destinations. Travelers use public resources when they visit; for example, they use roads and benefit from local policing and other services.

Increasing Money from Outside the Destination

One of the important things about tourism is that visitors bring their money from home and spend it in a destination. This is "new" money that expands the local economy. At a national level, international visitors spending money in a foreign destination are generating foreign exchange earnings for the host country. In this way, the money that international visitors spend in a destination can be considered "exports," in the same way as the money that is received when a company sells its products in a foreign country. It is perhaps easiest to think of this "new money" from the point of view of international travel and the foreign exchange earnings it generates. Even so, many of the principles discussed at a national level can be applied to smaller destinations where visitor spending merely comes from another part of the country.

Economic Leakage. One of the challenges of maximizing the benefits of tourism is *ensuring that money stays in the destination*. When small businesses buy from other local small businesses, they keep the money in the local economy. This is called reducing "economic leakage." Of course, any money spent on products and services from outside the community leaks out of the destination's economy. Some tourism operations are criticized for not engaging with the local economy and not ensuring that economic benefits stay with local people. *"Enclave"* tourism is when visitors stay on the cruise ship or at the all-inclusive resorts where all their needs are provided for and local businesses have little ability to interact with visitors. All-inclusive resorts and cruise companies can address these issues by developing supply-chain strategies that ensure local companies provide goods and services for the visitors.

Investment. In addition to the money spent by travelers, tourism can also encourage investment in the destination. This type of investment can be an important stimulant of economic activity. In some cases, this can include foreign direct investment. While such investment is often attractive to destinations, strategies to ensure that the investments meet the best practices of sustainable development are important. Many destinations seek to attract investment through tax rebates and commitment to infrastructure development—roads, airports, and the like. These commitments need to be carefully weighed against the benefits the new investment will generate.

Increasing Employment

A major argument for encouraging tourism development is that it produces many jobs. Tourism creates primary or *direct employment* in areas such as lodging, restaurants, attractions, transportation, and sightseeing operations. Secondary or *indirect employment* is also created in construction, agriculture, and manufacturing. The amount of indirect employment depends on the extent to which tourism is integrated with the rest of the

local economy. The more integration and diversification that occurs, the more indirect employment is generated.

Tourism is considered to be more *labor-intensive* than other industries. For this reason, it is often argued that tourism deserves special developmental support. The degree of labor intensity can be measured in terms of the cost per job created or the employment/output ratio. The employment/output ratio is the number of workers employed divided by the contribution of tourism to the national income. Although research conclusions are not unanimous, the cost per job created in tourism has been found to be no less than in other economic sectors. A major reason is because tourism is also *capital-intensive*. The heavy costs of providing necessary infrastructure and building structures drastically increase the costs of creating jobs.

At different stages of a tourism area's lifecycle—a topic we will discuss in more detail in Chapter 5—the costs of creating jobs change. In the early stages of tourism development, the cost per job created is likely to be high due to the capital costs required. Similarly, the capital/output ratio is high because of the low volume of visitors in the initial stages of tourism development. As the destination country develops and as more visitors are attracted, the capital/output ratio declines. The cost per job created is reduced due to the experience and organization of those in the destination.

FIGURE 2.2 A visitor's purchase of local handicrafts indirectly affects other sectors of the economy.

QUICK TRIP 2.2

The Impacts of Tourism on the United States

The U.S. Travel Association advocates for the travel industry in the United States. The *U.S. Travel Answer Sheet: Facts About A Leading American Industry That's More than Just Fun* provides a great overview of the value of tourism to the United States. It provides the following data on the impact of travel:

- $2.3 trillion: Economic output generated by domestic and international visitors
- 15.3 million: Jobs supported by travel expenditures
- $248.2 billion: Wages shared by American workers employed directly in tourism
- 2.7%: Percent of the nation's gross domestic product (GDP) attributed to travel and tourism.
- $1,250: Amount in additional taxes for each household without tax revenue from travel and tourism.

These benefits are impressive and it is the role of the USTA to make sure that the key stakeholders—including members of government, policy makers, and business people—are aware of the tourism industry. Tourism is sometimes called the "invisible industry" and it is the role of U.S. Travel to make it visible.

In addition to providing important research for the tourism industry, U.S. Travel has a number of advocacy campaigns and programs dealing with issues impacting tourism. Some advocacy campaigns target lawmakers and policy makers but others target business leaders. Some recent campaigns address the following:

- improved aviation and surface transportation infrastructure.
- improved customs and entry processes and visa reform.
- the importance of meetings. With pressure on the meetings industry following the financial crisis and the more meetings taking place virtually, U.S. Travel responded with a campaign that highlighted the value of face-to-face meetings. The ongoing campaign is called "**Meetings mean Business.**"

- the importance of taking time off. With the trend for Americans to take fewer vacations, Project: Time Off has stimulated a conversation about the importance of taking vacation and the benefits for individuals and families but also business profitability.

Empowering key stakeholders to act on these issues in concert with USTA is an important role of the organization. USTA brings together coalitions of stakeholders to work on addressing these issues. These advocacy campaigns often involve the development of special tools—like press kits, factsheets, talking points, websites, prepared social media postings, and infographics—for use by stakeholders.

Think about This

1. This is a good example of a carefully integrated communications program by a tourism association to increase awareness of the positive impacts of tourism. Why do you think it is necessary to have such a program to explain tourism's benefits?
2. Take a detailed look at the *Meetings Mean Business Coalition* website. How does the website explain the benefits of the meetings sector of tourism?
3. Take a detailed look at the Power of Travel Coalition website. What are the major purposes of this website and why is it needed?
4. Compared to other major nations of the world, the United States government does not place as high a priority on tourism. Why do you think this is so?

Sources

U.S. Travel Association. 2017. https://www.ustravel.org/programs/meetings-mean-business-coalition

U.S. Travel Association. 2017. https://www.ustravel.org/programs/power-travel-coalition

U.S. Travel Association. 2017. U.S. Travel Answer Sheet.

U.S. TRAVEL ANSWER SHEET
FACTS ABOUT A LEADING AMERICAN INDUSTRY THAT'S MORE THAN JUST FUN

 LEISURE TRAVEL

- Direct spending on leisure travel by domestic and international travelers totaled **$683.1 billion** in 2016.
- Spending on leisure travel generated **$106.4 billion** in tax revenue.
- **Nearly 4 out of 5** domestic trips taken are for leisure purposes (79%).
- U.S. residents logged **1.7 billion** person-trips* for leisure purposes in 2016.
- Top leisure travel activities for U.S. domestic travelers: (1) visiting relatives; (2) shopping; (3) visiting friends; (4) fine dining; and (5) rural sightseeing.

BUSINESS TRAVEL
(Including Meetings, Events and Incentive)

- Direct spending on business travel by domestic and international travelers, including expenditures on meetings, events and incentive programs (ME&I), totaled **$307.2 billion** in 2016.
- ME&I travel accounted for **$127.1 billion** of all business travel spending.
- U.S. residents logged **457.4 million** person-trips* for business purposes in 2016, with 38% for meetings and events.
- For every dollar invested in business travel, businesses benefit from an average of **$9.50** in increased revenue and **$2.90** in new profits *(2012)*.

*Person-trip defined as one person on a trip away from home overnight in paid accommodations or on a day or overnight trip to places 50 miles or more [one-way] away from home.

U.S. TRAVEL INDUSTRY IMPACT

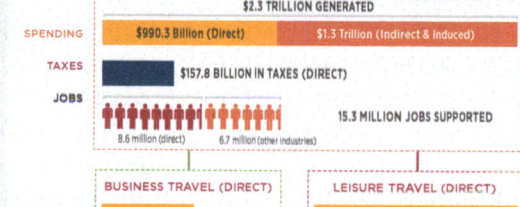

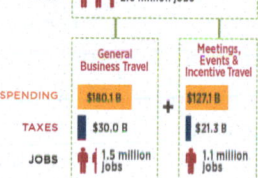

Each U.S. household would pay **$1,250** more in taxes without the tax revenue generated by travel and tourism.

Source: U.S. Travel Association
Note: Direct spending totals do not include international passenger fares.

 = 1 million jobs

SOURCES OF TRAVEL SPENDING

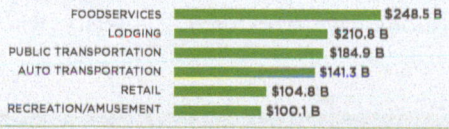

FOODSERVICES	$248.5 B
LODGING	$210.8 B
PUBLIC TRANSPORTATION	$184.9 B
AUTO TRANSPORTATION	$141.3 B
RETAIL	$104.8 B
RECREATION/AMUSEMENT	$100.1 B

TOTAL: $990.3 billion

Source: U.S. Travel Association

 ## INTERNATIONAL TRAVEL

- In 2016, U.S. Travel Exports (includes general travel spending, international passenger fares, as well as international traveler spending on medical, educational and cross-border/seasonal work-related activities) totaled **$246 billion**. International Travel Imports totaled **$159 billion**, creating a **$87 billion** travel trade surplus.
- International arrivals to the U.S. declined by **2.4 percent** and totaled **75.6 million** in 2016. Of those, approximately **37.6 million** came from overseas markets and **38.0 million** were from Canada and Mexico.
- The United States' share of total international arrivals is **6.1%** (down from **7.5%** in 2000).

- International travel spending directly supported about **1.2 million** U.S. jobs and **$32.4 billion** in wages.
- Each overseas traveler spends approximately **$4,360** when they visit the U.S. and stay on average **18 nights**.
- Overseas arrivals represent **50%** of all international arrivals, yet account for **85.3%** of total international travel spending.
- Top leisure travel activities for overseas visitors: (1) shopping; (2) sightseeing; (3) fine dining; (4) national parks/monuments; and (5) amusement/theme parks.

TOP 5 INTERNATIONAL MARKETS TO THE U.S. (2016 ARRIVALS)

ORIGIN OF VISITOR	2016
Canada	19.3 million
Mexico	18.7 million
United Kingdom	4.6 million
Japan	3.6 million
China	3.0 million

TOP 5 HIGH-GROWTH TRAVEL MARKETS THRU 2021 *(forecasted)*

ORIGIN OF VISITOR	ARRIVALS % CHANGE '21/'15
China	121%
India	72%
Argentina	50%
South Korea	43%
Taiwan	40%

Source: U.S. Department of Commerce – National Travel and Tourism Office

Direct spending by resident and international travelers in the U.S. averaged $2.7 billion a day, $113.1 million an hour, $1.9 million a minute and $31,400 a second.

1100 New York Avenue, NW Suite 450 Washington, D.C. 20005 | TEL 202.408.8422 | ustravel.org | CONNECT WITH US

BY THE NUMBERS
(all data 2016 unless indicated otherwise)

$2.3 trillion: Economic output generated by domestic and international visitors (includes $990.3 billion in direct travel expenditures that spurred an additional $1.3 trillion in other industries)

15.3 million: Jobs supported by travel expenditures (includes 8.6 million directly in the travel industry and 6.7 million in other industries)

$248.2 billion: Wages shared by American workers directly employed by travel

$157.8 billion: Tax revenue generated by travel spending for federal, state and local governments

2.7%: Percentage of nation's gross domestic product (GDP) attributed to travel and tourism

1 out of 9: U.S. jobs that depend on travel and tourism

No. 7: Where travel ranks in terms of employment compared to other major private industry sectors

84%: Percentage of travel companies that are considered small businesses *(2012)*

2.2 billion: Number of person-trips* that Americans took for business and leisure purposes

75.6 million: Estimated number of international arrivals in the U.S. in 2016, including 37.6 million from overseas markets

Travel is among the **top 10 industries** in 49 states and D.C. in terms of employment

In addition, as tourism increases, physical development takes place in facilities that require less investment than the construction of international-level hotels and resorts. Jobs are created at a lower average cost. In the third stage of tourism development, the average cost per job created may increase due to higher land prices and increased engineering costs because of the necessity of using sites that are more difficult to develop. In addition, as tourism increases in importance, more infrastructure (roads, electrical and sewerage services, etc.) may be necessary as the tourism plant becomes more spread out geographically. The increased demand for infrastructure may be caused by the larger numbers of visitors in the destination area.

The cost per job created depends on the type of facility constructed. For example, the cost is greater for a luxury hotel than for a smaller, more modest property. However, a luxury hotel offers more job opportunities per room and higher employment/output ratios than smaller properties. The larger properties are more inclined to use imported labor, especially for managerial positions. The key to maximizing the economic and job returns is to use materials and personnel indigenous to the destination area while maintaining standards of quality acceptable to visitors. To maximize employment benefits of tourism, many destinations have workforce development plans that ensure local people can contribute at all levels of the business—from entry level to senior management.

Tourism is a *highly seasonal business* in many destinations. To ensure a balance between market demand and staff requirements, tourism businesses tend to adopt one of two strategies. Employees are either laid off during the low season, or additional employees are imported from other regions during the high season. With the first approach, tourism cannot provide a meaningful job to a resident. With the second approach, there is an increased need for housing for employees who spend most of their wages outside of the destination area. Thus, jobs and income are lost to the local area. One of the challenges of sustainability in tourism destinations is developing strategies to mitigate seasonality and create year-round jobs.

One advantage of tourism-related jobs is that they are often *place-based* and *hard to outsource*. Tourism experiences are consumed in the destination, and people are needed to deliver that service. On the other hand, because tourism relies so heavily on people to deliver a service, productivity gains are difficult to come by. It may be difficult to improve the national output if tourism becomes a dominant part of the economy, particularly if the host destination lacks a strong industrial sector, where productivity gains are easier to obtain.

FIGURE 2.3 Tourism creates jobs in a variety of sectors including hotels and lodging.

Plugging "Leaks" to Maximize Economic Benefits

When people visit a destination and spend money, they add to the destination economy. But there are costs in other locations associated with attracting the visitors that are spent, and some of the money visitors spend leaves the destination economy to pay for things that aren't produced in the destination. The money that leaves the economy in this way is called "leakage." Leakage happens in all destination economies and the concept can be applied to all types of destination, but it is most clearly observed at the national level where countries monitor foreign exchange earnings. Economic leakage from tourism destination economies occurs from at least six factors. The extent to which a destination can minimize leakage will determine the size of the foreign exchange earnings.

1. Leakage occurs first from the cost of goods and services that must be purchased to satisfy the needs of visitors. If a Japanese visitor wants to eat sushi or sashimi, and if the fish and seafood have to be imported, the costs of the fish and seafood are import costs that must be deducted from earnings. Local manufacturing or handicraft industries may also import part of their raw materials to produce goods for visitors. This is a cost that needs to be subtracted from the foreign exchange earnings from souvenir sales and the sales of other locally produced products.

2. A second leakage occurs when importing goods and materials for infrastructure and buildings required for tourism development. The use of materials indigenous to the host destination not only reduces import costs but also adds a distinctive look to the local architecture and building interiors.

3. Payments to foreign *factors of production* represent a third leakage. Commissions have to be paid to overseas tour operators and travel agents. If foreign capital is invested in the country's tourism, interest payments, rent, and profits may have to be paid to those outside the country. The amount of local ownership and control is crucial in this regard. Foreign-owned chain hotels will often be staffed, stocked, and furnished by people, food, furnishings, fixtures, and equipment from the home country.

4. A fourth leakage is the expenditure for promotion, public relations, or publicity, and similar services abroad. The cost of maintaining a national tourist office (NTO) in an origin country can be substantial and needs to be set against the foreign exchange earnings from that country.

5. Fifth, there are several ways that *transfer pricing* can reduce foreign exchange earnings. If visitors make purchases in the country of origin for services to be delivered at the destination, the transfer payments need not be made for the services provided. If a tourism company is multinational, payments may be recorded in the country of visitor origin rather than in the destination country, thereby reducing profits and taxes in the destination country. As mentioned earlier, this has been the case with Japanese travelers to Australia who often purchase their packages from Japanese tour operators who buy services from Japanese-owned hotels, resorts, and attractions located in Australia. Purchases by a foreign-owned hotel within the host country may be made from a foreign-owned subsidiary at inflated rates to reduce the taxable income in the destination country. The use of credit cards and traveler's checks can mean that local banks are not able to participate in the exchange.

6. Sixth, foreign exchange earnings can be reduced when host governments exempt duties or taxes for foreign-owned companies or offer financial inducements to attract investment.

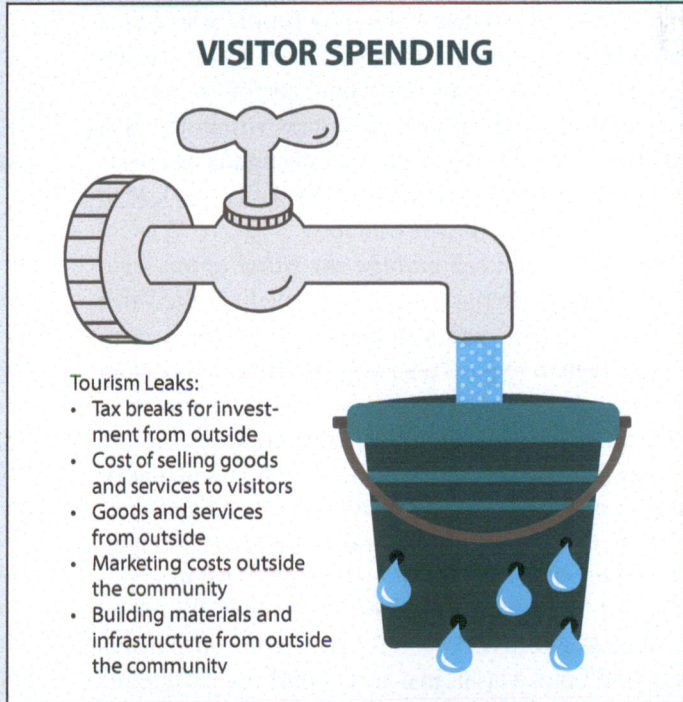

VISITOR SPENDING

Tourism Leaks:
- Tax breaks for investment from outside
- Cost of selling goods and services to visitors
- Goods and services from outside
- Marketing costs outside the community
- Building materials and infrastructure from outside the community

FIGURE 2.4   Sources of economic leakage.

TOURISM CHANGES SOCIETIES

Tourism development can change the economic structure of a destination area. Although such changes can easily be integrated into the economy of a developed nation, the effects in a lesser-developed country are more profound. Stresses can occur when the old and the new exist side by side. Traditional methods of farming and primitive industries contrast with modern hotels and polished entertainment for visitors. This may cause a movement away from traditional forms of employment. The fisherman turned tour-boat entrepreneur and farm girl turned waitress undergo not only a change in income but also a change in status. The fisherman's catch is lost to the local people, but his own income may increase. The waitress may view her task of serving as a throwback to earlier colonial times, or she may look at the newfound job as a cleaner and less arduous way to earn a living. The satisfaction for locals may depend on the range and type of jobs available and the opportunity for advancement.

As with any other economic development, tourism encourages *workforce migration*, with the corresponding possibility of breaking down the traditional family unit. It does appear that even though migration occurs, family ties and responsibilities are maintained.

Tourism development can cause profound changes within a society in terms of **economic power**. Tourism businesses attract women and young people who gain a higher level of economic independence. Great tension can occur, particularly in traditional societies, because of this shift in the economic resources within the host destination. This doesn't mean that change is necessarily bad—empowering women and minorities can lead to positive outcomes in the host society.

Finally, tourism can *change the value of land* and land ownership patterns. As tourism develops, the value of potential sites increases and land speculation occurs. Some destination regions take steps to prevent unhealthy land speculation. Land sold to outsiders results in a short-term profit to the local landowner. However, the land may be lost forever to agricultural production or local recreational use, and control of the land goes outside of the community. Tourism may force local indigenous people off of their traditional lands. Such has been the fate of the Masai tribes of Kenya and Tanzania. According to Krotz (1996) , "Tourism is the push that is chasing the Loita Masai, just as it is pushing indigenous local peoples in many places of the world."

Many impacts of tourism are direct (the raising of land values), whereas others are indirect (the demonstration effect when imports increase through local resident exposure to goods imported for visitor consumption). Many of these changes would occur no matter what type of economic development took place. Whether these changes are good or bad is often a value judgment. The important point is to realize that these impacts are likely to occur, decide whether or not they are desirable for the destination area, and plan accordingly.

SOCIAL AND CULTURAL IMPACTS OF TOURISM

Tourism impacts society—in particular, the people of the destination community. As we have mentioned, economic changes—even economic benefits—can affect elements of society. Tourism also brings together people from different backgrounds, and the interaction between host communities and visitors can create both benefits and conflicts.

In sociological terms, this means:

- Social relations between people who would not normally meet
- Confrontation of different cultures, ethnic and religious groups, values and lifestyles, languages and levels of prosperity
- Behavior of visitors, released from many of the social and economic constraints of everyday life
- The behavior of the host population, which has to reconcile economic gain and benefits with the costs of living with strangers

The interplay of these sociological factors leads to a variety of outcomes—some good and some not.

Clashing Cultures

One of the important reasons people travel is to meet new people and experience different cultures. Of course, the differences we seek when traveling can also be a source of friction between the host community and visitors. For instance, travelers may inadvertently *fail to respect local customs or moral values*, causing resentment in the destination community.

Many travelers visit countries or destinations with money in pocket, ready to find a good time, and they often behave in ways they wouldn't when they are at home. Travelers' *sense of entitlement* (but I should be able to do that—I'm on vacation!) may lead to resentment by the host community. The income disparity between visitors and the people of the host community can be significant and a source of tension.

Supporting Local Culture

Cultural assets—including intangible assets like dance, stories and legends, crafts, and styles of cooking—are important attractions in many destinations. In some cases, traditional ways and goods may be restored because willing buyers (visitors) can be found. The Aaraya women of Cuna, Panama, had to be taught to sew the traditional dress of their culture. The skill had been lost. In other areas, festivals are staged for visitors by the community—these festivals help to keep its culture alive. Thus, entertaining the visitor may be the impetus for the performing of cultural activities or the production of goods, but the effect on the local community is that of preserving part of the traditional culture. It is often hard to fully appreciate your own cultural assets—just ask anyone who has tried to hear their own accent. The process of considering the outsider can help local cultures more fully appreciate their own unique heritage. Recognizing that people from other parts of the world value your unique culture or local environment can stimulate community pride.

One challenge for destinations is maintaining their *cultural identity*. It is one of the ironies of tourism that we are attracted by things that are culturally different, but as tourism increases, many familiar elements of visitors' culture find their way to the destination community. Skyscrapers and highways, McDonalds, Starbucks, Hiltons, and Marriotts are all part of a *standardization* of destinations. As development takes place, destinations must work to ensure that the unique physical elements of their culture are maintained. Architecture, town planning, and the retail mix in shopping areas are all examples of areas that can be impacted by public policy to ensure cultural identity and "sense of place" is maintained.

Of course, there are challenges in representing culture for tourism. Sharing cultural rituals and festivals can lead to them being modified to appeal to visitors' sensibilities. This process is called *commodification*, where the cultural activity becomes a commodity to be sold. In preparing cultural activities to be shared with visitors, modifications are made to make them more

FIGURE 2.5 Cultural performances attract visitors and preserve local traditions.

HUMAN	SOCIAL	CULTURAL AND HERITAGE
Damage to family structures and subsistence food production	Encouragement of urbanization and emigration	Commercialization of traditional welcome and hospitality customs
Displacement of local people to make way for airports, resorts, nature reserves, historical and other attraction sites, and other tourism development projects	Friction between locals and visitors because of overcrowding and lack of access for residents to recreational areas	Loss of cultural authenticity (e.g., vulgarization of traditional crafts, importation of foreign cultural influences)
Encouragement of behaviors such as begging, touting, and other harassment of visitors	Increase in health risks through diseases such as AIDS and influenza	Overcrowding and damage to archaeological and historical sites and monuments
	Increase in drug abuse and prostitution	
	Open antagonism and crimes against visitors	

FIGURE 2.6 Potentially negative social and cultural impacts of tourism on a destination area.

QUICK TRIP 2.3

Tourism Breaking Down Barriers

Tourism has the ability to bring people together and to showcase the value of our unique cultural heritage. Despite being outlawed for decades, the caste system still has an impact on the people in countries like India and Nepal. People from the Dalit or Untouchable caste often face considerable hardship and exclusion even today. But in some places that is starting to change—in part because of the influence of tourism.

In the Aapsara Dalit Village, not far from the lakeside city of Pokhara, visitors can experience life in a traditional Nepalese village. Villagers welcome visitors into their homes and community and share aspects of traditional village life. Visitors meet the locals, share their foods, and learn farm skills and crafts. This is authentic, experiential travel at its best.

Preparing for visitors and gaining skills in providing quality homestay for visitors from around the world was part of a deliberate strategy by the people of the village to assist the economic development of the village. The group worked with a small NGO, Hands-On Institute, to develop their skills and the capacity of the village to meet the needs of their new guests. With the success of the program the villagers have found that they have benefited not only economically but socially as well. With the recognition of the program, Aapsara's villagers are being invited to participate in regional planning and governance activities.

Think about This

1. What challenges do community-based tourism products like this face?
2. In many places international visitors are often more interested in cultural activities—particularly involving indigenous or marginalized groups—than the locals. Why do you think that is?
3. After developing this product, the village must now attract visitors. How would you approach the promotion of this unique product?

Sources

https://sustainabletourismandresponsibletravel.com
http://www.onceinlife.org/

appealing to the visitors. Rituals that may have originally lasted for days may be reduced to forty-five minutes to accommodate visitors' time constraints. Some elements of the ritual may be maintained and the general approach could be considered "authentic," but not exactly as they happened. This modification is called "*staged authenticity*." Despite best intentions, authenticity of culture packaged for the visitor may be questionable. Many people feel that when a cultural event is prepared for visitor consumption, its original, often spiritual, meaning is lost. In some cases, adapting to tourism demands can lead to a *cultural involution*. The modernization of an area and a people can be halted due to visitor demand for the old ways. Tourism in essence can encourage local people to remain artisans at the expense of industrial modernization.

Ensuring that cultural *intellectual property*—the local knowledge of customs, remedies, and other heritage—is maintained by the host community is also important. Appropriation of cultural knowledge can rob local communities of their cultural heritage.

It is also important that planners of tourism ensure that the local community has *access to cultural assets*

and natural places. Local communities may be overwhelmed by visitor numbers at places that have special meaning or are sacred. Balancing travelers' desire to visit heritage sites as tourism attractions with locals' needs to use them for everyday life is a challenge that must be addressed.

While it is important to manage these issues, it is also important to remember that visitors can enrich the *quality of life of residents* in host communities. For instance, in London, England, many theaters can survive only because of the influx of visitors. In many destinations, restaurants that wouldn't be viable without visitors are enjoyed by locals. Infrastructure developed to serve tourism growth also improve the quality of life of residents.

Tourism can help communities by creating opportunities for residents and reducing the need for emigration from the destination community. For instance, tourism provides jobs for young people in rural destinations, thus reducing the need to leave home and go off to the city. This is true in rural locations all around the world, from small-town America to rural Nepal or Colombia.

© BLACKDAY/Shutterstock.com

FIGURE 2.7 Protecting heritage sites is an important part of sustainable tourism management.

Tourism and Crime

Tourism has the potential to increase levels of crime in destination communities. Certain types including theft and drug- and sex-related crimes are often prevalent in destinations attracting large numbers of visitors (and the criminals who cater to them). The sexual exploitation of women and children and people trafficking are significant issues in many destinations. Several international programs such as The Code, an industry-driven initiative designed to prevent the sexual exploitation of children, have become important tools in the reduction of these behaviors.

Some destinations recognize the specific needs of visitors and the types of crime that occur in places with large populations of visitors, so they have tourism-oriented policing programs. These police are trained to deal effectively with tourism-related crimes.

QUICK TRIP 2.4

Tourism Fighting Human Trafficking

Human trafficking, slavery, and the exploitation of children often seem like invisible problems but they are major concerns around the world—in both developed and developing countries. While tourism can be a force for good, it can also facilitate these activities and the members of the tourism system must be aware of the problems and be vigilant in preventing them.

Several sectors of the tourism system are working hard to address the problem. Frontline staff at hotels and transport providers are often the ones confronted by this problem. The American Hotel and Lodging Association (AHLA) is working with the Polaris Project to develop training for hotel workers to identify human trafficking. The Association of Flight Attendants is a partner in the US Department of Homeland Security's Blue Campaign—a program designed to end Human Trafficking.

The Code (Short for Code of Conduct for the protection of children from sexual exploitation on Travel in Tourism) is an international multi-stakeholder initiative to reduce sexual exploitation of children. They recommend companies in the tourism industry do the following six steps.

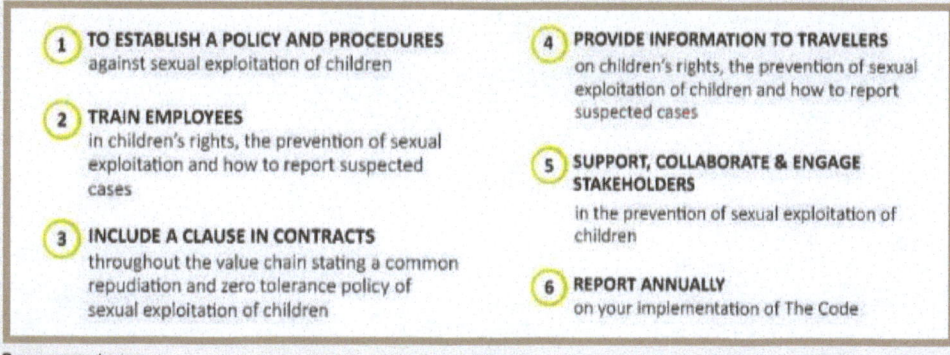

Source: code.org

Think about This

1. Why is the issue of human trafficking particularly important to the tourism system?
2. Go online and look at what major hotel companies are doing to eliminate human trafficking. Check out the Corporate Social Responsibility pages on the corporate websites. Do you think this is enough? What else do you think they should do?
3. If you were working in a hotel or transport provider how would you identify possible human trafficking and what would you do? Check your answers against recommendations from The Code or the Polaris Project.

Sources

http://www.thecode.org/about/
https://www.dhs.gov/blue-campaign#
https://polarisproject.org/

Tourism and Social Justice

Tourism can be a catalyst for social justice. Many tourism companies support social justice issues. For example, many hotel companies have corporate social responsibility programs that promote diversity and equality, provide job opportunities for at-risk youth, and support local philanthropy programs like Habitat for Humanity.

One special type of enterprise found on the tourism system are "*social enterprises*" that are established by social entrepreneurs to specifically address social issues in the destination community. These enterprises may be created to ensure "fair trade" prices to suppliers of tourism services or to provide opportunity for entrepreneurial members of the host community.

ENVIRONMENTAL IMPACTS OF TOURISM

Tourism impacts the environment in many ways. At a global level, tourism is known to contribute to climate change, and it is clear that tourism development often places pressure on ecosystems and biodiversity.

It is very difficult to "leave only footprints"—even for the most responsible of travelers. Providing services for travelers—from hotel rooms to transportation—requires use of resources that impact the environment. From the "big picture" perspective, the impact of tourism on energy use (particularly nonrenewable, carbon-based energy use), water use, and creation of waste are three core environmental concerns. Beyond these, specific destinations face important environmental issues.

Energy, Water, and Waste

Travelers tend to use more energy and water when they are "on the road" than when they are at home. As such, travelers tend to use more resources than non-travelers.

Some tourism system businesses, including hotels and restaurants, are heavy users of energy and water resources. Many tourism system companies are working hard to reduce their energy and water consumption. For example, most hotel companies have extensive programs to reduce energy consumption, with things like "linen reuse" programs that are just a small part of much larger programs.

Of course, companies undertake such programs for a variety of reasons, and reducing their operating costs is an important rationale for energy conservation and water reduction programs.

Greenhouse Gases

The use of carbon-based energy sources by the tourism system generates greenhouse gases (GHG) that are causing climate change. Tourism is believed to contribute approximately 5 percent of the GHG.

Aviation is the greatest source of GHG in the tourism system. Flying to your destination generates carbon and other GHG—some of which do more damage to the atmosphere than gases released on the ground. It is ironic that some of the "greenest" destinations require long-haul air travel. The second major source of GHG in the tourism system is buildings, including hotels (Day and Cai 2012).

Local Environmental Issues

It is true that often we "love our attractions to death." There are many cases around the world where tourism has been a direct contributor to environmental degradation. Often these negative impacts occur when the level of visitor use is greater than the environment's capacity to cope (known as the carrying capacity).

Researchers in the city of Sochi on Russia's Black Sea coast found that tourism was contributing to air and noise pollution in this resort area (Lukashina et al. 1996) Sewage pollution is a major problem for many older Mediterranean resort areas (Romeril 1989). The increasing popularity of trekking in Nepal's Annapurna region is leading to pollution along the trekking trails and contributing to deforestation. Further, the development of tourism is threatening the nesting sites of loggerhead turtles in Turkey and Greece (Doggart and Doggart 1996).

© Goncharovaia/Shutterstock.com

FIGURE 2.8 Tourism was found to contribute to pollution in Sochi, Russia.

FIGURE 2.9 Visitors visiting gorillas provide important resources to protect these beautiful apes.

Protecting Natural Ecosystems and Biodiversity

Tourism has a vested interest in the preservation of natural places and local biodiversity. Although tourism is increasingly being criticized for its adverse environmental effects, it can have positive impacts on the local ecology. For example, greater protection of specific ecosystems may ultimately support tourism. This may mean that other harmful economic activities, such as commercial fishing around reef systems, logging operations in forests, and excessive clearing and runoffs from agriculture may be limited or eliminated. Some of the visitor expenditures to enjoy natural environments may be reinvested in research and better conservation programs. A greater emphasis on the natural environment to support tourism may result in a greater understanding among local people of environmental issues.

MEASURING THE IMPACTS OF TOURISM

The saying goes, "you can't manage what you don't measure," and that is certainly true of tourism. As a complex system, measuring tourism impacts takes place at a number of levels within the system. Nations and destinations (macro-level) measure the impacts of tourism, as do corporations and individual businesses. Individuals like you can track their impacts and make improvements in their personal sustainability profile. In this chapter we'll focus on the macro-level measures of impact.

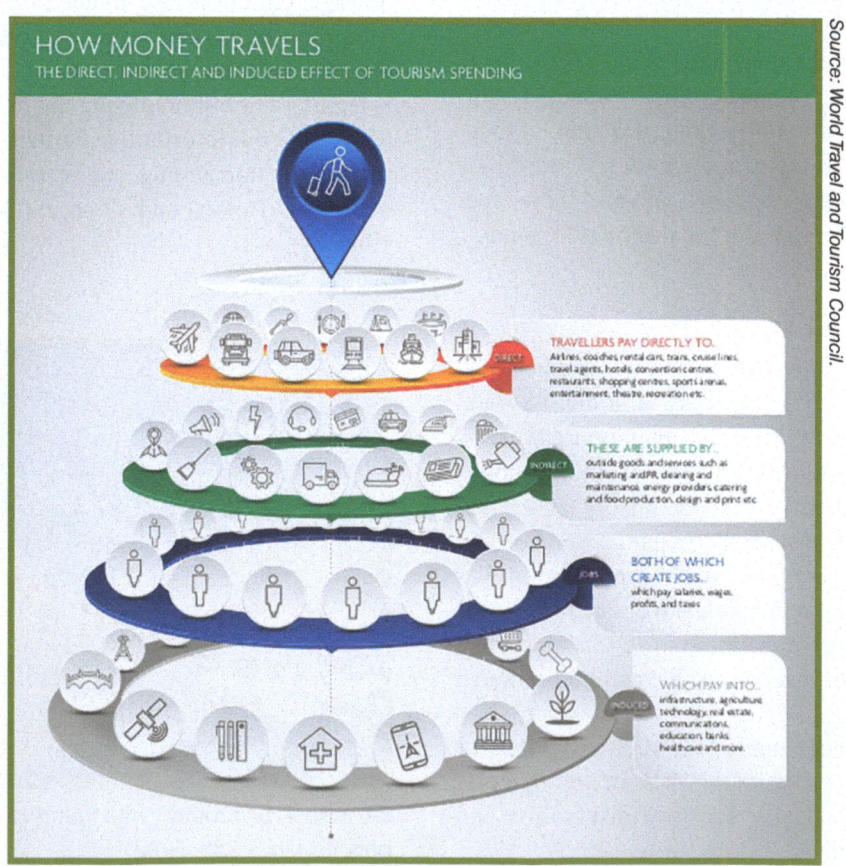

FIGURE 2.10 Money from tourism flows through the economy.

Measures of Economic Impact

When economists look at the value created by tourism, they look at more than just the money spent directly by visitors. In addition to direct spending, tourism spending stimulates other economic activity. There are a number of ways that economists measure this additional economic activity. The most popular method for estimating the income generated from tourism is to determine the income multiplier for the destination. *Income multipliers* measure the amount of local income generated per unit of visitor expenditure (Wanhill 1994). There are three main techniques used for measuring the multiplier effect: the *ad hoc* or *simple multiplier, input-output analysis,* and *economic impact models.*

• **Ad hoc or simple multiplier**

The important message that one gets from studying the multiplier effect is that it is wrong to just measure what visitors spend in the destination area. There are three levels of income that must be analyzed:

1. **Direct:** The first round of spending by visitors in the destination area
2. **Indirect:** The second round of expenditures by businesses who receive the first round of visitor spending
3. **Induced:** The third and subsequent rounds of expenditures after the second round

The total income impact of tourism equals the sum of the direct, indirect, and induced impacts. If the multiplier is found to be 2.0, then the indirect plus the induced are equal to 1.0. If the multiplier is calculated at 1.73, then the indirect plus the induced are 73 percent of the direct. In this example, for every dollar spent by a visitor, the destination generates $1.73 in economic benefit.

The size of the multiplier depends on the extent to which the various economic sectors are linked to one another. This is a function of the diversity of activities within the destination. When tourism operators buy goods and services mainly from other local economic sectors, the multiplier ratio will be higher than if tourism operators buy from outside the destination. The size of the destination has a great influence on the size of the income multiplier. For example, many smaller island economies have income multipliers of less than 1.0. Larger countries with developed economies, such as Turkey and the United Kingdom, have higher multipliers in the range of 1.5 to 2.0.

The simple multiplier has been criticized by some experts. It is best used in small countries with relatively small economies. The simple multiplier model does not take into account the fact that the destination country may increase export sales to other countries from which it presently imports. Although it may be necessary to import certain items to cater to visitors, once visitors return to their home countries they may want food, beverages, or other items from the destination country (e.g., wine from South Africa, cheese from the Netherlands). Second, the model fails to account for the new investment in the destination country resulting from the additional income generated.

• **Input-output analysis**

A more serious criticism of the simple multiplier model is the assumption that each type of income has the same effect. To remedy this it is necessary to break the increase in expenditures into component elements to analyze the effect of each element separately. This is done through a technique called *input-output analysis.* Input-output analysis is a method of looking at these interactions among different economic sectors and determining the effects of any possible changes. It is a means of analyzing interindustry relationships in the production process in a destination area's economy (Frechtling 1994). An input-output table shows how transactions flow through an economy in a given time period. A matrix is developed, the rows of which show the total value of all the sales made by each sector of the economy (or industry) to all the other sectors. The columns of the matrix show the purchases made by each sector from each of the other sectors.

There are also problems associated with input-output analysis. It is extremely difficult and expensive to get sufficient data for a detailed model, largely because visitor spending affects so many sectors of the economy. Analysis is suitable only for the short- and medium-terms. Last, it is argued that input-output analysis makes too many unrealistic assumptions. For example, it assumes that supply is elastic. Any increases in demand will require more output than can be met by purchases from the economic sectors that supplied the previous supply. It is unlikely that this will happen in the short run because of production hindrances. Input-output analysis assumes that production functions are linear in form and that trade patterns are stable. It assumes that when production increases, purchases of imports will be made in the same proportions and from the same sources as before, negating any thought of *economies of scale.*

Additionally, input-output analysis assumes that increases in income will be spent on the same items and in the same proportions as previously. In reality, none of these assumptions are likely. Certainly, input-output analysis can show the economic impacts of different kinds of visitors, which assists in target market selection. It can also show short-term economic effects compared with the effects of other sectors of the economy. However, other tools are needed to demonstrate the best long-term policy option for investment in the various available economic sectors.

- **Economic impact models**

In addition to the multiplier methods, some destination areas have developed *economic impact models* that reflect their specific needs. For example, the U.S. Travel Association has developed the Travel Economic Impact Model (TEIM). In Canada, the Conference Board's Canadian Tourism Research Institute (CTRI) has developed the Tourism Economic Assessment Model (TEAM). This model estimates the direct, indirect, and induced economic impact for around sixty measures, including employment, wages and salaries, gross domestic product (GDP), and by categorical industry output. TEAM is used by several Canadian convention and visitors bureaus (CVBs) and provincial tourism agencies. These models gather data on visitor expenditures and tourism employment and then simulate the economic impacts that follow from these direct effects.

- **Tourism satellite accounting**

The system nature of tourism—the way that it includes contributions across industries including lodging, transportation, restaurants, and a variety of other businesses—has created challenges for measuring tourism at a national level. One of the traditional problems in analyzing the true economic impacts of tourism is that it is not considered to be an industrial sector of its own in national accounting systems. In essence, this means adding up the impacts of tourism that have traditionally been allocated to other economic sectors. The development of tourism satellite accounts (TSA) was an important step forward for tourism. All industries have a standardized set of industry accounts, called Standardized National Accounts (SNA), that are used in determining economic contributions of those industries. The problem is there is no SNA for tourism. Tourism, a system of many types of business, includes contributions from many SNAs and so the TSA framework was designed to set an internationally accepted way of using SNA material to determine the value of tourism. According to the Organization for Economic Co-operation and Development (OECD), TSA reporting can be seen as a set of ten key tables and all the supporting data required to justify the findings. Those key reports include:

- Inbound, domestic tourism and outbound tourism expenditure
- Internal tourism expenditure
- Production accounts of tourism industries
- Gross Value Added (GVA) and Gross Domestic Product attributable to tourism
- Employment
- Investment
- Government consumption
- Non-monetary indicators

TSA reporting allows economists and other stakeholders to compare the performance of tourism to other industries and to results in other countries.

QUICK TRIP 2.5

The Tourism Satellite Account Results for New Zealand

Statistics New Zealand has adopted Tourism Satellite Accounting as a means of reporting on the value of tourism. The diagram on the following page shows the flow of tourism expenditures through the New Zealand economy.

In this report the term "value added" is the value businesses add to goods and services for the purchase and use in producing their own product. For example, a restaurant may buy buns, meat, and potatoes—add their own value—and sell a hamburger and fries. Direct value added looks at the value added by companies with direct relationships with visitors, indirect value added is created when companies without a direct relationship with the tourism supply to companies that do.

The highlights of the report are outlined as follows. (A couple of tips in comparing the diagram to the report—the highlights are rounded to one decimal place and 1,000 million is 1 billion. The currency is New Zealand Dollars.)

- Total tourism expenditure was $34.7 billion
- International tourism expenditures were $14.5 billion
- Domestic Tourism expenditure was $20.2 billion
- Tourism generated a direct contribution to GDP of $12.9 billion
- Indirect contribution to the GDP was an additional $9.8 billion
- 188,136 people were directly employed in tourism
- Tourism generated $2.8 billion in tax (Goods and service tax) revenues

This table shows the tourism expenditure by type of product. After determining the accounts to be used, economists must determine the proportion of the overall expenditure that is related to tourism.

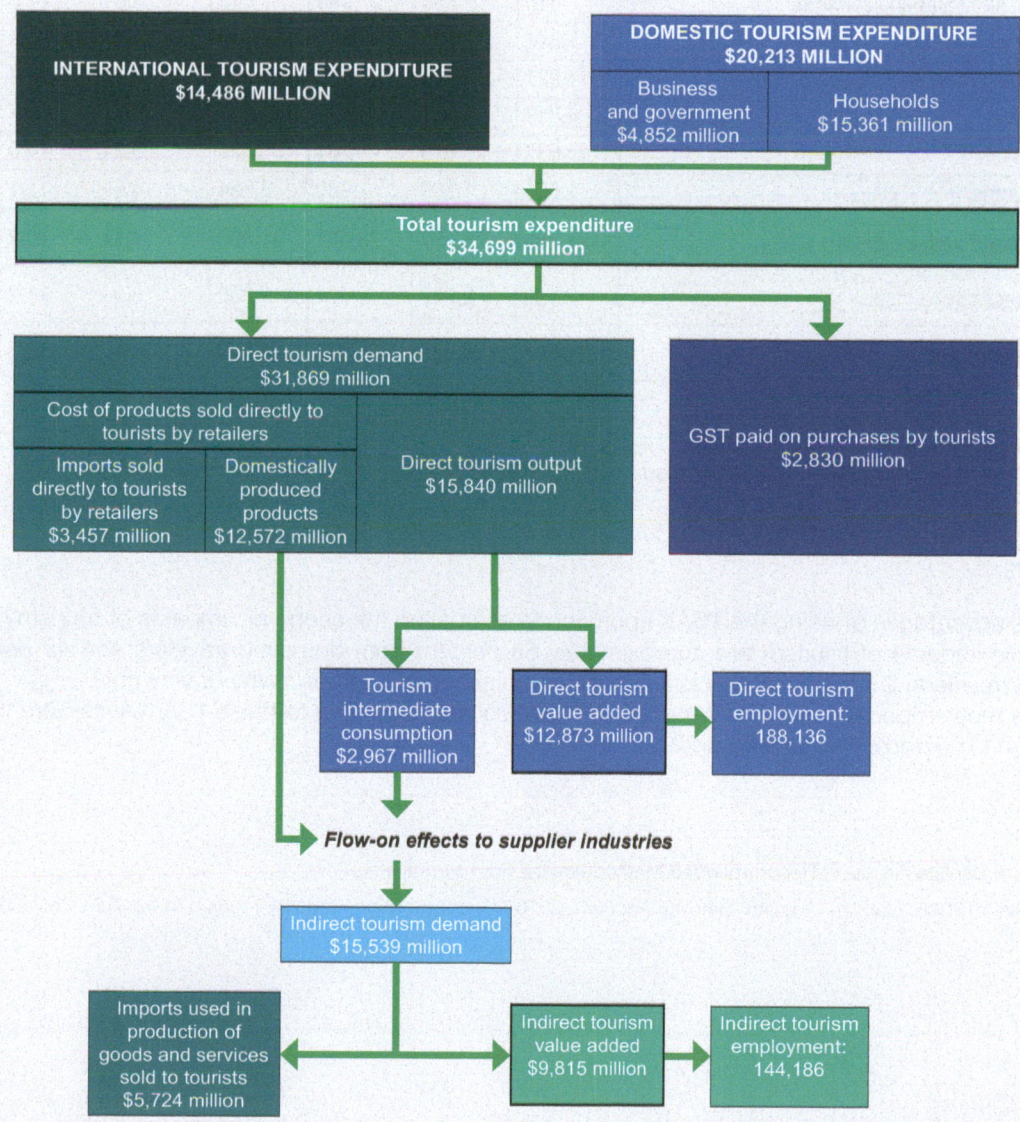

Flows of Tourism Expenditure through the New Zealand Economy [1,2]
Year ended March 2016

(1) Totals may not add to the stated totals, due to rounding.
(2) Tourism expenditure is measured in purchasers' prices. Other monetary aggregates are measured in producers' prices.

Source: Statistics New Zealand

Tourism Expenditure by Type of Product [1,2]

Product	Year ended March						
	2013	2014	2015	2016P	2014	2015	2016P
	$(million)				Annual Percentage Change		
Accommodation services	2,166	2,257	2,439	2,607	4.2	8.1	6.9
Food and beverage serving services	2,862	2,969	3,356	3,896	3.7	13.0	16.1
Air passenger transport	4,232	4,347	4,736	5,200	2.7	8.9	9.8
Other passenger transport	3,114	3,351	3,626	3,985	7.6	8.2	9.9
Imputed rental on holiday homes	699	719	739	776	2.9	2.8	5.0
Cultural recreation, and gambling services	815	869	995	1,145	6.6	14.5	15.1
Retail sales—alcohol, food, and beverages	1,840	1,911	2,119	2,410	3.9	10.9	13.7
Retail sales—fuel and other automotive products	1,921	1,943	2,076	2,256	1.1	6.8	8.7
Retail sales—other	4,812	4,991	5,625	6,469	3.7	12.7	15.0
Education services	637	670	764	871	5.2	14.0	14.0
Other tourism products	1,691	1,769	1,965	2,254	4.6	11.1	14.7
Total tourism demand and excluding GST	**24,788**	**25,797**	**28,441**	**31,869**	**4.1**	**10.2**	**12.1**
GST paid on purchases by tourists	2,159	2,242	2,494	2,830	3.8	11.2	13.5
Total Tourism Expenditure	**26,947**	**28,039**	**30,935**	**34,699**	**4.1**	**10.3**	**12.2**

1. All product values are in producers' prices.
2. Individual figures may not sum to stated totals due to rounding.
Note: Figures for all years prior to 2016 have been revised.

Think about This

1. What are the advantages of using the TSA's approach to estimating the economic impacts of tourism?
2. The economic impacts of tourism are approximately 58 percent from domestic travelers and 42 percent from international travelers. Do you think this is a healthy combination of sources? Why or why not?
3. What are the most important sectors of tourism in New Zealand according to these TSA results? Are these rankings what you expected? Why or why not?

Sources

OECD. 2008 Tourism satellite Account: Recommended Methodological Framework.

Statistics New Zealand. 2016. 5249.0—Tourism Satellite Account: 2016 The contribution made by tourism to the New Zealand economy.

• **Other economic considerations**

In addition to measuring the economic impact of tourism, economists also consider the trade-offs that tourism may require. For example, one issue that needs to be analyzed from an economic policy perspective is the attractiveness of tourism versus other forms of economic development. Another issue that needs to be measured and monitored is the long-term economic change that tourism brings.

Cost Benefit Analysis of Tourism

Imagine you have three opportunities but only enough money to choose one of the projects. How would you choose? Cost benefit analysis is a technique used to determine which economic sector produces the most benefit in terms of foreign exchange, employment, taxes, or income generated relative to the costs of development. The factors of production are valued at their *opportunity cost*—the marginal value of their next best use. It is then possible to compare several investment options. The social cost benefit analysis of a project determines the average annual rate at which benefits accrue to society. Critics of cost benefit analysis argue that the results are too dependent on the appropriateness of its assumptions. It is not possible to check actual performance against prediction.

Measures of Environmental Impact

While there is a long history of measuring the economic impacts of tourism, measuring the environmental and social impacts is less established.

Many communities require environmental impact studies to be conducted prior to development of new developments. We will examine this type of study in Chapter 6.

Some destinations also track their environmental performance. Capturing this information is the first step in undertaking a full environmental management program that encourages improvement in performance over time. What are the important measures for environmental performance management? Environmental management programs include measures of energy consumption, water consumption, and the effectiveness of recycling programs. For instance, Kaikoura District Council, New Zealand, Mount Huangshan, China, and Riviera Maya, Quintana Roo, Mexico, each have systematic programs that collect environmental performance data for their community.

While it is still not common for destinations to collect environmental performance data, many tourism operators collect this information and actively work to improve their environmental performance, often reducing operating costs.

Measuring Social Impacts

Measuring the social impacts and community perceptions of tourism is an important part of good destination management. Progressive destinations monitor community perceptions of tourism to ensure that the local host community understands and values the positive contributions of tourism while accepting the potential negatives.

A SYSTEM'S RESPONSE TO TOURISM IMPACTS

As we have seen, tourism creates a variety of impacts—some good, some bad. Each element of the tourism system has an important role in maximizing the benefits of tourism and minimizing the negative outcomes. Throughout The Tourism System you'll see ways that parts of the tourism system address the impacts of tourism.

Destinations

Many of the impacts of tourism take place in destination communities. It is important to remember that tourism, like any development activity, should be a choice for the community and that visitors come to a destination with the permission of the host community. Too often tourism development takes place without *effective consultation* with the members of the destination system or tracking of host community concerns or issues. This may ultimately lead to community backlash against tourism development and visitors.

The leaders of the destination system must ensure that the benefits of tourism are maximized and the negatives reduced or eliminated. This is a complex process requiring the work of many independent actors all working collaboratively. They must also work to communicate the benefits of the "invisible" industry to maintain awareness and support for the industry. You will learn more about the role of destinations in sustainable tourism development in Chapter 6.

QUICK TRIP 2.6

Using Tourism as a Tool for Development

Tourism can be used as a tool for development in developed and developing countries. In fact, 2017 was the International Year of Sustainable Tourism for Development. In recognition of the power of tourism to generate positive benefits for destination communities, Louise Twining-Ward, a senior specialist in sustainable tourism at the World Bank, shared the following **20 Reasons to integrate tourism in your development agenda.**

Sustainable Economic Growth

1. **Stimulates GDP Growth:** Worth USD7.6 trillion dollars, the travel and tourism sector accounts for more than 10% of global GDP, and represents 7% of all international trade and 30% of the world's export in services.
2. **Increases International Trade:** Worth USD1.4 trillion in export earnings, tourism is the third world's largest global export.
3. **Boosts International Investment:** Tourism and hospitality is now the second fastest-growing industry in terms of foreign direct investment (FDI).
4. **Drives Infrastructure Development:** Tourism sector development often results in improvements in basic infrastructure, such as airports, roads, water supply, energy, and medical services.
5. **Supports Low-Income Economies:** In 2015, the world's 48 lower income and lower middle income countries received 29 million international tourism arrivals (nearly a threefold increase in a decade) and earned USD21 billion from international tourism.

Social Inclusiveness, Employment, and Poverty Reduction

6. **Creates Jobs Efficiently:** The second largest-job generator, travel and tourism supported 292 million jobs, or one in ten jobs in 2016.
7. **Promotes Inclusive Growth:** Tourism is labor intensive and has the potential to reach and benefit large numbers of people thanks to its wide supply chain.
8. **Strengthens Rural Communities:** Rural tourism supports economic diversification and creates jobs for rural youth and ethnic minorities.
9. **Revitalizes Urban Areas:** As urban populations surge globally, many cities pursue tourism-based urban regeneration for its potential to create jobs, improve infrastructure, and attract investments.
10. **Improves Access to Income via Travel Tech:** Digital platforms are transforming the way travel is researched, purchased, provided, and experienced, which offers many new, more informal ways to earn money through tourism.
11. **Benefits Women:** Women make up 60 to 70% of tourism-industry workers and tourism is one of the few sectors where female labor participation is already above parity in some regions.
12. **Bolsters Artisans:** Artisans benefit from selling their crafts to visitors, which opens them up to the global market.

© Leonard Zhukovsky/Shutterstock.com

Local artisan at the Grand Anse Craft and Spice Market in Grenada generates income selling authentic, local art to visitors.

Resource Efficiency, Environmental Protection, and Climate Change

13. **Facilitates Conservation:** Nature-based tourism is in high demand, which not only increases the value placed on unspoiled nature and wildlife, it generates funds used for conservation.
14. **Raises Climate Change Awareness:** Tourism is often an innovator of sustainable consumption and production, and climate change awareness.
15. **Propels the Blue Economy:** Tourism accounts for an estimated 26% of ocean-based economic activity, making it a key driver of the blue economy and increasing the value of marine conservation.

Cultural Values, Diversity, and Heritage

16. **Protects Cultural Sites:** Visitor spending on entrance tickets, guides, and souvenirs contributes to capital needed for the protection of important cultural sites.
17. **Sustains Intangible Culture:** Tourism can protect or revive intangible cultural heritage, music, performing arts, and oral traditions.

Mutual Understanding, Peace, and Security

18. **Spreads Philanthropy:** Tourism can be an effective way to engage visitors in philanthropy.
19. **Cultivates Intercultural Understanding:** Meeting diverse peoples and experiencing other cultures via tourism play a critical role in promoting peace, security, and intercultural understanding.
20. **Aids Post-Conflict Recovery:** Tourism has served as a post-conflict recovery tool for many fragile and conflict situations (FCS).

Think about This

1. Tourism has the potential to be used in a positive way to meet development goals but it doesn't happen automatically. Consider one or two of the recommendations and consider what things would need to be in place for the best possible outcomes.
2. Consider destinations you have visited that seem to be doing a good job at protecting the environment. What were they doing right?

Source

20 Reasons You Should Integrate Tourism in Your Development Agenda. World Bank http://blogs.worldbank.org/psd/20-reasons-you-should-integrate-tourism-your-development-agenda

Travel Intermediaries and DMOs

Travel intermediaries play an important role in influencing the behavior of both consumers and suppliers of travel. In some markets, intermediaries like tour wholesalers are the most powerful members of the distribution system with the ability to significantly influence both consumers and suppliers of travel. TUI, for example, is a billion-dollar travel wholesaler that provides tour packages and a variety of other tourism services. TUI is committed to sustainability and works with its suppliers to ensure best practices of environmental and social and cultural business practices. In Chapter 16 you'll examine the important role of travel intermediaries in promoting sustainable tourism.

Destination management organizations (DMOs) are institutions like national tourism organizations or visitors and convention bureaus. These organizations are becoming increasingly aware of their role in developing sustainable tourism experiences as well as promoting destinations. You will see more on the role of DMOs in Chapter 3.

Travel Providers

The role of travel providers is critical to the tourism system's sustainability performance. Hotels and lodging organizations, tour operators, and transportation providers all have a role to play in ensuring the benefits of tourism outweigh the costs. While tourism is sometimes criticized as a wasteful industry, many of the largest companies in the system have committed to sustainability goals. When companies *go beyond the requirements of the law* to pursue environmental or social goals, it is called *Corporate Social Responsibility* or CSR. CSR programs often address environmental issues and social issues—both inside the company and in the community. Hotel companies provide a great example of the role in CSR in ensuring sustainability in the tourism system. The largest hotel companies have a variety of programs that address each element of the triple bottom line (i.e., people, planet, profit). For example, most major hotel brands have well-established diversity and inclusion programs. Many hotel companies have programs designed to provide entry-level jobs or internships to the industry for disadvantaged young people. Some hotels use the power of their *supply chain*—the organizations they buy from to deliver their services—to promote social values. They may set a goal of buying 25 percent of their supplies from businesses owned by women or commit to purchase on "fair trade" products like coffee or chocolate. Many hotel companies will support local charities as well as major national charities like Habitat for Humanity.

In recent years, hotel companies have worked to improve their environmental impacts. While linen recycling programs have become ubiquitous, they represent only a small part of many hotels' environmental programs. It is important to remember that many of these decisions are made for important business-related reasons. Energy can be a major cost for hotels. By increasing energy efficiency, companies reduce their costs—and improve their profitability. In addition to the focus on energy consumption, many hotel companies have water conservation and waste reduction programs. Some hotel companies engage with bigger environmental issues. For example, Marriott committed to protecting a specific part of the Amazon.

From an environmental perspective, the role of air travel is particularly important to the overall performance of the tourism system. Major airline companies are increasingly developing more fuel-efficient airplanes. The challenge is that demand for air travel is outpacing the improvements in fuel efficiency. You'll learn more about these issues in Chapter 17.

An important element of sustainability and CSR activities is the commitment to managing the process. It is an important task of companies that are committed to sustainability to measure their progress and manage for performance improvement. Developing a systematic approach to sustainability can be challenging, and some companies use certification programs as frameworks for guiding sustainability issues. The proliferation of sustainable tourism certifications leads to the establishment of the Global Sustainable Tourism Council (GSTC) and the creation of a set of criteria that represent the basic inclusions that all programs should incorporate.

While CSR is an important way that companies contribute to sustainability, some companies are set up to address social issues. *Social enterprises* are businesses that are set up to address social issues. Social enterprises use the operation of the business and its profits to address local social issues. Some *ecotourism* products are social enterprises, as are some *community-based tourism* operations. *Social entrepreneurs* are entrepreneurs who see that issue and build these businesses to help solve the problem.

Travelers Making a Difference

Travelers are an important part of the tourism system. Each of the billions of people who travel each year have the ability to maximize the benefits of their travel to destination communities. Travelers can contribute to the positives of each part of the triple bottom line. How? Here are some easy tips that will help you be a responsible traveler.

Economic Benefits You Can Provide. Use the power of your spending where it will do the most good. Buy local souvenirs and local foods when you can.

Environmental Benefits You Can Provide. Bring your good behaviors from home and make sure you conserve energy, save water, and recycle when you travel. "Leave no trace" when you visit natural places.

Social Benefits You Can Provide. Respect local customs and traditions, and remember you are a guest. Learn about the culture you are visiting—even if you're going to get some sun.

QUICK TRIP 2.7

Travel Care Code

The Travel Care Code promotes responsible travel and highlights ten things that every traveler can do to ensure their trip reduces the negative impacts of tourism and maximizes the benefits.

Think about This

1. Which Travel Care recommendations encourage good environmental behaviors? social and cultural behaviors? economic behaviors that support the destination community?
2. What activities would you add to this list?
3. Consider whether you believe an individual can make a difference in the face of global challenges. How does that impact your behaviors?

Source

TravelCarecode.org

Five Most Popular Ways to Travel Responsibly

In recognition of the first year with one billion tourists, the United Nations launched a campaign called "One Billion Tourists, One Billion Opportunities" to encourage individuals to make responsible travel decisions.

They launched the campaign by saying:

> *Small changes in travel behavior can contribute to positive change throughout the world. With one billion tourists traveling the world in a single year in 2012, transforming these one billion tourists into one billion opportunities is at the heart of the online campaign launched by UNWTO to celebrate this historic milestone.*

As part of that campaign, UNWTO conducted a survey on social media asking consumers to pick the most important thing individuals could do to travel more responsibly. The winning tip was to buy locally—a way to improve economic and social benefits to host communities.

Sources

http://1billiontourists.unwto.org/

http://www2.unwto.org/press-release/2012-11-06/one-billion-tourists-one-billion-opportunities-new-unwto-campaign-calls-one

SUMMARY

Tourism is a global phenomenon that has impacts. Tourism generates significant economic impacts—more than $US 1 trillion in international travel alone. Money from tourism flows through the economy, providing benefits for people not directly involved in tourism. Tourism can also have significant social and environmental benefits, allowing communities to share—and celebrate—their unique culture and providing an important rationale for protecting unique landscapes and biodiversity. But tourism can have negative impacts as well, such as increasing crime, commodifying culture, and destroying natural places. As a result, the members of the tourism system must actively work to maximize the benefits and reduce or eliminate the costs of tourism.

While all components of the tourism system must work to ensure the best possible outcomes from tourism, it is important to remember that individual travelers can contribute to sustainable outcomes for tourism. Over one billion international travelers—and many more traveling domestically—can make responsible choices to ensure tourism is a force for good in the world.

ACTIVITIES

You have been asked to do a presentation on the impacts of tourism in your local area.

1. Describe what steps you would take and whom you would consult to determine the economic impacts of tourism within your local area.
2. Which agencies would you contact to determine the extent and types of environmental and sociocultural impacts of tourism on the area?
3. Conduct a small survey of local area residents to find out their opinions on the most significant tourism impacts. What are your results and conclusions?
4. What are the major sources of online information about the economic impacts of tourism that you would analyze?
5. Which websites would provide you with the best sources of information of the environmental impacts of tourism?
6. Which websites would provide you with the best sources of information of the sociocultural impacts of tourism?
7. Identify ten ways that you can make a positive impact when you travel.

ACRONYMS

CTRI (Canadian Tourism Research Institute)
CVBs (Convention and Visitors Bureaus)
CSR (Corporate Social Responsibility)
DMO (destination management organizations)
GSTC (Global Sustainable Tourism Council)
GHG (Greenhouse Gas)
DGP (Gross Domestic Product)
OECD (Organization for Economic Co-operation and Development)
TEAM (Tourism Economic Assessment Model)
TSA (Tourism Satellite Accounts)
TEIM (Travel Economic Impact Model)
TBL (Triple Bottom Line)
UNWTO (United Nations World Tourism Organization)
USTA (United States Travel Association)

REFERENCES

Day, J., and L. Cai. 2012. "Environmental and Energy-Related Challenges to Sustainable Tourism in the United States and China." *International Journal of Sustainable Development and World Ecology 19* (5): 379–388. doi: http://dx.doi.org/10.1080/13504509.2012.675600

Doggart, C., and N. Doggart. 1996. "Environmental Impacts of Tourism in Developing Countries." *Travel and Tourism Analyst* 2:71–86.

Frechtling, D. 1994. "Assessing the Impacts of Travel and Tourism: Introduction to Travel Economic Estimation." In *Travel, Tourism, and Hospitality Research,* edited by J. R. B. Ritchie and C. R. Goeldner, 359–365. New York: John Wiley and Sons, Inc.

Krotz, L. 1996. Tourists: How Our Fastest Growing Industry Is Changing the World. Boston: Faber and Faber.

Lukashina, N. S., M. M. Amirkhanov, V. I. Anisimov, and A. Trunev. 1996. "Tourism and Environmental Degradation in Sochi, Russia." *Annals of Tourism Research* 23: 654–665.

Romeril, M. 1989. "Tourism: The Environmental Dimension." In *Progress in Tourism, Recreation and Hospitality Management* edited by C. Cooper, 103–113. London: Bellhaven Press.

UNWTO Tourism Highlights: 2017 Edition. Madrid: United Nations World Tourism Organization.

Wanhill, S. 1994. "The Measurement of Tourist Income Multipliers." *Tourism Management* 15: 281–283.

WCED. 1987. Our Common Future, World Commission on Environment and Development. Oxford: Oxford University Press.

CHAPTER THREE

Government Involvement, Tourism Policy, and Organizations

Guiding Tourism to a Better Future

The policy of being too cautious is the greatest risk of all

JAWAHARLAL NEHRU, *First Prime Minister of India*

YOUR LEARNING DESTINATION

You will be able to describe a tourism policy and the roles of governmental and other organizations at different geographic levels in the world.

WHAT YOU NEED TO KNOW

Having read this chapter, you will be able to:

- ✔ Describe reasons for government involvement in tourism.
- ✔ Elaborate on government roles in tourism.
- ✔ Define tourism policy and explain the tourism policy-setting process.
- ✔ Review the roles of global, multi-country, national, state, provincial, territorial, regional, and local tourism organizations.

BREAKING THE ICE

Think about the games you play—sports, board or video games, and so on. They all have rules, don't they? Sometimes the rules are changed; for example, soccer (football) introduced goal-line technology to determine if the ball has crossed the line and is a goal for the attacking team. Who sets and changes these rules? Usually it's someone in a position of authority like a sport-governing body or the game's manufacturer. From time to time, they review the "rules of the game" and make updates and changes.

Well, tourism is not a game, but an economic sector; so, that's where this metaphor ends. However, governments are usually the ultimate authority in tourism and the rules they set are known as tourism policies. Because of the impacts of tourism that you learned about in Chapter 2, governments must get involved in tourism. Usually, when they set and implement tourism policies, they have the legal right and resources to do so. However, with thousands of other tourism organizations, many private-sector and non-profit players, and residents also involved in tourism, government agencies can be more effective if they work with others in putting policies into action.

KEY TAKEAWAY POINTS

- There are eight potential roles for government in tourism (policy-setting and tourism destination planning; legislation and regulation; coordination; development stimulation and control; infrastructure and transportation development; operations; marketing and research; training and education).

- Tourism policy-setting should be done regularly and in a systematic way.

- A tourism policy is the basic framework for tourism in a destination expressed as policy guidelines, goals, and initiatives.

- Not all destinations have tourism policies.

REASONS FOR GOVERNMENT INVOLVEMENT IN TOURISM

You should know that governments are a major player in tourism around the world. Why do government agencies get involved in tourism? First, there are security and political reasons. International tourism involves travel across national boundaries. Governments must get involved with policies and procedures on the entry and exit of foreign travelers and nationals. The encouragement of tourism can be used for political purposes by furthering international relations among countries, as a way of enhancing the national and international image of a country, or because of political differences between countries. For example, several countries have introduced visa on arrival (VOA) programs to make it easier for foreign nationals to enter (Figure 3.1).

Second, there are sustainable development and environmental reasons for government involvement. Tourism is based on such things as the scenery, history, and cultural heritage of destinations. One of the dangers of tourism is, in making destinations more accessible to foreign and domestic markets, the integrity and authenticity of the physical, social, and cultural environments may be permanently damaged, altered, or lost. Therefore, among other things, governments must encourage adoption of the principles of sustainable tourism.

Third, there are economic reasons for government involvement in tourism. Tourism generates income, creates jobs, helps in economic diversification, complements certain local industries, is an export, and provides foreign exchange earnings. To enhance these economic advantages to destinations, government agencies get involved in tourism.

You should realize that the extent of government involvement in tourism varies from country to country.

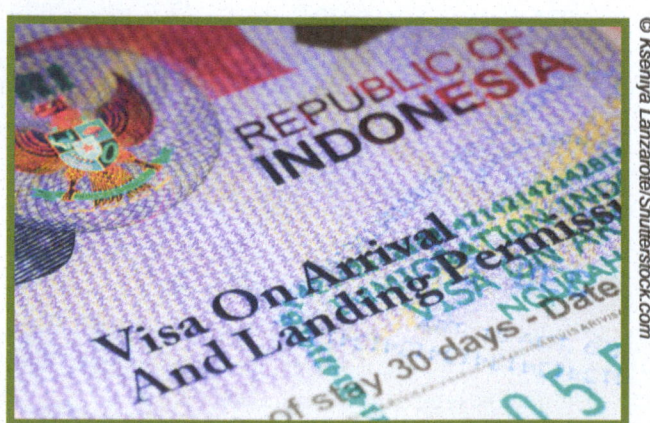

FIGURE 3.1 Indonesia offers VOAs to the citizens of many countries.

The greater the importance that the government attaches to tourism, the greater is the government involvement. For example, government involvement in tourism is much greater in the Maldives, where travel and tourism represented 79.4 percent of total GDP in 2016, than in the UK, which has a much more diverse economy and tourism is 10.8 percent of total GDP (WTTC 2017). The existing conditions in a country, including the political, economic, and constitutional system, also affect the type and amount of government involvement in tourism. For example, the level of involvement in socialist countries such as China, Vietnam, Cuba, and Laos is greater than in countries that are predominantly free-enterprise systems.

China Bans Travel to South Korea

The China National Tourism Administration, the government body responsible for Chinese tourism, has forbidden both online and offline travel agencies to sell trips to South Korea. The ban affects all types of Chinese tourism to South Korea (i.e., group travel, individual travel, and cruises). Some analysts have predicted that this will cause up to a 70 percent drop in Chinese arrivals.

Source: Meesak, D. 2017. China's South Korea travel ban: What you need to know. *Jing Daily*, March 16.

The level of economic development is another important factor determining the extent of government involvement. The greater the economic development of a country, the less is the need for government involvement. The maturity and financial capabilities of the private sector are important factors. The greater the capability of the private sector, the less is the need for government involvement. In the United States, politicians argue that tourism businesses are so highly developed, sophisticated, and resourceful that there is little need for the federal government to be involved in tourism development or marketing. This philosophy was clearly demonstrated through the closure of the U.S. Travel and Tourism Administration (USTTA) in 1996.

GOVERNMENT ROLES IN TOURISM

There are eight key roles that government agencies play in tourism (Figure 3.2). The extent of government involvement varies. In the United States, for example, government tourism organizations are mostly involved in tourism marketing and research. In Canada and

FIGURE 3.2 Eight potential roles of government in tourism.

Australia, they play a wider role and typically lead the process of tourism destination planning, while making extensive contributions in tourism training and education. In less-developed nations of the world, government tourism agencies play a more "hands-on" role in tourism development and operations.

Policy-Setting and Tourism Destination Planning

Government agencies are involved in setting tourism policies and in coordinating the preparation of tourism destination plans. Among other things, these policies and plans indicate the sectors of tourism to be developed, the appropriate rates of growth, sustainable tourism procedures, and the sources of capital needed for expansion. The key is to balance the development of supply (attractions and events, built facilities, transportation, infrastructure, and human resources) and the promotion of demand (the number of visitors) while maintaining the principles of sustainable tourism. Policy-setting is discussed in this chapter; government's tourism destination planning role is explained in Chapter 5.

Legislation and Regulation

An important role of government is as a legislator and regulator. Government legislation can affect the number of paid vacation days during the year and, hence, the amount of discretionary paid time available for vacations. Policies on passports and visas also directly affect tourism. Visitors are required to have official visas when traveling to several countries (e.g., China and India). Government influence may also be felt through regulations on operating a tourism business. In some countries, tour operators, travel agents, and guides must be licensed. Businesses have safety and health regulations to abide by; they also must meet zoning, building, and licensing requirements. The need to protect the environment and other resources that attract visitors may result in restrictions regarding the use of fragile natural resources. Visitors are no longer allowed to enter certain European monuments (e.g., Stonehenge in England, Figure 3.3), and park systems often have certain areas set aside as wilderness where use is severely limited. This legislative and regulatory role is fully reviewed in Chapter 4.

FIGURE 3.3 Built by English Heritage and opened in 2013, the Stonehenge Visitor Centre offers a virtual experience of standing among the stones.

Coordination

Government agencies often play a coordinating function. Coordination is necessary among the many governmental bodies concerned with different aspects of tourism. For example, immigration may decide to relax the frontier formalities to expedite the entry of visitors into the country. This helps tourism. The agency responsible for drug enforcement may be against this proposal for fear that it will increase the flow of drugs into the country. Coordination is also required among government agencies at the national, state, provincial, territorial, regional, and local levels. To be truly effective, tourism must be coordinated so that all areas are working toward the same tourism vision and goals. For the same reason, coordination is necessary among the government, private sector, and non-profit organizations. Many educational and cultural organizations, although they do not have tourism as a core focus, provide resources that attract visitors. The private sector is very

involved in tourism. To avoid duplication of effort, it is vital that goals and strategies be coordinated. The overall responsibility for tourism needs to be assigned to a specific agency dedicated to tourism, usually a destination management organization (DMO).

Development Stimulation and Control

Governments stimulate tourism development in different ways. Government agencies identify tourism project development opportunities and seek developers for these projects. Financial and fiscal incentives, such as low-interest loans or non-payment of taxes for a specified period ("tax holidays"), are offered to induce private-sector investment in tourism. Governments must also introduce and enforce development controls to ensure that the environment and cultural heritage are not harmed and that all other procedures and codes have been followed. This sustainable tourism development role is discussed in detail in Chapter 6.

Infrastructure and Transportation Development

Governments are expected to provide the infrastructure and transportation facilities (roads, airport facilities, sewage disposal, electricity, water, and other essential services) for tourism development in destinations. These services are crucial to tourism development and cannot be provided by private developers without government assistance. Again, there is a special need for this assistance from government in less-developed countries.

New Zealand Introduces Tourism Infrastructure Fund in 2017

"The Tourism Infrastructure Fund provides up to $25 million per year for the development of tourism-related infrastructure such as carparks, freedom camping facilities, sewerage and water works and transport projects. Announced as part of Budget 2017, the Tourism Infrastructure Fund supports local communities facing pressure from tourism growth and in need of assistance—areas with high visitor numbers but small ratepayer bases, for example."

Source: Ministry of Business, Innovation & Employment. 2017.

Operations

Many governments are involved through the ownership and operation of certain attractions, facilities, and services. Typically, this involvement is limited to national and state park systems, historic and government sites, monuments, and buildings. Many countries still operate state-owned airlines, but there is a definite trend toward the privatization of national carriers. Governments own and operate chains of hotels in India, Greece, Spain, and Portugal. Government ownership and operation of hotels and resorts is not very prevalent in the developed countries. An exception to this rule is found within certain national, state, and provincial parks in the United States and Canada. Governments also may own and operate travel agencies and inbound tour operators such as in China.

Marketing and Research

Governments sponsor research that benefits all tourism organizations and businesses. For example, research may be conducted on the characteristics of a foreign market. The results are made available to tourism businesses that develop plans to attract this market. Governments stimulate tourism by spending money on marketing. The marketing covers the entire country, state, province, territory, region, or local area. It consists of travel promotion aimed at generating visitor demand. In some cases, it may also involve promotion aimed at encouraging capital investment for tourism attractions and facilities. The marketing role of government is highlighted in Chapters 7 through 9.

Training and Education

Another important role played by government agencies is the provision of training and education programs for tourism. Some programs focus on training at the skill levels and this includes the many national governments that operate their own hotel and restaurant training schools, including Bahrain, Sri Lanka, and Indonesia. Other agencies, including Fáilte Ireland, assist with the development of training programs (courses, seminars, workshops) and materials (books, manuals, guides, videos, websites) for management. Some governments are concerned with the establishment of minimum standards or competencies that tourism employees must meet. This is a very common practice for tour guide qualification in several countries. In addition, some governments operate training programs for foreign retail travel agents including Tourism Australia, Tourism Ireland, and VisitScotland.

TOURISM POLICY AND POLICY-SETTING PROCESS

Because of the potential impacts of tourism on destinations, government involvement is required for setting, implementing, and evaluating tourism policies. To guide the government's own programs, along with the actions of private and non-profit organizations, it is essential that a top priority is the setting of a *comprehensive and integrated tourism policy*.

Definition of Tourism Policy

A simple definition of tourism policy is the basic statement on tourism in a destination expressed as policy guidelines, goals, and initiatives. Tourism policy gives guidance for all those directly and indirectly involved in tourism by creating a roadmap for the future. Despite the importance of having a tourism policy, many

Tourism Destination Aspects	Examples of Policy Questions
Tourism development	What to develop and on what scale? How to avoid environmental damage? How to protect cultural heritage? How to maintain or improve resident quality of life?
Destination marketing	Should the emphasis be on international tourism, domestic tourism, or both? How to market and to whom? How to improve marketing effectiveness?
Experience and activity design	How to ensure sufficient visitor experiences and activities are provided?
Human resource development	What is the status of current capacity and skill levels? What are the HR needs for the future?
Tourism organization	How to create the best structure for destination management and marketing?
Community relationships with and involvement in tourism	How to improve quality of life? How to get more involvement of residents in tourism?
Service quality and quality assurance	How to improve service quality?
Support services and activities	How to enhance the safety and security of visitors?

FIGURE 3.4 Potential policy questions for aspects of tourism.

government agencies and destinations have yet to develop such policies.

You need to know that a tourism policy is not the same as a tourism destination plan. Rather, policy is the first of 5 Ps in the tourism destination planning process, which you will learn about in Chapter 5.

Aspects of Tourism and Policy Questions

The authors recommend that all tourism policies reflect the principles of *sustainable tourism*. There are also several specific aspects of tourism that a new policy should address and these are shown in Figure 3.4, along with examples of policy questions.

Tourism Policy-Setting Process

Policy-setting should follow a regular and systematic process, meaning it should be planned to occur at certain predetermined times and be accomplished in a logical manner (Dredge and Jenkins 2007; Edgell and Swanson 2013). The process described below is designed for comprehensive and integrated tourism policies.

You should realize, however, that *specific tourism policies* are sometimes formulated by governments on an as-needed basis. For example, the Ministry of Tourism in Kerala, India (Figure 3.5) tabled a new adventure tourism policy in 2017. The Province of British Columbia, Canada, introduced a new Adventure Tourism Policy in 2015 (British Columbia Government 2015). In December 2016, the Japanese government changed a long-standing policy to allow the operation of casino resorts (The Economist 2017).

It is recommended that comprehensive tourism policies be updated at five- to ten-year intervals. However, due to unforeseen events (such as crises and disasters), government ruling party and leadership changes after elections, and unexpected rapidly development opportunities, tourism policy-setting can be triggered at previously unscheduled times.

The process illustrated in Figure 3.6 shows how a comprehensive and integrated tourism policy should be set. Effective tourism policies are formulated by following a step-by-step process; each step being comprised of several components that are described following the figure.

The comprehensive tourism policy-setting process shown in Figure 3.6 indicates that several drafts of the policy are prepared and that input is sought through successive rounds of consultation. As with tourism

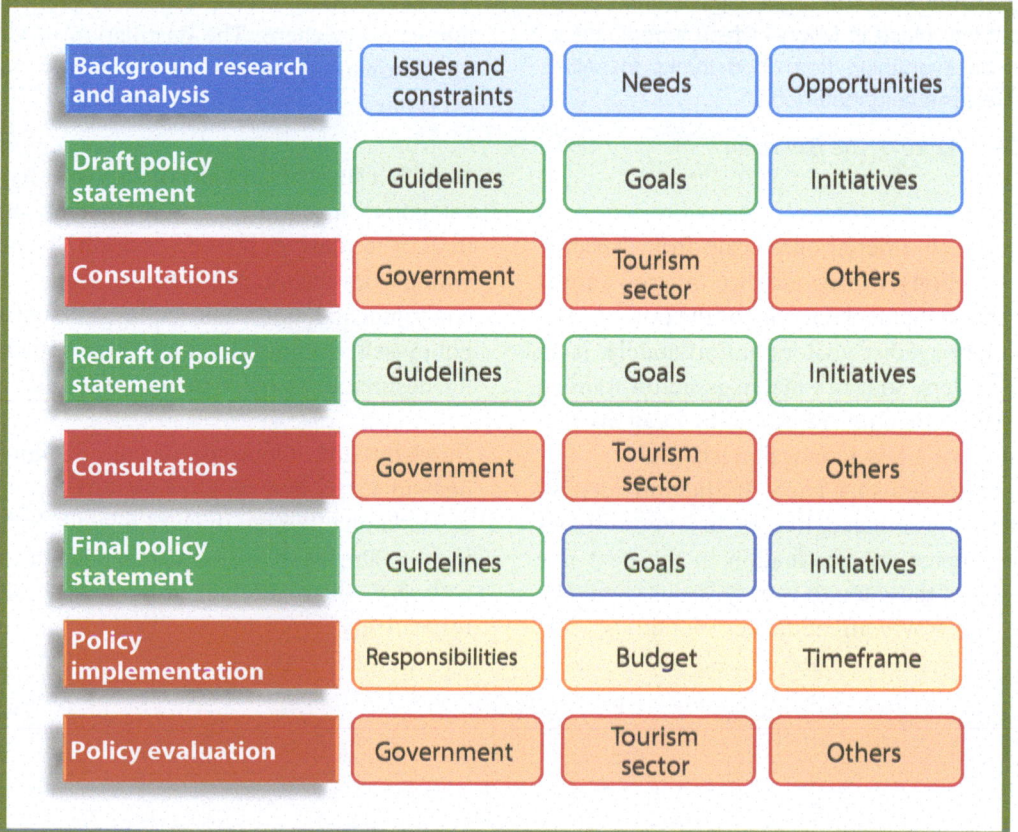

FIGURE 3.5 The Back Waters of Kerala, India, are famous for houseboat trips and other adventures.

Background research and analysis	Issues and constraints	Needs	Opportunities
Draft policy statement	Guidelines	Goals	Initiatives
Consultations	Government	Tourism sector	Others
Redraft of policy statement	Guidelines	Goals	Initiatives
Consultations	Government	Tourism sector	Others
Final policy statement	Guidelines	Goals	Initiatives
Policy implementation	Responsibilities	Budget	Timeframe
Policy evaluation	Government	Tourism sector	Others

FIGURE 3.6 A comprehensive tourism policy-setting process.

destination planning discussed in Chapter 5, setting a tourism policy should start with background research and analysis.

- **Background research and analysis**

Important factors to be analyzed include issues and constraints, needs, and opportunities.

Issues and Constraints. What is an issue? You know that it is an often-used word, but precisely what does it mean? The simplest definition is that an issue is a topic, theme, or problem that people are thinking and talking about. Tourism certainly has its fair share of current issues, including sustainability, climate change, terrorism, poor visitor behavior, sharing economy, taxation, entry requirements for citizens of specific countries, and many others. The backlash from residents in European cities over tourism volumes and visitor behavior is an example of an issue that is forcing local governments to set new tourism policies.

Italian Cities Move to Control Anti-Social Behavior of Tourists

"Italy has also been cracking down on anti-social behaviour in other tourist hotspots. In Rome, this means a ban on people eating or paddling in the city's fountains and drinking on the street at night. Similar measures have been put into place in Milan—which introduced a summer ban on everything from food trucks to selfie sticks in the Darsena neighbourhood."

Source: McCann, D. 2017. *The Guardian*.

Issues can be considered on a scale from "macro" (affect all destinations worldwide) to "micro" (affect only the destination that is the focus for the policy). The threat of terrorism against visitors, unfortunately, is an issue with no borders, so it is a macro-issue for tourism destinations. The protection of Komodo Dragons is a micro-issue only for a few Indonesian islands.

It is recommended that each destination identify five to ten macro-issues and five to ten micro-issues most likely to impact the destination in the next five years. Then each of these ten to twenty issues should be assessed as to how it will affect the destination.

Constraints are circumstances and factors that limit or hold back the actions of the tourism sector in all or specific destinations. Destinations have external and internal constraints; external constraints are those outside the direct control of the destination. For example, a destination cannot control fluctuations in currency exchange rates.

The Role of the Loonie

"What has fuelled the recent influx of international tourists to Canada? Destination Canada, as well as several provincial and destination management organizations, will justifiably point to enhanced marketing and targeting efforts, but currency is also a key factor. The relentless appreciation of the Greenback against the Loonie over the past three years has had a consistently positive impact on US visitation to Canada since 2014."

Source: TIAC. 2017. 2016 Annual Report on Canadian Tourism, p. 7.

Note: Loonie is the name given to the Canadian one-dollar coins; the Greenback is the US dollar.

Internal constraints influence tourism policy, but can be modified by the tourism policy that is established. The budget assigned for tourism is an internal constraint almost everywhere. The destination product constrains all destinations, since no place has "something for everyone."

Needs. The needs of a destination mostly fall into three categories: economic, environmental, and social-cultural. The tourism sector is not an "island unto itself" within a destination, but is part of a mosaic of economic, environmental, and socio-cultural systems. So, tourism policy-setting must consider "bigger picture" needs of the destination in these three categories.

Opportunities. Opportunities are windows of time that open to attract new types of visitors through developing or marketing tourism in certain ways. In two of the previous examples, Kerala and Japan are moving to capture a larger share of adventure and gaming tourism respectively.

QUICK TRIP 3.1

Policy Issues in Tourism in Belize

Belize is a small Central American country located on the Caribbean Sea between Mexico and Guatemala. It gained its independence from the UK in 1981. Belize has a population of around 354,000 and a land area of 23,000 square kilometers.

Tourism is a significant contributor to the economy of Belize and its major foreign exchange earner. WTTC (2017) estimates that the tourism sector contributed 38.1 percent of total GDP in 2016. It is known for its nature, ecotourism, and cultural-heritage, including the Belize Barrier Reef and significant Mayan ruins (Figure 3.7).

The last National Tourism Policy for Belize was developed in 2005 and the time came to update this policy in 2017. The new policy is designed to guide the tourism sector in Belize for the

FIGURE 3.7 The Mayan Mask Temple in Lamanai, Belize.

next five years. Based upon background research and a first round of consultation by the consultants (The Tourism Company, UK), the following sixteen issues were identified for consideration in the new National Tourism Policy:

1. The shape and balance of tourism in Belize
2. Target markets, positioning, and promotion
3. The product offer
4. Quality and standards
5. Cultural tourism
6. Natural heritage and protected areas
7. Cruise tourism
8. Social issues, safety, and security
9. Climate change and environmental management
10. Physical planning and development control
11. Investment and business support
12. Human resources and capacity building
13. Local destination areas and their management
14. Tourism transport and connectivity
15. Tourism data and evidence gathering
16. Governance and delivery structures

Having analyzed all sixteen of these issues, the Assessment Report outlined several recommendations that will lead to the development of a "draft policy framework." The recommendations included the following:

"The style of the new policy should be clear, accessible, confident, up-beat and challenging; it should be sufficiently short to be readable but have enough substance to be meaningful" (p. 36).

"This must be a policy for all tourism stakeholders, rather than just for the Government of Belize . . . it must be reflected in the way the policy is presented and in the requirement it places on everyone for its delivery" (p. 36).

These recommendations suggest that a policy statement should not be too long and complex, and should not only be implemented by government.

Think about This

1. Belize had not updated its tourism policy in twelve years. Chapter 3 suggests that it should have been updated before 2017. How many years should a tourism policy run before it is checked and revised? Why?
2. The consultants identified sixteen tourism policy issues for Belize. Do you believe these are too many or too few for policy-setting purposes? Why or why not?
3. It is recommended that the new Belize policy be short but also have substance. How can the policy statement accommodate these seemingly different requirements?
4. The recommendations suggest that the new Belize tourism policy should not overlap with the country's tourism destination plan. How best can these two documents dovetail together?

Sources

Belize Tourism Board. 2017. About BTB. http://www.belizetourismboard.org/about-btb/

Central Intelligence Agency. 2017. Belize. https://www.cia.gov/library/publications/the-world-factbook/geos/bh.html

Denman, R. 2017. Updating the National Tourism Policy of Belize. Assessment Report Final.

The Tourism Company. 2017. Belize National Tourism Policy. http://www.thetourismcompany.com/project.asp?type=2&projectid=1301

World Travel & Tourism Council. 2017. Travel & Tourism Economic Impact 2017 Belize. https://www.wttc.org/-/media/files/reports/economic-impact-research/countries-2017/belize2017.pdf

- **Draft policy statement**

A comprehensive tourism policy includes guidelines, goals, and initiatives. Governments themselves can prepare these guidelines or they may recruit the services of consultants to assist in drafting a *policy statement*.

Policy Guidelines. Policy guidelines express the government's top-most priority or priorities for tourism, and overall how the policy is to be implemented. The 2015 tourism policy for Ireland provides a good example. The top-most priority of the Irish government is to "*maximise the services export revenue*" of tourism. The "how" of implementation is "*achieving its full potential as a destination for overseas tourism.*"

Ireland's National Government Guidelines for Tourism

"The Government's primary objective in tourism is to maximise the services export revenue of the sector, and therefore, this policy statement is centred on Ireland achieving its full potential as a destination for overseas tourism. However, it is recognized that the domestic tourism market underpins the range of visitor accommodation and services that provide competitive advantage to Ireland in the international market and many of the measures contained in this Statement will similarly benefit the domestic tourism sector."

Source: Department of Transport, Sport and Tourism. 2015. *People, Place and Policy. Growing Tourism to 2025.* Dublin, Ireland.

Policy Goals. The policy goals should reflect sustainable tourism principles as well as considering all aspects of tourism in destinations. Typically, there is an economic growth element to the policy goals, as well as targets related to the environment and social-cultural factors. Goals indicate clear results the government wants to achieve from implementing the policy. A policy goal for tourism in Ireland is to have 10 million international visitors by 2025 (Department of Transport, Tourism and Sport 2015).

Policy Initiatives. Policy initiatives are drafted to implement the policy goals, serving as a platform for more detailed actions. For example, in Quick Trip 3.2 you will see that one of the four policy initiatives for tourism in Australia is to "*limit the tax, red tape and other regulatory burden industry faces*" (Australian Trade and Investment Commission 2017).

FIGURE 3.8 The beautiful scenery of Ireland attracts millions of international and domestic visitors.

QUICK TRIP 3.2

Australia's Tourism 2020

Tourism Australia describes Tourism 2020 in the following way:

"Tourism 2020 is a whole-of-government and industry long-term strategy to build the resilience and competitiveness of Australia's tourism industry and grow its economic contribution."

Although TA describes it as a strategy, the authors feel that it more resembles a tourism policy for Australia. Drawing a distinction among policies, plans, and strategies is a difficult issue in tourism practice today, as the terms seem to be used interchangeably.

According to Austrade, the mandate for Tourism 2020 is as follows:

"Tourism 2020 was developed to respond to ongoing challenges and emerging opportunities for the Australian tourism industry. Providing a framework for growth, Tourism 2020 will assist tourism businesses remain competitive into the future in a dynamic global environment."

Four policy initiatives (priorities) were identified in Tourism 2020:

- To encourage high-quality tourism experiences, including Indigenous tourism
- To limit the tax, red tape, and other regulatory burden industry faces
- To undertake coordinated and effective marketing campaigns to drive demand
- To work with industry to support the development of tourism infrastructure that can drive demand

The overall policy goal of Tourism 2020 is to double overnight domestic and international visitor expenditure to between $115 and $140 billion, requiring:

- High impact, effective, and coordinated international tourism marketing campaigns
- Facilitation of the existing development pipeline to deliver quality rooms to meet our target of 6,000 to 20,000 new rooms by 2020
- 40 to 50 percent more international aviation capacity and 23 to 30 percent more domestic aviation capacity by 2020. This means an additional 1.9 million (as at March 2016) more inbound seats by 2020—which equates to approximately seventy-eight more A380 flights per week
- An additional 152,000 persons employed by 2020 to meet demand

Six key reform areas are identified:

1. Increase cross portfolio collaboration within all levels of Australian Governments to plan and drive reform of the visitor economy.
2. Improve visa arrangements to make Australia's visitor visas easier, quicker, and competitive.
3. Improve aviation capacity and customer experience to improve access and flexibility to meet demand in the tourism transport environment.
4. Develop a skilled tourism workforce to better service the visitor economy.
5. Integrate national and state tourism plans into regional development and local government planning to generate effective infrastructure to service regional communities, services to the visitors, and encourage private investment in tourism infrastructure.
6. Identify partnerships, efficiencies, and opportunities to increase marketing spend to drive demand for travel to Australia and improve conversion.

Think about This

1. Do you think Tourism 2020 is a policy or a strategy? Why or why not?
2. Australia is a very large country with much diversity (Figures 3.9 and 3.20). What are the specific challenges facing a large country in developing a comprehensive and integrated tourism policy?

QUICK TRIP 3.2 CONTINUED

3. Governments have a major role to play as a coordinator in tourism; yet Tourism 2020 mentions the need to reduce the "red tape" (bureaucracy) in the future. How do you suggest that government agencies coordinate effectively without appearing bureaucratic to the tourism sector?

4. Are visas a significant impediment to inbound international tourism growth? Why or why not?

Sources

Australian Trade and Investment Commission. 2017. About Tourism 2020. https://www.austrade.gov.au/Australian/Tourism/Policy-and-Strategy/tourism-2020

Tourism Australia. Tourism 2020. 2017. Tourism 2020. http://www.tourism.australia.com/en/about/our-organisation/our-performance-and-reporting/tourism-2020.html

© Javen/Shutterstock.com

FIGURE 3.9 The Sydney Opera House is one of the most powerful icons of Australian tourism.

• **Consultations**

Draft policy recommendations in a policy statement are shared with other government agencies, the tourism sector, and others for review and feedback. This part of the policy-setting process is known as consultation. Consultations can be done in different ways, ranging from simple online distribution to full public meetings. These days, it is likely that "consultation documents" are placed on the coordinating government agency's website and submissions are invited in response to the contents of these documents. Another form of consultation is to present the draft policy statement in a public meeting or conference; for example, this is how the draft tourism policy for Belize was introduced during 2017 (Denman 2017).

• **Redraft of policy statement**

The government agency then analyzes and interprets the submissions received online and through other channels. Some submissions may require lengthier discussions with their authors.

Based upon the feedback to the first policy draft, the statement is revised accordingly. Changes to the first draft and the reasons for the revisions are noted.

• **Consultations**

After recirculating the revised draft tourism policy statement, a second round of consultations is initiated. Feedback is again invited either through online submissions, public meetings, or other channels.

• **Final policy statement**

When two or more rounds of consultations are completed, a final tourism policy statement is written; this becomes the framework for implementation and evaluation. Typically, the policy statement will be published online, and it may also be introduced at a public meeting or conference.

You should understand that the final tourism policy statement becomes a trigger for legislation and regulations (Chapter 4), tourism destination planning (Chapter 5), sustainable tourism development (Chapter 6), and destination marketing (Chapters 7–9).

• **Policy implementation**

Policies should not be just a few sheets of paper or several hundred words online. Tourism policy statements must be actionable, meaning they must be capable of implementation. A tourism policy implementation plan should be prepared that includes the required actions, assignment of responsibilities and budget for policy implementation, and have a specific time frame for accomplishment.

• **Policy evaluation**

The effectiveness of a tourism policy should be measured by the extent to which the policy goals are achieved. To measure policy success, policy goals that are quantified are better, as are policy initiatives that indicate specific rather than vague follow-up actions.

Tourism Policies Need a Team Approach

"Tourism policy development is an increasingly complex process, with longer time-scales and a wider scope than in the past. Developing the necessary tourism and related infrastructure to meet expected future demand requires an integrated long-term approach across departments and levels of government, with input and support from industry."

Source: Haxton, P. 2015.

TOURISM ORGANIZATIONS

Policy-setting is the responsibility of government, but tourism policies must involve all important shareholders. You should recognize that tourism policy is also shaped and implemented through the efforts of many tourism organizations at all geographic levels.

The number of tourism organizations involved in tourism around the world is growing and in the many thousands. There are tourism organizations worldwide that either set tourism policies or try to influence them. Figure 3.10 identifies tourism organizations by geography and scope. The first row of three sets of organizations is those whose scope is fully focused on tourism at the global, multi-country, and country levels. The second row is of organizations that are not only involved in tourism, but also engaged with other economic sectors (global airline organizations, multi-country economic organizations, and development agencies and banks).

You should know that there are other organizations not specifically identified in Figure 3.10. For example, there are many trade associations for hotels, travel agencies and tour operators, attractions, travel agents and tour operators, and so on.

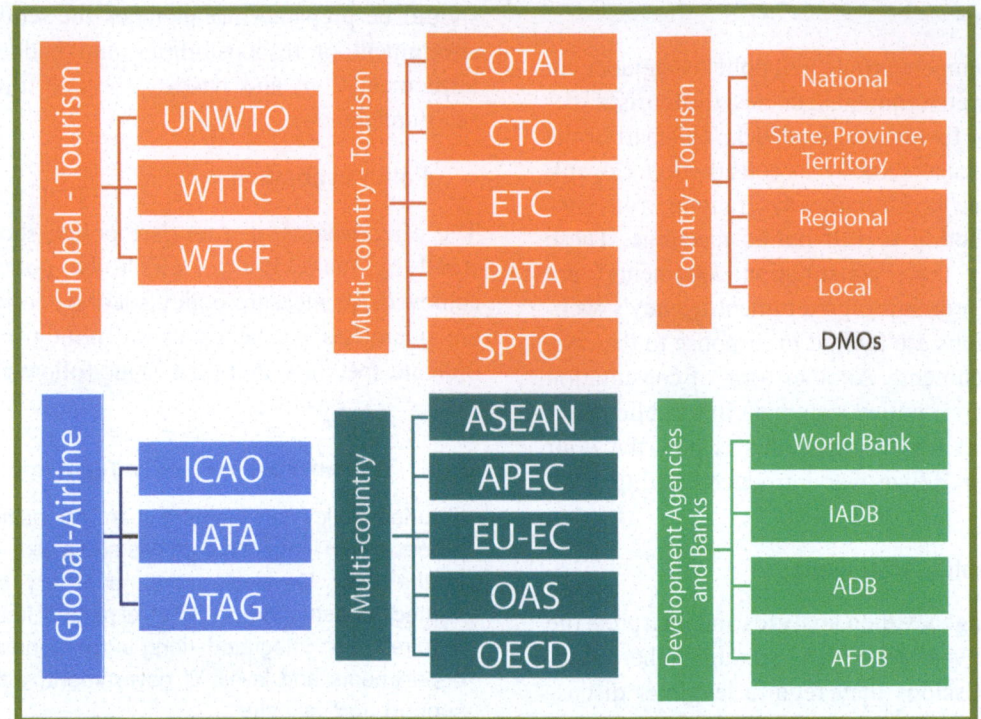

FIGURE 3.10 Organizations at various geographic levels and by scope.

• **Global tourism organizations**

The first group is global tourism organizations and they include the World Tourism Organization (UNWTO), World Travel & Tourism Council (WTTC), and World Tourism Cities Federation (WTCF).

World Tourism Organization (UNWTO). The only official organization that represents governmental interests on a worldwide basis is the World Tourism Organization (UNWTO). The World Tourism Organization is a specialized agency of the United Nations and the leading worldwide organization in tourism. It serves as a global forum for tourism policy issues and is a major source of tourism research and knowledge. A profile of UNWTO is provided in Figure 3.11.

Although its members include many developed countries, such as Canada, France, Germany, Italy, and Japan, the UNWTO places a special emphasis on tourism in developing countries. It is noteworthy that the United States, UK, Australia, New Zealand, Norway, Sweden, Denmark, and Finland are not UNWTO members (as of August 2016).

There are other United Nations agencies that have roles that affect tourism. These include UNESCO (UN Educational, Scientific and Cultural Organization); International Labour Organization (ILO); UN Environment Programme (UNEP); and the UN Conference on Trade and Development (UNCTAD).

World Travel & Tourism Council, London, England. WTTC is a private-sector organization that brings together major players in the tourism sector including airlines, hotels, cruise lines, car rental, travel agencies and tour operators, GDS and technology. Figure 3.12 has a profile of WTTC.

WTTC is an important provider of comprehensive statistics on the economic impact of tourism at global and country levels.

World Tourism Cities Federation, Beijing, China. WTCF is the newest global tourism organization, formed with the assistance of the Beijing Government. A profile of WTCF is provided in Figure 3.13.

• **Multi-country tourism organizations**

Several multi-country regional tourism organizations assist with the planning, development, and marketing of tourism in different parts of the world. Although these organizations are aimed at promoting tourism in specific geographic areas, they differ in their membership compositions and structures. For example, PATA is an industry association, while the SPTO is a grouping of national government tourism agencies.

World Tourism Organization (UNWTO)
A specialized agency of the United Nations (UN)

LOCATION
Madrid, Spain

WEBSITE
http://www2.unwto.org/

MISSION
"As the leading international organization in the field of tourism, UNWTO promotes tourism as a driver of economic growth, inclusive development and environmental sustainability and offers leadership and support to the sector in advancing knowledge and tourism policies worldwide."

HISTORY
The forerunners to UNWTO were the International Congress of Official Tourist Traffic Associations (ICOTTA) set up at The Hague (Netherlands) in 1925 and the International Union of Official Travel Organizations (IUOTO), established in 1947. UNWTO was transformed into a specialized agency of the UN in 2003.

GOALS
UNWTO is committed to promoting tourism to help achieve the Sustainable Development Goals (SDGs).

WHAT UNWTO DOES
(1) Mainstreaming tourism in the global agenda; (2) sustainable development of tourism; (3) ethics and social responsibility; (4) tourism and development; (5) competitiveness; and (6) fostering knowledge.

MEMBERSHIP
156 Member States (August 2016)
6 Associate Members and 2 Observers (2017)
493 Affiliate Members (July 2017)

FIGURE 3.11   Profile of the World Tourism Organization (UNWTO).

World Travel & Tourism Council (WTTC)
Private-sector membership organization

LOCATION
London, England

WEBSITE
https://www.wttc.org

MISSION
WTTC works to raise awareness of Travel & Tourism as one of the world's largest sectors, employing 1 in 10 people and generating approximately 10% of global GDP.

HISTORY
WTTC was founded in 1990 and is a private-sector membership organization that provides a forum for business leaders in the Travel & Tourism industry.

GOALS
WTTC has three priorities that underpin its mission: (1) Freedom to Travel; (2) Policies for Growth; and (3) Tourism for Tomorrow.

WHAT WTTC DOES
WTTC's programs fall into three broad categories: (1) research; (2) advocacy; and (3) summits.

MEMBERSHIP
More than 150 CEOs of major travel and tourism companies.
13 industry partners; 8 knowledge partners; and 25 media partners (August 2017)

FIGURE 3.12   Profile of the World Travel & Tourism Council (WTTC).

World Tourism Cities Federation (WTCF)

Non-profit organization

LOCATION
Beijing, People's Republic of China

WEBSITE
http://en.wtcf.org.cn/

MISSION
WTCF is committed to facilitating exchanges and cooperation between members and promoting sustainable growth in the tourism sector. WTCF aims to increase the appeal of tourism cities as international destinations, enhance the quality and efficiency of their services, boost the brand images of tourism cities and promote balanced economic and social progress in tourism cities and regions.

HISTORY
Established in September 2012 in Beijing.

GOALS
WTCF main goals are to promote greater cooperation among tourism cities and to increase the profile of and research on cities as tourism destinations.

WHAT WTCF DOES
(1) Fragrant Hills Summit (annual); (2) research; (3) member services; (4) investment platform

MEMBERSHIP
126 city members and 63 institutional members

FIGURE 3.13 Profile of the World Tourism Cities Federation (WTCF).

COTAL (Confederación de Organizaciones Turísticas de la América Latina), Buenos Aires, Argentina. Founded in 1957, COTAL has twenty members including all the nations of South America, Central America, Mexico, as well as three entities in the Caribbean: Puerto Rico, the Dominican Republic, and Haiti. COTAL's mission is "to solve the difficulties that impede the development of tourism in Latin America, promoting the care of natural, cultural, and historic resources as key elements." The Confederation's two main objectives are to: (1) raise awareness of Latin American tourism participants of the need to work together to overcome obstacles and achieve sustainable development; and (2) make Latin America a tourism destination par excellence based on its rich natural, historic, cultural, and human resources.

CTO (Caribbean Tourism Organization), Barbados, West Indies. A profile of the Caribbean Tourism Organization is shown in Figure 3.14.

ETC (European Travel Commission), Brussels, Belgium. ETC is a body that represents tourism in most European countries (excluding the UK). A profile of ETC is provided in Figure 3.15.

PATA (Pacific Asia Travel Association), Bangkok, Thailand. PATA is an important and influential multi-country tourism organization for the Asia-Pacific region. A profile of PATA is given in Figure 3.16.

SPTO (South Pacific Tourism Organisation), Suva, Fiji Islands. SPTO represents tourism in the countries of the South Pacific. Figure 3.17 provides a profile of SPTO.

There are other multi-country regional tourism organizations, including the Greater Mekong Subregion (GMS) (Mekong Tourism Coordinating Office 2017) and Mundo Maya (Mayan World) in Mexico and Central America (Mundo Maya 2017).

• **Country tourism organizations**

You learned earlier in this chapter about government involvement in tourism. Much of this direct involvement in tourism is done through destination management organizations (DMOs), which governments either operate or finance. Within individual countries, there are often many official DMOs at different geographic levels (Figure 3.10).

National Tourism Organizations. The tourism policy of a country is developed and implemented by its national DMO, the official national body responsible for the policy-setting, planning, development, and marketing of tourism.

Caribbean Tourism Organization (CTO)

The Caribbean's tourism development agency

LOCATION
Barbados, West Indies

WEBSITE
http://www.onecaribbean.org/

MISSION
The primary objective of CTO is to provide to and through its members the services and information necessary for the development of sustainable tourism for the economic and social benefit of the Caribbean people.

HISTORY
Established in 1989

GOALS
The CTO's vision is to position the Caribbean as the most desirable, year-round, warm weather destination by 2017 and our purpose is Leading Sustainable Tourism—One Sea, One Voice, One Caribbean.

WHAT CTO DOES
Advocacy; Caribbean Tourism Development Company; CTO Scholarship Foundation; CTO UK & Europe; CTO USA Inc.; human resource development; finance and resource management; research and information technology; sustainable tourism development; total visitor satisfaction

MEMBERSHIP
28 countries and territories

FIGURE 3.14 Profile of the Caribbean Tourism Organization (CTO).

European Travel Commission (ETC)

Non-profit organization, mainly funded by member contributions

LOCATION
Brussels, Belgium

WEBSITE
http://www.etc-corporate.org/

MISSION
The 32-member NTOs work together to build the value of tourism to all the beautiful and diverse countries of Europe through, in particular, cooperating in areas of sharing best practices, market intelligence, and promotion.

HISTORY
Established in 1948.

GOALS
(1) Promote Europe as an attractive tourist destination; (2) assist member NTOs to exchange knowledge and work collaboratively; (3) provide industry partners and other interested parties with easy access to material and statistics regarding inbound tourism to Europe.

WHAT ETC DOES
(1) Public relations; (2) consumer advertising in selected overseas markets; (3) trade promotions; (4) market research; (5) professional development for members; (6) liaison with other relevant agencies.

MEMBERSHIP
32 member NTOs, 9 Associate Members, and 7 Partners

FIGURE 3.15 Profile of the European Travel Commission (ETC).

Pacific Asia Travel Association (PATA)

Not-for-profit membership association

LOCATION
Bangkok, Thailand

WEBSITE
http://www.pata.org

MISSION
The Pacific Asia Travel Association (PATA) is a membership association acting as a catalyst for the responsible development of the Asia Pacific travel and tourism industry. In partnership with PATA's private and public sector members, we enhance the sustainable growth, value, and quality of travel and tourism to, from, and within the region. See more at: https://www.pata.org/about-pata/#mission

HISTORY
Established in 1951 to promote Pacific Asia's tourism destinations, products, and services.

GOALS
(1) Build the Business for members; (2) provide valuable insights, forecasts, and analysis to help members make better business decisions; (3) to take a lead position on travel industry issues that need to be addressed.

WHAT PATA DOES
Advocacy; PATA events (PATA Travel Mart, etc.); PATA Strategic Intelligence Center provides data and forecasts; PATA Foundation (contributes to sustainable and responsible tourism development, the protection of heritage, and education).

MEMBERSHIP
95 government, state, and city tourism bodies; 29 international airlines, airports and cruise lines, 63 educational institutions, and hundreds of travel industry companies. Operates 43 PATA Chapters. PATA also operates Student Chapters.

FIGURE 3.16 Profile of the Pacific Asia Travel Association (PATA).

South Pacific Tourism Organisation (SPTO)

Mandated organization representing tourism in the South Pacific

LOCATION
Suva, Fiji Islands

WEBSITE
https://corporate.southpacificislands.travel/

MISSION
Market and develop tourism in the South Pacific.

HISTORY
Established in 1983 as the Tourism Council of the South Pacific.

GOALS
(1) To improve air and sea access to islands; (2) to enhance brand "South Pacific"; (3) to develop capacity of government and private sector for sustainable tourism.

WHAT SPTO DOES
(1) Advocacy for tourism; (2) marketing; (3) research and planning; (4) sustainable tourism development

MEMBERSHIP
18 government and 200 private-sector members

FIGURE 3.17 Profile of the South Pacific Tourism Organisation (SPTO).

Most countries have just one national DMO, but some have split the roles between two different agencies (NTA and NTO). This happens when governments want to allow more flexibility in conducting destination marketing. In some destinations, all roles except for destination marketing, but including policy-setting, product development, planning, and research, are assigned to the NTA. Australia's NTA is the Australian Trade and Investment Commission (Austrade); Tourism Australia is the other national level office and is a statutory body responsible for the international marketing of Australia as a destination for leisure and business travel. In New Zealand, the NTO is Tourism New Zealand and the NTA is the Ministry of Business, Innovation & Employment. TA and TNZ are examples of *statutory bodies* or *quangos* (quasi-autonomous non-governmental organisation). One of the main advantages of statutory bodies is that they tend to offer a blend of public- and private-sector strengths, and are often called ***PPPs*** (public-private partnerships). These organizations are governed by independent boards of directors drawn from various sectors. Therefore, they have more management flexibility in dealing with the commercial aspects of marketing and promotion (Wight 2013). Additionally, they have closer relationships with the private sector and non-governmental organizations.

The roles of national DMOs vary based upon the governmental status they are given in specific countries. The national DMO may be governmental and part of the civil service system as an ***independent ministry***. Countries with an independent Ministry of Tourism consider tourism to be a highly important economic sector. The Bahamas, Croatia, Ghana, Kenya, Oman, India, Indonesia, Israel, Jamaica, Malaysia, Maldives, and Trinidad and Tobago, mostly developing countries, have a Ministry of Tourism.

Some countries assign tourism a lower priority and place it along with other government departments in a ***shared ministerial portfolio***. For example, it is often combined with economic development, as in the case of the Ministry of Economy, Development, and Tourism in Chile and Greece. Other popular combinations are tourism and culture (Turkey) and tourism and civil aviation (Bangladesh and Nepal). In some cases, the word "tourism" does not appear in the official name of the Ministry. An example of this is in New Zealand where tourism is just one of the industry ***sectoral units*** within the Ministry of Business, Innovation & Employment. In the UK, tourism is under the Department for Digital, Culture, Media & Sport. Brand USA is yet another example of national DMO structure, in which the operation is as a ***non-profit organization***, which receives no direct Federal Government funding.

QUICK TRIP 3.3

Brand USA

Brand USA is the USA's first public-private partnership "to spearhead a globally coordinated marketing effort to promote the United States as a premier travel destination and to communicate U.S. visa and entry policies." It commenced operations in 2011 as a nonprofit corporation after being officially established by the Travel Promotion Act of 2009.

There is also a unit called the National Travel & Tourism Office (NTTO) within the International Trade Administration (ITA) of the U.S. Department of Commerce. NTTO functions as the NTA and its responsibilities include tourism policy, research and statistics, export expansion activities, and technical assistance.

Brand USA has the following five objectives:

1. Drive results: Increase international visitation, spend, and global market share for the United States.
2. Create innovative marketing: Promote the entirety of the USA with innovative marketing that supports all fifty states, the District of Columbia, and five territories to, through, and beyond the gateways.
3. Market the welcome: Inspire, inform, welcome, and thank travelers while accurately communicating vital and compelling information about visa and entry policies.

QUICK TRIP 3.3 CONTINUED

4. Build and maintain trust: Build and maintain trusted relationships with stakeholders worldwide through inclusive, proactive, and transparent outreach with a commitment to compliance and integrity through words, actions, and results.
5. Add and create value: Pioneer cooperative marketing platforms and programs that leverage and grow the USA brand in ways our partners would be challenged or unable to do on their own.

Brand USA receives its funding from a variety of sources. According to Brand USA, its operations *"are supported by a combination of non-federal contributions from destinations, travel brands, and private-sector organizations plus matching funds collected by the U.S. government from international visitors who visit the United States under the Visa Waiver Program."* Brand USA's budget for Fiscal Year 2017 was $164.4 million, with 57 percent of this expected from the Visa Waiver Program.

Brand USA claims that its marketing efforts reach thirty different countries. The return on investment on Brand USA's marketing is impressive. Oxford Economics estimated that every $1 of Brand USA's marketing generated $30.70 in visitor spending. Despite its prodigious return, Brand USA's funding is threatened by a major budget cut in 2018 by President Trump.

Think about This

1. What are the major difficulties in marketing tourism in a country as large and diverse as the USA? (Figure 3.18)
2. What are the advantages to a country from separating its national DMO into an NTA and NTO?
3. The USA has a goal of 100 million international visitor arrivals by 2021. Do you believe this target will be attained? Why or why not?
4. Many experts and tourism sector operators argue that the U.S. Federal Government does not put enough money into tourism. Do you agree with this argument? Why or why not?

Sources

Brand USA. 2016. FY2017 Objectives, Summary Marketing Plan & Budget. https://www.thebrandusa.com/about/reports

Brand USA. 2017. Who we are. https://www.thebrandusa.com/about/whoweare

Fuller, E. 2017. Why the U.S. budget ax must spare Brand USA. *Forbes*, June 26.

ITA National Travel & Tourism Office. 2017. National Travel & Tourism Office. http://tinet.ita.doc.gov/about/overview.asp

Oxford Economics. 2017. The Return on Investment in Brand USA Marketing: Fiscal Year 2016.

Peltier, D. 2017. Brand USA is facing declining contributions from travel brands this year. *Skift*, July 13.

There is great variety in the naming of national DMOs. Historically, they were called boards, authorities, or commissions. In some countries, the national DMO is named as the National Tourism Administration, such as the China National Tourism Administration (CNTA). More recently, the country names are superseded with either "tourism" or "visit" or "destination," including Tourism Australia, Tourism New Zealand, VisitBritain, and Destination Canada.

The roles of national DMOs affect the supply and demand for all elements of tourism. On the supply side, programs include conducting inventories and assessments of the destination product prior to the development of a national tourism plan. National DMOs usually are principals in coordinating the national tourism destination planning process. National DMOs develop and operate programs to improve the quality of different elements of the destination product. This includes protecting the environment through a national park system, other protected areas, and policies and measures to encourage sustainable tourism. Governments may establish minimum standards for hotels, attractions, tour operators, and tour guides. National DMOs operate training and education programs to increase professionalism in tourism and improve hospitality skills. When another agency sets policy that affects tourism, the national DMO may have some advisory input into that policy.

FIGURE 3.18 The United States is a land of such great diversity.

Although the government's involvement in economic activities in free-market economies is generally confined to legislation and regulation, the role of the government in socialist countries is quite different, although the differences are now becoming less obvious. In socialist countries, governments have traditionally been involved in owning and operating visitor attractions and facilities, as well as in controlling domestic travel agencies and inbound tour operators. Developing countries lacking private capital and expertise also often find it necessary for the government to develop, own, and manage facilities and attractions. To further ensure the appropriate supply, governments provide financial incentives for the development of facilities and attractions (Chapter 6), and for human resources development to educate and train local residents for tourism.

On the demand side, national DMOs are involved in facilitation, marketing research, marketing, and representation in foreign countries. Their role in facilitation tends to be an advisory one, commenting on the effect of

Destination Canada

Destination Canada, formerly the Canadian Tourism Commission, is the official national DMO for Canada. Legally, Destination Canada is a federal Crown corporation wholly owned by the Government of Canada. It is mainly funded by the Government of Canada through parliamentary appropriations. During Calendar Year 2016, Destination Canada received a total of C$ 81.5 million from the Government of Canada. With headquarters in Vancouver, Destination Canada also has offices in Ottawa, Japan, China, and UK.

Destination Canada's mandate, by legislation, is:

- To sustain a vibrant and profitable tourism industry
- To market Canada as a desirable tourism destination
- To support a cooperative relationship between the private sector and the governments of Canada, the provinces, and the territories with respect to Canadian tourism
- To provide information about tourism to the Canadian private sector, the governments of Canada, the provinces, and the territories

Destination Canada's approach to marketing the nation abroad is summarized below:

"We use data-driven marketing strategies to stimulate international demand and tourism export revenue for Canada in 11 countries: Australia, Brazil, China, France, Germany, India, Japan, Mexico, South Korea, the UK and the USA."

Destination Canada, and its forerunners, has built a reputation as being an outstanding national DMO known for its detailed consumer market research, *Signature Experiences* program, and the *Explorer Quotient* psychographic segmentation scheme. With an area of almost 10 million square kilometers to cover, Destination Canada works in partnership with thirteen provincial and territorial DMOs, many RTOs/RTAs, and local DMOs (Figure 3.19).

Think about This

1. Destination Canada is considered by many experts to be one of the very best NTOs in the world. Using the sources supplied here, what are the main reasons for CTC's outstanding world ranking?
2. Destination Canada (then CTC) was moved in 2005 from Canada's capital, Ottawa, to Vancouver. This move was somewhat controversial in Canada. Do you think that a national tourism organization must always be in its capital city? Why or why not? What do you think were the advantages of moving Destination Canada to Vancouver on Canada's West Coast?
3. Canada for many years has fought against a limiting image of just having "Moose, Mountains and Mounties." One of Destination Canada's strategies is to broaden this perception by placing the focus on diversified visitor experiences, and to show the active involvement of people in its advertising. How can this change from "sightseeing" to "active and participatory experience" help Canada and other destinations improve and expand their tourism sectors?
4. Although Canada's population is almost ten times less than the United States', its Federal Government allocates significant direct funding to the national DMO, Destination Canada, while the US Government provides no direct funding to Brand USA. What does this tell you about the priorities attached to tourism in the two countries? What can the United States learn from the excellent programs developed by Destination Canada?

Sources

CIA World Factbook. 2017. Canada. https://www.cia.gov/library/publications/the-world-factbook/geos/ca.html

Destination Canada. 2016. *Seizing the Winning Conditions for Canada. 2016–2020 Corporate Plan Summary*. Vancouver: Destination Canada.

Destination Canada. 2016. *Welcoming the World. 2016 Annual Report*. Vancouver: Destination Canada.

Destination Canada. 2017. About us. https://www.destinationcanada.com/en/about-us

Destination Canada. Corporate Governance. 2017. https://www.destinationcanada.com/en/corporate-governance

FIGURE 3.19 Canada is a destination for explorers.

government policies regarding visas, passports, and customs formalities on visitor demand. National DMOs are traditionally known for their roles in marketing, especially in attracting foreign visitors to their respective countries, and in sponsoring or generating tourism marketing research data. Some agencies, including Tourism Australia, have no direct supply-side functions and are also not involved in the marketing of tourism to their own residents (domestic tourism). Others such as the Singapore Tourism Board have traditionally had both supply- and demand-side functions. The promotional role of national DMOs is reviewed in detail in Chapter 8.

State, Provincial, and Territorial Tourism Organizations.
Several larger countries have governmental systems below the national level. In these situations, DMOs operate at state, provincial, or territorial levels.

Different types of organizational structures are found. Many are governmental entities. For example, in New York, the Division of Marketing, Advertising and Tourism is within the State Government's Empire State Development Agency (Empire State Development 2017). The Department of Tourism, Government of

Kerala in India (Kerala, Department of Tourism 2017) and the Gauteng Tourism Authority in South Africa are other examples (Gauteng Tourism Authority 2017). All DMOs in China are government operated.

There has been a trend to create statutory bodies and other forms of non-profit organizations, particularly to handle the destination marketing at various levels. Tourism Northern Territory and Tourism & Events Queensland in Australia are examples of statutory bodies (Tourism Northern Territory 2017; Tourism & Events Queensland 2017). Visit California is a non-profit organization classified as a corporation (Visit California 2017).

The roles of these organizations tend to parallel those of their respective national DMOs. The fifty states in the United States, the ten Canadian provinces, and the three Canadian territories have an agency officially responsible for tourism. The six Australian states, the Northern Territory, and the ACT also have official tourism organizations. In the UK, VisitEngland, VisitScotland, VisitWales, and Tourism Northern Ireland support the efforts of VisitBritain by marketing their areas (VisitBritain 2017). A state tourism organization system is also found in India and a provincial tourism administration/bureau system is found in China.

The primary role of state, provincial, and territorial tourism organizations is *domestic tourism promotion*; promoting their destinations to their own residents and the residents of nearby states, provinces, or territories. However, these organizations are becoming more involved in international travel promotion and are spending more to attract foreign visitors. This is certainly the case with the state and territorial tourism organizations in Australia and the national agencies in the UK. Additionally, these organizations are playing an increasingly important role as a cooperative partner with their national DMOs.

A traditional marketing role of these DMOs has been in *generating and fulfilling inquiries* through social media, websites, and media advertising. Many of these organizations also provide travel information at *visitor/tourist information* or *welcome centers* that they operate. Some of them have marketing offices in other parts of the country and overseas. They set up promotional booths at *travel trade and consumer travel shows, fairs, or exhibitions*. They host travel writers, retail travel agents, and tour wholesalers visiting their state, province, or territory on *familiarization tours*.

These DMOs make significant investments in *tourism marketing research*, gathering statistics on ongoing visitor volumes and on other special tourism research studies. The level of research effort has been increasing as these organizations try to more precisely target marketing programs and to measure the effectiveness and impacts of their marketing activities.

Many state, provincial, and territorial DMOs play a role in *tourism development* and in the *training and education* of tourism employees. This is especially true in Australia, Canada, New Zealand, and the UK, where significant investments have been made in tourism planning and stimulating the development of new attractions and facilities, and in the improvement and expansion of existing ones. Australian, British, Canadian, and New Zealand organizations have also had a well-established role in educational and training programs to upgrade management and other employee skills.

Almost all these DMOs play some role in encouraging *package tour development and promotion*. In some cases, this has involved financial and/or technical assistance with package or tour development. Many of these organizations have cost-sharing programs that provide grants to local groups to promote tourism to their communities.

QUICK TRIP 3.5

Tourism Organizations in Queensland

Popularly known as the Sunshine State, Queensland's total area is almost two-and-a-half times greater than the state of Texas. Covering 1,727,000 square kilometers, it is the second largest state in Australia after Western Australia. Given such a large area with very diverse regions, it is not surprising that Queensland has quite an elaborate system of DMOs at the state, regional, and local levels (Figure 3.20).

Queensland has a population of over four million, and is the home of five of Australia's eleven UNESCO World Heritage natural areas (Scenic Rim National Parks, Fraser Island, Riversleigh Fossil Fields, the Wet Tropics, and the Great Barrier Reef).

For a large state, where tourism is an economic sector, Queensland has an extensive system of tourism organizations. At the state level, this includes a division of responsibilities between a State Government agency (DTESB) and Tourism and Events Queensland (TEQ).

- Tourism and Events Queensland (TEQ) is a statutory body of the Queensland Government and its lead marketing, destination, and experience development and major events agency.
- Department of Tourism, Major Events, Small Business, and the Commonwealth Games (DTESB) is the State Government agency with the oversight of tourism and major events in Queensland.
- Regional tourism organizations (RTOs): There are thirteen RTOs in Queensland (Brisbane Marketing; Bundaberg North Burnett Tourism; Capricorn Enterprise; Fraser Coast Tourism and Events; Gladstone Area Promotion & Development Ltd; Gold Coast Tourism; Mackay Tourism Ltd; Outback Queensland Tourism Association; South Queensland Country Tourism; Visit Sunshine Coast; Townsville Enterprise; Tropical North Queensland; Tourism Whitsundays).
- Local tourism organizations: There are also some local tourism organizations, including for example Business Events Cairns & Great Barrier Reef.

QUICK TRIP 3.5 CONTINUED

- Queensland Tourism Industry Council (QTIC): QTIC is a not-for-profit, private sector, membership-based organization representing the interests of Queensland's tourism and hospitality industry.
- DestinationQ: A partnership between the Queensland State Government and the tourism sector in Queensland.

Think about This

1. Why is it important in a large state like Queensland to have several levels of DMOs?
2. One of the roles of government in tourism is coordination. In Queensland, how do the two state-level DMOs (DTESB and TEQ) coordinate other players in the tourism sector?
3. There are thirteen tourism regions in Queensland. What is the value in having RTOs in Queensland and other destinations?
4. TEQ is an example of a state DMO that has both domestic and international offices doing domestic and international marketing. Given that Tourism Australia also markets Australian tourism abroad, how can TEQ justify having its own international marketing efforts?

Sources

Department of Tourism, Major Events, Small Business and the Commonwealth Games. 2017. DTESB. https://www.dtesb.qld.gov.au/

Queensland Tourism Industry Council. 2017. About us. https://www.qtic.com.au/qtic-peak-industry-body-tourism-queensland

The State of Queensland. 2017. Interesting facts about Queensland. https://www.qld.gov.au/about/about-queensland/statistics-facts/facts

The State of Queensland. 2017. What is DestinationQ? https://www.destq.com.au/about

Tourism and Events Queensland. 2017. About TEQ. https://teq.queensland.com/about-teq-new

Tourism and Events Queensland. 2017. Regional Tourism Organisations. https://teq.queensland.com/about-teq-new/contacts/rtos

© TellyVision/Shutterstock.com

FIGURE 3.20 The beautiful Mission Beach in topical North Queensland.

Regional Tourism Organizations. The next level of tourism organizations found in several countries is at the regional level. The definition of what a region constitutes varies and so does the meaning of a regional DMO. For example, smaller-sized countries such Italy have regional government agencies below the national level. Larger countries such as Canada and Australia have states, provincial, or territorial government agencies below the national level and then have regions under the states, provinces, or territories. The economic and social priorities and destination products are quite different from region to region. In these situations, it is very desirable for groups of communities to prepare their own policies and plans for tourism development and marketing. This may lead to the creation of a system of regional DMOs. These bodies are often referred to as *RTOs* (regional tourism organizations) or *RTAs* (regional tourism associations).

Regional DMO systems are found in Australia, Canada, New Zealand, and the UK. In many cases, these systems have been initiated by state and provincial DMOs to increase the effectiveness of regional tourism marketing and development. Often, regional DMOs are created as non-profit organizations or associations. Regional DMOs are generally partly funded by state or provincial grants and by membership dues from private-sector tourism businesses and local DMOs. Regional DMOs perform roles like the state, provincial, or territorial DMOs. Regional DMOs tend to be mainly involved in destination management, but in some cases, they also assume other roles, including planning, research, and product development.

Another broader definition of tourism regions is one that is composed of several countries. For example, European Cities Marketing represents several major cities in the European region (European Cities Marketing 2017).

Local Tourism Organizations. The final group of DMOs is found at the individual community level. Around the world, the number of communities forming these organizations is increasing rapidly. There are many different organizational formats for local DMOs. The DMO may be within the local government structure and be funded completely by local government. It may be a public-private partnership (PPP) with some funding from both the local government and private-sector tourism businesses. The local DMO may have little or no direct local government funding, but receive its budget from user taxes and private-sector memberships.

Local DMOs are mostly at the county and city levels. These exist in most countries in the largest metropolitan areas. In some countries and especially in the United States, there are extensive systems of county and city DMOs, where the introduction of room or bed taxes at county and city levels led to a rapid expansion of the number of DMOs. Guests at hotels and other forms of accommodation pay these taxes and then part or all the collections are distributed by local governments to DMOs. In the United States, these organizations are called *convention and visitors bureaus* (CVBs). They mainly focus on destination marketing but are gradually placing greater emphasis on other destination management roles.

States and provinces are often instrumental in the creation of local DMOs and in helping maintain their operations. States and provinces can assist local efforts by passing legislation enabling communities to collect taxes to support local promotional activities. In the United States, this is in the form of a *room or innkeeper's tax*, but some cities derive support from a tax on alcoholic beverages, car rentals, entertainment and gaming, or tickets, or from an earmarked sales tax. Room taxes are a common method of obtaining funding for local DMOs. This requires passage of a county or city ordinance after state- or provincial-enabling legislation has authorized counties or cities to establish such a tax. Room tax proposals are often resisted by local lodging groups as an unfair tax on only one segment of tourism. However, local residents are inclined to be supportive since these are taxes paid by the visitor, not the resident (i.e., they represent a *user-pay* approach).

States, provinces, and territories provide matching (cost-sharing) grant funds, either for general purposes or for activities specified by the state, provincial, or territorial government. The types of activities receiving such funding are usually such things as digital marketing, advertising, familiarization tours for tour wholesalers and travel writers, brochure preparation, public relations, festival and event marketing and development, tourism planning studies, and marketing research projects. Counties and cities in some cases also receive an allocation from the general funds of the city, county, or state or province.

Another common method of financing local DMOs is through *membership programs*, especially for those that are constituted as non-profit organizations. Often the membership-based local DMOs offer tiered membership program levels, based on the benefits that different member categories receive.

- **Global airline organizations**

As shown in Figure 3.10, there are three major global airline organizations that have an impact on tourism.

International Civil Aviation Organization, Montreal, Canada. ICAO is a specialized agency of the United Nations established in 1944 to administer and govern the Convention on International Civil Aviation (Chicago Convention). The ICAO is made up of representatives from the governments of 191 Member States (national governments). It works with these Member States and industry groups "to reach consensus on international civil aviation Standards and Recommended Practices (SARPs) and policies in support of a safe, efficient, secure, economically sustainable and environmentally responsible civil aviation sector."

International Air Transport Association, Montreal, Canada. IATA is the trade association for approximately 275 of the world's airlines with a mission "to represent, lead, and serve the airline industry." IATA's members represent 83 percent of total air traffic in the world. IATA's priorities, as expressed in 2017, were: (1) distribution and payment transformation; (2) reduce airport and ANSP (air navigation service provider) charges, fuel fees, and taxes; (3) fast travel; (4) safety in air cargo; (5) normal aircraft tracking and ICAO Annex Amendments; (6) IOSA (IATA Operational Safety Audit) transformation; (7) improving the regulatory and legal environment; (8) toward a global agreement on CNG 2020 (Carbon Neutral Growth by 2020); (9) supporting sustainable aviation fuel projects; and (10) membership.

IATA offers a variety of services for its members, including accreditation, research and statistics, financial services, consulting, safety and flight services solutions, advertising in IATA publications, and IATA codes.

Air Transport Action Group, Geneva, Switzerland. ATAG is a not-for-profit association that was established in 1990. Its funding members are Airports Council International, Airbus, ATR, Boeing, Bombardier, Civil Air Navigation Services Organisation (CANSO), CFM International, Embraer, GE, Honeywell Aerospace, International Air Transport Association (IATA), Pratt & Whitney, Rolls-Royce, and Safran. ATAG has fifty members from airlines, airports, aircraft manufacturers, and many other parts of tourism.

ATAG brings together "all aviation industry players so that they can speak with one voice—and it works to promote aviation's sustainable growth for the benefit of our global society." ATAG's mission is "to define common positions on issues and to make expert and constructive contributions to the industry and governmental consultation process." Its activities revolve around aviation industry collaboration, climate change, social and economic benefits of aviation, industry communications, intermodality, sustainable development, and sustainable aviation biofuels.

- **Multi-country economic organizations**

There are several multi-country organizations that have an emphasis on economic cooperation and trade among members. Some of these organizations are quite involved in tourism.

Association of Southeast Asian Nations, Jakarta, Indonesia. ASEAN was established in 1967 in Bangkok, Thailand, with the signing of the ASEAN Declaration (Bangkok Declaration). There are ten member countries (see Figure 3.21).

ASEAN is very active in tourism and has an ASEAN Tourism Ministers (M-ATM) group, involving meetings of the ASEAN NTOs. ASEAN has produced the *ASEAN Tourism Strategic Plan 2016–2025*. It periodically releases statistics on travel within its member countries. ASEAN has produced competency standards for tourism professionals within ASEAN (*ASEAN Mutual Recognition Arrangement—MRA—on Tourism Professionals*) and the *ASEAN Community Based Tourism Standard*. ASEAN also has a small ASEAN Tourism Marketing group, operating from Bangkok (Association of Southeast Asian Nations 2017).

Asia-Pacific Economic Cooperation (APEC), Singapore. APEC was created in 1989 and has since become a primary vehicle for promoting open trade and economic cooperation among the countries of the Asia-Pacific region. It has twenty-one members that include Australia, Canada, Chile, China, Japan, Mexico, New Zealand, United States, and several Southeast Asian countries. APEC's primary goal is to support sustainable economic growth and prosperity in the Asia-Pacific region.

APEC has the APEC Tourism Working Group (TWG) that serves as "a platform for tourism administrators of APEC economies, to share information, exchange views and develop areas of cooperation in tourism trade and policies."

The *APEC Tourism Charter*, endorsed at the 1st Tourism Ministerial Meeting in Seoul, Korea, in 2000, constitutes the basis for APEC tourism cooperation.

FIGURE 3.21 **ASEAN** Economic Community.

This Charter establishes four key policy goals and an agreed process for realizing these aims:

- Removal of impediments to tourism business and investment
- Increase mobility of visitors and demand for tourism goods and services
- Sustainable management of tourism outcomes and impacts
- Enhance recognition and understanding of tourism as a vehicle for economic and social development

European Commission, Brussels, Belgium. The European Union consists of twenty-eight countries (Figure 3.22); but this number will be reduced by one after the UK withdraws as a result of the much-publicized Brexit vote. There are also five Candidate Countries and two Potential Countries that may join in the future.

The European Commission (EC) is the executive institution of the European Union. It "promotes the general interest of the EU by proposing and enforcing legislation as well as by implementing policies and the EU budget." For tourism, EC has the following initiatives:

- Enhancing what European tourism has to offer (coastal and maritime tourism; sustainable tourism; cultural tourism; accessible tourism; low season tourism; European Destinations of Excellence, EDEN)
- Support to tourism businesses (digital tourism; professional skills; Enterprise Europe Network—tourism and cultural heritage)
- Promoting Destination Europe (simplifying visa rules)
- International cooperation
- Conferences and other events (live events and digital tourism; European Tourism Days; European Tourism Forum)

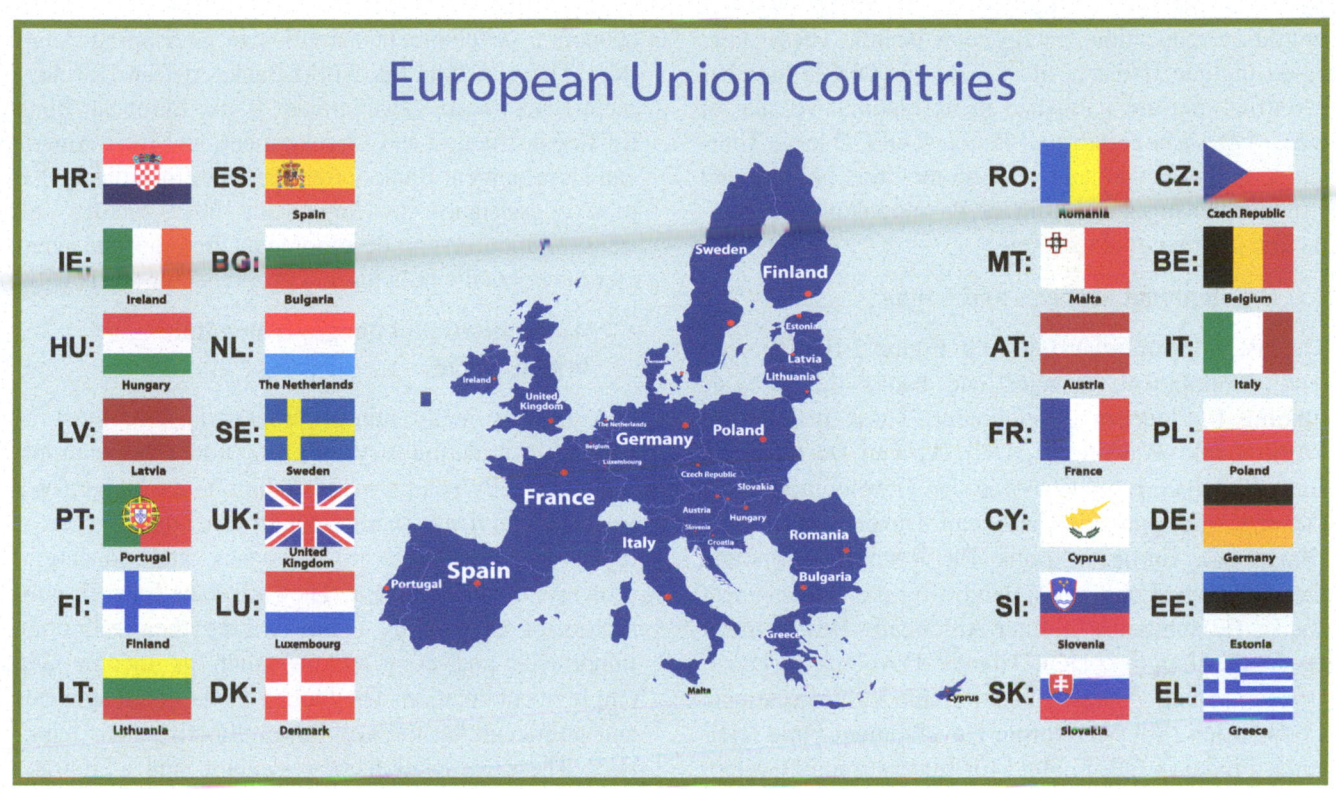

FIGURE 3.22 Member Countries of the European Union (as of August 2017).

The EU's Tourism Policy

"EU policy aims to maintain Europe's standing as a leading destination while maximising the industry's contribution to growth and employment and promoting cooperation between EU countries, particularly through the exchange of good practice. The EU's competence in the tourism is one of support and coordination to supplement the actions of member countries."

Source: European Commission. 2017. https://ec.europa.eu/growth/sectors/tourism/policy-overview_en

Organization of American States, Washington, DC, USA.
OAS was established in 1948 to achieve among its member states "an order of peace and justice, to promote their solidarity, to strengthen their collaboration, and to defend their sovereignty, their territorial integrity, and their independence."

The OAS has thirty-five member states and has granted permanent observer status to the European Union and around sixty-nine other countries. It has four pillar activities: (1) democracy; (2) human rights; (3) security; and (4) development.

OAS has a Culture and Tourism Section within its Department of Economic Development. This section: supports "the development of tangible and intangible cultural and tourism assets and cements new and established links between the tourism and culture sectors to enhance the contribution of both sectors to economic and social development" in OAS countries. It accomplishes this through training and capacity building; strengthening small and medium tourism enterprises; and promoting public policy dialogue in culture and tourism. The Section also acts as the technical secretariat for Inter-American Meeting of Ministers and High-Level Authorities on Tourism.

Organisation for Economic Co-operation and Development, Paris, France.
OECD was created in 1981 for reasons of general economic growth and stability. OECD's mission is "to promote policies that will improve the economic and social well-being of people around the world." It has thirty-five member countries.

OECD is one of the world's largest and most reliable sources of comparable statistical, economic, and social data. Its databases span areas as diverse as national accounts, economic indicators, trade, employment, migration, education, energy, and health. These databases include statistics of tourism for OECD member countries that are published in its biennial volume of *OECD Tourism Trends and Policies*. OECD has a Tourism Committee that analyzes and monitors policies and structural changes affecting the development of domestic and international tourism.

- **Development agencies and banks**

The last group of organizations in Figure 3.10 is specialized development agencies and banks that provide funding for tourism development. These include the World Bank (Washington, DC), African Development Bank (Abidjan, Ivory Coast), Asian Development Bank (Manila, Philippines), Caribbean Development Bank (Barbados), European Bank for Reconstruction and Development (London, England), European Investment Bank (Luxembourg), Inter-American Development Bank (Washington, DC), Islamic Development Bank (Jeddah, Saudi Arabia), Japan Bank for International Cooperation (Tokyo), Nordic Development Fund (Helsinki, Finland), OPEC Fund for International Development (Vienna, Austria), US AID (Washington, DC, USA) (US AID 2017), and many others.

Some of these banks are referred to as Multilateral Development Banks (MDBs) since they provide financial support and professional advice for social and economic development activities in developing countries. These include the World Bank, African Development Bank, Asian Development Bank, European Bank for Reconstruction and Development, and Inter-American Development Bank. Often the types of projects that receive assistance are large-scale infrastructure and transportation system developments. Some of the agencies have specific policies and programs for tourism.

- **Associations and nongovernmental organizations**

Tourism has many non-profit associations, most of which are trade/industry or professional associations. They normally charge memberships in exchange for a variety of services. The two major functions of trade or industry associations are advocacy and education/professional development. They advocate for their subsectors of tourism by demonstrating their economic importance and contributions, such as income and employment creation. They lobby government agencies and politicians on the key issues affecting their members. These associations also develop and administer education and training programs, and hold annual conferences and other meetings. Six examples are Destinations International (Figure 3.23), a Washington-based group that represents destination management organizations; Meeting Professionals International (Meeting

Destinations International
Non-profit trade association of DMOs

LOCATION
Washington DC, USA

WEBSITE
https://destinationsinternational.org/

MISSION
We empower our members so that their destinations excel.

HISTORY
Renamed to Destinations International from Destination Marketing Association International (DMAI) in 2017. Established originally in 1914, it was the International Association of Convention and Visitor Bureaus (IACVB), International Association of Convention Bureaus, and Association of Convention Secretaries.

GOALS
(1) Industry advocacy leadership; (2) international impact; (3) strategic partnerships; (4) next generation professional development

WHAT DESTINATIONS INTERNATIONAL DOES
(1) Community; (2) advocacy; (3) research; (4) education

MEMBERSHIP
Approximately 600 members.

FIGURE 3.23 Profile of Destinations International.

Professionals International [MPI] 2017), an association for the global meeting and event community; American Society of Travel Agents (American Society of Travel Agents [ASTA] 2017), the world's largest association of travel agents and other travel professionals; Cruise Lines International Association (CLIA), the leading authority for the global cruise community (Cruise Lines International Association 2017); the International Festival & Events Association (International Festival & Events Association, 2017); and the Society for Incentive Excellence (Society for Incentive Excellence [SITE] 2017).

There are several professional associations involved with tourism education and research. These include the Travel & Tourism Research Association, CHRIE, International Academy for the Study of Tourism, International Tourism Studies Association, International Society of Travel & Tourism Educators, ATLAS, Asia Pacific Tourism Association, and others. They provide a forum for educators and scholars to share best practices and research.

NGOs as private organizations characterized primarily by humanitarian or cooperative, rather than commercial, objectives that pursue activities to relieve suffering, promote the interests of the poor, protect the environment, provide basic social services, or undertake community development in developing countries (Werker and Ahmed 2008). NGOs are non-profit organizations that are involved with international development. Some well-recognized examples with strong conservation and sustainable tourism agendas are the Global Sustainable Tourism Council (GSTC), World Wide Fund for Nature (WWF), International Union for Conservation of Nature (IUCN), Rainforest Alliance, and Nature Conservancy.

QUICK TRIP 3.6

Influential International Industry Organizations in Tourism

There are other influential tourism organizations in the world that are not specifically described in this chapter, and they represent specific sectors of tourism. Four of these organizations are:

- European Cities Marketing (ECM)
- International Congress and Convention Association (ICCA)
- International Festival & Events Association (IFEA)
- Society for Incentive Travel Excellence (SITE)

European Cities Marketing (ECM), Dijon, France

ECM is an association of tourist boards, convention bureaux, and city marketing organizations in Europe. In its own words:

"European Cities Marketing is a non-profit organisation improving the competitiveness and performance of the leading cities of Europe. ECM provides a platform for leisure, meetings industry and city marketing professionals to exchange knowledge, best practices and widen their network to build new business."

European Cities Marketing (ECM) provides more than 120 members, representing upward of one hundred major cities in more than thirty countries. It runs the *ECM Summer School* each year and produces an annual version of the *ECM Benchmarking Report* on the status of European tourism.

International Congress and Convention Association (ICCA), Amsterdam, The Netherlands

ICCA is one of the most prominent organizations in the world of international meetings. It is the only association that comprises a membership representing the main specialists in handling, transporting, and accommodating international events. ICCA's network of over 1,000 member companies and organizations to the international meetings industry spans the globe, with members in one hundred countries. All companies and organizations which have a strategic commitment to provide top quality products and services for international meetings should consider ICCA membership as part of their long-term plans.

QUICK TRIP 3.6 CONTINUED

International Festival & Events Association (IFEA), Boise, Idaho, USA

IFEA is a not-for-profit association that represents major festivals and events around the world. As well as its HQ in the USA, IFEA has Global Affiliates in Africa, Asia, Australia and New Zealand, Europe, Latin America, and the Middle East. An Annual Convention, Expo & Retreat is organized by IFEA. The association offers a number of education and training programs including the CFEE (Certified Festival and Event Executive) designation.

Society for Incentive Travel Excellence (SITE), Chicago, USA

The Society for Incentive Travel Excellence (SITE), established in 1973, has 2,000-plus members and twenty-nine local chapters. SITE's members are incentive travel professionals who know from experience that incentive travel works. Incentive travel works to reward, retain, and motivate employees. The SITE global member community, covering eighty-four counties, has the mission to strengthen and inspire incentive travel. SITE offers the Certified Incentive Specialist (CIS) designation.

Think about This

1. These four influential tourism organizations have a strong focus on cities and counties. What are the major advantages to cities of belonging to associations such as ECM, ICCA, IFEA, and SITE?
2. Many of the members of ICCA, SITE, ECM, and IFEA rely heavily on business and association meetings. How can the networking among members help them to be more successful in the meetings market?
3. All four organizations have a high priority on education and on improving professional standards in their sectors. What are the advantages of industry-driven education and training over programs introduced by government agencies?
4. What are your suggestions about future avenues of cooperation among these four agencies to improve the professionalism and public recognition of tourism?

Sources

European Cities Marketing. 2017. *ECM Benchmarking Report 2017*. Dijon, France: European Cities Marketing.

European Cities Marketing. 2017. European Cities Marketing. http://www.europeancitiesmarketing.com/

International Congress and Convention Association. 2017. About ICCA. http://www.iccaworld.org/abouticca/

International Festival & Events Association. 2017. Who we are. http://www.ifea.com/p/about/whoweare

Society for Incentive Travel Excellence. 2017. About SITE. http://www.siteglobal.com/page/who-we-are

SUMMARY

Governments around the world have selected to take a leadership role in tourism policy-setting, planning, development, and marketing because of the potential economic, social-cultural, and environmental impacts of tourism. The amount of involvement depends upon such factors as the importance assigned to tourism, the political philosophy of the government, and the maturity of the destination. A comprehensive and integrated tourism policy must be established to guide the tourism destiny of the country, region, state, or province. Without a policy and a mechanism for implementing it, tourism will increase or decline in a haphazard and potentially negative manner within the destination.

To bring a tourism policy into effect, there must be an organization responsible for its implementation. There are various levels of tourism policy and, therefore, a variety of policy-implementing agencies spread throughout the world. For example, the UN World Tourism Organization (UNWTO) has a global responsibility for tourism, while there are several multi-country regional tourism organizations. Within an individual country, there is usually a national DMO, state, provincial, or territorial DMOs, regional tourism organizations (RTOs), and local DMOs.

ACTIVITIES

1. Select a group of DMOs in your country at the city/county, regional, or state/provincial/territorial level. Choose a group of up to ten of these with a good geographic distribution.
2. What are the tourism policies and goals of each of these DMOs?
3. What are the organizations' major programs and activities?
4. Find and analyze these organizations' websites and social media sites. What types of information are provided on the websites and social media?
5. Do these websites/social media provide information of the organizations' tourism policies and goals? Which websites/social media provide the best information on these topics, and why?
6. Overall, which of the websites/social media do you feel are the most effective? What are your reasons for this assessment?

ACRONYMS

APEC (Asian Pacific Economic Cooperation)

ATAG (Air Transport Action Group)

COTAL (Confederación de Organizaciones Turísticas de la América Latina)

CTO (Caribbean Tourism Organization)

CVB (convention and visitors bureau)

DC (Destination Canada)

DI (Destinations International)

EC (European Commission)

ECM (European Cities Marketing)

ETC (European Travel Commission)

EU (European Union)

GSTC (Global Sustainable Tourism Council)

IATA (International Air Transport Association)

ICAO (International Civil Aviation Organization)

ICCA (International Congress and Convention Association)

ILO (International Labour Organization)

IUCN (International Union for Conservation of Nature)

NTA (national tourism administration)

NTO (national tourism organization or national tourist office)

OAS (Organization of American States)

OECD (Organisation for Economic Co-operation and Development)

NGO (non-governmental organization)

PATA (Pacific Asia Travel Association)

RTA (regional tourism association)

RTO (regional tourism organization)

SME (small- and medium-size enterprises)

SPTO (South Pacific Tourism Organization)

TA (Tourism Australia)

TEQ (Tourism & Events Queensland)

UNCTAD (UN Conference on Trade and Development)

UNDP (UN Development Programme)

UNEP (UN Environment Programme)

UNESCO (UN Educational, Scientific and Cultural Organization)

UNWTO (UN World Tourism Organization)

WTCF (World Tourism Cities Federation)

WTTC (World Travel & Tourism Council)

REFERENCES

American Society of Travel Agents. 2017. About ASTA. https://www.asta.org/About/index.cfm?navItemNumber=11164

Association of Southeast Asian Nations. 2017. About ASEAN. http://asean.org/asean/about-asean/

Australian Trade and Investment Commission. 2017. About Tourism 2020. https://www.austrade.gov.au/Australian/Tourism/Policy-and-Strategy/tourism-2020

British Columbia Government. 2015. Adventure Tourism Policy. http://www2.gov.bc.ca/assets/gov/farming-natural-resources-and-industry/natural-resource-use/land-water-use/crown-land/adventure_tourism.pdf

Cruise Lines International Association. 2017. About CLIA. https://www.cruising.org/about-the-industry/about-clia

Denman, R. 2017. Updating the National Tourism Policy of Belize. Assessment Report Final.

Department of Transport, Sport and Tourism. 2015. *People, Place and Policy. Growing Tourism to 2025*. Dublin, Ireland.

Dredge, D., and Jenkins, D. 2007. *Tourism Planning and Policy*. Milton, Queensland: John Wiley & Sons Australia, Ltd.

The Economist. 2017. Japan's government has legalized casinos, but they are not popular. February 2.

Edgell, D. L., Sr., and Swanson, J. R. 2013. Tourism Policy and Planning, 2nd ed. London: Routledge.

Empire State Development. 2017. Exploring New York State is an amazing business. https://esd.ny.gov/industries/tourism

European Cities Marketing. 2017. European Cities Marketing. http://www.europeancitiesmarketing.com/

Gauteng Tourism Authority. 2017. About the Gauteng Tourism Authority. http://www.gauteng.net/pages/about-us

Haxton, P. 2015. A Review of Effective Policies for Tourism Growth. OECD Tourism Papers 2015/01.

International Festival & Events Association. 2017. Who we are. http://www.ifea.com/p/about/whoweare

Kerala, Department of Tourism. 2017. Welcome to God's Own Country. https://www.keralatourism.org/

McCann, D. 2017. First Venice and Barcelona: now anti-tourism marches spread across Europe. *The Guardian,* August 10. https://amp.theguardian.com/travel/2017/aug/10/anti-tourism-marches-spread-across-europe-venice-barcelona

Meeting Professionals International. 2017. About MPI. http://www.mpiweb.org/About

Mekong Tourism Coordinating Office. 2017. What is the Greater Mekong Subregion. http://www.mekongtourism.org/about/what-is-the-gms/

Mundo Maya. 2017. Mundo Maya. http://mundomaya.travel/

Society for Incentive Excellence. 2017. About SITE. http://www.siteglobal.com/page/who-we-are

Tourism & Events Queensland. 2017. About TEQ. https://teq.queensland.com/about-teq-new

Tourism Industry Association of Canada. 2017. 2016 Annual Report on Canadian Tourism. Ottawa: TIAC.

Tourism Northern Territory. 2017. Welcome to Tourism NT's Corporate Website. http://www.tourismnt.com.au/

US AID. 2017. What we do. https://www.usaid.gov/what-we-do

VisitBritain. 2017. What we do. https://www.visitbritain.org/what-we-do

Visit California. 2017. Industry Website. http://industry.visitcalifornia.com/

Werker, E., and Ahmed, F. Z. 2008. What do nongovernmental organizations do? *Journal of Economic Perspectives*, 22(2), 73–92.

Wight, A. C. 2013. Identifying best practice in national tourism organisations. *Journal of Vacation Marketing*, 19 (2), 133–148.

World Travel & Tourism Council. 2017. Economic Research. https://www.wttc.org/research/economic-research/

ADDITIONAL RESOURCES

Air Transport Action Group. 2017. Who we are. http://www.atag.org/about-us/who-we-are.html

Asia-Pacific Economic Cooperation. 2017. About APEC. https://www.apec.org/About-Us/About-APEC

Caribbean Tourism Organization. About CTO. http://www.onecaribbean.org/about-cto/

Destinations International. 2017. Who we are. https://destinationsinternational.org/

European Commission. 2017. Tourism. https://ec.europa.eu/growth/sectors/tourism_en

European Travel Commission. 2017. About ETC. http://www.etc-corporate.org/about-etc

International Air Transport Association. 2017. About us. http://www.iata.org/about/pages/index.aspx

International Civil Aviation Organization. 2017. About ICAO. https://www.icao.int/about-icao/Pages/default.aspx

New Zealand Ministry of Business, Innovation & Employment. 2017. Tourism Infrastructure Fund. http://www.mbie.govt.nz/info-services/sectors-industries/tourism/tourism-infrastructure-fund

Organisation for Economic Co-operation and Development. 2016. *OECD Tourism Trends and Highlights 2016 Highlights*. Paris: OECD.

Organisation for Economic Co-operation and Development. 2017. Tourism. https://www.oecd.org/industry/tourism/

Organization of American States. 2017. Who we are. http://www.oas.org/en/about/who_we_are.asp

Pacific Asia Travel Association. 2017. About PATA. https://www.pata.org/about-pata/

South Pacific Tourism Organisation. 2017. South Pacific Tourism Organisation. https://corporate.southpacificislands.travel/

UNWTO. 2017. Western Silk Road Tourism Initiative. http://silkroad.unwto.org/project/western-silk-road-tourism-initiative

World Tourism Cities Federation. 2017. Introduction of WTCF. http://en.wtcf.org.cn/About/WhoWeAre/

CHAPTER FOUR

Tourism Legislation and Regulation

Controlling Tourism

You do not examine legislation in the light of the benefits it will convey if properly administered, but in the light of the wrongs it would do and the harms it would cause if improperly administered.

LYNDON B. JOHNSON

YOUR LEARNING DESTINATION

Having learned the reasons for government laws and regulations, you can describe the classification and forms of tourism legislation and regulations.

WHAT YOU NEED TO KNOW

Having read this chapter, you will be able to:

- Explain why government laws and regulations are essential, but sometimes controversial.
- Review reasons for introducing tourism laws and regulations in destinations.
- Describe categories of tourism laws and regulations found in destinations.
- Pinpoint specific forms of destination legislation and regulations.
- Reveal what private-sector tourism organizations and consumers are doing to promote self-regulation.
- Elaborate on multilateral and bilateral agreements affecting tourism.

BREAKING THE ICE

You probably have heard of the expression "red tape" and there being too much of it. No, it is not what you use for wrapping presents, but about there being too much bureaucracy and regulations from government agencies. Peter Simpson is credited with saying, "There's far too much red tape and not enough red carpet" (FQ Quotes 2018). This quote seems to fit well for getting visitor visas to some countries.

KEY TAKEAWAY POINTS

- Government laws and regulations are needed in tourism, but they can cause conflict and resentment.

- Tourism businesses and their associations can self-regulate, and consumers can also be asked to manage their behaviors when traveling and within destinations.

GOVERNMENT ROLE IN CONTROLLING TOURISM

You learned in Chapter 3 about why and how governments get involved in tourism, and you know there are many good reasons for governments to have "hands-on" participation. Chapter 3 reviewed how governments set tourism policies; in this chapter, you will get to know how governments introduce and enforce tourism laws and regulations. This role of government is legitimate and needed in destinations. However, laws and regulations can be controversial and resented by tourism operators. Laws and regulations are essential because governments cannot totally rely on the private sector to effectively control and regulate tourism. They are often resented because the private sector feels that governments go too far in enforcing laws and regulations. This is where we get the expressions of "too much bureaucracy and red tape" and having to "swim in a sea of government paperwork" (Figure 4.1).

Government agencies around the world have many laws and regulations that directly or indirectly affect tourism. Countries with socialist or communist governments regulate tourism very comprehensively, such as in China and Vietnam. The complexity of the tourism regulatory framework in most destinations is a direct reflection of tourism itself. Visitors cross international borders; are exposed to all the cultural, historic, man-made, and natural resources of destinations; and must be catered to in a safe, secure, and hygienic fashion. It is no surprise that government agencies have assorted tourism-related laws and regulations.

You saw in Figure 3.2. that government roles in tourism include policy-setting and planning, legislation and regulation, coordination, development stimulation and control, infrastructure development, operations, marketing and research, and training and education. The emphasis given to each of these eight roles varies from destination to destination, but it is usually related to the importance attached to tourism as an economic sector. Government actions must be supported by laws (legislation) and specific regulations to have legitimacy in democratic societies. The greatest controversy often comes with governments' enforcement of laws and regulations. This causes friction between the private sector and government in the tourism system.

Tourism Industry Leaders Take Issue with U.S. Visa Rule Changes

"Warning of the 'economic ramifications' of the 'significant policy change,' 20 trade associations have asked the Trump administration to reconsider an executive order likely to lengthen the period international visitors must wait for visas to visit the U.S.

The June 21 executive order effectively reversed a 2012 policy mandating that 80 percent of nonimmigrant visa applicants be interviewed within three weeks of submitting an application. U.S. Travel praised the move at the time as a near-certain boost to U.S. economic and jobs growth."

Source: U.S. Travel Association. 2017.

In introducing laws and regulations, governments act in the perceived general interests of their citizens and visitors. They do so to protect and conserve their destination area's natural, historical, and cultural resources; to ensure the health, safety, and security of visitors; and to protect visitors from unscrupulous business practices and scams. From these perspectives, the value of the government role cannot be questioned.

However, the private sector frequently criticizes government agencies as being too bureaucratic, developing unnecessary "red tape," going too far in their policing efforts, and being uncoordinated. This is especially true when the political pendulum and public sentiment swing more toward the free enterprise ("right-wing") approach, as demonstrated in the privatization of state-owned enterprises (SOEs) such as airlines, airports, and railways.

Governments are most often chastised for taxation regimes, changes to visa policies, and for lowering budgets and resources allocated to tourism and DMOs. In addition, they are sharply criticized for hindering the development of tourism destinations because of lengthy and complex project approval processes.

FIGURE 4.1 A "swimming in a sea of government paperwork" visual metaphor.

© alphaspirit/Shutterstock.com

The lack of adequate coordination and cooperation among government agencies in policies, laws and regulations, and programs is quite prevalent in tourism. This reflects the diversity of interests within the tourism system and incompatibility of the goals of government agencies, such as natural resource conservation in protected areas versus tourism promotion and development agencies. Any destination with a high priority on tourism should ensure a significant level of coordination and cooperation among its government agencies.

You will hear the term *lobbying* often when the public sector is mentioned. It means trying to influence governments and politicians to remove, modify, or introduce policies, laws, and regulations that favor the lobbying economic sector, companies, or special-interest groups. You also will notice the word *advocacy* in this book and, although connected, it is not the same as lobbying.

Being an advocate is like performing the role of a lawyer and "arguing the case" for tourism or an industry sector of tourism. For example, the Caribbean Tourism Organization (CTO) is arguing that the Air Passenger Duty (APD) introduced by the UK Government is having a negative impact on Caribbean tourism as well as on the Caribbean diaspora in the UK (Caribbean Tourism Organization 2017).

REASONS FOR DESTINATION LEGISLATION AND REGULATIONS

Every country has laws and regulations that affect tourism. These are established by different levels of governments from national to local. Laws and regulations allow governments to control the impacts of tourism (Chapter 2); to implement tourism policies and plans, fulfill government roles in tourism, and create and modify DMOs (Chapters 3 and 5); implement sustainable tourism development principles (Chapter 6); and tourism marketing, promotion, and product development (Chapters 7–9).

Many of the laws that directly affect tourism are in the *statutory law* category. These are laws created by acts of lawmaking bodies (governments). There are *tort and criminal laws* that impact tourism; most often when frauds are committed against travelers and people buying land for recreational purposes. Some of the most common reasons for introducing tourism-related laws and regulations are as shown in Figure 4.2 and described below.

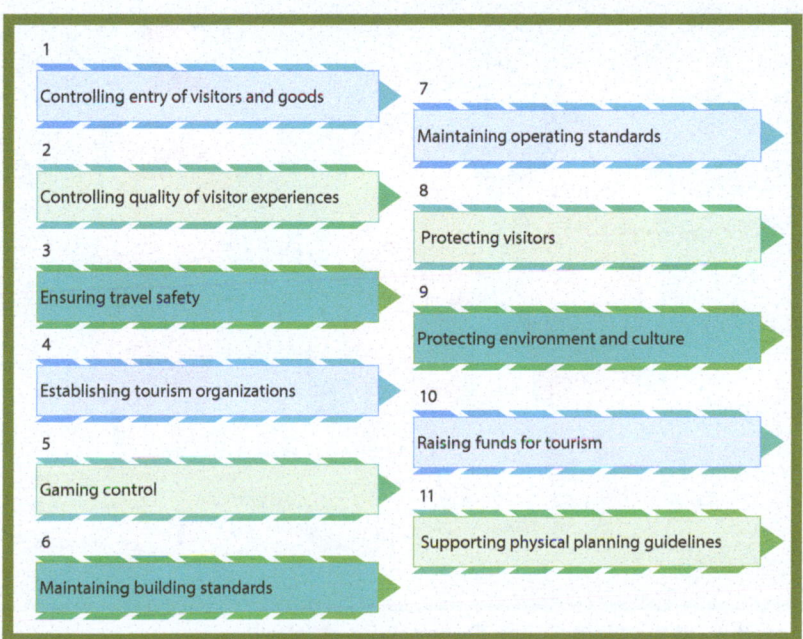

FIGURE 4.2 Reasons for tourism legislation and regulations.

FIGURE 4.3 Many countries require visas for the entry of foreign nationals.

Controlling the Entry of Foreign Visitors and Goods

There is a need in every country to introduce laws and regulations regarding the entry of foreign nationals and goods from other countries. Protecting the national health interest is one of the reasons for immigration regulations and procedures, as is the detection of the flow of illegal drugs and potential terrorist threats against a country. Most countries have a visa system for visitor entry (Figure 4.3), but it is harder to get into some countries than others.

Controlling the Quality of Visitor Experience

Laws and regulations may be introduced to ensure that visitors have a high-quality experience in the destination. For example, the use of some wilderness areas (e.g., scenic rivers) may be regulated so that the user's experience of the wild is not spoiled by there being too many other visitors. Laws may be introduced to protect foreign visitors from being harassed or abused by local people who are begging or touting services and products.

Ensuring Travel Safety

Many laws and regulations are in force to ensure the safety of people traveling by air, rail, road, and sea. Regulatory agencies are created within each country to control and enforce safety standards. For example, many countries have a maritime regulatory agency that ensures the safety of all watercraft through programs of licensing and regular inspections. Other nations and states have regulations and procedures to ensure safety in adventure travel activities and swimming/surfing areas on beaches (Figure 4.4).

FIGURE 4.4 Lifeguards on duty at the Gold Coast, Queensland, Australia.

QUICK TRIP 4.1

The Impacts of Government Travel Advisories

The U.S. Department of State warns U.S. citizens to avoid travel to Somalia because of wide-spread terrorist and criminal activity.

(U.S. Department of State, August 3, 2017).

Generally, governments cannot control where their citizens travel, unless there are legally-instituted bans on going to specific countries or regions. However, they do issue travel advisories in which citizens are warned about the potential dangers of traveling within certain countries. While many travelers ignore these notices posted on government websites, they do affect the perceptions of significant numbers of potential visitors.

Travel advisories are needed, but they can cause hardships for some destinations. Tourism sector stakeholders often argue that warnings are exaggerated or that they cover too extensive geographical areas. However, governments counter that it is their duty to warn their citizens of any threats of danger.

According to UNWTO,

"Governments have the right—and the duty—especially in a crisis, to inform their nationals of the difficult circumstances, or even the dangers they may encounter during their travels abroad; it is their responsibility however to issue such information without prejudicing in an unjustified or exaggerated manner the tourism industry of the host countries and the interests of their own operators; the contents of travel advisories should therefore be discussed beforehand with the authorities of the host countries and the professionals concerned; recommendations formulated should be strictly proportionate to the gravity of the situations encountered and confined to the geographical areas where the insecurity has arisen; such advisories should be qualified or cancelled as soon as a return to normality permits . . . " (UNWTO 2017).

UNWTO (2017) provides the following list of threats and risks that may be covered in government travel advisories:

- Political (due to political processes)
- Social (crime, delinquency, scams)
- Related to terrorism
- Environmental (natural disasters)
- Industrial (such as chemical or nuclear) hazards
- Health-related (communicable disease status and emergencies, such as epidemics)
- Transportation systems-related

While travel advisories are necessary, as confirmed by UNWTO, some in travel and tourism believe they go too far, especially for disadvantaged poorer countries and destinations that do not have the marketing budgets to counter the powerful influence of government information. Sir Richard Branson (2014) of Virgin, for example, argues that developing countries are treated unfairly in the issuance of travel advisories when compared to developed nations such as the UK and USA. He specifically cites Bali and Kenya as two destinations that have suffered from wide-ranging travel advisories.

However, travel advisories are not just limited to poorer countries as this travel advisory for Europe issued on May 1, 2017, indicates:

Extremists continue to focus on tourist locations, transportation hubs, markets/shopping malls, and local government facilities as viable targets. In addition, hotels, clubs, restaurants, places of worship, parks, high-profile events, educational institutions, airports, and other soft targets remain priority locations for possible attacks. U.S. citizens should exercise additional vigilance in these and similar locations, in particular during the upcoming summer travel season when large crowds may be common

(U.S. Department of State, May 1, 2017). Report of the World Committee on Tourism Ethics Addendum 1 Implementation of the Global Code of Ethics for Tourism

QUICK TRIP 4.1 CONTINUED

Think about This

1. What are the benefits to consumers from the travel advisories issued by governments?
2. If you were planning to travel to a new country, would you check with your government on any advisories for your destination? Why or why not?
3. Do you believe the information that people can get on social media is more up-to-date and accurate than travel advisories? Why or why not?
4. What can poorer countries do to combat the "negative publicity" contained in travel advisories?

Sources

Branson, Richard. 2014. Why advisories hurt countries and help terrorists. Virgin. https://www.virgin.com/richard-branson/why-travel-advisories-hurt-countries-and-help-terrorists

UNWTO. 2017. Travel Advisories. http://www2.unwto.org/en/risk-crisis-management/travel-advisories

U.S. Department of State. 2017. Europe Travel Alert.

U.S. Department of State. 2017. Somalia Travel Warning. https://travel.state.gov/content/passports/en/alertswarnings/somalia-travel-warning.html

Establishing Tourism Organizations

Laws are often passed to establish new tourism organizations. For example, the Tourism Australia Act of 2004 established Tourism Australia. Destination Canada (previously CTC) came into being because of the Canadian Tourism Commission Act of 2000. Local legislation in the United States and UK is paving the way for the creation of *tourism business improvement districts* (TBIDs) that have dedicated marketing funds from user-pay taxes on hotel rooms (Levine 2015; VisitBritain 2011).

Gaming Control

Laws are introduced at various levels of government to control the development of gaming operations including casinos and lotteries. Some countries and states strictly prohibit different forms of gaming due to social or religious reasons. Other governments allow only certain forms of gaming, such as casinos on riverboats or casino gaming on cruise ships outside of territorial waters.

Maintaining Building Standards

Building codes are introduced to ensure that building materials and specifications meet required standards (International Code Council 2017). For example, the City of Las Vegas (2017) publishes an extensive list of building Standards & Requirements online at its website.

Maintaining Operating Standards

Governments introduce licensing and registration systems to maintain the operating standards in different parts of tourism. These may include regular inspection programs to ensure continued conformance to standards. Accommodation grading or rating systems are an example of this type of system.

Protecting Visitors

A variety of laws and regulations are introduced to protect visitors. These include fire safety laws for hotels, regulations on the safe handling of food, and laws to protect travelers from frauds and scams and the financial failures of travel trade companies. Regulations may also be in force to protect the safety of visitors when engaging in certain activities (e.g., adventure travel activities such as white-water rafting and ballooning) and attending certain types of attractions (e.g., amusement parks with rides).

Protecting Environment and Culture

There are many laws and regulations dealing with environmental protection and conservation. These include

FIGURE 4.5 Wildlife sunset silhouettes in Kruger National Park, South Africa.

laws creating national or state park systems (Figure 4.5), shoreline protection systems, regulations on sewage disposal systems, and other measures to protect physical environments. For example, the Kingdom of Bhutan in the Himalaya Mountains strictly controls the number of foreign visitors into the country to control the impacts of tourism.

Raising Funds for Tourism

Some laws are introduced to institute taxes or other levies to provide for tourism marketing and development. In the United States, uniform innkeepers' laws at the state level provide the mechanism for funding local convention and visitors' bureaus (CVBs). The Travel Promotion Act of 2009 created the mechanism for funding Brand USA through allocating part of the fees that visa applicants from Visa Waiver Program (VWP) countries pay to the Electronic System for Travel Authorization (ESTA).

What Is the Purpose of the Travel Promotion Act of 2009?

"According to the Senate Report of the Travel Promotion Act of 2009 (Senate Report 111-025), the purpose of the Travel Promotion Act is to increase international travel to all areas of the United States, communicate United States travel policies overseas, and make entry procedures into the United States more efficient and welcoming."

Source: U.S. Customs and Border Protection. 2018.

Supporting Physical Planning Guidelines

Laws and regulations are introduced to control land use. The zoning regulations and building permit systems in force in many municipalities are a good example. The Center for Responsible Travel (CREST) says that mass

FIGURE 4.6 Sun and sea destinations like Acapulco, Mexico, can damage coastal ecology.

tourism has caused "loss of biodiversity including beach erosion, dredging, destruction of wetlands, mangroves, sea grasses, and corals, as well as displacement of coastal communities and alterations of local livelihoods" in many popular Mexican beach resort areas (Figure 4.6).

Recommendations for Tourism Land Use in Coastal Areas

"To avoid this pitfall, appropriate coastal management planning and land use policies supported by satellite imagery, geographical information systems and scientific environmental, social and cultural data framework is necessary, particularly if new coastal tourism zones or areas are to be developed in accordance with sustainable development principles. This action will ensure that the physical integrity of the coast and its natural resources are protected, while at the same time safeguarding local livelihoods by enabling them to continue to have direct access and management rights to the resources that are essential for their subsistence."

Source: Center for Responsible Travel. Undated.

DESTINATION AREA LEGISLATION AND REGULATIONS

Classifications of Legislation and Regulations

Before describing specific forms of tourism legislation and regulations, it is useful to classify them into different groups. One method of classification is to group the tourism legislation and regulations into *functional areas*, such as those related to the protection of the environment, those related to economic development, and those related to frontier controls. Another means of classification is to group on a *sector basis* by identifying the legislation and regulations that relate to airlines, hotels, travel agents, and other tourism businesses. *Horizontal legislation or regulations* are those items that affect every sector, whether it be a tourism or non-tourism one, such as income tax and labor legislation. *Specific legislation or regulations* are those items that relate directly to a specific sector. An example of this is a grading system for hotels. Figure 4.7 illustrates commonly found legislation and regulations classified on a sector-by-sector basis in tourism.

Accommodation and Food Services	Travel Agents, Tour Wholesalers, Tour Operators	Airlines, Railways, Buses, Ships, and Other Carriers	Attraction Operators, Adventure Travel Operators
• Alcohol sales and regulations • Building and zoning codes • Classification, grading, and rating of hotels and other establishment types • Fire safety regulations and codes • Health safety regulations and codes • Liability laws with respect to guests and their belongings • Labor and taxation legislation	• Definition of responsibilities and limitations • Regulations and licensing of travel agents, tour wholesalers and operators • Regulations of promotions • Labor and taxation legislation	• Control of fares and tariffs • Control of route entry and exit • Labor and taxation legislation • Licensing of carriers • Limitation of weights and capacities • Negotiation of services • Regulation of safety procedures • Subsidization of routes	• Regulation of safety procedures • Licensing or registration of operators • Inspection and licensing of equipment • Licensing or certification of guides

FIGURE 4.7 Specific legislation and regulations in tourism.

FIGURE 4.8 Forms of destination legislation and regulation.

Forms of Legislation and Regulations

There are certain forms of legislation and regulation that are encountered in most destinations, and several of these are shown in Figure 4.8.

Here now are the descriptions of these forms of legislation:

Accommodation Standards.

One of the aspects of tourism that receives much attention from governments around the world is the standards of accommodation facilities. Some countries have introduced mandatory *classification and grading systems* for accommodation, whereas others operate similar programs on a voluntary basis. For example, the Republic of Ireland operates a compulsory registration and classification system. Fáilte Ireland (the National Tourism Development Authority) operates the system, which covers hotels, guest houses, youth hostels, holiday camps, caravan and camping sites, holiday cottages, and holiday apartments.

Assuring Accommodation Standards in Ireland

All hotels must be classified using the Fáilte Ireland Hotel Classification Scheme, hotels must attain the Approval minimum entry level requirements in order to comply with the Registration and Renewal of Registration Regulations for Hotels 2016. The scheme was developed in close consultation with the Irish Hotels Federation (IHF). The objective of the scheme is to inform consumers to recognise quality and to differentiate levels of facilities and services, which as potential guests they can expect. This offers far greater information and transparency to the consumer.

Source: Fáilte Ireland. 2017.

Airport and Airline Security and Safety.

Airports and airplanes have been the targets of terrorists for many years, but it took the incidents of 9-11 to truly awaken most people to the need for tighter security at airport terminals and on planes. The incidents in Barcelona, Berlin, Brussels, London, Manchester, Munich, Nice, Paris, Stockholm, and other European cities in 2015–2017 (Figure 4.9) again sensitized the world that visitors and leisure-seekers are prime targets for extremists of all types. Previous research has shown a clear negative correlation between acts of terrorism and volumes of visitors to affected areas or sites. Therefore, government authorities and transportation companies must continue to introduce regulations, systems, and procedures that give further protection to the world's growing flow of visitors.

Alcohol Sales Laws and Regulations.

Regulations are required over the sale and consumption of alcohol. This is accomplished mainly through the licensing of establishments that can sell alcohol and where alcohol consumption is permitted. One of the main goals of licensing is to prevent injuries that can result from the abuse of alcohol through car accidents, fights, and other antisocial behavior. A second reason is to prevent the sale of alcohol to underage customers, to people who are already intoxicated, and to habitual drunkards. Typically, licenses to sell alcohol are granted by state, provincial, or territorial governments.

There are places in the world where the sales and consumption of alcohol are restricted or banned, and these are mainly for reasons of religious beliefs. For example, alcohol is banned in Saudi Arabia. Several airlines, including Saudi Arabian Airlines, Pakistan

FIGURE 4.9 Terrorist attacks in tourism destination cities made headlines in 2015–2017.

International, Kuwait Airways, and others do not allow alcohol consumption onboard their flights.

Civil Aviation Regulations. Almost every country in the world has a government regulatory agency that controls air travel. In the United States, this is the Federal Aviation Administration (FAA). Canada has Transport Canada, Australia has the Civil Aviation Safety Authority (CASA), and both the UK and New Zealand have a Civil Aviation Authority (CAA) (UK Government, 2017). One of the major roles of these regulatory agencies is to ensure the highest levels of safety when flying and when on the ground at airports.

Controlled Substances Laws. Most destinations have laws and regulations about the use and sales of controlled substances, including marijuana. These rules are designed to prevent the use of recreational drugs, especially among youth. The decriminalization of marijuana is a trend in some countries; for example, in 2012 Colorado allowed its use for recreational purposes and other US states did likewise later.

Health Regulations. Governments introduce rules to protect visitors and residents from the risk of disease and illness resulting from exposure to food, water, animals and insects, and infected people. Several countries insist that travelers from infected areas of other countries show proof of vaccination against certain diseases (e.g., yellow fever). The outbreak of severe acute respiratory syndrome (SARS) in 2003 in China and Hong Kong, which was spread by travelers to Canada and other countries, brought a new level of world awareness to the interaction of tourism, travel, and the spread of disease. This resulted in the screening of air passengers in many Asian airports. For example, an estimated CAD $7.55 million was spent on airport passenger screening in Canada from March 18 to July 5, 2003. The threat of the spread of avian (bird) flu (H5N1), swine flu (H1N1), MERS (Middle East Respiratory Syndrome), Ebola, and Foot and Mouth were other major health concerns in tourism (Figure 4.10). There is an obligation on the part of governments and tourism businesses to warn travelers of the risks of contracting certain diseases and precautions that are advisable to reduce such risks.

FIGURE 4.10 People wearing masks in Seoul, South Korea, during the MERS virus scare.

It is essential that governments protect people from foodborne illnesses when they eat in restaurants. This role is accomplished through regular inspections by health inspectors and rules regarding the storage, cooking, and handling of food and beverages. Often, this role is performed by local government agencies that have the right to close establishments that do not meet standards.

Innkeeper Liability Laws.   Most destinations have a variety of laws and regulations that indicate the extent of the liability of accommodation establishment operators for the personal injury of guests and the loss of guest possessions. These measures include fire safety laws that impose rules regarding the construction and operation of accommodation establishments. One of the major problems facing accommodation operators is how to protect guests' property when they are on the premises. Thefts from guest rooms and vehicles are quite common in tourism. In some countries, under common law, innkeepers have "absolute liability" for any loss of guest property. Other accommodation operators install elaborate security systems including guest room safes and electronic door card key systems.

Protected Area Laws and Regulations.   Governments at all levels have introduced laws and regulations aimed at promoting environmental protection and conservation. These measures help support the role of governments in sustainable tourism. Among the most important laws are those that have initiated systems of national parks and other protected areas (International Union for Conservation of Nature 2017). Two of the landmark pieces of such legislation in the world are the Yellowstone National Park Act of 1872 in the United States and the Rocky Mountain Parks Act of 1887 in Canada, which established its first national park surrounding Banff, Alberta. The National Parks Act followed in Canada in 1930 and in 1953 the Historic Sites and Monuments Act was passed. The 1930 Act stated that only such uses would be permitted within national parks that would "leave them unimpaired for the enjoyment of future generations" (Parks Canada Agency 2000). This clause has been quite controversial since some of Canada's national parks such as Banff, Lake Louise, and Jasper are among the nation's major tourism attractions and most favored destinations, particularly for foreign visitors.

In England in 2006, the government created Natural England to protect England's nature and landscapes for people to enjoy and for the services they provide (Natural England 2017). Natural England has the responsibility for designating national parks and areas of outstanding natural beauty.

State, regional, county, and municipal governments usually have the authority to regulate land uses and to acquire land within their jurisdictions. Historically, these powers have been passed on to local governments at the city, town, and county levels. Cities, towns, and counties exercise these powers through the development of municipal plans, the enforcement of zoning regulations, and the operation of building permit systems.

QUICK TRIP 4.2

IUCN Protected Area Classification

The International Union for Conservation of Nature (IUCN) is a membership union of government agencies, NGOs, and other organizations. IUCN's mission is to "Influence, encourage and assist societies throughout the world to conserve the integrity and diversity of nature and to ensure that any use of natural resources is equitable and ecologically sustainable." It has 1,300 member organizations and its headquarters are in Gland, Switzerland.

IUCN is one of the world's most authoritative sources on protected areas and their classification. The following table shows the protected area categories according to IUCN:

Codes	Protected Area Classifications
Ia	**Strict nature reserve**: set aside to protect biodiversity and also possibly geological/geomorphological features, where human visitation, use and impacts are strictly controlled and limited to ensure protection of the conservation values.
Ib	**Wilderness area**: usually largely unmodified or slightly modified areas, retaining their natural character and influence, without permanent or significant human habitation, protected and managed to preserve their natural condition.
II	**National Park**: protect large-scale ecological processes, along with the complement of species and ecosystems characteristic of the area, which also provide a foundation for environmentally and culturally compatible spiritual, scientific, educational, recreational and visitor opportunities.
III	**Natural monument or feature**: protect a specific natural monument, which can be a land form, sea mount, submarine cavern, geological feature such as a cave, or even a living feature, such as a grove.
IV	**Habitat/species management area**: protect specific species or habitats, where management reflects this priority. Many will need active interventions to address the requirements of particular species or to maintain habitats, but this is not a requirement of the category.
V	**Protected landscape/seascape**: protected areas where the interaction of people and nature over time has produced an area of distinct character with significant ecological, biological, cultural and scenic value and where safeguarding the integrity of this interaction is vital to protecting and sustaining the area and its associated values.
VI	**Protected area with sustainable use of natural resources**: protects ecosystems and habitats, and associated cultural values and traditional natural resource management systems. Generally large areas, with most of the area in natural condition, where a proportion is under natural resource sustainable management and with low-level industrial use of natural resources compatible with nature conservation.

QUICK TRIP 4.2 CONTINUED

IUCN says the following about the application of this classification of protected areas:

"IUCN protected area management categories classify protected areas according to their management objectives. The categories are recognised by international bodies such as the United Nations and by many national governments as the global standard for defining and recording protected areas and as such are increasingly being incorporated into government legislation."

Think about This

1. Why are protected areas important to tourism and destinations?
2. IUCN says it is a "union" and "network" of organizations that are interested in the conservation of nature. How does IUCN's protected area classification influence government legislation and the management of protected areas?
3. How do national parks balance the need for the conservation of nature with the demand for recreation and tourism within their boundaries?
4. What can destinations do to sensitize visitors about conserving nature?

Sources

IUCN. 2012. What is IUCN? https://www.youtube.com/watch?v=0uf5e9vsXWo

IUCN. 2017. About IUCN. https://www.iucn.org/about

IUCN. 2017. Protected Areas Categories. https://www.iucn.org/theme/protected-areas/about/protected-areas-categories

Safety Regulations in Activities.   There are many situations around the world in which travelers are exposed to danger within destinations. These include when people are traveling by road, rail, and by water, and when visitors are engaging in certain activities that may result in injuries or death. Scenic boat trips, motor coach tours, scenic rail trips, and guided four-wheel drive trips are examples of tourism offerings where travelers are exposed to a certain level of physical danger. An element of danger is also present when riding on rollercoasters and other equipment at theme and amusement parks. The trend toward the increasing popularity of adventure tourism destinations is placing more people in situations of personal risk.

The rapidly increasing popularity of adventure tourism in many parts of the world has inevitably led to an increase in accidents involving visitors. These have occurred in activities including ballooning, kayaking, jetboating, and whitewater rafting. Some destinations that are quite dependent on adventure tourism are concerned about the negative publicity these incidents create for tourism. New Zealand is one of these countries and it is well-known for its adventure activities (Figure

© Chameleons Eye/Shutterstock.com

FIGURE 4.11 Jetboating is an adventure activity in Queenstown, New Zealand.

4.11). In 2016, the New Zealand Government introduced *The Health and Safety at Work (Adventure Activities) Regulations 2016* (New Zealand Government 2016). This shows that the government not only has a responsibility to protect the safety of visitors, but that failure to perform this role may have a negative effect on destination marketing.

FIGURE 4.12 Timesharing apartments near Marbella, Spain.

Timesharing Laws and Regulations. Another part of tourism that has received considerable attention has been the condominium real estate developments within resort areas, particularly *timesharing* or *vacation ownership* projects. The early history of these projects in many countries involved several cases of fraud and misleading sales claims. Several governments moved to protect customers from such abuses. For example, the European Commission in 2009 issued a directive to control the sales of timesharing units (European Commission 2017a) (Figure 4.12).

Travel Agency/Tour Operator Laws. Travel trade intermediaries are another part of tourism that is frequently covered by tourism legislation and regulations. These measures are introduced to protect consumers from fraudulent practices and "scams," and from the financial failure of tour wholesalers and operators, retail travel agencies, and other organizations that sell travel

services. There is a definite trend toward more regulation in this area as the numbers of travel-related frauds are increasing, especially with the growing reliance on the Internet and social media. Often these programs require travel companies to be licensed or register with a government agency before they can operate. They may also be required to post a bond or pay into a compensation fund.

The province of Ontario in Canada provides a good example of the regulation of travel trade intermediaries. The Travel Industry Act of 2002 required all travel agencies and wholesalers operating in Ontario to be registered. The Travel Industry Council of Ontario (TICO) was established by the Ontario Government to administer the 2002 Act that covers all travel agencies and wholesalers registered in Ontario.

In the UK, the Civil Aviation Authority (CAA) grants licenses to companies that provide package vacations that include flights. These are called Air Travel

QUICK TRIP 4.3

The Ontario Travel Industry Compensation Fund

The travel and tourism business can be very volatile and there is a need to protect consumers when a travel company fails. The Province of Ontario represents a good example of government intervening by introducing legislation and regulations to protect travelers. The Ontario Travel Industry Compensation Fund was established under the *Travel Industry Act, 2002*. Registered travel agencies and travel wholesalers contribute to the Compensation Fund, which is administered by the Travel Industry Council of Ontario (TICO).

TICO's mission is

> "to promote a fair and informed marketplace where consumers can be confident in their travel purchases. We also support the mission of the Ontario Ministry of Consumer Services to maintain a fair, safe and informed marketplace as it relates to Ontario's Travel Industry Act, 2002" (TICO 2011).

The Chateau Laurier Hotel and Cenotaph in Ottawa, Ontario.

The Compensation Fund provides reimbursement to consumers for monies paid to an Ontario registered travel agency for travel services that are not provided due to the bankruptcy or insolvency of either an Ontario registered travel retailer (agency), registered travel wholesaler (tour operator), or due to the cessation of an airline or cruise line.

Think about This

1. What are the major reasons that some travel agencies and tour operators run into serious financial difficulties?
2. What steps should destinations follow to take care of visitors who are left stranded by bankrupt or insolvent travel companies and airlines?
3. Do you think it is better for government to introduce this type of legislation or to have the travel industry self-regulate itself? What are your reasons?
4. These types of unfortunate situations are usually not caused by the travelers' destination but they may result in bad publicity for the destination. What can destinations do to counter such negative publicity?

Source

Travel Industry Council of Ontario. 2011. http://www.tico.ca/. Courtesy of Travel Industry Council of Ontario (TICO).

Organisers' Licenses (ATOLs). Every ATOL holder is examined each year to ensure that it is financially sound. The Travel Compensation Fund is Australia's "primary means of providing compensation to eligible travellers who suffer loss as a result of the financial collapse of a participating travel agency business" (Travel Compensation Fund 2017).

Truth in Advertising Laws. Governments are concerned about what advertisers say and promise, and have introduced truth in advertising laws to control this aspect of marketing. The legislation is designed to stop misleading, false, or deceptive promotions that trick consumers into buying products or services that do not live up to their promises.

Other Forms of Tourism Legislation and Regulations

Recently, other forms of legislation and regulation have come into being due to the Internet and social media, the sharing economy, and the social conditions of people. These include privacy laws and policies, sharing economy provider registration and taxation schemes, and protection against the increasing number of travel scams being perpetrated on visitors (Li and Pearce 2016).

- **Privacy laws and policies**

The arrival of the Internet and social media brought many efforts to protect the privacy of information that consumers share online with organizations. Privacy laws are now in force in many countries and most organizations have also established their own privacy policies (Figure 4.13).

- **Sharing economy provider registration and taxation**

The sharing economy is having a major impact on destinations through companies such as Airbnb, Uber, and others (Figure 4.14). The huge popularity of Airbnb has increased the numbers of visitors in certain destinations, and this has attracted the attention of commercial accommodation operators and local governments. Iceland is one of the destinations in which the added sharing-economy accommodations has significantly increased visitor arrivals and government agencies are requiring Airbnb and other private rental accommodations to be registered (Adam 2017).

- **Travel scams**

The variety of scams involving visitors to destinations seems to be on the increase, especially in cities and resort areas in Europe. A scam is a deceptive act or fraudulent scheme perpetrated on visitors that results in a loss of money or possessions. You can find many lists of potential scams online and the following is one that the authors themselves have experienced in Asia:

© One Photo/Shutterstock.com.

FIGURE 4.13 Privacy laws and policies are protecting consumers' personal information.

FIGURE 4.14 Protest against Uber in Toronto, Canada.

Arthouse or Rug Sale Scam

"A young 'art student' will approach a visitor (often at large tourist sites) and ask if s/he likes artwork created by local students. The student invites the visitor to view the artwork at an art studio or gallery and will pour tea and provide snacks while introducing their art. The art student will then pressure the visitor to buy artwork and demand compensation for the hospitality shown. The same scam is used by rug salesman in many countries."

Source: U.S. Department of State 2018.

SELF-REGULATION IN TOURISM

A government's main control over individual tourism business operators is through mandatory licensing or registration, which may or may not be supported by a system of regular inspections or reviews. Government licensing or registration systems operated by government protect travelers from tourism operators or operations that are unsafe, incompetent, or financially unstable. An alternative to this type of government control is to have tourism businesses and consumers regulate themselves. This may be done through private sector associations, specially created institutes, or NGOs. There is a definite trend around the world toward more self-regulation in tourism. The types of programs that can be used to maintain professional and other standards in tourism include the following:

Accreditation

Accreditation is a process by which an association or agency evaluates and recognizes a business or non-profit organization as meeting certain predetermined standards. For example, Destinations International (2017) operates the *Destination Marketing Accreditation Program* (DMAP) which accredits DMOs. The appointment of travel agents by organizations such as IATA is another example of this approach.

Destination Marketing Accreditation Program of Destinations International

It is important for individual sub-sectors of tourism to establish their own professional standards. This is preferable to having government intervention and helps the sub-sector plant the seeds to upgrading the profession. Destinations International showed great vision in creating the Destination Marketing Accreditation Program (DMAP) for the following reasons:

"The globally recognized Destination Marketing Accreditation Program (DMAP) serves as a visible industry distinction that defines quality and performance standards in destination marketing and management. Achieving DMAP accreditation positions a destination organization or CVB as a valued and respected organization in your community and increases your credibility among stakeholders."

Sixteen domains provide the main framework for the DMAP program:

1. Governance	9. Communications
2. Finance	10. Membership
3. Human resources	11. Management and facilities
4. Technology	12. Brand management
5. Marketing	13. Destination development
6. Visitor services (Individual/Leisure Market)	14. Research/marketing intelligence
7. Group services	15. Innovation
8. Sales	16. Stakeholder relationships

For each domain, three sets of guidelines have been defined: (1) mandatory standards, (2) essential elements, and (3) voluntary standards.

There is also a DMAP Code of Ethics that all accredited DMOs must abide by:

1. Provide exceptional customer service and detailed information on destination products and services.
2. Treat all stakeholders, including members of Destinations International, courteously, ethically, and professionally.
3. Actively encourage the integration of ethics into all aspects of management of the DMO activities.
4. Build collaborative relationships with other DMO industry professionals and others for the advancement of the profession of destination marketing.
5. Handle all inquiries, requests, transactions, correspondence, and complaints promptly, courteously, and fairly.
6. Provide clean and well-maintained facilities and equipment for the enjoyment of their customers (members and clients).
7. Exercise truth in all promotional materials concerning facilities, services, and amenities provided and advise the public in a reasonable manner if and when unable to provide the level of services or facilities as advertised. Promotional material supplied by the member must be appropriate for all audiences.
8. Provide customers with complete details on prices, cancellation policies, and services and ensure customers receive fair exchange for their foreign currency where appropriate.
9. Promote responsible and sustainable use of environmental resource base when providing services and products to customers.
10. Abide by all applicable federal, provincial, and municipal laws.

Courtesy of Destinations International.

DMAP was launched in January 2007 and by July 2017 over 200 DMOs had received the DMAP accreditation; these were mostly CVBs in the United States. Several DMOs in Canada, one DMO in Europe, and one in Puerto Rico were accredited. Accreditation lasts for four years.

Think about This

1. What are the benefits to a DMO that will accrue from being DMAP accredited?
2. Do you think that other sectors of tourism should also introduce accreditation programs? Which sectors and why should they introduce accreditation programs?
3. Destinations International suggests that DMAP will improve the overall credibility and recognition of DMOs. Do you agree with this assertion? Why or why not?
4. What are the benefits for consumers and the citizens and governments of the destinations in having a DMO accredited under DMAP?

Source

Destinations International. 2017. Destination Marketing Accreditation Program (DMAP). https://destinationsinternational.org/destination-marketing-accreditation-program-dmap

Certification

Certification applies to individuals who work for tourism organizations. It is a process by which people are tested and evaluated to determine mastery of specific skills or a field of knowledge. Certification usually follows a course of study and after the individual has gained a prescribed number of years of experience. In the United States, for example, the National Restaurant Association offers certification programs on food sanitation standards and alcohol service (ServSafe™ programs).

There has been a proliferation of professional certification programs in tourism worldwide. These now cover corporate travel managers, DMO executives, hotel managers and sales executives, incentive travel and meeting planners, retail travel agents, and tour planners. The *Certified Travel Counselor* (CTC) program offered for retail travel agents by The Travel Institute is one of the oldest of these programs. However, programs such as these are most effective if all members of the group participate in the program, and many of these programs in tourism are voluntary. Associations are often reluctant to enforce mandatory conditions of membership for fear that organizations will not join and membership revenues will be lost. In addition, it is essential that visitors understand the program objectives and the value of using organizations participating in the program.

Codes of Ethics or Practice, and Bills of Rights

Trade associations may develop codes of ethics or codes of practice to which they require members to adhere. Several travel agency associations (including ASTA, AFTA, and ABTA) have developed codes of ethics for their members (American Society of Travel Agents 2017; Association of British Travel Agents 2017; Australian Federation of Travel Agents 2017).

Another example of this is the bill of rights bestowed upon customers of tourism businesses. The Cruise Lines International Association (CLIA) has established the *Cruise Passenger Bill of Rights* and all its members must voluntarily adopt this.

Cruise Industry Passenger Bill of Rights

CLIA member lines have voluntarily adopted the *Cruise Industry Passenger Bill of Rights*, an explicitly stated, publicly available set of policies that provides transparency, consistency, and accountability for cruise passengers detailing CLIA members' commitment to the safety, comfort, and care of guests in the rare event of a mechanical failure or shipboard emergency.

Source: CLIA. 2017

QUICK TRIP 4.5

The Global Code of Ethics for Tourism

The Global Code of Ethics for Tourism (GCET) were adopted first in 1999 thanks to the efforts of UNWTO. They were introduced to promote an equitable, responsible, and sustainable world tourism order, whose benefits will be shared by all sectors of society in the context of an open and liberalized international economy.

The Code's ten principles amply cover the economic, social, cultural, and environmental components of travel and tourism:

- Article 1: Tourism's contribution to mutual understanding and respect between peoples and societies
- Article 2: Tourism as a vehicle for individual and collective fulfilment
- Article 3: Tourism, a factor of sustainable development
- Article 4: Tourism, a user of the cultural heritage of mankind and contributor to its enhancement
- Article 5: Tourism, a beneficial activity for host countries and communities
- Article 6: Obligations of stakeholders in tourism development
- Article 7: Right to tourism
- Article 8: Liberty of tourist movements
- Article 9: Rights of the workers and entrepreneurs in the tourism industry
- Article 10: Implementation of the principles of the Global Code of Ethics for Tourism

Detailed descriptions on each article are available in English in this document: http://cf.cdn.unwto.org/sites/all/files/docpdf/gcetbrochureglobalcodeen.pdf

How is the CGET to be implemented? Article 10.1 says the following about GCET implementation:

"The public and private stakeholders in tourism development should cooperate in the implementation of these principles and monitor their effective application."

Think about This

1. How do the GCET communicate and support the principles of sustainable tourism?
2. The GCET are excellent guidelines for how destinations should conduct tourism in a sustainable and responsible way. How can governments apply the GCET within their destinations?
3. The private sector in tourism has a major role in implementing the GCET. How should tourism businesses incorporate these ethics within their operations?
4. Ethics are not laws or regulations, but they are guidelines for professional practice. What difficulties does this present for governments and businesses in ensuring that the GCET guidelines are being followed?

Sources

UNWTO. 2015. Report of the World Committee on Tourism Ethics. Addendum 1. Implementation of the Global Code of Ethics for Tourism. http://cf.cdn.unwto.org/sites/all/files/docpdf/a2110reportoftheworldcommitteeontourismethicsadd1en0.pdf

UNWTO. 2017. Global Code of Ethics for Tourism. http://ethics.unwto.org/content/implementation-reports-global-code-ethics-tourism

UNWTO. Undated. Global Code of Ethics for Tourism (brochure). http://cf.cdn.unwto.org/sites/all/files/docpdf/gcetbrochureglobalcodeen.pdf

Consumer Protection Programs

A trade association establishes a program to protect travelers in the event of the bankruptcy or insolvency of any of its members. All members are required to participate in this program. A self-imposed program may obviate the need for a government agency to introduce one. The *USTOA $1 Million Travelers Assistance Program* operated by the U.S. Tour Operators Association (USTOA) is a good example of this.

Responsible Traveler Ethics and Consumer Conduct

Consumers can also be requested and reminded to manage their own behaviors; and the burden of self-regulation falls not only on tourism businesses and their trade associations. One of the areas where these programs are well articulated is with responsible travel. For example, UNWTO has suggested *Tips for a Responsible Traveller*:

Tips for a Responsible Traveller from UNWTO

- Honour your hosts and our common heritage
- Protect our planet
- Support the local economy
- Be an informed traveller
- Be a respectful traveller

Source: UNWTO. 2017

Another example of an effort to have consumers behave more appropriately is in the *Etiquette Guidelines* published by the China National Tourism Administration (CNTA) in 2017.

MULTILATERAL AND BILATERAL AGREEMENTS

In addition to the layers of national, state, provincial, territorial, regional, county, and municipal legislation and regulations, there are certain agreements that have been reached among foreign countries which have a direct impact on tourism. These are called *multilateral agreements*, meaning that several countries have signed and agreed to abide by the codes of conduct in the agreements. These agreements are increasingly leading to the liberalization of trade and travel among countries; a trend that will be beneficial to tourism in the future.

Multilateral Air Agreements

Perhaps the most significant multilateral agreements for tourism are those that relate to commercial air travel. The embryonic period for these air travel agreements was during World War II. The *five freedoms* of international air travel were first discussed at an international civil aviation conference in Chicago in 1944 (the *Chicago Convention*) and were (International Civil Aviation Organization 2017):

1. **Right of transit:** The freedom to fly over another country without stopping.
2. **Right of technical stop:** The right to stop at another country's airport for fuel and servicing.
3. **Right to discharge passengers:** The right to discharge passengers at another country's airport.
4. **Right to pick up passengers:** The right to pick up passengers from another country's airport and return them to their homes.
5. **Right to discharge and load passengers:** The right to discharge passengers at another country's airport and to then load passengers for countries farther on.

Although these freedoms had considerable support, especially from the United States, they were never agreed to universally. This meant that there was a need to establish bilateral agreements between pairs of countries. The formation of the International Civil Aviation Organization (ICAO) in 1944 and the International Air Transport Association (IATA) in 1945 paved the way for the development of bilateral agreements (International Air Transport Association 2017). You learned in Chapter 3 that ICAO is an organization of national governments and an agency of the United Nations; IATA is a trade association that represents the airlines.

In 1979, IATA was reorganized into a "two tier" organization. First, IATA is a trade association that represents airlines. Second, IATA handles *tariff coordination* for passenger fares, cargo rates, and travel agent commissions for international air travel. More than 110 of IATA's members are tariff coordination members including most of the major airlines in North America, Europe, and the Asia-Pacific region. IATA sets rates on international routes to which all member airlines agree. IATA operates a *Clearing House* for air ticket coupons that allow passengers to fly internationally on several airlines while requiring only one flight coupon. When a passenger travels on two or more airlines on a trip, this is called *interlining*.

Many multilateral agreements have been agreed to by countries on airlines' liabilities for passenger injuries and damage or loss of baggage. Three of the major agreements are the *Warsaw Convention*, The Hague *Protocol*, and the *Montreal Agreement*. The Warsaw Convention dates to 1929 and constitutes the main body of international rules in this respect. The United States accepted the Warsaw Convention regulations in 1934; Canada and the UK are other adherents to it. The Hague Protocol and the Montreal Agreement represent international agreements that have raised the dollar limit on an airline's liability to an individual passenger. In 1999, the Montreal Convention was signed into existence and replaced the Warsaw Convention. The Montreal Convention partially removed the previous limits of liability of airlines in aircraft accidents where passengers are injured or killed. A two-tier system of compensation was approved: (1) the airline is found to be at fault in the

QUICK TRIP 4.6

Regulating and Managing Inappropriate and Disruptive Visitor Behavior

One of the trickiest problems for government authorities to deal with in destinations is when visitors do not behave appropriately. Destination managers must decide how to handle visitor behavior while the visitors are present. Some regulations and monitoring of visitor behavior are required in all destinations.

The most difficult situation for destination managers is dealing with inappropriate, disruptive, unusual, and rude visitor behavior. Certain groups of visitors have gained notoriety for questionable behavior in recent times including the Chinese and Russians. These two groups are, however, not alone in behaving inappropriately as the "naked tourist photo" incidents on Mount Kinabalu (Sabah, Malaysia), Angkor Wat (Cambodia), and Machu Picchu (Peru) demonstrates. Two visitors from the United States were caught carving their names into the wall of the Colosseum in Rome, a World Heritage List cultural property. Destination managers must be careful and sensitive not to stereotype all visitors from certain countries, cultures, or ethnic groups.

The use of selfie-sticks to take photos using smartphones is very popular. This practice is widespread at major tourism sightseeing spots and attractions, but poses potential dangers to the visitors themselves, other visitors, and to the upkeep and maintenance of facilities. Due to the potential damage from selfie-sticks and reduction in the quality of visitor experiences, several famous museums have completely banned their use.

Problems with public intoxication, fights, and disturbances in hotel rooms and restaurants, and excessive noise are traditional problems with visitors in destinations. Often, ordinances are introduced by local governments to deal with these situations.

There are different approaches that a destination can use to manage visitor behavior:

- Rules or "house rules"
- Codes of conduct
- Monitoring behavior
- Regulations
- Police enforcement

Think about This

1. How has social media and the taking of photos with smartphones changed the behavior of visitors within destinations?
2. What can destinations do to better prepare for people with different cultural and social backgrounds?
3. Rudeness offends other visitors, local people, and tourism staff members, but it cannot be regulated. Do you agree with this statement or not? What can governments do to encourage their citizens to behave appropriately when they travel abroad?
4. Inappropriate behavior by visitors appears to be increasing worldwide. What do you believe are the major reasons for this upward trend?

Sources

BBC News Magazine. 2015. How prevalent is the naked tourist photo? June 11. http://www.bbc.com/news/magazine-33091556

Li, A. 2016. Why are Chinese tourists so rude? A few insights. *South China Morning Post,* August 10. http://www.scmp.com/news/china/article/1251239/why-are-chinese-tourists-so-rude

Pile, T. 2017. Who are the world's worst tourists? Six nations that stand out—you may be surprised? *South China Morning Post Magazine,* July 14. http://www.scmp.com/magazines/post-magazine/travel/article/2102308/who-are-worlds-worst-tourists-six-nations-stand-out

Scammell, R. 2015. US tourists caught carving names into Rome's Colosseum. *The Guardian,* March 8. https://www.theguardian.com/world/2015/mar/08/us-tourists-caught-carving-names-into-colosseum-rome

accident (unlimited liability applies); (2) a payment of around $160,000 per passenger irrespective of the airline's fault.

In more recent times, governments, especially the United States, have been advocating more liberalization of international air travel through the signing of bilateral and multilateral *open skies agreements* (U.S. Department of State, 2018). A discussion of these follows, but in general they are an attempt to lessen the regulations in international air travel.

Bilateral and Plurilateral Air Agreements

A *bilateral agreement* is an agreement struck between two national governments. The UK–U.S. *Bermuda Agreement* of 1946 was the benchmark bilateral air travel agreement. Bilateral air service agreements (ASAs) mainly address the questions of which airlines can fly between two countries and to which airports they can fly. Since 1946, thousands of bilateral air agreements have been signed and registered with ICAO. Bilateral air services agreements usually contain provisions on:

- **Traffic rights:** Routes airlines can fly, including cities that can be served within, between, and beyond the bilateral partners
- **Capacity:** Number of flights that can be operated or passengers that can be carried between the bilateral partners
- **Designation, ownership, and control:** Number of airlines the bilateral partners can nominate to operate services and the ownership criteria airlines must meet to be designated under the bilateral agreement (this clause sometimes includes foreign ownership restrictions)
- **Tariffs (prices):** Some agreements require airlines to submit ticket prices to aeronautical authorities for approval
- Other clauses address competition policy, safety, and security (Department of Infrastructure and Regional Development, Australian Government, 2014).

Plurilateral air services agreements are used in situations in which groups of countries get together to negotiate and sign such agreements (European Commission 2017b).

Airlines are increasingly forming *strategic alliances* with foreign airlines to gain greater access to foreign countries (e.g., Star Alliance, One World Alliance, and Sky Team Alliance). This strategy allows the airlines to avoid the intergovernmental restrictions imposed by bilateral and plurilateral agreements. These alliances have been very popular in the United States, where outbound international passenger volumes have increased. *Code sharing* is one of the facets of these alliances. This arrangement allows one airline to use its own two-character code (e.g., AA for American Airlines) to advertise a flight as its own in travel agent computer reservation systems, when the flight is being operated by its partner airline (e.g., China Eastern Airlines).

Historically, one of the reasons for restrictions of airline operations was the protection of government-owned airlines (also known as *national flag carriers*). The need for these restrictions is becoming less as more countries are *privatizing* national carriers. There has also been a trend in airports to allow these to be operated by companies and authorities that are autonomous of government.

World Trade Organization, GATT, and GATS

The General Agreement on Tariffs and Trade (GATT) is a treaty and represents the world's only multilateral agreement on the rules for international trade. The first agreement was signed in 1947. Generally, the purpose of GATT is to remove barriers to international trade. There have been several rounds of negotiations since 1947, with the latest known as the Uruguay Round in 1986 to 1994. The final stages of the Uruguay Round resulted in an agreement to create the World Trade Organization. Today, the World Trade Organization (WTO), established in 1995 and headquartered in Geneva, deals "with the rules of trade between nations" (World Trade Organization 2017). In 2016, the WTO had 164 member countries (including Australia, Canada, China, the UK, and the United States).

Another outcome of the Uruguay Round was the General Agreement on Trade in Services (GATS). The accord, which came into force in January 1995, is the first set of multilateral rules covering international trade in services. GATS liberates trade in services and could have a major impact on tourism. GATS applies in principle to all services, except government services and air transportation services.

Criteria for the World Heritage List

The World Heritage List (WHL) includes many of the world's best-known tourism attractions including the Pyramids in Egypt, the Great Wall and Terracotta Warriors in China, the Great Barrier Reef and Kakadu National Park in Australia, the Acropolis in Greece, Vatican City, Canada's Rocky Mountain National Parks, Britain's Stonehenge and the Tower of London, Yellowstone National Park and the Statue of Liberty in the United States, and Japan's Himeji Castle (Figure 4.15). Many other listed sites may not be household names but fit UNESCO's definition of global, cultural, and natural treasures.

To be included on the WHL, sites must be of outstanding universal value and meet at least one out of ten selection criteria:

1. To represent a masterpiece of human creative genius;
2. To exhibit an important interchange of human values, over a span of time or within a cultural area of the world, on developments in architecture or technology, monumental arts, town-planning or landscape design;
3. To bear a unique or at least exceptional testimony to a cultural tradition or to a civilization which is living or which has disappeared;
4. To be an outstanding example of a type of building, architectural, or technological ensemble or landscape which illustrates (a) significant stage(s) in human history;
5. To be an outstanding example of a traditional human settlement, land-use, or sea-use which is representative of a culture (or cultures), or human interaction with the environment especially when it has become vulnerable under the impact of irreversible change;
6. To be directly or tangibly associated with events or living traditions, with ideas, or with beliefs, with artistic and literary works of outstanding universal significance. (The Committee considers that this criterion should preferably be used in conjunction with other criteria);
7. To contain superlative natural phenomena or areas of exceptional natural beauty and aesthetic importance;
8. To be outstanding examples representing major stages of earth's history, including the record of life, significant ongoing geological processes in the development of landforms, or significant geomorphic or physiographic features;
9. To be outstanding examples representing significant ongoing ecological and biological processes in the evolution and development of terrestrial, fresh water, coastal and marine ecosystems, and communities of plants and animals;
10. To contain the most important and significant natural habitats for in situ conservation of biological diversity, including those containing threatened species of outstanding universal value from the point of view of science or conservation.

Think about This

1. What are the potential advantages to a destination if it receives a World Heritage Listing from UNESCO?
2. Are there any dangers that receiving such a listing might pose and, if so, what are these?
3. What steps can a destination take to ensure that these sites are protected from environmental damage from human impacts?
4. What evidence is there that receiving a World Heritage Listing has increased visitor volumes to the sites?

Source

UNESCO WHL website. 2017. http://whc.unesco.org/en/criteria

World Heritage List, UNESCO

The United Nations Educational, Scientific and Cultural Organization (UNESCO) is an agency of the United Nations concerned with education, science, and cultural and natural heritage. At its 1972 General Conference, an international agreement was signed titled the *Convention Concerning the Protection of the World Cultural and Natural Heritage*. In 2017, there were 1,073 sites around the world on the UNESCO *World Heritage List* (832 cultural, 206 natural, and 35 mixed) (Figure 4.15). Some of the well-known tourism attractions on the list include the Canadian Rocky Mountain National Parks; Ayers Rock-The Olgas, and the Wet Tropics of Queensland (Australia); the Galapagos Islands (Ecuador); the Cathedral of Notre Dame in Paris; the Taj Mahal; Machu Picchu (Peru); the Kremlin and Red Square (Russia); the Old and New Towns of Edinburgh (United Kingdom); and Grand Canyon National Park (United States).

UNESCO maintains another list called the *List of World Heritage in Danger*. This list includes sites that are placed in danger because of civil disturbances or through environmental threats. For example, in 2017 these sites included 54 of the 1,073 on the World Heritage List, including the Historic Centre of Vienna, Liverpool—Maritime Mercantile City; Belize Barrier Reef Reserve System; Everglades National Park in the United States; and the Tropical Rainforest Heritage of Sumatra, Indonesia.

Free Trade Agreements

There are many other treaties and agreements governing trade and travel procedures among countries. These also play a key role in the tourism regulatory framework of destination areas. One of the major forces here in recent years has been the creation of *free trade areas* such as the European Community (EC) and the ASEAN Economic Community (AEC) (Association of Southeast Asian Nations 2017). Australia and New Zealand have signed a Trans-Tasman Mutual Recognition Arrangement (TTMRA).

Figure 4.16 provides you with a visual summary of what you have learned in this chapter. It indicates the laws and regulations at the national and country levels; then shows the self-regulatory programs at three levels (association-institute-NGO, organizations, and consumers). There is an important conclusion that you can draw from considering this diagram about legislation and regulation in destinations. This is that governments are not alone in their concern for the proper behaviors of economic sectors, companies, and visitors. In fact, it takes a multi-level effort to ensure that visitors have safe, secure, and worry-free experiences on their trips.

© supavamin yaisoon/Shutterstock.com

FIGURE 4.15   Himeji Castle in Japan is a UNESCO World Heritage List cultural property.

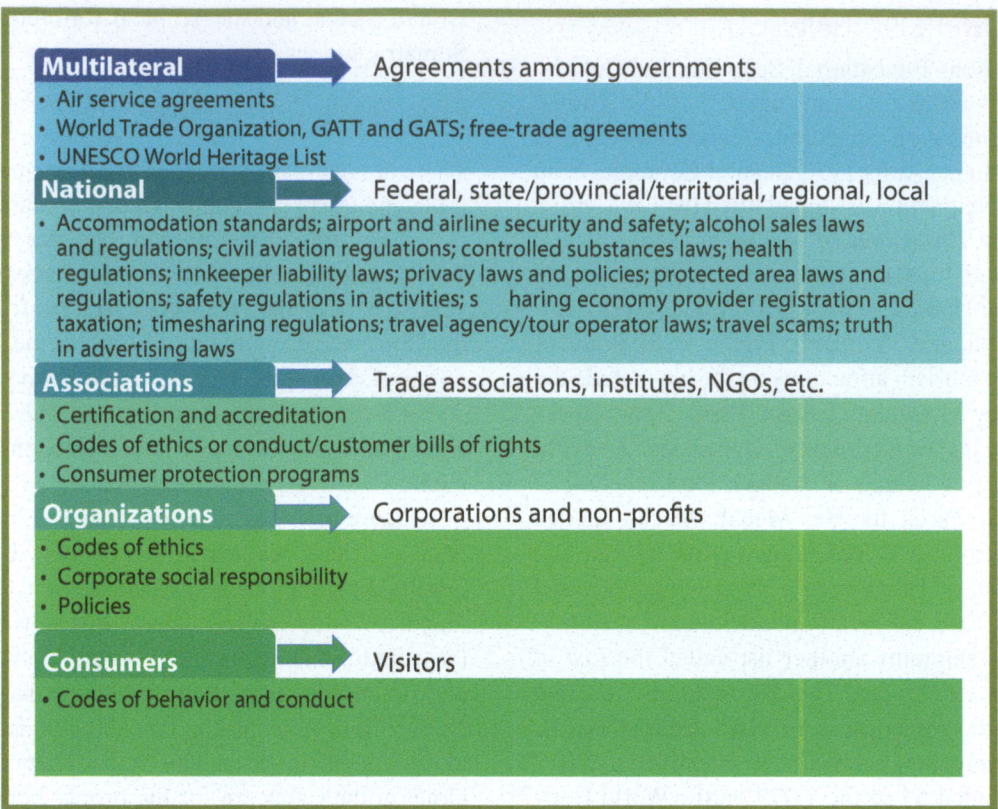

FIGURE 4.16 Levels of legislation and regulation in destinations.

SUMMARY

Experience has shown that tourism development can have both positive and negative impacts on destinations. Tourism also affects and is influenced by the national interests of a country including its natural and cultural resources and its immigration laws and policies. For these and other reasons, it is essential that governments play a role in developing legislation and in regulating specific parts of tourism.

All destinations have laws and regulations that affect tourism. Many of these are introduced to protect visitors and residents, as well as the environmental and cultural heritage of the destination.

There has been a strong global trend toward freer trade and travel among countries. This will continue to have a positive influence on world tourism in the future. There is also a trend toward deregulating parts of tourism and toward the privatization of previously government-operated organizations (Organisation for Economic Co-operation and Development 2015). Another trend that shows the increasing maturity and professionalism in tourism is the move toward greater self-regulation through accreditation, certification, and consumer protection programs. The development of programs such as these, along with more deregulation and privatization, may mean that the government influence on tourism will diminish in the future. Finally, consumers themselves are taking more responsibility for how their actions impact upon destinations, and that is welcome in promoting sustainable tourism.

ACTIVITIES

1. Analyze the strategic alliances among airlines in your region of the world. Which airlines are involved in these partnerships? What are the benefits to the partner airlines?
2. In what ways are the airlines cooperating (e.g., code-sharing, sharing of equipment and facilities)?
3. What are the potential benefits of these partnerships to airline passengers? Do you think that the number of strategic alliances will grow in the next five years? Why or why not?
4. Find the web and social media sites of these strategic airline alliances. What passenger services and benefits are offered through these websites?
5. What are the benefits to each of the strategic alliance partners in having its airline's information on these web and social media sites?
6. For those airlines that do not belong to the strategic alliances, what are the major challenges of not being part of these cooperative programs both offline and online?

ACRONYMS

ABTA (Association of British Travel Agents)
AFTA (Australian Federation of Travel Agents)
ASTA (American Society of Travel Agents)
ATOL (Air Travel Organizer's License)
CAA (Civil Aviation Authority, UK)
CAB (Civil Aeronautics Board, USA)
CASA (Civil Aviation Safety Authority, Australia)
EU (European Union)
FAA (Federal Aviation Administration, USA)
GATS (General Agreement on Trade in Services)
GATT (General Agreement on Tariffs and Trade)
IATA (International Air Transport Association)
ICAO (International Civil Aviation Organization)
SOE (state-owned enterprise)

TBID (tourism business improvement districts)
TC (Transport Canada)
TICO (Travel Industry Council of Ontario)
TID (Tourism Improvement District)
TSB (Transportation Safety Board of Canada)
TTI (The Travel Institute)
UNESCO (United Nations Educational Scientific and Cultural Organization)
UNWTO (United Nations World Tourism Organization)
USTA (U.S. Travel Association)
USTOA (U.S. Tour Operators Association)
WTO (World Trade Organization)

REFERENCES

Adam, N. 2017. Tourism Saved Iceland, but Now It's a Headache. *Wall Street Journal*, August 20.

American Society of Travel Agents (ASTA). 2017. ASTA Code of Ethics. https://www.asta.org/About/content.cfm?ItemNumber=745

Association of British Travel Agents (ABTA). 2017. ABTA Code of Conduct. https://abta.com/about-us/code-of-conduct

Association of Southeast Asian Nations. 2017. ASEAN Economic Community. http://asean.org/asean-economic-community/

Australian Federation of Travel Agents (AFTA). 2017. AFTA Travel Accreditation Scheme (ATAS). Code of Conduct. http://www.afta.com.au/uploads/atas-code-of-conduct.pdf

Caribbean Tourism Organization. 2017. Advocacy. http://www.onecaribbean.org/our-work/advocacy/

Center for Responsible Travel (CREST). Undated. Fact Sheet #4: Land Use and Tourism. http://www.responsible-travel.org/projects/documents/Fact%20_Sheet_4_Land_Use_and_Tourism.pdf

China National Tourism Organization, New York. 2017. For Chinese Tourists. http://www.cnto.org/better-behavior-urged-chinese-tourists/

City of Las Vegas. 2017. Standards & Requirements. https://www.lasvegasnevada.gov/portal/faces/wcnav_externalId/bp-standards-requirements

Cruise Lines International Association. 2017. Cruise Industry Passenger Bill of Rights. https://www.cruising.org/about-the-industry/regulatory/industry-policies/other/pbor

Department of Infrastructure and Regional Development, Australian Government, 2014. The Bilateral System—how international air services work. https://infrastructure.gov.au/aviation/international/bilateral_system.aspx

Destinations International. 2017. Destination Marketing Accreditation Program (DMAP). https://destinations international.org/destination-marketing-accreditation-program-dmap

European Commission. 2017a. Timeshare. http://ec.europa.eu/consumers/consumer_rights/travel/timeshare/index_en.htm

European Commission. 2017b. Aviation: 10 years of EU-US Air Transport Agreement. https://ec.europa.eu/transport/modes/air/news/2017-07-10-aviation-10-years-eu-us-air-transport-agreement_en

Fáilte Ireland. 2017. Hotels. http://www.failteireland.ie/Supports/Get-quality-assured/Hotels.aspx

Federal Trade Commission. 2017. Truth in advertising. https://www.ftc.gov/news-events/media-resources/truth-advertising

FQ Quotes. 2018. Quote from Peter Simpson—There's far too much red tape and not enough red carpet. https://fquotes.com/quote/peter-simpson-552698

International Air Transport Association (IATA). 2017. Accreditation of IATA Agents. http://www.iata.org/services/accreditation/accreditation-travel/Pages/index.aspx

International Air Transport Association. 2017. Fact Sheet. Montreal Convention 1999 (MC99). https://www.iata.org/pressroom/facts_figures/fact_sheets/Documents/fact-sheet-mc99.pdf

International Civil Aviation Organization. 2017. Freedoms of the Air. https://www.icao.int/Pages/freedomsAir.aspx

International Code Council. 2017. About ICC. https://www.iccsafe.org/about-icc/overview/about-international-code-council/

International Union for Conservation of Nature (IUCN). 2017. Protected Areas. https://www.iucn.org/theme/protected-areas

Levine, A. 2015. The TBID Revolution: New Dollars for Tourism Marketing. *Forbes*, December 1.

Li, J., and Pearce, P. 2016. Tourist scams in the city: challenges for domestic travellers in urban China. *International Journal of Tourism Cities*, 2(4), 294–308.

National Restaurant Association Educational Foundation. 2017. Welcome to ServSafe! https://www.servsafe.com/

Natural England. 2017. Natural England. About us. https://www.gov.uk/government/organisations/natural-england/about

New Zealand Government. 2016. Health and Safety at Work (Adventure Activities) Regulations 2016. http://www.legislation.govt.nz/regulation/public/2016/0019/latest/DLM6725703.html

New Zealand Legislation. 2017. Trans-Tasman Mutual Recognition Act 1997. Reprint as at 27 July 2017. http://legislation.govt.nz/act/public/1997/0060/latest/DLM410793.html

Organisation for Economic Co-operation and Development. 2015. *OECD Guidelines on Corporate Governance of State-Owned Enterprises. 2015 Edition*. Paris: OECD.

Parks Canada Agency. 2000. Unimpaired for Future Generations? Protecting Ecological Integrity with Canada's National Parks. http://publications.gc.ca/collections/collection_2017/pc/R62-323-2000-2-eng.pdf

Tourism Australia. 2017. Privacy Policy. http://www.australia.com/en-us/privacypolicy.html

Travel Compensation Fund. 2017. TCF. http://tcf.org.au/

Travel Industry Council of Ontario. 2017. Ontario Travel Industry Act, 2002. https://www.tico.ca/consumers/travel-industry-act-2002.html

The Travel Institute. 2017. CTC Certification. https://www.thetravelinstitute.com/product/ctc/

UK Government. 2017. Civil Aviation (Air Travel Organisers' Licensing) Regulations 2012. https://www.gov.uk/government/publications/civil-aviation-air-travel-organisers-licensing-regulations-2012

UNESCO. 2017. List of World Heritage in Danger. http://whc.unesco.org/en/danger/

UNESCO. 2017. World Heritage List Statistics. http://whc.unesco.org/en/list/stat#s6

UNWTO. 2017. The Responsible Tourist. Tips for a Responsible Traveller. http://ethics.unwto.org/content/responsible-tourist

U.S. Customs and Border Protection. 2018. What is the purpose of the Travel Promotion Act of 2009? https://www.cbp.gov/faqs/what-purpose-travel-promotion-act-2009

U.S. Department of State. 2018. Air Service/Open Skies Agreements. https://www.state.gov/e/eb/tra/ata/

U.S. Department of State. 2018. International Financial Scams. https://travel.state.gov/content/passports/en/emergencies/scams.html

U.S. Tour Operators Association. 2017. USTO $1 Million Travelers Assistance Program. https://www.ustoa.com/travelers-assistance

U.S. Travel Association. 2017. Business Groups Raise Alarm on Trump Changes to Obama Visa Policy. July 20. https://www.ustravel.org/press/business-groups-raise-alarm-trump-changes-obama-visa-policy

VisitBritain. 2011. Tourism Business Improvement Districts. https://www.visitbritain.org/sites/default/files/vb-corporate/Documents-Library/documents/England-documents/intro_to_tbids.pdf

World Trade Organization. 2017. The General Agreement on Trade in Services (GATS): Objectives, coverage and disciplines. https://www.wto.org/english/tratop_e/serv_e/gatsqa_e.htm

World Trade Organization. 2017. The WTO. https://www.wto.org/english/thewto_e/thewto_e.htm

CHAPTER FIVE

Tourism Destination Planning

Envisioning and Charting the Future

He who fails to plan is planning to fail.

SIR WINSTON CHURCHILL

YOUR LEARNING DESTINATION

You will be able to explain the reasons for tourism destination planning and the process used to conduct tourism destination planning.

WHAT YOU NEED TO KNOW

Having read this chapter, you will be able to:

✓ Review the reasons for tourism destination planning.
✓ Pinpoint the potential barriers to tourism destination planning.
✓ Explain the purposes of tourism destination planning.
✓ Describe an effective framework for tourism destination planning.
✓ Detail a step-by-step process for preparing a tourism destination plan.

BREAKING THE ICE

Imagine if you set out on a hike in a huge wilderness area without your phone, a GPS device, or a map. You probably would get very lost and be in danger of doing serious physical harm to yourself. Similarly, destinations without tourism plans may not get to where they want to go and are endangering irreplaceable natural and cultural treasures. Just like you hiking in the wilderness area, a destination needs to envision where it is going to go and then chart a route for getting there.

KEY TAKEAWAY POINTS

*   Every tourism destination should have a tourism destination plan, but not all destinations have plans.

*   An effective tourism destination planning framework includes policy, principals, participants, process, and plan (5 Ps).

*   There is a tourism destination planning process that includes seven steps (background analysis; detailed research and analysis; synthesis and visioning; goal-setting, strategy selection, and objective setting; plan development; plan implementation and monitoring; and plan evaluation).

*   There are eight aspects of a tourism destination that need to be planned (tourism development; destination marketing; experience and activity design; human resource development; tourism organization; community awareness of and involvement in tourism; service quality and quality assurance; and support services and activities).

REASONS FOR TOURISM DESTINATION PLANNING

Why Tourism Destination Planning Is Needed

Tourism can benefit or damage destinations. The positive economic impacts of tourism development are the most lucrative to many destinations. However, tourism has damaged many natural and cultural heritage resources. Moreover, tourism affects everyone in destination communities, and does not just involve the visitors and tourism businesses. For example, you may have heard that the residents of Barcelona, Palma (Majorca, Spain), Venice, and some other European cities are complaining about there being too much tourism in their communities (now called "overtourism") (Figure 5.1).

The pace of tourism development is rapid, especially in regions with fast-developing economies. Globally, tourism is more competitive than ever before and

FIGURE 5.1 Local residents' graffiti about too much tourism.

there is much more marketing of tourism destinations. Additionally, tourism is a more complicated phenomenon than it was previously thought to be.

Tourism is very dynamic and constantly changing, and travelers' needs, expectations, and requirements are

FIGURE 5.2 Overcrowded beaches may result from inadequate tourism planning. A crowded beach in Costinesti, Romania.

continuously evolving. So, it is important for destinations to plan ahead and envision what future consumers will be wanting.

What Can Happen without Tourism Destination Planning

What are the consequences of having no tourism destination planning? There are many examples of tourism's damaging impacts on physical environments, cultural heritage, and local communities. These negative impacts include damage to coral reefs, disturbing wildlife, tramping of vegetation, littering, carving of initials on priceless heritage structures, overcrowding, various forms of pollution, inappropriate behavior, and others.

Often, but not always, the lack of adequate tourism destination planning is as much to blame for these problems as tourism itself. Some of the consequences and symptoms of a lack of tourism destination planning are shown in Figure 5.3.

Impacts	Consequences and Symptoms of a Lack of Tourism Planning
Physical	• Damage or permanent alteration of the physical environment • Harming of historical and cultural landmarks and resources • Overcrowding • Traffic congestion • Water, air, and solid waste pollution
Human	• Deficient community awareness of the costs and benefits of tourism • Dislike and resentment of visitors among local people • Inadequate involvement of local people in tourism • Insufficient education of tourism employees in skills and hospitality • Loss of cultural identities and traditional lifestyles • Reduced accessibility to services and visitor attractions for local people resulting in local resentment of tourism activity
Marketing	• Erosion of market shares by competitive destinations • Failure to capitalize on new marketing opportunities • Inaccurate image of destination in potential markets • Inadequate visitor activities, experiences, and packages • Insufficient awareness in prime markets • Minimal partnership marketing among tourism businesses • Poorly conceived destination branding • Unfocused target marketing
Organizational	• Failure to act upon important issues, challenges, problems, and opportunities of common interest to tourism • Fragmented approach to the marketing and development of tourism, often involving "competitive" splinter groups • Inadequate representation (advocacy) of tourism's interests • Infrequent cooperation among tourism businesses • Insufficient support from local government agencies
Other	• High seasonality and short lengths of stay • Inadequate interpretation and guiding services • Incomplete directional signage programs • Insufficient attractions and events • Poor or deteriorating quality of facilities and services • Not enough travel information services

FIGURE 5.3 Consequences and symptoms of a lack of tourism planning.

QUICK TRIP 5.1

A Tourism Plan to Tackle Seasonality at Punta del Este

Seasonality is a major challenge for many destinations and persists without adequate tourism planning. It occurs in destinations that are weather-dependent outside of the Tropics, including summer beach and winter sport resorts. Seasonality also happens because of the holiday-making times of visitors, being influenced by such factors as school holidays. The availability of transportation and the presence of certain natural phenomena (e.g., wildlife, celestial occurrences) are other causes of seasonality.

UNWTO says this about the impact of seasonality on tourism destination planning:

> "Seasonality affects negatively the planning capacity of the destination, its ability to attract investments and employment stability in the region, which in turn weakens the overall ability of destinations to adapt to changes in demand."

Destinations suffering from seasonality often require diversification of their tourism product offerings. This means developing a plan for adding new attractions, events, experiences, and activities in other parts of the year than the peak season.

Punta del Este is a popular seaside resort destination in Uruguay, South America (Figure 5.4). With the help of UNWTO, a plan was developed to lessen the seasonality problem of the Atlantic coast city. Punta del Este 365 is the name of the UNWTO's Programme Prototype to help the destination overcome its seasonality problem. A short video on the plan can be viewed at https://vimeo.com/110980259. This plan put an emphasis on innovations in visitor experiences, with a guiding theme of energy. New product development in the following areas was recommended:

- Wellness
- Gastronomy
- Art and culture
- Agricultural tourism
- Sports tourism
- Meetings
- Language training and academic training specializing in tourism

UNWTO used the suggestions and inputs of its affiliate members to shape the plan for Punta del Este.

Think about This

1. How can tourism destination planning help alleviate the problems associated with seasonality?
2. Can you identify some destinations that suffer from seasonality and explain the reasons for their seasonality?
3. What have other destinations planned and done to combat seasonality?
4. What are the benefits of the approach used by UNWTO in Prototype 365 for Punta del Este?

Sources

UNWTO. 2014. Punta del Este 365—UNWTO launches first prototype to overcome seasonality. http://media.unwto.org/press-release/2014-11-06/punta-del-este-365-unwto-launches-first-prototype-overcome-seasonality

UNWTO. 2014. UNWTO Affiliate Members Programme Prototype: Punta del Este 365 Vimeo. https://vimeo.com/110980259

UNWTO. 2017. Prototype 365. http://affiliatemembers.unwto.org/content/prototype-365

UNWTO. Undated. UNWTO Seasonality Prototype. Punta del Este 365. Madrid: UNWTO.

FIGURE 5.4 Hand sculpture symbol of Punta del Este in Uruguay.

POTENTIAL BARRIERS TO TOURISM DESTINATION PLANNING

Not every place has a tourism destination plan. With so many good reasons for tourism planning, you might wonder why not. Here are seven potential barriers to tourism destination planning:

Objections to the Principle of Tourism Destination Planning

The first potential barrier is that some people are against tourism planning in principle, particularly within the developed countries. This is especially true in parts of the Asia-Pacific region, Europe, and North America, where tourism has existed for many years without any formal tourism destination planning. Many business-people view tourism planning as an encroachment, mainly by government agencies, into a private-sector domain of activity and they are skeptical of its ultimate value to them. They argue that tourism has already succeeded without a formal tourism destination plan.

High Costs of Tourism Destination Planning

The high cost is a second potential barrier to tourism destination planning. Because effective tourism destination planning must be based upon detailed resource analysis, primary market research, and extensive local consultations, it often becomes a very time-consuming and expensive process. Governments generally are required to fund tourism destination planning efforts on behalf of everyone involved. Private-sector tourism businesses may object to this, believing that the money is better spent on more marketing or promotion of the destination.

Complexity of Tourism and the Large Number of Government Agencies Involved

A third potential barrier is the complexity of tourism and the large number of government agencies whose activities affect tourism, directly and indirectly. Tourism destination planning is often made more difficult because the policies of these departments are not coordinated and indeed are sometimes in direct conflict with one another. Additionally, tourism is not a readily identifiable sector; it cuts across many other economic activities. Although the front-line recipients of visitors' expenditures, such as hotels and resorts, attractions, restaurants, airlines, car rental agencies, and RV parks are obvious, others including retail shops, banks, and municipal governments are not normally seen as being part of tourism. Another complication is that some tourism businesses receive their income both from visitors and from local residents.

Diversity of Tourism Businesses

A fourth potential barrier to planning is that tourism is often characterized by having a few very large and a multitude of smaller- and medium-sized businesses (SMEs). There is also a tendency for individual operators to categorize themselves as being in particular business segments (e.g., "hospitality" or "foodservice" or "entertainment") rather than acknowledging their broader role in tourism.

Seasonality of Tourism

The seasonality of tourism in many destinations can make it difficult to contact, involve, and observe certain types of tourism and tourism businesses. Because of climatic conditions, tourism seasons may be very short.

High Ownership and Management Turnover in Tourism

Tourism destination plans are usually implemented over five to ten years. It is helpful if the people involved in implementing plans stay the same as this means greater continuity. However, tourism is a sector that experiences frequent ownership and management turnover, and this is a sixth potential barrier to effective tourism destination planning.

Unpredictability of Tourism

The seventh potential barrier is the unpredictability of tourism in destinations due to crises, disasters, and other disruptions caused by a variety of external factors including nature, economic trends, political policies, and terrorism. Some people argue that, since tourism is so easily influenced by external factors, there is no point in planning tourism for many years ahead.

Despite these seven barriers to tourism destination planning, an increasing number of plans are produced each year around the world. Indications are that tourism destination planning will be given a higher priority in the future and that more destinations will become involved in planning. As they become involved, they will have at their disposal the prior planning experience and "templates" of many other areas and thus a more refined "technology" of tourism destination planning.

PURPOSES OF TOURISM DESTINATION PLANNING

Tourism depends on the existence of unique attractions, events, activities, and experiences. These may include beaches, natural scenery, parks, historical buildings and landmarks, unique cultural characteristics, one-of-a-kind local events and festivals, and outdoor sports and recreation activities. If destinations want to sustain tourism as a long-term economic activity, they must use tourism destination planning to preserve and enhance these special factors that make them different from other destinations. Destinations must follow sustainable tourism principles. Tourism development planning has five basic purposes that are detailed in Figure 5.5.

One of the most important of these purposes of tourism destination planning is to avoid the negative physical, human, marketing, organizational, and other impacts that can occur when planning is not practiced. Tourism is not the answer to every destination's economic, socio-cultural, and environmental issues, and all communities should not pursue tourism. However, where the decision is made to develop tourism, it is much more likely to be successful if destination planning is done.

FRAMEWORK FOR TOURISM DESTINATION PLANNING

Tourism destination planning requires an effective overall framework. There are five major components of this framework and they all start with the letter "P" (Figure 5.6):

- *Policy:* The basic guidelines for tourism expressed as policy statements, goals, and initiatives.
- *Principals:* The groups of people that coordinate the long-term planning process for tourism in the destination.

Identifying Alternative Approaches	Adapting to the Unexpected	Maintaining Uniqueness
• Marketing • Development • Organization of tourism • Community awareness of and involvement in tourism • Support services and activities	• General economic conditions • Energy supply and demand • Values and lifestyles • Economic performance of local industries • Government legislation and regulations • Technological advancements • Crises and disasters	• Natural features and resources • Cultural and social fabric • Architecture and heritage • Historical monuments and landmarks • Festivals, events, and activities • Parks and outdoor sports areas

Creating the Desirable	Avoiding the Undesirable
• Sustainable tourism • High community awareness of the benefits of tourism • Clear and positive image of tourism destination • Effective organization of tourism • Frequent cooperation among tourism organizations and businesses • Effective marketing, directional signage, and travel information programs	• Friction and unnecessary competition • Hostile and unfriendly attitudes of local residents toward visitors • Undesirable permanent alteration of natural features • Damage to cultural heritage resources • Loss of cultural identities • Declining market share • Stoppage of unique local events and festivals • Overcrowding, congestion, and traffic problems • Pollution • High seasonality

FIGURE 5.5 Purposes of tourism planning.

- *Participants:* The organizations and individuals invited to participate in the tourism destination planning process.
- *Process:* The heart of tourism destination planning and the overall approach followed to develop, implement, monitor, and evaluate the tourism plan.
- *Plans and communicating about plans:* The planning documents and associated media, and how they are communicated.

Policy

As indicated in Chapter 3, tourism policies provide the basic guidelines for tourism in a destination that are typically set by government agencies. Policy goals and initiatives are the initial inputs for tourism destination planning (as shown in Figure 5.6).

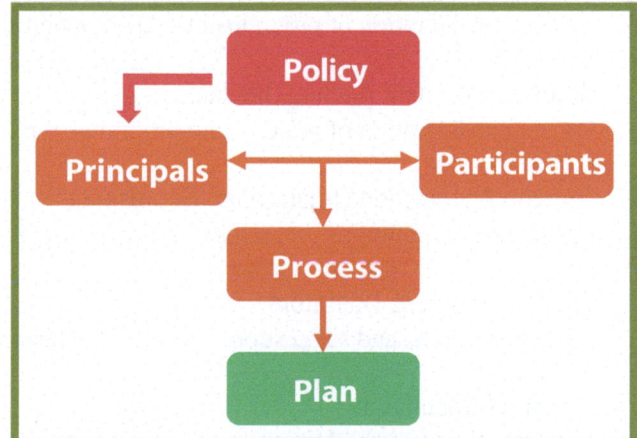

FIGURE 5.6 The 5 Ps framework for tourism destination planning.

Principals

The principals are the people who coordinate the tourism destination planning process. Often, it is a government agency performing the coordination role in preparing a tourism destination plan. In some cases, a destination management organization (DMO) plays this role and forms a public-private Steering or Coordinating Committee.

Independent consultants and planning companies are usually hired to conduct the analysis required for a tourism destination plan and to facilitate the planning process. There are consulting companies that specialize in this type of planning work.

Participants

The principals decide which organizations and individuals should be invited to participate in the tourism destination planning process. The invitees should represent all groups of stakeholders including government, tourism sector organizations, community, environment, and visitors (Figure 5.7). The input from visitors must also be gathered either through surveys, focus groups, or independent in-depth interviews.

For the *Vancouver Tourism Master Plan* in British Columbia, residents, local businesses, and other interested parties were invited to complete an online survey. The *Macao Tourism Industry Development Master Plan* also included the gathering of local community resident opinions and attitudes; however, these surveys were completed face-to-face. Another technique to encourage greater participation is exemplified with the circulation of a *Consultation Paper* during the preparation of the *Macao Tourism Industry Development Master Plan*.

Process

The process is the heart of tourism destination planning and requires great forethought about how best to accomplish the tasks involved. There is no standardized template for a tourism destination planning process. In actual practice, many different approaches are used. You will learn about one of these processes later in this chapter.

Government Tourism Officials
Coordinate the tourism planning process; fund tourism planning; provide liaison among all parties involved.

Local Community Residents
Identify community values; indicate satisfaction levels with tourism and acceptable future changes in tourism; provide opinions and suggestions.

Nonprofit Organization Representatives
Ensure consideration of programs of related nonprofit organizations; provide opinions and suggestions.

Other Government Agency Officials
Ensure consideration of policies and programs of related government agencies.

Tourism Association/Organization Representatives
Ensure consideration of programs of tourism associations/organizations; provide opinions and suggestions.

Tourism Business Operators
Provide opinions and suggestions. Ensure plan recommendations are practical and realistic.

Tourism Consultants
Facilitate the tourism planning process; conduct research and analysis; write tourism plan.

Developers and Investors
Develop project conceptual plans; fund feasibility studies; provide investment funds.

FIGURE 5.7 Tourism planning participants and roles.

QUICK TRIP 5.2

Communicating the Kuala Lumpur Tourism Master Plan

How a tourism destination plan is communicated can be vitally important to its ultimate success. Traditionally, tourism plan communications are through written reports and public meetings. However, in the age of the Internet and social media, there are other ways to share the information about tourism destination planning. One of the options is to videotape presentations on the tourism destination plan.

Kuala Lumpur, the capital city of Malaysia (Figure 5.8), is a destination that produced a video to more broadly and visually communicate its new Tourism Master Plan. The 3:32-minute video showcases the highlights of the plan. The contents of the Kuala Lumpur Tourism Master Plan 2015–2025 are as follows:

Executive Summary
Chapter 1: Diagnostic
State of tourism in KL
Performance of KL tourism
Overall tourist perception of KL
KL's offerings—nine key segments
Supporting infrastructure and enablers for tourism
Potential opportunities for KL tourism
Chapter 2: Vision
KL tourism vision
KL tourism strategic framework
KL tourism strategic targets
Chapter 3: Strategy
Designing the master plan
Initiatives
Culture, heritage & places of interest
Shopping
Entertainment
Nature & adventure
Luxury travel
Sports
Business & MICE
Medical & wellness
Education
Enablers
Chapter 4: Impact
Expected impact of KL Tourism Master Plan
Funding requirements
Chapter 5: Conclusion
Conclusion
Chapter 6: Collaboration
Appendices
Abbreviations and definitions
List of stakeholders engaged

QUICK TRIP 5.2 CONTINUED

Think about This

1. What are the advantages for a destination in preparing a video presentation of its tourism plan?
2. Producing videos can be costly. How should a destination justify the investment in a tourism plan video presentation?
3. Are there any potential dangers in revealing plans so publicly, or do the advantages outweigh the potential dangers?
4. What are your overall thoughts on the KL video and how could it be improved?

Sources

Kuala Lumpur City Hall. 2015. Kuala Lumpur Tourism Master Plan 2015–2025. http://www.kltourismmasterplan.com/

Visitklofficial. 2015. KL Tourism Master Plan 2015–2025. https://www.youtube.com/watch?v=3X70QCTKqtl

© ESB Professional/Shutterstock.com

FIGURE 5.8 Kuala Lumpur chose an innovative video presentation approach to communicating its Tourism Master Plan.

The end product of tourism destination planning is the plan itself which will remain as the record of what was proposed and what was done. However, the planning process can be equally important as the written plan since, if developed in a participatory way, the process creates a shared sense of ownership of the plan, its vision, goals, and objectives, and implementation programs and actions.

Plans and Communicating about Plans

A tourism destination plan is a written document that describes what will be done by the destination to achieve the tourism vision, goals, and objectives. Planning documents vary greatly in style and length, and they may be produced in different versions aimed at distinct audiences. Typically, a shorter document, often called an Executive Summary, is prepared for general distribution and a longer, detailed report is designed for a more selective audience.

Communicating the essential contents of tourism destination plans has become more important and careful attention must be given to this task. Tourism planning processes can be long and it may even take up to one year to prepare a plan. With so much time and effort going into the planning process and all the associated research, analysis, meetings, and discussions, it can be easy to forget that the plan is a "beginning" and not "the end."

LEVELS OF TOURISM PLANNING

Tourism planning for destinations is conducted at multiple levels within a country (Figure 5.9). The highest level is at the national level with the planning process being coordinated by the country's national DMO. At the sub-national level, there can be plans for states, provinces, territories, and regions (if applicable). Quick Trips 5.3, 5.4, and 5.6 provide examples from these levels.

The local level is the third tier for tourism planning and there can be several types of plans here depending on how local authorities are structured. In many countries, there will be counties, cities, and towns, and tourism plans may be prepared for each of these. Quick Trips 5.1, 5.2, and 5.5 are examples at these levels. A fourth tier is area tourism planning; for example, this could be a tourism plan for a protected area such as a national park or for a resort destination.

TOURISM DESTINATION PLANNING PROCESS

Although tourism planning takes place at a variety of levels in a destination, the approaches used in producing the plans should follow a similar step-by-step pattern. There are seven steps in the tourism planning process (Figure 5.10).

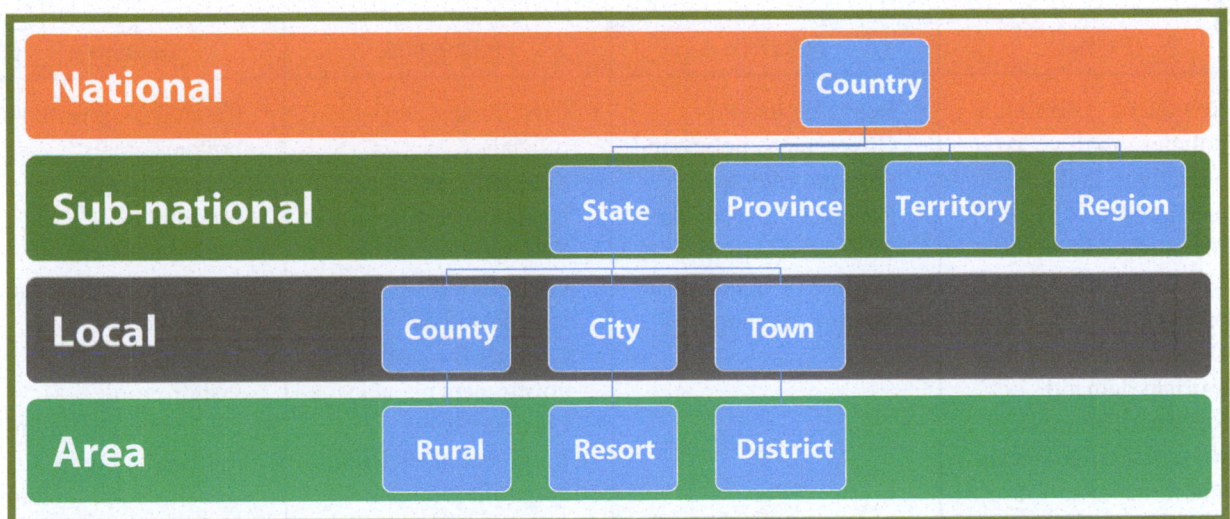

FIGURE 5.9 Levels of tourism planning in a country.

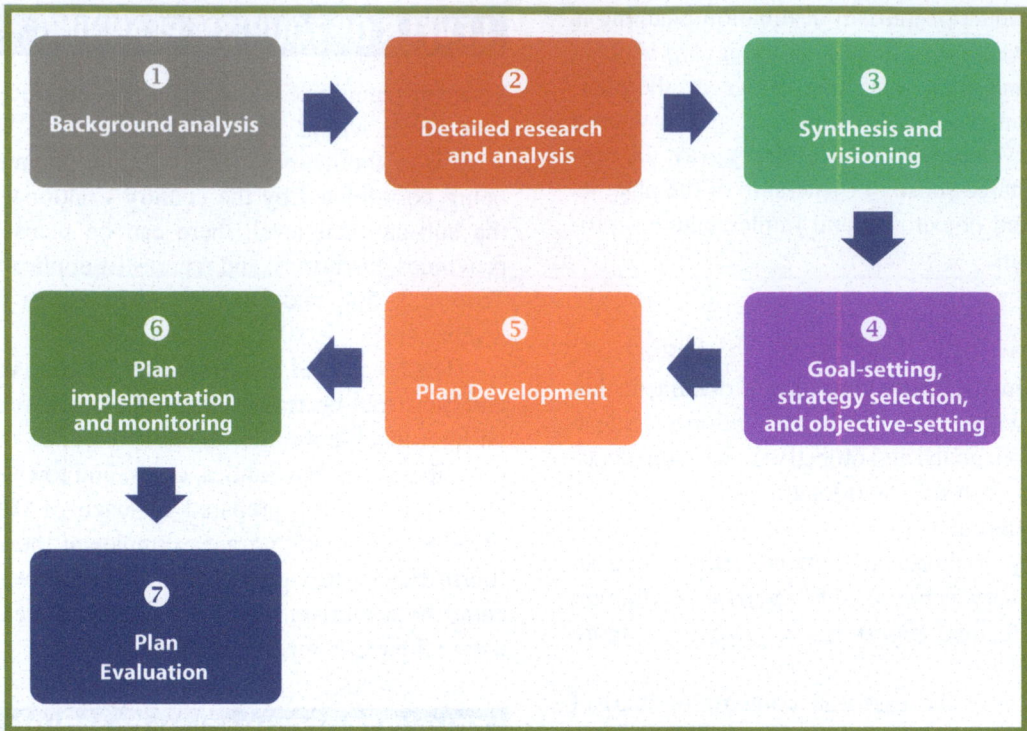

FIGURE 5.10 Tourism destination planning step-by-step process.

Step 1: Background Analysis

The first step in the tourism destination planning process is a situation or SWOT analysis that produces the direction for the succeeding steps. This is a logical starting point because most destinations have some level of existing tourism activity, as well as tourism policies and legislation. The parts, activities, participants, and outcomes for the Background Analysis step are shown in Figure 5.11.

Parts	Activities	Participants	Outcomes
• Review of government policies, goals, objectives, and programs • Inventory and analysis of existing destination product • Description of existing tourism demand • Review of strengths, weaknesses, problems, and issues with tourism	• Resource inventory • Government policy and program review • Research of secondary sources of information • Pooling of opinions and group workshops	• Government tourism officials • Selected tourism business operators • Selected tourism organization representatives • Officials from other key government agencies • Local residents • Representatives from nonprofit groups • Tourism consultants	• Catalog of government policies, goals, objectives, and programs • List of destination product elements and components • Description of past visitor profiles • Description of major tourism strengths, weaknesses, problems, and issues

FIGURE 5.11 Tourism destination planning process, Step 1: Background analysis.

- **Review of government policies, goals, objectives, and programs**

Government policies should be considered first, as you saw earlier in the 5 Ps framework. Other government agencies, apart from those directly involved in tourism, have policies, goals, and objectives that affect tourism. These should also be considered in the Background Analysis step. Existing tourism-related programs or activities of government and private-sector tourism associations and organizations should be identified as well.

- **Inventory and analysis of existing destination product**

An inventory and analysis of the destination's destination product should be completed next. Figure 5.12 provides a description of the destination product elements and their components.

- **Description of existing tourism demand**

The existing tourism demand in the destination is described using published secondary sources of information. This information provides a profile of the major

Attractions, Events, Experiences, and Activities
- Accessibility (proximity to markets)
- Climate (contrasts with market areas' climates)
- Culture (beliefs, attitudes, habits, traditions, customs, forms of behavior)
- Historic resources (government, habitation, religious, war)
- Natural resources (landscapes, scenery, beaches, lakes and rivers, flora and fauna, other unique natural features)
- Experiences and activities offered for visitor participation

Built Tourism Facilities
- Hotels, resorts, and other accommodation properties
- Food and beverage
- Support services (souvenir and handicraft shops, duty-free shops, guides, festival areas, recreational facilities, laundries, visitor/tourist information centers)

Infrastructure
- Telecommunication networks
- Health care facilities
- Power sources and systems
- Sewage disposal and drainage systems
- Water resources and systems
- Internet/Wi-Fi services

Transportation Systems, Terminals, and Equipment
- Transportation terminals
- Roads, streets, highways, and parking systems
- Railway systems, water transportation systems, public transportation systems

Service Quality and Friendliness
- Community attitudes toward tourism
- Hospitality and service quality training programs
- Population and workforce
- Travel information centers

FIGURE 5.12 Inventory of destination product.

Activity and Experience Participation and Facility Use
Activity and experience participation, usage of facilities (accommodation, attractions, events, recreational facilities, information centers, etc.)

Demographic and Socioeconomic
Age, gender, income, education, occupation, family life cycle stage

Geographic
Geographic origins, geographic destinations

Psychographics
Attitudes, interests, and opinions

Information Sources and Media Use
Sources of travel information used, media habits

Travel Planning and Arrangements
Length of trip planning period, types of travel arrangements preferred (e.g., group versus independent travel)

Travel Trip Characteristics
Expenditures, length of stay, number of previous visits, timing of visit, transportation used, trip purposes, travel party composition, travel party type (e.g., families with children, singles, tour groups, business groups)

FIGURE 5.13 Visitor profile factors and characteristics.

characteristics of past visitors (Figure 5.13). The quantity and quality of this information is determined by the priority the destination gives to tourism market research. Gaps found in the available information are identified and are filled later in Step 2 (Detailed Research and Analysis).

- **Review of strengths, weaknesses, problems, and issues with tourism**

The fourth and final part of the Background Analysis is a review of the major strengths, weaknesses, problems, and issues of tourism within the destination. This is an important scene-setter for the remainder of the tourism destination planning process. It needs to be introspective, critical, and objective. Those involved in this review should be government tourism leaders, officials from other key government agencies, selected tourism business operators, selected tourism association/organization representatives, and local residents. The review will be more objective and productive if a broad variety of opinions and interests are represented. Private consulting

organizations specializing in tourism are often used as facilitators for these discussions. The consultants bring objectivity and broad tourism experience that may not be readily available in the destination.

Another initiative that is taken in some tourism destination plans at this point is staging a series of public meetings with local resident groups. These sessions determine community resident attitudes and awareness levels of tourism, and the types of future directions that residents want for tourism and the involvement that they desire.

Step 2: Detailed Research and Analysis
An effective tourism destination plan cannot be developed without primary or original research. Tourism destination plans that are prepared without primary research tend to reflect the subjective opinions of their authors and to perpetuate existing situations. Research is conducted in four areas: resources, activities, markets, and competition. The basic level of research during the

QUICK TRIP 5.3

Baseline Analysis of Macao's Tourism

Macao became a Special Administrative Region (SAR) of the People's Republic of China in 1987, ending colonization by Portugal since the sixteenth century. It has a local population of around 600,000 in a land area of just 28.2 square kilometers. Macao welcomed 30.95 million visitors in 2016; of whom 66.1 percent were from Mainland China and 20.7 percent from Hong Kong (Figure 5.14).

The Macao Government Office of Tourism (MGOT) in 2015 commissioned the *Macao Tourism Industry Development Master Plan*. This planning process is being coordinated by a government agency, MGOT, and a consulting company, AECOM, was selected after a bidding process to prepare the plan. In this case, the principals are MGOT and AECOM. The plan includes the following components:

- Analysis of the situation of Macao tourism development
- Objectives and strategies for Macao tourism development
- Analysis of tourism resources
- Tourism products planning
- Tourist market promotion strategies
- Tourism branding and image building
- Tourism and the application of innovative technology
- Tourism quality and service system planning
- Tourism industry and city development planning
- Tourism industry cooperation system
- International and regional cooperation
- Possible scenario analysis
- Suggestions for the implementation of the plan

The Background Analysis for this plan included the "baseline analysis and challenges" for nine factors:

- City competitiveness: The average length of visitor stay in Macao is shorter than in competitive destinations.
- Tourism resources and products: There is an opportunity to develop tourism products and services other than gaming, including MICE facilities, shopping, and festivals and events.
- Tourism source markets and target markets: Macao is overdependent on Greater China markets and especially Mainland China.
- Tourism branding and city positioning: Gaming is exerting too much influence on the positioning and branding of Macao.
- Innovative technology and smart tourism: Macao is not yet fully applying innovative information technologies and smart tourism approaches.
- Tourism quality and service: Macao needs to further improve its service quality in tourism.
- Regional tourism cooperation: There are significant future opportunities for promoting multi-destination travel through more regional cooperation.
- City development: Waterfront resources are underutilized and urban regeneration is needed in older parts of Macao.
- Transportation and accessibility: Public transportation in Macao needs to be improved and the capacity of the airport is being challenged.

© Sean Hsu/Shutterstock.com

FIGURE 5.14 Macao's Tourism Industry Development Master Plan aims to diversify tourism products and resources.

QUICK TRIP 5.3 CONTINUED

Think about This

1. How important is it to conduct a thorough background analysis on tourism in a place like Macao as the foundation for the tourism destination plan?
2. What are the special challenges facing Macao, given its current dependence on gaming and on visitors from Mainland China?
3. Are there examples of regional tourism cooperation in other parts of the world from which Macao can learn? What are these examples?
4. The Consultation Paper asserts that Macao's image is too much influenced by gaming at the current time. How should Macao diversify its tourism positioning and branding?

Sources

Central Intelligence Agency. 2017. Macau. https://www.cia.gov/library/publications/the-world-factbook/geos/mc.html

Macao Government Tourism Office. 2016. Macao Tourism Industry Development Master Plan Consultation Paper.

Macao Government Tourism Office. 2017. Macao Tourism Industry Development Master Plan Public Consultation. http://masterplan.macaotourism.gov.mo/home-en/index.html

Statistics and Census Service (DSEC). 2017. Tourism and Gaming. http://www.dsec.gov.mo/home_enus.aspx#

Background Analysis step helps to pinpoint where the more detailed research needs to be focused (Figure 5.15).

- **Resource mapping and analysis**

Using the inventory of the destination product (Figure 5.12), maps are prepared showing the location of key resources. With the mapping completed, the carrying capacities of the resources are then measured. Although the capacities of some of the tourism resource components are easily measured (such as in guest rooms, restaurant seats, camp sites, and golf courses), the capacities of others (such as boating lakes/rivers, beaches, and historical landmarks) are not.

The final stage of the resource analysis is resource classification. This represents a ranking or grading of

Parts	Activities	Participants	Outcomes
• Resource mapping and analysis • Activity and experience analysis • Market analysis • Competitive analysis • Other analyses	• Resource mapping • Resource capacity measurement • Limits of acceptable change process • Resource classification • Primary market research and experience • Activity and experience identification and evaluation • Identification and evaluation of competition	• Government tourism officials • Physical planners • Market researchers or survey specialists • Tourism consultants	• Maps showing the disposition of tourism resources • Capacity measurements for resources • LAC standards • Description of scope of appeal of resources • Research results on potential markets • Inventory of tourism and recreation activities • Competitive strengths and weaknesses

FIGURE 5.15 Tourism destination planning process, Step 2: Detailed research and analysis.

the scope of appeal of the tourism resources of the destination area. Thus, individual resources or zones within the destination are normally defined as being of international, national, regional, or local significance, or as having international, national, regional, or local market appeal.

- **Activity and experience analysis**

Activities and experiences include all of the things that the visitor can do in the destination, ranging from active outdoor recreational pursuits, such as alpine skiing, to more passive activities, such as shopping and viewing scenery. Every destination has a variety of existing and potential activities and experiences. As the activities available at the destination are often a prime motivating factor to travel, this exercise can be useful in identifying new demand generation opportunities. The activities and experiences are classified by range of appeal (local, regional, state, national, or international). It also is essential to identify the seasons and months of the year in which the activities and experiences can be pursued. Because many destinations suffer from seasonality of demand, this helps to pinpoint those activities and experiences that will generate demand outside of peak periods.

- **Market analysis**

A good tourism plan incorporates primary research on the destination's existing and potential markets. The market research carried out in the Background Analysis step was based upon already available information (secondary research). The primary research is done by conducting one or more surveys of existing and potential visitors. Surveys of existing visitors are normally done while the visitors are within the destination. Most often, the personal interview technique is used in these surveys of existing visitors, either at exit or entry points, or at

key tourism facilities, attractions, and events. In addition to gathering visitor profile data as shown in Figure 5.13, visitor surveys are useful in producing the following information:

- Awareness of destination attractions and other product elements and components
- Constraints or barriers to return visits
- Expenditures within the destination
- Images of the destination
- Attractions and other items that will increase the likelihood of return visits
- Likelihood of return visit
- Motivations for travel
- Ratings of attractions, facilities, services, and other destination mix elements
- Satisfaction with trips
- Sources of information used in planning trips and during trips

The first two steps in the tourism planning process provide clues as to the sources of potential new market demand for the destination. The eight main components of a destination's market potential are shown in Figure 5.16, using trip purpose and visitor origin sources. In addition to the potential markets shown in Figure 5.16, the destination may concentrate on attracting current pleasure travelers as future pleasure travelers (i.e., encouraging repeat visits), and vice versa. Another potential market may be in attracting current business travelers as future pleasure travelers, or to convince them to combine business and pleasure (bleisure trips).

A variety of techniques are available to research potential visitor markets. These include online surveys, personal interviews, focus groups, telephone interviews, and mailed questionnaires. Research can be directed toward the individual pleasure travelers in a specific geographic market or be aimed at travel trade

Pleasure Travelers		
Existing geographic markets • Increase market penetration • Develop new market segments	↓	**New geographic markets** • Attract existing market segments • Attract new market segments
Business Travelers		
Existing geographic markets • Increase market penetration • Develop new market segments	↑	**New geographic markets** • Attract existing market segments • Attract new market segments
Similar potential may exist for VFR, personal travelers, and other market segments.		

FIGURE 5.16 Components of a destination's market potential.

intermediaries (retail travel agents, online travel agencies or OTAs, tour wholesalers, tour operators, incentive travel planners, corporate travel departments, and convention and meeting planners) and other travel opinion leaders (travel bloggers/vloggers, club, association, and affinity group executives). This research helps to determine:

- Awareness of destination attractions, events, activities and experiences, and other destination product elements
- Competitive destinations
- Images of the destination
- Likelihood of future visits to the destination
- Steps needed to generate business from these potential visitors

Research also provides an opportunity to "market test" new ideas for tourism attractions and events, tours or packages, hotel and resort developments, and new activity and experience ideas that have been identified earlier in the plan.

Another important aspect of the market analysis is an evaluation of the likely impact of future travel trends on the destination. The information on these trends comes from a variety of available futures research studies and ongoing tracking research programs on travel trends. It is a common practice at this point in the tourism destination planning process to forecast tourism demand volumes for the duration of the plan.

When the forecasts are ready, a supply (capacities of resource components) and demand (forecast demand volumes) matching exercise is carried out. This step helps those in the destination determine where there are likely to be shortfalls in different tourism resources and where there could be problems in preserving tourism resources due to excessive demand levels.

QUICK TRIP 5.4

A Research-Based Approach to Curaçao's Tourism Master Plan

Curaçao is a constituent country within the Kingdom of the Netherlands that is in the Caribbean and a popular tourism destination (Figure 5.17). In 2014, the process was initiated to develop a Tourism Master Plan that was led by the Dick Pope Institute for Tourism Studies (DPITS) at the University of Central Florida in Orlando. Chapter 5 stressed the importance of conducting research when preparing tourism destination plans, and especially primary research. Curaçao's Tourism Master Plan represents an outstanding example of this recommended research-based approach:

"Eleven surveys were created and nearly 7,000 respondents completed the surveys, including stay-over tourists, cruise tourists, Caribbean tourists who had never visited the island, employees, and the local population at-large."

Some 250 stakeholders were interviewed face-to-face, and 50,000 comments about Curaçao on TripAdvisor were analyzed. Surveys were conducted with residents and with employees in the tourism sector. In addition, the following three market surveys were completed

- Visitors to Curaçao (exit survey at airport)
- Cruise passengers (survey at cruise harbor)
- People who had never visited Curaçao

Think about This

1. What are the benefits of conducting primary research when preparing tourism destination plans?
2. What are the major challenges facing tourism in smaller island countries such as Curaçao?
3. What can be learned from comparing the research on existing visitors versus people who have never visited Curaçao?
4. Curaçao invited a university to assist it with preparing its tourism plan. What are the advantages of involving academic researchers in tourism destination planning?

Sources

Central Intelligence Agency. 2017. Curaçao. The World Factbook. Washington, DC: CIA.

University of Central Florida. 2015. *Curaçao: Building on the Power of the Past.* Orlando, Florida: Rosen College of Hospitality Management.

FIGURE 5.17 Curaçao offers great diving opportunities.

- **Competitive analysis**

No destination is without competition and a tourism plan must consider the competitive advantages and future plans of competitors. It is useful to define competitors in terms of their relative distance from prime geographic markets. Those destinations closer to a prime market are intervening opportunities; the visitor must pass them to reach the destination being planned. For example, Hawaii is an intervening opportunity for tourism in Australia, while Canada's Yukon Territory and British Columbia are intervening opportunities for tourism in Alaska. The research described earlier assists in identifying the most competitive destinations, their strengths and weaknesses, and the steps that can be taken to make the subject destination different from these competitors.

- **Other analyses**

Other types of research and analysis may be needed. This includes an evaluation of the destination management organization, community tourism awareness and involvement levels, and destination marketing programs. For example, in some areas, organizational problems or conflicts may be so acute that they require detailed research and evaluation.

It is also important to consider the human resource requirements of the destination in the future, and the capacity of people in the destination to deliver on the service quality and specific requirements of future visitors.

Step 3: Synthesis and Visioning

The third step of the tourism destination planning process represents the point in which the major conclusions from all previous work are formulated (Figure 5.18). Some consider this to be one of the most important and creative steps in the process.

- **Preparation of preliminary position statements**

The first stage is the preparation of position statements for each of the eight aspects of tourism shown in Figure 5.19. The position statement describes the existing situation (*Where are we now?*) with respect to each of the aspects. One of the participating groups is given the responsibility for preparing preliminary position statements, usually either the tourism consultants or government tourism officials. These are then reviewed and discussed by all participants, and a consensus is reached on the final wording of the statements. Position statements may be simply expressed in one sentence or be

Parts	Activities	Participants	Outcomes
• Preparation of preliminary position statements • Preparation of vision statements • Identification of critical success factors (CSFs)	• Information assembly • Writing of position statements • Writing of vision statements • Group workshops	• Government tourism officials • Selected tourism business operators • Selected tourism organization representatives • Officials from other key government agencies • Local residents • Tourism consultants	• Position statements on current conditions • Vision statements of desired future situations • Critical success factors (CSFs)

FIGURE 5.18 Tourism destination planning process, Step 3: Synthesis and visioning.

Tourism Destination Aspects	Recommended Changes, Improvements, or Additions
1. Tourism development	Physical changes in the destination including new attractions, facilities, infrastructure, travel information and interpretive centers, and transportation systems.
2. Destination marketing	Modifications to past marketing programs involving new marketing strategies, positioning and branding approaches, packaging and tours, distribution, and promotional programs.
3. Experience and activity design	New and enhanced visitor experiences that can be provided within the destination.
4. Human resource development	Programs needed to increase the number and capabilities of people prepared to work within tourism in the destination.
5. Tourism organization	Refocusing of government and non-government organizations involved in tourism, including destination management organizations (DMOs).
6. Community relationships with and involvement in tourism	Programs to increase community resident awareness of the benefits of tourism and their involvement in tourism and decision-making about tourism.
7. Service quality and quality assurance	Improvements needed in service quality and programs to ensure that certain quality levels are delivered within the destination.
8. Support services and activities	Changes in travel information center systems, directional sign programs, scenic tour systems, interpretive services, hospitality, and service training programs.

FIGURE 5.19 Tourism plan recommendations on aspects of tourism.

documented in several pages of text. A simple position statement on development could be "our destination has historically been developed to appeal to a summer/warm weather market; activities and experiences to attract tourism at other times of the year have not been constructed."

• **Preparation of vision statements**

The second stage is visioning in which the desired future situation for tourism is determined (Where would we like to be?) (Figure 5.20). The desired future states are

expressed in terms of vision statements for each of the eight aspects of tourism. In our simple example this could be "it is our desire to have year-round tourism facilities in our destination." Tourism plans provide the "bridge" between the present and desired future situations in a destination. They provide the means to the end.

• **Identification of critical success factors (CSFs)**

To accompany the vision statements, there should be critical success factors (CSFs) or conditions that must be met for the vision to be realized.

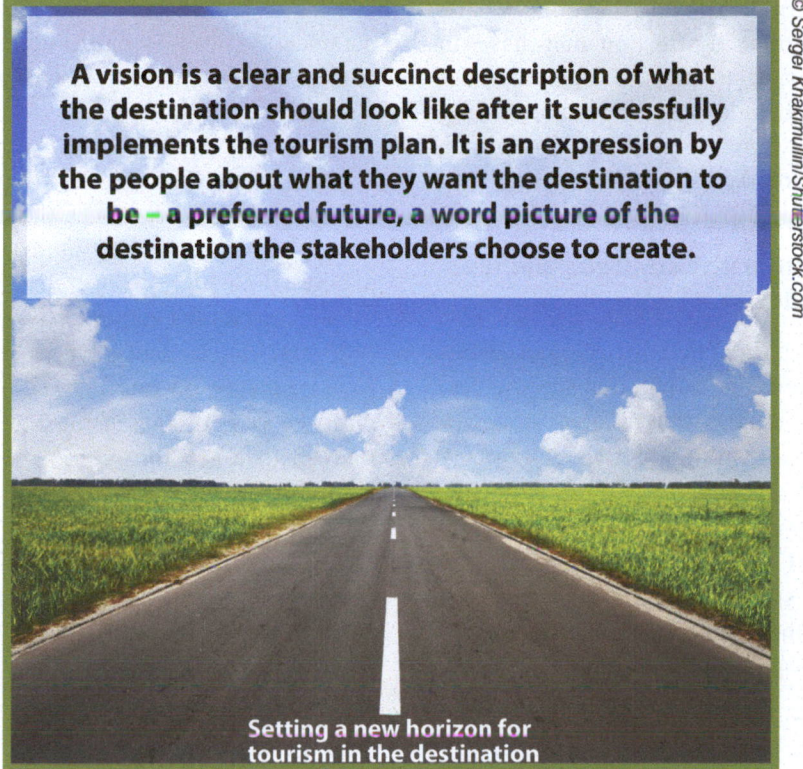

A vision is a clear and succinct description of what the destination should look like after it successfully implements the tourism plan. It is an expression by the people about what they want the destination to be – a preferred future, a word picture of the destination the stakeholders choose to create.

Setting a new horizon for tourism in the destination

© Sergei Khakimullin/Shutterstock.com

FIGURE 5.20 Horizon metaphor for visioning in a tourism destination.

Step 4: Goal-Setting, Strategy Selection, and Objective-Setting

Now that the future vision for tourism in the destination is defined, goals, strategies, and objectives are identified (Figure 5.21).

- **Definition of tourism goals**

Tourism plan goals, strategies, and objectives must support and be consistent with the overall tourism policy goals and initiatives. The major policy goal for tourism may be to stimulate employment, income, and economic development through tourism; an economy-oriented policy approach to tourism. Another destination suffering from overcrowding or an already too rapid pace of development may select a more conservation-oriented approach. Remember that a tourism plan has a relatively short life span, usually up to five or not more than ten years, and its goals should be achievable within that period. A destination with an economy-oriented policy approach may wish to obtain the maximum economic impact from tourism within the term of the plan. This area will probably adopt a goal that emphasizes the development and marketing of those regions or specific resources likely to produce the greatest economic return

Parts	Activities	Participants	Outcomes
• Definition of tourism goals • Identification of alternative strategies and selection of desired strategies • Definition of tourism objectives	• Goal-setting • Strategy mapping • Writing of goals, strategy statements, and objectives • Group workshops	• Government tourism officials • Selected tourism business operators • Selected tourism organization representatives • Officials from other key government agencies • Local residents • Tourism consultants	• Statements of tourism goals • Maps or other visual presentations of alternative strategies • Strategy statements • Rationale for selected strategies • Statement of tourism objectives

FIGURE 5.21 Tourism destination planning process, Step 4: Goal-setting, strategy selection, and objective-setting.

within the planning period; it will concentrate on its major strengths. Yet another destination may have an economy-oriented approach but be more concerned with spreading the economic benefits of tourism more evenly throughout its regions. Its goal might be to concentrate on the development and marketing of those regions with the lowest levels of existing tourism activity.

- **Identification of alternative strategies and selection of desired strategies**

Once the tourism goals are defined, a variety of strategies can be used to achieve them. Within a specific destination, it should also be realized that different strategies may be used for the regions within it. Some regions may have economy-oriented strategies and some may have conservation-oriented strategies.

A commonly found tourism development strategy involves dividing the destination into destination zones, touring corridors, and other areas. This can be applied to many geographic areas, including countries, states, provinces or territories, counties, and regions within counties. As well as being visually displayed through maps, a strategy is verbalized in a series of strategy statements.

A comprehensive strategy incorporates in these statements the eight aspects of tourism identified earlier. Again, a strategy translates the existing conditions for these aspects into desired future situations. For example, a destination highly dependent on one specific geographic market for visitors may wish to adopt a strategy of diversifying its geographic markets, thereby reducing its dependence on one market. Those in a destination with the goal of increasing the economic benefits of tourism to a specific region may select a strategy to increase visitation to that region.

- **Definition of tourism objectives**

Tourism objectives flow from the selected strategy and support specific tourism goals. The objectives are more short-term than the goals and are more measurable.

QUICK TRIP 5.5

Goals and Strategies for Tourism in Minneapolis

During 2016, Meet Minneapolis, the DMO for Minneapolis, Minnesota, in the United States (Figure 5.22), developed the city's first-ever Tourism Master Plan *(Destination Transformation 2030)* together with its partners. The planning process used is described as follows:

"Throughout the 12-month planning process, more than 3,000 people weighed in, including tourists, travel writers, meeting planners, local stakeholders and industry experts. Six subcommittees worked to develop the plan, which will guide us toward a bold future for tourism in Minneapolis."

Five different research methods were used in preparing the plan and 3,026 interviews with twenty-six different audiences. The plan's contents are:

Executive Summary
Introduction
Chapter 1: A history of looking ahead
Chapter 2: Investigation and analysis
Chapter 3: Assessing Minneapolis' current condition and tourism potential
Chapter 4: Saying "yes" to tourism
Chapter 5: Eight big initiatives for 2030

The *Destination Transformation 2030* document set out four quantified tourism goals to be achieved:

- Attract 50 million visitors
- Annual marketing campaign budget of $10 million
- 11 million visitors in winter
- 40,000 hospitality jobs

QUICK TRIP 5.5 CONTINUED

Eight "big initiatives" are identified for 2030 as follows; most of these can be considered as strategies:

1.   Attract 50 million visitors to the metro area annually by 2030.
2.   Launch a metro-wide branding and marketing campaign.
3.   Build an iconic visitors center on downtown's central riverfront.
4.   Implement a unified transportation, wayfinding, and information program for Minneapolis.
5.   Adopt a comprehensive place-making plan to drive Minneapolis' tourism priorities and investments.
6.   Accentuate winter as a novel tourism adventure.
7.   Grow and emphasize hospitality jobs as important to social equity and the metro economy.
8.   Identify and secure ongoing resources to implement the Tourism Master Plan.

Think about This

1.   What are the advantages for Minneapolis in having such specific goals and strategies (initiatives) for the future of tourism?
2.   How have other countries, regions, and cities successfully dealt with the perception that they are cold places in winter? What could Minneapolis learn from these cases?
3.   Are there other aspects of tourism that Minneapolis should have included in its goals and strategies?
4.   What are the potential challenges in a large city like Minneapolis in getting a higher priority attached to tourism?

Source

Meet Minneapolis. 2017. Destination Transformation 2030. Aiming for a Bold Future. http://www.minneapolis.org/partners-and-community/meet-minneapolis/destination-transformation-2030/

© Scrugglegreen/Shutterstock.com

FIGURE 5.22 Spectacular view of the Mississippi River and Stone Arch Bridge in Minneapolis.

Step 5: Plan Development

The next step is the development of the plan itself. The plan details the programs and activities needed to achieve the goals, implement the strategy, and attain the objectives (Figure 5.23).

- **Description of programs, activities, roles, budgets, and funding**

A comprehensive plan deals with all eight aspects of tourism. The tourism plan takes the objectives and specifies the activities, programs, and other initiatives required to achieve them (Figure 5.24).

- **Writing of tourism plan reports**

Once it has been laid out in this detail, the tourism destination plan is then written up in formal reports, either by a private tourism consulting firm or by government tourism officials. The tourism plan reports are often presented in two parts. The first is a summary report containing the plan itself, and the second is a more detailed technical report providing all of the research, findings, and conclusions. The reports are usually prepared in draft and are reviewed and revised by government and tourism business representatives prior to being finalized for publication and for public presentations.

Step 6: Plan Implementation and Monitoring

Many tourism plans have been written but never implemented. Why would so much good work and money be wasted? The answer is that plan implementation has been given inadequate attention. Responsibilities for the tourism objectives must be clearly allocated to specific organizations or people. The funds must be available to carry out the activities and programs in the plan (Figure 5.25).

- **Plan implementation**

The implementation of the plan occurs according to its schedule. The overall responsibility for coordinating its implementation is usually given to a governmental tourism agency or the DMO. Proposed development projects and other proposals requiring physical changes are reviewed in feasibility studies and environmental impact assessments (EIAs). The principles of sustainable tourism are discussed in Chapter 6.

- **Plan monitoring**

While the plan is being implemented the coordinating agency continually checks to ensure that progress is made as was originally planned. Monitoring is done for each tourism goal and for every objective that supports this goal. Modifications to the plan may be required if inadequate progress is made toward achieving certain goals and objectives.

Stages	Activities	Participants	Outcomes
• Description of programs, activities, roles, budgets, and funding • Writing of tourism plan reports	• Plan detailing • Report writing • Report presentations • Report review and revisions	• Government tourism officials • Selected tourism business operators • Selected tourism organization representatives • Officials from other key government agencies • Local residents • Tourism consultants	• List of programs and activities • Description of government and private-sector roles and responsibilities • Funding requirements and sources • Description of specific development projects and marketing initiatives • Plan schedule and timetable • Tourism plan reports

FIGURE 5.23 Tourism destination planning process, Step 5: Plan development.

Outcomes and Results
Expected results and outcomes of the tourism destination plan.

Activities and Programs
Programs and activities required to achieve each objective.

Tourism Development
Specific development projects needed to achieve certain objectives.

Destination Marketing
Specific marketing initiatives needed to achieve certain objectives.

Other Destination Aspects
Initiatives to be taken for experience and activity design; human resource development; tourism organization; community relationships with and involvement in tourism; service quality and quality assurance; and support services and activities.

Budget and Funding
Money required to carry out specific programs and actions and the sources of these funds.

Monitoring and Evaluation Procedures
Monitoring and evaluation procedures for judging the success of the plan.

Roles and Responsibilities
Roles and responsibilities of government, tourism businesses and organizations, and others.

Schedule and Timetable
Schedule and timetable for carrying out specific programs and activities.

FIGURE 5.24 Tourism destination plan elements.

Stages	Activities	Participants	Outcomes
• Plan implementation • Plan monitoring	• Feasibility studies • Environmental impact assessments • Marketing plan development • Implementation of development projects • Improvements to infrastructure and transportation • Improvements in hospitality resources and community awareness programs • Organizational changes	• Government tourism officials • Selected tourism business operators • Selected tourism organization representatives • Officials from other key government agencies • Developers • Tourism consultants	• Feasibility studies • Environmental impact assessments • Marketing plans • New organizational structures in place • New developments • New hospitality resource and community awareness programs • New support services and activities • Progress reports on plan implementation

FIGURE 5.25 Tourism destination planning process, Step 6: Plan implementation and monitoring.

Step 7: Plan Evaluation

Plan evaluation occurs after the term of the tourism destination plan has expired. The basic purpose of plan evaluation is to determine if the goals and objectives of the tourism destination plan were achieved. If they were not achieved, an analysis is conducted to determine the reasons for non-performance (Figure 5.26).

- **Measure performance against each goal and objective**

The actual performance related to each individual goal and objective is measured. A variety of indicators may be used that involve evaluation research of different types.

This might include surveys of visitors, local residents, and tourism business operators to determine their attitudes to the changes resulting from the plan's implementation. Specific measurement indicators such as visitor numbers and expenditures may also be used in the evaluation. Meetings are scheduled to discuss the findings of the tourism plan evaluation.

- **Analyze reasons for non-performance**

It is likely that not all tourism goals and objectives will be achieved. The important consideration here is to determine the reasons for non-performance on specific goals and objectives. Non-performance may result for many reasons such as unexpected changes in world events, the inability to attract private development funding, or unanticipated competitive strategies and programs.

- **Prepare recommendations for future tourism destination planning**

It is beneficial at this point to rewrite the position statements that were prepared earlier in the Synthesis and Visioning step. This allows the participants to evaluate if the vision statements were realized.

The final outcome of evaluation becomes a major input into the next round of tourism destination planning. Specific recommendations are made based upon the lessons of this tourism destination planning process. The most important questions that need to be answered are:

- What goals and objectives were achieved?
- What goals and objectives were not achieved?
- Why were these goals and objectives not achieved?
- What should be done differently the next time tourism destination planning is done?

The tourism destination planning process has come full cycle.

Stages	Activities	Participants	Outcomes
• Measure performance against each goal and objective • Analyze reasons for non-performance • Prepare recommendations for future tourism destination planning	• Gathering of performance indicators • Surveys of local residents • Surveys of local tourism business operators • LAC measurements • Marketing plan evaluation	• Government tourism officials • Selected tourism business operators • Selected tourism organization representatives • Officials from other key government agencies • Local residents • Tourism consultants	• Performance indicators for each goal and objective • Local resident attitude surveys • Tourism business operator surveys • LAC results • Marketing plan evaluation results • Suggestions for future tourism planning processes

FIGURE 5.26 Tourism destination planning process, Step 7: Plan evaluation.

Key Performance Measures for Murray Region (Australia) Strategic Plan

The Murray tourism region is in southeastern Australia along the Murray River (Figure 5.27). The Murray Regional Tourism Board (MRT) is a regional tourism organization representing communities along the river in Victoria and New South Wales. MRT prepared a Strategic Plan for regional tourism for 2015–2020, identifying four strategic priorities of product development, advocacy and leadership, regional marketing, and industry development.

It is essential that measures be set in advance for monitoring and evaluating tourism destination plans, and the Strategic Plan 2015–2020 for MRT provides a good example of this. For each of the plan's four strategic priorities, three key performance measures are set, as shown below:

Product Development

Facilitate investment in infrastructure, new products, and experiences that revitalize the Region's tourism offer.

- Increase in investment in tourism assets and infrastructure measured by local government area
- Grow the economic contribution of the events sector by 10 percent
- Shift the comparative product strengths of our key experiences through the product life-cycle stages

Advocacy and Leadership

Provide a clear direction for growth and development for the Murray Region through strong leadership, advocacy, and industry engagement.

- Long-term funding agreements in place with local government areas and government partners to 2020
- Diversification of revenue source to 20 percent from non-government entities
- Increase the employment contribution of the sector by 1,100 jobs

Regional Marketing

Promote the Murray Region in partnership with key stakeholders and industry.

- Increase Visitation to 5.72 million visitors and Expenditure to $2.27 billion tracked by National Visitor Survey (NVS) and International Visitor Survey (IVS) data
- Increase in online enquiries and conversion to bookings by 30 percent from current benchmark
- Increase industry participation rates in marketing services by 20 percent

© River kwest/Shutterstock.com

FIGURE 5.27 Paddle steamer on the Murray River.

QUICK TRIP 5.6 CONTINUED

Industry Development

Improve the supply and quality of tourism experiences in the Region through industry training and development.

- Minimum 25 percent of operators in the Murray Region participated in training programs delivered by Murray Regional Tourism and our partners over the life of this plan
- Growth of industry engagement from current benchmark
- Achieve a satisfaction rating of minimum 70 percent by training attendees

Think about This

1. What are the benefits of having key performance measures like those included in the Murray Region Strategic Plan?
2. What are the likely problems if a tourism destination plan does not include measures for monitoring and evaluation?
3. What are the potential difficulties in implementing a tourism destination plan for a region that straddles two states and several local government areas?
4. Are there aspects of tourism not covered in the MRT's strategic priorities that could have been considered, but were not? Why do you think these aspects were not included?

Sources

Murray Regional Tourism Board. Strategic Plan 2015–2020. http://www.murrayregionaltourism.com.au/research-resources/strategies-plans/

Murray Regional Tourism Board. 2017. Corporate website. http://www.murrayregionaltourism.com.au/

SUMMARY

Every destination interested in tourism should adopt the tourism destination planning process. Although tourism destination planning can be hard work, time-consuming, costly, and sometimes difficult to justify, it is an essential activity in today's rapidly changing business environments. The absence of tourism planning in a destination can lead to irreversible economic, socio-cultural, and environmental damage and to loss of market share. There are several barriers to tourism destination planning, but the rewards resulting from an effective tourism destination planning process far outweigh the efforts needed to surmount these. Empirical evidence throughout the world clearly shows that the "model" destinations for successful tourism are those that have embraced the tourism destination planning concept.

ACTIVITIES

1. Arrange an interview with an official of a local DMO to discuss the topic of tourism destination planning. Begin the discussion by asking this person about the perceived value of tourism destination planning for the local area. Has a tourism destination plan ever been completed for the area? If not, why has a plan never been prepared? Ask the person to describe how he or she thinks a tourism destination plan could be developed.
2. If a tourism destination plan has been completed, what process was used for its development? Who coordinated the tourism destination planning process and what other parties were involved?
3. Has the implementation of the tourism destination plan been successful? Why or why not?
4. Do an Internet search and collect information on an assortment of tourism destination plans for a variety of different geographic areas.
5. What are the most effective tourism destination plans and what is the reason for your evaluation?
6. What can your local area learn and apply based on your review of these tourism destination plans?

ACRONYMS

CSF (critical success factor)
DMO (destination management organization)
EIA (environmental impact assessment)
KPI (key performance indicator)
LAC (limits of acceptable change)

REFERENCES

Dredge, D., and Jenkins, D. 2007. *Tourism Planning and Policy*. Milton, Queensland: John Wiley & Sons Australia, Ltd.

Gunn, C. A. 1994. *Tourism Planning: Basics, Concepts, Cases*, 3rd ed. Washington, DC: Taylor & Francis.

Hall, C. M. Tourism Planning. 2008. *Policies, Processes and Relationships*, 2nd ed. Harlow, England: Pearson Education Limited.

Kuala Lumpur City Hall. 2015. *Kuala Lumpur Tourism Master Plan 2015–2025*. http://www.kltourismmasterplan.com/

Macao Government Tourism Office. 2016. *Macao Tourism Industry Development Master Plan Consultation Paper*.

Mason, P. 2008. *Tourism Impacts, Planning and Management*, 2nd ed. Abingdon, England: Routledge.

Meet Minneapolis. 2017. *Destination Transformation 2030. Aiming for a Bold Future*. http://www.minneapolis.org/partners-and-community/meet-minneapolis/destination-transformation-2030/

Morrison, A. M. 2013. *Marketing and Managing Tourism Destinations*. London: Routledge.

Murray Regional Tourism. 2015. *Strategic Plan 2015–2020*. http://www.murrayregionaltourism.com.au/research-resources/strategies-plans/

Tourism Vancouver. 2017. *Vancouver Tourism Master Plan*. https://www.tourismvancouver.com/about/tourism-master-plan/

Tourism Winnipeg. 2016. *Master Tourism Plan for Winnipeg 2016–2018*. https://www.tourismwinnipeg.com/industry/master-tourism-plan

University of Central Florida. 2015. *Curaçao: Building on the Power of the Past*. Orlando, Florida: Rosen College of Hospitality Management.

UNWTO. 2017. Prototype 365. http://affiliatemembers.unwto.org/content/prototype-365

CHAPTER SIX

Sustainable Tourism Development

Building a Sustainable Future for Tourism

Sustainability is the pathway to the future we want for all.

BAN KI-MOON, Secretary-General of the United Nations

YOUR LEARNING DESTINATION

You will explain the concept and principles of sustainable tourism, and describe a process for evaluating individual tourism project development opportunities.

WHAT YOU NEED TO KNOW

Having read this chapter, you will be able to:

✓ Explain sustainable development and sustainable tourism.
✓ Overview the triple bottom line concept.
✓ Describe various types of tourism developments by their functions.
✓ Elaborate on the realms of tourism development.
✓ Discuss government, private-sector, community, and non-profit organization roles in tourism development.
✓ Identify the role and types of government incentives for tourism development.
✓ Describe the steps in completing pre-feasibility and economic feasibility studies.
✓ Review the cost/benefit analysis technique.
✓ Explain the purposes of an environmental impact assessment.

BREAKING THE ICE

You have heard of global warming and climate change. Chances are you also know there are poverty, health, education, gender equality, and water quality issues in many parts of our world. Tourism can be a force in helping to reduce the impact of some of these issues; however, tourism can also cause damage to the environment and local communities. Following sustainable tourism principles, destinations are confident that tourism will not damage physical environments, and will make positive contributions to economic prosperity and the quality of life of local people. Tourism development following sustainability principles is the way to go.

KEY TAKEAWAY POINTS

• Tourism should be conducted in a sustainable way.

• The triple bottom line considers people, planet, and prosperity.

• Tourism development is not just physical; people, programs, and packages are also realms for tourism development.

• The absence of tourism destination planning is one of the causes of unsustainable tourism development.

• Pre-feasibility and economic feasibility should be done on individual tourism development projects.

• Large-scale tourism development projects should be subject to environmental impact analyses.

BUILDING A SUSTAINABLE FUTURE FOR TOURISM

Sustainable Development

The beginning of sustainable development is with the 1980 World Conservation Strategy and the 1987 World Commission on Environment and Development (Brundtland Commission), which defined sustainable development as "development that meets the needs of the present without compromising the ability of future generations to meet their own needs" (United Nations 1987).

The United Nations in 2015 outlined seventeen sustainable development goals for the world in a new sustainable development agenda (Figure 6.1).

This new agenda was adopted by UN countries with the overall goals of ending poverty, protecting the planet, and ensuring prosperity for all.

Sustainable Tourism

Sustainable tourism is the application of the principles of sustainable development to tourism and UNWTO (2017) provides a simple definition of sustainable tourism as:

"**Tourism** that takes full account of its current and future economic, social and environmental impacts, addressing the needs of visitors, the industry, the environment and host communities."

You should notice that sustainable tourism is not just about natural and physical environments, but recognizes the need to maintain the cultures and lifestyles of local peoples. UNWTO states that sustainable tourism should meet three principles:

FIGURE 6.1 UN Sustainable Development goals.

1. Make optimal use of environmental resources that constitute a key element in tourism development, maintaining essential ecological processes and helping to conserve natural heritage and biodiversity.
2. Respect the socio-cultural authenticity of host communities, conserve their built and living cultural heritage and traditional values, and contribute to intercultural understanding and tolerance.
3. Ensure viable, long-term economic operations, providing socio-economic benefits to all stakeholders that are fairly distributed, including stable employment and income-earning opportunities and social services to host communities, and contributing to poverty alleviation.

The International Year of Sustainable Tourism for Development was celebrated in 2017 and five potential contributions of sustainable tourism were identified as (UNWTO 2016):

- Inclusive and sustainable economic growth
- Social inclusiveness, employment, and poverty reduction
- Resource efficiency, environmental protection, and climate change
- Cultural values, diversity, and heritage
- Mutual understanding, peace, and security

The Triple Bottom Line

The three priorities of sustainable development and sustainable tourism are often called the "triple bottom line" or "3BL." Figure 6.2 gives you an idea of what is included in the triple bottom line concept.

Tourism development should respect these principles of sustainable tourism. The sustainable tourism concept highlights the need for careful tourism development planning that assesses all the potential impacts (social, environmental, and economic) of a tourism project development opportunity.

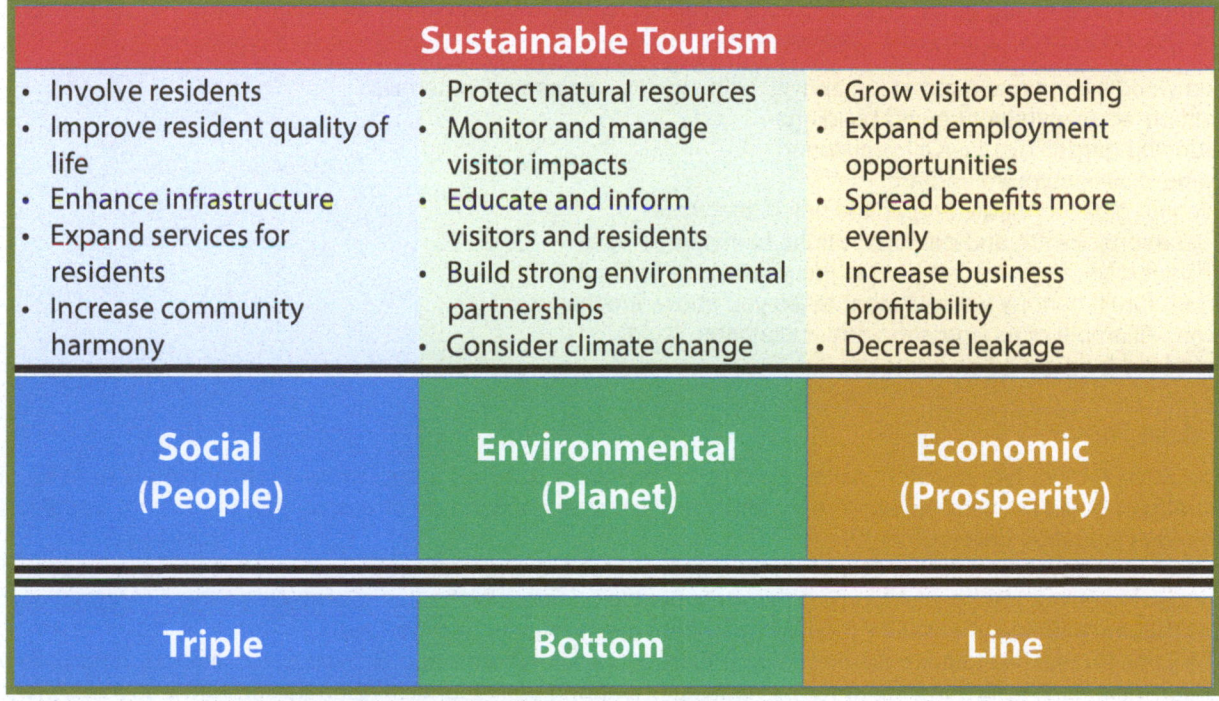

FIGURE 6.2 The triple bottom line applied to sustainable tourism.

QUICK TRIP 6.1

Eden Project Sustainability Policy

You might have heard of the old saying, "you can't make a silk purse out of a sow's ear." This is a strange saying that is attributed to Jonathon Swift and it means that you cannot make something good out of something that is bad. How about transforming an ugly and abandoned China clay pit into a beautifully-designed tourism attraction? As a matter of fact, this has been accomplished in the UK. This "silk purse" is the Eden Project located in Cornwall in the south-west of England. It is an education charity that serves as a visitor attraction and hosted just over one million guests in 2016. The Eden Project consists of several "biomes" as shown in Figure 6.3.

Apart from the amazing landscape transformation, the Eden Project is an excellent example of sustainable tourism for you to know about, as the following statement from the organization confirms:

"Sustainability is at the heart of what the Eden Project is all about. It is a major part of the message we hope to convey."

The Sustainability Policy of the Eden Project in 2017 includes the following sections:

- **Education:** these initiatives include, among others, promoting sustainability through informal learning.
- **Consistency:** ensuring that sustainability pervades everything that the Eden Project does.
- **Measurement:** tracking the social, environmental, and economic indicators for the Eden Project.
- **Transparency:** publishing information on the Eden Project's sustainability performance.
- **Behaviour:** acting with sustainability in mind in all areas of the Eden Project's practices.

These are just a sampling of the Eden Project's initiatives for the five sections of its Sustainability Policy. The ten reasons to visit Eden Project are (Visit Cornwall 2017):

1. The world's largest rain forest in captivity with steamy jungles and waterfalls
2. Cutting-edge architecture and buildings
3. Stunning garden displays all year-round
4. World-class sculpture and art
5. Evening gigs, concerts, and an ice rink in the winter
6. Educational centre and demonstrations to inspire all ages
7. Brilliant local, fairly-traded food in the restaurants and cafes
8. A rain forest canopy walkway that takes you above the treetops
9. Living example of regeneration and sustainable living
10. Free land train pulled by a tractor

Think about This

1. The Eden Project has transformed an eyesore on the landscape into a popular tourism attraction. In what other situations could tourism developments improve the visual appearance of places that have been damaged by previous industrial development?
2. For tourism development, the Eden Project demonstrates the great importance of creative thinking, especially in conceiving new attractions. Assuming this statement to be true, which other examples are there of attractions like this that have been successfully located away from major tourism destinations?
3. The Eden Project is a tourism development with a deep environmental and social mission. In 2016, it had over one million visitors. Why is it that an attraction with such a strong educational mission can still draw so many visitors?
4. In contrast to the integrated resort developments, the Eden Project is more of a demonstration in natural simplicity. To which types of people and market segments do you think the Eden Project appeals the most?

Sources

edenprojecttv. 2015. Eden Project: an overview. https://www.youtube.com/watch?v=f8unx8-pZxg

Eden Project. 2017. Sustainability Policy. http://www.edenproject.com/eden-story/about-us/sustainability-policy

Visit Cornwall. 2017. Eden Project. https://www.visitcornwall.com/things-to-do/attractions/south-coast/st-austell/eden-project

FIGURE 6.3 The Eden Project in Cornwall, England.

CATEGORIES OF TOURISM DEVELOPMENTS

Types and Functions of Tourism Developments

Good tourism development planning in a destination should follow sustainable tourism guidelines, and that includes considering the functions of each development project. You should realize that there are different types of tourism developments that perform specific functions within their destinations. Six types of tourism developments by function are:

• **Flagship**

Flagships are major tourism attractions or resort areas that provide a primary reason for people to visit a destination. You already learned about the Eden Project, which is a flagship visitor attraction for Cornwall in England. It is an example of a single-entity flagship that is man-made, and you know it has a strong sustainability mission (Eden Project 2017). A multiple-entity flagship tourism development is a resort or destination area with several tourism attractions, hotels, and other tourism businesses. The development of Sentosa Island in Singapore is a good example of this, comprised of integrated resorts, theme parks, and multiple other attractions and tourism facilities.

The Gardens by the Bay shown in Figure 6.4 is one component of a multiple-entity flagship tourism development on Sentosa Island. This amazing attraction, like the Eden Project, has a strong sustainability ethic. Its two glass biomes and the Supertrees were designed to have environmentally sustainable functions (Gardens by the Bay 2017).

Not all flagships are man-made, like the Eden Project and the Gardens by the Bay. In fact, many are based on nature, including the Grand Canyon and the Rocky Mountains in North America, and Uluru (Ayers Rock) and the 12 Apostles in Australia (Figure 6.5). Others are cultural-heritage treasures such as the Terracotta Warriors and Horses in Xi'an, China; Taj Mahal of India; and Chichen Itza in Mexico. These natural and cultural-heritage flagships require special care to ensure their sustainability, and they are generally within protected areas.

FIGURE 6.4 Supertree Grove at Gardens by the Bay, Sentosa Island, Singapore.

FIGURE 6.5 The 12 Apostles in Victoria, Australia, are a nature-based flagship.

- **Hub**

You already know that the hub is the middle section of a bike or car wheel. A hub plays a central role in these systems, as it also does in a tourism hub. Large airports with many international and domestic flights serve as transportation hubs, including Chicago O'Hare, London Heathrow, Tokyo Haneda, Incheon in South Korea, and Amsterdam Schiphol. Other tourism hubs are gateways or "jumping off" points to major attractions. Inverness, for example, is considered to be the gateway to the Scottish Highlands. Cairns, in the north of Queensland, Australia, is a popular hub from which to access the Great Barrier Reef. Siem Reap in Cambodia is the gateway to Angkor Wat (Figure 6.6).

FIGURE 6.6 Angkor Archaeological Park UNESCO World Cultural Heritage Centre.

- **Cluster**

A cluster is a combination of tourism developments with similar or related functions or themes. You will quickly grasp this type if you know that an area with many vineyards and wineries is a cluster. Mendoza Province's wine region is one of the most famous in Argentina, encompassing around 1,500 wineries (Figure 6.7).

Cultural districts in cities are another example of clustering in tourism.

The advantages of clustering to tourism destination not only include specialization, but also increasing the "drawing power" or critical mass. Think about farmers' markets and night markets, and you will understand that generally the larger they are, the more people they attract.

FIGURE 6.7 The Mendoza wine region of Argentina.

- **Circuit and trail**

A tourism or tourist circuit is usually a driving, biking, or hiking itinerary in a more or less circular pattern. These include, for example, the Lake Superior Circle Tour that has areas both in the United States and Canada, and the Lake Zurich Circular Tour (Zürichsee-Rundweg) in Switzerland.

A trail is a point-to-point configuration, in which the visitor may not return to the starting point. For example, the Overland Track in Tasmania, Australia, and the West Highland Way in Scotland (Figure 6.8) are popular hiking trails that draw many visitors each year. Other examples are the Southern Literary Trail and the Robert Trent Jones Golf Trail, both in the south of the United States (Robert Trent Jones Golf Trail 2017; Southern Literary Trail 2017).

- **Event or festival**

Festivals and events come in all sizes and varieties; however, they are popular in tourism for promoting destination images and themes, and in attracting visitors in off-seasons. Hallmark events or festivals are a little like flagships, as they are major occasions that draw international audiences. Oktoberfest held each year in Munich, Germany, is an example of a hallmark event and fair. Others include the Fringe Festival in Edinburgh, Scotland; White Nights in St. Petersburg,

FIGURE 6.8 Hiking the West Highland Way in Scotland.

Russia; and the Rio Carnival in Brazil. The Holi Festivals held in India and Nepal are drawing more visitors from abroad (Figure 6.9).

- **Support**

Flagships, hubs, clusters, circuits and trails, and events and festivals create the need and demand for other facilities and services. These facilities and services are essential in a supporting role, and without them destinations would not be complete in meeting all the needs and requirements of visitors. Tourist or visitor information centers are a good example of support facilities and services (Figure 6.10).

FIGURE 6.9 Celebrating the Holi Festival in India.

FIGURE 6.10 Tourism information center in Shibuya, Tokyo, Japan.

QUICK TRIP 6.2

Product Clubs: A Trend in Tourism Development

Newer cooperative models of tourism development have emerged in recent years. One of these models is the "product club" concept. A tourism product club is a group of companies that have agreed to work together to develop new tourism products or increase the value of existing products and collectively review the existing problems that hinder profitable development of tourism.

The European Commission (2014) identifies the following benefits for product club members:

- Greater market opportunities
- Income at a lower cost
- More market penetration with less effort
- Increased forecasting of seasonal demand
- Increased certainty for market shares
- Increased competitiveness
- Increased credibility
- Improved business image

According to Del Campo Gomis et al. (2010), the following types of activities can be carried out by a tourism product club:

- Businessmen's association in joint projects
- Research of specific markets' needs
- Identification of potential markets and segments

QUICK TRIP 6.2 CONTINUED

- Evaluation of successful initiatives in other places (benchmarking)
- Implementation of a development strategy and marketing of the activity concerned
- Creation of new packages
- Seminars
- Production of newsletters and other communications (business to business: B2B)

Tourism product clubs bring together businesses, organizations, and places that share similar products or have an interest in the same types of target markets. These are typically small- and medium-sized enterprises. For example, in Spain tourism product clubs were established for marinas, wine routes, spas, incentives, congresses, idiomatic tourism, and camping. The Fassa Valley of Northern Italy has created product clubs for gastronomy, hikes, motor tourism, and wellness treatments. The Wineries of Niagara Lake in Ontario, Canada, is another example of a product club.

A good example of a specific product club concept is provided in The Wine Routes of Spain Products Club. This project began in 2001 and now there are twenty-six "routes" that are members. It is operated by ACEVIN (Associación Española de Ciudades del Vino) with support from the Ministry of Energy, Tourism and Digital Agenda and the Ministry of Agriculture and Fishing, Food and Environment. This product club is designed to "help the traveller discover a 'different' Spain and enjoy some unique experiences" based upon the culture of wine.

Think about This

1. What are the major advantages of belonging to tourism product clubs for small- and medium-sized businesses?
2. How can the product club idea assist a destination with its tourism development strategies and plans?
3. Other than the product club themes mentioned in this Quick Trip, what other types of product clubs can be established?
4. When product clubs form in a destination, this makes destination marketing easier and opens up the potential of attracting more special-interest visitors. Do you agree with this statement and why?

Sources

Del Campo Gomis, F. J., Lluch, D. L, Civera, J. M. S., Torres, A. M. A., Mollá-Bauzá, M. B., Poveda, A. M., de los Ríos, F. C., and Pedregal, A. M. N. 2010. Wine tourism product clubs as a way to increase wine added value: the case of Spain. *International Journal of Wine Research*, 2, 27–34.

European Commission. 2014. Tourism product club. https://www.youtube.com/watch?v=Hg4Xl4Nlmn0

Hashimoto, A., and Telfer, D. J. 2006. Selling Canadian culinary tourism: Branding the global and the regional product. *Tourism Geographies*, 8(1), 31–55.

Stipanović C., and Rudan E. 2016. Tourism product club in generating the value chain. *Polish Journal of Management Studies*, 14(2), 214–223.

Telfer, D. J. 2000. Tastes of Niagara. *International Journal of Hospitality and Tourism Administration*, 1(1), 71–88.

Val di Fassa. 2017. Product Club. http://www.fassa.com/EN/Product-club/

Wine Routes of Spain. 2017. Rutas Vino de España. http://en.wineroutesofspain.com/

Wineries of Niagara on the Lake. 2017. About us. http://www.wineriesofniagaraonthelake.com/about-us/

Realms of Tourism Development

Another way of looking at types of tourism developments is illustrated in Figure 6.11, showing that not all are physical or tangible. In addition to physical products, holistic tourism development planning should contain programs, packages, and people (guests and hosts). There is a tendency to think of tourism development as just being physical construction, transportation, and infrastructure; however, a more holistic approach requires that careful attention be given to intangible aspects of tourism.

Hard and Soft Tourism Developments

You can experience many different forms of development in tourism destinations around the world. These range from high-impact or "hard" (mass) to low-impact or "soft" developments. Hard tourism developments typically involve large-scale physical construction and

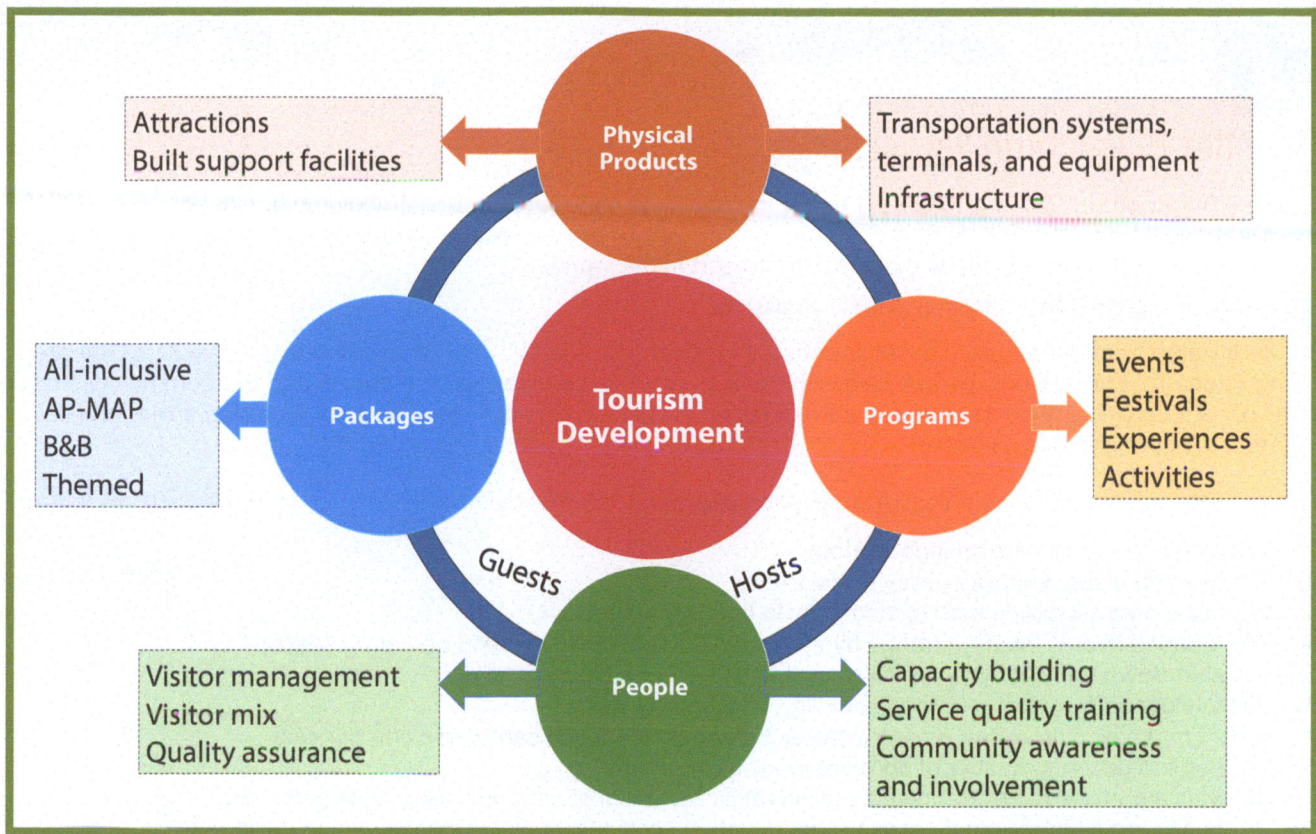

FIGURE 6.11 Physical products, programs, packages, and people are four realms of tourism development.

extensive tracts of land designed for hosting major volumes of visitors. They are often associated with package tours (Pollock 2013).

Mass tourism is where thousands of visitors congregate and this requires large-scale investment in accommodation, transportation, infrastructure, and services. Examples include parts of Florida (e.g., Orlando and Miami); Bali in Indonesia; Pattaya and Phuket in Thailand; Sentosa Island in Singapore; the beach areas of France, Italy, and Spain; and the Surfers Paradise area of Australia's Gold Coast. Resort tourism includes self-contained or integrated projects like the typical Club Med village, often referred to as "enclave" tourism. On the one hand, high-impact tourism development projects and mass tourism have the potential of causing major transformations in local environments and peoples. On the other hand, they often generate significant economic impact and benefits.

Soft tourism developments are for individual or small groups of visitors, and require limited construction and land (Figure 6.12). Low-impact or "soft" tourism developments are smaller-scale and are often referred to as alternative tourism, boutique tourism, or ecotourism experiences (The Nature Conservancy 2017;

FIGURE 6.12 Eco-resort in Koh Phayam, Thailand.

Theng, Qiong, and Tatar 2015; Tourism & More 2016). They are considered to be more sustainable, as they have a smaller "footprint" on the land and are more likely to involve local community residents.

While many argue that soft tourism developments are more sustainable, you should not conclude that all hard tourism developments are not sustainable. For example, the top eight theme parks in the world in 2016 all had over 10 million visitors and they have existed for several decades (AECOM 2017).

QUICK TRIP 6.3

Whistler Blackcomb Targets a Zero Footprint

Whistler Blackcomb (WB) is a major ski resort located near Vancouver in British Columbia, Canada (Figure 6.13). *Ski Magazine* rated WB first in three categories for 2017—overall resort, terrain variety, and off-hill activities. *The Telegraph* in the UK rated it as the "Best Ski Resort in the World."

WB has a strong environmental sustainability mission:

> "Zero waste, zero carbon, zero net emissions—this is our goal—for Whistler Blackcomb to achieve Zero Operating Footprint. This will only be possible with the support of our employees, our guests and our community. For all of us, Every Step Counts. This collective mission inspires guests to visit us who are factoring environmental impacts into their travel choices."

This is a refreshing outlook from such a large resort operation. WB has defined its "Environmental Top 10" as follows:

1. WB has a 7-step climate change strategy.
2. WB has had a sustainability policy since 1999.
3. WB has saved 14 million kWh of electricity in the past 10 years.
4. WB reduced overall landfill garbage by 70% from 2000 to its 2015–2016 operating season.
5. WB shut down the electricity for both mountains for Earth Hour in 2017.
6. WB tracks and reports grooming fleet idling on a weekly basis.
7. WB's Employee Carpooling program saves 360 metric tonnes of carbon dioxide per year.
8. WB participates in a number of social responsibility programs.
9. WB runs a number of environmental conservation educational programs for guests and staff.
10. WB builds recreational experiences within mountain ecosystems rather than changing them.

© Pierre Leclerc/Shutterstock.com

FIGURE 6.13 The Whistler-Blackcomb resort area, near Vancouver, British Columbia, Canada.

Think about This

1. What can other resorts and destinations learn from the example set by Whistler Blackcomb in terms of its environmental management programs?
2. For ski resorts, what are the special challenges faced with environmental management programs?
3. What are the long-term benefits for Whistler Blackcomb in following its principles of environmental management?
4. Which other tourism developments have exemplary environmental management programs and what are these programs?

Sources

Vail Resorts. 2017. Epic Promise. http://www.epicpromise.com/environment/zero-footprint/

Whistler Blackcomb. 2015. 50 Years of Going Beyond—Full Movie. https://www.youtube.com/watch?v=OJTh-dDA4yY

Whistler Blackcomb. 2017. Environment. https://www.whistlerblackcomb.com/about-us/environment

Whistler Blackcomb. 2017. Whistler Blackcomb's Environmental Top 10. https://www.whistlerblackcomb.com/about-us/environment/environmental-top-10

However, too many visitors can overload destinations. The Responsible Tourism Partnership (2017) explains an issue with there being too many visitors within a destination as follows:

> **Overtourism** describes destinations where hosts or guests, locals or visitors, feel that there are too many visitors and that the quality of life in the area or the quality of the experience has deteriorated unacceptably.

A Jumble of Tourism Development Terminology

The authors do not want to confuse you with too much bewildering terminology. However, tourism, and especially sustainable tourism, seems to be a jumble of overlapping terms. You already heard about alternative, boutique, and ecotourism; but there are more. Figure 6.14 provides the definitions of twelve terms that express forms of tourism that are related to sustainable tourism.

Terminology	Definition	Source
Alternative	Involves travel that is personal and authentic and encourages interaction with the local environment, people, and communities.	Bulgarian Association of Alternative Tourism. 2018.
Boutique	Caters more to smaller groups of families or intimate friends. It allows for spontaneity in site/sight selection. Boutique tourists often seek the more unusual and are not afraid of language or cultural difficulties.	Tourism & More. 2016.
Community-based	Controlling, managing, and developing their own tourism industry, whereby tourists and travelers can experience the community's way of life and consider their social, economic, and environmental impacts upon the destination they are visiting.	CBT Vietnam. 2017.
Ecotourism	Environmentally responsible travel to natural areas, in order to enjoy and appreciate nature (and accompanying cultural features, both past and present) that promote conservation, have a low visitor impact and provide for beneficially active socio-economic involvement of local peoples.	The Nature Conservancy. 2017.
Ethical	Tourism which benefits people and the environments in different destinations.	Tourism Concern. 2018.
Geotourism	Tourism that sustains or enhances the distinctive geographical character of a place—its environment, heritage, aesthetics, culture, and the well-being of its residents.	National Geographic. 2018.
Green	Any tourism activity operating in an environmentally friendly manner.	Pintassilgo, P. 2016.
Low-carbon	The reduction of "carbon" emissions, mainly carbon dioxide, during travel.	Yang, Y. 2015.
Overtourism	Describes destinations where hosts or guests, locals or visitors, feel that there are too many visitors and that the quality of life in the area or the quality of the experience has deteriorated unacceptably.	Responsible Tourism Partnership. 2017.
Responsible	Making better places for people to live in and better places for people to visit.	Responsible Tourism Partnership. 2018.
Slow	Moving at a pace that allows rediscovery.	Callot, P. 2013.
Sustainable	Takes full account of its current and future economic, social, and environmental impacts, addressing the needs of visitors, the industry, the environment, and host communities.	UNWTO. 2017.

FIGURE 6.14 Definitions of forms of tourism associated with sustainable tourism.

TOURISM PLANNING AND TOURISM DEVELOPMENT

An absence of tourism planning can lead to unsustainable tourism development. As you learned in Chapter 5, tourism destination planning produces goals, strategies, and objectives for tourism development. The tourism development portion of the plan provides overall guidelines for development and outlines broad development concepts. These overall tourism development guidelines ensure that when development occurs it supports the area's economic, social and cultural, and environmental policies and goals. Specific guidelines describing the basic characteristics of the scale, quality, and types of development are written.

The tourism planning process also identifies individual project development opportunities worthy of in-depth research through feasibility studies and environmental impact analyses (EIAs). The term "tourism or destination product" is used for all categories of project development opportunities, both commercial and non-commercial. The economic feasibility and environmental impact of commercial (profit-making) project development opportunities is established with the techniques described in this chapter. The non-commercial development opportunities may include support facilities like travel information centers, infrastructure, transportation, and non-profit attractions such as museums and other historic landmarks. The advisability of proceeding with these projects cannot be measured through an economic feasibility study since they may produce little or no revenue. These projects may be analyzed using a technique known as cost/benefit analysis, or are assessed for their contributions to the achievement of the tourism plan's goals and objectives.

ROLES IN TOURISM DEVELOPMENT

Governments, the private sector, non-profits, and communities have important roles to play in sustainable tourism development. The following materials help you better understand how each of them get involved.

Private-Sector Roles

The private sector's main role is to invest in, develop, market, and operate tourism facilities and services for visitors while maximizing financial returns. In today's more enlightened times, companies accept that they have corporate social (CSR) and environmental responsibilities that they must uphold in achieving profit goals.

You should know that not all tourism project development opportunities are identified in the tourism destination planning process, described in Chapter 5. Many project ideas emerge from the private sector through sponsored research studies and assessments of supply and demand relationships. Idea generation is, therefore, a key role of the private sector.

The entrepreneurial role is the heart of the private sector's involvement in tourism development. This role embraces idea generation, development project implementation, financial risk-taking and investment, marketing, and the management of operations. The private sector also provides the specialized technical skills required in the development process through tourism consultants, market research firms, economists, environmental and social impact experts, architects, landscape architects, engineers, designers, lawyers, project managers, and builders. The private sector, through its financial institutions, other corporate lenders, and individual citizens, provides a large proportion of the financing for the investment in tourism development projects.

Non-Profit Organizations and NGO Roles

Non-profit organizations play an important role in tourism development in most destinations. These organizations include many DMOs (including convention and visitors bureaus, CVBs), chambers of commerce, travel associations, foundations, historical and cultural societies, recreation and sports associations, service clubs, community associations, and religious groups. While their roles vary, non-profits typically are involved in operating attractions (such as pioneer villages, historic buildings, museums, and art galleries); creating and running festivals, events, and special meals; providing travel information services; and financing the development of community-oriented facilities (such as recreation and community halls, historical and cultural centers, and trail systems).

NGO is short for non-governmental organization, and many NGOs worldwide are directly or indirectly involved with tourism development. You will recognize one of these as the World Wide Fund for Nature (WWF), an NGO that is trying to reduce the marine impacts of tourism (WWF 2017). NGOs often are involved in capacity building (developing and strengthening skills) and helping local communities to gain benefits from tourism in other ways through direct participation, as in community-based tourism (CBT), discussed below.

Community Roles

Local communities should not be "silent partners" in tourism development and indeed can play an active role in delivering the authentic experiences that visitors are seeking. CBT is one of the strategies for delivering the benefits of tourism directly to local communities (Figure 6.15). CBT Vietnam (2017) defines CBT as involving communities in "controlling, managing and developing their own tourism industry, whereby tourists and travellers can experience the community's way of life and consider their social, economic, and environmental impacts upon the destination they are visiting."

Even in situations where communities are not direct participants in tourism development, local residents should be consulted when there are large projects proposed that will affect their quality of life.

FIGURE 6.15 Community-based tourism in the Mekong Delta of Vietnam.

QUICK TRIP 6.4

The "Battle" of Benoa Bay, Bali, Indonesia

A luxury resort and theme park development is proposed on reclaimed land in Benoa Bay, Bali (Figure 6.16). One journalist has characterized the $3 billion project, called Nusa Benoa, as a mass tourism development (Langenheim 2016). Some local residents are strongly opposed to the new venture and are publicly protesting against it. An organization (ForBALI—The Bali Forum against Reclamation) has been formed to lobby against the tourism development project.

The developers, Pt Tirta Wahana Bali Internasional (TWBI) (2015) provide this overall description of the proposed project:

> "A sustainable development project that integrates the origins of Balinese culture and traditional customs in the development of resorts, theme parks, community areas, residential clusters to become the new iconic tourist-destination in Bali."

The company first proposed the project in 2014 after Benoa Bay was reclassified from a conservation area into a revitalization zone by the government. Nusa Benoa would reclaim land in the bay into a series of islands that would house the tourism developments.

These types of situations tend to be a dilemma for governments. Large-scale projects can generate significant economic benefits; however, they may lead to irreversible environmental change and alter the lifestyles of local residents. The developers claim that Nusa Benoa will create around 150,000 new jobs; those who oppose say that reclaiming a significant portion of the bay will result in not being able to perform its natural functions and side effects, such as flooding, will occur. Locals also argue that the project will disrupt their religious practices and other aspects of their daily lives.

According to media coverage, TWBI has had an environmental impact analysis (EIA) conducted, but it is yet to be approved by the relevant government agency. Even with the EIA completed, the local opposition to the project remains strong. Those who are not in favor of Nusa Benoa are suggesting that it is located in a part of southern Bali that is already struggling to cope with the pressures of too much tourism.

QUICK TRIP 6.4 CONTINUED

Think about This

1. What should the Bali government do in this situation when there is such great public opposition to this large-scale tourism development?
2. Does this situation suggest that there can be conflict within the triple bottom line concept? Why or why not?
3. How can the capacity of an area such as southern Bali to handle a certain number of visitors be determined?
4. Do you believe that it is more important for locals to maintain their lifestyles rather than to sanction large-scale tourism development? Why or why not?

Sources

ForBALI (The Bali Forum against Reclamation). 2017. ForBALI. http://www.forbali.org/id/

Juniarta, I. W. 2017. Government orders another study into Benoa Bay reclamation project. *The Jakarta Post,* February 23. http://www.thejakartapost.com/news/2017/02/23/government-orders-another-study-into-benoa-bay-reclamation-project.html

Langenheim, J. 2016. Mounting opposition to Bali mass tourism project. *The Guardian,* March 22. https://www.theguardian.com/environment/the-coral-triangle/2016/mar/22/mounting-opposition-to-bali-mass-tourism-project

Pt Tirta Wahana Bali Internasional. 2015. Nusa Benoa. http://nusabenoa.com/

TWBI. 2017. A Catalyst for Sustainable Growth, Embracing the Environment towards the Community and Tourism Development in Bali. http://twbi.co.id/index.php?page=home&sid=

© Avtk/Shutterstock.com

FIGURE 6.16 Benoa Bay, Bali, Indonesia.

Government Roles

The most widely-accepted function of government in tourism development is as a stimulator or catalyst for development. Governments complement the efforts of the private sector, non-profit organizations, and local residents. UNWTO recommends as a general principle that governments should not try to do what the private sector is able and willing to do. Although this is a generally accepted principle in many countries, there are still many cases of overlapping activities and conflict between the government and the private sector. In some countries, the federal, state or provincial, and local governments are involved in the operation of parks, most of which include camping facilities. Many private campground operators feel that the government-operated facilities offer unfair competition and that the government should not be in the campground business. Another area of contention often found is in the provision of boat-docking facilities where both the private sector and government agencies operate competitive facilities. A further area of direct competition is that of government-owned airlines versus private air carriers.

There are several valid reasons behind the reversal in the government and private-sector roles in tourism development. The most important is that it is not always reasonable to expect tourism to develop in the manner and at the speed contemplated in the tourism destination plan if left entirely to the private sector. Government agencies often find themselves with a more direct role in tourism development for the reasons shown in Figure 6.17.

Due to profitability concerns, several countries and states are directly involved in the hotel and resort business. These include the Paradores of Spain and the states of Indiana and Kentucky in the United States, where inns have been developed within certain state parks. In these parks, the inns are owned by the state government and are either operated by the state government or by the private sector through a management contract or lease arrangement (Indiana Department of Natural Resources 2017; Kentucky State Parks 2017; Paradores 2017).

Reasons	Direct Government Involvement in Tourism Development
Bankruptcy	Existing tourism facility becomes bankrupt and cannot be sold on the market; the government is obliged to acquire the facility.
Conservation of cultural heritage	Government decides to adapt cultural heritage properties for tourism and local leisure and recreation.
Pilots or demonstration projects	Government wants to encourage private-sector development by pioneering new types of development through "demonstration" or "pilot" projects.
Profitability concerns	Private sector is unwilling to finance a project because of limited profit potential; the government has given this project a high priority due to its regional economic contributions or its pivotal role in stimulating tourism.
Regional tourism	Underdeveloped regions are unable to attract private-sector investors, developers, and operators.
Social tourism	Government wants to provide low-cost vacation opportunities for disadvantaged groups within the population, such as the poor, the sick, and the aged.

FIGURE 6.17 Reasons for direct government involvement in tourism development.

QUICK TRIP 6.5

Paradores de Turismo de España, S.A.—A Model of Sustainable Tourism

Generally, hotel operations are the domain of the private sector. However, Paradores de Turismo de España, S.A. is an example of a hotel chain that is 100 percent owned and operated by government. The organization was first established in 1928, long before sustainable development and sustainable tourism came into being. However, the mission of Paradores well reflects the principles of sustainable tourism:

> "Paradores is an instrument of State tourism policy. The company presents an image of modern, high-quality tourism abroad and contributes to geographical integration, recovery and maintenance of our country's cultural and artistic heritage, and the preservation and enjoyment of natural spaces. It also serves as the driving force behind stimulus actions for areas with limited tourism or economic activity."

When the company began operations in the 1920s, tourism was just beginning in Spain and no hotel chains were active in the market. However, the government wanted to communicate the message that tourism was of a high quality in Spain. The refurbishing of historic buildings into hotels became the "trademark" of the Paradores in those days. In 2015, Paradores had sixteen castles and walled sites (Figure 6.18), fourteen convents and monasteries, twelve palaces, six unique historic buildings, and forty-seven newly-built and traditional buildings. Paradores asserts that adapting historic buildings to become hotels links heritage and tourism. Without such renovation, many of the properties could not have been sustained and might eventually have ended in ruins.

Paradores (2015) lists eight reasons why it is a model for sustainable tourism management as follows:

- Developing a high-quality tourism product which acts as the national and international image of the Spanish hotel industry.
- Facilitating the reclaiming of cultural heritage for the purposes of tourism, enabling it to be preserved and maintained.
- Providing stimulus for non-industrial areas with the aim of creating economic opportunities.
- Lending value and recognition to regional gastronomy, rediscovering traditional recipes, while also making the most of latest trends.
- Promoting more even distribution of tourism by channeling demand into areas of interest which are more unknown and less exploited.
- Showcasing destinations and cultural activities.
- Preservation and use of natural areas.
- Encouraging environmentally friendly development.

Think about This

1. How can direct government involvement in hotel and resort operations contribute to sustainable tourism, as exemplified in the Paradores case?
2. Why might the private sector be reluctant to renovate historic or heritage buildings into hotels?
3. What are the potential advantages and disadvantages of government-operated hotels and resorts?
4. What lessons can other countries and regions gain from the development and operation of the Paradores in Spain?

Sources

Paradores. 2015. Paradores de Turismo de España: A model of sustainable hotel management.

Responsible Tourism Inc. 2017. 17 Sustainable Tourism Ideas for This 2017. https://www.biospheretourism.com/en/blog/17-sustainable-tourism-examples-for-this-2017/2

FIGURE 6.18 Castle of Cardona Hotel Parador, Spain.

The social tourism function of governments is a widely-accepted phenomenon in several countries in Europe and elsewhere. For example, France has established a network of "village de vacances" (family-oriented resorts) and "gites familiaux" (family homes in resort settings) for its disadvantaged citizens. The International Social Tourism Organisations defines social tourism as "any activities contributing, in a fair and sustainable way, to a greater access to holidays and tourism activities for everyone" (ISTO 2017).

Another major role of governments is as a regulator of tourism developments. Governments must ensure that developers follow all the laws, procedures, and codes in planning and constructing projects. This may mean that developers are required to conduct environmental impact analyses and to involve local residents in a process of consultation.

Role of Government Financial Incentives

One of the major hurdles that all tourism projects face is securing the financing needed for their development. Many tourism projects have been economically feasible but have not been developed because the developers were not able to attract the right amount or types of financing. The number of government agencies providing specific financial incentives for tourism projects has greatly increased on a worldwide basis. This is part of government's role as stimulators of tourism development.

Government financial incentives for tourism projects can be classified into two broad categories. Fiscal incentives are special allowances for income tax or other tax purposes. Direct and indirect incentives constitute the second main category, and include a wide variety of programs aimed at easing the financing requirements of projects. The basic objective of most of these incentive programs is to help businesses implement tourism development projects that, without assistance, may be abandoned or seriously delayed. On a global basis, all levels of government are involved in providing these types of incentive programs. Figure 6.19 provides a description of the types of financial incentive programs provided by government agencies to tourism development projects.

Fiscal Incentives
• Tax holidays or deferrals. Government agency defers the payment of income taxes or other taxes for a predetermined time.
• Remission of tariffs. Government agency relaxes or removes import duties on goods and services required by the project.
• Tax reductions. Government agency lowers the normal tax rates that would be paid by the project.
Direct and Indirect Incentives
• Nonrefundable grants. Reduces a project's capital budget.
• Low-interest loans. Reduces the amount of interest that the project must pay during its operating life.
• Interest rebates. Government agency rebates a portion of the project's interest costs during its operating life.
• Forgivable loans. Government agency loans funds to the project and then "forgives" all or part of these over an agreed-upon time period; this acts like a phased nonrefundable grant.
• Loan guarantees. Government agency guarantees a loan given to a project by a private financial institution.
• Working capital loans. Government agency loans funds to meet the working capital needs of a project.
• Equity participation. Government agency purchases some of the available shares in the project, and becomes an equity investor.
• Training grants. Government agency provides a nonrefundable grant to the project for staff training purposes.
• Infrastructure assistance. Government agency assumes the costs of some or all of the infrastructure required for the project.
• Leasebacks. Government agency purchases land, buildings, or equipment and then leases them to the project.
• Land donations. Government agency donates land free of charge to the project.

FIGURE 6.19 Categories and types of government incentives.

Because most government departments providing these financial incentives receive more applications for assistance than their budgets can handle, it is inevitable that not all projects that request monetary help receive it. In certain cases, this results in these projects not proceeding any further. A government agency involved in providing financial incentives, technical, or other assistance to individual tourism projects establishes a set of project selection criteria. These criteria assist the agency in identifying those projects that merit assistance and screening out other projects that are not as desirable. Typically, criteria fall into the nine categories shown in Figure 6.20.

Private Sector Financing

Although governments play a significant role in providing financing to tourism development projects, it is the private sector that supplies the majority of the financing. These private sources range from individual citizens to major institutional lenders such as banks, trust companies, credit unions, insurance companies, and other commercial finance companies. Typically, a private financing source requires that the following five criteria be met before lending money to tourism developers:

1. Previous management experience in tourism and an established credit record within the management development team
2. Proof of economic feasibility via an independent economic feasibility study
3. Adequate collateral or security for the funds to be borrowed
4. Adequate equity invested by the owners of the project
5. Proof of stability in the tourism destination in which the project will operate

Tourism development projects require equity from owners and investors as well as borrowed capital (debt). These individuals are the true "risk takers" in the development, and they are rewarded with profits for a return on their investments. Not all projects are able to secure the types and amounts of private financing that they require, although they may have successfully survived all of the earlier screening mechanisms.

Criteria	Description of Criteria
Competitive impact	Project complements, rather than competes with, existing tourism businesses and does not seriously jeopardize the financial viability of any individual business.
Compliance with policies and plans	Project complies with the destination's tourism policies and plans.
Developer and operator capabilities	Project developers and operators are capable of successfully developing and operating the business.
Economic contributions	Project creates significant levels of income and employment benefits.
Environmental impacts	Project is developed in compliance with existing legislation and regulations governing the conservation and protection of the environment (sustainability guidelines).
Equity contributions	Where the project is profit-making, the investors have sufficient equity to inject into the venture.
Feasibility	Where the project is profit-making, it is economically feasible.
Socio-cultural impact	Project does not jeopardize the social well-being of local residents.
Tourism impact	Project adds to the destination's tourism potential by creating an attraction, by improving the area's capacity to receive and cater to visitors, or by being beneficial to tourism in some other way.

FIGURE 6.20 Criteria for government financial assistance.

QUICK TRIP 6.6

Unsustainable Tourism: White Elephants on the Landscape

There are plenty of examples of unsustainable tourism developments around the world, including abandoned Olympic Games' buildings and facilities, failed theme and amusement parks, derelict and unfinished hotels and resorts, convention centers with no delegates (except real and furry mice), and airports where no planes fly (Figure 6.21). These can be called "white elephants" since they are expensive to maintain and nobody knows what to do with them. Thankfully, some have already been demolished and at least there is no visible reminder of the mistakes that were made.

Tourism experts like to talk about sustainable tourism, especially from the perspective of the environment, but few have a focus on all aspects of "unsustainable tourism." In fact, there are many reasons why tourism developments fail and are not sustainable, and they are not all environmental. Some of these failures result from:

- Bankruptcy of private-sector operators
- Insufficient financing during construction
- No or inadequate market and feasibility studies
- Poor locations
- Lack of market demand
- Changes in consumer preferences
- Changes in government policy
- No alternative uses (e.g., after an Olympic Games or other mega-event)
- Obsolescence or inadequate capacity and design for contemporary needs
- Uncontrollable external factors, including natural disasters, wars, and other civil conflicts

QUICK TRIP 6.6 CONTINUED

A few interesting "white elephant" case examples are highlighted below:

- Gulliver's Kingdom theme park, Japan. Built near Mount Fuji, this theme park opened in 1997, but was closed in 2001. Its demise is blamed on a poor location near Aokigahara, Japan's "suicide forest," and a strange theme park concept that attracted too few visitors.
- Mirabel Airport, Montréal, Canada. This airport was opened in 1975 with the intention of eventually replacing the Montréal Dorval Airport (now Pierre Elliott Trudeau International Airport). The last passenger flight to use Mirabel was in 2004. Mirabel's location, at approximately 50 kilometers north of the city, and the introduction of longer-range jets are thought to be the main reasons for its failure.
- Olympic Games' venues. *Business Insider* (Knowlton 2015), in an article containing many photos of dilapidated buildings and facilities, highlighted the difficulties in repurposing Olympic Games' venues in Athens, Atlanta, Beijing, and Sarajevo.
- River Country, Lake Buena Vista, Florida. This was the first water park operated by Disney and it was opened in 1976. It operated for twenty-five years, but was shut down in 2001. The park's demise is attributed to declining attendance figures.
- Riviera Hotel and Casino, Las Vegas, Nevada. This famous property was demolished in 2016 after its owners went bankrupt a year earlier. It was the location for several movies, including *Diamonds Are Forever* (1971).

These five short examples represent a very minor proportion of tourism developments that failed or were abandoned. Some of them enjoyed success, but that was not sustained for a variety of reasons.

To ensure that you have a balanced viewpoint on the topic of "tourism white elephants," it must be said that tourism has saved many historic or heritage buildings and facilities from destruction. There are many examples worldwide of places such as factories or mills being converted into hotels or attractions. In these cases, tourism has prolonged the lifespan of precious community resources.

Think about This

1. When new tourism development projects are being considered, what steps can be taken to ensure they are sustainable?
2. How can thorough primary research on potential market demand and consumer expectations improve the sustainability of tourism development projects?
3. Mega-events like the Olympic Games pose a dilemma for their hosts in sustaining the use of venues after the events have closed. What successful plans and measures have hosts implemented to overcome the challenge of repurposing buildings and facilities?
4. There are situations in which tourism has had the opposite effect and turned disused or abandoned buildings and sites into thriving businesses. Can you find and document three or four examples of this phenomenon?

Sources

Atlas Obscura. 2017. Abandoned Amusement Parks. http://www.atlasobscura.com/categories/abandoned-amusement-parks

AviationCV.com. 2017. World's Most Amazing Abandoned Airports. https://www.aviationcv.com/aviation-blog/2016/worlds-most-amazing-abandoned-airports

CBC News. 2014. Mirabel airport terminal, Trudeau's white elephant, to be torn down. http://www.cbc.ca/news/canada/montreal/mirabel-airport-terminal-trudeau-s-white-elephant-to-be-torn-down-1.2628421

Foote, K. 2015. These Historical Buildings Have Been Repurposed into Amazing Accommodations & Cultural Spaces. *Epicure & Culture,* March 26. https://epicureandculture.com/historical-buildings-accommdation-cultural-spaces/

Haines, G. 2016. 14 fascinating abandoned hotels. *The Telegraph,* August 17. http://www.telegraph.co.uk/travel/news/abandoned-hotels-around-the-world/

Knowlton, E. 2015. What abandoned Olympic venues from around the world look like today. *Business Insider,* August 24. http://www.businessinsider.com/abandoned-olympic-venues-around-the-world-photos-2015-8/#this-is-whats-left-of-the-figure-skating-facility-zetra-hall-14

Pleasance, C. 2014. The Lilliput that's now kaput: Japanese theme park based on Gulliver's Travels that has been left to rot. *Daily Mail,* February 13. http://www.dailymail.co.uk/news/article-2558813/The-Lilliput-thats-just-kaput-Japanese-theme-park-based-Gullivers-Travels-left-rot.html

Sim, N. 2015. Abandoned: The Rise, Fall and Decay of Disney's River Country. *Theme Park Tourist,* http://www.themeparktourist.com/features/20150323/30074/abandoned-rise-fall-and-decay-disney-s-river-country

FIGURE 6.21 Abandoned resort hotel on Hachijojima Island, Japan.

ANALYSIS OF INDIVIDUAL PROJECT DEVELOPMENT OPPORTUNITIES

Individual project development opportunities in tourism are either generated through the tourism destination planning process or by the private sector independent of this process. In destinations without tourism destination plans, governments may also be involved in identifying development opportunities for private-sector investment. Although these development opportunities can have the potential of satisfying tourism destination planning goals and considerable initial appeal to those in the private sector, they may be undesirable due to financial, environmental, social, cultural, or other reasons. All individual tourism project development opportunities must be carefully analyzed before proceeding with construction.

There are many types of tourism project development opportunities. Projects differ in their ability to generate financial profits. Projects such as hotels and commercial attractions are inherent profit-generators. Profit-generating projects are analyzed in economic feasibility studies. Other projects, such as travel information centers and infrastructure, generate no direct financial returns. However, these projects are essential to destinations. Other projects are the subject of cost/benefit analyses or other types of contribution analysis studies. Some tourism projects involve building construction (superstructure) or the development of transportation and essential public services (infrastructure); others require only human resources and equipment (such as guided canoe or ecotourism trips).

Despite differences in the tourism project ingredients, individual project opportunities should be analyzed by using similar techniques. Figure 6.22 shows a tourism project evaluation system. There are several decision points in project analysis in which further consideration of a tourism development project may be terminated. These include:

- A pre-feasibility study produces negative results.
- The site for the project is unsuitable and no alternative site is available.
- The market analysis indicates that the market is not large enough to support the project.

- The project is not economically feasible.
- The environmental, social, or cultural impacts are unacceptable.
- The results of a cost/benefit analysis are negative.

- The government decides the project does not qualify for financial assistance and it is not feasible without these government incentives.
- Sufficient financing from the private sector cannot be secured.

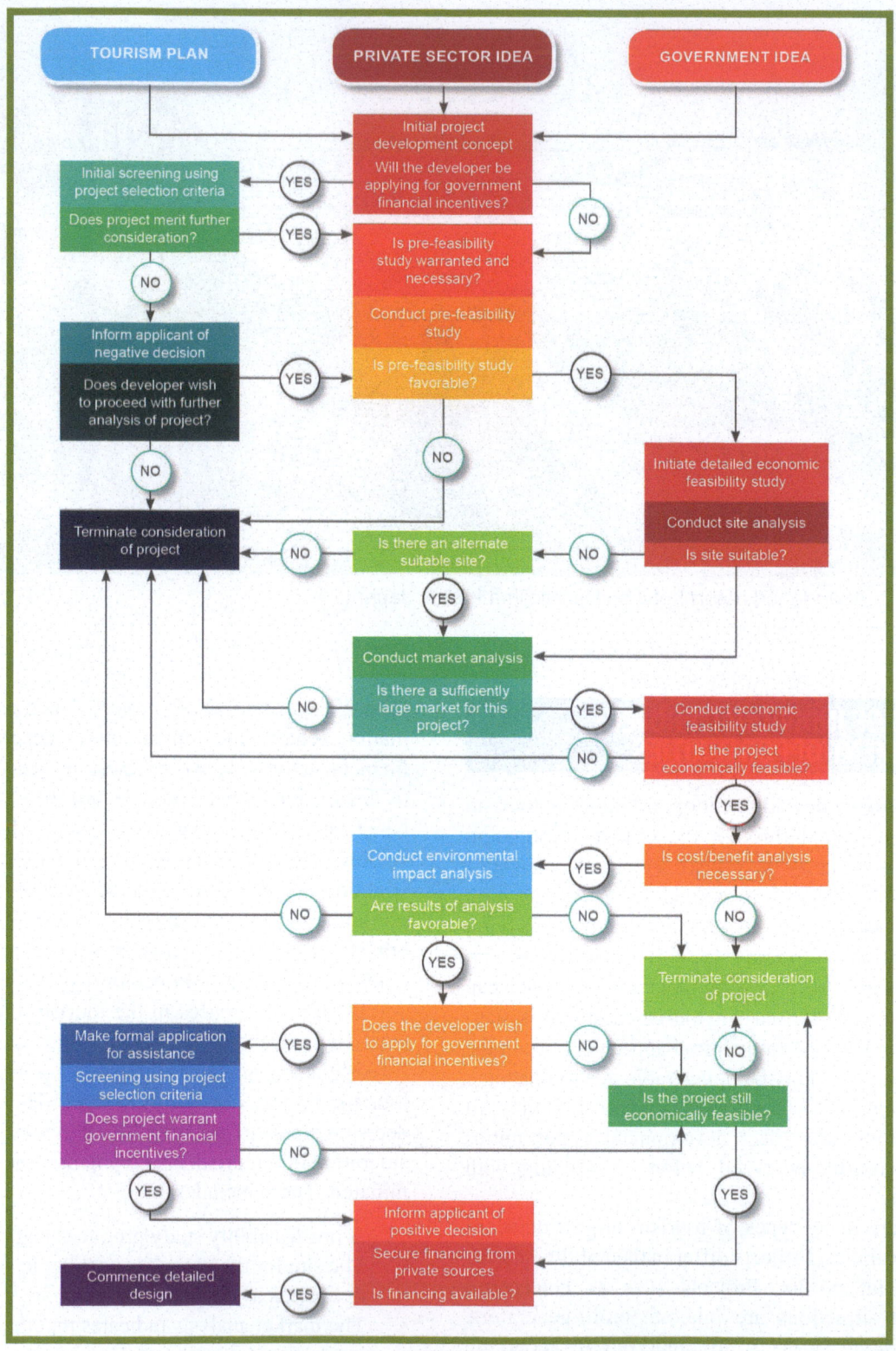

FIGURE 6.22 Conceptual model of a tourism project evaluation system.

Pre-Feasibility Study

A pre-feasibility study determines whether a detailed economic feasibility study is justified and which topics this detailed study should address. Because detailed economic feasibility studies are costly and time-consuming, pre-feasibility studies can be extremely valuable to developers. The objectives of a pre-feasibility study are to determine whether:

- The information available is adequate to show the project will not be viable or will not be attractive to investors or lenders.
- The information available indicates that the project is so promising that an investment decision can be made on the basis of the pre-feasibility study itself; that is, a detailed study is not needed.
- A preliminary assessment of potential environmental, social, or cultural impacts shows that these potential impacts are significant and unacceptable to the local community.
- Aspects of the project are so critical to its viability that they must be analyzed as part of the detailed economic feasibility study.

- The availability of factors critical to the viability of the project (such as the availability of a specific site) must be confirmed prior to doing a detailed economic feasibility study.

Pre-feasibility studies can be completed by private developers, by government agencies considering financing projects, or by private consulting organizations on behalf of the developers or government agencies. In some cases, the tourism development component of the tourism destination planning process produces pre-feasibility analyses of key tourism project development opportunities.

Detailed Economic Feasibility Study

If a project survives the pre-feasibility screening, it should then be analyzed through a detailed economic feasibility study. The majority of tourism development project economic feasibility studies are carried out by private consulting organizations on behalf of private developers, investors, or government agencies, or a combination of these parties (Figure 6.23).

FIGURE 6.23 Feasibility studies are usually a team effort.

Although many successful tourism development projects have been developed without detailed economic feasibility studies, as have many that have not proven successful, these analyses are vital to many people involved in the development process including the developers, investors, potential lenders, and government agencies. Other players involved in the process may include management companies interested in operating the projects on behalf of the developers and investors under management contracts or leases. The potential lenders may fall into two groups: those providing the construction (interim) financing and those providing the long-term (permanent) financing.

An economic feasibility study is a study to determine the economic feasibility of a tourism development project opportunity. A project is economically feasible if it provides a rate of return acceptable to the investors in the project. A market study is one component of an economic feasibility study which analyzes the project's market potential. Because of the need to acquire an unbiased opinion on a project's viability, economic feasibility studies are prepared by an independent third party and not by the developers, investors, or the potential lenders. Many lenders, including both private financial institutions and government agencies providing financial assistance programs, require that these independent studies be completed before they will seriously consider projects.

An economic feasibility study is designed to answer the questions, shown in Figure 6.24, that are of concern to the participants in the development process. The economic feasibility study has another important use for developers. It produces recommendations on the scale, sizes, facility types, and quality levels of operation. These recommendations are based upon the size and expectations of the market from the market study. At a later date in the development process, these findings will be used as the basis for the architect's preliminary drawings.

- **Site analysis**

Although not all tourism development project opportunities require physical site locations, a very large proportion do. An economic feasibility study can either specify a site (site specific), if a specific site location has been chosen for the project, or determine if an appropriate site exists within a given geographic area.

A tourism project site usually requires specific characteristics to be successful. This is not true of all sectors of an economy, as there are many "footloose" enterprises that are not location-dependent. In tourism, location has an extremely important bearing upon financial viability. The characteristics or criteria for site selection and evaluation vary with the type of tourism project under consideration. For example, a proposed new alpine ski area is dependent on the snow conditions and

Feasibility Study Questions
Developers and Investors
• Which of several alternative site locations is the most appropriate?
• Is a specific site appropriate for the development?
• If not, is there another site available that would be suitable?
• Is market demand large enough to support the project?
• What are the optimum scale and components of the project?
• What style of operation and quality levels should be provided?
• What revenues and expenses will the project experience?
• What will the capital costs be?
• Will the project produce a satisfactory return on investment?
• Should the developers and investors proceed with further analysis?
Lenders
All the above questions should be of concern to the lenders, and:
• How much money will be loaned to the developers and investors?
• Do the developers and investors have sufficient equity to invest in the project, given the financing required?
• Will the project produce sufficient operating profits and cash flow to cover the interest and principal payments when they become due?

FIGURE 6.24 Questions addressed in a feasibility study.

slope characteristics in a given location, while an urban hotel requires proximity to a concentration of industry and commerce. Similarly, a motor hotel requires ease of access and proximity to highways, while the placement of tennis courts is dictated by the wind and sun conditions at the site. The first step in the site analysis is to identify the criteria that are crucial to the project.

Tourism development project site criteria or characteristics can be divided into three categories. Figure 6.25 provides a master list of individual criteria within each of these categories. The identification of the most important site characteristics for a project is crucial. This requires a familiarity and experience with the particular project type, and a broad knowledge of construction and

Market-Related Criteria	
Proximity and Accessibility to: • Attractions and events • Competitors • Facilities (accommodations, restaurants, shopping) • Potential visitor markets • Transportation facilities	**Visibility:** • If required, is site visible to potential visitors? • If required, is site sufficiently private?

Physical Characteristics	

Aesthetics:
• Adjoining lands and land uses
• Focal points
• Noise
• Scale
• Variety (features, forms, colors)
• Views
 	
Geology and Geomorphology:
• Bedrock type
• Geologic history
• Water-table level and quality
• Infrastructure availability:
  • Energy sources
  • Sewage disposal system
  • Transportation facilities and systems
  • Water supply (drainage and flooding problems, lakes and seas, natural springs, rivers and streams, waterfalls and cascades)
 	
Natural Conditions:
• Ability to support specific types of recreational activities
• Climate and micro-climate (humidity, precipitation, purity of air, seasons, sunshine and clouds, temperatures, winds)
	Soils and Topography:
	• Depths
	• Slopes
	• Soil types
	• Vegetation:
	  • Clearing problems
	  • Ground cover type
	  • Tree types
	  • Visual and physical condition
	
	Wildlife and Fish:
	• Effects of development on these
	• Species and types
	
	Other Site Characteristics:
	• Dimensions and shape
	• Geographical orientation
	• Height above sea level
	• Length of shoreline
	• Rights of way and easements

Other Criteria	
• Availability of a suitable quality of land for project • Availability of staff accommodation • Cost of land • Labor laws and labor relations history	• Manpower availability • Social and economic characteristics of host area • Sources and types of financial assistance in host area • Zoning laws and other government regulations

FIGURE 6.25 Master list of site selection criteria.

site engineering. Ideally, a multidisciplinary team consisting of a specialized tourism consultant, engineer, environmental and social impact experts, landscape architect, architect, and transportation planner should be used.

When a specific site has not been selected, a "long list" of potentially suitable sites is identified; these sites are ranked on their compatibility with the project. This ranking can be done by attaching a weighting factor to each site selection characteristic and giving each site a numerical score for that characteristic. The weighting factor reflects the relative importance of each site characteristic, and the numerical score (say on a 0 to 10 basis) indicates the quality or quantity of that characteristic for the site. The multiplication of the weighting factor and the numerical score provides a final score for each characteristic at each alternative site. The final scores for all characteristics are added to give a total score for each alternative site. The most appropriate site for the project is the one earning the highest total score.

The evaluation of sites for certain tourism projects requires a high degree of specific technical expertise. Generally, these projects are highly dependent on the characteristics of the natural resource base and have high construction costs, such as alpine skiing areas, golf courses, and large full-service marina projects. Private organizations specializing in site evaluations for projects are normally contracted to perform these analyses.

An economic feasibility study may be terminated after the site analysis if an essential site characteristic is missing or if some insurmountable legal or zoning restriction or other barrier to development is found. The study moves on to the market analysis if this is not the case.

- **Market analysis**

The market analysis portion of an economic feasibility study is often the most costly and time-consuming element. The costs and time required are dependent on the mix of primary and secondary research conducted. Secondary research is the analysis of available, published sources of information and is far less expensive than primary research. Market surveys aimed at producing new information and conclusions for the project are classified as primary research. Although pre-feasibility studies are often based only on secondary research, detailed economic feasibility studies must contain a mixture of both secondary and primary research.

Secondary Research. The market analysis starts with the collection and review of secondary sources of information since this provides a clearer focus on the type and scope of primary market research needed. With the growing attention being given to tourism on a worldwide basis, the amount of available tourism research is enormous. An analysis of secondary sources in tourism can be time-consuming and exhausting, unless the researcher knows about the major tourism journals, reference centers, libraries, and online sources of information.

Primary Research. When the review of secondary sources of information is complete, a primary research plan is drawn up and implemented. This may involve conducting surveys or using other research methods. It requires that the researchers have a thorough understanding of market research techniques.

1. *Survey questionnaires*: Questionnaires are the most frequently used instruments in tourism project feasibility studies. Researchers direct their questions to potential visitors or to the managers of competitive or similar operations. In the latter case, the questions are aimed at gathering information on the facilities and services offered, and on the existing market volumes and characteristics through such competitive performance statistics as room occupancy rates or attendance figures. The common factor in all questionnaires is that they require responses (written or oral) to questions (written or oral). The three major advantages of questionnaires are versatility, speed, and cost. Questionnaires are versatile because almost every research problem can be addressed, including the respondent's knowledge, opinions, motivations, and intentions. The use of questionnaires is usually faster and cheaper than the observational method of research. The observational method is a process of observing and studying the behavior of people, objects, and occurrences rather than of questioning people to get the same information.

   The questionnaire method has recognized limitations. Respondents may be unwilling to provide the information. They may not agree to be interviewed or refuse to answer specific questions. Mail surveys typically have low response rates with sometimes as many as 90 percent of the questionnaires not being returned. Skilled and experienced researchers can bring the response rates up to 40 percent or more. Online surveys also typically have low response rates. Personal and telephone surveys have higher response rates. A second disadvantage of questionnaires is that the respondent may be willing to cooperate but is unable to provide accurate answers to some questions. For example, the respondents may not have thought through their motivations for particular purchases or activities. A third limitation of questionnaires is that the respondent may intentionally supply incorrect or inaccurate information. Some respondents may give the types of answers that they think the researchers want, or they may deliberately give misleading information. Others may answer in a particular way so as not to be embarrassed or to have their egos damaged. Respondents may also wrongly interpret the meanings of particular questions and may give less than satisfactory answers.

Broad-scale questionnaire surveys, although relatively inexpensive when compared to other market research techniques, can be very expensive if they are conducted at the individual household level. This is particularly true if the potential users reside in countries distant from the destination area. Unlike consumer product research, market research using broad-scale questionnaires may encounter difficulties in determining the exact geographical origins of potential users of a tourism project and their relative proportions. Because there are these problems in defining the statistical universe, it is also extremely difficult to accurately state what the size and structure of a sample should be.

Due to the unique challenges in conducting surveys of potential users of proposed tourism projects, it is common to survey people in the channels of distribution (retail travel agencies, tour wholesalers, and tour operators) and other travel decision-makers (such as convention-meeting planners, corporate travel managers, and association executives) or to utilize the focus group, Delphi, or case study methods as a supplement to questionnaire surveys.

2. *Focus groups:* The focus-group method involves bringing together a small group of people (ideally eight to twelve) in one place and asking them to focus upon the research topic. The research team supplies an experienced focus group moderator. The objectives of these sessions are to get the group to reach consensus on questions posed by the moderator. The focus group can be drawn from householders in general, or each participant may have common characteristics, such as being convention-meeting planners, retail travel agents, tour operators, tour wholesalers, or club executives. Because focus-group participants tend to interact with one another and because there is a greater opportunity to explore individual preferences and attitudes, this method overcomes some of

the drawbacks of questionnaires. Focus-group participants are often prescreened before being invited to the meetings.

3. *Delphi method:* The Delphi method is often used for forecasting and future exercises in tourism, but it can be applied to a tourism development project. It can be called the "knowledgeable panel" method since it involves recruiting a team of experts on a particular topic. The team acts as a sounding board on alternative approaches, ideas, or concepts. The Delphi group participants do not have to meet in person, but each one is required to give responses to a variety of written propositions prepared by the researchers, such as "What probability do you attach to this resort succeeding at this location?" (Provide a probability percentage between 0 percent and 100 percent.)

4. *Case studies*: Another method that has been used for some tourism projects is analogy or case study research. This does not involve any surveying of potential visitors; it means doing detailed research on the performance of comparable (or analogous) operations. By studying the success of comparable projects, conclusions are drawn on the likely success of the proposed project. Because many factors contribute to a tourism business' success, analogy research must be applied with great caution.

5. *Forecasting:* In economic feasibility studies, it is often necessary to forecast demand for either the project itself or for the destination area in general, or for both. There are many forecasting techniques available to the researcher. Forecasts are divided into time spans that are considered to be accurate. There is general agreement that there are four basic forecasting horizons: short-term (one day to two years), medium-term (between three and five years), long-term (more than five to fifteen years), and futurism (more than fifteen years). For example, the extrapolation method is thought only to be useful for short-term forecasts, while correlation techniques are considered to be good for short-, medium-, and long-term forecasting.

The forecasting of potential market demand for a project usually covers the medium-term to long-term forecasts, that is, the initial five to fifteen years of operation. This seems appropriate since the critical financial years of a purely commercial project are its first one to ten years. Most commercial tourism projects are expected to reach their full financial and operating potential within their first five years of operation and to pay back their investor's equity within ten years. Also the present value concept dictates that the earlier the financial returns are received from a project the greater is their contribution to economic feasibility.

The actual forecasting of potential demand levels for a tourism development project can be approached through several different methods. It is advisable to use two or more of the methods shown in Figure 6.26 and then to cross-check their results. Once a technically acceptable potential market demand forecast has been developed, an initial judgment can be made as to whether the market is of sufficient size with the appropriate characteristics to support the project. This requires considerable experience with the business type being considered. It has to be very clear that the potential demand levels are large enough to make the project viable. For example, if a hotel requires an annual occupancy percentage of 70 percent to be viable, and the potential demand generates an occupancy rate of only 30 percent in the project's fifth year, the proposed hotel will not be viable. In most cases, this judgment is not so obvious, and more analysis needs to be done to determine if the demand levels justify the investment.

• **Economic feasibility analysis**

The economic feasibility analysis determines if a tourism development project can produce a satisfactory financial return for investors. It is composed of the following seven steps:

1. *Project description:* The forecasts of potential market demand and the desires and expectations of people interviewed provide the key inputs for detailing the project concept. The project concept describes the components, scale, sizes, and quality levels of facilities and services needed to satisfy the potential demand. Unit prices and rates are then prepared.

2. *Pricing:* The next two steps are referred to as the production of forecast or *pro forma* income statements indicating the estimated revenues, operating expenses, and operating profits for the project.

3. *Revenues:* When estimating revenues, the total potential demand is broken down into segments, and the applicable unit prices and rates are multiplied by the resulting volumes in each segment.

4. *Expenses and profits:* The operating expenses include the costs of operating the project, such as the cost of food and other merchandise for resale, labor, marketing, energy, and repairs and maintenance. Publications containing average business performance statistics can be helpful in estimating these operating costs. Greater individual accuracy occurs when the forecaster is familiar with the type of business under consideration, and when detailed staffing schedules and other operating standards are developed for the project.

5. *Capital costs:* There are other ongoing expenses that the project will encounter, and these all relate to the capital investment in the development. To estimate these expenses requires that a capital budget be prepared first. A capital budget is a detailed, itemized forecast of the capital investment required by the project. For a tourism development project, these costs include building construction, professional fees, infrastructure, recreational facilities, furniture,

Methods	Description of Approaches
Alternative scenario	Uses the calculation, market share/penetration, or survey/potential demand quantification methods and produces optimistic, realistic, and pessimistic scenarios of potential demand levels.
Analogy	Assumes that the project will achieve certain demand levels based upon the known performances and penetration levels of similar projects elsewhere.
Calculation	Projects potential demand by using "rules-of-thumb" or consumer expenditures and behavior patterns.
Market share or market penetration	Calculates total market demand and the project's share of total demand by using information from competitive facilities, historic demand growth rates, and anticipated future occurrences, or other forecasting techniques.
Survey and potential demand	Quantifies total potential demand by using the results from questionnaire or other survey methods, by "grossing up" from the sample size taken.

FIGURE 6.26 Forecasting methods and approaches.

fixtures and equipment, interim financing, contingencies, and miscellaneous other items. The most realistic capital budgets are produced by a multidisciplinary team consisting of specialized tourism consultants, civil engineers, quantity surveyors, interior designers, architects, landscape architects, and transportation planners. The capital budget is prepared by identifying all of the capital costs that will be encountered, and then pricing each item. A contingency factor, normally between 10 and 20 percent, is added to cover unforeseen cost overruns or overlooked items. Once the capital budget is complete, the capital-related expenses for the project are calculated. These expenses include financing charges on long-term debt, depreciation, municipal/local government taxes, and insurance premiums on fixed assets.

6. *Cash flow:* The capital-related expenses are deducted from the operating profits to give net income figures (after tax profit) and cash flow forecasts. The net income and cash flow projections cover the useful life of the project.

7. *Return on investment (ROI):* One or more financial analysis techniques are used to measure the rate of return produced by these forecast net income and cash flow levels. Most experts in the field favor present value yardsticks that use the discounted cash flow (DCF) method, especially the net present value (NPV) and internal rate of return (IRR) techniques. The present value concept implies that money has a time value. Thus, a dollar, euro, or pound received today is worth more than a dollar, euro, or pound received a year from now, since the cash received today can be reinvested to produce a higher overall return. With present value methods, the cash received in profits in the earlier years are more valuable than those earned in later years. Both the NPV and IRR techniques use cash flow figures as a basis for projections and discount the value of future cash flows at certain assumed rates of return. Based upon the rates of return predicted, a decision is made as to whether the tourism development project is economically feasible. If the rate is less than what the investors require, the project is not economically feasible.

The positive impact of government financial incentives upon a project's economic feasibility has not been discussed. Many tourism projects, which are not economically feasible with only private-sector financing, are developed because of the injection of government financial assistance. These incentives increase the rates of return for investors by reducing the interest burden on projects or reducing financing costs in some other way. In many cases, the increases are great enough to change a project into a feasible venture. However, if a project is not feasible and there is no possibility of receiving government financial assistance, it will probably be terminated at this point.

Cost/Benefit Analysis

Profit-making projects that are found to be economically feasible may or may not have to be further analyzed using cost/benefit analysis. Cost/benefit analyses are useful for evaluating non-commercial tourism projects that generate no direct revenues or that have, at best, operating revenues equaling operating expenses. Cost/benefit analyses are done by or on behalf of government agencies. They help these agencies measure and weigh all of the costs and benefits of alternative projects. The agencies are then able to determine which project will produce the largest net economic benefits for society as a whole.

Economic feasibility analyses are just one aspect of cost/benefit analysis. There are several financial analyses or capital budgeting techniques available that permit comparisons between alternative projects. In purely financial terms, the project that creates the highest rate of return for its investors is the best alternative. However, from a government viewpoint, the size of the return on private investors' capital cannot be the only criterion for support. A government agency has broad-scale economic, environmental, social, and cultural responsibilities that have to be considered before giving financial assistance or other support to a project. For example, a proposed casino may generate spectacular returns for investors, but a government agency may feel that such a project will undermine the social well-being of the destination area.

A cost/benefit analysis attempts to weigh the quantifiable and non-quantifiable costs and benefits of a tourism project against each other. Some subjectivity and judgment has to enter into this because there can be no single measurement or set of measurements of a project's overall worth to a destination. Assuming that the cost/benefit analysis results are positive, the project can progress to the next level of evaluation. Some project developers may wish to apply for government financial assistance, while others may go ahead without such assistance.

Environmental Impact Analysis

An environmental impact analysis is "a process of evaluating the likely environmental impacts of a proposed project or development, taking into account inter-related socio-economic, cultural and human-health impacts, both beneficial and adverse" (Convention on Biological Diversity 2017). According to UNEP-CBD, the following steps should be included in an EIA:

1. *Screening:* Which projects require a full or partial EIA?
2. *Scoping:* Which potential impacts should be assessed?
3. *Assessment and evaluation of impacts and development of alternatives:* What are the likely environmental impacts, and which alternative approaches can be followed?
4. *Reporting the Environmental Impact Statement (EIS) or EIA report:* What are the contents of the EIS or EIA? This must include an Environment Management Plan.
5. *Review of the Environmental Impact Statement (EIS) or EIA report:* Who should be consulted and how should the EIS/EIA results be shared?
6. *Decision-making:* Should the development be approved or not?
7. *Monitoring, compliance, enforcement and environmental auditing:* How successful was the Environmental Management? (EMP)

Many countries require that EIAs be conducted before final government approval is given. These analyses are usually paid for by the developers and conducted by expert consultants. The consultants attempt to predict and evaluate the impact of the tourism development project on various environmental attributes (e.g., beaches and coastlines, wetlands, flora, and fauna). They also recommend environmental safeguards that must be taken to ensure that the development does not cause the adverse impacts that have been predicted. Governments often require that the developer and their consultants establish a process of public input into the EIA.

There is growing public concern for the impact of developments on the environment. Around the world, several proposed tourism projects have been vigorously opposed by conservation and other interest groups (see Quick Trip 6.4 about Benoa Bay, Bali) (Langenheim 2016). So great has been the protests that the developers have given up on the projects. There can be no doubt that these types of public opposition on environmental grounds will continue in the future as society becomes more environmentally sensitive. This will place an even greater premium on careful planning by developers and the adoption of "best environmental practices."

Detailed Design and Construction

In the final stages of realizing a tourism development project, various levels of architectural designs and drawings are prepared. Normally, this procedure includes:

- Preparation of preliminary architectural concepts
- Preparation of a preliminary architectural design
- Preparation of a final architectural design
- Construction

At each of the first three stages, the drawings become increasingly more detailed and exact. When the final drawings have been approved, the project moves into construction.

SUMMARY

Tourism development must be sustainable and in harmony with the local environment and residents' quality of life. This means that all tourism developments must consider environmental, economic, and social-cultural impacts (the triple bottom line).

The tourism destination plan provides overall guidelines for development, and identifies project development opportunities worthy of more in-depth analysis through economic feasibility studies, cost/benefit analyses, and environmental impact assessments. Governments play a key role in ensuring that developers abide by the overall guidelines and the broad development concepts are realized. Government agencies are also playing an ever-increasing role in stimulating the development of tourism project opportunities through many types of financial incentive programs.

Only a small proportion of tourism project development opportunities actually reach the construction stage, as most are unable to meet certain criteria or to secure the necessary financing. Many are screened out because they are not economically feasible or due to environmental impacts that are expected to be adverse and unacceptable.

ACTIVITIES

1. You are asked to prepare an economic feasibility study on a new tourism development project in your area. What are the major steps that you would include in this economic feasibility study?
2. What secondary sources of information would be the most useful in doing this study?
3. What primary research would you conduct in preparing the study (e.g., surveys, focus groups)?
4. How would you use the Internet to gather information on the potential markets for the new tourism development project?
5. Identify up to five comparable projects that you could analyze online that would provide good benchmark information for your project. Analyze these comparable projects and prepare your results.
6. How would you use online sources to get information on the likely capital costs of this project?

ACRONYMS

3BL (triple bottom line)
CBT (community-based tourism)
CSR (corporate social responsibility)
DMO (destination management organization)
EIA (environmental impact assessment)
IRR (internal rate of return)
NGO (non-governmental organization)
NPV (net present value)
ROI (return on investment)
UNESCO (United Nationals Educational, Scientific and Cultural Organization)
UNWTO (United Nations World Tourism Organization)
WWF (World Wide Fund for Nature)

REFERENCES

AECOM. 2017. Global Attractions Attendance Report.

Bulgarian Association of Alternative Tourism. 2018. What is alternative tourism? http://www.baatbg.org/?lang=2

Callot, P. 2013. Slow Tourism. In: Idowu, S. O., Capaldi, N., Zu, L., Gupta, A. D. (Eds). Encyclopedia of Corporate Social Responsibility. Heidelberg; Springer.

CBT Vietnam. 2017. What is community based tourism? http://www.cbtvietnam.com/communitybasedtourism/

Convention on Biological Diversity. 2017. What is impact assessment? https://www.cbd.int/impact/whatis.shtml

Eden Project. 2017. Sustainability Policy. http://www.edenproject.com/eden-story/about-us/sustainability-policy

Gardens by the Bay. 2017. Sustainability Efforts. http://www.gardensbythebay.com.sg/en/the-gardens/sustainability-efforts.html

Indiana Department of Natural Resources. 2017. Indiana State Park Inns. http://www.in.gov/dnr/parklake/2435.htm

International Social Tourism Organisation. 2017. Definitions. http://www.oits-isto.org/oits/public/section.jsf?id=39

Kentucky State Parks. 2017. Lodges. http://parks.ky.gov/places_to_stay/lodges/

Langenheim, J. 2016. Mounting opposition to Bali mass tourism project. *The Guardian*, March 22. https://www.theguardian.com/environment/the-coral-triangle/2016/mar/22/mounting-opposition-to-bali-mass-tourism-project

National Geographic. 2018. Geotourism. https://www.nationalgeographic.com/maps/geotourism/

The Nature Conservancy. 2017. Eco-trips and travel. What is ecotourism? https://www.nature.org/greenliving/what-is-ecotourism.xml

Paradores. 2017. Corporate information. http://www.parador.es/en/corporate-information

Pintassilgo, P. 2016. Green Tourism. In: Jafari, J., Xiao, H. (Eds). Encyclopedia of Tourism. Cham, Switzerland: Springer. https://link.springer.com/referenceworkentry/10.1007%2F978-3-319-01384-8_264

Pollock, A. 2013. Six reasons why mass tourism is unsustainable. *The Guardian*, August 21.

Responsible Tourism Partnership. 2017. OverTourism. http://responsibletourismpartnership.org/overtourism/

Responsible Tourism Partnership. 2018. Cape Town Declaration on Responsible Tourism. http://responsible tourismpartnership.org/cape-town-declaration-on-responsible-tourism/

Robert Trent Jones Golf Trail. 2017. Robert Trent Jones Golf Trail. https://www.rtjgolf.com/

Southern Literary Trail. 2017. Southern Literary Trail. http://www.southernliterarytrail.org/

Theng, S., Qiong, X., and Tatar, C. 2015. Mass tourism vs. alternative tourism: Challenges and new positionings. *Etudes caribéenes*. https://etudescaribeennes.revues.org/7708?lang=en

Tourism Concern. 2018. About Tourism Concern. https://www.tourismconcern.org.uk/about/

Tourism & More. 2016. Mass versus boutique tourism: The advantages and disadvantages of both. http://www.tourismandmore.com/tidbits/mass-versus-boutique-tourism-the-advantages-and-disadvantages-of-both/

United Nations. 1987. Report of the World Commission on Environment and Development: Our Common Future. http://www.un-documents.net/wced-ocf.htm

United Nations. 2015. *Sustainable Development Goals: 17 Goals to Transform Our World*. http://www.un.org/sustainabledevelopment/sustainable-development-goals/

UNWTO. 2016. Why tourism? http://www.tourism4development2017.org/

UNWTO. 2017. Sustainable Development of Tourism. http://sdt.unwto.org/content/about-us-5

UNWTO and European Travel Commission. 2011. Handbook on Tourism Product Development. Madrid, Spain.

WWF. 2017. Reducing the impacts of tourism. http://wwf.panda.org/what_we_do/how_we_work/our_global_goals/oceans/solutions/reducing_tourism_impact/

Yang, Y. 2015. Implementation strategies of low-carbon tourism. The Open Cybernetics & Systemics Journal, 9, 2003-2007

PART TWO

Marketing
Strategy, Planning, Branding, and Promotion

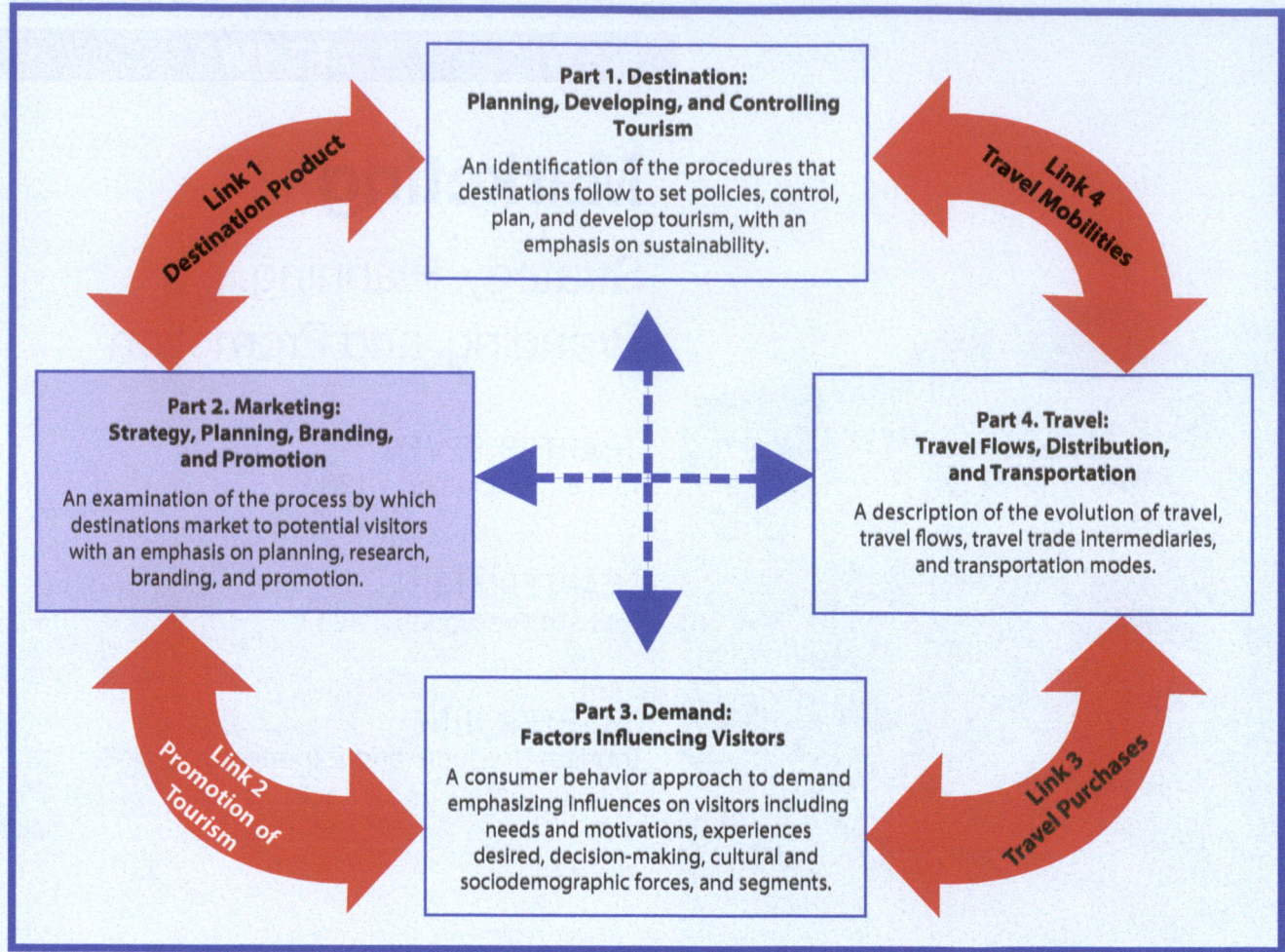

**Part 1. Destination:
Planning, Developing, and Controlling
Tourism**

An identification of the procedures that destinations follow to set policies, control, plan, and develop tourism, with an emphasis on sustainability.

**Part 2. Marketing:
Strategy, Planning, Branding,
and Promotion**

An examination of the process by which destinations market to potential visitors with an emphasis on planning, research, branding, and promotion.

**Part 4. Travel:
Travel Flows, Distribution,
and Transportation**

A description of the evolution of travel, travel flows, travel trade intermediaries, and transportation modes.

**Part 3. Demand:
Factors Influencing Visitors**

A consumer behavior approach to demand emphasizing influences on visitors including needs and motivations, experiences desired, decision-making, cultural and sociodemographic forces, and segments.

Link 1
Destination Product

Link 4
Travel Mobilities

Link 2
Promotion of Tourism

Link 3
Travel Purchases

An examination of the process by which destinations market to potential visitors with an emphasis on planning, research, branding, and promotion.

Now in the second part of the system, destinations must reach people in the market and encourage them to travel by using marketing principles and techniques. The uniqueness of tourism marketing is explained. The processes of *market segmentation* and *positioning*, and the application of the *product life cycle*, are described. A step-by-step procedure for marketing is introduced. Destination *positioning* and *branding* are reviewed.

Marketing success depends to a large extent on effective communications through *promotion*.

LINK 2: PROMOTION OF TOURISM

The link between Parts 2 and 3 (Marketing and Demand) is called the *promotion of tourism*. A change in the marketing approach may cause a change in the market. Often, it is the other way around, there is a shift in demand, and marketing is changed accordingly. When people started to take shorter vacations (Demand), tourism destinations and suppliers began to offer short-break and weekend getaway packages (Marketing).

CHAPTER SEVEN

Tourism Marketing

Bringing All of the Parts of Tourism Together

To lift a destination brand from the pages of a strategic plan, put meaning behind words of a promise and bring it into existence requires a unique plan of action.

DESTINATION BRANDSCIENCE, *Courtesy of Destination Marketing Association International*

YOUR LEARNING DESTINATION

You'll be able to describe tourism marketing, how it is different from traditional product marketing, and how it is planned and executed.

WHAT YOU NEED TO KNOW

Having read this chapter, you will be able to:

- ✔ Describe the differences between the marketing of tourism services and traditional product marketing.
- ✔ Compare and contrast the different approaches to marketing associated with production, sales, marketing, and societal marketing orientations.
- ✔ Explain the concept of market segmentation and how target markets are selected.
- ✔ Define branding and positioning and explain how they are used in tourism.
- ✔ List and describe the elements of the marketing mix.
- ✔ Describe each of the steps of the marketing planning process in tourism.

BREAKING THE ICE

Do you have a bucket list of places that you'd like to visit or tourism experiences that you'd like to do? How did you find out about these things? Did you read about them online or see an interesting advertisement in a magazine? How far along are you in your planning? Is it just a vague idea at the moment or have you started planning in earnest? Tourism marketers work to ensure you are aware of their products and services and excited to use them. They work to help move you along the buying process and to ensure that you have a great experience when you do actually take that bucket list trip. In this chapter we'll look at how they do it.

KEY TAKEAWAY POINTS

- Marketing is a management process that creates value for consumers by satisfying their wants and needs and achieves the organization's objectives.
- Understanding the customer is critical for marketers. Analysis of "big data" is providing new insights for marketers.
- Market segmentation, choosing a target market, and positioning are important concepts in marketing.
- Markets may be segmented in a variety of ways. Common ways of segmenting the market include demographic, socio-economic, family life cycle, geographic, purpose-of-trip, behavioral, psychographic, benefit or attribute, product-related, or channel of distribution.
- Target markets must be viable—they must be s ubstantial, accessible, measurable, defensible, durable, competitive, homogeneous, and compatible with the company's objectives.

- Companies market to groups beyond consumers. They may market to internal stakeholders, like their employees, or external stakeholders, like special interest group or the government.

- Marketers create value using a wide variety of activities and processes. These activities are sometimes categorized as the eight Ps of marketing—Place, Price, Promotion, Product, Partnerships, Packaging, Programming, and People. Within each of these categories are a wide range of techniques and activities.

- Brands—the set of associations people have of a product or service—can be an important asset for a company or destination. Strategies to develop brands are an important task of marketers.

- The marketing planning process follows the five-step planning cycle and answers the key questions—Where are we now? Where would we like to be? How do we get there? How do we make sure we get there? How do we know we got there?

WHAT IS TOURISM MARKETING?

"Tourism marketing" is one of those terms that everyone uses but each person seems to have a slightly different definition. To help get us "on the same page" it is worthwhile to review some definitions of marketing and then to examine ways these definitions have been applied to tourism. Kotler, an influential marketing professor, defines marketing as the "art and science of exploring, creating, and delivering value to satisfy the needs of a target market at a profit" (Kotler, Bowen, and Makens 2015). This definition captures the importance of focusing on delivering value to the consumer. In 2013 the American Marketing Association (AMA) revealed their updated definition of marketing. Marketing is "the activity, set of institutions and processes for creating, communicating, delivering and exchanging offerings that have value for customers, clients, partners and society at large" (American Marketing Association 2013). It is worth noting that while customers come first, marketers are creating, communicating, delivering, and exchanging offerings for other stakeholders including partners and society at-large. It is easy to see the AMA definition being applied to tourism.

Tourism marketing has also been defined as a "continuous, sequential process through which management in the hospitality and travel industry plans, researches, implements, controls and evaluates activities designed to satisfy both customer needs and wants and their own organization's objectives" (Morrison 2010).

In this book you'll apply key concepts from both definitions. Our focus will recognize that:

- Marketing is primarily consumer focused. It creates value by meeting the needs of consumers and other stakeholders. This consumer focus is the foundation of a marketing orientation.

- Marketing is applied to stakeholders beyond customers. Marketing can be applied to internal stakeholders and external stakeholders including the distribution network.

- Marketing is a management process. It requires planning, organizing, and controlling actions to meet specific goals. It is a continuous, sequential process to create value for consumers and for the company.

MARKETING ORIENTATION

As an essential first step in marketing, an overall marketing orientation must be developed to guide marketing efforts. This philosophy sets the tone for every subsequent decision. Although several different orientations are possible, experience has shown that they are not all equally effective.

Production Orientation. Some organizations' marketing efforts are guided by a ***production orientation***. With a production orientation, the greatest emphasis is placed on the services or products provided to the visitor. For example, a destination area may have many physical, heritage, and cultural resources. The extent to which the destination's resources are better than those of its competitors determines, in part, how many people visit the destination. This orientation was used at one time by the local authorities in a town on the south coast of England. They decided in the late 1960s to print brochures only in English. It was pointed out that a major potential market was the French residents across the English Channel, but their reply was that if the French wanted to visit, then they should be interested enough to learn to read English in order to understand what was available. Although it cannot be denied that resources are important, a total emphasis on tourism supply fails to recognize the visitor's needs and expectations. A production orientation is only successful if there is a surplus of demand over supply (which rarely happens in the modern, highly competitive tourism environment). In this case, the destination or company that offers the best product will get the visitor. An old adage says, "Build a better mousetrap, and the world will beat a path to your door." Often referred to as the "better-mousetrap fallacy," this form of competitive advantage is normally short-lived in today's business climate.

It can be challenging for suppliers of travel to look beyond their product and consider the consumer needs they are satisfying. For example, a hotelier may be excited about specific attributes of the room and focus their marketing message on the product attributes, forgetting the main benefit of their hotel is the view outside the window.

Sales Orientation. When supply exceeds demand, the problem becomes, "How can I sell all these mousetraps?" The number of destinations actively seeking tourism has increased as has the number of travel destinations throughout the world with easy accessibility. The emergence of more professional destination management organizations, tour operators, travel agencies, the Internet, and social media has increased the intensity of competition for the visitor dollar, euro, and pound. It has meant that destination areas can no longer sit back and wait for visitors to come to them. Visitors must be convinced of the benefits of traveling to a particular destination. This has caused a shift in orientation from emphasizing the product to intensified selling. The emphasis in this orientation is on promoting what is available for sale. Yet, this *sales orientation* still focuses on the needs of the seller—How can we sell more product?—rather than on the visitor's needs and wants— What will satisfy the visitor? The first priority here is to convince potential visitors that what is available for sale will please them.

Marketing Orientation. A newer development is an orientation in which the needs and wants of the visitors are the first priority for the marketer. This is called a *marketing orientation*. A tourism organization begins with the needs and wants of the visitor and attempts to provide the services to satisfy them. It involves being open when the visitor wants it to be open; serving breakfast when the visitor wants it rather than when it is convenient for management; providing the kind of experiences that visitors want rather than what we feel they should have. It is more prudent to say that, using the

earlier metaphor, an individual does not want to buy a mousetrap; rather, he or she wants to kill mice. Some say this is an exercise in "putting yourself in the visitor's shoes"; always try to see things from the visitor's viewpoint. If and when a better way is developed of satisfying a need, people are likely to try it. This marketing orientation will be reinforced later when an emphasis will be placed on the satisfaction of needs and wants.

Societal Marketing Orientation. Many tourism organizations have come to realize that they have a responsibility to society and local communities as well as to their visitors. Strictly concentrating on their visitors' needs and wants may cause long-term damage to the environment, society, and local communities. This contemporary view of marketing is consistent with the sustainable tourism development concept, or what others call responsible tourism.

Having a sense of social and community responsibility is especially important in tourism. A marketing orientation that concentrates solely on visitors' needs is not the ideal philosophy, even for the visitors themselves. A tourism destination relies on the resources of its community, which both visitors and residents share. To become totally marketing oriented, all aspects of the community would have to be oriented toward satisfying visitors' needs and wants. The risk for the community is that by orienting totally for visitors' needs, the needs, integrity, and long-term interests of the community and local residents may be harmed. Consider the situations explored in previous chapters of destination areas that have adapted to the needs of the visitor and, in the process, have lost their uniqueness, heritage, and natural resources while receiving a relatively poor economic return on investment. Destination areas that adapt their resources to satisfy visitors' needs may lose the very thing that makes them attractive and unique in the first place. The visitor is the ultimate loser, as more and more destinations take on an increasingly similar and familiar appearance.

The best solution to these potential problems with tourism is to develop a marketing approach that focuses on the satisfaction of visitor needs and wants while respecting the long-term interests of the community. This approach is referred to as a *societal marketing orientation*. This orientation provides for planning, development, and marketing activities that focus on the needs of the visitor, but that also consider the effects of these activities on the long-term interests of the community before any action is taken. It is also known as encouraging *sustainable tourism development* (as discussed in Chapter 5).

All marketing activities are influenced by the orientations of those people directly responsible for marketing. It is essential that these individuals' decisions reflect a predetermined philosophy or corporate culture that provides an overall guide for the development and marketing efforts of the destination or organization.

UNDERSTANDING YOUR CONSUMER

If marketing is about creating value by meeting the needs of the consumer, then understanding your consumer is a core task of the marketer. Ultimately, as a marketer you want to know the people who may buy from you, the consumers, so well that you can anticipate their needs and provide them with what they need—perhaps even before they have asked for it. This idea reminds me of the old-time storekeeper who knew his customers so well that he would have what they needed waiting in the store ready for them to ask for it—or would suggest a product he thought they could use based on his knowledge of their needs. He probably threw in a candy just to leave a smile on their faces. The storekeeper's clients were loyal to him and always bought from him because he really understood them and they had a personal relationship.

Big Data and Profiling the Consumer

Although many years have passed since the days of the old-time storekeeper, companies still want to achieve that level of customer loyalty. In recent years, the use of "big data" and profiling of individual consumers has replaced the memory-based system of the old-time storekeeper.

Every time you go online, or make a transaction, you leave information about yourself—your interests and wants. As you can imagine, there is an incredible amount of information being captured, which is why the information is called *"big data."* It's been only recently that our ability to analyze this data has caught up with our ability to collect it. The analysis of this information has become more sophisticated, allowing businesses to understand not only what you have done but also to develop projections of what you may be interested in and suggest it to you—just like the old-time storekeeper. You can see applications of big data everywhere if you look for it. It is in the suggestions Netflix gives you for shows you may like based on the shows you have watched, and it is in the coupons Target gives you when you check out.

The application of big data is moving marketers **to** the ideal of a *"one to one"* relationship with their customers. Many companies in the tourism system, including hotel companies, cruise companies, and gaming operations develop detailed consumer profiles on customers, combining spending behavior and shared consumer preferences with social media behavior and other sources of information. Marketers from some of tourism's largest intermediaries, including online travel agencies, develop sophisticated *algorithms* that anticipate consumer preferences and offer suggestions based on past purchases.

Despite the move to big data and customer profiling, the traditional marketing model of market segmentation, targeting, and positioning is still relevant and provides useful insights.

Market Segmentation

The application of big data is not universal. Many tourism companies lack the resources or market reach to take full advantage of big data. Another approach to building a deeper understanding of consumers is through building deep understanding of target markets through a process of market segmentation. *Market segmentation* is a recognized and universally accepted way of analyzing tourism markets and selecting from among them. Indeed, even companies using big data may also use market segmentation and target marketing techniques. Market segmentation is a process through which people with similar needs, wants, and characteristics are grouped together so that a tourism organization can use greater precision in serving and communicating with these people. Market segmentation is a two-step process: (1) deciding how to group all potential visitors (the *market segments*), and (2) selecting specific groups from among these (the *target markets*) to pursue.

The process of segmenting the tourism market should be the basis for *strategic* (long-term) marketing decisions. Market segmentation is more than a process for analyzing demand. It is a management tool that leads to specific marketing decisions. The development of a marketing strategy begins with the identification of market segments and their characteristics. With unlimited resources, a tourism company or destination may decide to develop unique offerings for every potential visitor market segment. However, no company has unlimited resources. Identifying a target market segment allows the company to focus its resources where it believes it can be most successful. Hotel companies like Marriott provide a great example of this approach. Marriott has thirty hotel brands that target market segments including the luxury market (Ritz-Carlton, St. Regis), leisure drive travelers and business traveling road warriors (Courtyard, Springhill Suites), and upscale business travelers (JW Marriott) to name just a few.

Segmenting the Market

Looking at all the ways of segmenting a market can be confusing. If there is just one market how can there be so many market segments? Morrison (2010) gives the analogy that it's a bit like shuffling a deck of cards in different ways—it's always the same deck but the cards are grouped in different ways. How a marketer segments the market is dependent on a number of factors including the resources available, the information that can be collected, and the sophistication of the marketer. Why marketers segment is more straightforward. They want to improve the efficiency and effectiveness of their marketing.

Seven Ways to Segment the Market

There are a number of methods that marketers use to segment the market. In the following section we will highlight seven of the most common techniques.

Demographic and Socioeconomic Segmentation. Many early segmentation studies in tourism used demographic and socioeconomic statistics as the basis for forming market segments. These remain the most commonly used today due to the relative ease of acquiring the statistical data, the comparability of the information through census as well as media-generated data, and the fact that the data are easy to understand and apply. For example, age and income have been very successful predictors of recreation participation. However, the use of only demographic data to segment markets has come under attack. The rapidly changing nature of society makes it impossible to rely solely on these data as a means of developing a marketing strategy. Just because a segment of people is of a particular age or income group does not necessarily mean they have similar travel preferences. Also, socioeconomic information does not give the marketer sufficient information about likes and dislikes to position the tourism destination or organization properly in the marketplace.

Greater success has been found in using demographic criteria that are *multivariate* (using two or more demographic variables). Status, for example, includes dimensions of income, education, and occupation.

© Monkey Business Images/Shutterstock.com

FIGURE 7.1 A vacation destination is marketed very differently to families with children than to young, single people.

Family life cycle is a composite of marital status, age, and the numbers and ages of children at home. Life cycle segmentation has proven to be an effective way of segmenting in a number of tourism and recreation cases.

It is unlikely that segmentation on the basis of demographics will ever be abandoned. Although other segmentation bases provide information useful for strategic decisions on what to offer in the way of tourism services, it is still necessary to communicate with an individual market segment. For all its shortcomings, demographic segmentation offers one of the best ways to access a specific segment of the market.

Geographic Segmentation.
Geographic considerations are very important to tourism. Much of the attractiveness of a visitor destination is based on contrasting cultures, climates, or scenery. This implies there being a certain distance between origin and destination. This book has already discussed the crucial role in tourism that the accessibility of a destination plays. In a simple example, many tourism organizations collect postcode or zip code information to understand where their current clients are coming from and then market to those postcodes. The logic goes that it can be effective to market to my current customers and their neighbors. The rationale that "birds of a feather flock together" is the basis of very sophisticated marketing based on geocoding. The VALS study described in detail in the psychographic section uses geocoding to identify where people in the segments they identify can be found. National and state tourism organizations tend to use geographic segmentation for the purposes of guiding promotional efforts. National tourism statistics have traditionally been collected by country of origin, and marketing priorities are set according to the contributions of each country to total arrivals.

Purpose-of-Trip Segmentation.
The established tradition in tourism is to divide the market into two broad purpose-of-trip segments: (1) business and (2) pleasure/personal travel markets. A modified version of this approach was used in a segmentation study of a hotel located in Singapore. Two broad segments were first defined: (1) the group segment and (2) the individual segment. The group segment was then further subdivided into group tours, conventions, corporate meetings, and airline crews. The individual segment consisted of corporate, full-rate and miscellaneous, frequent travelers, and group-inclusive tours. The research for this study showed that purpose of trip was a better way of

Demographic and Socioeconomic

Age, education, gender, income, family size and composition, family life cycle stage, social class, type of residence/home ownership status, second home ownership, race or ethnic group, occupation

Geographic

Country, region, market area, urban/suburban/rural, city size, population density, ZIP code or postal code, neighborhood

Purpose of Trip

Regular business travel; business travel related to meetings, conventions, exhibitions, and congresses; incentive travel; visiting friends and relatives; close-to-home leisure trips; touring vacation; city trip; outdoors vacation; resort vacation; cruise trip; visit to theme park; festival or event visit

Behavioral

Volume of use, frequency of use, usage status, use occasions, brand loyalty, benefits sought, lengths of stay, transportation modes used, expenditure levels, experience preferences, activity participation patterns

Psychographic

Lifestyle, attitudes/interests/opinions, values

Product-Related

Recreation activity, equipment type, price level, type of hotel/resort property

Channel-of-Distribution

Principal function, area of specialization, size and structure, geographic location

FIGURE 7.2 Tourism market segmentation bases and characteristics.

differentiating segments than nationality or income (Mehta and Vera 1990).

Behavioral Segmentation.
Behavioral segmentation divides customers by their usage rates, benefits sought, use occasions, usage status and potential, and brand loyalty (Kotler, Bowen, and Makens 2015). Usage rate was increasingly used by the tourism industry in the 1980s and 1990s, especially as greater attention was focused on frequent travelers.

QUICK TRIP 7.1

Marketing Trends in Latin America

Tracking market trends is an important task for any marketer. Sabre, the largest Global Distribution System (GDS), provides information services to airlines, and the travel industry. Many travel agents book travel products through Sabre. In 2017 Sabre released its report "The Latin American Traveler" that identified six trends of particular importance to hoteliers. The trends identified were:

1. **Status Seekers:** The Pursuit of Status Travel stories are a great way to gain status and as travel opportunities have increased, many Latin Americans are ready to share their experiences on social media.
2. **Local Love:** The Importance of Local Context. Latin American travelers are seeking authenticity, culture, and environmentally friendly experiences. They are celebratory of all things "local."
3. **Post Demographic:** The Death of Demographic Segmentation. Economic, social, and technological forces are shifting traditional demographic segments and Latin Americans are constructing identities more freely than ever before. One particular important change is the role of women and their increasing freedom to travel and explore.
4. **Ubitech:** Technology is everywhere and Latin Americans, like people from all over the world, expect service "on demand" via technology. Technology is helping many Latin Americans feel safer than ever before when traveling.
5. **InfoLust:** The need for relevant and actionable information. The growth of smartphone technology means travelers are seeking the right information at the right time—in digestible, intuitive, and actionable formats.
6. **Playsumers:** The Ageless Quest for Fun. Latin Americans are expecting their brands to adopt a playfulness as consumers seek less constrained and "proper" experiences. Latin Americans want to experience—not just observe.

This about This

1. This list of trends describes trends in Latin America. To what extent do you feel they represent global trends?
2. If demographic segmentation is "dead," what techniques would you suggest marketers use to segment the markets in Latin America?
3. In your opinion—what are the most important drivers of these trends? What is causing these changes?

Source

Sabre: The Latin American Traveler 2017.

Latin Americans are embracing local culture and fun.

FIGURE 7.3 Adventure seekers are an important market for nature-based tourism.

Heavy-half segmentation is an example of usage-rate or use frequency segmentation. Some attempts have been made in recreation and tourism to use this segmentation base. Heavy-half segmentation refers to the idea of segmenting a market on the basis of quantity purchased or consumed. As with other types of products, however, heavy-half segmentation has been found lacking. The major problem is that the characteristics of the heavy half (the major purchasers) have been found to be similar to those of the light half. Similar difficulties have been found with segmentation on the basis of brand loyalty.

Benefit or Attribute Segmentation is becoming a popular segmentation base in tourism. It involves segmenting a market according to the relative importance assigned to benefits that visitors expect to realize after purchasing the product. The relative importance of specific product benefits to prospective visitors is determined. Clusters of people are formed who attach similar degrees of importance to the same product benefits. The results can have important ramifications for developing new products and advertising messages. However, it is necessary to develop demographic profiles of the benefit clusters to reach them.

Use-occasion Segmentation is enjoying greater popularity in tourism. Perhaps the best example of this is the growing number of resorts and destinations pursuing the honeymooner market. Here, the use-occasion is a honeymoon. The Japanese and Korean honeymooner market has drawn special attention among destinations in the Asia-Pacific region. Destinations such as Australia, Hawaii, Hong Kong, and Singapore have been particularly successful in appealing to these honeymooners.

Psychographic Segmentation. Although expensive to use and difficult to carry out, this newer technique of market segmentation can be helpful in describing visitors. It is especially useful in highly specialized and extensively developed markets where psychographic profiles supplement the information gained from simpler analyses. Demographic data may be likened to the bones of a skeleton; psychographic data represents the flesh. The bones form the basis of the structure, but it is only by covering the form with flesh that the features become recognizable. Information about an individual's attitudes, interests, and opinions gives a much clearer picture of the people in a market segment.

The VALS™ (Values and Life Styles) program is one of the most widely recognized applications of psychographic segmentation in the United States. There are other psychographic or lifestyle segmentation methods available, including the Prizm NE and Acorn system.

Product-Related Segmentation. A major advantage of segmenting by means of product-related variables is that the information gained is directly related to the particular tourism service under consideration. Indeed, a major flaw in some studies is that information is sought from the potential visitor that deals with general benefits sought or, in the case of psychographic segmentation, general attitudes about types of products and services, rather than about specific products and services.

Channel-of-Distribution Segmentation. This chapter has already indicated that tourism's distribution channels are unique and play a more powerful role than the intermediaries in other industries. Chapter 16 provides a detailed description of these distribution channels. It is important to recognize that these intermediaries should be segmented by the other tourism organizations that depend on them for business. Intermediaries vary according to their principal function (e.g., retailing versus wholesaling travel services), area of specialization by travel service, market segment, destination (e.g., cruise-only travel agents, corporate and ethnic travel agencies), size and structure (e.g., large franchised travel agency chains versus the small independent retailer), online versus offline, and, of course, geographic location.

While segmentation schemes for distribution channels have received little attention from tourism researchers, the traditional and newer online intermediaries are of great importance to tourism. Most organizations that target travel intermediaries in their marketing use a two-step process that includes first identifying the target market of travelers and then selecting the intermediaries who serve these target markets. Channel of distribution segmentation should be considered separately from marketing within the distribution channel.

QUICK TRIP 7.2

Trapping the MICE: Business Events Are Very Important in Tourism Marketing

The term "MICE" has been around for a long time in tourism and now some prefer to use the terms "business events" or the "meetings industry." However, you will see MICE used often, and it is better to know what the acronym means:

- **Meetings:** The most general term and includes groups of all sizes and types coming together to achieve specific purposes.
- **Incentives:** These are meetings held when groups of people receive travel as a reward for outstanding work performance.
- **Conferences:** Usually organized by associations and allow attendees to participate in the meeting process.
- **Exhibitions:** Shows held by specific industry sectors to display and merchandise various products and services.

You should also know that "convention" is often used instead of "conference" in defining MICE. Also "exposition" is sometimes substituted for "exhibition" or "event." While MICE is common, other acronyms are also common. For instance MEEC—Meetings, Expositions, Events, and Conventions—is also quite common.

The MICE markets are tremendously important to many destinations around the world and form an important part of the tourism system. There are several industry associations that help destinations with MICE marketing:

- **Event Industry Council** The Event Industry Council (EIC), formally known as the Convention Industry Council (CIC), is an association of associations. It has thirty-three meeting-, incentive-, and convention-related associations as its members and represents all parts of the sector. The EIC plays an important role in setting standards across the industry through its accepted practices exchange (APEX) and certification programs. The CIC has been an important promoter of green practices in the meeting industry and Green Meetings Industry Council is an EIC initiative (www.eventscouncil.org).

QUICK TRIP 7.2 CONTINUED

- **Destinations International** (DI), Washington, DC. As the world's largest and most reliable resource for official DMOs, DI is dedicated to improving the effectiveness of over 3,300 professionals from nearly 650 DMOs in over thirty countries. DI advocates for the professionalism, effectiveness, and significance of destination management organizations worldwide (www.destinationsinternational.org).
- **European Cities Marketing** (ECM), Dijon, France. ECM's mission is to be the preferred instrument of Europe's leading cities for the exchange—by their city tourist offices, convention bureaus, and city marketing organizations—of best practice and information within a city marketing framework (www.europeancitiesmarketing.com).
- **International Congress and Convention Association** (ICCA), Amsterdam, The Netherlands. ICCA is the global community for the meetings industry, enabling its members to generate and maintain significant competitive advantage (www.iccaworld.com/abouticca.cfm).

Business events are crucial to the tourism in many destinations.

Think about This

1. What are some of the key differences between MICE marketing and marketing aimed at pleasure travelers?
2. Some experts like the term "MICE," but others do not. What are the benefits and disadvantages of using the MICE terminology?
3. Which destinations are especially effective in attracting the MICE markets? What are the reasons for their above-average performance in attracting these groups?

Sources

www.destinationsinternational.org

www.europeancitiesmarketing.com

www.eventscouncil.org

www.iccaworld.com

FIGURE 7.4 Meetings are an important part of the tourism system.

Selecting Viable Target Market Segments

The process of identifying possible market segments varies by company or destination. How the organization decides to segment the market may be determined by the financial resources, available data, and other factors. No matter how the process is done, the goal of the process is to identify segments that are worthwhile to focus on. How can you tell if it's worthwhile to focus on a segment?

A viable visitor market segment must meet the following criteria by being:

- **Measurable.** Can the number of potential visitors within the segment be estimated with a reasonable degree of accuracy?
- **Accessible.** Can these visitors be reached with specific promotional techniques or media? Can they be reached and influenced by existing or potential travel trade distribution channels, or by the Internet?
- **Substantial.** Are there sufficient numbers of visitors in this visitor market segment to justify a tailor-made marketing effort?
- **Defensible.** Are the visitor market segment's characteristics different enough to justify separate marketing activities and expenditures just for them, or can they be grouped with one or more other target markets? If competitors decide to use more of a mass-marketing approach, will this have an adverse effect on us?
- **Durable.** As the market develops, will this visitor market segment maintain its uniqueness, or will these differences disappear with time?
- **Competitive.** Do we have a relative advantage over the competition in serving this visitor market segment?
- **Homogeneous.** Are the people within the visitor market segment similar enough?
- **Compatible.** Is the visitor market segment compatible with the other visitor market segments that the organization or destination attracts?

Once market segments have been identified and profiled, the tourism destination or organization must select the target market or markets that it wants to attract and serve. This decision is based upon analysis to determine which segments will produce the greatest benefits and which segments the destination or organization can serve best. The analysis involves four concerns:

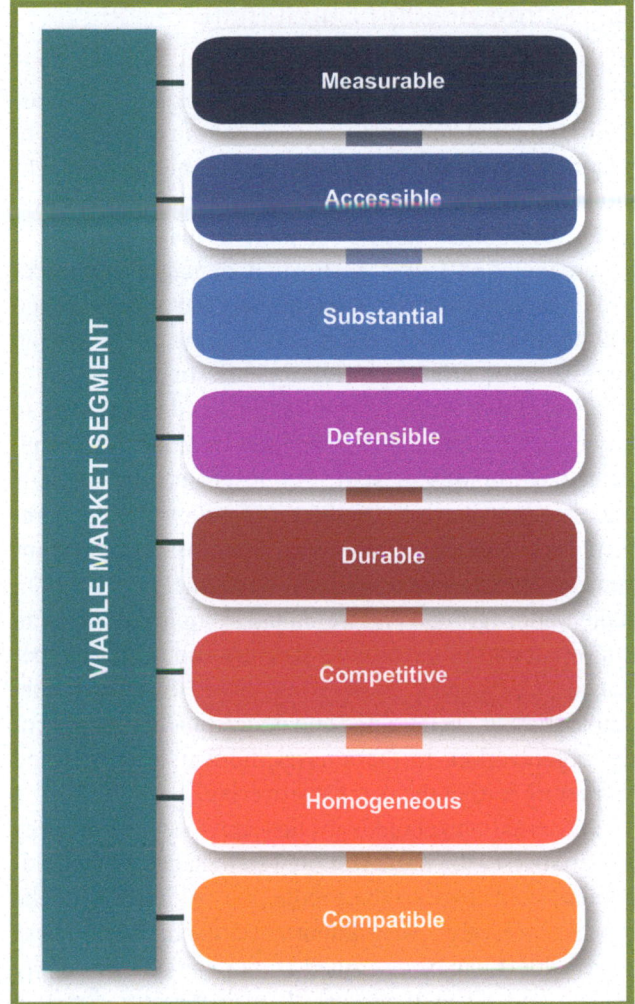

FIGURE 7.5 Viable market segment.

1. **Income potential and yield:** What is the current and future potential for income from this segment? Income is a combination of the number of current and potential visitors and their current and potential per-person spending.
2. **Competition:** To what extent does competition exist for the segment in question? How strong is our advantage compared to that of competitors?
3. **Cost:** How much investment is required to develop services to attract this segment and to communicate with its members?
4. **Ability to serve:** Are the financial and managerial capabilities in place to design, promote, and distribute the appropriate services and satisfactorily serve this market segment? The segments chosen become the destination's or organization's target markets.

Marketing Beyond Consumers—The Importance of Marketing to Stakeholders

While target markets are the primary focus of the marketing oriented company, they are not the only group to which organizations need to apply marketing techniques. Many of the other members of the tourism system are important targets for tourism marketing. From an organization's or a destination manager's perspective, these other tourism system members will be called **stakeholders.** Stakeholders are anyone who has an interest in the firm, organization, or destination.

Stakeholders can be both internal and external to an organization. Internal stakeholders include staff and, indeed, groupings of staff. For instance, women staff members may have a specific set of issues that the company is committed to improving. For most tourism companies, employees are an extremely important stakeholder group. As we noted, employees are an important part of the product delivery and the user experience. Companies must work hard to ensure that employees are well trained and understand the culture of the organization. In these cases, human resources and marketing within the company overlap.

External stakeholder groups may vary in level of importance to the organization. For instance, stakeholders that contribute to the production or delivery of the product are often very important stakeholders. These stakeholders can be described as members of the supply chain—and we will discuss them in greater detail in Chapter 16.

Tourism organizations will also apply tourism marketing techniques to other stakeholder groups as well. Destinations may market to the destination's host community, not only to tell them about visitor-related attractions and activities, but also to share the benefits of tourism with them and their community. Just as organizations will develop marketing plans—with specific goals and activities to achieve those goals—for the target market, they develop marketing plans for select stakeholder groups. Some of these plans may be described in other ways. For instance, marketing plans addressing government officials may be called advocacy plans. But they will follow the same principles as other marketing plans.

Destinations may consider "internal" stakeholders as the members of the destination system and external stakeholders as intermediaries, travel suppliers, and media outlets. Internal marketing for the destination includes engaging with members of the destination system closely tied to the delivery of tourism products and organizations that are important to tourism but may not consider themselves as "in tourism," such as political leaders and utility and social service (police, health care, etc.) providers. It also means marketing to system members impacted by tourism, including community members in the host destination.

THE MARKETING TOOLBOX

If the role of marketing is to create value for consumers, then it is reasonable to ask: how do we create that value? Marketers have a wide range of tools and techniques they can use to create value for their customers. That set of tools and techniques is often called the marketing mix, and traditional approaches to marketing suggest that a *marketing mix* is comprised of four components: product, price, promotion, and place (distribution). These are called the *four Ps of marketing* (Perreault and McCarthy 2000). Some authors have suggested that there are additional components to the tourism marketing mix. Because of the uniqueness of tourism marketing, it is recommended that packaging, programming, people, and partnership be considered as four additional marketing mix components (Morrison 2010). The traditional four Ps then expand to eight Ps (product, price, promotion, place, packaging, programming, people, and partnership). It is essential that each address the needs and characteristics of people in the selected target markets.

Product. Travel experiences consist of several different services and products ranging from transportation and lodging to sightseeing and souvenirs. These services and products are usually offered by a variety of tourism organizations. Each organization is dependent on the others to offer an attractive and satisfying overall travel experience. A marketing orientation suggests that services and products be designed to match the needs and wants of the targeted visitors.

In Chapter 9 we will look closely at how product—and the related marketing mix components of packaging, partnerships, programming, and people—come together to create value for consumers and profits for tourism organizations.

Packaging. Packaging can be described as the ways that individual products can be brought together to create a more comprehensive—and often better—tourism experience. Packaging aggregates products. Consumers' travel experiences almost always incorporate a variety of product/service offerings. Packaging recognizes the value created when experts bring those products together in anticipation of the needs of visitors. Packag-

FIGURE 7.6 Tourism marketing mix.

ing is undertaken by products working together in partnership; it is also the foundation of the business model of many intermediaries including tour operators and travel wholesalers.

Programming. Programming leverages the ability of travel products to offer new and different products by changing themes, service delivery, and scheduling. Programming leverages the flexibility of the core tourism product enabling the delivery of new experiences. At an individual product level, examples of programming include special Christmas activities at Disneyland—decorations, Santa joining Mickey on the parade, carol singers in the park, or high tea at an upmarket hotel. Destinations use programming to provide a reason to travel. For instance, the Edinburgh Festival or the Macau International Fireworks Display Contest provide additional, time-sensitive reasons to go to these great cities.

People. Tourism is a people business and people are a fundamental part of the product delivered to the visitor. In addition to ensuring that people are carefully trained and empowered to deliver high-quality visitor experiences, tourism organizations can work with people in a variety of ways to ensure great experiences. It is often the people that you meet that are the most important part of any travel memory.

Partnership. Partnership means working with other organizations to deliver experiences to visitors. These partnerships may be loose collaborations or highly structured, legally binding partnerships. Ideally, tourism partnerships—like any great teamwork—create **synergy**, where the combination of the two companies is worth much more than just the sum of each company's individual offering.

Price. In pure economic terms, price is a result of supply and demand. When supply exceeds demand, prices will tend to decrease. The reverse is also true. Of greater importance is the extent to which demand changes (as measured by the amount purchased) as price changes—the elasticity of demand. A 5 percent reduction in price may result in a corresponding 10 percent increase in the number of buyers and a subsequent increase in total sales revenue. Demand in this case is elastic. Generally, products aimed at the luxury end of the customer scale are less susceptible to changes in price and tend to be

QUICK TRIP 7.3

Virtual and Augmented Reality in the Tourism System

Virtual and Augmented Reality are new but they are already making a mark on the tourism system. The arrival of new technologies can impact many aspects of marketing including product development and promotion.

Pokemon Go was one of the first large-scale uses of augmented reality. The game, played on a mobile phone, used augmented reality to project Pokémon to locations throughout the world, via your smartphone. In essence, augmented reality provides additional information to a real situation. Pokemon Go launched in summer (northern hemisphere) of 2017 and was an immediate hit: it seemed like everyone was in the race to catch the little critters (Tsukayama 2017). Agile, opportunistic marketers used the fad to promote their businesses and there was some backlash from destinations that didn't want smartphone-wielding Pokémon Go players looking for Pokémon in their locations. The popularity of the game lasted much of 2016 and left many marketers thinking about how they could incorporate the technology into their products and marketing. While Pokémon Go may have been a fad, the use of augmented reality is expected to be widely adopted by museums and attractions to provide additional information to visitors. Even destinations are examining how to add augmented reality services.

Virtual reality allows travelers to try before they buy, reducing the risk of travel purchases.

If augmented reality adds information to reality, virtual reality provides immersive sensory input that creates reality. Virtual reality currently requires use of headsets to create the impression of reality for the user. Virtual reality is already being used in many parts of the tourism system. Some meeting venues are already using virtual reality to help meeting planners visualize the spaces they will be using. The technology is also being used to build demand for products and destinations. In Wales, tourism businesses are being encouraged to use virtual reality to attract visitors and to provide a new dimension to their real-world experience. "Dolphin Dive" and "Flight of the Kingfisher" are raising awareness of the wildlife in Wales and encouraging visitors to come and see it for themselves (Gidley 2017). Marriott believes that virtual reality can help sell their hotels. As Michael Dail, VP of Marriott Hotels Brand Marketing, says "Every virtual trip increases the demand for physical travel (Adamson 2015).

Think about This

1. Consider ways that augmented reality could be applied to tourism from either a promotion or product development perspective.
2. There are often concerns that new technologies will reduce the demand for travel. For instance, many worried that videoconferencing would reduce demand for in-person meetings. Do you think virtual reality will increase or decrease demand for travel? Explain your answer.
3. Find five ways that augmented reality is being applied in the tourism system. What's your favorite application so far?

Sources

Adamson, A. 2015. "Virtual Reality: Not Right for All Marketers, but brilliant for Marriott." *Forbes.*

Gidley, S. 2017 "Virtual Reality: Tourism Firms use VR to attract visitors." BBC. http://www.bbc.com/news/uk-wales-41635746.

Tsukayama, H. 2017 "Pokemon Go and teh lifespan of fads in the internet age." *Washington Post,* https://www.washingtonpost.com/news/the-switch/wp/2016/08/31/pokemon-go-and-the-lifespan-of-fads-in-the-internet-age/?utm_term=.b2eaa27cbdae.

FIGURE 7.7 The Macau International fireworks display is an example of programming.

price inelastic. For businesses that are open only part of the year, supply is limited and prices have to be higher (everything else being equal) than businesses open year-round. Because demand is not often uniform throughout the year, it is common to charge higher prices during the peak season and lower prices when demand slackens.

The expected length of the PLC and the destination's or company's position on it also affect pricing decisions. A fad item with an expected short life cycle will have to charge high prices to recoup the investment in a relatively short period of time. A product that expects a longer life can be priced lower.

The price charged is influenced by competition. If a destination's facilities and services are very similar to competitors, its prices must be similar to theirs. The extent to which the destination area or other tourism service is unique influences whether it can charge more than the competition. Related to the influence of competition is the management policy regarding market share. If the decision is made to increase market share, prices will probably be lower than if we decide to "skim" a small number of visitors from several market segments.

Pricing policy is also influenced by the needs of the selected target market. If a tourism destination or organization serves the needs and wants of the market and if those needs and wants are perceived as being important to the members of the market segment, those people will be willing to pay a higher price. The price charged must also be perceived by the market as less than or at least equal to the value received. In some situations, the influence of the market seems to go against economic principles. With certain luxury items, demand may increase as price increases. This phenomenon reflects a degree of snobbishness on the part of the market. The feeling may be that the higher the price, the greater the perceived value and the greater the demand. But the actual value in the minds of the buyers must still equal or exceed the price paid.

Promotion. The topic of promotion is covered in detail in Chapter 8. Promotion is the most visible part of the marketing mix, apart from the services or products themselves. Many people fall into the trap of confusing marketing and promotion, thinking of them as being exactly the same. However, there is much more to marketing than just promotion. The *promotional mix* consists of several elements including advertising, sales promotion, merchandising, personal selling and sales, public relations and publicity, along with Internet marketing. All promotions involve some form of communications with potential customers.

Place (Distribution). Tourism distribution is unique. In the absence of a physical distribution system, tourism has developed a unique set of *distribution channels* and travel trade intermediaries. These intermediaries influence visitors' choices of tourism destinations and businesses, and require separate attention by the tourism marketer. The choice of specific channels of distribution and intermediaries is influenced by several factors including the target market, type of tourism service or destination, and the location of the services relative to the customers' residences. Chapter 16 provides detailed information on tourism distribution and individual categories of travel trade intermediaries.

BRANDING IN THE TOURISM SYSTEM

Brands and Branding

You are probably very familiar with many consumer brands. Apple, McDonald's, and Coca-Cola are some of the most recognized companies in the world. Elements of the Disney brand may be some of your earliest memories. Brands create great value for their companies. It has been said that the Apple brand is worth over $178 billion (IBISWorld 2017). With a value like that, a brand can be considered an important intangible asset of the company. The most successful brands are built over the years through consistent marketing—not just ad campaigns but product experience, pricing, and many other elements of the marketing mix.

So what is a brand—from a marketing perspective?

Brand can mean a couple of things. At the simplest level, brand refers to a logo, sign, symbol, or design used to identify a product and differentiate it from competitors. But just as the BMW logo is only a small part of the consumer's brand experience, brands are much more than just a logo. A brand is the set of associations that consumers have of a product or service. Those associations are created in a variety of ways from promotional strategies to user experience. For example, the quality of the physical product influences how you perceive the brand. Starbucks works hard on the design of their stores to ensure a consistent feel in the physical environment they create for visitors. At the essence of their brand is the idea of the "third place" for drinking coffee. Brand associations can also be built through consumers' experience of corporate culture and customer interaction with staff—think of the "ladies and gentlemen of Ritz Carlton" delivering high-quality service.

Brand Strategy. Of course, some of the things we know about brands aren't that positive. For instance, we know that fast-food can have negative impacts on health and we may associate fast-food with McDonald's. But this is not what McDonald's wants you to think about when you first think of them. **Brand strategists** want you to think about what they consider the brand identity as they define it—the things they want their brand to be known for—and overlook, forget, or never learn the negatives. David Aaker, one of the foremost experts on branding, explains that brand strategists create a *brand identity*—a key set of factors that they want the product or organization to be known for—and then choose elements of the identity that they will use to attract specific consumers (Aaker 1996). The elements of the brand identity they choose for a given target market will add the most value for those customers but will also be true to the overall reputation they want to develop. For example, a brand may have a number of elements that it considers important to its brand identity but only a few are relevant to the specific consumer group. McDonald's once again provides a good example. McDonald's may have as part of its brand identity: value food, quality and consistency, and family-friendly, with some premium products like coffee. In the ads they run on Saturday morning during the kids' cartoons the ads will focus on value foods, quality and consistency, and family-friendly. The ads they run at night targeting adults will focus on value food, consistency and quality, and premium products. In targeting each market they highlight the most relevant parts of their brand identity. But they don't ever stray from the brand identity.

Brand strategists use those elements of the brand identity to **position** a product in the minds of the target consumer. Positioning was first introduced by two advertising executives, Al Reis and Jack Trout, in the book titled, *Positioning: The Battle for Your Mind.* In these authors' own words, "Positioning is what you do to the mind of the prospect" (Ries and Trout 2001). Other authors have elaborated on this original definition, including Lewis and Chambers (2000) who say that position is "the consumer's mental perception of a product, which may or may not differ from the actual characteristics of a product or brand." Most experts agree that the purpose of positioning is to create a perception or *image*—to establish a position—in the targeted visitor's mind. The marketers, guided by the brand identity, use the marketing mix to position the organization in the minds of the consumer. While it may seem that "branding" is all about advertising campaigns and taglines, positioning uses the full marketing mix. For instance, the Apple brand is built not just on their advertising but on the user experience, the performance of the technology, and so on. A strong positioning is valuable to an organization. If you are an Apple devotee then not only do you happily pay more for the product than other similar products, but you probably don't even think about buying another product in the first place. Apple may be the only thing that comes to mind when devotees think of computers—Apple is firmly **positioned** in the minds of these consumers when they think of computers. Because the objective is to influence the individual visitor's perception of the destination or organization, there is a clear link to the psychological dimensions of perception discussed in Chapter 12.

Brand Equity. So when we say the Apple brand is worth $178 billion, what does that really mean? The value of the brand is not physical or tangible like other assets. While physical assets include hotel buildings and cruise ships, this type of asset is intangible. We call the value of the brand *brand equity*. You may recall from your accounting classes that equity is a thing of value and this value rests firmly in the minds and hearts of the consumer. Brand equity is the value consumers give to a product because of the associations with the brand. Brand strategists may categorize these associations in a number of ways.

Brand Strategies and Destination Branding

Branding is an important activity for many tourism companies. Hotel companies have been very aggressive in creating brands for specific markets. After Marriott's acquisition of Starwood it managed no less than thirty brands. But Marriott is not alone—it is common for tourism companies to create separate brands for separate markets. For instance, The Travel Corporation operates both Contiki Tours, a wholesaler targeting eighteen- to thirty-five-year-olds and Grand European vacations that markets guided tours to more mature travelers. By separating the brands, the Travel Corporation is able to clearly communicate with two target markets.

Destination Brands and Branding. While product branding has been around for millennia, in recent years there has been a growing realization that branding approaches can be applied more broadly. Many DMOs consider destination branding to be a core function of their operation. Until recently, destination branding

meant developing promotional campaigns to reinforce a brand image in the marketplace. In more recent years, DMOs have recognized that brand building includes working to develop and enhance the destination experience as well as conduct promotional campaigns.

Marketing Is Too Important To Be Left To the Marketing Department

While many companies have marketing departments, marketing activities—activities that create value for consumers—can be found in a wide variety of places in most companies. In fact, there are many people working in tourism companies that are working in marketing—and probably don't know it!

People providing services to visitors are an important part of the product provided by the company. Revenue managers setting prices are doing a marketing activity. The sales department—often separate from the marketing department in many companies—is performing an important marketing function. These people are all part of the marketing team.

MARKETING PLANNING PROCESS

Marketing: Strategic or Tactical?

If strategic goals look at the long-term and tactical plans address short-term goals, is marketing strategic or tactical?

In business, **strategic** *activities* are activities that address long-term goals. For many companies, strategic planning is developing plans to achieve goals three to five years in the future. As you have seen in Chapter 5, strategic planning for destinations can be based on long time frames. Marketing may be a strategic activity; it creates long-term value. Building strong brands and developing strong relationships take time and contribute lasting value for the organization. Marketing is an important component of the strategic planning process.

Once long-term goals are established, organizations develop plans to achieve these strategic goals. An annual marketing plan typically covers actions to be completed within a twelve-month period. These shorter time frame plans may be called *tactical plans,* and contribute to the longer-term goals. An important challenge for marketers is aligning long-term goals with short-term activities

QUICK TRIP 7.4

Destination Next and the Future of Destination Management Organizations

As the tourism system changes, Destination Management Organizations—Convention and Visitor Bureaus, State and National Tourism Offices—must respond to new technologies, new consumer preferences, and new expectations from their key stakeholders. How they respond to these challenges is an existential problem for these organizations. To prepare for the challenge, Destinations International (DI), formally Destination Marketing Association International, has led a strategic planning program—Destination Next—to identify the challenges facing DMOs and determine the future role of these organizations.

The Destination Next identifies a wide range of issues facing DMOs. The Top 10 Major Trends identified in the 2017 Destination Next report are:

Rank	Trend
1	Social media's prominence in reaching the travel market (e.g., Facebook, Pinterest, Twitter, Weibo).
2	Content creation and dissemination by the public across all platforms drives the destination brand and experience.
3	Customers increasingly seeking authentic and personalized travel experience.
4	Mobile platforms and communication will become increasingly important to engage leisure customers from the destination consideration stage through to the trip experience stage.
5	Mobile platforms and apps becoming the primary engagement platform for travelers.
6	Video becomes the new currency of destination marketing and storytelling.
7	Harvesting data and developing business analytics differentiate successful tourism enterprises and destinations.
8	Smart technology (e.g., phones, bag tags, and cards) creating new opportunities for innovative new services and processes.
9	Technology enabling faster decision-making by customers.
10	Geotargeting and localization becoming more prevalent.

How DMOs respond to the changing marketplace has been a major focus of the Destination Next project. In 2014, during the first phase of the Destination Next study, three transformational opportunities were identified.

1. Sales and Marketing: Shifting from broadcast to engagement and transactional to strategic.
2. Destination Management: playing a greater role in product development.
3. Business Model: greater emphasis on partnerships and collaboration.

and ensuring the plans for each of the functional specialties work together in a cohesive manner toward the goals of the organization.

Marketing can also incorporate the plans of a variety of specialist functional areas. For instance, there may be a public relations plan, a sales plan, and a social media plan. Ideally these plans will be developed to ensure a cohesive, consumer-based plan. Of course, that is not always the case. It has been said that one of the great challenges of the Chief Marketing Officer is breaking down barriers with the organization and ensuring the marketing departments work as a team.

Marketing Planning Process

A tourism destination or company must segment the market using the most appropriate methods and bases and select target markets; taking into account the PLC stages of the industry and its own offerings, it must position these effectively within the minds of the targeted

The 2017 Destination report recommends that DMOs of the future should adopt five key roles:

- Curators of destination content
- Adopters of business intelligence and data science
- Catalysts of economic development
- Activists in community place making
- Collaborators in strategic networks

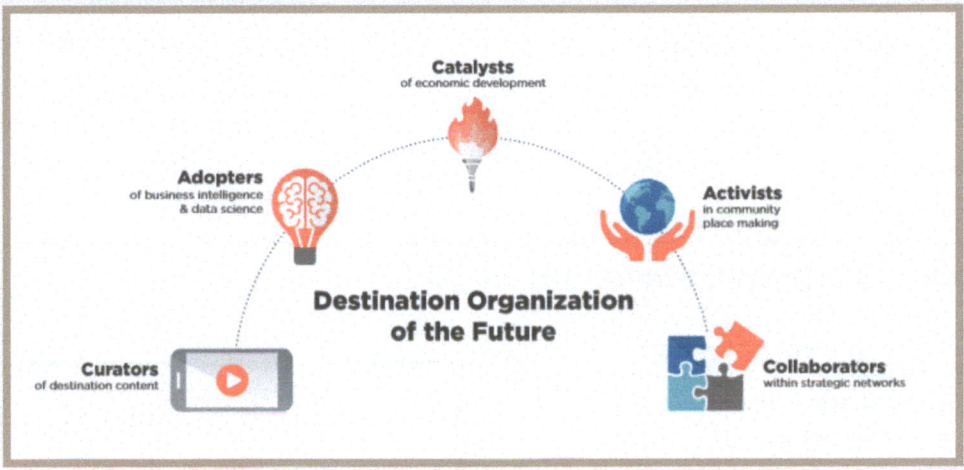

Think about This

1. Consider the Major Trends identified in the Destination Next report. How would you categorize them? What patterns do you see?
2. DMOs are an important part of the tourism system but they can sometimes be less visible than other system members, particularly in their own destination because some of their activity is undertaken in other markets. What exposure have you had with DMOs? Based on your experience, how would you value the contribution of DMOs?
3. What role do DMOs have in economic development?

Source

potential visitors. Having made these decisions, specific marketing programs using pricing, services and products, promotions, and distribution channels (marketing mixes) are designed. The process used to develop marketing mixes should be systematic; it should follow a step-by-step procedure known as the ***marketing planning process***.

Marketing planning implies a future orientation. It involves identifying suitable marketing goals and objectives as well as determining the most appropriate marketing strategies to achieve these goals and objectives.

Marketing planning takes place at two levels: ***strategic marketing planning*** for three to five years or more in the future, and ***tactical marketing planning*** for the next year. Tactical plans should flow logically from strategic plans and the vision.

A model of the marketing planning process containing five basic questions has been suggested by Morrison (2010) (see Figures 7.8 and 7.9). The five questions are:

1. Where are we now?
2. Where would we like to be?

Marketing Planning Process Steps	Techniques and Concepts	Outcomes and Results
1. Where are we now?	Environmental scan Situation analysis	Strengths and weaknesses Challenges, opportunities, and threats Visitor market profile Competitive analysis
2. Where would we like to be?	Visioning market Segmentation positioning	Vision, goals, and objectives Marketing strategy Target markets Positioning approach
3. How do we get there?	Marketing mix	Marketing plan (eight Ps)
4. How do we make sure we get there?	Control	Progress reports Marketing plan modifications
5. How do we know if we got there?	Evaluation	Marketing effectiveness or accountability

FIGURE 7.8 Tourism marketing planning process model.

3. How do we get there?
4. How do we make sure we get there?
5. How do we know if we got there?

It is important to note that the marketing planning process is an ongoing process. A start-up business may start at step one but ongoing businesses should be continuously working through these steps. Marketing plans should be referred to frequently and guide the businesses activities each day.

Where Are We Now?

The planning of marketing must begin by addressing the question, "Where are we now?" This involves a thorough analysis of the existing situation. Marketing goals, strategies, and objectives should not be defined until this analysis has been completed. Many marketing experts refer to this step as a *situation analysis* or *SWOT* (strengths, weaknesses, opportunities, threats) analysis. The factors that should be analyzed include the marketing environment, development goals and strategies, services, products and destination mix, market profile, and competition.

Scan the Marketing Environment. Planning must be accomplished within the framework of the external environment that is constantly changing but over which the marketing manager has little or no control. The technique of identifying and analyzing the impact of external environmental forces is known as *environmental scanning*. The basic reason for doing an environmental

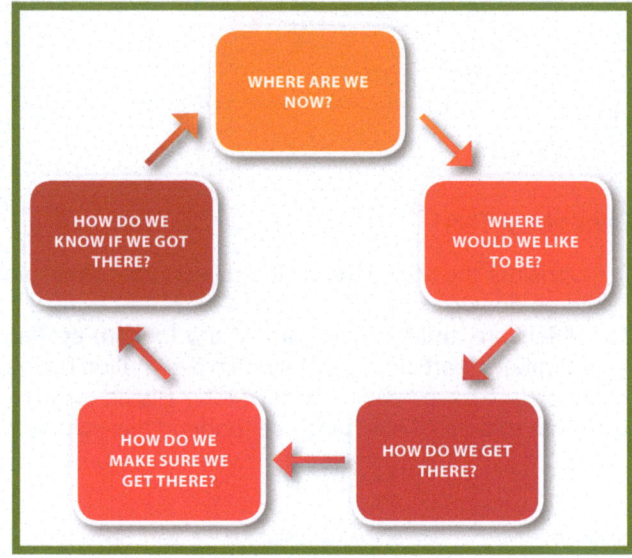

FIGURE 7.9 Planning process—marketing.

scan is that it is better to anticipate change before it happens than to react to change after it has happened. This can be accomplished by answering these key questions: What are the major trends? Will they affect us, and how will they affect us? How much will they affect us? How will they affect our closest competitors? What should we do differently in the future to adapt to these trends and their likely impacts?

The environmental forces to be scanned should include legislation and regulation, political situations, social and cultural characteristics, economic conditions, technology, transportation, and competition at a macro level. For a tourism company or destination that attracts visitors from several countries, an environmental scan is needed for each individual visitor-generating country.

The first of the forces to be considered is the *legal and regulatory environment*. Certain countries, including South Korea and China, have in the past placed legal restrictions on their residents that have hampered the flow of outbound tourism. Residents may be restricted from traveling, or they may be unable to take more than a certain sum of money out of the country. Political factors must also be considered. Tensions or hostilities between the country of origin and the country of destination will affect marketing success. A good example of this is the uneasy relationship between Cuba and the United States. It is important to consider the social and cultural characteristics of the host destination's residents including educational backgrounds, traditions, religions, and the overall way of life. Most international travel is generated from countries with higher educational standards, from societies regarded as more cultured, and from countries having a higher degree of industrialization.

The pace of *technological change* within tourism and society in general is accelerating. Profound changes are resulting from the direct and indirect impacts of new technologies, including the use of the Internet and particularly the web. Tourism is rapidly transforming from dependence on paper-based information to dependence on electronic information (e.g., e-tickets). Other technologies that are having a significant impact are mobile phone or smartphone technologies (m-commerce), global distribution systems, and video- and teleconferencing using satellite and other technologies.

Another important factor is *transportation* and other aspects of *accessibility*, such as documentation requirements. The destination must be accessible to visitors from generating countries or regions. The current and projected *economic conditions* in generating countries are a factor of great importance in tourism. It is essential that there are enough people in the country who can afford to travel. China's increasing affluence, for example, has attracted much greater attention from destinations in the Asia-Pacific region and elsewhere. The *exchange rate* between the host country and generating countries is another key economic concern. Past history has shown that major exchange rate shifts have a direct impact on travel volumes between specific pairs of countries.

Although commonly overlooked, the destination or organization's *macro-competition* should be analyzed. These are not head-to-head competitors, but represent the other products and services competing for the same

disposable income. For example, the purchase of an expensive home entertainment system may take the place of a foreign vacation trip. A new car purchase may result in less frequent and shorter vacations being taken. There are potential substitutes for travel, and they should be taken into consideration in marketing planning.

Consider the Development Goals and Strategies. The marketing plan should be just one part of the overall *strategic plan* for the destination or organization, and just one element in the comprehensive tourism plan for a destination area. Tourism is one, and only one, strategy for development. As noted in Chapter 2, tourism can be used as a political, social, and economic force. Yet, other alternatives are available. A comprehensive plan for tourism must be consistent with the overall planning and development goals and strategies for the destination area.

Evaluate Services, Products, and the Destination Mix. One of the principal outcomes of a situation analysis is the determination of the destination's or organization's strengths and weaknesses, especially when compared to its closest competition. Competition is defined as anyone who serves the same target market or markets. The situation analysis reviews the destination's or organization's services and products, target markets, and competition. A tourism destination should compare the five components of its *destination mix* against those of its closest competitors:

- Attractions (natural resources, climate, cultural and historical resources, ethnic attractions, accessibility, manmade attractions)
- Facilities (lodging, food and beverage, support industries)
- Infrastructure (fresh water supply, sewage disposal systems, communications systems, road systems, health care facilities, energy systems, security systems)
- Transportation (airports, railway systems, cruise ship terminals, bus transportation)
- Hospitality (hospitality training programs, friendliness of local residents, overall service levels)

Prepare a Visitor Market Profile. The crucial task is to develop a profile of the visitor and then to project that profile into the future by considering trends in the country or region of origin. The profiling task should address the questions and provide the visitor characteristics shown in Figure 7.10.

When the existing target markets have been profiled, consideration is then given to new visitor target markets. Jones (1995) suggests that four categories of potential new visitors should be analyzed:

1. **Existing market segments:** Other people from existing target markets that have not yet visited the destination or used the service. For example, if most people in the existing market come from within a 500-mile radius, potential markets may be discovered from areas within 500 miles from which visitors do not yet come (e.g., specific cities or communities).

2. **Proximate potential market segments:** Past visitors to nearby destinations who have similar characteristics to existing target markets. These people have used a region and have demonstrated an interest in what it has to offer.

3. **Expanded potential market segments:** Travelers who want similar products and services to that offered by the destination, but who have not yet visited the region. These might include special-interest markets such as adventure travel, golf, and scuba diving.

4. **Potential market segments for additional/enhanced products:** New visitors that would be attracted if new attractions or facilities were added. Examples might include a casino operation, convention center, golf courses, or guided nature tours.

Analyze Competition. It is important to analyze the marketing programs, positioning, and overall management of competing destinations or companies, and to compare this with those of the subject destination or company. What image do competitors have in the minds of potential customers? How successful were their past marketing programs? What have been their most successful marketing efforts? Do they have a cohesive, experienced, and marketing-oriented management team?

Determine Strengths and Weaknesses. The culmination of this analysis is the identification of competitive strengths and weaknesses (what is there that is better than competitors?). The typical broad approach in marketing is to build upon and enhance competitive strengths and to take steps to address and improve upon weaknesses.

Topics	Questions	Characteristics
Who?	Who are they? Who makes the travel decision? Who helps them with travel decisions?	Behavioral characteristics Demographic/socioeconomic Influence of travel trade intermediaries Psychographic
Where?	Where do they live? Where do they travel within the destination? What other destinations do they visit?	Geographic characteristics Travel routes and patterns
What?	What do they buy?	Services, products, facilities Usage of packages or tours
Why?	Why do they travel? What do they like to do?	Activity preferences Motivations
When?	When do they travel? When is the travel decision made? How long do they stay?	Length of stay Planning or "lead" time Seasonality of demand
How many?	How many of them are there? What are the sizes and composition of travel parties?	Market size Trip party size
How?	How do they make travel plans?	Booking preferences Use of travel trade

FIGURE 7.10 Components of a visitor market profile.

Where Would We Like to Be?

The second step in marketing planning is to define what the tourism destination or company wants to achieve in the future. This is accomplished by considering alternative approaches to marketing for the next three to five years. The process involves defining a vision, establishing marketing goals, selecting target markets, creating a positioning approach, and setting marketing objectives.

Define a Vision and Vision Statement. When the situation analysis is completed, the tourism organization or destination now must describe where it wants to be in the future. The first step in sketching the desired future situation should be the determination of a *vision* and *vision statement* for the destination or organization. According to Ritchie (1993), the visioning process consists of three distinct stages:

1. Envisioning an image of a desired future organizational state, which
2. When effectively communicated to followers,
3. Serves to empower those followers so they can enact the vision.

In some ways, a vision is like a *super-long-term goal* that becomes the foundation for defining the whole program of marketing action.

While there are few specific guidelines as to what a vision statement should include, it should at a minimum be measurable. The following are examples of vision statements for tourism destinations:

- **London, England:** London and Partners describe the vision for London as "visitors will be able to unlock the best version of London for them by tailoring their experience to meet their needs. They will be provided with better online and offline information to help them navigate the city more effectively and make more informed choices. They will be encouraged to do more and see more of London, which will step up their overall satisfaction and increase their likelihood of returning as visitors or to work, invest, trade or study. The tourism industry will work together to manage the expected significant growth in visitor numbers in a sustainable way. And we will achieve our vision by balancing the needs of Londoners and visitors, with more Londoners recognizing the importance of the visitor economy and benefiting from its social and economic impact" (2017, 9).

- **Canada:** Canada's New Tourism Vision sets out concrete targets for growth: Canada will compete to be one of the Top Ten most visited countries in the world by 2025; the number of international overnight visits to Canada will increase by 30 percent by 2021; and the number of visitors from China will double by 2021 (2017).

- **South Africa:** South Africa's National Tourism Sector Strategy Vision is "rapidly and inclusively growing tourism economy that leverages South Africa's competitive edge in nature, culture, and heritage, underpinned by Ubuntu and supported by innovation and service excellence. A top world responsible tourism destination" (NTTS 2017).

- **Mexico:** Be a leading organization in the promotion of tourism, encouraging participation and joint efforts by the various stakeholders in the industry (MTB 2015).

Establish Tourism Marketing Goals. A set of *marketing goals* are now required to translate the vision into a program of marketing activities for the next three to five years. Marketing goals describe the overall purposes and desired outcomes of future marketing programs. Marketing goals may be statements about the types of target markets to be attracted, images and perceptions to be communicated, marketing partnerships to be created, and forms of tourism development desired. They may set targets for visitor arrivals, expenditures, and foreign exchange earnings. Marketing goals provide the framework for the selection of target markets and the identification of more specific marketing objectives.

Select Target Markets. For marketing goals to be realized, there must be a clear strategy about which segments of the tourism market will be targeted in the next three to five years. This involves the use of the *market segmentation analysis*. First, market segments are defined using one or more of the seven segmentation bases discussed previously: demographic and socioeconomic, product-related, psychographic, geographic, purpose of trip, behavioral, or channel of distribution. The segments selected as target markets must meet the criteria of being measurable, accessible, substantial, defensible, durable, homogeneous, and compatible. The size (substantiality) of the market can be measured in terms of the number of visitors, the number of visitor nights, or the amount of visitor expenditures. Market segments that are large offer less risk than ones that are relatively small. Other factors that should be considered are the income potential, competition, cost, and the abil-

QUICK TRIP 7.5

Nova Scotia's Strategic Planning for Tourism

Tourism is of great importance to the province of Nova Scotia in Canada, generating an estimated $2.6 billion in income in 2016, and the new strategic plan for tourism plans on increasing that number to $4 billion by 2024. The new plan, *Driving Export Revenue: 2017–2022 Strategic Plan* (TNS 2017), is an important part of the future of Nova Scotia. In 2014, a commission on *Building our New Economy,* with the goal of identifying ways to create a brighter, more sustainable economic future for the region, named tourism as a critical industry for the future. A new crown corporation, Tourism Nova Scotia, with a private sector board of directors was established. The goals of Tourism Nova Scotia include growing tourism, implementing long-term strategies for sustainable tourism, and to collaborate with communities, private industry, and tourism organizations. The mission of the new organization is to market Nova Scotia's tourism experience to the world through innovation and collaboration; its vision is to be recognized globally as the leading Destination Management Organization.

Nova Scotia recognizes that tourism requires support from a variety of stakeholders. The plan carefully outlines the roles of tourism industry operators, the community, government, the tourism industry association, and Tourism Nova Scotia in achieving the goals for the destination.

The famous Peggy's Cove in Nova Scotia.

Nova Scotia has four strategic pillars on which to achieve its goals:

- Attract first-time visitors
- Invest in markets of highest return
- Focus on world-class experiences
- Build tourism confidence

Tourism Nova Scotia uses Destination Canada's traveler segmentation approach, Explorer Quotient (EQ), to identify high potential markets. The three target segments are:

- Authentic Experiencers: "Authentic Experiencers understated travelers looking for authentic, tangible engagement with the destinations they visit."
- Cultural Explorers: "Cultural Explorers are defined by their love of constant travel and continuous opportunities to embrace, discover, and immerse themselves in the culture, people and settings of the place they visit."
- Free Spirits: "Free Spirits are highly social and open minded . . . experimental and adventurous, they indulge in high-end experiences shared with others."

Tourism Nova Scotia focuses on world-class experiences to satisfy these markets is careful not to confuse "world-class" with "luxury" products. Tourism Nova Scotia promotes experiences that differentiate the destination and that are authentic to the culture, heritage, and coastal landscapes of the maritime province.

Think about This

1. What are the strengths of Nova Scotia's tourism approach and strategic pillars?
2. Nova Scotia places the greatest emphasis on visitor experiences rather than specific products. What are the major advantages of putting so much focus on experiences?
3. Why is it important for the Nova Scotia Strategic Plan to describe the roles of the stakeholders?
4. How does the Explorer Quotient (EQ) segmentation help inform the product (or experience) development process?

Sources

TNS. 2017 Driving Export Revenue: 2017–2022 Strategic Plan Tourism Nova Scotia.

www.tourismns.ca/research/explorer-quotient

ity to serve potential target markets. The destination or organization should also have some advantage over one or more competitors in serving the target market.

The Fiji Visitors Bureau (FVB) and the Hawaii Visitors and Convention Bureau (HVCB) provide good examples of targeting a specific market segment. The FVB has developed special and attractive pages on its website dedicated to the theme of weddings and honeymoons. The HVCB, again using its website, takes aim at MICE planners in trying to position Hawaii as an attractive MICE destination. An excellent example of a highly targeted marketing strategy is that used by Contiki Holidays. This tour operator provides escorted tours to various parts of the world for people between ages eighteen and thirty-five.

Create a Positioning Approach. Next, the positioning of the destination or organization for each selected target market must be developed. Positioning should involve answering the following questions: Is there an existing image or perception in potential visitors' minds? What is this image or perception? Is there a need to create, change, or reinforce this image or perception? How should objective or subjective positioning be used to create the desired future positioning? Which positioning approach should be used?

Tourism New Zealand is considered to be one of the best national visitor offices in the world. With its *100% Pure New Zealand* program, it set new standards for positioning and branding a country tourism destination. This positioning emphasizes the unique and spectacular natural scenery in the country's North and South Islands.

Set Marketing Objectives. *Objectives* are established for the next year and should meet four tests. First, they must be capable of being measured. Second, they must address a specific target market. Third, they must be stated in terms of a desired result or outcome that relates directly to either the environmental scan, situation analysis, or development goals and strategies. Finally, a specific deadline for achievement must be stated. The accountability for marketing should be measured against the degree to which objectives are achieved "How do we know if we got there?").

The Fiji Visitors Bureau (FVB) and Business Events Sydney (BESydney) in Australia provide good examples of targeting a specific market segment. FVB has developed special and very attractive pages on its website dedicated to the theme of weddings and honeymoons. BESydney, again using its website, takes aim at planners of corporate meetings, conferences, and incentive trips, positioning Sydney as an attractive business event destination. An excellent example of a highly targeted marketing strategy is that used by Contiki Holidays. This tour operator provided escorted tours to various parts of the world for people between ages eighteen and thirty-five.

How Do We Get There?

The third step is to prepare an action or implementation plan to achieve the marketing goals and objectives. Using the marketing objectives for each selected target market as a starting point, marketing mixes are designed and detailed in a written *marketing plan*. Remember, marketing is about creating value for your consumers and you have a full marketing toolkit that you can use to create that value. Marketing plans will use a variety of marketing tools and techniques to achieve their goals.

How Do We Make Sure We Get There?

Marketing does not stop after the marketing plan has been written. Steps must be taken to ensure that the plan is successful in achieving its objectives. Progress toward the achievement of objectives must be made as the plan is being implemented. This is done by checking progress at predetermined times to see if things are going as planned. If significant deviations from the expected results are found, it may be necessary to modify the marketing plan. This process is often referred to as *marketing control*.

How Do We Know If We Got There?

The last step in the marketing planning process is to determine *marketing effectiveness*. Results and outcomes are evaluated to determine if the marketing goals and objectives have been attained. It has become popular to refer to this as a procedure to ensure the *accountability* of those responsible for tourism marketing. Marketing effectiveness is measured by accountability or evaluation research.

SUMMARY

Marketing focuses organizations on their consumers and recognizes that profits come from serving the needs of those visitors. In the long-term, without customers there is no business. Marketers rely heavily on their understanding of the market and use a variety of techniques including the development of sophisticated consumer profiles and utilizing segmentation and targeting techniques.

Perhaps because of its importance to the success of the whole organization, marketing often involves more than just the marketing and sales departments. Product development, operations and quality control, pricing and revenue management, and human resources are a few of the additional departments in a typical business that are important contributors to marketing. The marketing mix—price, place, promotion, product, packaging, people, programming, and partnerships—provide marketers with a great set of tools for creating value for consumers. Planning for tourism marketing is an ongoing process. Tourism businesses must continually assess and reassess their marketing activities, making course corrections as new technologies arrive and consumer tastes change.

ACTIVITIES

1. Pick a segment of the tourism market in which you have an interest. This could be a special-interest market (scuba diving, cuisine, health/spa, etc.) or another type of segment (e.g., families, MICE). Visit a local library or bookstore and try to find as much information as you can in printed format on destinations and travel activities for your chosen market segment.
2. Visit a selection of local travel agencies and ask for information on travel for your chosen market segment. How comprehensive and appealing was the information that the agencies provided?
3. Interview a variety of tourism companies and organizations that are actively marketing to this segment. What types of marketing strategies are they applying in appealing to this segment?
4. Identify a set of up to ten tourism websites that specifically address your selected market segment.
5. What specific activities and experiences do these websites feature for the market segment?
6. In your opinion, which websites are the best in appealing to and providing information for the market segment? Why?

ACRONYMS

DMAI (Destination Marketing Association International)
DMO (destination management organization)
ECM (European Cities Marketing)
FVB (Fiji Visitors Bureau)
GPS (global positioning system)
HKTB (Hong Kong Tourism Board)
HVCB (Hawaii Visitors and Convention Bureau)
ICCA (International Congress and Convention Association)
ICT (information communication technology)
ITE (International Travel Expo)
MCVB (Melbourne Convention and Visitors Bureau)
MICE (meetings, incentives, conventions, exhibitions)
PLC (product life cycle)
STO (state tourism office)
SWOT (strengths, weaknesses, opportunities, threats)
VTC (Virginia Tourism Corporation)

REFERENCES

Aaker, D. 1996. *Building Strong Brands.* New York: Free Press.

American Marketing Association. 2013. "Definition of Marketing." https://www.ama.org/AboutAMA/Pages/Definition-of-Marketing.aspx.

Government of Canada. 2017. "Canada's New Tourism Vision." https://www.ic.gc.ca/eic/site/095.nsf/eng/00002.html.

IBISWorld. 2017. Car Rentals in China–August 2017 In IBISWorld Industry Report IBISWorld.com

Jones, C. B. 1995. Destination Databases as Keys to Effective Marketing. San Francisco Economic Research Associates.

Kotler, P, J. Bowen, and J. Makens. 2015. *Marketing for Hospitality and Tourism.* 6th ed. Boston, MA: Pearson.

Lewis, R. C., and R. E. Chambers. 2000. *Marketing Leadership in Hospitality,* 3rd ed. New York: Van Nostrand Reinhold.

London & Partners. 2017. A Tourism Vision for London.

Mehta, S. C., and A. Vera. 1990. "Segmentation in Singapore." *Cornell HRA Quarterly 31* (1): 80–87.

Morrison, A. 2010. *Hospitality and Tourism Marketing*, 4th ed. Clifton Park, New York: Delmar.

MTB. 2015. "About Mexico Tourism Board: Mission and Vision." Mexico Tourism Board. http://www.cptm.com.mx/mision-vision-y-estrategias.

NTTS. 2017. National Tourism Sector Strategy 2016–2026 edited by Department of Tourism. Pretoria, South Africa Republic of South Africa.

Perreault, W. D., Jr., and E. J. McCarthy. 2000. *Essentials of Marketing: A Global Managerial Approach,* 12th ed. Homeward, II: Irwin.

Ries, A., and J. Trout. 2001. Positioning: The Battle for Your Mind. New York: McGraw Hill.

Ritchie, B. W. 1993. "Crafting a destination vision: Putting the concept of resident-responsive tourism into practice." *Tourism Management* 14:379–389.

CHAPTER EIGHT

Tourism Promotion

Communicating with Target Markets

If you look at what Brand USA is doing, it is an opportunity to welcome the world.

CATHY TULL, *Senior Vice President of Marketing, Las Vegas Convention and Visitors Authority.*

YOUR LEARNING DESTINATION

Having learned about the general principles of communications, and having explored the toolbox of promotional techniques available to marketers, you'll be able to describe a program for implementing a promotion in a tourism destination or company. You will also be able to explain the roles of destination management organizations (DMOs).

WHAT YOU NEED TO KNOW

Having read this chapter, you will be able to:

- Identify and describe which promotional methods are most effective during the various stages of a visitor's buying process.
- Distinguish between informative promotion, persuasive promotion, and reminder messages, and identify when the use of these techniques is most appropriate.
- List and describe the main elements in the communication process.
- List and describe the elements of the promotional mix.

- Explain the increasing role of the Internet, social media networks, and mobile telephones in tourism information and promotion.
- Identify and explain the procedures involved in implementing a promotional program.
- Describe the roles and activities of national tourist offices (NTOs) related to promotion.
- Describe the promotional programs operated by agencies at the state, provincial, territorial, regional, and local levels.

BREAKING THE ICE

Do you get anxious when you are separated from your phone? In a recent survey by Pew Research, 46 percent of Americans say they "couldn't live without" their smartphone (Smith 2015). For many people, checking messages on their mobile is the first thing they do in the morning and the last thing they do at night. And many of the messages they receive are marketing messages. Some experts say we receive over 5,000 marketing messages each day—most of which we never even notice or forget as soon as we have seen them. This chapter will look at the ways marketing managers try to get your attention and get you to act.

KEY TAKEAWAY POINTS

- Promotions is a core element of the marketing mix.
- Promotional activities communicate to a select audience
- Promotions inform, persuade or remind consumers.
- There are many types of promotional activities. Personal Selling, Advertising, Digital and Social Media marketing, direct marketing, sales promo- tions, and public relations, just to name a few, are all types of promotion.
- Integrated Marketing Communication ensures each element of the promotional mix integrates and works to a common goal.
- The promotional planning process follows the 5 step planning process.
- Destination Management Organizations are responsible for promotional programs for destinations

PROMOTIONS = COMMUNICATIONS

Promotions is an exercise in communications. Tourism marketers communicate with consumers and key stakeholders through a wide range of promotional techniques to achieve marketing goals. No matter what the technique, it is useful to understand the communication process. Figure 8.1 provides an overview of the communications process as it pertains to tourism promotion.

Creating the Message

For the company preparing marketing communication, the first step in the communication process is deciding what needs to be communicated and then deciding the way you will communicate it. Anyone who has had an e-mail message misinterpreted or realized that they needed to talk to someone in person rather than send them a text knows that how you decide to encode your message is important. At this stage in marketing communications, several decisions need to be considered. What medium will be used? Is it most effective to say this message (oral), write it (written), or show it (visual)? What channel of communication will you use? A personal conversation, a banner ad, a traditional TV advertisement, or something else?

Barriers, Filters, Noise, and Permission

One of the great challenges of marketers in communicating to consumers or other stakeholders is just getting your message to people. In many cases, consumers don't want the message, so they put up **barriers** to many marketing messages. One of the popular government programs is the Do Not Call Registry that limits telemarketers' ability to call your number after you've signed up to the program. Consumers that record TV programs using their DVRs and then skip all the ads are putting up barriers as well. On many apps, people will pay money in the form of subscription fees to avoid getting unwanted ads. Other consumers *filter* many of the messages sent by marketers. A simple example of filtering is when you go to the mailbox and skip through a pile of direct mail and throw out 90 percent of it without even reading it. No matter how well the letter is written, if you don't read it, communication won't happen. **Noise** refers to everything in the environment that distracts us from a message. While it can be actual audible noise stopping you from hearing a message, this idea covers other noise as well. If you are stressed and don't have time to listen, that's noise. If you are multitasking and miss a message—noise.

Not all marketing communication is stopped, filtered out, or drowned out by noise. Some marketing messages we actually want to receive, and we'll ask for them. Marketing expert Seth Godin (1999) called this *permission marketing*. Sometimes we give our permission *explicitly*. If you subscribe to the movie previews channel, then you have given permission for the movie studios to market to you. If you sign up for special offers from your favorite clothing store, you are explicitly giving them permission to send you information. Many organizations have extensive consumer relationship management (CRM) systems to effectively deliver information. In other cases, the permission may be more *implicit*. Many services we receive online are paid for, either completely or partially, by advertising. Network television works this way, as do most radio stations. By using the service, you are implicitly giving permission for the company to market to you and for them to share your information with other marketers. However, while traditional broadcasters had little information on you personally and had to do surveys to be able to profile their viewers, companies now can capture much more information directly from users of digital media. For instance, Facebook is an example of a service that we get for free where we implicitly give them permission to send us ads. Once that implicit permission is given, digital media companies like Facebook work really hard to analyze your data and deliver messages that you won't filter. The better these companies cater to our interests, the more valuable we find their marketing communication. And, the more they know about you, the more valuable you are to them as they sell that information to their advertising clients.

DECODING THE MESSAGE AND ACTION

Once the consumer receives the message, there is still no guarantee that effective communication has occurred. The receiver must decode the message and interpret it as it was intended. There are a couple of factors to be considered here. First—did the receiver "get it"? The receiver assigns meaning to the message based on their own perceptions and psychology. Even when someone hears what you say, it doesn't mean that they understood you the way you intended. Second—did the receiver believe it? If you receive a message and decode it to be unbelievable or insincere, effective communication hasn't happened.

Marketing communication is often designed to elicit a response or to encourage some other form of action. As communication experts Thill and Bovee (2013) note, the receiver must remember the message long enough to act, to be able to act on it, and to be motivated to act on it.

Feedback

The final step in the communication process is receiving feedback. This is a critical step in being sure that the message was received as intended. In a personal conversation, you may check in with the person to whom you are talking to ensure they understood what you meant.

Many forms of traditional promotions had little opportunity for detailed feedback. While managers may

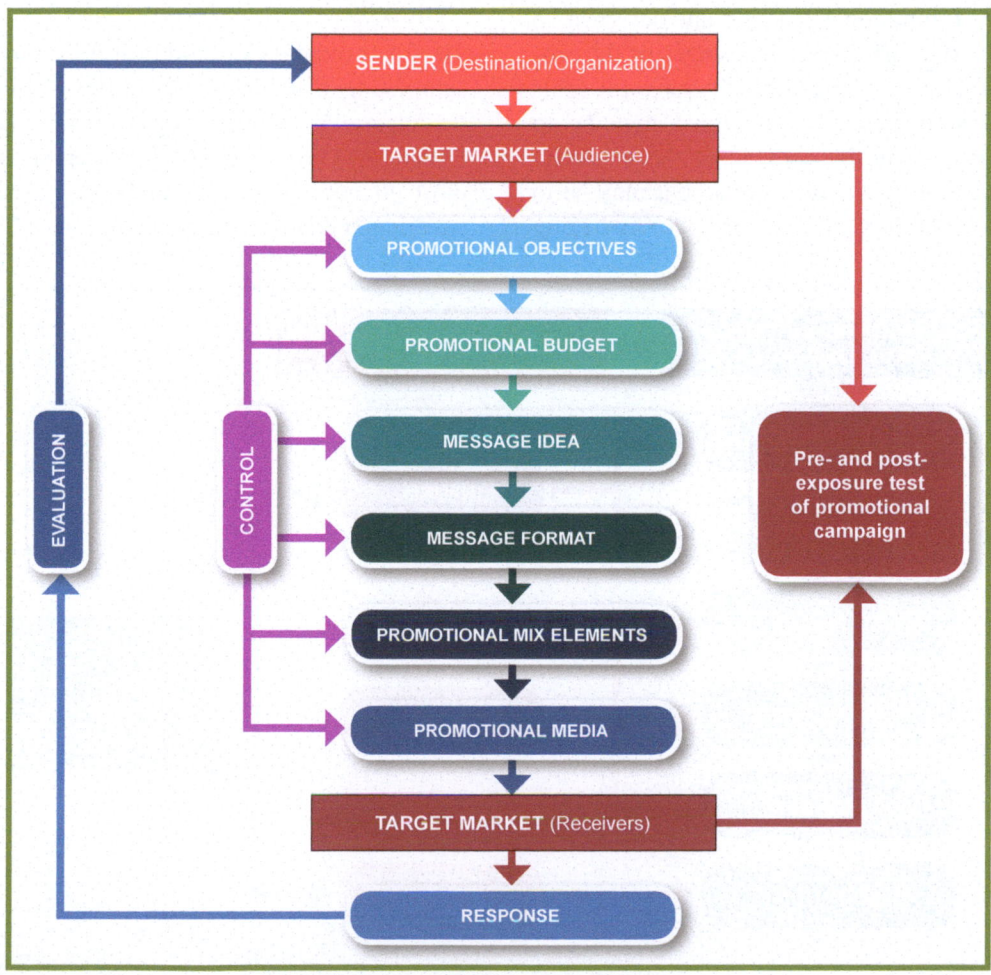

FIGURE 8.1 The communications process in tourism.

measure the effectiveness of the communication by responses or sales, understanding how the ads were received required market research, which included surveys and focus groups. Today, technology provides consumers with many more ways to provide immediate feedback about products. Indeed, the challenge for marketers today is to be able to utilize the information they receive.

GOALS AND TYPES OF PROMOTION

If promotion is communication, why are we communicating with our target market? The ultimate goal of promotion is behavior modification: the marketer uses promotion to change your behavior in some way. Promotions are designed to encourage you to do something. Whether it is stopping you from just dreaming about the experience and encouraging you to seek out information, or moving you to commit to buying, or reminding you to tell your friends about the great experience—the promotion is changing your behavior.

In Chapter 12 you will learn about the consumer buying process. Promotion strategies are designed to move consumers through the various stages of the process. In general, there are three broad behavioral goals of promotional strategies. The first goal may be to *create a booking* or sale by convincing the visitor to purchase for the first time. The second goal may be to modify the repeat visitor's purchase behavior by having

them *switch* to another destination, package, or service. The third goal may be to reinforce existing behavior by having the repeat visitor continue to purchase the same destination, package, or other service. Promotion accomplishes this by *informing*, *persuading*, or *reminding* the visitor about the promoter's services. Figure 8.2 shows the relationship between these three communication goals and the visitor's buying process.

Of course, each of these goals may require the use of multiple promotional techniques working together to achieve a goal. A consumer may be persuaded to purchase a vacation by a series of messages delivered through a variety of mediums over a period of time. For example, a television advertisement they happened to notice while they were thinking about taking a vacation, a blog post talking about the destination, or a great discount offer just as they were ready to buy may help move a consumer through the buying process toward a travel purchase.

Promotion and the Visitor's Buying Process

The goals of behavior modification are more effectively achieved by matching the three types of promotion with the stages of the visitor's buying process (as discussed in Chapter 11). For example, *informative promotions* are most effective at the earlier buying process stages of attention and comprehension (Figure 8.2). Promotional

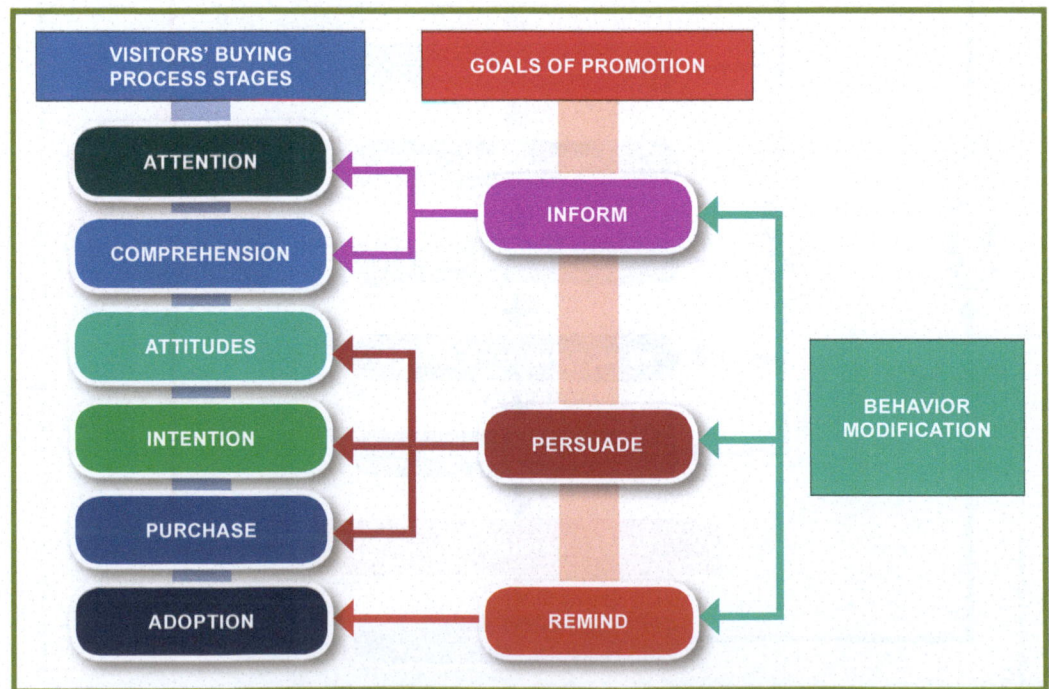

FIGURE 8.2 Goals of promotion and the visitor's buying process.

messages must grab the visitor's attention, while providing enough information and convincing arguments to assist with comprehension. Destination Canada does a great job of this in its "Canada: Keep Exploring" promotional campaign (2018). Instead of showing just the spectacular Canadian scenery, these promotions show people actively enjoying certain types of experiences in these beautiful destinations.

Persuasive promotions work more effectively at intermediate buying process stages (attitudes, intentions, and purchases). They can be used to change attitudes, develop intentions to buy, and to initiate purchases. Tourism New Zealand provides a good example of this on its website. Videos of inspirational experiences in New Zealand can be watched on the website. Tourism New Zealand also uses testimonials from celebrities, like Bryce Dallas Howard, who share their love of the destination (2017). These are a powerful testimonial for other people considering similar trips to an exciting long-haul destination such as New Zealand.

Reminder promotions are more effective after the first visit to the destination or after the first use of the organization's services. These promotions help stimulate repeat visits or purchases. A process known as *database marketing* is used in tourism to encourage repeat usage. Computer technology that allows for the manipulation of relational databases on past and potential visitors is facilitating this process. Cruise line companies and casino operators have been especially successful in building databases and using reminder promotions.

THE PROMOTIONAL TOOLBOX

The tools available to marketers to promote are many and varied. As with any well-stocked toolbox, there are tools that can be used for specialized purposes. Some activities are best used for long-term brand building. Other promotional techniques elicit immediate responses. Some are best for reminding consumers of the good time they had on their last trip.

FIGURE 8.3 Meeting planners secure sales through personal communication and problem–solving.

There are a number of major elements of the promotional mix that can be used. These categories are a little "fuzzy," and some techniques fit equally well in two categories of activity. For instance, when you pay a blogger to write an article to support your business, it could be described as advertising—or at least advertorial or digital marketing.

Personal Selling. Oral conversations, either by telephone or face-to-face, between salespeople and prospective customers.

Advertising. Any paid form of non-personal presentation and ideas, goods, or services by an identified sponsor. Advertising takes many forms and remains a mainstay of promotion. It can be found in a variety of mediums—from banner ads on websites to television, to newspapers, to glossy magazines. Different types of advertising are effective in achieving different goals. For instance, newspaper advertising focusing on today's specials may be designed to encourage immediate action; television advertising may be designed to raise awareness or interest and build brand equity.

Consumers recognize that the advertising message is controlled by the organization. In order to overcome consumer skepticism, advertisers may use *advertorial magazine* sections that look like regular articles but are written by the advertisers, not independent journalists.

Merchandising. Materials used in-house to stimulate sales including brochures in display racks, signs, posters, photographs, displays, tent cards, and other point-of-sale promotional items. Visitor guides are important marketing communications tools used by DMOs to provide detailed information to consumers.

Digital Marketing. This has rapidly become the major marketing and promotional venue for most DMOs and tourism companies. The main tools being used include websites, social media, and e-mail. Marketing through mobile phones, especially smartphones (iPhones, Android, etc.), is closely connected with these Internet marketing efforts. Together, these are often called *information and communications technologies.*

Hotel Brand Loyalty Programs are Strong

A recent study by Kalibri Labs (Estis-Green and Mazzocco 2017) found that the power of hotel loyalty programs is significant and growing. They attribute between 4 and 6 out of every 10 room nights were driven by loyalty program members in upper midscale, upscale, and upper upscale hotels.

Direct Marketing and Customer Relationship Management (CRM). CRM is an increasingly sophisticated marketing technique. Marketers collect data on customers' preferences and purchases in order to anticipate needs. While even small businesses can undertake CRM, larger data driven organizations are taking customer relationship management to new levels with advanced analytical approaches.

Sales Promotion. Approaches other than personal selling, advertising, and public relations and publicity where customers are given a short-term inducement to make an immediate purchase or booking, or to communicate with potential visitors or travel trade intermediaries. Sales promotion is the "and everything else" category.

Public Relations and Publicity. All the activities that maintain or improve relationships with other organizations and individuals. Publicity is one public relations technique that involves unpaid communication of information about a destination's or organization's services.

The Challenge of Believability

One of the important issues in communication is whether the message is believable. Consumers have become increasingly skeptical of marketing.

One of the important observations in tourism marketing communications is that a consumer's belief in a message increases as the marketer's control of the message reduces. Glossy advertisements are less likely to be believed than consumer-generated reviews.

This is a good reminder that effective marketing is more than just a promotional campaign. The promotions and marketing communications must be true to the consumer experience.

QUICK TRIP 8.1

I AM OUTSTANDING: A Model for Effective Tourism Websites

What are the characteristics of the world's best DMO websites? To demonstrate these characteristics, the "I AM OUTSTANDING" model was developed by Professor Alastair Morrison. While there are undoubtedly more characteristics than included in this model, it does cover many of the most important required features of tourism destination websites. There are at least fourteen important characteristics of excellent international DMO websites and taken one-by-one they spell out "I AM OUTSTANDING." They reflect online features that are not only important to visitors, but also are critical to effective DMO marketing communications.

- International: Communicate with global markets
- Address travelers as individuals: Personalize the website experience
- Monitored: Constantly check and evaluate
- Outstanding: Strive to be the best
- Up-to-date: Include timely information
- Targeted: Pinpoint different target markets
- Social media: Engage in conversations about the destination
- Telephone-ready: Make mobile phone applications available
- Attractive: Design eye-catching home pages
- Networked: Partner with others for greater success
- Dynamic: Create interactive online environments
- Integrated: Link all marketing communications together
- Niche markets: Capitalize on special interests
- Great contents: Provide detailed and useful information

Websites give tourism organizations and companies global reach.

© Toria/Shutterstock.com

If you take a look at www.webbyawards.com, you will find many outstanding tourism and travel websites that have been nominated. For example, the 21st Annual Webby Awards in 2017 included awards for websites of Qantas, Conde Nast Traveler, Snap Traveler, Travel Hacks, and New Orleans Tourism Marketing.

Think about This

1. What other criteria are important for effective destination websites in addition to those in the "I AM OUTSTANDING" model?
2. Do you think it is sufficient today for a tourism destination or company just to have a website, or do they also need to have sites/pages on the most important social media channels? Why or why not?
3. How do you think tourism websites compare to the sites for other services and products? What can tourism website designers learn from sites for other sectors of the economy?
4. Prepare a Top 10 list of your favorite tourism and travel websites. Which sites would you include and what were your selection criteria?

Sources

Morrison, A. M. 2009. *Hospitality and Travel Marketing,* 4th ed. Boston, MA: Cengage Learning.

Webby Awards. 2011. www.webbyawards.com/webbys/current.php#webby_entry_tourism

QUICK TRIP 8.2

The New Influencers

Could you be paid $200,000 a year to travel? With the rise of social media there is a new breed of travel influencers that marketing companies are reaching out to help promote their businesses.

Scott and Collette Stohler travel around the world for six months a year and are paid to post videos, photos, newsletters, and blogs on their website and social media channel. But getting paid doesn't just happen. In a recent story on the BBC, the Stoehlers were quick to point that it takes work to live this lifestyle (Holland 2017). The Stoehlers are paid for their posts by sponsoring companies, including DMOs, hotels, and attractions. Once they have secured a client, they will work on the logistics. Their income includes expense-paid trips with a "content creation fee," sponsorships, and product placement fees. "You need to hustle. For every 50 pitches we'll only hear a couple of yeses. You have to have that grit and that passion." While the client decides how many posts they will pay for, the Stoehlers maintain control on the content—what they write and post. That's important because they must maintain the relationship and trust with their followers—after all that is what they are paid for.

Digital nomads blog from their travels source.

The Stohler's work from their Los Angeles home, but there are influencers traveling further afield and blogging about exotic travel closer to the source of the story. Digital nomads are people who use technology to support their nomadic lifestyles. With Wi-Fi, a laptop, and a decent camera a digital nomad can blog from anywhere. Of course, to earn an income, they must have a following on social media.

With trust in traditional marketing at all-time lows, marketers are looking for credible sources to tell their story. Major public relations companies like Edelman provide corporations with advice on managing influencer marketing strategies. As Pauline Linton of Edelman points out "influence no longer comes from the top" and the most credible source of information is "a person like yourself." With this trend in place, the role of social media influencers in tourism marketing will continue to grow (Linton 2017).

Think about This

1. One of the challenges of modern consumers is finding reliable sources of information. Does this article make you more or less likely to believe things you read on blogs or see in your Instagram feed?
2. What ethical issues do influencers like the Stohler's face when recommending products that they are paid to promote? Is this different from more traditional media?
3. There is a growing awareness that many social media posts are staged and that people's lives are often very different from what they post on Facebook or Instagram. Does the possibility that images are staged influence how you view the post. Why or why not?

Sources

Holland, J. 2017. "The Couple Paid $200K a year to travel." BBC. http://www.bbc.com/capital/story/20171019-the-couple-paid-200k-a-year-to-travel.

Linton, P. 2017. "Building an Influencer Marketing Strategy." Edelman. https://www.edelman.com/post/building-an-influencer-marketing-strategy/

INTEGRATED MARKETING COMMUNICATION

While the marketer has many promotional "tools" in their toolbox, it is important that each of the tools is used in a coordinated way to achieve desired outcomes. As Figure 8.4 signifies, it is important to integrate the design and application of all promotional mix elements. This integration leads to more consistent communications across all channels and makes promotion much more effective. The term *integrated marketing communications* is commonly used for this process of ensuring uniformity in design and messages.

PLANNING PROMOTIONS

Big P and little p promotions. The promotion planning process is an important component of the marketing planning process. Even so, it shouldn't be a surprise if there isn't a "promotions" plan or, if there is, that it only deals with certain elements of the promotional mix. It's common for elements of the promotional mix to work independently while still contributing to the marketing plan. It's more common for the advertising department to report to a marketing manager than to a promotions manager. Specialists in aspects of promotion work to develop their own plans. For instance, many organizations will have a sales department and will develop sales plans to meet specific sales goals. Similarly, specialists in digital marketing, social marketing, public relations, advertising, and any of the other promotional mix elements may very well have their own plans.

PROMOTIONS PLANNING PROCESS

The promotions planning process follows the same general planning model (Morrison 2010) discussed in Chapter 7.

Where Are We Now?

The promotions planning process should be built on a foundation of market intelligence. Much of the information used by those building the promotions plan will be shared with other marketing departments. At a time when media is changing rapidly, particularly digital marketing, it is critical to stay ahead of the new ways people receive information. As with all managers involved in building marketing plans, one of the most important tasks of promotions planners is to gain a deep understanding of the target market—including the market's buying behavior and media consumption.

Select the Target Audience

The process of *target market selection* was explained in Chapter 7. This should include an analysis of published (secondary research) market data and primary research results from such techniques as surveys or focus groups. A target market must be accessible through one or more promotional mix elements, or through a specific type of media. Certain basic information must be available on a target market's demographics and geographic origins (place of residence or business). A target market may be more finely pinpointed by overlaying demographic and

FIGURE 8.4 Integrated Marketing Communication ensures the messages from each type of promotional activity work to a common goal.

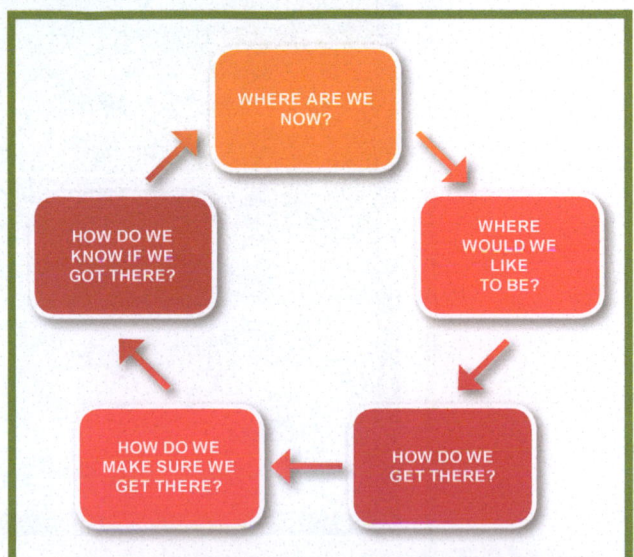

FIGURE 8.5 Planning Process–Promotions. The planning process used for marketing and destination development can also be applied to developing promotional plans.

geographic characteristics with one or more of five other segmentation bases (psychographics or lifestyles, purpose of trip, product-related, behavioral, or channel of distribution). The target market must also include people with similar characteristics who are the best prospects for future business. This first element of the tourism communication process can only be effective if a complete market segmentation analysis has been completed.

No matter how the market is segmented, it is useful to have information of the target market's media consumption profile and buying process. This type of information allows the marketer to target the promotional messages in a way that will impact behavior and through a medium that is effective. The current level of awareness of the tourism destination or service must be established. If people in the target market are at the intention stage of the buying process, then informative messages are a poor use of time and money. By conducting an awareness study, either through a survey or focus groups, the buying process stage of the targeted visitors can be determined.

To achieve marketing goals, some promotional campaigns are directed not to target markets but to other stakeholder groups. Promotional campaigns can focus on members of the companies' supply chain, internal stakeholders like host community members for destinations or staff for organizations, and even the media. DMOs and tourism companies have four principal groups to which they need to direct promotional messages, as shown in Figure 8.6.

Two of these branches of promotion are called consumer promotions (visitors) and trade promotions (travel trade intermediaries). Consumer promotions can be further categorized into potential visitors, past visitors, and present visitors. Messages also need to be directed to the media (Internet news services, newspapers, magazines, television, and radio stations) and the local community (residents, elected officials, and government agencies).

The effectiveness of specific promotional tools varies according to which of the four groups are being targeted (Figure 8.6). For example, sales promotions and educational workshops or seminars can be very effective when promoting to retail travel agencies. Advertising on television or in a consumer travel magazine may be more effective in communicating with potential visitors. However, the emergence of the web and social media networks has provided a vehicle for reaching all four groups.

Where Would We Like to Be? Developing Promotional Objectives

The next step is to establish the objectives for the promotional campaign. Promotions and marketing communications objectives will contribute to strategic marketing goals. To be effective, objectives must be target-market specific, stated as a desired result or outcome,

FIGURE 8.6 Promotional target groups of DMOs and tourism companies.

measurable, realistically attainable, and have a deadline for achievement.

When setting promotional objectives, it is important to consider the targeted visitors' buying process stage, as well as the destination or organization's product life cycle (PLC) stage. In the attention or awareness stages, the objective may be to expose the message to a specified number of target market members within a specific time period. In the intention stage, the objective may be oriented toward increasing purchases.

How Do We Get There? Developing Action Plans to Achieve Goals

By first establishing the objectives, the promotions planner can "begin with the end in mind." Working backward from the outcomes they expect, they can identify the activities that need to happen to achieve the desired outcome.

Activities and Campaigns.

An activity may be undertaken to achieve specific, often tactical objectives. More commonly, a series of activities may be identified to achieve a specific promotional objective. So for instance, if the promotional objective is to raise awareness of the brand 5 percent in the core target market, the marketer may use a combination of advertising—television and magazine, public relations and a social media–based image competition that encourages people to post brand-consistent images on the site.

A *promotional campaign* may be a set of activities designed to achieve a set of promotional goals within a specific *time frame*. For instance, a fall campaign may contribute to several major promotional objectives, such as raising brand awareness, generating leads, and generating specific sales. The fall campaign may utilize a variety of promotional mix tools to achieve these goals. Campaigns may contribute significantly to achieving promotional objectives during the course of a year.

Establish the Promotional Budget

The promotional objectives must provide the basic foundation for establishing the promotional budget. This is called the *objective-and-task budgeting method,* which uses a "bottom-up" or zero-based budgeting approach. Only by planning what is required (the tasks or activities) to achieve objectives can an accurate estimate be made of how much to spend on promotions. Often, objectives are based upon how much money the destination or company has to spend, which is "top-

down" budgeting or the *affordable budgeting method*. Tourism destinations and companies do not have unlimited funds for marketing, and many operate with very small promotional budgets. Despite this, setting marketing objectives after the budget is established (rather than before) can produce objectives that will never be achieved. When a tentative budget amount has been estimated based upon the objectives and tasks (promotional activities), other factors need to be considered. These include the promotional budgets of competitors and the funds available to the tourism destination or organization. All marketing plans and budgets must be flexible enough to allow for changing market conditions and competitive activities; therefore, a contingency amount needs to be attached to the promotional budget.

When preparing the budget, consideration is given to cooperative promotions (*partnerships*) with other organizations. Many DMOs have extensive cooperative marketing programs, especially with efforts to attract international visitors. The pooling of promotional dollars creates great synergy for all parties involved; in effect, it increases everyone's promotional budget.

Determine the Message Idea

Marketers must determine the key message, or the message they need to convey to achieve their promotional objectives. Marketers may hone the message, seeking feedback from the target audience, to ensure that the message is being received and decoded exactly as intended. In the sales process, salespeople may use probing questions and careful listening to ensure that meaning is conveyed correctly. In advertising, other techniques with the same goals may be undertaken. Primary research techniques such as focus groups, one-to-one interviews, and surveys can be used to pinpoint the target market's perceptions (images), needs, wants, motives, and expectations. The findings may be used to determine what to communicate in the message (the message idea). Alternative message ideas can be developed and discussed with a sample of people from the target market, perhaps in a small-group setting like a focus group. Based on people's ratings of the alternative approaches, the most effective message idea is chosen. Message ideas must support the positioning approach (image to be communicated) selected by the tourism destination or organization. Control is achieved through the process of pretesting alternative message ideas by choosing a message idea that communicates best to representatives of the targeted visitors.

Select the Message Format

Message ideas can be communicated in many different ways. How a message is communicated to the target market is called the message format or creative format. The objective is to choose a format that effectively communicates the message idea in a way that is understandable, distinctive, and believable for the target market. Advertising agencies are often used to assist with this creative task.

Select Promotional Mix Elements

As we have seen, there are many possible tools that a marketing manager can use in developing a promotional campaign. Indeed, there is an almost infinite set of combinations of uses of these tools to achieve marketing objectives.

The selection of promotional mix elements varies with the characteristics of the target market, the type of destination or company service, and the promotional funds available. Different promotional tools or techniques will be more appropriate in some situations than others. For example, the more expensive and complex the service or destination being promoted, the greater the need for some form of personal selling. While an advertisement may induce a couple to spend a weekend at a resort, a meeting planner choosing a site location for a convention of more than a thousand delegates will require more detailed information and some personal selling. Likewise, a couple planning to take a cruise or an extensive foreign tour may need the advice of an experienced travel agent.

Most promotional budgets in tourism include amounts for each of the promotional mix elements. However, the relative proportions of each mix element will vary according to the absolute size of the budget. For example, maintaining a large sales force and placing national-level advertising require a large minimum investment. Many forms of advertising are relatively expensive, and advertising typically represents a large share of all promotion spending. For example, a four-color advertisement in a national consumer travel magazine may cost more than $50,000.

Select Promotional Media

Decisions about the specific media to use will be tied closely to your decision on what promotional mix elements to use. Media used in tourism include the Internet and social media channels, mobile phones, newspapers, magazines, television (network and cable), radio, outdoor/transit, and direct mail. Each medium has distinct advantages and disadvantages. The crucial part of media selection is choosing those that will be seen, read, or heard by the intended target market.

Most media companies provide market research statistics on the profiles of their readers, viewers, or listeners. In addition, there are general criteria against which media can be compared to determine which is the most appropriate:

- **Cost per contact:** The cost of reaching one person in the target market
- **Cost per inquiry:** The cost of an advertisement divided by the total number of inquiries it generates
- **Cost per thousand:** The cost of reaching 1,000 people in the target market
- **Geographic selectivity:** The ability to target specific geographic areas
- **Life span:** The length of time the target market will be exposed to the message
- **Market selectivity:** The ability to communicate with specific target markets
- **Noise level:** The amount of competitive advertising in the medium
- **Pass-along rate:** The rate at which people pass along materials (e.g., magazines) to other people
- **Reach:** The total number of people who are exposed to the message
- **Source credibility:** The credibility or reputation of the medium for accuracy and lack of bias
- **Timing flexibility:** The amount of lead time required to place the message (shorter lead times give greater flexibility)
- **Total cost:** The total cost of developing and communicating the message
- **Visual quality:** The level of quality of the visual presentation, especially when in color

Although the cost per contact is low for *television advertising,* the total cost is very high. Television allows the tourism advertiser to be geographically selective and choose the target market by the specific type of shows or programs. The visual quality of television advertisements can be extremely high. However, television suffers from a rather low level of credibility and trust among viewers. Because of the tendency to watch television with other people, the noise level tends to be higher than average. Because advertising schedules often have to be decided far in advance, the timing flexibility for television is below average.

Radio offers a medium that is low in total cost and cost per contact. Like television, radio is selective for

Visitors	Travel Trade, Media/Press, and Local Community
Potential Visitors	**Travel Trade Intermediaries**
Consumer travel, sports, recreation shows Help desks Inquiry handling and fulfillment Media advertising Telemarketing Travel videos and films Web site Social media sites and networks Blogs and microblogs Mobile phone apps Mobile phone messaging (SMS/MMS) Travel review websites (e.g., TripAdvisor)	Collateral materials (visitor guides, calendars of events, maps, etc.) Direct mail and direct fax advertising Display materials (maps, posters, brochures) Destination "expert" programs Familiarization trips Inquiry handling and fulfillment Newsletters Preferred supplier programs Press releases Recognition and award programs Telemarketing Trade journal advertising Travel trade fairs, shows, exhibitions Workshops and seminars Website Social media sites and networks Blogs and microblogs Mobile phone apps Mobile phone messaging (SMS/MMS)
Past Visitors	**Media and Press**
Direct mail and direct fax advertising Frequent traveler clubs Newsletters Telemarketing Website Social media sites and networks Blogs and microblogs Mobile phone Aapps	Editorials/feature stories Familiarization trips for travel writers Newsletters Photo galleries Press conferences and releases Website Social media sites and networks Blogs and microblogs Mobile phone messaging (SMS/MMS)
Present Visitors	**Local Community**
Hospitality and service training programs Reception and welcoming services Travel maps and literature Travel information centers Websites Social media sites and networks Blogs and microblogs Mobile phone apps Mobile phone messaging (SMS/MMS) Travel review websites (e.g., TripAdvisor)	Community tourism awareness programs Newsletters Hospitality/service quality award programs Website Social media sites and networks Blogs and microblogs Mobile phone apps Mobile phone messaging (SMS/MMS)

FIGURE 8.7 Promotional target groups and communications tools.

broad market groups and has high geographic selectivity. The credibility and noise level are similar to those for television. However, the timing flexibility is far greater; radio advertisements can be placed on very short notice.

Newspapers also offer a low total cost and cost per contact. Market selectivity is low, but geographic selectivity is good because it is possible to target specific cities and towns. Certain nationally distributed newspapers allow tourism marketers to pinpoint business travelers, such as *The Wall Street Journal, Globe & Mail, The Australian, London Times,* and the *Daily Telegraph.* The trust factor for newspapers seems to be low, and the visual quality is less than average. To compensate for a

QUICK TRIP 8.3

GoPro and Australia: Creating Compelling Promotional Messages

In a world awash with marketing messages, how do you create content that captures people's attention? Gather one hundred extreme athletes from around the world, give them GoPro cameras, and ask them to capture the fun of one of Australia's iconic tourism destinations—the Gold Coast.

In 2016 Tourism Australia, Tourism and Events Queensland, Gold Coast Tourism, and GoPro partnered to create the GoPro Athlete Summit (Keen and McElroy 2016). The athletes were popular influencers in their own fields—many with their own large presence on social media—and had a combined 10 million social media followers. There were Olympians, endurance and adventure athletes, skydivers, swimmers, surfers, snowboarders, wakeboarders, skateboarders, BMX riders, motorcyclists, and rally drivers. The video and images they created and edited were shared with their own followers and then amplified by the campaign partners including GoPro and Tourism Australia.

> "What better way to create compelling content for our new aquatic and coastal campaign than by hosting 100 of the world's top action sports athletes at one of Australia's most iconic coastal destinations and for them to then share their adventures and experiences with their fans around the world," said Tourism Australia Managing Director, John O'Sullivan.

What sort of things did the athletes show? The local newspaper, the *Gold Coast Bulletin* captured the news this way:

- England's world champion freeride mountain biker Sam Pilgrim has been tweeting his 90,000 followers about having a great time surfing and getting up close to a kangaroo.
- "Got in the ocean today here on the Gold Coast!" he tweeted after arriving yesterday afternoon.
- "Board shorts surfing is the best!"
- In a Facebook photo shared with his 213,000 followers, Pilgrim posted shots of a kangaroo and noted: "Stoked to have gotten this close to a wild kangaroo today on the Gold Coast Australia!!"
- Professional Canadian BMX rider Drew Bezanson went exploring waterfalls with fellow BMX rider Mike Escamilla who is also a stuntman, tweeting: "Epic first day exploring @Australia on @GoPro athlete summit with @MikeEscamilla. #seeAustralia #gopro." (2016)

The promotion created immediate impact and provided resources that could be used in ongoing campaigns promoting coastal experiences. In fact, footage created during the GoPro Athlete Summit was shown at Australia's largest international tourism tradeshow, the Australian Tourism Exchange, the very next week.

Think about This

1. How much control do you think Tourism Australia had over the messages shared by the athletes? Do you think that was an advantage or a risk for the sponsors?
2. Credibility is a challenge for marketers. Would you be more likely to believe the reactions of these athletes than traditional television advertising?
3. Would this type of promotion capture your attention? Why or why not?

Sources

Tourism Australia. 2016. "Tourism Australia Teams Up With GoPro to Showcase Queensland's Gold Coast". http://www.tourism. australia.com/en/news-and-industry-tools/latest-news/tourism-australia-teams-up-with-gopro-to-showcase-gold-coast.html. Used with permission.

Keen, R., and N. McElroy. 2016 "Tourism Australia hails Gold Coast as GoPro Athlete Summit and Australian Tourism Exchange loom." *Gold Coast Bulletin.* http://www.goldcoastbulletin.com.au/entertainment/tourism-australia-hails-gold-coast-as-gopro-athlete-summit-and-australian-tourism-exchange-loom/news-story/5afb0a7cddb0ab29381fd9341ef8308d

---

high noise level, short life span, and low pass-along rate, newspapers offer a great deal of flexibility in the timing of advertisements. Although market selectivity is low with newspapers, the total cost, cost per contact, and geographic selectivity are good.

Magazines have a much higher cost per contact and total cost than newspapers. However, due to the specialized nature of magazines, the market selectivity can be very high. The regional editions available for certain magazines offer some geographic selectivity. The visual quality of magazines is much higher than for newspapers, and the noise level is usually much lower. Both the life span and pass-along rate are above average. The timing flexibility is low with magazines as they have relatively long lead times for placing advertisements.

Although the total cost of a *direct mail* campaign tends to be rather high, the cost per contact varies widely depending upon the quality of the materials to be sent. Market selectivity and geographic selectivity are the highest of all media; direct mailings can be highly personalized. The source credibility is below average due to the ever-increasing volume of junk mail that most people receive. The life span of a direct mail piece tends to be short, especially if the mailing is not highly personalized. The visual quality can be very high, and the noise level is low but increasing. A direct mail piece can have a strong impact on a purchase decision, again if the message is highly personalized. Timing flexibility can be good with direct mail but is dependent on the type of items to be included in the mailing and on their production times.

All of these media types, except direct mail, suffer from a lack of personalization; they are mass media. With the emergence of the concept of relationship marketing (building and enhancing long-term relationships with individual visitors and other organizations), a greater emphasis is now being placed on one-to-one communications. Media that provide for individualized messages are fast growing in popularity in tourism. These include all forms of direct marketing, including direct mail and telemarketing (telephone selling).

The print media (newspapers and magazines) are popular with travel, hotel, and resort organizations. Although newspapers are expected to continue to be the most used advertising medium for tourism, their effectiveness is eroding. The travel sections of newspapers tend to be read only after the decision to travel has been made. People who read the travel sections are highly motivated to travel. In order to expand the travel market, other media such as television, radio, direct mail, and the web will get greater use in the future.

Restaurant companies (especially fast-food chains), hotel chains, and airlines tend to spend the largest amounts on media advertising. Restaurants spend the largest proportion of their media advertising budgets on the electronic media, especially on television. Hotels and airlines tend to favor the print media (newspapers and magazines). DMOs appear to make the greatest use of magazines and television for their advertising.

The interactive potential of using the web and other types of Internet marketing has attracted great attention from tourism marketers in the past fifteen to twenty years. The major advantages of Internet marketing are:

- The global reach of the Internet and the twenty-four-hour availability of travel information
- The increased speed of transactions
- The capacity to instantly update information
- The ability to gather research information and build customer databases
- The ease of forming virtual partnerships with related organizations
- The greater ability to build and maintain relationships through improved communications and personalization
- The availability of instant feedback for customers
- The relatively low cost of Internet marketing

How Do We Make Sure We Get There? Measure Promotional Effectiveness

One of the great challenges of promotional campaigns is to prove their effectiveness. John Wanamaker, who was a successful merchant in the late nineteenth and early twentieth century and was considered by some as a pioneer of marketing, is quoted as saying, "Half the money I spend on advertising is wasted; the trouble is I don't know which half." Determining promotional campaign effectiveness has improved since Wanamaker's time. In particular, the growth of digital marketing has increased marketers' ability to track consumer progress through the buying process. Nevertheless, the challenge to measure promotional effectiveness remains.

The response to a promotion can be measured in terms of changes in the awareness levels of the tourism destination or organization, the way the message is perceived by visitors (see Chapter 11), the number of responses, and, if appropriate, the conversion rates. Potential problems are minimized if campaigns are controlled and effectiveness is tested at each step in the promotional program. However, the measurement of promotional effectiveness appears to be something that needs to be improved among tourism organizations.

Each type of promotional activity will have its own *specific metrics*. Television advertising metrics will be different for online marketing. In order to effectively control the marketing activities over time, tourism marketers may use a variety of metrics. Some of these metrics will be performance indicators, measures that give you a sense of how the program is progressing, and others will be results. For example, in an advertising campaign responses may be a *performance indicator* because you need responses if you want to convert people who have shown some interest in your product to be actual paid customers. The *result* is the number of customers who convert from the responses. Tourism promoters must be careful not to confuse KPIs with actual results.

QUICK TRIP 8.4

Google and Tourism Marketing

There is no doubt that Google has changed tourism marketing. Across the tourism industry, specialists in search engine optimization work to ensure their websites come up first when someone searches for a hotel, destination, or attraction like theirs. Google has also upended the advertising industry, allowing companies to pay just a few dollars for prequalified leads. Google certainly changed the information search process for consumers. Today, more information is available on more places than ever before When traveling, Google Maps is often the first place that people go to plan a trip—or check on directions while they travel. New features on Google Maps allow consumers to buy travel products as they travel along. Google Earth allows many potential travelers to walk the streets they plan to visit, or relive the experience when they return.

In recent years, Google has added a number of travel-related products including Google Flights which provides information on flights including the ability to track prices, notifications on price rises, and flight availability. Of course, you can book through Google as well. The hotel search feature on Google has similar features. Both have easy options to check different dates and length of stay at the move of a fingertip. Google Trips is a new service that keeps all your travel information in one place, provides updates on changes in schedules, book buses and trains, and checks trending destinations. Google Trip information can be downloaded so you have it on your phone even when not connected to the Internet. Skift Research calculates that Google's travel business generates over $11 billion annually, making the value of this part of the business alone more than $100 billion. That's a valuation higher than the leading OTA (Wein 2017).

Google and mobile technology are enabling travelers to explore new places.

Google continues to innovate in ways that create value for consumers in the tourism system. In late 2017 they introduced Google Pixel Buds—earphones that when combined with Google Translate and Google Assistant (Google's equivalent of Apple's Siri) have real-time translation for over forty languages. The system is powered by machine learning and gets better as it learns. If Google can deliver on the promise of this technology it will reduce another important barrier to international travel (Sheivachman 2017).

So what does Google say is the future of travel? In a recent posting they highlighted three important trends:

- Travel purchasers are increasingly impulsive and 60 percent of United States travelers would book a trip on a whim if they could get a good deal.
- People want information fast—and customized in a way that is meaningful to them. Fifty-seven percent of United States travelers tailored information to their personal preferences or past experiences.
- Voice and digital assistants are becoming increasingly important. One in three travels used digital assistants to research or book travel.

Behind many of these services is a growing use of artificial intelligence and machine learning.

In a recent Google blog (Loo 2017), Oliver Heckman, Google's VP of Engineering for travel and shopping, explained "Our goal is to make sure that travelers have a great user experience when they come to Google for answers, and I see our role in the travel ecosystem as one that helps connect users to partners. Where we can help is in providing data and insights around traveler intent, identity, and context," he said. "At the end of the day, it's all about making people's lives easier, and machine learning accelerates all of these opportunities to engage travelers at the right time and place."

Think about This

1. Consider the last time you traveled. How many times did you use a Google product during the process of preparing for the trip, traveling, and returning?
2. Consider how Google and mobile technology has changed tourism. Make a list of the ways these technologies are used.
3. Is language a barrier to travel? How do you think Google Translate will change the tourism system?

Sources

Loo, J. 2017. The future of travel: New consumer behavior and technology giving it flight. https://www.thinkwithgoogle.com/marketing-resources/new-consumer-travel-assistance

Sheivachman, A. 2017. Google's New Earbuds with real-time translation have huge implications for travel. https://skift.com/2017/10/05/googles-new-earbuds-with-real-time-translation-have-huge-implications-for-travel/

Wein, J. 2017. Google Travel is worth $100 billion—even more than priceline. https://skift.com/2017/09/18/google-travel-is-worth-100-billion-even-more-than-priceline/

Measuring Promotional Activities

The techniques used to measure the effectiveness of promotional activities will be contingent on the type of promotion. Here is a sampling of techniques that can be used to measure promotional efficiency and effectiveness. These include (Davidson 1994, Koth 1988, Perdue and Pitegoff 1994, Pizam 1994, Siegel and Ziff-Levine 1994, Woodside and Ronkainen 1994).

- **Advertising tracking studies:** These studies track the awareness levels and images of the tourism destination or organization before and after the placement of the advertising.
- **Cost-comparison method:** This method calculates ratios such as cost per inquiry, cost per visitor, and return on investment. These ratios may be produced in a conversion study.
- **Concept testing:** These are small-scale, qualitative studies of rough drawings of message ideas or campaigns.
- **Conversion studies:** These studies determine how many inquirers from tourism advertising convert to visitors as well as the converted visitors' demographic and travel-behavior characteristics, including length of stay, travel-party size, destination activities, and expenditures.
- **Inquiry and lead tracking:** These are measures of promotional efficiency in which records are kept of direct-response advertising inquiries or sales leads (from sales calls or travel and trade shows).
- **Pretesting:** Studies that expose samples of the target market to preliminary or finished versions of the proposed promotions.
- **Post-testing:** Studies done after the promotional campaign has ended to determine changes in images, awareness, attitudes, and recall.
- **Travel or trade show audits:** Studies on the past attendance and characteristics of the people who attend consumer travel and travel trade shows.

Many DMOs and tourism companies now are setting key performance indicators to set targets and then to measure the results of all marketing and promotional activities.

How Do We Know We Got There? Evaluating Marketing Communications

Promotional effectiveness is determined by the ability of the campaign to achieve the goals outlined. Evaluation is an important part of the managerial process of control. Failure to achieve a communication goal may be the result of a partial or complete failure in any aspect of the communication process. Marketers may use feedback from effective marketing evaluations to further refine their strategies.

DMOS AND TOURISM PROMOTION

In Chapter 3 we saw the important role DMOs play in destination development and policy creation. DMOs also promote their destinations.

Destinations Systems and DMOs

Destinations systems can be defined by their geographic scope. A destination can exist at a local level; for instance, a destination can be a city like New York. It can even be as small as a neighborhood like SoHo. A destination can be a region like Tuscany. A state—California. A country or nation, like Australia or Britain. Systems theories remind us that systems are often embedded in other systems, and this is true for destinations. Destinations can simultaneously be in several destination systems. So, when you stand on North Michigan Avenue, you are simultaneously on the Magnificent Mile (neighborhood), in the city of Chicago, in the state of Illinois, and in the nation of the United States. For each of these destination systems there are DMOs. While each of these DMOs share similar goals and undertake similar activities, each one frames the market slightly differently and adds value in a unique way.

National Tourism Organizations (NTO)

An NTO is the organization officially responsible for the marketing and promotion of tourism for a country. Many NTOs are charged with marketing the country internationally. As you will recall from Chapter 2, when visitors from other countries spend money in a destination, it is an export and generates valuable foreign exchange earnings. Brand USA is an example of an NTO that only markets internationally. Most NTOs maintain head offices in their own countries and operate a network of offices in other countries. NTOs are located in countries that generate most of their international visitor arrivals.

Some NTOs also conduct marketing within their home country to stimulate travel by locals and to support the domestic tourism market. This approach is designed to stimulate economic activity within the sector and to reduce leakage from the system as locals travel and spend money overseas.

There are now several hundred NTOs abroad. A relatively small country, New Zealand, operates fifteen overseas offices. With the arrival of the Internet, it became possible to operate overseas marketing campaigns from a head office. Smaller countries with low NTO budgets are forced to do this. Some NTOs contract with sales representative firms or public relations consultants to handle their promotional efforts. Others work through the offices of their national airlines. Some use their embassies or consulates to represent the NTO, but this tends not to be an effective solution. One explanation is that embassies located in the country's capital are often not in the best places for promoting to potential visitors and travel trade intermediaries (e.g., Canberra in Australia, Ottawa in Canada, and Washington, DC, in the United States). It is much more effective to locate NTOs in the country's largest cities (e.g., Sydney, Melbourne, Toronto, Montreal, Vancouver, New York, and Los Angeles). NTOs staff their foreign offices mainly with their own citizens.

Regional Tourism Organizations

Another level of tourism promotion agencies is at the regional level (within states, provinces, or territories). The format of these agencies varies by country, mainly due to the organizational structure of government and the physical size of the country, state, province, or territory. In smaller countries such as Scotland and Ireland, there tends to be a structure of regional tourism agencies under the NTO. For example, in Scotland there are six regions (Aberdeen City and Shire, East Central Scotland, Highlands and Islands, South of Scotland, Tayside, and West Central Scotland). Within these six regions, there are a total of fourteen local offices of VisitScotland.

In larger states and provinces like Ontario in Canada and Queensland in Australia, systems of regional tourism offices or organizations have been established. The Province of Ontario has twelve regional tourism organizations in the OTAP program (Essex, Southwest Ontario, Niagara Region, South Central Ontario, Toronto and Region, Central Ontario, St. Lawrence Corridor, Ottawa Region, Eastern Ontario, North-Central, North-East, and North-West). Queensland, Australia, has fourteen regional tourism organizations (Brisbane Marketing, Bundaberg North Burnett

Tourism, Capricorn Tourism and Economic Development Organisation, Tourism Fraser Coast, Gladstone Area Promotion and Development, Gold Coast Tourism, Mackay Tourism, Outback Queensland Tourism Association, Southern Downs and Granite Belt Regional Tourism, Toowoomba Golden West Tourism and South Burnett Tourism, Sunshine Coast Destination, Tourism Tropical North Queensland, Tourism Whitsundays, and Townsville Enterprise).

There are other interpretations of "region," and it is good to be aware of these as well. In the United States, there are tourism regions consisting of several states. For example, Travel South USA is the official regional marketing organization for the Southern United States. Travel South's mission is to promote, foster, and encourage travel to and within the states of Alabama, Arkansas, Georgia, Kentucky, Louisiana, Mississippi, North Carolina, South Carolina, Tennessee, Virginia, and West Virginia.

Another interpretation of the term "region" in tourism is that this represents an area encompassing several different countries and NTOs. For example, the NTOs in the Scandinavian region in Northern Europe operate their international travel promotions in a regional partnership called the Scandinavian Tourist Boards. Other regional partnerships in tourism include El Mundo Maya (the Mayan World), involving the countries of Belize, El Salvador, Guatemala, Honduras, and Mexico in Central America, and the Greater Mekong region (Cambodia, China, Laos, Myanmar, Thailand, and Vietnam). The Caribbean Tourism Organization, European Travel Commission, and the Pacific Asia Travel Association are all examples of permanent organizations that have been created to encourage the development and promotion of tourism in their multi-country regions.

County, City, and Other Local Tourism Organizations

Many cities and towns have their own local DMOs. Some of the larger countries in the world, including the United States, Australia, and China, have strong local tourism organizations at the county, city, or other local levels.

In the United States, the introduction of room taxes by city and county governments has helped to finance an extensive network of local CVBs. The first CVB was opened more than one hundred years ago in Detroit, Michigan. Most of the larger CVBs in the world are members of the Destination International located in Washington, DC. A traditional role of CVBs, as their name suggests, has been to attract business from the MICE markets (meetings, incentives, conventions, and exhibitions). Recently, CVBs have been placing more emphasis on attracting group tours and individual pleasure travelers.

Destination Marketing Communications

DMOs undertake a wide variety of activities. The seven major goals of an NTO are:

1. **Image creation and enhancement role:** To promote a favorable image of the country as a tourism destination, and to maintain or enhance this image.
2. **Literature distribution and fulfillment role:** To increase and make more effective the supply of information on the tourism services and products of the destination.
3. **Marketing research and database development role:** To collect information and create databases that help to increase the effectiveness of marketing decisions.
4. **Package and tour development role:** To increase the availability of the tourism products of the destination by increasing the number of new tour programs and packaged vacations and the capacity of existing ones, or to maintain at targeted levels the number and capacity of such programs.
5. **Partnership development role:** To play a leadership role in the development of marketing and promotional partnerships between transportation carriers, suppliers, travel trade intermediaries, and other businesses in the host country and the originating countries.
6. **Consumer marketing and promotional role:** To secure maximum promotional exposure for the destination mix of the country.
7. **Travel trade marketing and promotional role:** To familiarize travel trade distribution channels with the destination's services and products and stimulate them to increase sales.

Of the seven major roles of the NTOs, all require the use of marketing communication and promotional activities.

Image Creation and Destination Branding

Through its promotional programs, an NTO must communicate a distinctive and favorable image (positioning) of the country as a destination. It must seek to maintain and enhance this image, even in the face of adverse publicity.

Literature Distribution and Fulfillment

Printed literature distribution has been a traditional role of all NTOs. However, since around 1995, much greater emphasis has been placed by NTOs on the development of digital media contents for websites, social media networks, mobile phones, and in DVD format. Most NTO websites include interactive maps, lists of attractions, festival and event calendars, hotel guides, visitor guides, information on packages and tours, and much more.

Marketing Research and Database Development

NTOs abroad are used to gather marketing research information and to build databases of travel trade intermediaries, business event groups, and other types of visitors. The generation of inquiries as a result of website visits and direct-response advertising is a good source of databases. Databases may also be bought from magazines and mailing list brokers when special-interest markets are to be targeted.

Package and Tour Development

One way to increase the flow of visitors to a country is to increase the number of tour programs and packaged vacations to that destination.

Partnership Development

Many NTOs try to create marketing and promotional partnerships with tourism and non-tourism organizations. The CTC has an extensive cooperative marketing partnership program that involves other DMOs and the private sector.

Consumer Marketing and Promotion

A full range of promotional activities was shown in Figure 8.7. Advertising to potential visitors is important in creating awareness of the country and generating enough interest so that visitors want more information. However, traditional consumer advertising tends to be relatively expensive. The NTOs with larger budgets are able to mount substantial consumer campaigns in certain markets using mainly magazine and television advertising. Smaller-budget NTOs are forced to concentrate on Internet marketing, travel trade marketing, and the use of public relations and publicity to promote to the consumer.

Travel Trade Marketing and Promotion

An important NTO role is to inform travel trade intermediaries about the country and to familiarize them with its tourism attractions, events, and other resources. One effective way of doing this is through familiarization tours (also called "fams" for short). NTOs organize these educational tours for selected tour wholesalers, retail travel agencies, and travel writers. Having experienced the country firsthand, the intermediaries are in a much better position to sell it as a tourism destination. During familiarization tours, the foreign travel trade intermediaries inspect facilities, visit tourism attractions, and make contacts with the local travel trade, who may act as their partners in channeling visitors to the country. Such tours may be conducted in small groups or on an individual basis.

Another major activity of NTOs is exhibiting at travel trade exhibitions or shows. Two of the largest shows in the world are ITB Berlin (held in March each year in Germany) and the World Travel Market (held in November each year in London, England).

© Adriano Castelli/Shutterstock.com

FIGURE 8.8 Trade shows provide channel members a chance to renew relationships and talk in person.

QUICK TRIP 8.5

California YouTube Campaign and Dream365TV

If a picture is worth a thousand words then a great video is almost priceless. California's Dream365 Project included the development of inspirational videos highlighting the California brand's essence and a twenty-four-hour "take-over" of YouTube.

Why video? In a recent interview with Skift, Visit California VP of Marketing Lynn Carpenter said "Part of what makes California attractive is the people, the lifestyle, and the attitude. And nothing conveys that better than video." (Shankman 2014)

As the Internet, and social media in particular, is embracing new mediums including video and virtual reality there is increasing focus on creating and distributing interesting content—video, imagery, stories.

The Dream365 campaign began with a global launch that included debuting twenty-four new videos in twenty-four hours on YouTube. The launch tracked around the world with YouTube promotions in UK, United States and Canada, and Australia. Each video showcased California's Dreamers—and featured both iconic and off the beaten track destinations.

> "Consumers are no longer only looking at official sources of travel information but they also want to be inspired and interested in what other people are saying," said Caroline Beteta, the President and CEO of Visit California, to *Fast Company* magazine. "We felt to demonstrate the breadth and depth of California, in terms of endless experiences, how many destinations could pull off this much content? The beauty of it is, [with YouTube] it will have an extremely long shelf life, not just 30 seconds during a broadcast show." (Beer 2014)

The videos are still available at www.visitcalifornia.com/dream365tv

The campaign generated over 136.6 million impressions in just one day and the results aligned nicely with Visit California's target audience. As a bonus, some of the videos went viral. One video, of skateboarder Bob Burnquist on a floating ramp on Lake Tahoe, has been seen more than 800,000 times. The campaign increased California's travel search volume on Google by 21 percent. The increased awareness generated by the campaign led to a 17 percent increase in likelihood to visit and a 7 percent lift in consideration (2014).

Think about This

1. Video production is often more expensive than still photography. From a marketing perspective, do you think it is worth it?
2. The videos in Dream365 are not traditional travelogues. Instead they capture the brand through human interest stories. If you were developing a video for your destination, what would it be about?
3. Why do you think that Visit California invested in the twenty-four-hour takeover of YouTube, rather than just releasing the videos as they were produced?

Sources

think with Google. 2014. "Visit California Lifts Intent to Travel to California with Unique Experience on YouTube." https://www.thinkwithgoogle.com/advertising-channels/video/visit-california-increases-traveler-interest-with-youtube-campaign/

Beer, J. 2014. "California Tourism Dreams Big with Google, Releasing 24 videos in 24 hours." *Fast Company*.

Shankman, S. 2014. "Visit California Gets Into Content marketing with 24-hour YouTube takeover." Skift. https://skift.com/2014/02/28/visit-california-gets-into-content-marketing-with-24-hour-youtube-takeover/

Educational workshops and seminars are organized and staged in overseas countries. They bring together all the main components of tourism, such as hotels, travel agents, airlines, and providers of tourism services, from both the generating and the destination country. The main objective of these workshops and seminars is to promote the destination mix of the country to the travel trade and other principals of the generating country. They motivate travel trade intermediaries to increase sales of group tours and fully independent tour travel. They familiarize travel trade intermediaries with the country's facilities and services and the latest developments in tourism. They provide an opportunity for the travel principals of the destination and generating countries to establish working relationships.

Several NTOs have gone further with their trade education efforts to set up training programs that lead to travel agent accreditations. These include the Shamrock Club operated by Tourism Ireland, the Aussie Specialist Program operated by Tourism Australia, the Kiwi Specialist program operated by Tourism New Zealand, and the Canada Specialist program.

Sales calls are made by NTO staff to retail travel agencies and tour wholesalers. The aim of these calls is to assist the travel trade in selling the country by providing them with information, advice, and promotional collateral materials. To keep the travel trade well stocked with promotional materials on the country, NTOs have regular direct e-mailings and traditional mailings of brochures and other collateral materials. With this information, the travel trade is in a better position to effectively service client inquiries and promote the country.

Many NTOs establish a permanent channel of communications with the travel trade through the regular distribution of e-newsletters. The e-newsletters inform the travel trade about upcoming events, developments in the destination's facilities and services, and other interesting facets of its tourism. As well as maintaining an ongoing relationship, these e-newsletters also attempt to promote sales by the travel trade to the country.

Some NTOs provide incentives or bonuses in the form of free vacations or gifts. These incentives are sometimes linked with promotional contests or games. These sales promotions are usually done in partnership with the main tourism principals of the country (hotel and airline companies, inbound tour operators, attractions, etc.). "Road shows" or promotional events may be organized for members of the travel trade and media or press; they are basically public relations exercises. These are often staged in hotels or resorts. Food, beverages, and entertainment, often imported from the NTO's country, are provided.

SUMMARY

Promotion is an important component of the marketing mix. Promotion is communicating with consumers about how your products and services will create value for them. It is about informing, persuading them, and reminding them. Planning for promotions, like other parts of the marketing function, is an ongoing process in the life of a company or destination.

In the tourism system there are organizations that specialize in marketing functions, particularly promotions. Destination Management Organizations play an important role in marketing destination systems.

ACTIVITIES

1. Select a set of countries or cities that you would most like to visit, and analyze their offline and online promotions. Telephone a selection of travel agencies and ask them for information on the countries or cities you selected. How comprehensive and appealing was the information that the agencies provided?
2. Telephone the DMOs of the countries or cities and ask them to send you more travel information on their destinations. Which of the DMOs were the most responsive and helpful? How comprehensive and appealing was the information that the DMOs provided?
3. Search for advertisements and other promotions done by the countries or cities in magazines, newspapers, on television, and elsewhere.
4. Find the official tourism websites of the countries or cities and rank them according to their attractiveness from your point of view.
5. Which websites are the most user-friendly and easy to navigate? Why?
6. Which websites provide the most comprehensive and useful information?

ACRONYMS

CVB (convention and visitors bureau)
DMO (destination management organization)
MICE (meetings, incentives, conventions, and exhibitions)
NTO (national tourist office)
PLC (product life cycle)
RTO (regional tourist office)
STO (state tourism office)

REFERENCES

Tourism New Zealand. 2017. "100% Pure New Zealand: Bryce's New Zealand Videos." https://www.newzealand.com/us/feature/bryces-nz-videos/.

Destination Canada. 2018. "Canada–Keep Exploring." https://us-keepexploring.canada.travel/.

Davidson, T. L. 1994. "Assessing the effectiveness of persuasive communication in tourism." In *Travel, Tourism and Hospitality Research: A Handbook for Managers and Researchers,* edited by J. R. B Ritchie and C. R. Goeldner. New York: John Wiley and Sons.

Estis-Green, C., and M. Mazzocco. 2017. *Book Direct Campaigns: The Costs and Benefits of Loyalty.* Rockville, MD: Kalibri Labs.

Godin, Seth. 1999. *Permission marketing: turning strangers into friends, and friends into customers.* New York: Simon & Schuster.

Koth, B. A. 1988. *Evaluating Tourism Advertising with Cost-Comparison Methods.* St Paul, MN: Minnesota Extension Service.

Morrison, A. 2010. *Hospitality and Tourism Marketing,* 4th ed. Clifton Park, New York: Delmar.

Perdue, R., and B. Pitegoff. 1994. "Methods of accountability research for destination marketing." In *Travel, Tourism, and Hospitality Research for Destination Marketing* edited by J. R. B Ritchie and C. R. Goeldner. New York: John Wiley & Sons.

Pizam, A. 1994. "Methods of accountability research for destination marketing." In *Travel. Tourism, and Hospitality Research: A Handbook for Managers and Researchers* edited by J. R. B. Ritchie. New York: John Wiley & Sons.

Schaal, D. "10 Top Quotes About Brand USA, Tourism's Future from Destination Marketing Officials." Skift.com

Siegel, W., and W. Ziff-Levine. 1994 "Evaluating Tourism Advertising Campaigns: Conversion vs Advertising Tracking Studies." In *Travel, Tourism, and Hospitality Research: A Handbook for Managers and Researchers* edited by J. R. B. Ritchie and C. R. Goeldner. New York: John Wiley & Sons, Inc.

Smith, A. 2015. "U.S. Smartphone Use in 2015." *Pew Research Center.* http://www.pewinternet.org/2015/04/01/us-smartphone-use-in-2015/

Thill, J, and C Bovee. 2013. *Excellence In Business Communications.* Boston: Rearson.

Tull, Cathy. Senior Vice President of Marketing, Las Vegas Convention and Visitors Authority. "10 Top Quotes About Brand USA, Tourism's Future from Destination Marketing Officials." Schaal, D. Skift.com

Woodside, A. G., and I. Ronkainen. 1994. "Improving Advertising Conversion Studies." In *Travel, Tourism, and Hospitality Research: A Handbook for Managers and Researchers* edited by J. R. B. Ritchie and C. R. Goeldner. New York: John Wiley & Sons, Inc.

CHAPTER NINE

Tourism Products and Experience Development

The Business of Making Memories

Work is theatre and every business is a stage.

JOSEPH PINE AND JAMES GILMORE

YOUR LEARNING DESTINATION

You'll learn about tourism products and the rise of experiential travel. You'll explore how tourism products are unique and how the tourism planning process can be applied to product development.

WHAT YOU NEED TO KNOW

Having read this chapter, you will be able to:

- ✔ Describe the unique characteristics of tourism products.
- ✔ Explain the importance of experiences and the value they create for both consumers and tourism businesses.
- ✔ Detail the process of product development planning.
- ✔ Explain the role of DMOs in product development.

BREAKING THE ICE

It was a perfect fall morning—the sky clear and blue, the air brisk. My boys were on break, so we took a family trip to Chicago, one of our favorite cities. We got up early and walked a couple of blocks to one of the city's iconic pizza restaurants, Uno Pizzeria and Grill. Over the next couple of hours, we learned how to make authentic Chicago-style pizza. In the same booths where

diners would sit in later in the day we learned about Uno's founding seventy-five years ago. With prepared ingredients and great stories from our chef guide, we built our own personal deep-dish pizza. We shaped the dough, crushed tomatoes—one of the very special ingredients—layered our cheese, and added the toppings. Along the way we laughed at our own little mistakes and enjoyed stories that walked us through years of Chicago history. We explored the storied kitchen as

FIGURE 9.1 Pizzeria Uno has created a unique experience for visitors by providing cooking lessons in the iconic restaurant.

our pizzas cooked in the professional ovens. Our pizza wasn't the prettiest thing you ever saw, but it tasted great and was ours. No matter how much we paid for the morning—it wasn't a lot, but it was more than just a pizza—it was worth it. The experience of that morning will remain one of my favorite Chicago memories.

Uno has created a unique tourism product by recognizing the importance of crafting an iconic location with great storytelling and excellent service into an experience. In this chapter we'll look at products, services, and experiences in the tourism system.

KEY TAKEAWAY POINTS

- Tourism products and services are unique in several ways. They are intangible, perishable, produced "on demand" with the consumer, often involve multiple providers, tourism intermediaries can play an important role in product creation, travel demand is elastic and seasonal, and service is a critical part of most tourism products.

- Describing tourism products and services in terms of experiences is becoming increasingly common. The use of the word "experience" focuses product and service delivery on the consumer. Experiential travel, travel that provides unique experiences to travelers, is growing in importance in the tourism system.

- Tourism experiences are created by the interaction of physical elements of the product, services provided by the people of the tourism company and the traveler.

- Marketers create tourism experiences by using a variety of techniques. The product "toolbox" includes packaging, partnering, programming, and people.

- The product development follows the same five-step process discussed in other chapters.

- Products may follow a lifecycle that includes introduction, growth, maturity, and decline. Products may avoid decline by a focus on renewal and innovation.

PRODUCTS AND SERVICES

It can be hard to put your finger on what makes a tourism product. Is it a hotel stay or visit to an attraction? Or is a tourism product the package you purchased that included flights and accommodations and tickets to the play? Does a tourism product include the massage on the spa table set up by the beach? Of course the answer is yes, all of the above.

Products are described by the American Marketing Association as bundles of attributes (features, functions, benefits, and uses) capable of exchange or use. In other words, on one level we can think about a product as anything that can be sold or used. A product can be something physical—a good—like a car, a computer, an idea, or a service. Services can be considered a specific type of product. The AMA describes a service as an intangible product. Tourism system products are often services ("AMA Dictionary.").

Tourism is part of the "service sector." Most tourism products include a combination of both goods and services, but it is the delivery of *service* products that defines tourism. Sure, some physical goods are required to deliver tourism experiences. For instance, the airline had to buy an airplane in order to deliver you the service

of air travel; the hotel company had to build a hotel so you can enjoy a good night's sleep in another city. But it is the services associated with those physical goods—the pilot flying the plane, the flight attendants ensuring in-flight safety and comfort, the luggage management systems, and the computer systems that enable the flight purchase—which are the components of the product.

As we've noted, tourism is unique in many ways—some of which are related to the special nature of services.

TOURISM PRODUCTS ARE UNIQUE

The challenges of tourism marketing are unique and different from those of traditional product marketing. These differences (see Figure 9.2) are due to the nature of a tourism product and how travel experiences are created and consumed.

Tourism Experiences Are Intangible. The first important characteristic of travel is that an *intangible experience* is offered, not a physical good that can be inspected before it is bought (Kotler, Bowen, and Makens 2015). Sure, there may be elements of the product that are

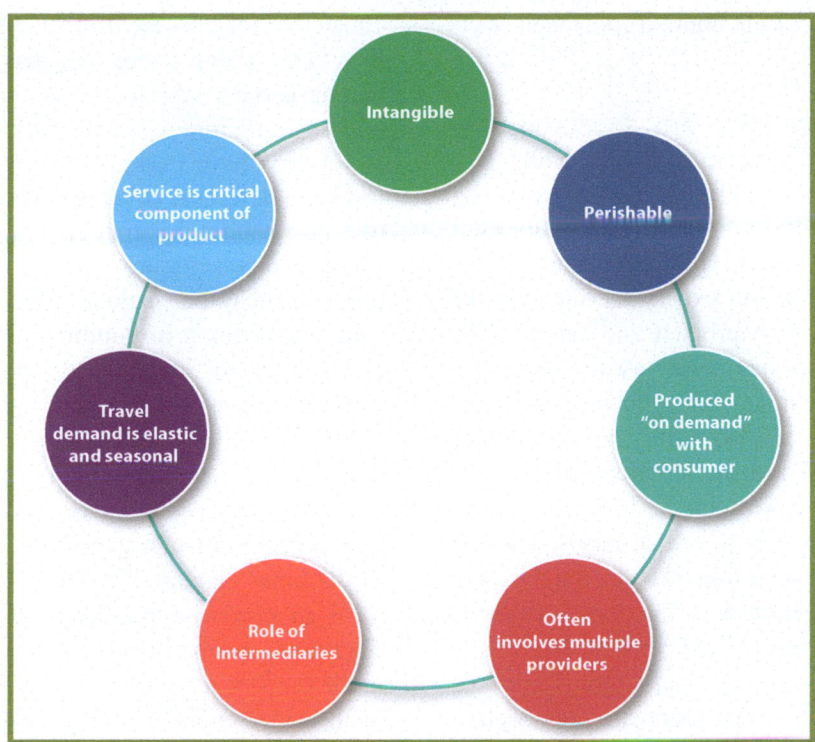

FIGURE 9.2 Unique features of tourism marketing tourism products.

physical—like the cruise ship cabin—but the cruise experience includes many services that are more than the cabin itself. The intangible nature of a tourism product adds risk to the purchase—you are paying for your trip without being able to "kick the tires."

The intangible nature of tourism services means that the visitor's travel experiences exist only in memory after the trip is over. Many products can be reused several times after they are bought. While vacation blogs, photographs, videos, and souvenirs help visitors remember their trips, a re-purchase is necessary to enjoy a similar trip experience again. This places a greater onus on tourism organizations to deliver satisfactory experiences to their customers.

Tourism Products are Perishable.
A second important characteristic is that tourism is a highly *perishable* commodity (Kotler et al. 2015). In manufacturing, goods are produced, stored, and sold. The inventory process for products serves as a way of linking these stages of production and consumption. However, tourism supply cannot be stored. Unlike a can of food that if not sold one day can be sold the next, airline seats, hotel rooms, cruise ship berths, places on an escorted tour, and restaurant seats not sold today are lost forever. While the "tourism inventory" cannot be stored and adjusted to changes in demand, the capacity to produce tourism services must be developed ahead of time. This puts great pressure on tourism developers to effectively plan the

proper amounts of facilities and to keep them as fully used as possible. The perishability of tourism products is the driving factor behind many marketing strategies—from last-minute booking websites to sophisticated revenue management strategies that lead to variable pricing of airline seats and hotel room. This creates another kind of challenge: In many cases, tourism supply is relatively fixed. The resources and infrastructure of a destination, cruise ship, or theme park cannot change as quickly as can visitor demand.

Tourism Experiences Are the Combination of Physical Product and Personal Service.
A third important characteristic in the guest's satisfaction is a *function of the staff providing the service.* Tourism is a people business: people providing personal services to other people. Because of the great amount of variation in human personalities, it is difficult to always provide a consistent quality of service. It is impossible to fully standardize tourism services. As one person has said, although we may want to, "You can't paint a smile on a human being's face." The tourism organizations that invest most heavily in hospitality skills and other types of service training are the ones most likely to enjoy the greatest success.

This combination of physical and personal service is often described as "inseparability," which means that the product and service can't be delivered separately. A hotel room can't be sold unless it is combined with a set of services including check-in, housekeeping, and reservation services.

Many Tourism Experiences Are Produced "On Demand" and with the Consumer.

Fourth, while tourism companies may develop the physical product and work diligently on training staff, there is one element of the tourism product that is out of the direct control of the tourism provider. The tourism experience includes the consumer's interaction with product and service. The tourism experience is "*co-produced*" or *co-created* with the staff. Think of the interaction you have with the white-water guide when you go rafting or with Mickey when dining at Disney World. Part of the experience was the way you interacted with them. It is also worth remembering that tourism is a service business where both production and consumption take place at the same time. Some service products come into existence at the same time that they are bought and consumed.

For instance, a massage at a spa exists while it is happening. Tourism experience production takes place in real time.

Tourism Experiences Often Involve More Than One Provider.

A fifth factor that makes tourism unique is that the service provided is a *mixture of several services and some facilities and products*. For example, most travel trips have information, transportation, lodging, food and beverage, attraction, and activity components (the destination mix concept discussed in Chapter 1). These components are offered by different organizations and may be marketed directly to the visitor by each organization or combined into a package where the services are supplied by a group of organizations. This lack of one single organization's control over the entire travel trip experience means that a great deal of *interdependence* exists among tourism organizations. For the visitor to leave having had a satisfactory experience, every tourism organization must have performed to the same standard. One bad service experience can spoil an otherwise perfect vacation or business trip. Therefore, the marketing success of each organization in the tourism service chain is dependent on the efforts of the other organizations providing all the other trip components.

FIGURE 9.3 On demand product creation.

Consumers Travel to the Destination-It Doesn't Come to Them—And Travel Intermediaries Have an Important Role. There is no physical distribution process in tourism. In the place of *physical distribution* is a network of professional travel trade intermediaries and the Internet. A fifth factor that makes tourism different from other industries is the role of *travel trade intermediaries*. Because visitor services are located at a distance from potential customers, specialized intermediaries—organizations that operate between the producer and the visitor—are required to bridge the gap. These skilled, knowledgeable travel trade intermediaries can influence, if not determine, which services are offered, to whom, when, and at what price.

Tourism Demand Is Elastic and Seasonal. The final factor that makes tourism different from other industries relates to demand. Tourism demand is highly elastic and seasonal in nature, and is influenced by subjective factors such as taste and fashion as well as more objective factors such as price and the physical attractions at the destination. In many cases, the services and experiences sought can be provided by any number of destinations or organizations. For example, many destinations around the world offer unique natural environments together with interesting flora and fauna. For example, from the late 1980s to 2011, the Central American countries of Costa Rica and Belize became very popular and somewhat "fashionable" nature-based tourism destinations.

Destination Management Organizations

Destination Management Organizations have their own unique product challenge. The DMO's product is the destination but DMOs Destinations usually have **little control over the quality and quantity of services provided.** Destination Management Organizations (DMOs), such as convention and visitors bureaus and state tourism offices (STOs) and national tourism organizations are seldom directly involved with the operation of tourism businesses providing visitor services. While these organizations are held accountable for the successful marketing of all the destination's tourism offerings, they must rely on the other tourism organizations to provide satisfactory experiences for visitors. For these reasons, in recent years DMOs have become more involved in product and experience delivery in the destination.

EXPERIENCES

A tourism product is what you buy. A tourism experience is what you remember.

CANADIAN TOURISM COMMISSION

In recent years the focus in tourism has switched from goods and services to experiences. There is greater awareness that tourism is not just about the service you receive but the experience you have engaging with the tourism product or destination. Tourism has been at the cutting edge of a trend in marketing to understand and manage the *user experience*.

The growth of *experiential travel* has been an important trend in the tourism system in recent years. While sightseeing and relaxing by the beach are still important, many visitors now seek ways to actively participate in their travel. Today many travelers are looking to have authentic experiences in their travels.

It has been said that "work is a stage" and that is particularly true for tourism experiences. It is easy to imagine this at a place like Disneyland, where the language of performance is an important part of the corporate culture. At Disney, service workers are cast members, and when they are in a public place they are "on stage." But many great tourism products recognize the truth that tourism is about "putting on a show."

FIGURE 9.4 Horseback riding in the Costa Rican cloud forest.

© creatista/Shutterstock.com

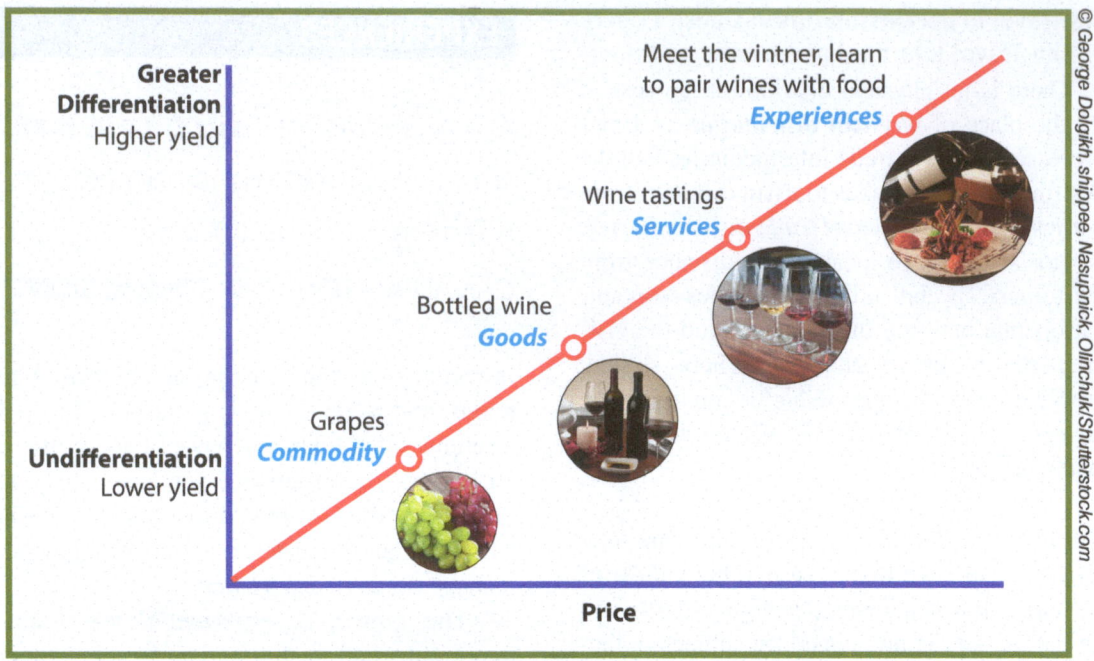

FIGURE 9.5 The progression of economic value. | © 2011 Tourism Cafe. Reprinted by permission.

Workers at a luxury hotel are "on stage" delivering great service.

In addition to the consumer demand for experiential travel, tourism operators have come to the realization that tourism products that focus on experiences can deliver greater returns. By creating experiences that consumers value, marketers are able to generate more value for themselves. The idea that experiences create greater value and generate better returns has been popularized by Pine and Gilmore (1999). Figure 9.5 shows how value is created as basic products move toward experiences.

THE ELEMENTS OF THE EXPERIENCE

Many products include some service component, and services are sometime categorized by the level of service provided to meet the customer need.

Using this framework, it is clear that there are at least two elements of a service product: the *physical elements* of the product and the service elements of the product provided by the *staff*. A third element of the product is the *consumer* themselves. Consumers interact with both service staff and the physical elements to *co-create* or *co-produce* products. For example, each morning customers create their own customized breakfasts with the buffet at the Courtyard hotel. Similarly, trekking guides sit down with their clients and decide what they will do during the day. In both cases, the

AirBnb and Experiences

In late 2016 Airbnb moved beyond providing accommodation and introduced a new product offering based on experiences. The new product allows hosts to offer visitors local trips and experiences. The products offered range from everyday activities like cooking and painting lessons to unique offerings like following a truffle hunter through a forest in Italy. Growth in the experience business has been very strong—from a small base. Brian Chesky, one of the founders of Airbnb and its CEO advised experience growth grew twelve times from January and earned the company about half a million dollars. "We've purposefully kept it small—a lesson I learned from the core business" Chesky reported. "Our strategy is to do for travel what Amazon did for retail—which is to be a one stop shop."

Sources: *Fortune,* Nov 1, 2017, "Airbnb's conquest is just getting started"; *New York Times,* Nov 28, 2016, "Navigating the New Airbnb."

consumer is playing an important role in the creation of the product.

While these three elements are most directly related to the consumer experience, other elements may have an impact on the experience. For instance, other guests may impact the experience. The interaction between the staff may also have an impact on the experience. Finally, the destination itself may impact the experience.

QUICK TRIP 9.1

Canada Embraces Experiential Travel

Keep Exploring. That is the tagline for the Canadian Tourism Commission's (CTC) brand campaign and it captures the CTC's commitment to the importance of experiential travel. CTC is working closely to support its industry to adopt experience economy values. In "Experiences: A toolkit for partners of the CTC" they explain experiential travel and the importance of great experiences.

Experiential travel engages visitors in a series of memorable travel activities that are inherently personal. It involves all senses, and makes connections on a physical, emotional, spiritual, social or intellectual level. It is travel designed to engage visitors with the locals, set the stage for conversations, tap the senses and celebrate what is unique in Canada.

From yoga on the docks of the Discovery Centre overlooking the UNESCO-designated landscapes of Gros Morne National Park to the intriguing culinary dining adventures in complete darkness at O'Noir, to digging for dinosaurs in the badlands of Alberta or learning to mush a dogsled in Canada's North, captivating visitor experiences engage travelers in memorable and relevant ways that go beyond viewpoints, interpretive talks or serving a tasty meal.

Experiential travel represents an opportunity for the tourism industry to inspire visitation by creating authentic experiences designed to connect travelers to the special places, people and cultures within communities across this nation.

The CTC highlights the benefits for their tourism partners of adopting a product creation process focused on experiences.

Over the past decade, increasingly, companies have embraced experiences as an opportunity for their businesses because of the benefits, which include:

- a new value proposition that can be developed in almost any community
- a response to domestic and international market demand that generates new revenue
- an opportunity to be innovative, creative and truly responsive to the reasons why people travel
- a competitive advantage over those in service industries
- a lower-cost investment because experiences don't involve capital infrastructure changes or upgrades
- the ability to leverage your marketing budget through partnerships
- an opportunity to create advocates for your business with guests that rave online or via word-of-mouth about their time with you
- a decision to be "stronger together" in working with community partners and other businesses to create a more holistic destination experience, particularly in rural communities
- expanding your network of suppliers and partners and working with new people who may never have realized they have something wonderful to share with travellers
- an opportunity to introduce value-based pricing and attract higher-yield customers

Businesses that succeed in developing and delivering experiential travel have one thing in common: it is rewarding to both staff and visitors.

Think about This

1. Identify examples of experiential travel you have experienced. Did it live up to the ideals outlined in the Quick Trip?
2. Can the benefits associated with experiential travel be achieved without embracing this new way of doing business? What makes experiential travel products different from regular products?
3. Changing how an industry thinks about product development is challenging. If you believed that you had found a better way to market, how would you encourage change in the system?

Source

From "Experiences: A Toolkit for Partners of the CTC" by Destination Canada. Copyright © 2011 by Government of Canada. Reprinted by permission.

FIGURE 9.6 Enjoying social experiences.

With each of these elements impacting the visitor experience, tourism marketers need to market to not only their consumers but also their staff and other stakeholders. *Internal marketing* focuses on the company's staff and includes marketing communication and training. Internal marketing can contribute to the corporate culture of an organization. *Corporate culture* within an organization can guide staff members on what is expected of them, even when no one is there to tell them what to do.

Companies also direct marketing techniques at consumers to ensure they have the best consumer experience. Companies apply marketing techniques to consumers to "teach" them how to interact with the product and service; they also teach them about the product as they consume it. In addition, consumers "socialize" knowledge between themselves. Proactive marketing companies will influence this process of peer socialization in ways that lead to the best possible outcomes.

THE PRODUCT TOOLBOX

Tourism marketers creating tourism experiences have a wide variety of tools available to them. While the physical elements of creating a tourism product can be capital intensive and have long lead times, many other product-related factors are more flexible and can be introduced to the marketplace quickly. For instance, changes in service training or different mixes of product and services can substantially change the product offering. How products are combined with other products can also change the product offering. Morrison (2010) expanded on the 4Ps of marketing—Promotion, Place, Price, and Product—with an additional 4 Ps—Packaging, Partnership, Programming, and People—in recognition of how important these additional components are in the marketing mix. Each of these new Ps relates directly to product. In particular, the components Product, Packaging, Partnership, Programming, and People give marketers a powerful toolbox for creating tourism experiences.

Product

From the marketing perspective, a product creates value by meeting the needs of the consumer. At the most fundamental level, every marketer must understand the *core benefit* that the customer is buying and create an offering that delivers that benefit. This is an important point as too often tourism marketers get so tied up in the physical attributes of their product that they lose sight of the core benefits they are providing. Kotler and Keller (2016), two preeminent marketing experts, provide a useful hierarchy to understand products. Once the core benefit is identified, the marketer must create a *basic product*. So, if the benefit is nourishment, then the basic product may be food, drink, tables and chairs, and eating utensils. This offering must at least meet customer expectations for a product of this type. Beyond this expected product, the marketer may provide additional differentiation—new services or additional features—creating an *augmented product*. In the case of a restaurant the augmented product may take the form of a sports bar—with big screen TVs, sporting paraphernalia around the walls, and casual wait staff that encourage a relaxed, friendly environment; or a five-star fine dining experience with decor of dark wood tones, fine wines and the highest quality dishes, and a highly trained, formal serving staff.

In the development of the augmented, differentiated product, marketers have a variety of tools and techniques. Morrison's (2010) 8 Ps of marketing focuses on several important elements of the marketing mix that relate closely to the development of products that meet the needs of consumers.

Packaging

A travel package brings together a set of tourism products in a way that creates additional value for the consumer. Some travel marketers *aggregate* or *combine* products in new ways that create something new, in the same way that building blocks can be put together to create a toy house or tower. For example, a tourism marketer may bring together a luxury hotel stay, tickets to a play, a spa treatment, and a horse carriage ride through the local park into a luxury weekend escape package. The consumer values the creativity of the experience that is created, the knowledgeable choices the marketer makes about what to include—and what to leave out—and the ease of booking.

Packaging is significant because it brings together many of the elements of the destination mix. Packages combine the services and products of several tourism organizations. The package is more convenient for visitors because it includes several services and products at an all-inclusive price. Other advantages of packages are listed in Figure 9.7.

Packages in tourism are unique. They are especially important because they can be used to help cope with the problems of the immediate perishability of services and the difficulties of matching demand volumes with

Group	Reasons
Visitors	• Greater convenience (saves time) • Greater economy (saves money) • Ability to budget for trips (makes planning easier) • Implicit assurance of consistent quality (less risk) • Satisfaction of specialized interests • Added dimension to traveling
Participating Businesses	• Increased business in off-peak periods • Enhanced appeal to specific target markets • Attraction of new target markets • Easier business forecasting and improved efficiency • Use of complementary facilities, attractions, and events • Flexibility to capitalize on new market trends • Stimulation of repeat and more frequent usage • Increased per capita spending and lengths of stay • Public relations and publicity value of unique packages • Increased customer satisfaction

FIGURE 9.7 **Reasons for the Popularity of Vacation/Holiday Packages** | *Adapted from Morrison (2009).*

supply capacities. Packaging also provides a way to match tourism services and products with visitors' needs. For example, tourism businesses now offer many packages for special-interest groups ranging from anthropologists to zoologists.

Packaging of travel experiences is the very foundation of the business models of travel wholesalers and travel agents.

Partnership

Partnership can mean a variety of ways that members of the tourism system join together to work—from loose collaborations to legally binding partnership arrangements.

Partnership can mean *collaborative or cooperative marketing* programs involving two or more tourism destinations or individual organizations. In an increasingly competitive tourism industry, the pooling of resources with other organizations may provide the added edge necessary for success. Packaging, when it involves two or more organizations, represents one important application of the partnership concept. While packaging often includes contractual commitments between the

organizations involved, it doesn't always have to. In some cases, simply by identifying an appealing itinerary and promoting it, a tourism product is created. A group of wineries may publish a "weekend wine trail" that suggests a route to take from one winery to another and makes recommendations for local B&Bs.

Cooperative advertising is another common example of cooperative marketing. For example, the Central American countries of Belize, El Salvador, Guatemala, and Honduras have linked up with Mexico in promoting the Mayan World region (*El Mundo Maya*). This joint marketing program is based on the remaining archaeological sites of the Mayan civilization, which are found in these five countries. Another example of a regional partnership is the joint promotion by the countries of Europe sharing the Alps (Austria, France, Germany, Italy, and Switzerland).

Strategic alliances are another form of partnership in tourism. These are long-term agreements between companies or countries to invest in joint marketing programs. Strategic alliances have been especially popular among airline companies. Alliances are also being formed among hotels, airlines, and car rental companies to gain competitive advantages through reciprocal

FIGURE 9.8 **The airlines of the Oneworld Alliance.**

frequent traveler award programs and to provide travelers with greater speed and flexibility (Dev, Klein, and Fisher 1996). Good examples of these are the three major airline strategic alliances (Star Alliance, One-World Alliance, and SkyTeam Alliance) and the cooperation between the Scandinavian countries in tourism promotion (Denmark, Finland, Iceland, Norway, and Sweden are represented by the Scandinavian Tourist Boards).

Programming

Programming involves special activities, events, or other types of programs to increase customer spending or to give added appeal to a package or other tourism service. Disneyland at Christmas time provides a good example of programming. Each year at Christmas time, Disneyland decks its park in Christmas decorations, provides special uniforms for the staff, adds Santa Claus to the parade, and changes the fireworks so they have a Christmas theme. Many vacation packages include some form of programming such as escorted ground tours, sports instruction, and entertainment events.

Even destinations use programming. A popular approach among travel destinations is to designate particular years for special celebrations and to focus attention on programs that support specific themes. For example, the China National Tourism Administration introduced "China World Expo Tourism Year" in 2010 to mark the holding of the 2010 Shanghai World Expo. Other destinations make a special effort to promote their festivals. The Edinburgh office of VisitScotland (www.edinburgh.org) promotes the Edinburgh Festival held in Scotland's capital in August annually. The Macau International Fireworks Display Contest is a great example of programming. Held over five separate evenings in September, this is a contest in fireworks displays among several countries.

People (Human Resources)

Tourism is a people business. No amount or quality of facilities can make up for poor service. A tourism marketer must ensure that employees are adequately trained in their specific functions and that tourism employees and local residents have hospitable attitudes toward visitors.

It is important to remember that in many cases, the services provided by people are the product—or the most important part of it. The success of the walking ghost tour on the streets of London is completely determined by the storytelling of the guide. The river guide will almost always be one of the most memorable parts of the white-water rafting trip.

© Ammit Jack/Shutterstock.com

FIGURE 9.9 Guide helps visitors spot animals in the Ecuadorian Jungle. Guides—the stories they tell and the information they share—are an important part of the travel experience.

QUICK TRIP 9.2

Creating Customer Experiences

Tourism and Events Queensland (TEQ), the DMO for the state of Queensland, Australia, is a leader in destination marketing. TEQ provides valuable tips for creating customer experiences in "The Bib Marketing Book," their guide for tourism operators. Here are ten tips they recommend:

1. Only in your destination
- Nowhere else on earth.
- No one does it better.
- If travellers want to have this experience, your destination is the best place in the world for it.
- This experience makes your destination truly unique, puts Queensland on a global stage and attracts visitors on its own merits.
- Contributing factors could include a unique setting, unique wildlife, local customers or food.

2. An inspirational story
Does the experience:
- Feature an inspirational story or theme?
- Tell the story of local characters, customs and culture, or flora and fauna?
- Provide the visitor with an opportunity to interact with and learn about your destination?

3. The customer in the 'lead role'
- Would travellers from all over the globe want to come to your destination to be part of this experience?
- It is a 'must-do' draw card that will excite and attract your target audience?
- Will the experience exceed your customers' expectations?

4. Touch, smell, taste, sight, sound
Is the experience:
- Multisensory and provokes emotion?
- Interactive with hands-on elements?

5. A 'backstage pass'
Does the experience:
- Provide a special insight into how your operation ticks?

- Make your visitors feel truly special?
- Give visitors a feeling of exclusivity?
- Deliver a once-in-a-lifetime feel, bragging rights?

6. Feel like a local
- Does the experience make your visitors feel like they are part of your local way of life?
- Do you make your visitors feel really welcome, like an old friend and not just like another tourist?

7. Authentic and genuine
- The experience is real, does not have a staged mass-market feel and is not commericalized or superficial.

8. Your destination brand and brand Queensland
Is the experience an embodiment of your destination brand? Does your experience deliver on any of the following brand Queensland themes:
- Adventure?
- Natural encounters?
- Island and beaches?
- Queensland lifestyle?

9. Surprise
- Does the experience feature an element of surprise and create the unexpected?

10. Create lasting memories
Ultimately, does the experience:
- Engage visitors emotionally, adding meaning to their personal lives?
- Allow visitors to take home lasting memories that they will share with families and friends?

Think about This

1. Design a tourism experience using the ten tips. For tip number 8, substitute your destination for Queensland. Make sure you take some time to think about the brand of your destination.
2. Each of the tips contributes in a different way to the consumer experience. Which tip do you think would add the most to your experience? Why?
3. Why does Tourism and Events Queensland produce a marketing guide?

Source

From *The Big Marketing Guide* by Tourism & Events Queensland. Copyright © 2017 by Tourism & Events Queensland. Reprinted by permission.

PRODUCT DEVELOPMENT PLANNING PROCESS

Developing products, services, and experiences that meet the needs of consumers is a critical role of the tourism organization. In tourism, some products are capital intensive and require long lead times. A cruise ship, a new hotel, and a major new attraction at a theme park all require major investments. On the other hand, some new products and services can be introduced relatively quickly and easily through programming or packaging. No matter the type of new product, its development follows a predictable process.

Where Are We Now?

Product development begins with deep understanding of the capabilities of both the organization and its partners, appreciation for the destination in which the product will be embedded, and knowledge of the organization's customers.

Understanding the Market. Product development should begin with a deep understanding of the needs of the target market. There should be strong demand for the service or product from at least one core market segment, with the possibility of additional business from other market segments. It may be that the product can expect to break even on the basis of business from the major market segment and produce profit from business from the rest of the market. There may, of course, be a period of time before sales of a new attraction or service reach the point of breakeven.

Capacity of the Company. New products and services should match the positioning or image of the tourism

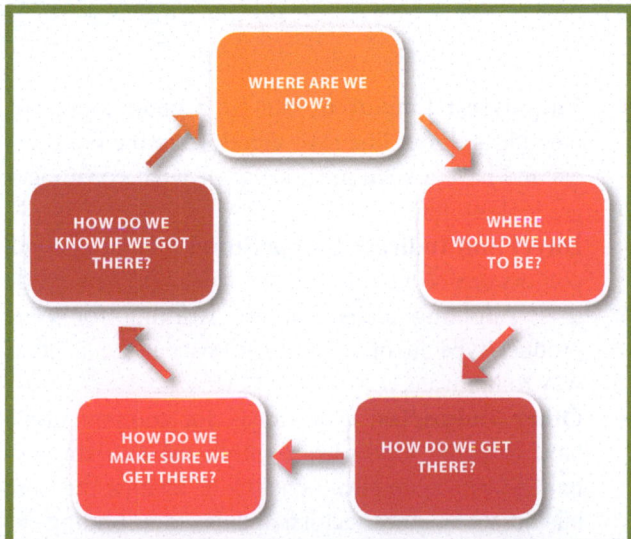

FIGURE 9.10 Planning Process—Product. The planning process used in destination marketing and promotion is also applied to product development.

destination area or organization. They should also complement existing offerings. This does not mean that a destination area must appeal only to one segment of the market and that all its services and products must meet the needs of that market segment. A great deal obviously depends on the size of the destination area. One part of a destination area may appeal to the younger singles and couples, while another part may be more attractive to seniors. It is important, however, that each individual part of the destination area develop the services, products, and positioning to fit one or more selected target markets.

New services and products must be adequately supported by the available supply of human resources, capital, management expertise, and natural resources. Although new services and products should be based on an identified competitive advantage, they may not be feasible due to a lack of the right quality or quantity of human or financial resources. For example, a destination area may have magnificent mountain terrain suitable for skiing but lack management knowledge in ski-area operations. Experienced management may have to be hired on a permanent or temporary basis before a ski area can be proposed. In tourism it is also possible that certain new services or products may be undesirable for social, cultural, or environmental reasons.

Capturing a Sense of Place. Destination Management Organizations advocate that product developers within tourism organizations work to capture the unique "sense of place" of a destination.

Where Would We Like To Go?

Establishing goals and setting expectations for the product is an important first step in the product development process. New services and products should contribute to the profit and/or growth of the entire tourism destination or company. In some cases, the new offering may bring in no profit itself, but its provision may contribute to growth. The hotel pool, for example, may cost the operation money while bringing in no direct revenue. However, its availability may generate additional room business. If the pool is eliminated, this may cause guests to use another hotel or resort. Similarly, a destination may introduce its own airline, not as a revenue-producing venture but as part of a strategy to attract more visitors.

Developing new products can have strategic implications for a company. The new product may enhance an existing product line, or meet the needs of a new market. If the consumer is the first thing marketers think about, developing and enhancing the product to meet the needs of those consumers is the next thing to consider.

QUICK TRIP 9.3

Hotels Meet the Needs of Millennials

The Millennial Market, now one of the largest consumer segments, is influencing the design of hotels as hotel companies adapt their products to meet changing preferences. Brands like Hyatt Centric, Radisson RED, Marriott's Moxy and AC hotels, are developing products that appeal to millennials. But marketers insist that this is not demographic segmentation but more concerned with attitude and psychographics. In a recent article in the *Washington Post,* Rose Anderson, VP of Global Branding and Innovation with Carlson Rezidor, describes her approach as "It's not so much about the age; it's more about the behaviors that have been kind of pegged to the millennials: very social, online, connected. We are very much targeting a millennial mind-set versus a generational audience." (Silver 2017)

Product changes you may notice next time you visit a hotel catering to the younger "vibe":

- Many hotels are including art and design values into their décor. The idea is to be "Instagram worthy." Other hotels are ensuring they incorporate the essence of the destination in their design.
- Menus are changing and food options are greater than ever before. There's greater variety including more vegan and healthful options.
- High-tech approaches include apps that allow you to not only access the room, but order room service, chat with other guests, and ask for more towels. This technology accommodates the needs of the "on-demand" generation.
- Hotel lobbies are changing form and function with more workspaces for connected workers, more places to just hang out, and less formal front desks.

Think about This

1. Do you think that segmenting by attitude and behavior is a better approach than demographic segmentation?
2. Do these changes appeal to you? Why or why not?
3. Using your understanding of the product toolbox, what other product changes would you suggest to hotel companies to meet the needs of your market?

Source

Silver, K. 2017. Six Ways hotels are targetting the Millenial market (and benefiting us all). *Washington Post.* https://www.washington post.com/lifestyle/travel/six-ways-hotels-are-targeting-the-millennial-market-and-benefiting-us-all/2017/06/29/244c0646-5852-11e7-a204-ad706461fa4f_story.html?utm_term=.8be87cdf517b

How Do We Get There?

Idea Generation. The development of a new product begins with an idea. Companies can get new product ideas from a variety of places. Here are some of the places where new ideas for products can be identified:

- **Customers:** Customers can be a great source of ideas for innovation. One of the important roles of great Market Intelligence Systems (MIS) is identifying new ideas and opportunities.
- **Market Research:** Market research can identify opportunities for new development. Deeply understanding the needs of your target market can reveal opportunities to serve them with products and services.
- **Employees:** Employees can be a great source of new ideas. Front line staff are close to the consumers and have a keen great sense of what consumers are looking for.
- **Direct and Indirect Competitors:** Watching competitors can be a great source of ideas for new products. Adopting ideas that are working for your product type in other destinations can be a great way to innovate.
- **Other Industries:** New ideas for tourism don't have to come solely from within the tourism system. Many companies benchmark against the best businesses in other sectors, and use their findings to generate new product ideas.

- **Trend watching:** Watching the trends in our industry and in society in general can be a great way to get ideas that can be applied to tourism experiences. Advertising agencies and other marketing firms create trend reports—which are sometimes free—that can inspire.

Techniques to encourage creativity, such as *brainstorming* and *nominal group technique*, encourage delaying idea evaluation until after the list is developed. By ensuring that all the ideas are included—even the whacky ones—people are encouraged to share ideas and, on occasion, two off-the-wall ideas will come together as one great new idea. Once the ideas are gathered, it will be necessary to screen the ideas and narrow the field to the products most likely to succeed.

Concept Development and Testing. Once an idea has been generated and an initial screening has determined it is worthwhile to pursue, the product concept must be developed and tested with consumers. New products in the tourism system can range from multimillion-dollar investments to simple programming changes. As a result, a wide range of concept testing tools are used. For example, Marriott used conjoint analysis—a process that determined consumers' preferences in a set of choices on product attributes—when they developed the Courtyard brand. Tourism operators may test-market new product ideas by offering them to consumers and seeking immediate feedback. It is important to remember that, as the concept develops, the marketer is developing not only a physical product but a complete *customer experience*.

> **Fast Prototyping** is an approach to manufacturing in which companies create a new product quickly—often using new technologies like 3D printing. The new product can be tested and adapted based on real user feedback. Tour operators are able to fast prototype new products and test them in the marketplace—adjusting with feedback as they go. While some products take a low-tech approach to this type of product development, OTAs and other technology-driven companies can undertake sophisticated testing of "test products."

When the concept is tested and the product developed, the marketers will develop **market entry strategies** to introduce the product to consumers. One common technique for market entry is the "soft opening." Many tourism organizations, including hotels and restaurants,

will welcome guests before the "official opening" in order to "get the kinks out" and make final adjustments to policies and service standards prior to opening. This is a great way to introduce the product to the market and build interest in the product.

How Do We Make Sure We Get There?

Once a new product has been identified it is important for the company to determine whether it is viable. The detailed product planning should include:

Feasibility Studies and Budgeting. As the concept develops, marketers will develop detailed projections of the financial viability of the product. These projections will provide a benchmark against which the company can judge the success of the product compared to a set of predetermined goals. Budgets set the financial goals against which the product can be assessed.

Benchmarks. In addition to financial goals, the new product developers may have additional targets—or benchmarks—that they expect the product to reach. Customer satisfaction scores are an important indicator of long-term success, and marketers may set benchmarks against which they will judge success on this dimension. There are many criteria that may be benchmarked. For instance, a company may set benchmarks for positive social media, word of mouth, or environmental performance.

How Do We Know We Got There?

Whether the product is new—or has been in that market for some time—it is critical that marketers measure progress against the budgets and benchmarks established. Many companies will use a set of criteria to judge the overall success of the product. Performance against these criteria may be presented in a variety of ways, but modified *balanced-scorecard* approaches or a *dashboard* of key metrics, are becoming increasingly popular by tourism managers.

Kaizen and Continuous Improvement. It is important to remember that the marketing planning process and the promotional planning and product development processes are ongoing. In product planning and delivery good marketers are always looking to improve the quality of the product and the visitor experience. *Kaizen* is a Japanese term that translates to continuous improvement. Kaizen, or continuous improvement, became

QUICK TRIP 9.4

Experiential Travelers and "Agile Tours"

Tour operators are adapting to deliver experiential travel in the digital age. A recent article in *Skift* examined the ways tour operators are incorporating flexibility and agile strategies in their programs (Sheivachman 2015).

> "The whole experiential movement continues to grow as an industry segment," said Terry Dale, president of the U.S. Tour Operators Association. "We've got access to the people in communities that can put that package together that can be extremely difficult to do on your own."

Skift reports that tour operators are increasing the amount of unscheduled time in tours to allow time for customization on the fly. This flexibility creates the space for impromptu activities to take place. With deep relationships in destination communities, tour operators are able to create experiences to meet the needs of their customers.

G Adventures, a tour operator that specializes in responsible travel, is an organization that exemplifies this trend. As Jeff Russill, vice president of product and innovation at G Adventure says in the *Skift* interview "There's a whole lot of free time in our trips; we customize what's going to happen on the ground by taking advantage of what's happening on the ground, you can't really do that in a resort or on a cruise ship. The more structure there is, the further travelers get from the magic needed to make things actually happen."

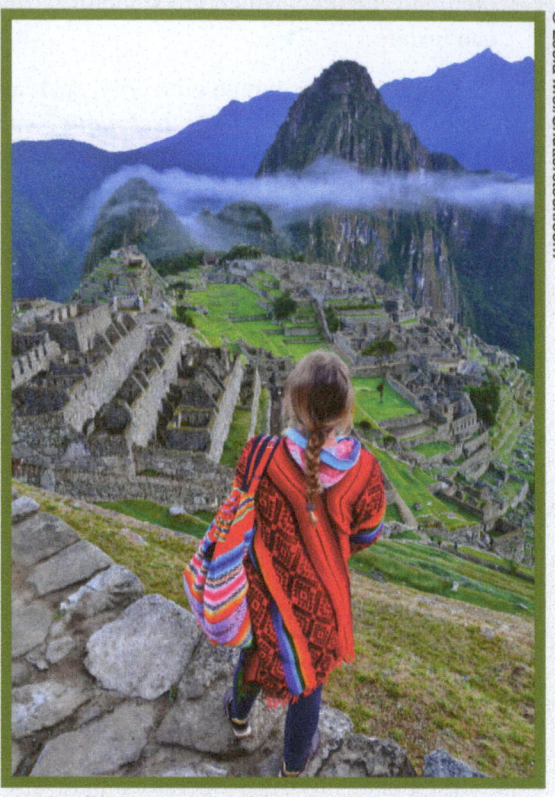

Machu Pichu is one of the destinations G Adventures visits.

Think about This

1. What are the advantages of booking travel through a tour operator like G Adventures?
2. How do G Adventures' relationships with the tourism supply chain impact their ability to deliver special experiences?
3. How can tour operators overcome perceptions that their product is just sitting on coaches passively sightseeing?

Source

Sheivachman, A. 2015. "Experiential Travel Trend Suits Tour Operators Just Fine." *Skift*. https://skift.com/2015/10/27/experiential-travel-trend-suits-tour-operators-just-fine/

popular during the 1980s when manufacturing companies realized the value of producing high quality products. The concept applies to tourism as well.

One way tourism companies commit to quality is by adopting industry standards or participating in certification programs. A certification is not something that just hangs on the wall. The best certification programs require a long-term commitment to not only meeting minimum criteria but to reaching higher levels of performance over time. High quality certification programs have broadly recognized standards, clearly articulated criteria, third-party verification, and a commitment to continuous improvement. Many criteria have levels of recognition—for instance, bronze, silver, gold—as new levels of performance are met. Those levels can motivate better performance in the company and provide assurance to the consumer. You may recall that things like intangibility raise the risk when choosing a tourism product; certification can help reduce that risk and support a buying decision.

PRODUCT RENEWAL AND THE PRODUCT LIFE CYCLE

An important concept in product management is the idea of the product life cycle (PLC). The concept behind PLC is that products have distinct characteristics and needs when they are introduced and as they become more familiar to consumers. Throughout this life cycle the product may have different customers and different marketing needs and different sales, and those sales may generate different levels of profitability.

A simple model of the product life cycle includes four stages of "life":

- **Introduction:** The product is new and sales must be built. At this stage costs of the product development and launch marketing may limit profitability.
- **Growth:** Awareness of the product is increasing. Profitability may be increasing even though marketing expenses are still relatively high.
- **Maturity:** This is the stage when the product has become familiar. It is during this stage that the product must ensure it remains appealing to the market by undertaking action that renews the product.
- **Decline:** As the product reaches decline, there are many competitors. New technologies or changing trends may make the product less profitable.

Of course, each product follows its own path through the life cycle (Kotler & Keller 2016). Some products are fads and have short life cycles; others (e.g., trains or cruises), have long life cycles with periods of product change and renewal.

The tourism industry as a whole is characterized as a mature industry and, while innovative products come along frequently, one of the greatest challenges for products is maintaining sales and profitability of mature products. Many of the capital-intensive parts of the industry have established guidelines or, at the very least, rules of thumb for renewal. For instance, it may be part of the brand guidelines for a hotel to have a "soft refurbishment" every three years and a "hard refurb" every ten to fifteen years. Theme parks "stay fresh" by adding a variety of product-related changes. For instance, they may add major attractions within the park every five to seven years and minor changes to established products more frequently, and throughout the year have programming that keeps the product new and fresh.

Life cycles have been identified in destinations as well. We have examined that phenomenon in Chapter 5.

PRODUCT/MARKET PORTFOLIOS

One useful concept in managing products is **portfolio management**. A portfolio is a set of products managed by the company. Managing the portfolio is a way to lower the risk of relying too heavily on a single product. Some companies will develop a product portfolio that includes vertical integration—buying members of the distribution or supply chain or horizontal integration. Even small companies can consider their products in terms of a portfolio. For instance, a small hotel may have a standard business product, a weekend romance product, and a small meeting product. Developing and maintaining each product may reduce the reliance on a single product/market.

Product/Market Compatibility. Products must ensure that their portfolio includes products—and the markets they serve—are compatible. For instance, some hotels that target the romance market discourage the family market.

QUICK TRIP 9.5

Qualmark Is New Zealand Tourism's Official Quality Assurance Program

Tourism contributes about 10 percent of New Zealand's gross domestic product and employs about one in ten New Zealanders. The country has enjoyed great success with its *100% Pure New Zealand* destination branding approach. According to Tourism New Zealand, however, "living up to that reputation and planning ahead are vital to the continued growth of tourism in New Zealand."

Tourism does not have a comprehensive system for quality control. The great number of services and products used by visitors, and the need to constantly create unique experiences, increase the difficulty of quality management. New Zealand, with its Qualmark program, increases the probability of guaranteeing quality. Qualmark is the official quality assurance system for the New Zealand tourism industry.

Qualmark is owned by Tourism New Zealand and backed by leading industry organizations; it was established in 1993. The program assesses accommodation, venues, transport, activities, and services. Qualmark focuses on ensuring the delivery of quality tourism experiences. Qualmark evaluation is conducted in line with sustainable tourism practices. In assessing businesses, it focuses on criteria in the categories including health and safety, environment, business operations and economic issues, and social/people-related issues including customer satisfaction and community engagement. The system is regularly reviewed to ensure it adapts to changing industry standards and customer expectations. As a high-quality certification program, New Zealand's Qualmark program is designed to support continued improvement of participating companies.

The high-speed jet boat ride is committed to delivering quality experiences.

In today's tourism system, this program demonstrates New Zealand's commitment to provide the best possible experiences, products, and services for all the involved stakeholders.

Think about This

1. Will initiatives like Qualmark redress the assumption that quality management in the tourism industry is impossible? Why or why not?
2. In an industry that is constantly growing, there are many companies directing their products to visitors. How can quality labels affect buying processes? Are they truly worthwhile?
3. This quality label is a result of New Zealand's identification of a need expressed by the market. Which are the other labels and destinations that have shown this kind of program?
4. Are there any underlying advantages for marketing a destination with a quality label?

Source

Tourism New Zealand and Qualmark Official websites. 2011. www.newzealand.com/travel/trade/marketing-toolbox/qualmark/qualmark-quality-assurance.cfm and http://www.qualmark.co.nz/. Used with permission of Tourism New Zealand & Qualmark®.

SUMMARY

Tourism is an important part of the service sector and our products typically include a mix of both physical product and service. Tourism products are unique in a variety of ways—in part because of the nature of service products. They are intangible, perishable, often created "on demand," and frequently created along with the consumer. Experiential travel has been a significant trend in the tourism system, and the recognition that consumers highly value experiences is impacting many aspects of product development.

Tourism marketers have a large tool kit for developing new products. In addition to the core product, tourism marketers can work with people, programming, and packaging to create new experiences for consumers. While some tourism products are capital intensive, other products can be quickly—and cheaply—introduced to the marketplace. The product planning process—like the marketing planning process—is an ongoing process that can extend throughout the life of the product. Maintaining and enhancing product and service quality is a critical element in maintaining the vitality of the product in the marketplace. The flexible nature of tourism products means that many products—even relatively simple products—can be managed as portfolios of products and services, delivering a variety of experiences to the market.

ACTIVITIES

1. Think about your most memorable tourism experiences. What made these experiences special? Consider how the travel provider designed the experience for you.
2. Design a three-day itinerary that capture the character of your destination. What would be the highlight experience of each day? Where would you have your guests stay? What would they do? How could you design the trip to make it special?
3. Visit the website of a travel wholesaler and look at seven or fourteen-night packages to a country you'd like to visit. What is included in the package? What is the advantage of buying a package?
4. Think of a tourism product that has been around for a while. It may be a classic hotel or an attraction like Disneyland. How has the product kept itself "fresh"?
5. Discuss with a small group or in class the products and innovations that are likely to impact tourism experiences in the coming years. What new products do you think will make the biggest impact on the tourism system in the next ten years?

ACRONYMS

AMA (American Marketing Association)
CTC (Canadian Tourism Commission)
DMO (destination management organization)
MIS (Market Intelligence System)
PLC (Product Life Cycle)

REFERENCES

AMA Dictionary. https://www.ama.org/resources/Pages/Dictionary.aspx?dLetter=P

Dev, C. S., Klein, S., and Fisher, R. A. 1996. A Market Based Approach to Partner Selection in Marketing Alliances Journal of Travel Research, 35 (1), 11–17.

Kotler, P., Bowen, J., and Makens, J. 2015. *Marketing for Hospitality and Tourism*, 6th ed. Boston, MA: Pearson.

Kotler, P., & Keller, K. 2016. *Marketing Management*, 15th ed. Boston: Pearson.

Morrison, A. 2010. *Hospitality and Tourism Marketing*, 4th ed. Clifton Park, New York: Delmar.

Pine, B., & Gilmore, J. 1999. *The Experience Economy: Work is Theatre and Every Business a Stage*. Boston: Harvard Business School Press.

PART THREE

Demand

Factors Influencing Visitors

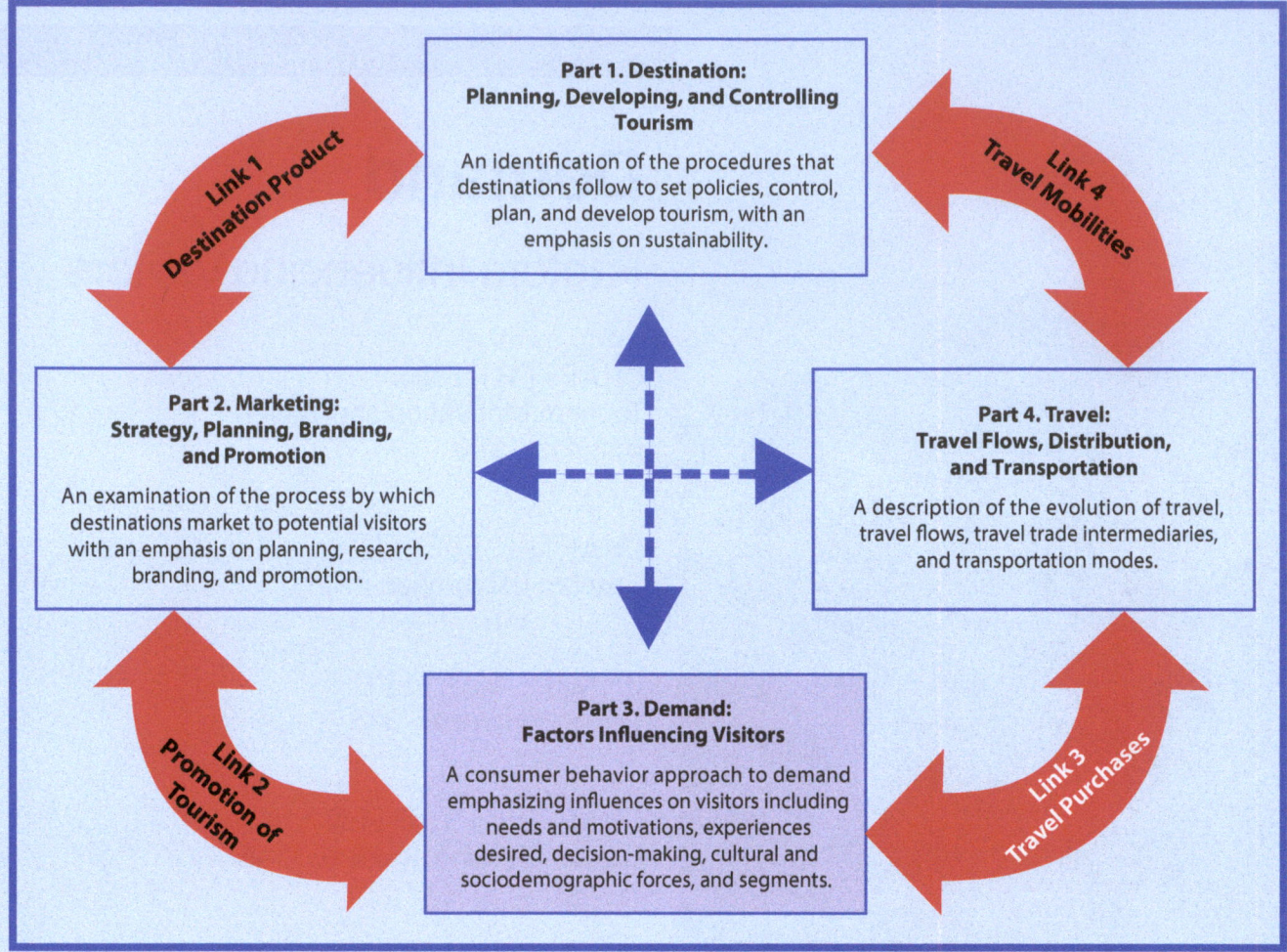

A consumer behavior approach to demand emphasizing influences on visitors including needs and motivations, experiences desired, decision-making, cultural and sociodemographic forces, and segments.

Part 3 of the book is devoted to demand and the factors that influence people in making travel decisions. A consumer behavior approach is used to describe the travel decision-making process. People decide to travel if they have learned that travel satisfies their *needs and motives,* if they can get the *experiences* they want, and if they can travel based on their external constraints (culture and sociodemographics). Travelers' *buying decision processes* and *market segments* are described.

LINK 3: TRAVEL PURCHASE

The linkage between Parts 3 and 4 (Demand and Travel) is called *travel purchase*. An arrow pointing in both directions, clockwise and counterclockwise, characterizes it. This means that each of the two parts (Demand and Travel) may influence the other part. For example, new segments in the market may emerge based on special interests or characteristics of groups of people (Demand). These people may decide to take advantage of exploring these special interests or mixing with other people of similar characteristics while traveling (Travel). A new travel mode may be introduced or become more popular (Travel). Space tourism is clearly an example of this, but as of now only the wealthiest of people (Demand) have been able to afford it.

CHAPTER TEN

Tourism Motivation and Travel Benefits

Why Do People Take Vacations?

If our life is dominated by the search of happiness, few activities reveal as much about the dynamics of this quest for happiness—in all this ardour and paradoxes—than our travels.

ALAIN DE BOTTON

YOUR LEARNING DESTINATION

Based on an understanding of what motivates people to travel and how travel benefits visitors, you will be able to suggest vacation products and communications that will appeal to travelers' needs and wants.

WHAT YOU NEED TO KNOW

Having read this chapter, you will be able to:

✓ Describe the role of travel as a satisfier for fundamental human needs.
✓ Explain, and give appropriate examples of, the role of travel marketers in motivating people to take vacations.
✓ Suggest strategies to combat people's given reasons for not taking vacations.
✓ Explain, and give appropriate examples of, how vacations can benefit people.
✓ Describe the role of tourism in contributing to consumer well-being.

BREAKING THE ICE

Person A: How was your trip?

Person B: Oh well, it was somewhat of a disappointment. I was expecting to roam around the city and discover places that only a few would get to see. Well, everywhere I went was full of tourists. It wasn't really what I was looking for.

If you overhear this conversation, you know that Person B is dissatisfied about his trip. This is the case of not so much about the place he visited being bad but about his expectations being not met. This travel episode underscores the importance of understanding traveler's expectations. Do you know what shapes traveler expectations? Although there may not be a clear one-line answer to this question, research has shown that a major factor connected with expectation formation has to do with motivation. In other words, why Person B traveled to the place he went in the first place significantly influenced what he expected to see, which in turn resulted in the let-down of his actual experience.

The gap between travel motivation, expectation, and reality can be better bridged if a destination considers people's motivations in their experience planning and marketing. Motivation sets in motion the formation of expectations, and influences how a person judges destination products and services as well as how satisfying they find their experience to be. Chapter 10 addresses this topic by presenting theories of motivation that help explain why people travel and how travel benefits them. It explains how destinations can utilize this knowledge in developing effective products and marketing communication strategies.

KEY TAKEAWAY POINTS

- Travel can satisfy one or multiple fundamental human needs.
- Travel needs, wants, motivations, and benefits are overlapping terms that are not conceptually equivalent.
- People's physiological, relational, and developmental needs motivate them to travel.
- People's innate curiosity for the unknown motivates them to travel.
- People travel to escape undesirable situations and seek desirable situations.
- Rest and relaxation is a baseline travel motivation.
- Preconditions, orientations, strength, and tangibilization of travel motivation can explain the development of travel motives, the nature of these motives, the psychological potencies of these motives, and action-oriented goals.
- Benefits from travel can be viewed from both physiological and mental aspects.
- Mood enhancement, bodily stimulation, hedonic pleasure, wellness/fitness, knowledge, skills, creativity, productivity, perspectives, and spiritual growth are some typical travel outcomes.
- Destinations often possess restorative properties.
- De-motivational factors are often related to nativistic tendencies.

FUNDAMENTAL HUMAN NEEDS

The starting point for understanding travel behavior is knowledge related to why people take trips. From a psychological perspective, travel is simply a form of behavior that satisfies fundamental human needs. Knowledge of these needs will help professionals in the tourism field to gain better understanding of the consumer psychology that underlies the exhibited travel behavior. This follows because the motivation to travel is driven by unsatisfied internal needs of the potential traveler and the extent to which the potential traveler perceives these needs will be satisfied by travel.

A potential travel consumer, however, may not be clearly aware of their internal needs and often will articulate their desires in more concrete terms such as what they want or what benefits they are seeking. For tourism destinations to effectively market to travel consumers and serve them well, it is essential to understand the underlying deep-seated needs that people wish to satisfy through vacations.

Much of our conceptual understanding regarding why people travel is grounded in early theorizations in psychology regarding fundamental human needs.

Psychologists agree that there are a set of fundamental human needs that come with humans being human. People across cultural and historical boundaries are known to share a number of inherent needs and traits, although the manifestations and fulfillments of these needs may vary.

This section intends to provide a brief discussion of these basic human needs before proceeding to address what drives consumers to take on the action of travel as a way to fulfill fundamental human needs. The overview of these theoretical propositions in this chapter is not intended to be comprehensive but rather be illustrative of foundational theories that are in position to contribute to your understanding of why people travel and how these baseline human needs play a key role in driving the choices consumers make.

Murray's Classification of Needs

Henry Murray (1893–1988), one of the early famous American psychologists, suggested that there are a set of universal human needs. These needs can be understood as primary or secondary. Primary human needs pertain to human biological needs such as food, water, and oxygen. Secondary needs are generally psychological needs such as the need to achieve or the need for independence. According to Murray, these universal needs can be classified into five categories including Ambition, Materialism, Power, Affection, and Information. Travel is regarded as a means to satisfy both primary and secondary fundamental human needs.

Maslow's Hierarchy of Needs

The most well-known need theorist is Abraham Maslow (1908–1970). His theory of a hierarchy of needs denotes that human beings possess five ordered innate needs with self-actualization at the top and survival at the bottom of a hierarchy:

1. Survival—hunger, thirst, rest, activity
2. Safety—security, freedom from fear and anxiety
3. Belonging and love—affection, giving and receiving love
4. Esteem—personal achievement, self-esteem, and esteem from others
5. Self-actualization—personal self-fulfillment

The lower levels of Maslow's need hierarchy correspond to Murray's physiological needs necessary for human survival, while the higher-level needs are of a psychological nature. This hierarchy suggests that lower level needs demand more immediate attention and satisfaction before a person turns to the satisfaction of higher level needs. It might be better to think of the hierarchy as a series of nested triangles. This nested representation emphasizes the fact that higher level needs encompass all lower level needs.

To this original need conceptualization, Maslow later added two intellectual needs:

6. To know and understand—acquiring knowledge
7. Aesthetics—appreciation of beauty

The relationship between the physical, psychological, and intellectual needs is unclear. It is thought that the intellectual needs exist independently of the other needs.

The decision to travel and selection of a destination can be understood as a function of a complex mixture of fundamental needs motivating an individual to set and prioritize goals with the belief that achieving these goals will satisfy the perceived needs. Maslow's hierarchy of needs has shed light for tourism scholars to later develop a systematic understanding of consumer travel motivation.

Alderfer's ERG Theory

Clayton Alderfer (1940–2015) further conceptualized Maslow's need hierarchy into three categories, that of existence, relatedness, and growth. Alderfer's existence category is comprised of the human survival and human subsistence needs, and closely corresponds to Maslow's physiological and safety needs. Alderfer's second category of relatedness needs corresponds to human's social and interpersonal needs. This includes the needs of belonging and esteem from others in Maslow's theorization. Alderfer's growth need category refers to human being's intrinsic need for personal development. This aligns with Maslow's self-actualization, intellectual, and aesthetic needs. Alderfer suggested that when growth needs are unmet, an individual would exert more efforts to satisfy their relatedness needs. When relatedness needs are not met, an individual will apply an extra effort in fulfilling the physiological needs.

Max-Neef's Need Classification Scheme

In the context of nation development, Chilean economist Max-Neef classified fundamental human needs into nine non-hierarchical dimensions: subsistence, protection, affection, understanding, participation, leisure, creation, identity, and freedom. Max-Neef's scheme does not distinguish foundational or manifest needs nor does it assume an orderly or hierarchy structure of needs. Rather his classification scheme aims at provision of a more operationable set of need parameters for communities and nations to consider to provide for their citizens.

Max-Neef also suggested that human needs are characterized by simultaneities, complementarities, and trade-offs. These needs are interrelated and interactive, functioning similar to that of a system. Communities and nations can measure against how well they are able to satisfy their citizens' needs and identify deficiency or underperforming areas. In Max-Neef's need taxonomy, leisure and recreation, of which travel and especially leisure travel is a part of, becomes a distinct baseline human need.

It is within the context of these inherent human need propositions that we will discuss travel need. Is travel an inherent need for a human being? Do we have the travel genes in us? Most would say no. Travel generally is regarded as a means to an end, rather than an end itself. In other words, travel is not a fundamental human need itself, but it can satisfy one or multiple fundamental human needs.

You may have expressed your desire to travel as a travel need or have heard others use this term when they discuss their travel intent (e.g., "I need to travel"). In this case, people essentially are expressing their desire to use travel as a way to satisfy certain felt fundamental needs. When one or multiple fundamental human needs can be fulfilled by travel, a consumer becomes motivated to take such an action. In the following sections, when we use the term "travel need(s)," we intend not to treat travel as a fundamental human need, but as a manifestation of fundamental human needs.

TRAVEL NEED, WANT, MOTIVATION, AND BENEFIT

Why do people travel? People can travel for business (e.g., attending a convention) or personal reasons (e.g., attending a wedding or for medical treatments). For trips of this nature, the traveler is obligated to take on such an action. However, when it comes to leisure-oriented trips, travel becomes an activity of voluntary choice. Therefore, it becomes valuable for tourism professionals to understand why people choose to spend their free time to travel from among all leisure options.

Furthermore, tourism professionals need to understand questions such as: why does a consumer travel to a specific place from among so many available destinations? Why do people elect to be engaged in a certain set of activities among the various available activity options? Why do they select their chosen restaurants and lodging services? What benefits are they looking for? What comes out of leisure trips? Are there universal reasons that drive consumers to travel or are they culturally or situationally influenced? Answers to these questions can include a multitude of factors that determine people's behavioral tendencies. Travel needs, motivation, and benefits are especially significant factors because they are related to underlying psychological mechanisms explaining choices and satisfaction, as expanded upon below.

A starting point is that when fundamental human needs are not adequately met, a person feels deprived. This individual is said to be not in homeostasis, and becomes motivated to take action. This action may or may not be taken in the form of travel. When it does manifest into the choice of travel, consumers tend to express their travel desire in more concrete terms such as what they want to do or what benefits they are seeking from making a certain trip.

For example, an individual may decide to resort to a cruise trip as a way to combat mental boredom or fatigue. Most likely this person will not be able to clearly articulate his or her psychological motive but rather simply proclaim that "I want to take a cruise trip." In fact, consumers may not even be fully aware of their deep-seated needs and motives. For the cruise industry, however, it would be valuable to know what motivates consumers to choose to take a cruise instead of other alternative travel options. Although travel motives may not be directly observable, they can be inferred or understood via expressed wants or benefits sought on the part of the consumers.

The above discussion leads us to various travel motivation and benefit theories, but before discussing them, we would like to introduce four related concepts pertaining to tourism's role in satisfying human needs: travel need, motivation, want, and benefit. These terms are often used interchangeably by consumers. They are, however, not conceptually equivalent terms.

Travel Need

Travel need can be understood as a manifest human need, expressible in terms of fundamental needs such as Maslow's self-actualization, intellectual and aesthetic needs, or Alderfer's growth needs, discussed earlier. Travel need is sometimes articulated by consumers interchangeably with travel wants.

Travel Motivation

Travel motivation is defined as consumers' psychological impetuses for using travel to satisfy fundamental human needs. Travel motivation serves the function to intervene between a stimulus (need deficiency) and a response (travel).

Travel Want

A want is a tangible articulation for consumers to express their travel need and motivation.

Travel Benefit

Travel benefit refers to the positive personal outcomes brought upon consumers as a result of travel, or one's general beliefs about such positive outcomes. When it is anticipated, it is termed travel benefit belief. When it is remunerated, it becomes a fulfilled travel benefit.

It is important to realize that these four elements are not independent of each other. Figure 10.1 contains a model illustrating the relationships between travel need, want, motivation, and benefit, and how destination marketing activities should be aligned with these concepts. Marketing activities can awake one's travel need. Once

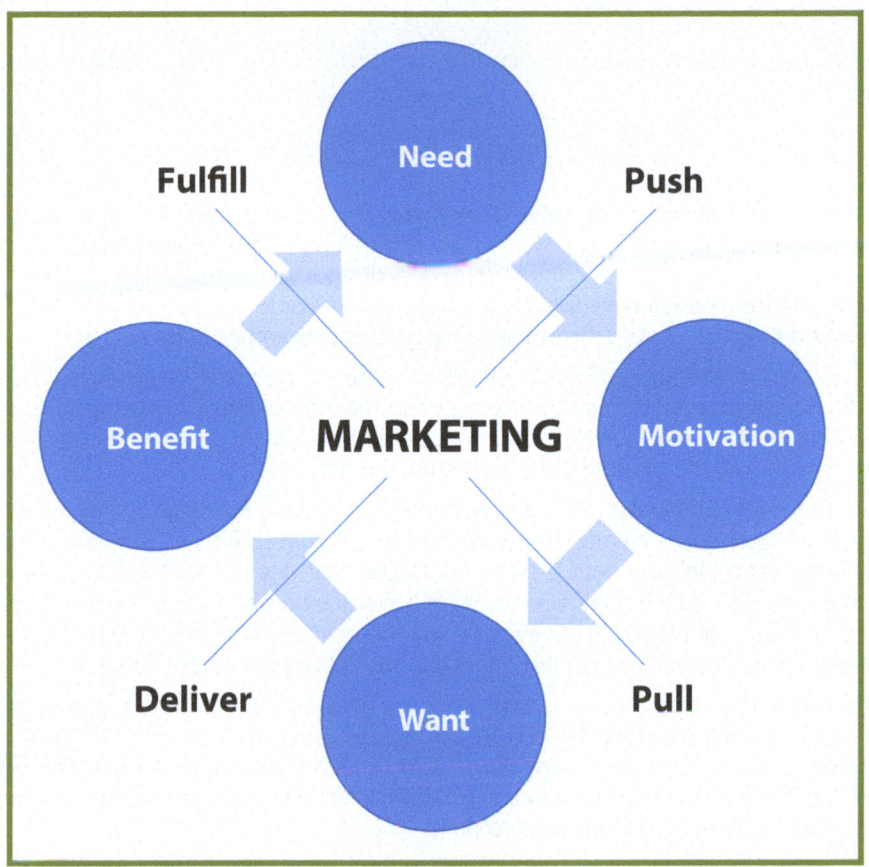

FIGURE 10.1 Marketing activities corresponding to travel need, want, motivation, and benefit.

someone's travel need is awaken/felt, it (NEED) creates a mental state of arousal called drive. This psychological drive will push us to travel (MOTIVATION). Marketing activities oriented toward specific traits and attractiveness of a certain destination or hospitality business will pull the consumer toward one particular destination or business selection. The consumer will then express in tangible terms what specifically he/she desires (WANT). Marketers then deliver to consumers consumptive benefits promised (BENEFIT). Finally, marketers engage consumers in the process of post-trip evaluation. When benefit anticipated is perceived as fulfilled, that cognition will be factored into the consumer's future patronization decisions. In this context, marketers are responsible for:

1. Arousing need
2. Generating interest
3. Sustaining interest
4. Motivating action-taking
5. Delivering on promises
6. Engaging renewed interest

TRAVEL MOTIVATION THEORIES

If you have traveled to another country, you probably have had experiences filling out an entry form requested by the country's immigration authority at the entry point. One common question employed by almost all countries is "What is the purpose of your trip?" The choices given usually include broad categories of reasons such as "business," "leisure," and "visiting friends and relatives." Similarly, market research surveys conducted by destination management organizations at various levels routinely ask trip purpose-related questions. These questions are designed to collect baseline market information as to why travelers visit a place. This information is deemed useful for marketing purpose because it provides a broad view of market segments for a destination. However, it is far from sufficient in understanding consumers' psychological drives underlying the broadly stated purposes. This is where motivational information can come in to provide a more nuanced picture of reasons for why people travel.

QUICK TRIP 10.1

How Does Airbnb Motivate People to Stay with Them?

Curiosity about others and the unknown can drive consumers to go see places. A major motivator for travel is the desire to explore and experience novelty and uniqueness. Airbnb's rapid growth and success is largely attributed to their ability to provide just that. They promote the uniqueness of their accommodations as a contrast to the cookie-cutter hotel room layout. As they can claim—and they do—every one of their host's listings is one of a kind. Accordingly, travelers are ensured they will never stay in the same type of accommodation twice.

Many travelers desire to explore the authentic side of a destination. Airbnb has long pushed their mantra of "live like a local" that represents how Airbnb immerses the traveler into the local community rather than just a visitor observing it. Aside from living in actual homes in real neighborhoods, Airbnb guests can also access hosts' custom-curated experiences and sites that showcase the authentic elements of a destination.

So how does Airbnb promote these benefit propositions in their marketing activities? They, in fact, make use of similar tactics that many other companies employ. For instance, they target traditionalists who always stay at hotels by including banner advertisements on hotel and OTA booking sites with the hope of enticing them with an alternative lodging option. Airbnb is also strategic in their search result advertisements by ensuring that keyword searches relating to lodging prompts a link to their website. They have also been increasing the number of commercials and video content over the last few years, even having a thirty-second slot in the 2017 Super Bowl.

Social media is an effective outlet for showcasing one's brand with potential customers and Airbnb is one of the most popular brands with a big social media presence. For comparison purposes, currently Airbnb's Facebook page has three times as many likes as Marriott Hotel's page (6.3 million vs. 2.3 million), and almost two times as many Twitter followers (595k vs. 254k). This suggests Airbnb has a greater potential for one of their followers to share or like their content, allowing a greater reach to attract new customers.

Their online presence extends beyond social media as they have also won awards for their excellent website and smartphone application, further ensuring that they seal the deal with prospective guests. Finally, Airbnb is also known for pulling various PR stunts such as the Floating House where people enter a competition for the opportunity to stay the night in the extraordinary accommodation. Campaigns like this are truly the essence of a pull marketing strategy, as the Floating House competition sent over 70,000 people to their site, of whom one-third had never visited the site before.

Think about This

1. What challenges may Airbnb face that other hospitality companies do not have to deal with when marketing their products?
2. What challenges may Airbnb face when delivering the benefits they promise?
3. What do you think major hotel brands would do to counter Airbnb's unique value proposition?
4. Of the two streams of marketing strategies (conventional and social media-based), which was probably most important in Airbnb's early years?
5. Of the specific strategies mentioned, which do you think is the most effective in the long run?

Sources

https://www.airbnb.com/night-at/floating-house

https://econsultancy.com/blog/68225-10-examples-of-great-airbnb-marketing-creative/

http://www.webbyawards.com/winners/2014/web/general-website/travel/airbnb/

http://www.webbyawards.com/winners/2014/mobile-apps/handheld-devices/travel-handheld-devices/airbnb-ios-app/

Characteristics of Motivation

Travel motivation represents a psychological driving force for consumer action. Motivational forces can play a major role in shaping individual interests and desires, framing the possibilities and directions for action and influencing whether travel behaviors result in persistence or change.

It is worth noting travel motivation can be understood at two levels. The first level is a global level when people express why they travel in general and broad terms. These generic motivational statements are sometimes called travel benefit beliefs or travel values, as they represent a person's general beliefs about travel's beneficial aspects and what travel can mean or do to one's life. For example, one may believe that travel is a great way to help one get out of one's comfort zone and expand one's life horizon, or that travel allows a person to get in touch with oneself. Someone else may feel that travel can help improve interpersonal relationships.

In other cases, consumer motives are more situation- or occasion-driven, usually articulated through wants and desires. For example, if someone is deprived of connections with their loved ones, they may express a desire/want to spend more time with family and take a family trip to the Canadian Rockies. This level of motivation is tied to a person's life situation and state of mind at a particular point of time. At this level, although a consumer may have a primary or dominant motive for a particular trip, it is plausible that they may have multiple motives simultaneously for taking a particular trip.

Additionally, although people can be motivated differently, travel motives at the situation or occasion level are almost always triggered by their life circumstances. In other words, understanding consumers' current life status and mental state can be important, as life situation variables can reveal why consumers are motivated in a certain way.

Another characteristic associated with travel motivation is that while fundamental human needs are finite and are consistent in all cultures and historical periods, travel's role as a means to satisfy these baseline human needs can vary across cultures and historical periods. In other words, people with different cultural backgrounds and people living in different generational cohorts may be motivated differently when they resort to travel to satisfy their needs.

Travel Career Ladder

Early tourism scholars have proposed various tourism motivation models that consider travel needs and other factors discussed above. A notable example is Pearce's Travel Career Ladder (TLC) (1982). Pearce organized travel motivation into a five-level hierarchy in which people move from level to level over time. This model, which is based on Maslow's hierarchy of needs theory, argues that each person has a "travel career" just as they have a "work career." The five levels of the Travel Career Ladder are:

1. Relaxation
2. Stimulation
3. Relationship
4. Self-esteem and development
5. Fulfillment

Pearce notes that travel motivation can be self-directed or other-directed. On the left side of the ladder represents self-directed motivations and the right side pertains to other-directed motivations. People start their travel careers at different levels and may change their levels during their travel careers. Some people "ascend" the ladder predominantly on the left side. Others may go through all the steps on both sides of the ladder. The main point that Pearce's career ladder emphasizes is that the psychological driving forces behind people's travel decisions and decision-making processes are not static; they change over a person's lifetime. For example, the more experienced travelers become, the more likely they may act on higher level needs in the ladder such as fulfillment, self-esteem, and development.

As with a career at work, people start at different levels and are likely to change levels during their lifetime. They do not always seek the same type of fulfillment from travel and people can descend as well as ascend on the ladder depending on situational and life circumstances. Although TCL is useful in facilitating our understanding of general travel motivation tendencies over a person's life timeline, it has also met with criticism. One such criticism is that a traveler does not necessarily follow this trajectory over their lifetime. They may also be predominantly motivated by one or two types of travel motivation and never develop other types of motivation.

QUICK TRIP 10.2

Why Do People Take Family Reunion Trips?

As today's family ties are sustained less through economic connections and more by personal and social bonds, and modern families continue to become increasing geographically scattered, family reunion travel has become increasingly popular. Family reunion is an occasion when members from an extended family congregate. About a third of United States adults travel to attend a family reunion every three years. Consequently, convention and visitor bureaus and hospitality businesses are paying increasing attention to this travel segment.

Knowledge about family reunion travel motivation in this context becomes very helpful because it will provide parameters for developing programs, activities, and other offerings that are geared toward fulfilling the needs of multiple generations. Below is a summary of what consumers say they want when they travel to see their extended family (Kluin & Lehto 2012):

Family History and Togetherness
- We like to listen to life stories of family members in person.
- We like to share life stories/feelings together at our family reunions.
- Through family reunions, we want to maintain our family's history.
- Doing things together is the most meaningful during our family reunions.
- Family togetherness is the most important while attending family reunions.
- It is fun to sit around remembering our family's history.

Immediate Family Cohesion
- I feel closer to my children after attending family reunions.
- I want my spouse/partner to spend time with my extended family.
- Through family reunions, I want my children to know their extended family.
- I want to show my life path to my family (spouse/partner and/or children).

Family Communication
- It is easier to express my true feelings to my family while attending family reunions.
- Tensions within my family are relaxed while attending family reunions.
- Family reunions help my family talk more freely and openly with each other.
- Family members openly discuss any topic with each other during family reunions.

Family Adaptability
- Family members' roles could change while attending family reunions.
- Our family does things together as a group even though it might have been more efficient to work separately.
- When attending family reunions, our family does not hesitate to try new things.

Personal Relaxation
- I am able to rest and relax at family reunions.
- While attending family reunions, I forget about the day-to-day stresses of my life.

Think about This
1. What may be challenges for extended families regarding travel? How can the industry help?
2. How can the understanding of these family reunion motives help industry practitioners?
3. What might be ideal locations to satisfy the family reunion needs?
4. Would other reunion travelers (e.g., class reunion) share similar needs with family reunion travelers?

Sources

Kluin, J., and Lehto, X. 2012. Measuring family reunion travel motivations. *Annals of Tourism Research,* 39 (2), 820–841. https://doi.org/10.1016/j.annals.2011.09.008

http://www.familytreemagazine.com/

QUICK TRIP 10.3

Why Volunteer While on Vacation?

Volunteer tourism, a form of travel where individuals spend their own vacation time and money to do volunteer work, has gained popularity in recent years. There are a large number of well-established organizations that offer structured volunteer tourism programs. They offer a wide spectrum of volunteer vacation experiences. Volunteer vacation destinations range from local to regional to global reach. Volunteer Vacation costs range from $100 and under to $3,000 and more, with project length from under one week to six months or more. While summer appears to be the most predominant travel season, there are packages and programs provided in all seasons.

Why do people spend their vacation time to travel to places for the sake of doing volunteer work? Voluntourism, as it has been called, offers people fulfilling experiences by providing them opportunities to have a direct and long-term impact on local communities. Volunteers are motivated by self-actualization-related needs. When travelers travel to contribute to something bigger than themselves, their needs are met. Research has shown that volunteering benefits people themselves as much as or more than the voluntourism destinations. Key motivators for volunteer vacationers include:

- Cultural immersion
- Giving back and making a difference
- Seeking camaraderie
- Seeking educational and learning opportunities
- Seeking bonding opportunities

Some of the top organizations include Global Vision International, International Volunteer Headquarters, and Cross-Cultural Solutions, to name a few. In particular, Projects Abroad is renowned for offering hundreds of various types of volunteer projects that are utilized by 10,000 annual volunteers whom are supported by 700 trained staff. Some of the top destinations that Project Abroad and most other voluntourism organizations have presence in include Nepal, Thailand, Fiji, India, Ghana, South Africa, and Peru. Collectively, the many organizations, destinations, and programs present people desiring to fulfill higher-order needs a large number of opportunities to do so.

Think about This

1. Are volunteer vacationers the heroes or the beneficiaries? Are their motivations self-directed or other-directed?
2. What are some specific benefits that voluntourism presents people that would otherwise not be available to non-volunteer vacationers?
3. What should any marketing campaign intended on encouraging voluntourism include?
4. What may be important elements for volunteer tourism providers to consider to provide a satisfactory experience?
5. Would you consider travel for volunteering purposes? Why or why not?

Sources

Brown, S., and Lehto, X. Y. 2005. Traveling with a purpose: Understanding the motives and benefits of volunteer vacationers. *Current Issues in Tourism*, 8 (6), 479–496.

http://www.projects-abroad.org/voluntourism/

When it comes to travel motivation for a specific trip, people may have multiple motives simultaneously. Pearce and his colleagues have recently modified the travel career ladder model and suggest that motivation can be better understood without a hierarchical order. Rather, travelers in general have a set of core motivations and a set of peripheral motivations (Pearce and Lee 2005). For example, relaxation and stimulation may be core or predominant travel motivations driving the behavior of most people much of the time. In fact, rest and relaxation is regarded as a baseline travel need that is important to almost all contemporary travelers. However, young travelers, such as college students on Spring Break tend to be driven by a desire for high stimulation, while other motivations such as nostalgia or self-discovery needs may not be as prevalent. The main point is that any given type of motivation may be drivers for some on certain occasions, not for others.

Travel Motivation POST Scheme

Lehto proposes a Travel Motivation POST Scheme that illustrates travel motivation's *Preconditions, Orientations, Strength, and Tangibilization* (POST) (Figure 10.2). This model explains psychological drives that propel the development of travel motives, the nature of these travel motives, the psychological potencies of these travel motives, and action-oriented goals that people derive from these travel motives (Figure 10.3a, b, c, d).

• **Preconditions**

The *Travel Motivation POST Scheme* suggests that a person can develop travel motivations based on two broad preconditions: need deficiency and man's innate curiosity. The *first* precondition is when people experience fundamental need deficiencies. In other words, consumers' undesirable or subpar personal circumstances in work life, personal life, or health/wellness status can dictate how they are motivated to travel. These undesirable life situations can be derived from three unmet foundational needs:

1. One's *physiological resource imbalance* (e.g., sub-health and sensory deprivation).
2. One's *relational resource* imbalance (e.g., lack of quality family time, social entanglement, lack of social engagement).

3. One's *personal growth resource* imbalance (e.g., self-identity crisis, existential anxiety, self-development barriers).

The second precondition is curiosity, a quintessential human quality. The curious nature of human beings can lead people to wonder, ponder, and voyage. These two broad preconditions will motivate consumers to travel, to escape undesirable situations in life, and to seek desirable situations.

• **Motivational Orientation**

Motivation orientation explains the nature of travel motives. The Travel Motivation POST Scheme suggests there are two general orientations: **escape-orientation and seek-orientation.** There are specific motivational themes corresponding to each of these orientations. Travel preconditions can drive these motivational themes.

For example, a person's subpar mental or physical health conditions can lead to the development of the motive to travel to escape their existing lifestyle and seek physical activities not available at home. A lack of alone time may drive the individual to travel to escape social engagements and to seek solitary times. In other cases, existential anxieties may stimulate a person to travel to escape from their inauthentic way of life and seek self-understanding. Curiosity for the unknown may also lead to a desire to travel to exotic or beautiful places to enjoy and learn about things.

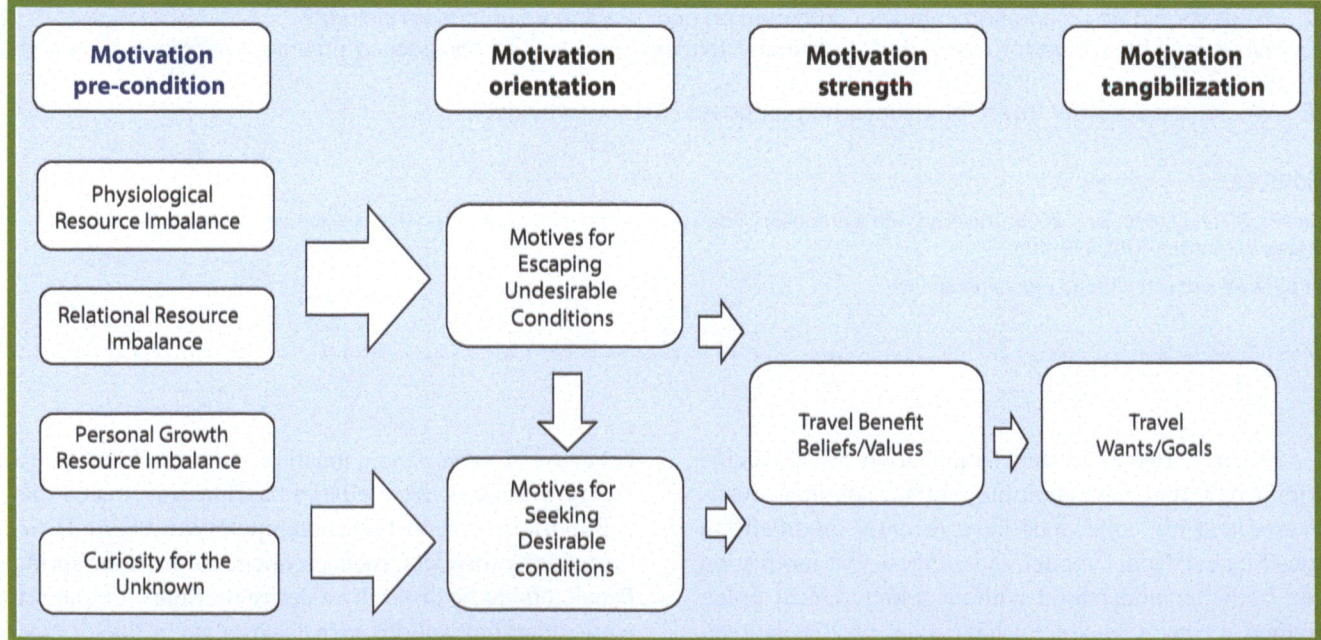

FIGURE 10.2 Travel Motivation POST Scheme.

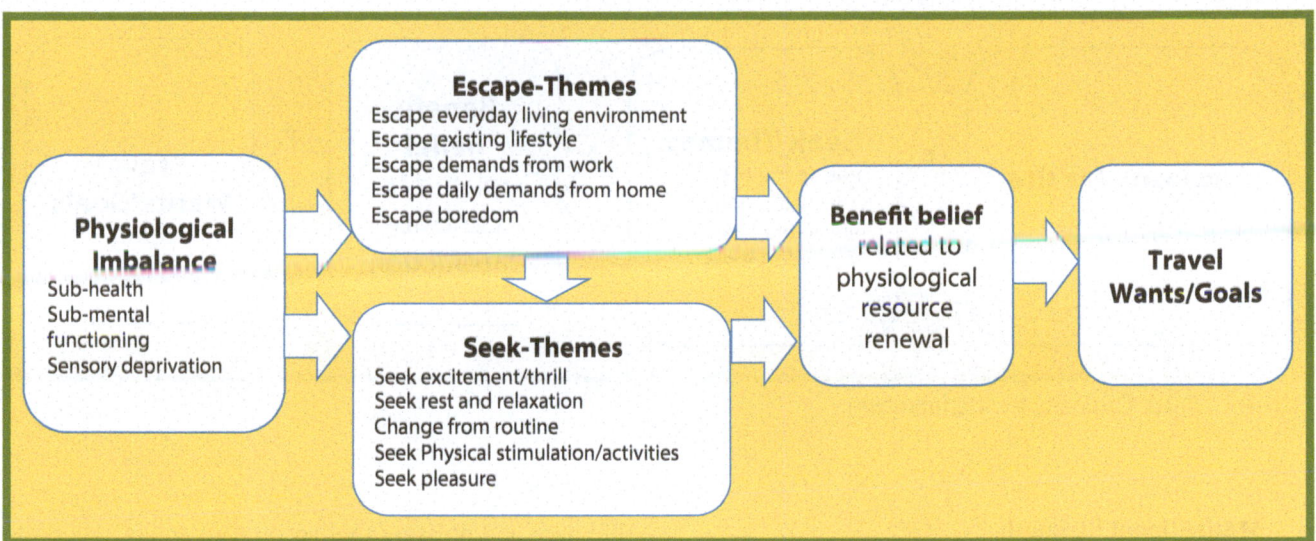

FIGURE 10.3A Physiological imbalance.

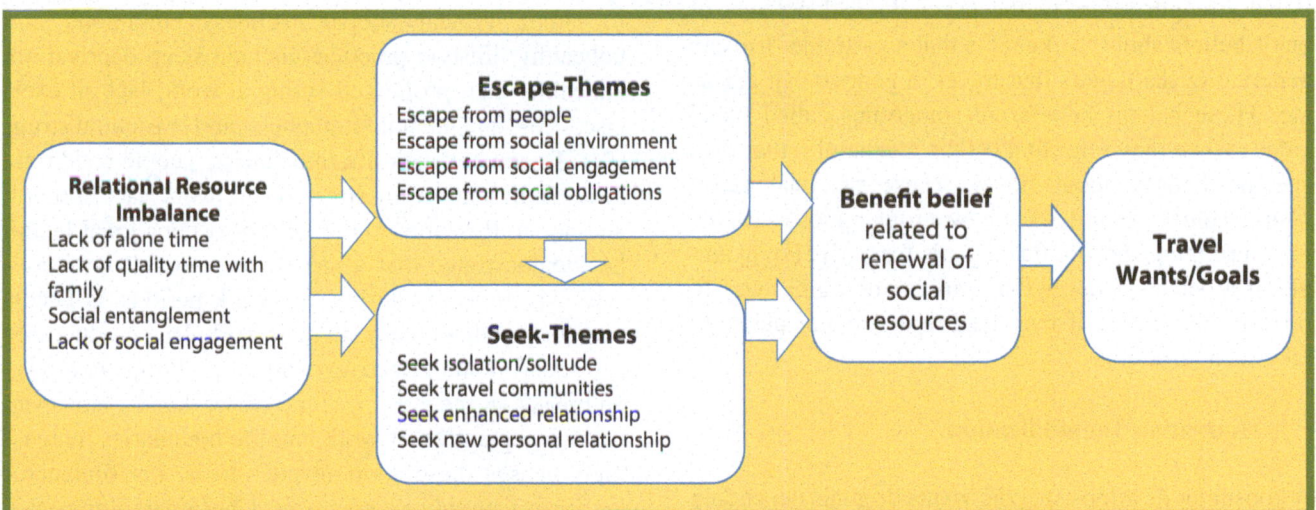

FIGURE 10.3B Relational resource imbalance.

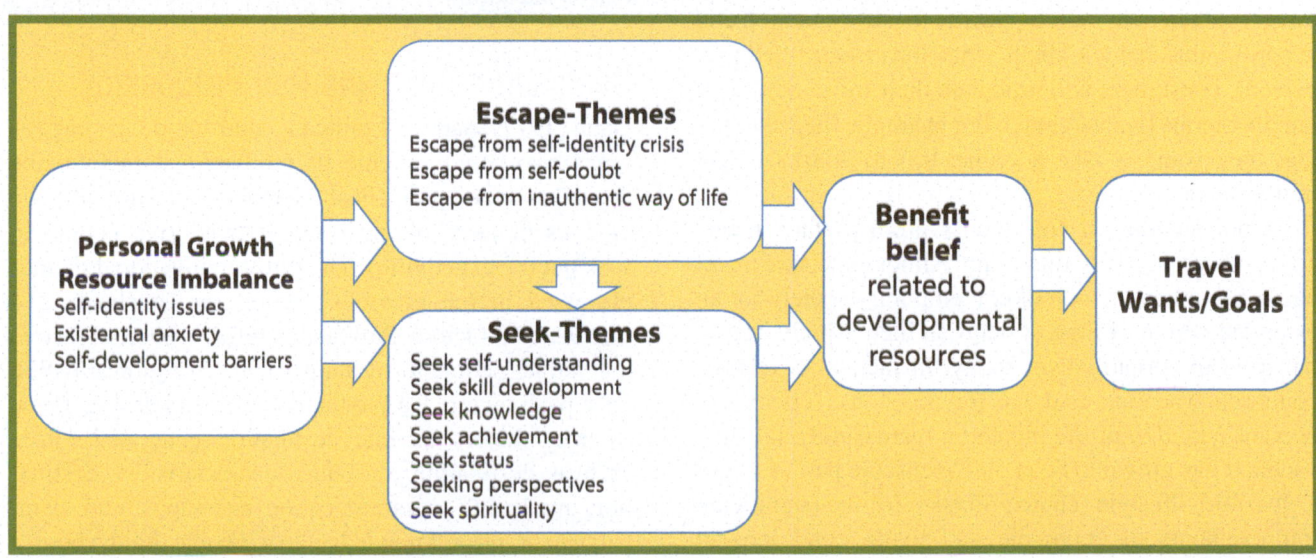

FIGURE 10.3C Personal growth resource imbalance.

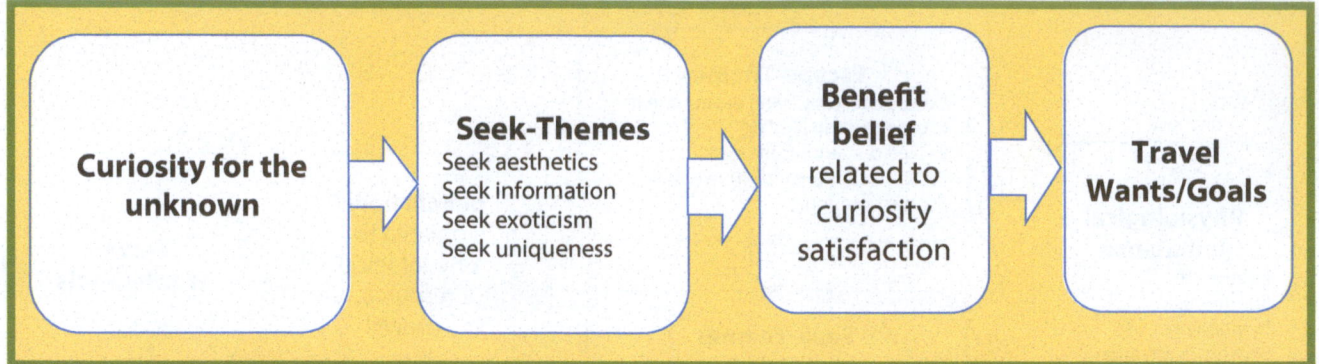

FIGURE 10.3D Curiosity for the unknown.

- **Motivational Strength**

In the Travel Motivation POST Scheme, travel motivational strength refers to the psychological potency of one's beliefs about the benefits that a particular trip can generate or the beliefs that travel in general can generate. These benefit beliefs are sometimes called travel values when they refer to a person's general rather than specific beliefs about travel. These personal travel beliefs/values can influence how strong a motive can be in determining specific travel goals for a trip. For example, if a person believes that cruises are a great way to refresh themselves, it may lead to a stronger desire to take such an action.

- **Motivation Tangibilization**

A consumer develops specific wants or goals depending on his or her travel motives and beliefs. Depending upon the strength of consumers' benefit beliefs with regard to travel (both benefit beliefs specific to a life situation and general value beliefs about what travel can offer to a person), consumers will articulate their travel desires in tangible terms (wants/goals). For example, they may say that they want to take a cruise trip to Alaska to get rejuvenated.

Understanding a consumer's pre-trip state in this context becomes very important. Although leisure travel has been a phenomenon of contemporary society for an extended period of time, it plays an increasingly important role in people's lives today. In fact, in developed countries, vacation and leisure travel has effectively become a quality of life indicator. Increasingly, taking a vacation has grown to be an indispensable part of life or a feasible lifestyle choice thanks to the significant improvements of economic and living conditions in these countries. In the meantime, the increasing work-

life pace and pressure that accompany today's working population also propel consumers to increasingly resort to travel for health and well-being considerations.

Some typical subpar wellness conditions and unhealthy lifestyle practices include sleep deprivation, unhealthy diet, prolonged sitting at work, lack of exercise, stress and mental fatigueness, and existential struggles. To combat such life imbalances, people need time away from sources of stress in the workplace, school, and home. Research in the field of occupational health has demonstrated that a mental process called "recovery," which occurs during non-work periods, is necessary for people to maintain their workplace productivity and social capital. Recovery can occur during workdays on breaks, in the evenings, and on weekends. However, the non-separation of work and life boundaries increasingly causes these short respites to be insufficient or ineffective to achieve recovery. Consumers are consequently increasingly seeking longer respite opportunities on vacation.

Destination Push and Pull Proposition

Dann (1977) made a significant contribution in suggesting a two-tiered scheme of motivational factors: the "push" and the "pull." Push factors refer to the intrinsic motives or psychological forces that drive people to seek out travel activities. The travel motivational themes discussed in the previous sections are push-oriented motivational factors. Pull factors refer to external factors that attract people toward a particular travel destination once push factors lead to the rise of travel desire. These external factors include destination generated forces such as destination attributes, characteristics, destination marketing communication messages and campaigns, or prior knowledge that people hold about a destination (Gnoth 1997).

QUICK TRIP 10.4

Sandals: All You Need Is Love

"Sandals is the most completely original place on Earth created for two people in love." This punch line found on their website represents Sandals' concentrated effort of going all in on the "couples" market. While other resort brands cater to a similar traveler segment, Sandals has uniquely created their product offering to exclusively satisfy a couple's need for relationship building. That is, unlike other resort brands that tailor experiences for a broader traveler audience, everything in a Sandals resort is distinctively created for romance.

This romance-oriented approach is clearly reflected in both the resort infrastructure as well as the services and activities offered at each resort. Over thirty years of experience in specializing on crafting the perfect couple's resort experience has made Sandals an expert in this area. For instance, each of their twenty-four properties includes any of the following features: (1) secluded and private areas for "romantic rendezvous"; (2) private pools "to spend time in each other's arms"; 3) fire pits "for igniting the passion." To complement these features, Sandals also provides highly trained butlers whose sole purpose is to alleviate any undue stress and worry, so a couple can simply enjoy each other's company. Rounding off these features and services are the extensive activities and amenities available. From private candlelight dinners, to tantalizing spa treatments, every offering at a Sandals Resort property is intended on enhancing the couple's togetherness.

Sandals Resorts International is a perfect example of a hospitality brand that has recognized and singled out one particular travel motivation, and created an experience centered around fulfilling that need. The founder and chairman of Sandals, Gordon Stewart, also known as the "Master of Marketing," has spent his career promoting his resort as the ultimate place "for two people in love."

Think about This

1. What are the advantages of focusing on satisfying one specific travel motivation?
2. In addition to the resort features, services, and activities offered, how else can Sandals demonstrate they are satisfying the romantic needs of travelers?
3. Can you think of another specific travel motivation that is being targeted by a travel/hospitality brand in the same way?

Sources

http://www.sandals.com/all-inclusive/

http://www.sandals.com/news/article/id/73/

While the push factors drive the desire to travel, the pull factors play an important role in impacting where a person travels to fulfill the identified desires. Pull factors emerge due to the attractiveness of a destination, examples of which can be unique natural environment, safety, sunshine, superior accessibility, entertainment options, novel cultures, sightseeing, or local cultural attractions and cuisines. Common characteristics of destination attractiveness can come from place properties such as aesthetic traits, expressive traits (e.g., unique or exotic landmarks), or utilitarian traits (e.g., proximity, convenience).

Although pull factors can be resource-based, they can also be influenced by marketing activities, because a person's perceived attractiveness of a destination is also a function of the alignment between a destination's own attributes and the person's intrinsic motivations. In other words, pull factors can be factored effectively into destination marketing schemes. As discussed previously, consumer beliefs about what benefits a trip to a destination can offer influences their motivation strength and their eventual goal articulation. In this sense, marketers can play an instrumental role in designing and communicating travel experiences that deliver benefits that best align with consumers' motivations. Destination attributes as pull factors will further be elaborated upon in Chapter 12 in the context of traveler decision-making.

It is important to know that motivation and tourism product are usually not in a one-to-one relationship. A tourism destination product can cater to people with

The Historically Motivated Traveler

As you've gathered, people are motivated to travel for different reasons. Some travel for business, some travel to get away from it all, some travel to jump into a hustle and bustle of a place other than home. Then there are those who travel for the deeply rooted need to expand their own knowledge. Travelers such as these are going to be attracted to places that can offer them a great deal of intellectual enrichment. Athens (Greece), Argos (Greece), Plovdiv (Bulgaria), Chania (Crete, Greece), and Larnaca (Cyprus) are some of the oldest known European cities. These treasured destinations bring in hundreds of thousands of visitors every day. Some hotels have tried to bring the destination to the visitor rather than the visitor to the destination by decorating in ways that give the hotel a museum-like feel. Take, for example, the Luxor Hotel in Las Vegas where there are Egyptian relics and a makeshift Nile River. Why would a person visit this hotel rather than the actual destination itself?

Think about This

1. Why are people attracted to ancient relics and ruins?
2. What age group(s) does this sort of travel appeal to? Why?

Source

http://www.tourism-review.com/europe-top-oldest-cities-news2761

---

varying motives. A person can also travel with more than one motive and goal. It is, therefore, important to carefully strategize destination marketing and planning activities based on a nuanced understanding of the dynamics of market segment characteristics and the destination's role in fulfilling the multiplicity of consumer needs that are co-present.

TRAVEL BENEFITS

Researchers have attempted to understand from a scientific standpoint what benefits travel actually brings to consumers. For example, it has been acknowledged that consumers are increasingly motivated by the health and wellness benefits from travel. This has led to efforts to answer questions pertinent to tourism service providers such as: How does taking a vacation bring benefits to a person's health and well-being? How long can the vacation effects last? Why do some people feel well-charged and energized after taking a vacation while others feel exhausted and overwhelmed? What types of vacation benefits do travelers want the most? How can destinations best facilitate such outcomes?

When answering such questions, it becomes clear that the positive outcomes or benefits of travel vary greatly. A simple model, or traveler gain framework, is given in Figure 10.4 that conceptualizes the benefits of travel. Mood enhancement, bodily stimulation, hedonic

pleasure, wellness/fitness, knowledge, skills, creativity, productivity, perspectives, and spiritual growth are some typical benefits of travel that have been noted by researchers. These travel benefits can be understood along two dimensions: the durability or endurance of changes (momentary-enduring) and the nature of changes (physiological–spiritual) brought upon travelers.

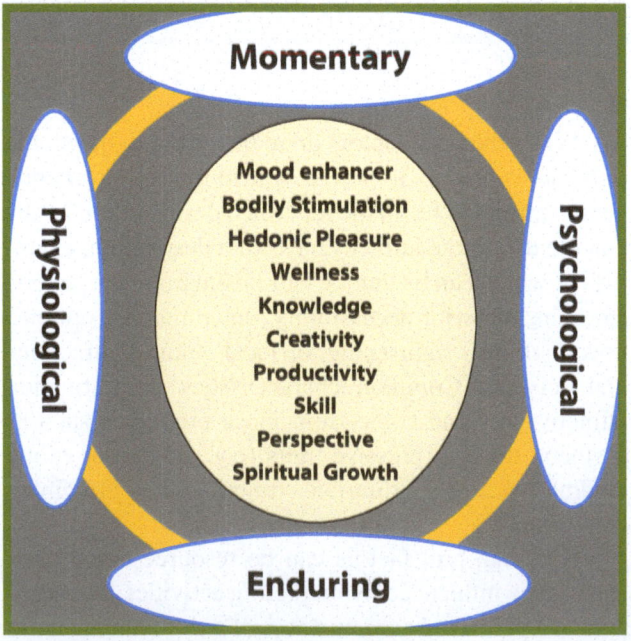

FIGURE 10:4 Traveler gain framework.

QUICK TRIP 10.6

Feel the Pull: Is a Great Place to Live a Good Place to Visit?

As pull factors, attractive characteristics and attributes of a destination can entice people to visit. A first time New York City visitor describes what he wants from his upcoming visit this way in a post in TripAdvisor: "I'm going to New York for the first time next week . . . My favorite thing to do when I travel is just to walk around and marvel, stopping at a nice bakery or ice cream shop along the way. I'm not a big fan of just checking off all the big attractions . . . So my question is, what are the best neighborhoods for a mid-20's couple to wander around in?" Clearly this visitor simply wants to wander around and explore in neighborhoods. Places like Greenwich Village, Soho, or Brooklyn Heights may just be the ideal places to be for them. These neighborhoods and places have become popular destinations. What is interesting is that many such communities and neighborhoods were built for and by their own residents without overt considerations for potential visitors.

Place is vital to human well-being. A well-planned place with its own unique texture and vitality serves its residents well. The American Planning Association (APA) provides various planning guidelines for places and neighborhoods with the overarching goal of creating memorability and fostering social engagement. They recommend consideration of the following functional place attributes in order to facilitate a resident's day-to-day living:

- Accommodates multi-modal transportation (i.e., pedestrians, bicyclists, drivers).
- Has design and architectural features that are visually interesting.
- Encourages human contact and social activities.
- Promotes community involvement and maintains a secure environment.
- Promotes sustainability and responds to climatic demands.
- Has a memorable character.

Think about This

1. Why do some say a good place to live is a good place to visit?
2. What neighborhood attributes will be appreciated by visitors?
3. Do visitors and residents want the same things? Why or why not?
4. Do residents really want to rub shoulders with visitors?
5. Think about your hometown. What may be some of the characteristics that can potentially appeal to visitors and why?

Sources

American Planning Association. https://www.planning.org/

http://wikitravel.org/en/Manhattan/Greenwich_Village

Travel Gain Durability

The endurance or durability the impact travel has on the person is an important parameter studied by tourism professionals. Some benefits are fleeting, while others are of a more enduring nature (Figure 10.4). Benefits that are momentary in nature are often received during a consumptive moment. For example, travel can be an instant mood enhancer. You may have travel moments when your mood is instantly lifted. Many of the hedonic gains associated with travel belong to this category of benefits.

Emotional reactions to scenery, foods, a conversation with a stranger, a sense of freedom and happiness can be felt at a moment onsite a destination. Hedonic pleasures such as joyfulness, thrill, peacefulness, comfort, clear-headedness, and other sensory stimulations can be brief. The sense of eupherism may last the entire trip or even days or weeks post-vacation, but they will eventually disipate. The traveler may return to an emotive set point.

Longer lasting benefits of travel, such as better focus and mental functioning due to the therapeutic effects of rest and recreation, may stay for days or weeks. Other benefits can be much more enduring, including personal growth outcomes such as change of lifestyle, change of life perspectives, change of self value, and spirtualility pursuits.

Nature of Change

The benefits of travel also vary depending on the nature of the changes to the traveler brought about by the travel experience. Some changes and associated benefits are trivial in nature, while others may be much more central to life. For example, a feeling of tranquility as a result of visiting a spa may not be as central to one's life as a change in spiritual belief system. These benefits gained from travel can vary on a spectrum from being entirely physiological, to psychological, or even spiritual. For example, sensual pleasure or weight loss as a result of traveling are physiological benefits, whereas enhanced work productivity may be a result of better mental functioning or creativity gained due to travel. Other gains can be transformative, such as feeling a connection to the home of one's ancestors.

Although people may be motivated by the benefits they expect to gain from travel, not all gains are expected. Some occur at surrendipicious moments. Some are completely unexpected. It is worth noting that not all travelers will make gains along the entire spectrum of benefits. For some, enduring gains or transformational gains will not occur.

Travel benefits can come from one particular moment or one particular trip, but can also be accumulative. They also can vary greatly. These benefits at the end of the day will be dependent on the quality of a vacation experience, an individual's specific life circumstances, and social demographic/psychographic traits. It is very benefical for destinations and other providers to understand these tourism benefit parameters as this helps ensure that they provide relevant and meaningful vacation services that help consumers to optimize their gain from travel.

Vacation Outcome Variability

Although we know that taking a vacation may have a positive impact on one's well-being and work performance, not every vacation results in such a desirable mental and physical state for vacationers. In fact, an increasing amount of travelers share the sentiment that their vacations exhaust them and that they need another vacation to recover from their vacation taken.

This begs the supposition that simply taking a vacation is enough. The question is, what types of vacation would be the most effective in restoring people? It is important to take a closer look at consumers' vacation content and consider the various elements and characteristics of a vacation destination to see how they may be conducive toward resting and restoring consumers. For example, how do different destination settings, characteristics, and activities recharge a visitor? Figure 10.5, Figure 10.6, and Figure 10.7 are examples of ways visitors spend time on a beach relaxing. Is the beach setting

FIGURE 10.5 **Young woman using smartphone on a beach.**

© Kite_rin/Shutterstock.com

superior to a city setting in recharging and resting a visitor? Do the activities visitors follow make a difference in how they feel physically at the end of the trip? These are questions that destinations and resorts are concerned with when considering and designing programs and activities for their customers.

FIGURE 10.6 Man doing a handstand on the beach.

FIGURE 10.7 An excited family riding Jet Ski.

DESTINATION RESTORATIVE QUALITIES

It is common for individuals to resort to taking a trip when feeling fatigued and worn out from work and daily routine. We know from the previous discussion that escape from daily routine, rest, and relaxation are dominant motivational drivers for travel. Rest and relaxation is a baseline motivation that either single-handedly drives consumers to taking vacation trips or, along with other factors, becomes one of the motives that influence consumers' decisions on whether to take a vacation and in the selection of vacation destinations. Theories from environmental psychology and recent tourism studies lend some insights regarding the attributes and characteristics of a vacation destination that effectively rest and restore consumers. Knowledge of these attributes and characteristics can guide destination and service providers seeking to market and improve the product they provide to vacationers.

Much of what we know regarding the general attributes and characteristics of a restorative environment has been given to us by environmental psychologists who have extensively studied the linkages between environmental qualities and health. Environmental psychologists suggest that performing activities such as work or study, to a large extent, require a type of attention called voluntary attention or directed attention. When a person suffers from deficient voluntary attention capacity, the person will not have normal functioning of the prefrontal cortex, which is a part of the brain responsible for mental functions. When someone has insufficient voluntary attention capacity, the person is said to be in a state of mental fatigue (Rothbart and Posner 1985). Kaplan (1995) suggests that placing a fatigued person in a physical environment that triggers one's involuntary attention will help the person to regain the needed voluntary attention capacity for daily work or study. Voluntary

FIGURE 10.8 Young businessman juggling a million things at once: time to have a vacation.

attention is the act of the will, taking place when the selection of an object of activity is made with a previously set goal. Many of the tasks associated with work or study require voluntary attention. Involuntary attention is a form of attention that is unintentional or unconscious.

Based on Kaplan's theory and other findings in environmental psychology, Lehto (2013) developed a model called *Destination Restorative Qualities* (DRQS) (see Figure 10.9). The DRQS model systematically addresses the attributes and characteristics of a destination that are restorative to visitors. It identifies six different restorative aspects of a destination, which are called *compatibility, extent, mental away-ness, physical away-ness, orientation,* and *fascination*. Lehto suggests that a destination or setting needs to consider each of these six aspects to optimally serve visitor needs for recuperation and rejuvenation.

One advantage of applying the Destination Restorative Qualities model is that it provides meaningful parameters for destinations targeting consumers who seek a restorative vacation experience. It explains features and characteristics of a destination that can best foster efficient renewal of diminished functional resources of visitors. The following section explains all six parameters and management implications.

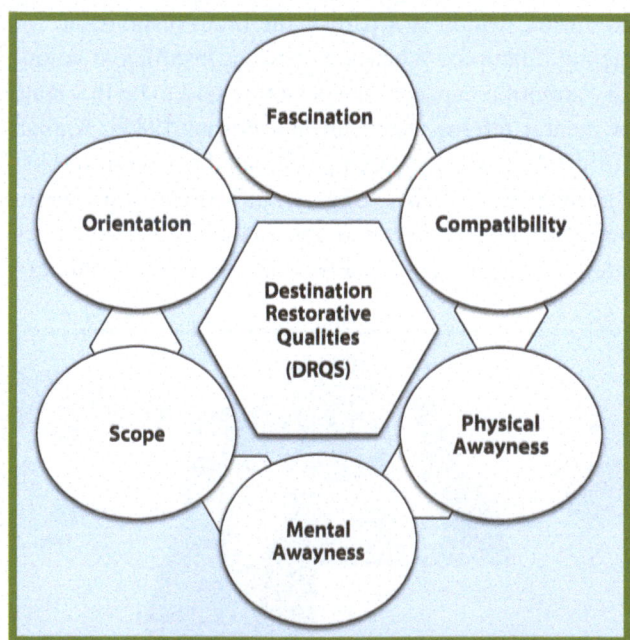

FIGURE 10.9 Destination Restorative Qualities. |
Adapted from Lehto 2013.

Compatibility

Compatibility refers to a sense of congruence or match between a visitor and the place he/she visits. Compatibility is an important parameter that a destination needs to consider, because a strong sense of compatibility makes a visitor feel more at ease, which allows them to more effectively rest themselves. The sense of compatibility comes from three sets of perceived congruence on the part of the visitor.

- **There needs to be a natural alignment between the visitor's self-image and a place's image.**

The visitor needs to feel companionable with the place they visit. They need to feel "This is my kind of place" and "This place suits my personality." They cannot feel out of place, so to speak. For example, mental tension can arise when a couple seeks to unwind in a resort with sophistication and a mature vibe, only to find themselves situated in a setting dotted with youthful mannerisms and personalities.

- **There is a need for alignment between a visitor's expectation and what the destination and its service providers can offer.**

A visitor needs to feel the things they can do at a destination are the things they were looking forward to doing prior to the trip. For example, if a destination promises pristine terrains for cross-country skiing and yet the person cannot actually do so due to overcrowding or insufficient snow, this will stress the visitor. Or if a place is said to be a destination for foodies, and yet there aren't quality choices, the visitor may feel underwhelmed or at odds with the place. They are not what they say they are, so to speak.

- **A destination's attractions, activity offerings, and hospitality services need to be well-suited for the larger natural and cultural surroundings.**

A destination needs to embrace its inherent natural and cultural characteristics. The various elements of attractions and facilities need to be attuned with each other and with its inherent geo-cultural locale characteristics. If a destination can manage to possess these harmonizing qualities, the destination will afford visitors a better chance of developing a sense of compatibility and harmony with the place they visit.

Traveler-place congruency can help create a sense of belongingness. A strong sense of compatibility necessitates little voluntary attention on the part of the visitors and, therefore, facilitates the restoration process. One challenge is with a destination that usually welcomes travelers with multiple cultural and social backgrounds and preferences, how does it create that sense of compatibility? It will require strategic and creative thinking.

Fascination

Fascination refers to a state of feeling an intense interest in a place. A destination's ability to hold visitor attention effortlessly because of certain environmental stimuli or patterns is important. The feeling of fascination aroused can contribute to a restorative vacation. Visitors need to be readily and effortlessly absorbed by things they see and do at a vacation destination.

What triggers a sense of fascination in visitors is not well-known, but there are destination qualities that may play a role. For example, visitors can be captivated by qualities that are mythical, unique, unusual, intriguing, sensual, and aesthetically inspiring. Figure 10.10 is an image of a pink lake in Western Australia that possesses such fascinating qualities (Quick Trip 10.7).

How to activate a sense of fascination on the part of the visitors is a question worthy of investigation. Kaplan believes that a natural setting has the best potential to possess what he calls *soft fascination* as people can be captivated by such features effortlessly. Soft fascination refers to a moderate intensity of fascination toward an object, activity, setting, or place (Kaplan 1995). Soft fascination has two important characteristics according to Kaplan. First, its intensity is sufficient to hold one's attention effortlessly but not so intense as to preclude reflection. The second trait of soft fascination is that settings or places that evoke soft fascination tend to be aesthetically pleasing and, therefore, helps offset the exertion that may accompany reflection.

The goal is to rest voluntary attention by activating involuntary attention through one's exchange with the environment. For the consumers to effectively recover from fatigue and its associated mental inhibitions, it is essential for a destination to provide environments (places and services) and activities that can pique visitors' imagination and curiosity without requiring them to exert the mental energy associated with their everyday life.

QUICK TRIP 10.7

Traveler Fascination with Islands

Islands are found to have a particular lure to travelers. Many islands are prominently promoted and featured. Although it is debatable whether islands are predisposed to be more suitable destinations than other forms of landscapes, people's fascination with islands have been well documented. You may wonder what traits and qualities of islands make this form of landscape fascinating to visitors. Bounded by water, islands are detached and self-contained. To the visitor, they project opportunities for more direct contact with native natural elements such as water, land, vegetation, and wildlife as well as human qualities of islanders such as resilience, self-reliance, and life contentment. The juxtaposition of the physicality of places, events, and people defines signature of an island. They promise mystery, adventure, romance, and mental restoration.

© wvita/Shutterstock.com

FIGURE 10.10 Pink Lake in Western Australia.

QUICK TRIP 10.7 CONTINUED

One such example is the Pink Lake Hillier of Western Australia. You may have not heard about the *Middle Island* in the Recherche Archipelago off the south coast of Western Australia but you may have heard about this pink-colored lake on the island. Resembling a solid bubble gum pink, this lake has enchanted both visitors and scientists. Scientists don't fully know why the lake takes on its permanently pink hue, but it is thought to be caused possibly by a combination of such natural phenomena as the lake's high salinity, the pigments of bacteria in the salt crusts, and the pigments in the water's algae.

People near and far take scenic flight tours to Middle Island to see this remarkable lake. It is also popular to take a cruise to appreciate the abundant wildlife and spectacular coastal scenery on the islands of Recherche Archipelago.

Think about This

1. Why are people fascinated with Pink Lake Hillier on Middle Island?
2. What may be some of the motivational factors for people to visit island destinations?
3. Are there unique benefits island visits may potentially offer to people compared to other geolocations?
4. What may be effective marketing communication messages to draw visitors to an island destination?
5. Are there potential perceived barriers for people to visit islands?

Sources

http://hillierlake.com/

http://www.australia.com/en-us/places/wa/pink-lake.html

QUICK TRIP 10.8

Food as Vehicle in Creating Perceptual Distance in Tourism

Food is not only an essential activity for travelers on the road. Food can be a major motivating force for travelers who are "foodies." Even when food is not a dominant motivator, food services should not be treated as an afterthought or haphazardly put together to serve.

Food elements can be carefully orchestrated to represent a tangible destination cultural domain as food can become part of a cultural landscape that helps cultivate in visitors a heightened sense of distance between their hometown and a destination they visit.

In many cases, local food represents a strong locale-based aura to the visitors, not only visually through uniforms, menus, table setup, decorations, displays, music, cooking materials, cooking methods, but also other sensory stimulations such as taste, olfaction, and the audible such as background music and language used by service providers. They can provide a more embodied experience through people's multisensory engagements when compared to other visual elements such as architecture. Think about this: how can a destination effectively utilize food and food-related elements to their advantage in cultivating a sense of away-ness in visitors? Take a quick trip to the website of a restaurant located in a popular destination and then visit the official website of the destination where the restaurant is located.

Think about This

1. Does the website of the restaurant effectively communicate its locale-specific features and characteristics?
2. If not, what makes you think so?
3. If yes, how does it do it through its website contents? Can they do better?
4. Would this restaurant help diners create a sense of away-ness from their usual living environment?
5. Does the official tourism website promote locale-specific food and food-related elements?

Physical Away-ness

A sense of away-ness is another essential parameter to consider for effectively fostering optimal restorative outcomes from taking a vacation. Away-ness provides a sense of escapism from peoples' daily routine and environment. There are two elements of this parameter that a destination and its service providers need to take into account: physical away-ness and mental away-ness.

For people seeking rejuvenation benefits, traveling to places that physically contrast their everyday living environment in geographic or locale characteristics such as contrasting climate, physical terrains, or tangible cultural and built landscapes may be conducive to gaining such vacation benefits.

For destinations, it would be useful to carefully consider the unique characteristics a destination has, preserving and accentuating those elements through visual, aural, and other sensory presentations. Research has demonstrated that striking aesthetics and aesthetic distance between a hometown environment and a destination environment contribute to perceptual seclusion and perceptual distance, which in turn significantly impact how well people feel rested and rejuvenated from a vacation trip. Chapter 11 will further elaborate upon the role aesthetics and aesthetic distance can play in engendering an invigorating vacation experience.

Mental Away-ness

Mental away-ness refers to a sense of psychological distance between one's usual routine or regular or ongoing pursuit of activities and purposes. Kaplan (1995) believes that mental away-ness can come from one's removal of distractions from their routine settings, distancing themselves from usual demands and duties, or temporarily suspending the pursuit of ongoing goals.

Mental away-ness may become harder to achieve in today's social media environment and omnipresence of Internet connectivity. Consumers may not truly feel they have left their everyday routine behind when vacationing. In fact, in the age of mobility enabled by electronic and wireless connections, many feel obligated to stay connected with work contents and contacts. Some even plan to work remotely while traveling. In the meantime, staying connected with family and friends through social media has become a new normal for many people. Some even feel that the lack of social media connectivity would make them feel they are cut off from their usual social circle.

Figure 10.11 is illustrative of the hate-to-love-smartphone "Stockholm Syndrome" of contemporary travelers. Ubiquitous connectivity enabled by modern smartphones and tablets may run contrary to the mental away-ness condition that is necessary for people to gain a sense of renewal and rejuvenation. Taking work on vacation can potentially reduce a person's intended function of restoration.

How best to create a balance for people in their simultaneous need to be away and to be connected? How best to encourage visitors to be more fully engaged with the place they visit, with each other, rather than the Internet and social media? What vacation products, settings, activities, and services may help create optimal restorative environment for visitors? There are opportunities for destinations to satisfy people's restoration needs with creative solutions both in marketing communications as well as product offerings. Away-ness should be a design parameter for destinations and tourism service providers to consider in a mindful manner.

Destination Orientation

Destination orientation refers to the cues that will help orient a visitor. A sense of disorientation, confusion, or even bewilderment can be negatively impacting a visitor's mental rejuvenation because it will increase the need for voluntary attention instead of resting it. People who feel disoriented will feel that they are cognitively exerting rather than resting.

A practical implication is that a destination needs to avoid to appear being too busy and/or too confusing. When a place is busy or disorganized, it can be mentally strenuous for the visitors as they will need to call upon voluntary attention to resolve the confusion. These discord elements can be distracting and taxing, and thus impede a person's ability to restore and regain sufficient mental capacity to function. Providing visitors with a sense of orientation and ease at a destination or hospitality service environment is imperative. Destinations need to provide good mental orientation for visitors through mechanisms such as

- Good road sign designs and placements
- Effective site configuration and orientation
- Timely information and guiding services
- Interpretive programs
- Effective crowd management

QUICK TRIP 10.9

Smartphone Obsession on a Trip

Can you imagine going on a trip without ready access to wireless Internet or phone connections? Today, electronic connectivity seems to be so prevalent that it has become a part of one's life, without which anxiety arises for many. However, for someone to effectively replenish diminished cognitive functions, it may be wise to leave work and other online activities behind or keep them at a minimal. This, however, appears to be increasingly challenging. The traditional distinction of work and leisure, the separation of daily and vacation spaces are increasingly being redefined.

How should tourism service providers cater to this new reality for travelers? This is a double-edged phenomenon. On the one hand, because of the increasing availability of online-based information and services, travelers increasingly resort to online sources for onsite and real-time trip plan-

© Lannaorchid/Shutterstock.com

FIGURE 10.11 Scissors trying to cut rusty iron chain that ties together hand and smartphone.

ning (e.g., what to do on a particular day or what's available nearby a hotel to eat). Travelers also enjoy social media activities such as real-time video and photo sharing and real-time chatting with one's social network. These online activities in the meantime may alter how a person engages in other destination activities and how active travelers will be. Online activities may become an impediment for a more direct and sustained contact with nature and, thus, adversely impact the renewal effect that a leisure trip can bring to travelers.

You may all have had experiences where everybody at a family dinner table is looking at his or her phone instead of talking to each other. Well that tendency has been extended to travel scenarios. As a result of almost obsessive cell phone use, family travelers talk to each other face-to-face less, running contrary to their motivation to do so. The travel benefit of physiological and social resource replenishment may be in jeopardy. Or even worse, travel might drain people mentally and physically.

You may notice that most businesses readily promote their free in-room Wi-Fi services and smartphone-based services such as room services, check-in, and check-out services through social media platforms. On occasions, you may also notice that restaurants have communication messages encouraging people to talk: we don't have Wi-Fi. Pretend you live in the 80s and talk to people.

Think about This

1. What may be the upsides and downsides of smartphone use on a trip?
2. How can a tourism destination help travelers with smartphone obsessions?
3. What may be effective strategies to encourage travelers to be mindful of potential pitfalls of overuse of smartphones on a trip?

Destination Scope

Destination scope is another important aspect of a destination that determines its restorative qualities. This aspect of a destination refers to the richness and extent of the activities, sights, and programs provided to engage visitors at a destination.

A destination needs to provide enough content variability for a vacationer. The variety of the activities, sights, and programs provided should be sufficient to allow exploration in many directions on the part of the vacationer and be rich enough for an individual to sustain his or her interests. The objective here is to engage the five senses of a visitor to the extent that they do not need use their voluntary attention. In this sense, a vacation that is static and one-dimensional may not be optimal for facilitating one's mental renewal.

It is useful to treat a person's visit to a place as a visit to separate settings, including the larger environmental settings such as natural and cultural landscapes and the service settings such as restaurants, hotels, shopping malls, and airports. Although destinations have lesser control over the characteristics of the larger setting, they do have much more direct influence on recreational areas and other business entities' environmental feature designs.

A rejuvenated visitor is a happy person. To effectively assist in people's renewal, tourism professionals need to carefully consider the destination restorative quality parameters in space design and sensory engagement because restorative qualities directly impact visitor satisfaction with a vacation destination as well as their loyalty. Service providers need to carefully consider how to create environments with optimal restorative qualities.

Vacation as a National Health Strategy

Leisure is well known as a coping strategy for combating the effects of stress and mental fatigue. From a societal perspective, leisure is being seen as possessing two beneficial restorative functions. That is, leisure provides an opportunity for people to exercise their own free will and an opportunity to receive social support and build family ties. For example, taking a vacation allows an individual to have an extended period of time for engaging in non-work-related leisure activities of their own choice, and being physically in a setting away from his or her routine environment. As a result of these two characteristics, vacation travel can potentially become a more effective recovery opportunity than regular free evenings and weekends spent in a home environment.

Because travel can be a healing mechanism and can be a mechanism for improved productivity and creativity at workplaces, vacation strategy has become a national health and wellness strategy for many countries. Paid vacation is a strategy that has been weaved into governmental and corporate policymaking. Some commonly seen practices are paid vacation time and paid holidays.

- Paid vacation refers to paid annual leaves, mandated by a government or voluntarily provided by a company.

- Paid holidays is also called paid national holidays, which are organized around particular dates in the calendar. Employers are required to pay workers at a premium rate if they work during national holidays.

Paid, legally-protected vacation days and holidays vary significantly across nations. Workers in European Union (EU) for instance are entitled to at least four weeks of vacation days as mandated by EU. American workers lag behind other developed countries in protected vacation days. The United States doesn't have legally required paid vacation days or holidays, and so do a large number of developing countries.

QUICK TRIP 10.10

Have Time, Will Vacation

Vacation days can be spent at home, which is termed staycation. Many people, however, spent part of their vacation days for pleasure travel (holiday making). Below is a list of countries with the most vacation days (which include national holidays and paid vacation days) according to a study conducted by the Center for Economic Policies in Washington, DC. The United States does not have a legal requirement for vacation and paid holidays—about a quarter of the United States workforce has no paid vacation or paid holiday. In Canada, provincial law governs annual paid leave. The number of statutory paid holidays varies by provinces. Most follow a pattern of two week's paid annual leave.

	COUNTRY	DAYS OFF	ANNUAL HOURS WORKED	LABOR PRODUCTIVITY	GDP PER CAPITA
1	Austria	35	1,598 hours	$51.60 per hour	$42,409
2	Portugal	35	1,711 hours	$32.40 per hour	$23,385
3	Germany	34	1,406 hours	$55.80 per hour	$30,028
4	Spain	34	1,685 hours	$47.50 per hour	$30,557
5	France	31	1,476 hours	$57.70 per hour	$35,548
6	Belgium	30	1,577 hours	$59.50 per hour	$37,883
7	Italy	30	1,774 hours	$46.60 per hour	$30,136

Think about This

1. Why do some countries mandate paid vacation time for workers and some don't? What may be the reasons for both policy decisions?
2. Why do most countries have paid public holidays?
3. Some argue that vacation reduces workforce productivity, while others argue that vacation can improve productivity. Do you agree? Why or why not?
4. What do you think may be a good vacation for a mentally stressed worker?
5. Why do people sometimes elect to stay home (staycation) during their vacation days off?

Source

Table adapted from https://www.usatoday.com/story/money/business/2013/06/08/countries-most-vacation-days/2400193/

QUICK TRIP 10.11

Can People Be De-Motivated to Travel?

On occasion, people may be de-motivated to travel despite the fact that they have the needed monetary or time budgetary resources. Understanding these psychological de-motivating factors can be useful for tourism professionals.

Hurvich and Jameson (1974)'s opponent process theory suggests that every psychological process can trigger its opposite. Human neural organization follows such opponent processes. In the context of travel, people can be motivated to travel but can also exhibit what researchers term as nativistic (as opposed to touristic) motivations, which serve as de-motivators for one to take on travel. According to George, Inbakaran, and Poyyamoli (2010), there are five main de-motivational factors:

- **Nativistic functionality:** People have motivations to stay in their home environment because of compulsions associated with home-based functioning such as caretaking at home, or perceived self-doubt about navigating outside their home environment.
- **Nativistic certainty:** People's sense of predictability and manageability of issues at their home environment will discourage them from travel. A sense of uncertainty and risk associated with a foreign environment can dissuade them from taking on travel.
- **Nativistic habituality:** People are inclined to follow habits. The need to learn or unlearn codes of public conduct at unfamiliar environments may de-motivate people from traveling.
- **Nativistic identity:** Individuals can be motivated to be in their home environment because of their established self-identify which is associated with values and beliefs. People could be de-motivated to travel when they perceive their self-identities may be challenged at a new environment.
- **Nativistic culturality:** The need to follow certain cultural codes of one's home environment may de-motivate him/her from travel because travel may require acclimatization or adaptation of new cultural codes.

Think about This

1. Why is it helpful for tourism professionals to understand travel de-motivators?
2. Are there strategies that destinations can use to encourage travel?
3. Would the increasing availability of virtual travel products dissuade people from travel?
4. Can people benefit just as much when they use virtual travel products instead of physically travel to a destination? Why or why not?

Sources

George, B. P., Inbakaran, R., and Poyyamoli, G. 2010. To travel or not to travel: towards understanding the theory of nativistic motivation. *Tourism, 58*(4), 395–407.

Hurvich L. M., and Jameson, D. 1974. Opponent processes as a model of neural organizations. *American Psychologist,* 29, 88–102.

SUMMARY

Vacation trips are a way of satisfying various needs. There are, however, ways other than taking vacations to satisfy those same needs. An individual will purchase a vacation to satisfy a need or needs if he perceives that the vacation will satisfy needs considered important.

It is essential for tourism destinations and businesses to have a firm grasp of what traveler needs and motivations may be and how these needs and motivations may be communicated by consumers in the name of wants and benefits. These conceptual understandings will assist destination organizations and their stakeholders to understand their target markets, improve their products and services, and develop effective marketing strategies.

Equally important is the recognition that leisure travel can be an important contributor to consumers' well-being. Destinations and tourism service providers need to mindfully take into consideration destination qualities in their tourism experience planning and marketing so as to deliver the most beneficial travel products to visitors.

ACTIVITIES

1. Assess your community from the perspective of potential visitors and answer the following questions:
   a. What may be the motivating factors for visitors to visit your community? Use the Travel Motivation POST Scheme model to explain these motivational factors and their psychological potency in attracting people to visit.
   b. Discuss the restorative properties of your community based on the Destination Restorative Qualities Model. How does your community do in marketing these properties to visitors?
2. You are a manager of a resort that has a golf course onsite. Create a "green" plan for your golf course. How do these specific sustainability practices motivate people to patronize this resort?
3. Create a full-page spread for a magazine including images and phrases that encourage people to travel abroad with their families. Attempt to grab someone's attention, and inspire that person to seek further information.
4. Call a few popular hotels in Mexico. Ask them about their security onsite and what they have done to make travelers feel comfortable about visiting there. Ask them about their policies with crime onsite and how they attempt to solve and make up for crime situations that occur.

REFERENCES

Alderfer, Clayton P. 1969. An empirical test of a new theory of human needs. *Organizational Behavior and Human Performance* 4 (2): 142–75.

Dann, G. (1977). Anomie, ego-enhancement and tourism. *Annals of Tourism Research*, (4): 184–194.

Gnoth, J. 1997. Tourism motivation and expectation formation. *Annals of Tourism Research* 24 (2): 283–340.

Kaplan, S. 1995. The restorative benefits of nature—toward an integrative framework. *Journal of Environmental Psychology* 15: 169–182.

Lehto, X. Y. 2013. Assessing the perceived restorative qualities of vacation destinations. *Journal of Travel Research* 52 (3): 325–33.

Max-Neef, Manfred A., Antonio Elizalde, and Martin Hopenhayn. 1989. Human scale development: conception, application and further reflections. New York: Apex. Chpt. 2. *Development and Human Needs*, 18.

Murray, H. A. 1938. *Explorations in Personality*. New York: Oxford University Press.

Maslow, A. H. 1943. "A theory of human motivation." *Psychological Review* 50 (4): 370–96.

Pearce, P. L. 1982. *The Social Psychology of Tourist Behavior*. Oxford: Pergamon.

Rothbart, M. K., and M. I. Posner. 1985. Temperament and the development of self-regulation. In *The Neuropsychology of Individual Differences, A Developmental Perspective*, edited by Lawrence C. Hartlage and Cathy F. Telzrow.

ADDITIONAL READINGS

Bansal, H., and H. A. Eiselt. 2004. Exploratory research of tourist motivations and planning. *Tourism Management* 25: 387–396.

Brown, S., and X. Y. Lehto. 2005. Traveling with a purpose: Understanding the motives and benefits of volunteer vacationers. *Current Issues in Tourism* 8 (6): 479–496.

Bushnell, R., and P. Sheldon. 2009. *Wellness and Tourism: Mind, Body, Spirit.* New York, NY: Cognizant Communication Corporation.

Cook, S., and S. Hopkins. 2007. *The Ideal American Vacation Trip.* Washington, DC: Travel Industry Association.

Crompton, J. 1979. Motivations for pleasure travel. *Annals of Tourism Research* 6: 408–424.

George, B. P., R. Inbakaran, and G. Poyyamoli. 2010. To travel or not to travel: towards understanding the theory of nativistic motivation. *Tourism* 58 (4): 395–407.

Hettler, W. 1984. Encouraging a lifetime pursuit of excellence. *Health Values: Achieving High Level Wellness* 8: 13–17.

Hurvich, L. M., and D. Jameson. 1974. Opponent processes as a model of neural organizations. *American Psychologist* 29: 88–102.

Kaplan, R., and S. Kaplan. 1989. *The Experience of Nature: A Psychological Perspective.* Cambridge: Cambridge University Press.

Kaplan, S. 2001. Meditation, restoration, and the management of mental fatigue. *Environmental Behavior* 33: 480–506.

Kirillova, K., X. Y. Lehto, and L. Cai. 2017. Existential Authenticity and Anxiety as Outcomes: The Tourist in the Experience Economy. *International Journal of Tourism Research* 19 (1): 13–26.

Klenosky, D. 2002. The "pull" of tourism destinations: A means-end investigation. *Journal of Travel Research* 40: 385–395.

Kluin, J., and X. Y. Lehto. 2012. Measuring family reunion travel motivations. *Annals of Tourism Research* 39 (2): 820–847.

Lehto, X. Y., X. Fu, H. Li, and L. Zhou. 2017. Vacation benefits and activities: Understanding Chinese family travelers. *Journal of Hospitality & Tourism Research* 4 (3): 301–328.

Lehto, X., K. Kirillova, H. Li, and W. Wu. 2016. A cross-cultural validation of the perceived destination restorative qualities scale: the Chinese perspective. *Asia Pacific Journal of Tourism Research*, 1–15.

McClelland, D. 1953. *The Achievement Motive.* New York: Appleton-Century-Crofts.

Norman, W. C., and M. N. Carlson. 1999. An investigation of the seeking-escaping theory as a segmentation tool in tourism marketing. 30th Annual Conference Proceedings of the Travel and Tourism Research Association, 10–18.

Pearce, P. L., and U.-I. Lee. 2005. Developing the travel career approach to tourist motivation. *Journal of Travel Research* 43: 226–237.

Prayag, G., and R. Chris. 2011. The relationship between the "push" and "pull" factors of a tourist destination: the role of nationality—an analytical qualitative research approach. *Current Issues in Tourism* 14: 121–143.

Snepenger, D., J. King, E. Marshall, and M. Uysal. 2006. Modeling Iso-Ahola's motivation theory in the tourism context. *Journal of Travel Research* 45: 140–149.

Yuan, S., and C. McDonald. 1990. Motivational determinates of international pleasure time. *Journal of Travel Research* 29 (1): 43.

CHAPTER ELEVEN

Tourism Experience

How Do Travelers Consume a Place Product?

The use of traveling is to regulate imagination by reality, and instead of thinking how things may be, to see them as they are.

SAMUEL JOHNSON

YOUR LEARNING DESTINATION

You will be able to explain how visitors consume an experience-based product such as travel and the implications for tourism experience management.

WHAT YOU NEED TO KNOW

Having read this chapter, you will be able to:

- ✔ Know the definition of tourism experience.
- ✔ Describe the process view of tourism experience.
- ✔ Describe the component view of tourism experience.
- ✔ Explain the role of aesthetics in tourism experience.
- ✔ Understand the role of authenticity and localness in tourism experience.
- ✔ Describe flow in tourism experience.
- ✔ Explain the role of experience theming and cueing in tourism experience management.
- ✔ Explain the importance of destination activities in tourism experience management.
- ✔ Explain how traveler-friendly technologies influence tourism experience.

BREAKING THE ICE

Iceland is known for its dramatic landscapes such as breathtaking glacier fjords and lava formations. One traveler, after visiting the jagged lava fields in the Snæfellsjökull National Park in western Iceland, was awestruck by the sheer powerfulness and vulnerability of the naked earth. He went on to proclaim that the experience rendered him wordless and that it has changed how he understands life itself. Travelers spend time at a destination, create memories, and tell stories. Memorable travel episodes such as this can become part of a colorful fabric of a person's life. What is in a trip? This traveler narrative is illustrative of what a memorable tourism experience is and what a trip can mean to an individual. It is, however, likely that another traveler who visits and enjoys Snæfellsjökull National Park may tell a somewhat different story about the trip.

Travelers encounter a mixture of physical and social elements of a destination such as natural and man-made sceneries and landscapes, artifacts, and services. They usually leave a destination with memorabilia and memories made of stories and narratives. It is important to recognize, however, that the memories that travelers create and moments they proclaim to be unforgettable may be divergent even if they partake in a similar set of activities at a destination. This is because experience is at the heart of travel and tourism.

This chapter introduces various theories that explain how individuals experience a destination and what factors can play a part in inducing visitor delight. Knowledge of these principles can inform industry practices and enable tourism destinations and service providers to strategically design, plan, market, and deliver intrinsically experiential offerings. Remember, destinations that deliver awe-inspiring consumptive moments not only can create raving fans but also can potentially transform visitors.

KEY TAKEAWAY POINTS

- Understanding how visitors experience a destination is imperative for destinations and tourism service providers.

- A tourism experience encompasses multiple stages and processes.

- A tourism experience journey starts prior to a trip and will not necessarily end when the trip is complete.

- A tourism experience can provide eight value components: entertainment, education, aesthetics, escapist, localness, spontaneity, personalization, and communitas.

- Although visitors interact with a destination through engaging in activities and utilizing hospitality services, their interpretation of an experience is subjective.

- Experience themes and cues can be developed by destinations and hospitality businesses.

- Sensory aspects of a tourism experience should be carefully considered.

- Local and authentic elements of a destination are valuable in tourism experience design.

- Tourism experience design needs to take into account traveler cultural and personal dispositions.

- Leisure activities and programming play an important role in the creation of memorable experiences.

WHAT IS A TOURISM EXPERIENCE?

Experience has become a cornerstone concept for tourism management as it provides not only insights into travelers' behavioral tendencies but also parameters for destinations and tourism service providers to consider when crafting, planning, and marketing tourism as an experience product. Tourism experience is a distinct type of consumptive experience. While sharing similar characteristics of an everyday consumptive experience, it exhibits unique characteristics stemming from the fact that travel represents a disengagement from one's daily routine and engagement with novel environments, and is ephemeral in nature.

> **A tourism experience** occurs when an individual engages with, participates in, and makes sense of events and activities pertaining to a tourism destination.

The notion of experience has garnered much attention in tourism management and beyond. Experience is thought to be a complex phenomenon. Holbrook and Hirschman (1982) are heralded as the pioneers who introduced this concept to the field of marketing. They posit that an experience is above all a personal or private event that occurs in response to stimuli from consumptive scenarios of products or services.

An experience often results from direct observation and/or participation, is holistic in nature, and involves the entire being of a person. Emotions and reflections are considered an integral part of such an occurrence.

A tourism experience can be understood as a subjective event created when a visitor sees, senses, feels, and evaluates happenings in the travel scenario. Visitors can have:

- sensory experiences (sense),
- emotional experiences (feel),
- physical experiences (do),
- mental experiences (judge, relate, reflect), and
- social experiences (interact).

Tourism experiences occur within physical and social spaces; the characteristics of these spaces and their management influence visitor satisfaction. Tourism experiences are created by visitors but facilitated by a destination and service providers. In a nutshell, a tourism experience occurs when a traveler is engaged with a place they visit emotionally, physically, intellectually, and spiritually.

The Process View of Tourism Experience

A tourism experience as a consumptive event is said to encompass multiple stages. Viewing it as a process and understanding these stages can be useful. From a *timeline* perspective, a tourism experience includes three broad phases: prior to the trip, the trip itself, and after the trip. From a *geo-location* perspective, a tourism experience contains multiple locales including the home setting, the on-route setting, the destination setting, and the virtual setting.

Multiple occurrences along the time and setting line make up a tourism experience. Planning, anticipating, receiving, savoring, reacting, reflecting, reminiscing, and re-creating represent stages and processes of events corresponding to important visitor experience elements. Together, they make a tourism experience complete. Visitor interaction with a destination essentially begins, albeit from a distance and virtually, when a traveler's interest in visiting a destination is aroused. For some, it continues long after a trip is completed.

Aho (2001) suggests that there are essentially seven stages of a tourism experience, consisting of multiple processes, spaces, and time frames (Figure 11.1):

1. The journey starts with an *Orientation* stage when an individual's interest in a place is piqued ("This place seems cool").
2. The individual then goes through an *Attachment* stage where the said interest is sustained and strengthened leading to a go-decision.
3. The third stage is the *Visiting* stage which includes activities and mental processes and on route to and onsite a destination.
4. The fourth stage of *Evaluation* pertains to how the visitor reacts, savors, judges, compares, and decides on future actions. This stage itself can involve multiple moments, episodes, and settings.
5. The fifth stage of *Storing* refers to the visitor attempt to document trip moments and episodes (through photos, videos, blogs, and souvenirs) as well mental processes to imprint a scenery or a trip moment on the brain (conversations, impressions, affections, and meaning-making). Figure 11.2 is a selfie documenting a happy moment on a sailing trip of a group of friends.

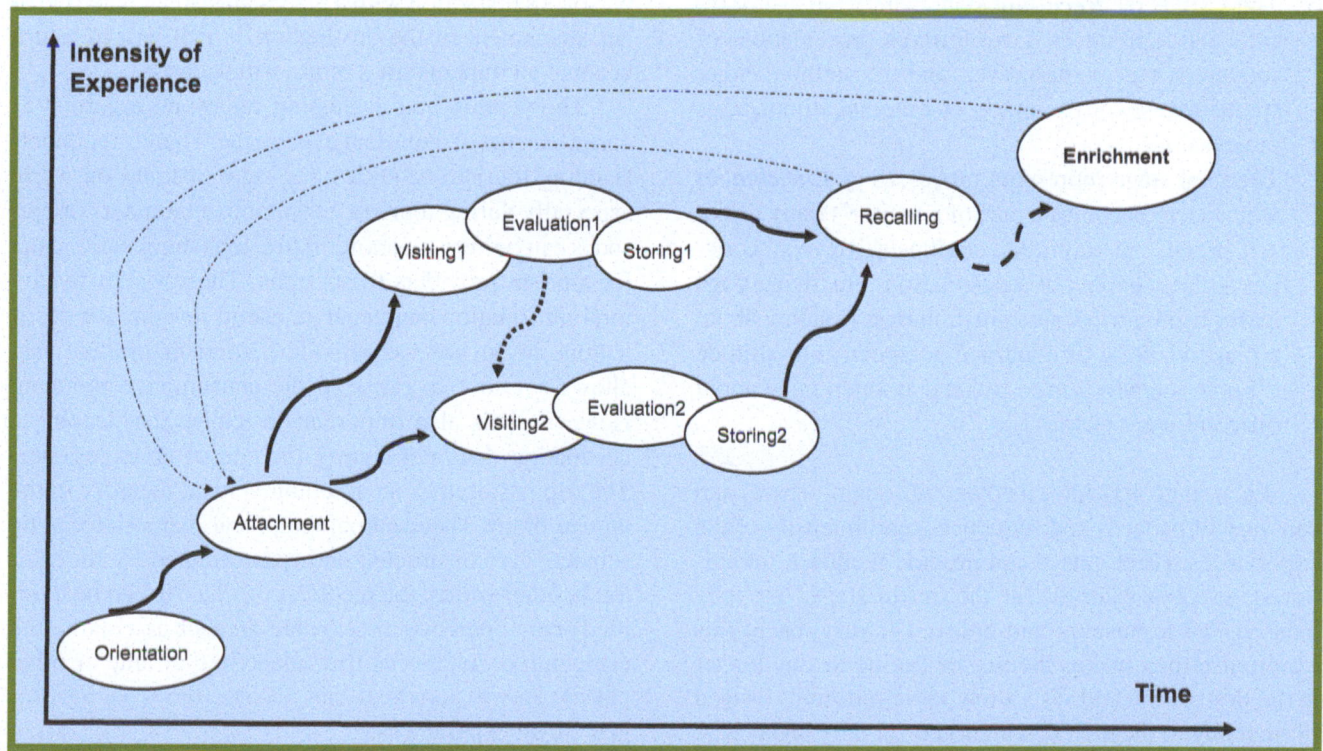

FIGURE 11.1 **Process view of tourism experience.** | Adapted from Aho 2001.

FIGURE 11.2 A selfie documenting a happy trip moment.

6. The sixth is the *Recalling* stage where the visitor recalls and reproduces a trip through presentations of souvenirs, videos, narratives, and storytelling, either spontaneously or prompted by external stimulations or occasions.

7. The final stage represents processes of *Enrichment* when a trip becomes a part of a visitor's daily life or self because of acquired activities/skills (e.g., cooking a dish sampled at a destination, practicing yoga learnt from a trip), sustained interest (reading about a place visited), or a learned perspective or attitude ("I now see why I need to keep an open mind about different ways of life").

Each stage may have its own multiple processes and can vary in patterns and sequences, and intensity of the experiences. Later stages can provide feedback for earlier stages. For example, at the onsite stage, one may have visited a museum and enjoyed it very much; this experience then makes the visitor decide to stay longer at the destination and visit a few more museums instead of traveling to the next destination originally planned. A person's satisfaction with a place can also increase his or her attachment of the destination, which will in return become an impetus for a return trip decision.

The visiting and evaluating stages are regarded as core elements of a tourism experience. Therefore, understanding tourism activities and state of mind on a trip especially during tourism consumptive moments or episodes can be very meaningful in establishing parameters for tourism providers to act upon. These visitor behavioral information can generate useful insights for destinations as to how to provide a tourism product that allows a visitor to relish in the consumptive moment. However, it is also important to realize that leaving a destination does not signify the end of an experience. The trip is stored as an autobiographical memory in the human brain. These autobiographical memories can be subjectively constructed and reconstructed by the visitor. In other words, the recollection of a trip can be modified or distorted over time by factors such as a marketing campaign or additional trips made to the same or other places. Past experiences can become the resources for new travel experiences.

The final stage of enrichment is considered as a stage with the highest intensity for a tourism experience. All first six stages of a tourism experience are said to play a role in the formation of the seventh stage of enrichment although not all visitors reach this stage for all trips. All stages can contribute to the formation of a complete tourism experience.

The Component View of Tourism Experience

Rather than focusing on the process, the component view of the tourism experience provides an alternative approach toward understanding this concept. This view holds that a tourism experience contains multiple value domains. Pine and Gilmore (1999) suggest that experience can be classified into four broad value realms: *entertainment*, *education*, *escapism*, and *esthetics*.

- *Entertainment* is one of the oldest forms of experience.
- *Esthetics* speaks to customers' interpretation of the physical environment around them.
- The *educational* realm appeals to the customer's desire to learn something new.
- *Escapist* experiences satisfy one's need to escape daily mandates and routines.

These four realms of experience engage consumers along the spectra of two dimensions: consumer participation and consumer connection with the environment. Depending on consumer relational positions (e.g., how the consumer and the consumptive environment interact) and product characteristics (e.g., the characteristics of the product or service being consumed), a consumer can be passive or active, and they can be in absorption or immersion modes. Experience providers can consider what realms of experience best suit their offerings and customer desires to form a "sweet spot" to gratify consumers. Pine and Gilmore's four realms of experience proposition has provided theoretical parameters for propelling businesses to move away from a functional orientation toward a conscious adoption of a consumer-centric orientation of experience engineering.

The four-realm experience framework can impart useful information for the various industry sectors within the tourism system to design and market the experiential values of their offerings. However, researchers have noted the need to identify specific experience characteristics that encompass both everyday consumptive situations as well as travel-induced situations because travel embodies both continuation of and departure from everydayness.

Based on evidences obtained from hotel and Airbnb guests, and building upon Pine and Gilmore's four realms of experience supposition, Mody, Suess, and Lehto (2017) propose an eight-dimensional experiencescape model to better encompass the specificities of a travel experience. In addition to the four dimensions suggested by Pine and Gilmore, an additional four experience components can be important to consider when planning a travel product: *serendipity*, *localness*, *communitas*, and *personalization*.

- *Serendipity* alludes to encounters and moments of a trip that are unplanned, unexpected, and spontaneous. Surprise situations and elements in a tourism product can create opportunities for unique visitor-environment exchange, and generate special connections with a place for the traveler. In fact, serendipitous moments are the most recalled highlights of a trip in travel stories shared online.
- *Localness* as a component of experience represents traveler quest for authenticity in a consumptive scenario.
- *Communitas* attests to an important social element of a travel experience—that of a sense of temporary community because of unstructured relationships and momentary emotional bonds formed. The communitas moments in tourism consumption can induce a potentially extraordinary tourism experience.
- The final component of *personalization* reflects travelers' desire for individuality and uniqueness in a travel consumptive situation.

Together, the eight dimensions of the **Tourism Experiencescape** (Figure 11.3) can engender gratifying travel experiences. How best to facilitate the interactions between the visitor, the service environment, and the larger destination environment is of importance for tourism providers because the travel and tourism products are inherently holistic and experiential. Given the diversity of traveler background, tourism providers need to carefully consider these experiential specificities and qualities to optimally situate the visitor to fully enjoy a trip. It is important to know that not all dimensions of the experiencescape are of equal value to all visitors. Depending on what motivates visitors to visit a destination (please refer to Chapter 10 for discussions related to tourism motivations) and what tourism resources a destination has, visitors may have varying valuations.

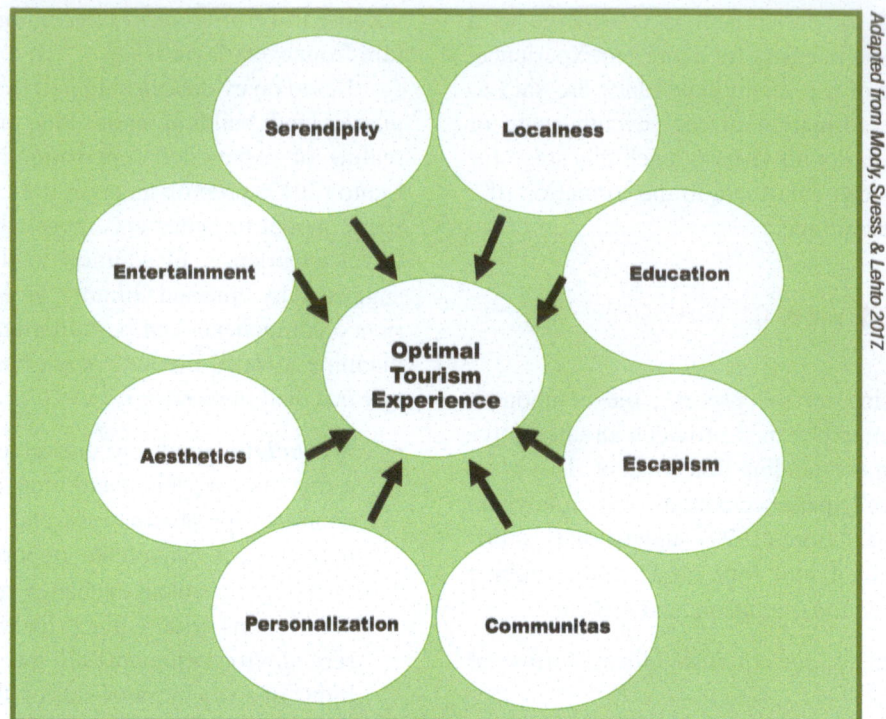

Adapted from Mody, Suess, & Lehto 2017

FIGURE 11.3 Tourism Experiencescape.

AESTHETICS AND TOURISM EXPERIENCE

There is a serene and settled majesty to woodland scenery that enters into the soul and delights and elevates it, and fills it with noble inclinations.

WASHINGTON IRVING

Aesthetics is an integral component of a travel experience because a vacation is in many ways a heightened aesthetic rather than utilitarian experience. When a traveler visits a destination, aesthetics is a significant source of pleasure. In fact, visitor aesthetic judgment of a place could critically influence their overall travel satisfaction. Aesthetic experience for a visitor can be quite unique because the individual is physically relocated and immersed in places that could be drastically different from his or her everyday environment. The change of environment implies a unique process of aesthetic appreciation on the part of visitors. A destination experience necessitates visitors' bodily and mental immersion, engagement, and appreciation of non-routine environments and thus entails a holistic and global judgment. Aesthetic pleasure is a natural human response. We describe a place as beautiful, breathtaking, picturesque, pretty, or quaint. Visually attractive landscapes and natural wonders can induce aesthetic experiences that result in not only awe-inspiring affective responses but sentimental associations.

Does the Beauty of a Place Lie In the Eyes of the Beholder?

The consensus is that there are two domains of factors at work when it comes to visitor aesthetic judgment. The first domain pertains to the universal appeal of an object, natural or man-made. A landscape can possess a set of features that prompt any individual to judge it as picturesque or otherwise. The second domain refers to that of the subjective sentiments prompted by the internalization and imagination on the part of the visitor. A visitor would judge a landscape from a learned and universally translatable picturesque to one much more hospitable to what Dixon Hunt (1992) describes as "the vague, the local, the sentimental, and the subjective." In other words, the relatively more objective and universal aspects of picturesque scenery can be taken in and appreciated by a visitor based on his or her cultural and personal dispositions, tastes, and associations. Because visitors have diverse backgrounds, they can form varying aesthetic judgments on a destination.

What Makes a Destination Beautiful?

The beauty of a tourism destination is uniquely judged and appreciated, and the assessment of the beauty goes beyond the visual aspects and engages all senses. There are various aesthetic themes. In general, visitors consider nine aspects of a destination when forming their judgments: Scale, Time, Condition, Sound, Balance, Diversity, Novelty, Shape, and Uniqueness. Figure 11.4 presents the various sub-elements within each aesthetic aspect. These aspects and elements explain how a place is taken in aesthetically by a visitor and how a destination's aesthetic qualities are being judged. Knowledge of these aesthetic components can assist tourism providers to capture opportunities to influence visitors' aesthetic judgment.

An optimal level of aesthetic stimuli needs to be orchestrated for favorable aesthetic judgment to occur. One practice for a tourism destination can be to develop its aesthetic reservoir of its aesthetic qualities and assess the relative importance of aesthetic dimensions in influencing its visitors' satisfaction. Some destinations already have several place-specific features in their inventory, others are yet to identify attributes readily identifiable with the locale. Destinations should also ensure that these features are diverse and captivating enough for visitors to sustain their admiration for the duration of a trip.

In general, authentic, well-maintained, diverse, and unique features that are in harmony with natural and cultural surroundings can positively influence visitors' aesthetic judgment of a destination. Scope (variety of offerings and richness of a destination environment) is found to be conducive to aesthetic pleasure and an enjoyable tourism experience. As such, the destination allows visitors to have a sense of complete immersion and experience the place in its richest and most expansive form.

Scale	Balance
Colorful–Dull (intensity of color) Grand–Quaint (physical proportion) Presence of People–Absence of People (crowdedness) Abundance–Scarcity (amount of visual cues) Openness–Narrowness (spatial characteristics)	Human touch–No human touch (suitability of visual cues to setting) Authentic–Artificial (extent of perceived integrity) Cohesive–Out of place (flow of visual cues)
Time Modern–Historic (age of a destination) Young–Old (age of people observed)	**Diversity** Diverse–Alike (variety of cues)
Condition Clean–Dirty (hygienic condition) Well-kept–Rundown (upkeep of physical attributes)	**Novelty** Novel–Typical (contrast of familiar and new environment)
Sound Lively–Peaceful (pace of sound) Man-made–Nature-made (source of sound) Loud–Quiet (volume of sound)	**Shape** Sophisticated–Simplistic (degree of complexity)
Uniqueness Unique–Ordinary (amount of uniquely identifiable features)	

FIGURE 11.4 **Themes of tourist aesthetic judgment.** | Adapted from Kirillova, Fu, Lehto, and Cai 2014.

QUICK TRIP 11.1

Aesthetic Appreciation

Figure 11.5 and Figure 11.6 depict aesthetically pleasing sights. Figure 11.5 is an aerial view from a helicopter of the Niagara Falls. Figure 11.6 depicts a coastal landscape of Vernazza village of Cinque Terre, Italy. Both sites possess aesthetic qualities that are awe-inspiring for visitors. Referencing Figure 11.4, we are able to develop a reservoir of aesthetic qualities of tourism places such as these. It will help us understand not only how visitors appreciate sights and sounds of places but also how tourism professionals can design tourism experiences based on aesthetic configurations, and deliver unforgettable moments. Take a virtual trip to each of the two sites at https://www.niagarafallstourism.com/ and http://www.cinque-terre-tourism.com/en/ to gather more tourism information about these two places.

Think about This

1. What are the prominent aesthetic qualities present at Niagara Falls?
2. What are the prominent aesthetic qualities present at Vernazza, Cinque Terre?
3. What are the differences in aesthetic elements and qualities of these two sights showcased through Figure 11.5 and Figure 11.6?
4. Aesthetics of a place is vital to tourism. How sustainable are these aesthetic qualities?
5. How can destinations accommodate visitors' aesthetic appreciation needs through its activity planning?
6. Have the websites of these destination management organizations done adequate work projecting their respective aesthetic qualities?

Sources

http://www.cinque-terre-tourism.com/en/

https://www.niagarafallstourism.com/

FIGURE 11.5 Niagara Falls Aerial View from helicopter, Canadian Falls, Canada.

FIGURE 11.6 Landscape view of Vernazza, Cinque Terre, Italy.

Home Environment Influence

The visitor's home environment can impact how a destination is perceived, admired, and evaluated. Distance between the aesthetic features of a visitor's home and those of a destination environment could have some bearing on how a visitor judges a destination. As a visitor moves from home environment to a destination surrounding, he leaves behind his usual geographical and institutional environments. However, one's home environment cues can be strong contextual cues in that visitors consciously and subconsciously compare and contrast what they see and sense at a destination with their home landscapes, sounds, aromas, weather, décor, and other configurations.

Visitor origin can be good proximate information to use to understand a person's evaluative judgment of a place. For example, those living in coastal areas could appraise mountainous destinations more favorably than beach vacations, simply because they tend to find the former of more novelty value. Or a person living in a coastal community can judge another coastal destination as inferior simply because the visitor believes that back home they have superior beaches. A visitor's home reference points can either positively or negatively affect his judgment of a visited destination.

Aesthetics and Visitor Home Culture

Visitor home environment is not simply a geographical concept, however. It possesses a cultural layer. The characteristic qualities of color, sound, texture, light, movement, smell, taste, perceptual patterns, space, and size can be culturally judged. In other words, distance between a home environment and a destination environment can influence a visitor's aesthetic judgment because of culturally oriented preferences (Kirillova and Lehto 2015). Visitor origin may also be a proxy variable to explain why one's cultural orientations and tastes can exert influence on how a visitor derives judgment on a destination. It is possible that a subpar impression of a destination's aesthetics is attributed to cultural differences.

Cultural contrasts between home and destination can result in either increased fascination and delight or increased anxiety. For example, the smell of cooked foods can be appetizing to one group of visitors but can also be repulsive to another as a result of dispositional differences of the visitors. What is music to one set of ears can be perceptions of crowdedness and unbearable noises to another.

It is also important to know that natural landscapes in many cases are not purely natural; human touches guided by cultural habits and local traditions can be found in not only buildings and roadways in the cities and countryside but also in remote and wildness areas. What is being perceived as harmonious coexistence between man and nature by one culture can be judged as intrusive to another. Therefore, home environment factors can become either a propeller of or hindrance to a good travel experience.

AUTHENTICITY AND LOCALNESS IN TOURISM EXPERIENCE

We went out to dinner in an authentic Italian restaurant off the tourist track where a lot of the students and artists live. The atmosphere in this part of town was very different. I can't explain this without sounding extremely clichéd, but it all seemed so alive and cheerful. There were so many sounds and smells and things to see, the people on scooters, kids playing soccer in these tiny streets, music drifting out all the windows. It was just great. — from an anonymous visitor

We frequently see travel accounts like the above, where a visitor's sense of authenticity and localness marks a cherished travel episode. Visitors frequently make judgments about an object, a setting, or an event they encounter at a destination as either authentic or inauthentic. These evaluations become an important part of visitor experience quality judgment. When a person visits a place, he/she comes in direct contact with a place's cultural and social spaces through activities that they engage in and symbols that denote what the place represents. These cultural and social spaces become de-facto tourism spaces.

Theoretically tourism spaces can manifest almost everywhere. Some are designed with tourism in mind while others are social spaces that a visitor shares with the locals. Typical tourism products which allow a visitor to encounter and experience the local element of a place are festivals, rituals, cuisine, dress, architecture, works of art, and crafts. Visitors form a sense of the genuine, the real, the original, the unique. Regardless of whether they are enacted or produced for the visitors or not, people's perception of authenticity is rooted in traditional and living culture.

Front and Back Regions

Based on American sociologist Irving Goffman's dramaturgical perspective, Dean MacCannell (1973) classifies tourism spaces into six settings including three *front regions* and three *back regions*. The front regions signify spaces that are, to a varying degree, set up for visitors. The back regions refer to spaces that represent, to a varying degree, what is native or local to the destination that travelers visit.

The first, called *Goffman's front region*, is set up completely for visitors with no considerations of authenticity. A Greek architecture style resort in a rural China region represents this form of tourism space. The second space represents *a touristic front region*; the kind of space that has been decorated with mementos or reminders of backstage activities. For example, to create the atmosphere of a beach setting, a hotel room uses a seashell theme for its decorations.

The third refers to a type of front stage that simulates the backstage. For example, Hawaiian hula performances are routinely staged for tourism entertainment. The fourth region represents a back region that is open to outsiders. For example, a tourism brochure that explains the facts and traditions visitors may not know about the Hawaiian Hula dance (i.e., the fact that a Hula dance is usually accompanied by Hawaiian music called *Mele* or a traditional Hawaiian chant).

The fifth space is a back region that may have been altered somewhat for visitors to see or visit. One such example may be a traditional ceremony or ritual simplified for visitors to participate in. The final space is called *Goffman's back region,* representing the kind of space that is in its native or original state. One example is a back alley local bar that rarely has visitor sighting. Dhobi Ghat, the world's biggest open air laundry place in the slums of Mumbai (Figure 11.7), is another such example. In fact, slum tourism where visitors visit poverty stricken areas of a city is a form of tourism experiences that appeal to some cultural travelers.

Authenticity in Experience Planning

Do all visitors want to do as the Romans do? A visitor's desire experience or to see what is really lived in places they visit can vary. Some visitors may seek out the back regions while others may perceive those regions as obtrusive. Although there is much debate about what constitutes authenticity and whether a visitor can experience it, authenticity and localness are important design parameters for destinations to consider. Conceptualizing tourism spaces in theatrical terms can be helpful in understanding how visitors interact with various destination environments and settings and what may be considerations and configurations conducive to visitor positive responses.

Local elements can be intentionally designed into a tourism experience. Consumer quests for authentic

FIGURE 11. 7 Dhobi Ghat, Mumbai, India.

experiences have inspired tourism and hospitality businesses to embrace local elements in their product offerings. Localness can be designed into service. Frequently visitors take note of local elements in their recollection of trips. Local culture oriented elements can be intentionally incorporated in facility decorations, tours, and interpretive and guiding services.

When planning and developing tourism in a community, a destination should be mindful of what unique locale specific features it can offer to and how it will be received by the visitors, while also ensuring this is done in a manner that is true to the local culture. It is important to understand that due to the short-term nature of touristic encounters and the diversity in visitors' personal, social, and cultural backgrounds, there is bound to be variations in visitor preferences and sense-making.

While authentic and local elements can enrich visitor experiences, not every traveler wants to venture into the back regions of a destination (just like not every host wants to place his or her life in plain sight of visitors). On occasion, visitors can be just as satisfied to stay at a distance for a glimpse of the local view. One practice frequently seen is to allow flexibility and freedom in tourism experience offerings. For example, the creation of the impression of temporal and perceptual distances between visitors (the viewing subjects) and the consumable objects (e.g., local way of life performed in a theatre) may help project a sense of welcomed authenticity and enable visitors to enjoy themselves. Enclave tourism, the all-inclusive resort experiences on many islands of developing countries, is one such example.

SENSE OF PLACE

When a traveler visits a place, they form an understanding of and relationship with the visited locality—a sense of place. Understanding this people-place relationship is important in tourism experience management because a strong sense of place a visitor forms can lead to a highly-involved traveler and a richer destination experience as a result.

Sense of place refers to the association or connection that a visitor develops with a particular destination. A place becomes distinct and unique in the mind of the visitor when one forms a strong connection with a place.

Sense of place has a cognitive domain that can be understood as **sense of place identity** (What is this place all about?); it also has an emotive domain that can be understood as **sense of place attachment** (Is this place special?). Sentiments of attachment can come from the social element related to the cultural landscape (Is its people special?); it can also have a physical dimension that is composed of environmental features and locale characteristics (How is the place special ecologically?). When a visitor develops stronger connections with a place, he or she will be more likely to have a rich experience and potential for revisit.

Role of Native Species

Tourism attractions are developed around such environmental elements as climate, physical or cultural landscape, and physical terrain. A characteristic physical setting is important for the development of sense of place. A destination's physical setting includes both the natural environment, (i.e., plants, animals, minerals, and the geography) and the built environment (i.e., architecture, streets). The two environments are often intertwined.

Two key elements of the physical setting are sight and sound, or visibility and audibility. These are vital sensory components for the development of sense of place. Visitors can develop a strong connection with a place they visit through their interactions and encounters with native species. Native species are defined as indigenous flora and fauna. What is native to a destination contributes to creating regional boundaries and inherent uniqueness. Native species can also help differentiate a destination from its competitors, and becomes an impetus for travel. Some native species have better potential than others to help in shaping a strong destination sense of place. Quick Trip 11.2 explains three baseline preconditions.

FLOW IN VISITOR EXPERIENCE

The notion of flow helps explain why or why not a visitor enjoys an activity he or she partakes in and a place he or she visits. The idea of flow is synonymous to the feeling of being in the zone. Mihaly Csikszentmihalyi, one of the best-known positive psychologists, is credited as the architect of the notion (2014). The concept is useful to understand optimal experiences. Its central tenet is that in order for people to have a best experience, they need to be in a state of "flow," a state of mental concentration or complete absorption with the activity at hand and the situation.

When in flow, an individual will operate at full capacity. A flow experience occurs when a person's actual skills and action capabilities are in perfect alignment with performance requirements or action opportunities presented. When the balance is not there, a person can feel either bored (under-stimulation) or anxious (over-stimulation). Based on the challenges presented and skills a recreationist possesses, Csikszentmihalyi (1990) classifies recreational consumptive situations into eight different mental states: **anxiety, worry, empathy, arousal, boredom, flow, control, relaxation**. People are the happiest when they are in the *flow* state. Based upon Csikszentmihalyi's idea, there are eight prerequisite conditions for a flow visitor experience to occur:

- Skills and knowledge a visitor may have about an activity or a place.
- The visitor has a sense of merging of action and awareness.
- The visitor has clear goals and receives real-time feedback.
- The visitor has a sense of absorption.
- The visitor feels he or she has personal control over the act.
- The visitor has a loss of self-consciousness.
- The visitor has a loss of sense of time.
- There are intrinsic rewards.

Flow in Visitor Experience Design

The flow concept is important for tourism experience management because it provides guiding parameters for destinations and other service providers in designing user-centric recreational activities, leisure programs, and travel itineraries. The state of flow is intrinsically rewarding to a visitor as it can induce a strong sense of accomplishment and enjoyment. Knowledge of optimal experience conditions will allow tourism providers to design activities and programs that are best brought in line with visitor skill levels or capabilities.

For example, local foods can provide visitors with a taste of local ways of life. Yet it could also be an overwhelming experience when a first-time visitor to China is treated with such local delicacies such as fish heads or chicken feet. Anxiety rises when visitors are not equipped to venture into spaces that they are not capable of navigating (Figure 11.9). A ski resort offering varying terrains and lessons based on its visitor skill level is

What Is in a Native Species?

Indigenous flora and fauna make up a substantial proportion of any physical setting. Native or indigenous species can contribute to the distinctiveness of a place. Most native species have a well-defined natural range and are automatically bound to a locality and therefore have the potential to represent a place. We can find interesting applications in tourism using native species as a national symbol to create a strong sense of destination place. Kiwi of New Zealand, Canadian maple leaf, Chinese panda (Figure 11.8), and Australian kangaroo are some examples.

Native species can contribute to a destination identity by encapsulating the essence of the place and engendering favorable connections with visitors. For a native species to become part of the tourism landscape of its native land and be utilized by a destination to enhance tourism destination sense of place, it needs to bear certain traits and have certain pre-conditions (Forristal, Lehto, and Lee 2014). Broadly, there are three such pre-conditions:

Figure 11.8 A panda baby cub sitting in a tree in China.

- Native species can play a unique role in the formation of destination sense of place if they have strong biological foundation in the natural environment (i.e., this native species is a dominant, keystone, or flagship species of the destination). As such, this native species is visible or audible to visitors in the physical setting.
- This native species has been weaved into the historical, social, and cultural fabric of a destination. When it finds representation of significance in literature, rituals/heritage traditions, and art works, it can signify mythical and symbolic qualities of a destination, leaving a unique imprint on the destination's built environment and imparts cultural depth.
- There need to be human interaction and/or activity in real time and on a personal level with the native species. Visitors' sensing of a destination is largely shaped through their participation in activities and interactions with the destination. Therefore, the higher the opportunities for a native species to be part of the visitor activity set such as in the form of museums, arts and crafts, movies, music, or food ways, the stronger sense of place visitors can develop.

Think about This

1. Why is it important for a destination to understand how visitors develop their sense of place?
2. What may be strategies for destinations to use to effectively develop a strong destination sense of place?
3. Why do native species contribute to sense of place development?
4. Discuss the use of or potentials for native species from your home town to be utilized for destination sense of place.

Source

Forristal, L. J., Lehto, X.Y., & Lee, G. 2014. Native species and sense of place: The case of the Provençal Cicada. *Current Issues in Tourism*, 17 (5), 414–433.

QUICK TRIP 11.3

Flow on the Water

White-water rafting is a very involving activity. Tourism research has shown that in order to induce flow in a white-water rafting experience, providers must strike a balance between a travelers' perceived level of *skill* and *challenge*.

White-water rafting outfitters in Colorado accomplish this by segmenting would-be rafters based on their level of prior experience (skill) with white-water rafting. Coloradorafting.net, for example, offers four levels of rafting trips: Beginner trips, family and intermediate trips, advanced trips, and advanced+ trips. The beginner trips ranged from float trips with a few small ripples to introductory white-water trips with easy rapids while the advanced+ trips are adrenaline rushing with almost continuous rapids and the biggest drops. This segmentation based on degree of difficulties allows rafters to align their skill level with a corresponding degree of challenge, thus avoiding anxiety or boredom.

Echo Canyon River Expeditions has a similar experience design. For inexperienced travelers, the rafting company provides training on how to row, specific life-saving knowledge, and other rafting maneuvers. In doing so, they are increasing this group's knowledge and self-confidence. Travelers with prior rafting experience possess a higher level of skill. Travelers in this group may skip the training and focus on ensuring they have access to rivers with a higher class rating to increase the *challenge* and thus aligning well with their high skill.

Ultimately, both companies increase the likelihood of engendering optimal (flow) white-water rafting experiences by ensuring all rafters are capable of meeting the challenge of the activity at hand. They, as a result, cater well to the adventure needs of travelers with varying degree of rafting comfort by offerings ranging from extreme white-water rafting to calm family floats.

Think about This

1. Why is it important to understand travelers' comfort level with an activity?
2. Why are the two rafting outfitters successful in providing memorable white-water rafting experiences to their customers?
3. Can you think of an episode of an activity that you participated in on a trip that stressed you out? What could have been done differently by the service provider?
4. Can you provide other examples to illustrate how Csikszentmihalyi's conditions for flow can inform tourism practitioners?

Sources

www.coloradorafting.net

www.raftecho.com/

FIGURE 11.9 **A fallen skier.**

Let's Take a Ride with the Tour Guide to See the Real Thing

Visitors may be inquisitive and want to venture into a culturally foreign back region of a destination. However, they may experience anxiety as experiencing such local spaces can be mentally exerting for visitors due to their lack of information about whereabouts or proper local protocols. Or they may experience boredom because they do not have adequate knowledge about the sites they visit and are not mentally aroused enough to appreciate what they see.

Tour guiding and interpretive services can come in play in such scenarios to help visitors to generate a sense of flow. Tour guides are storytellers. Their stories can help visitors develop a better understanding and appreciation for culturally distant sites. These services can guide visitors into the back regions of a destination, help ease an anxious mind, or arouse visitor curiosity. As a result, visitors can internalize what they see and develop a better sense of place and appreciation for the place.

Think about This

1. Why is the sense of flow important for a cultural visitor?
2. Have you ever utilized tour guiding services at a destination? How was it?
3. Think about a great trip you have made to a foreign destination in the past. Are you able to use Csikzentmihalyi's flow theory to explain why you had such a good time?

another example of following such parameters. When a recreational coordinator/coach or a tour guide provides encouragement or offers information, it allows visitors to be in position to feel more confident about taking on the challenges presented to them. This assistance and encouragement can help engender feelings of success and in control, and the loss of sense of time or self-consciousness, and thus a sense of enjoyment. Being mindful of a visitor's capacity to take on certain activities can lead to designs that generate the most intriguing, enlightening, and engaging visitor encounters.

Tourism activity programming can adopt the strategy of supportive design to foster a visitor sense of control with respect to physical-social surroundings. Situations or conditions that are uncontrollable by the participants are perceived as stressful. A spa environment for instance will likely support dealing with stress and thereby promote wellness if it is designed in such a fashion that the users can have a sense of control with respect to their physical-social surroundings. Here, customers can turn off the "music" or "noise" if they want to, or socialize if they prefer. Providing access to social support, but allowing freedom for solitude, can be seen as supportive design. It is optimal in the sense that a wellness seeker is given the freedom to rest, relax, and not be obliged to engage in any activities.

EXPERIENCE THEMING

Pine and Gilmore (1999) posit that an experience is not amorphous and that designing an engaging experience is vital for experience delivery. One important principle emphasized by Pine and Gilmore for experience design has to do with theming an experience. Theming is imperative in experience design because it serves to coalesce the various environmental cues for the users. It is a technique that has seen applications in hotels, resorts, restaurants, and other tourism businesses.

Theming refers to the practice of designing an experience that has identifiable characteristics such as distinguishable features, specific materials, and recognizable spatial configurations.

A compelling theme can drive all the design elements of an experience product toward a cohesive story line that is captivating and help unify the sensory stimulations, services, activities, and programs that a destination, a resort, or other businesses in tourism offer. Experience creation is not simply a show; it takes mindful orchestration and design that represents a nuanced undercurrent of substance. There are some central themes that tourism providers gravitate toward based on what visitors desire.

Entertainment Theme

Entertainment anchors one realm of any experience. For tourism and leisure services, entertainment is a dominant theme. Perhaps none is more illustrative than the destination city of Las Vegas when it comes to thematic experience design ranging from sensory stimulations to actual program and activity offerings.

Las Vegas' cityscape employs dramatic architecture and lights. The rapidly evolving skyline of the Las Vegas Strip has the highest concentration of mega resorts and casinos unified under the entertainment theme. One example is the Caesars Palace. First opened in the summer of 1966, it was the first true themed resort in Vegas on the Las Vegas Strip. For more than five decades, it has been the embodiment of a Roman theme, corralling all its entertainment elements in its façade and public spaces, and events on this theme. Today it is known as Las Vegas' *Grande Dame of Resorts*.

Cruise lines are offering entertainment themed cruises. Royal Caribbean's *Stars on Board* is one such example. Royal Caribbean describes this entertainment theme as such: "*You are not a fan. You are a boot scootin', sleng teng jamming, rhapsody seeker. And this is not a concert. This is an immersive aural experience. Come seek adventure and innovation on a Royal Caribbean cruise that will have you moving to the soundtracks of some of today's hottest artists and DJ's. Enjoy live entertainment all day long and dance parties long into the night on the ultimate vacation experience.*" For many music lovers, this is an enticing offering.

Wellness Theme

Aligning with today's traveler baseline need for rest and restoration, wellness is another thematic domain that has seen lively applications. For a wellness-oriented destination, the central theme is obviously centering on wellness. However, for one wellness provider to differentiate itself from another, it needs to consider creating a unique theme upon which it builds its identity. A central theme threads the disparate/array of activities, events, and programs that a wellness service provider offers into a unique experience.

For example, distinctive themes of various hot spring destinations help position themselves among differentiated and uniquely appreciated by visitors among a multitude of similar competing hot spring experience providers. The European model traditionally emphasizes the curative treatments of a wellness experience, while the American model may be oriented toward preventive therapy. Southeast Asia seems to focus more on Zen-ness and spiritual actuality, while East Asia (e.g., Korea and China) tends to have more of a hedonistic or social theme. These differing perspectives do not advocate against some degree of adaptive integration or cross-adoption on the part of wellness resorts and destinations. The point is that it is important to layer meanings and special benefits on top of the experience product and create an identity that cannot be rivaled by competitors.

The growing attractiveness and economic significance of wellness tourism presents an intriguing prospect for tourism marketers. Destinations at various levels are captivated by this market opportunity. In fact, promoting vacations to achieve wellness has evolved from what was originally more of a single business enterprise or product venture (such as day spa, hotel spa, spa resort) to broader strategic initiatives at the destination level (such as state- or city/county-wide wellness branding initiatives). Ultimately wellness-themed experiences are created to make visitors feel well and alive. Although it may not have been directly programmed into tourism business offerings, environmental quality is vital as it is difficult to imagine that visitors seeking physical wellness will patronize a healing center located in a heavily industrialized and populated area.

Collaboration among destination management organizations, spa and wellness operations, and cultural and recreational suppliers is essential in creating a positive wellness tourism experience. Every component of a wellness destination is an integral part of the bigger picture in servicing the wellness-seeking visitors. In fact, the strategic leadership at the destination level is critical as tourism authorities at a higher level have traditionally played a key role in channeling resources and coordinating initiatives toward projecting a positive wellness destination experience.

One such example is the Tourism Authority of Thailand. The national tourism organization has been successfully rallying "wellness troops" to make a concerted effort in marketing Thailand's wellness services. Using the campaign slogan "Find Your Fabulous," the tourism authority has teamed with Thai Airways International, Asia Website Direct, and thirty leading providers of health, beauty, and spa treatments to jointly launch a digital marketing campaign with more than 150 exclusive experience packages of health, wellness, beauty, and hotel deals for wellness visitors all over the world. Their annual wellness tradeshow "Thailand Health and Wellness Tourism Showcase" routinely attracts many medical tourism providers and travel agencies, international press, and social media influencers. One example of utilizing social influencers to promote the health and wellness campaign is the "You Care You Share" campaign to encourage online influencers to share their Thai wellness experiences and win wellness and spa travel packages provided by top spas, resorts, and hotels in Thailand. Four desirable market segments identified under the wellness theme by the Thai spa and wellness providers included high-end spenders from Russia, China, Germany, and India (www.thailandmedtourism. tourismthailand.org/).

Social Theme

A tourism experience has an inherent social domain as visitors encounter new social configurations. Spaces and events can be designed with social interaction as a central thematic orientation. Spurred by the rise of the sharing economy with successful business concepts such as Airbnb, more hotels have embraced the themes that address the social needs of a traveler.

Accor Hotels, for example, has developed a new brand concept in its latest brand offering of Jo&Joe. Jo&Joe's first two properties are slated to open in 2018, with plans to expand to fifty hotels worldwide by 2020. This is a product designed around the communal-driven "open-house" concept to fulfill traveler socializing and co-creating/sharing needs. As noted by the Accor Hotels CEO, "socialness is part of the design" (www.accorhotels.com).

Accor Hotels is very intentional in utilizing theming to project their focus and priorities. First, Jo&Joe is centered on the overall theme of an "open-house" that reflects a deliberate reimagining of a hotel not simply as a bed and a shower, but as a communal place to live. Every Jo&Joe property has a collaborative kitchen where guests can cook meals alongside each other. Additionally, within this "open-house" concept, they have also themed the various ways they provide overnight accommodations. As a potential guest, you have the option of sleeping in any of the following themed options: "Yours," "Together," and "OOO (Out Of the Ordinary)." These themes allow guests to stay in private rooms, shared areas, or unique sleeping arrangements (e.g., hammocks). Jo&Joe also features an area called "Happy House" where guests can "relax, work, cook, or wash their clothes—just like at home." Through the communal theme, Accor Hotels can accentuate its social and communal benefits to guests through this eclectic new accommodation brand. This social centric themed design of Jo&Joe appeals to travelers who value sharing, spontaneity, and experience.

EXPERIENCE CUEING

Tourism offers a multi-sensory experience. Visitors take in visual, aural, and other sensory cues/clues to derive pleasure and satisfaction. While the larger destination environment contains cultural and natural landscapes that have been perhaps organically formed independent of tourism considerations, there are other elements especially in the service arena that can be mindfully designed with visitor experience in mind.

Tourism and leisure service providers can strategize as to how to facilitate visitor experience through cueing to optimally engage their sensory reservoir. For example, the Japanese Garden in Portland (Oregon) is a popular visitor attraction (Figure 11.10). It is thought to be the most authentic Japanese garden outside Japan. The garden is designed with design styles that are recognizably Japanese: the strolling pond, the flat garden, the tea garden, the natural garden, and the sand and stone garden.

Broadly speaking, there are two elements of contextual cues to consider: a physical element and a relational element. Carbone and Haeckel (1994) refer to cues from the physical context as "*mechanics*" cues (e.g., sights, sounds, olfactory stimuli, and textures). Relational context cues are referred to as "humanics" cues. They are showcased in human behaviors such as service encounters, host and guest interactions, and visitor to visitor interactions. Both sets of contextual cues can be carefully orchestrated. Servicescape for example, is a management concept pertaining to tourism experience cueing.

© Hitman Sharon/Shutterstock.com

FIGURE 11.10 Footbridge over a pond at the Japanese Gardens in Portland, Oregon.

Servicescape

A tourism consumptive experience usually entails a visitor to spend extended periods of time in the physical surroundings of the service provider. Servicescape design can help tourism service providers to define and unify the characteristics of the physical surroundings and thus cueing and stimulating visitors about the experiences offered. Servicescape encompasses four environmental domains:

- The first domain to consider is ambience such as air quality, temperature, noise, music, and aroma.
- The second domain is related to space including such factors as facility layout, equipment, furnishings, and locale features.
- The third domain refers to signs and symbols used for the setting such as artifacts, decors, and signage.
- The last element pertains to humanics such as uniforms, service provider interactional protocols, and so forth.

The servicescape of a service environment carefully designed can signal visitors about an experience, a brand, and a destination in general. If unmanaged, these cues can leave no lasting impressions or negative impressions on the consumers.

Macro and Micro Cue Elements

Designing tourism experience products can be about making choices. Micro-scale environmental elements such as color, shape, line, music, facility material, architecture, cuisine presentation style as well as larger-scale elements such as scenery, landscape, sights, and sounds, can be intentionally orchestrated to provide tangible cues for the visitors.

Visual cues are necessary to project and reflect the experience theme. For instance, to serve as a visual cue of their intention to incorporate local/authentic living within the Jo&Joe hotel brand, several design cues stand out. First, their hotel bars are centrally placed in locales with high street visibility, which encourages locals to visit the bar, increasing the opportunity of guest-local interactions. To cue the sense of authenticity in dining, local cuisines are featured in all in-house restaurant menus. Jo&Joe properties also elect to use more traditional cooking methods such as grills, open flame barbeques, woks, and wood-fired ovens. Collectively, these visual cues serve as clear signals that the hotel is designed primarily with communal and local experiences in mind.

Disney Parks and Resorts is another example of a leisure business masterful in utilizing visual cues to enrich visual depth and visitor experiences. Serving as visual cues, Disney's employees become cast members in popular Disney characters. Visitors essentially immerse themselves in a three-dimensional movie-like reality, becoming part of a fantasy-like setting. The visitors are right in the middle of the action, experiencing fully the show scene-by-scene in a preplanned sequence. These intentional cue designs can condition visitors toward desired participation and interactions with various elements of a destination. They can be effective in triggering an internationalization process on the part of the visitors and engender emotional and cognitive connections with the destination.

Negative Cues

Bestowing a place with positive cues is, however, not enough for maintaining the integrity of the visitor experience. In addition to harmonizing impressions with positive cues, eliminating inconsistency in cues or negative cues is just as imperative, according to the design principles of Pine and Gilmore (1999). A destination needs to eliminate distracting or contradicting cues that may detract from the central theme.

Visitors take cues from the smallest signs. An unkempt bathroom, for instance, can send a visitor's imagination soaring, and associations such as unsanitary food and water may be made. Distractive elements can assert their presence and be difficult for visitors to ignore. These elements are more likely to be perceived as distractions if they are imposed on visitors without the possibility of personal choice or control. The visitor will take these unpleasant cues and utilize them negatively in the interpretation of their overall experience. For example, a visit to a restaurant bathroom is the most telling moment for a customer. Restaurant patrons usually associate a dirty bathroom with a dirty kitchen and unsanitary food. Because of this negative cue, customers are more likely to engage in Negative Word of Mouth on social media (e.g., negative reviews and photo sharing). They will be unlikely to re-patronize such restaurants.

Culturally Sensitive Design

Sensory stimulants of the tourism experience product need to be carefully thought out to support the central theme. Customer engagement, however, needs to be culturally sensitive. A physical-social environment perceived by one group as "enjoyable, happy, and friendly" may well be interpreted as "noisy, stressful, and invasive" by others. The needs and desires of inner-directed visitors can clash with those of outer-directed visitors. What cultivates a sense of enjoyment on the part of one group may impede the formation of that sense for another group. Cultural sensitivity should be incorporated into tourism experience design since tourism inherently implies visitor-environment exchanges cross-regional or cross-cultural boundaries. Not every traveler will experience the same sights and sites in the same manner. The degree of acculturation and preparedness is commensurate with the options open to individuals.

QUICK TRIP 11.5

Youth Hostels and Local Elements

Distinct local elements of a travel destination can become the highlight of a traveler's autographical memory of a trip. Hostels in particular can be places that allow travelers to enjoy the local element. Many hostels try to imbed local culture into their services. Visitors frequently take notice of and respond favorably about the local element being infused.

Given the increasing rise in the millennial travel segment and their desire for authentic local experiences, youth hostels around the world stand to benefit from ensuring their hostels reflect the local essence of its culture and location. To do so, there are several local elements that appear to be most cherished.

1. First, travelers crave genuine social interactions with locals. So, hostels find ways in which to entice local residents to visit the hostel such as adding a public bar or having an open communal area where travelers and locals alike can interact. Considering the hotel staff are essentially an extension of the local community, they are encouraged to socialize with travelers outside of their work hours.
2. Secondly, travelers recognize visual cues of their surroundings that suggest localness. As such, hostels' physical buildings and infrastructure, as well as their décor, present tangible evidence of their localness. When buildings appear to look less commercialized and showcase a design that matches the typical local residents' housing (e.g., mud hut), travelers take in the cues and recognize the authenticity of their living space. Likewise, hostels decorate their inside space with art and furnishings that reflect the local culture, such as colorfully decorated blankets and sheets.
3. Local-oriented hostels also strive to provide food offerings that ring true to the local cuisines of the area, rather than offering generic cookie-cutter menu options.

These are just a few examples of local elements that hostels leverage, but there are many other subtle ways that authentic localness is showcased. For instance, the Shoestring Backpackers Hostel in Zimbabwe is known for allowing an assortment of animals to roam freely throughout their property, and travelers come to appreciate this small but important quirk. Thus, hostels that don't try to cleanse out the localness of their establishment, and instead embrace everything that is true to their destination, recognize that "Local is Gold."

Think about This

1. What do you believe to be the single most important local element that can be leveraged?
2. What other local elements can hostels utilize to cue visitors an authentic representation of localness?
3. Do you think it is possible for a hostel or any service establishment to try too hard to present themselves as being locally-oriented?

Source

http://www.shoestringsvicfalls.com/shoestrings/shoestrings-about.html

Do As the Romans Do or Not? Or Does It Matter?

Experience is a subjective and private event. There is diversity in how visitors prefer to enjoy a place. Some may seek authentic and unique experiences, others may choose the popular and conventional activities. Two of the biggest technology companies in the world recognize this distinction in travel experience preferences, and have developed smartphone apps to satisfy the need for either pursuit.

Airbnb, originally the well-known peer-to-peer lodging platform, has recently added an entirely new destination-focused element to their service. Within their smartphone application, Airbnb users have exclusive access to experiences and places specially curated by the local hosts of the destination. With this service, Airbnb travelers are presented with "unique experiences" and "thousands of secret spots" to discover within any destination. Airbnb's ultimate goal is to ensure travelers have more genuinely-local tourism experiences.

Within the same year, Google released a stand-alone application called "Google Trips" which serves to appeal to the traveler seeking the more traditional or popular tourism experiences within a destination. Google Trips is a travel planner that makes it easy to organize day-to-day trip activities. In particular, Google touts their application's ability to help discover "must-see" or popular sights, attractions, restaurants, or activities at the destination. In some way, Google Trips is designed with the principle that travelers do not always prefer to do as the locals do, but desire an application that permits them to efficiently identify the most popular and highly-recommended experiences.

Collectively, these two services address diverse preferences for how to experience a destination. Whether a traveler wants to identify top things to do near Times Square, or seeks to discover the bars locals go to, or both. There is something for everyone. Suit your own needs!

Think about This

1. What may be reasons for travelers to enjoy a destination differently?
2. How would repeat visitors do things differently from first-time visitors?
3. When promoting a destination, how do you accommodate visitors' diverse tastes and preferences?

Sources

https://get.google.com/trips/

https://www.airbnb.com/new

DESTINATION ACTIVITY PARTICIPATION

As the preceding discussions illustrate, the travel product is experiential and holistic in nature. However, what visitors engage themselves in doing is instrumental in shaping visitor experience judgment. What a person does at a destination makes up the crux of their memories and narratives about a trip. Planning and configurations of these activities also provide a destination room for experience design, transforming resources into consumptive scenarios for visitors. Therefore, when we discuss how best to provide a memorable experience for visitors, we need to have an intimate understanding of visitor activity participation patterns and preferences.

Activities are a core component of tourism experience as they play a central role in the traveler-destination environment exchange. Destination activities allow a visitor to interact with a destination's physical environment, socio-cultural environment, and service environment. They are conduits allowing a destination to interface with visitors and engage their five senses.

Typology of Activities

Travel can be seen as a special type of leisure and recreational activity consumed away from home environment. Destination activities bear similarities with daily leisure activities. Visitor activity pursuits can be either active or passive activities. Active activities usually necessitate the visitor to exert physical or mental energy while passive activities require less physical or mental energy. Surfing, snowboarding, rafting, and skiing are some examples of active pursuits. Dining in a restaurant, attending a local event, and people-watching on the streets can be examples of more passive activities.

QUICK TRIP 11.7

Mt. Hood Adventure Activity Development Scheme

Mt. Hood Adventure in Oregon is one of the oldest ski resorts in the country. This mountain-based resort operates as two different adventure parks—Winter Adventure and Summer Adventure—and offers a wide variety of activities and services year-round. In terms of breadth, there are five notable categories of offerings that the resort groups their activities around. These include Summer, Winter, Lessons, Events, and Rentals. Within these categories, the resort also offers great depth in activities as well within each category of offerings. Figure 11.11 denotes the various activities under each category.

Think about This

1. Given the resort has access to rich natural resources on the mountain, do you think they are taking full advantage (in terms of activities) of what the mountain offers? Are there any new activity categories that the company could create?

2. Do you have specific suggestions for new activities?

Source

http://www.mthoodadventure.com/

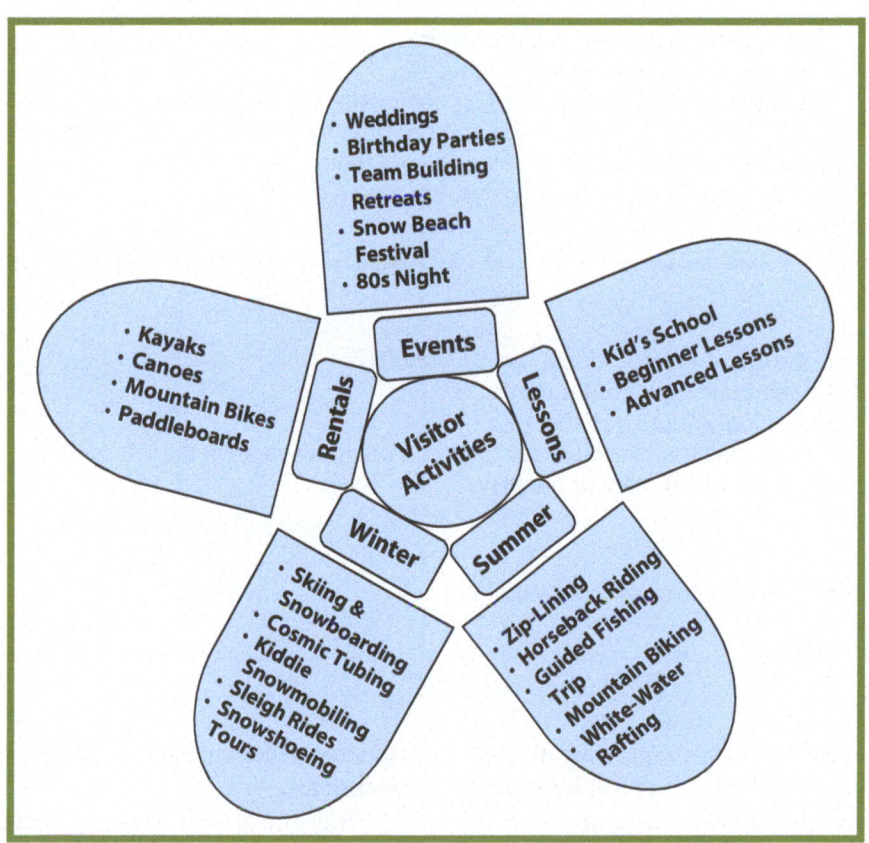

FIGURE 11.11 Mt. Hood Adventure activity development scheme.

QUICK TRIP 11.8

Bundling for a Good Experience for the Visitors

Bundling refers to the business practice of combining a collection of complementary places and experiences within a region together to offer to tourists. Bundling offers several benefits for the tourism destination and tourist alike. First and foremost, bundling allows destinations to leverage their businesses' and operators' core activities/offerings. When small tourism operators and suppliers come together to offer their respective bests to tourists, bundling assures the destination's product remains fresh, interesting, and enticing, while improving the profile and visibility of the destination. As a result, bundling helps in growing visitor arrivals, length of stay, and spending, while also encouraging WOM.

Tourists also benefit when destinations bundle their experiential products. Tourists often spend a great deal of time and effort conducting extensive research to identify isolated experiences in a destination. With bundled products, destinations alleviate this by curating only the most appealing activities and experiences to offer. Bundles are also often categorized and themed according to the type of experiences offered, which means tourists have experiences personalized to their preferences. Ultimately, bundling gives tourists confidence when identifying and determining how to best experience a destination.

You can view an explanation of how bundling works from this YouTube video produced by Tourism Australia: https://www.youtube.com/watch?v=zCVAaxFIDkA

How to Identify Experiences Worth Bundling

Identify:

- The experiences your business offers
- The experiences your region offers
- What's unique to your business, your local area, or your region
- What your local area or region can promote as a unique selling point
- What experience category you and your region can "own" and promote
- What visitors really want to get out of your experience

Think about This

1. What specific types of experiences/products can be bundled?
2. What other benefits does bundling offer tourists?
3. How does bundling save individual operators money?
4. How does bundling help small tourism business to gain a competitive advantage?
5. What are some possible disadvantages of bundling?

Source

Tourism Australia. https://www.youtube.com/watch?v=zCVAaxFIDkA

Visitor activities can be indoor (e.g., weightlifting in a hotel fitness center) or outdoor (e.g., strolling around town). They can be individual-based (e.g., snowboarding) or group-oriented (e.g., beach volleyball). They can be natural resource-based (mountain trekking) or cultural resource-based (visit a museum or a local market). They can be resource-consuming (e.g., shopping) or resource-generating/rejuvenating (attending an art workshop).

Tourism activities can be either *core* activities—activities central to a visitor's interest, or activities that are *complimentary* to the central interest, or *incidental* (activities that are spontaneous), or *essential* (activities that are necessary). For example, a visitor may visit

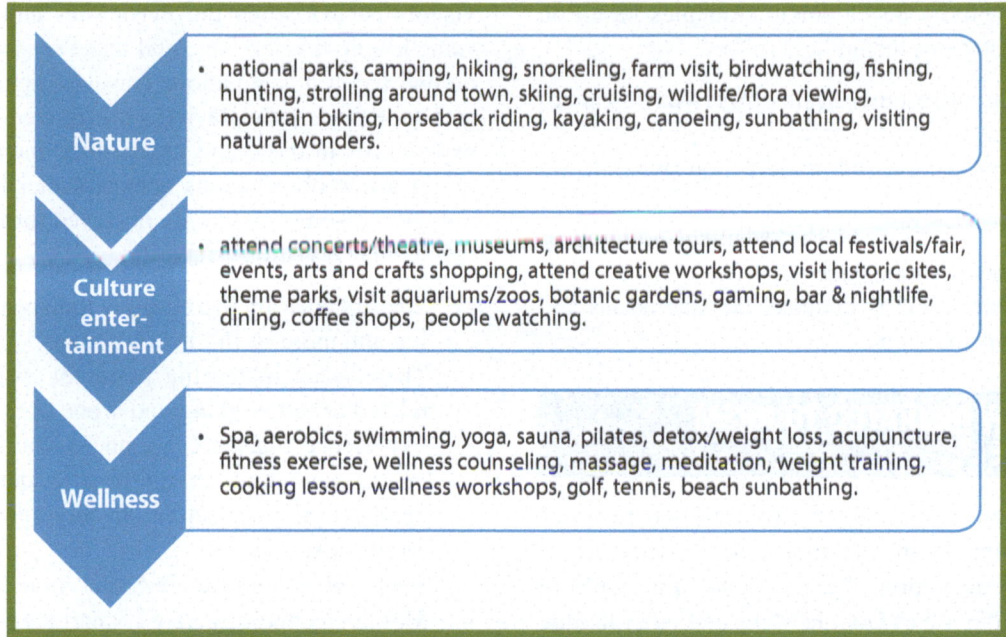

FIGURE 11.12 **A sample of activity breadth and depth development.**

New Orleans in late April or early May for the annual New Orleans Jazz & Heritage Festival. The core activities in this case may be to enjoy the world famous live music performances of various genres: jazz, rock, hip-hop, pop, funk, indie, blues, or zydeco. The visitor may also choose to do a New Orleans architectural tour visiting historical homes and buildings (complimentary). He may chance a good football game and decide to watch it (incidental). And of course, he will patronize local restaurants and bars (essential).

Destination Activity Design

Visitor's personal factors (such as age, gender, preferences, habits, income) and trip specific situations (e.g., destination setting and activity availability, number of trips made prior, travel companionship, time availability) influence how they engage in activity pursuits.

Prior experience is a strong predictor of visitor activity participation patterns. First-time visitors to a destination tend to participate in a wider variety of activities available at a destination. As a visitor returns to a destination for a repeat visit, their choices of activities tend to be narrower. The most frequent visitors tend to have the most focused activity choice sets.

Of course, other factors may exert influence on how visitors select activities. A visitor may consider activities based on time constraints or considerations related to travel companionship. When a visitor returns to Disney for a repeat trip with their children, they may do activities like those they did as a child themselves simply because they may want to experience the activities with their children.

Therefore, tourism destinations can benefit from knowledge as to who does what and with whom? Or who would be interested in doing what? They need to consider factors that may exert influence on how visitors make activity decisions and their activity skill level. It is important to provide ample leisure activity choices to suit visitor needs.

Activity Breadth and Depth Development

When planning activities, one approach for a destination or leisure service provider is to classify existing activities based on the activity breadth and depth development scheme. *Activity breadth* refers to the number of available activity categories (e.g., broader categories such as nature-oriented, cultural-oriented, entertainment-oriented, recreation-oriented, wellness-oriented). Activity category classification can be flexible but in general broader schemes. *Activity depth* refers to the number of available activities within each broad scheme or category. Figure 11.12 is an illustration of such a classification for a destination. Figure 11.11 is another example of such a schematic development of activities by a mountain-based resort in Oregon (see Quick Trip 11.7).

A destination or a leisure provider such as a resort can first take an inventory of available activities and cluster them into schemes. Then the destination may decide on its activity development strategies based on several considerations including:

- Its own tourism resource availability (what resources do we have?)
- Its image projection and brand vision (what do we want to be known for?)
- Its current and future market segment preferences (what do our visitors want?)
- Other factors such as financial considerations and competitive situations.

TECHNOLOGY MEDIATED TOURISM EXPERIENCE

Technology has always played a role in modern travel in ways varying from enabling long-distance travel because of the invention of cars, trains, and planes in early times to the use of Google Maps and other mobile applications today. The recent advances in communication technology, especially mobile technology, has even more significantly impacted why people travel (see discussions of technology induced travel motivations in Chapter 10), how people make travel decisions (see discussions of technology assisted information search and decision-making in Chapter 12), and the way people experience a destination.

Mobile technologies such as smartphones and tablets as well as the omnipresence of wireless connections in many parts of the world have made a clear mark on how visitors take in sights and sounds at a destination. These technologies also have greatly influenced how visitors behave when they visit sites and places, consume hospitality services, and make sense of what they do and see at a destination. Traveler friendly technologies are increasingly playing a role in mediating tourism experiences in these and many other ways. Below is a list of a few observations about traveler friendly technology and some commonly observed forms of technology mediated visitor behavior:

- Smartphones are increasingly indispensable in daily life and more so in travel for many.
- There is an increasing trend for visitor activities related to selfie-taking and drone use.
- Experience sharing (e.g., photo sharing, blogging, messaging/online chatting) at a destination and upon return has become an important part of the tourism experience.
- Visitor behavior often becomes more spontaneous.
- Mobile technology (e.g., smartphones) and real-time social media interactions mediate how visitors make sense of what they do and see.
- Virtual reality and augmented reality is changing how visitors enjoy activities and a vacation. Free Virtual Reality apps like YouVisit VR, Ascape VR, Discovery VR, and Google Street View provide people an immersive travel experience on their smartphones.
- Technology (e.g., mobile applications, use of robots, Marriott's 4-D teleporter) at service settings (e.g., hotels, restaurants, and airports) is changing visitors' perception of and interface with hospitality services.

SUMMARY

Experience is at the heart of travel. An engaging experience can potentially lead to much more than satisfaction. It can extend itself into the realm of loyalty. Knowledge of the ways in which visitors consume a place product is fundamental to tourism management.

Tourism experience is a multi-stage and multifaceted concept. Visitors derive eight different values from such a product: entertainment, education, aesthetics, escapist, localness, spontaneity, personalization, and communitas.

Visitors may internalize and appreciate what a destination offers differently based on their personal dispositions, tastes, needs, and trip-related characteristics. A destination needs to work with tourism businesses and co-create with visitors themselves such an experience product.

It is important for tourism destinations and service providers to establish a focal theme with supportive features and positive cues. Local and authentic elements in experience design are appreciated by visitors. Quality is ideally delivered through a carefully designed experience product that is optimally engaging. Given the diverse backgrounds of visitors, it is important to heed principles of universality and flexibility, thus allowing visitors to fully engage themselves with activities of their choices and have a sense of flow in what they do.

Provision of a quality experience requires a system's approach where all sectors of a destination work together to deliver the consistency that visitors desire. Visitors' cultural and demographic dispositions play a major role in their evaluation of a tourism experience. It is important to be culturally sensitive and understand market segment specificities in tourism experience. Travel-friendly technology is increasingly mediating how visitors experience a destination product and needs to be carefully considered by destinations and tourism service providers.

ACTIVITIES

1. Select a destination that you are familiar with and answer the following questions:
   a. Utilize the Tourism Experiencescape Model to conduct an analysis on what this destination can offer. What experience value dimension(s) should be highlighted in its marketing communications?
   b. Chart out a hypothetical but typical visitor's experience journey for this destination. What does an optimal experience looks like?
   c. Visit the website of this destination and at least one of its social media sites. Do you think this destination has done a good job communicating to visitors what it has to offer?
   d. Does the destination project a consistent and appealing destination image?

2. Take a walking tour in the community where you currently live.
   a. Take an inventory of its sensory and aesthetic qualities.
   b. Who might be attracted to these characteristics?
   c. Describe the typical visitor. Factors you can look at include his/her possible key motive to visit, his/her home environment characteristics, and his/her demographics and preferences.
   d. What are the existing activities in your community that may be appealing to this visitor?
   e. What may be possible negative cues for a visitor?
   f. Are there new activities and services that you can design to improve this visitor's experience?
   g. What local elements can be further utilized for tourism development?
   h. Can this community's leisure offerings be bundled with other communities to make the region more attractive?

REFERENCES

Accor Hotels. (www.accorhotels.com)

Aho, S. K. 2001. Towards a general theory of touristic experiences: Modelling experience process in tourism. *Tourism Review* 56 (3/4): 33–37. https://doi.org/10.1108/eb058368

Carbone, Lewis P., and Stephan H. Haeckel. 1994. Engineering customer experiences. *Marketing Management* 3.3 (Winter 1994): 8.

Csikszentmihalyi, Mihaly. 1990. *Flow: The Psychology of Optimal Experience*. New York: Harper and Row.

Csikszentmihalyi, Mihaly. 2014. *Flow and the Foundations of Positive Psychology: The Collected Works of Mihaly Csikszentmihalyi*. Dordrecht: Springer.

Holbrook, M. B., and E. C. Hirschman, 1983. The experiential aspects of consumption: consumer fantasies, feelings, and fun. *Journal of Consumer Research* 9 (2), 132–140.

Hunt, J. D. 1992. *Gardens and the Picturesque: Studies in the History of Landscape Architecture*. MIT Press.

Kirillova, K., X. Fu, X. Lehto, and L. Cai. 2014. What makes a destination beautiful? Dimensions of tourist aesthetic judment. *Tourism Management 42* (June), 282–293. https://doi.org/10.1016/j.tourman.2013.12.006

Kirillova, K., and X. Lehto. 2015. Destination Aesthetics and Aesthetic Distance in Tourism Experience. *Journal of Travel & Tourism Marketing* 32 (8), 1051–1068.

MacCannell, D. 1973. Stag authenticity: Arrangements of social space in tourist settings. *The American Joural of Sociology* 79 (3), 589–603.

Mody, M. A., C. Suess, and X. Lehto. 2017. The accommodation experiencescape: a comparative assessment of hotels and Airbnb. *International Journal of Contemporary Hospitality Management*. https://doi.org/10.1108/IJCHM-09-2016-0501

Pine, J., and J. Gilmore. 1999. *The experience economy: Work is theatre & every business a stage*. Harvard Business Press.

ADDITIONAL READINGS

Forristal, L., and X. Lehto. 2009. Place branding with native species: Personality as a criterion. *Place Branding and Public Diplomacy* 5 (3): 213–225.

Forristal, L. J., X. Y. Lehto, and G. Lee. 2014. Native species and sense of place: The case of the Provençal Cicada. *Current Issues in Tourism* 17 (5), 414–433.

https://www.imtj.com/news/thailand-promotes-health-and-wellness-tourism/

http://www.thaispaassociation.com/

Ritchie, B., V. Tung, and R. Ritchie. 2011. Tourism experience management research: Emergence, evolution and future directions. *International Journal of Contemporary Hospitality Management, 23* (4), 419–438.

Rossiter, J. R., and S. Bellman. 2005. *Marketing communications: Theory and applications*. Prentice-Hall.

Sherry, J. F. (Ed.). 1998. *Servicescapes: the concept of place in contemporary markets*. NTC Business Books.

Tourism Authority of Thailand. http://thailandmedtourism.tourismthailand.org/

Tsai, C. S. 2016. "Memorable Tourist Experiences and Place Attachment When Consuming Local Food." *International Journal of Tourism Research*. http://doi.org/10.1002/jtr

Tucker, H., and P. Lynch. 2005. "Host-Guest Dating: The Potential of Improving the Customer Experience Through Host-Guest Psychographic Matching." *Journal of Quality Assurance in Hospitality & Tourism* 5 (2–4): 11–32.

Tung, V., and J. R. B. Ritchie. 2011. "Exploring the essence of memorable tourism experiences." *Annals of Tourism Research* 38 (4): 1367–1386.

Tussyadiah, I. P. 2014. "Toward a Theoretical Foundation for Experience Design in Tourism." *Journal of Travel Research* 53 (5): 543–564.

Walls, A. R., F. Okumus, Y. Raymond, and D. J. Kwun. 2011. "International Journal of Hospitality Management An epistemological view of consumer experiences." *International Journal of Hospitality Management*, Elsevier Ltd 30 (1): 10–21.

Wang, N. 2004. Rethinking authenticity in tourism experience. *Annals of Tourism Research* 26 (2): 349–370.

Yiannakis, A., and H. Gibson. 1992. Roles tourists play. *Annals of Tourism Research* 19 (2), 287–303.

CHAPTER TWELVE

Travel Purchase
Traveler Decision-Making and Travel Information

Most travel, and certainly the rewarding kind,
involves depending on the kindness of strangers,
putting yourself into the hands of people
you don't know and trusting them with your life

American writer PAUL THEROUX

YOUR LEARNING DESTINATION

Having learned about how people make destination and other trip-related purchase decisions, students will be able to suggest appropriate marketing communication strategies.

WHAT YOU NEED TO KNOW

Having read this chapter, you will be able to:

- ✓ Describe the various travel decision models.
- ✓ Explain the nature and importance of travel information.
- ✓ Explain the role of risk in traveler decision-making.
- ✓ Explain the role of traveler-generated information.
- ✓ Explain how to use the factors that influence people's sensitivity to information to increase the chances of a message being noticed.
- ✓ Explain the effectiveness of different communication strategies at each stage of the buying process.

BREAKING THE ICE

How do travelers make purchase decisions? Why do they make the choices they do? How can we as tourism practitioners appeal to and serve travelers effectively in the traveler decision-making process? This chapter introduces you to decision factors and models that elucidate how consumers make travel decisions and purchase travel products. There is no one magic decision-making formula that can account for a travelers decision behavior but together these various models will provide useful insights for tourism professionals. You will be able to not only gain an understanding of the theoretical underpinnings of traveler decision–making, but also utilize knowledge of decision-related psychological processes to formulate effective marketing communication strategies.

KEY TAKEAWAY POINTS

- Traveler purchase decision is tied to value perceptions.

- Travel decisions are not as defined and are more spontaneous compared to other product purchases.

- Travel decisions have a high degree of risk and uncertainty.

- Monitoring traveler risk perceptions and developing safety and security mechanisms to protect visitors are important for destinations in engendering favorable travel decisions.

- Consumers can employ both automatic and controlled processes in making travel decisions.

- The traveler decision-making process involves multiple stages, of which marketers can utilize various strategies to exert influence.

- Travel information fulfills multi-dimensional needs including functional, hedonic, aesthetic, sign, and innovation needs.

- Traveler information search is expansive, continuous, and involves multi-platforms and multi-media.

- Travel-generated information is gaining increasing importance.

- Destinations can follow the 3Cs and 4Ps strategies for content strategy formulation.

TRAVELER DECISION-MAKING

Travel Decision Characteristics

Consumers' travel motivation is an important factor in channeling decisions to travel and subsequent decision choices (Please reference Chapter 10). Once an individual is motivated, how do they make purchase decisions? In a nutshell, visitors select destinations, travel services, and products that they judge as best meeting their needs. The question is "How and why do they derive such judgments?" What factors influence such judgments? Various theories have been proposed to explain such traveler behavior. Before getting familiar with these decision models, it is important to have a baseline understanding of the unique characteristics of travel decisions. What makes travel decisions different from other product purchases? Broadly speaking, there are five traits uniquely associated with travel decisions:

1. Travel products are inherently experiential. Because of this characteristic of what travelers buy, a majority of travel decisions are not as well defined choice situations as those for other more tangible or more defined products and services.
2. Travel purchase decision-making can encompass multiple phases defined by a timeline (e.g., pre-trip, on-route, and onsite purchases).
3. Travel decisions involve multiple decision components (e.g., destination selections, travel itinerary selections, transportation choices, lodging choices, restaurant choices, activity choices, and shopping choices).
4. Because travel entails one's relocation to physical and social environments that are different from one's everyday living environment, travel purchases can be associated with significant uncertainty a creating risky choice situations where the outcomes cannot be easily controlled or calculated with known probabilities.
5. There is a higher degree of openness and spontaneity about travel purchase behavior thanks to travel's inherent association with exploration, play, and curiosity. Therefore, what visitors seek to purchase and experience can be constructed in situ and spur-of-the-moment (Smallman and Moore 2010).

Classic consumer decision theories have been advanced to delineate an optimal choice, among an array of product options, based on models pertaining to uncertainty, risk, and utility. These theories describe the choice of an ideal hypothetical decision-maker who is logical, rational, and omniscient. These models are prescriptive in nature and can be somewhat limited in real life because consumers as decision-makers do not always do what they "should" nor do they have the omnipotent computational power that many of such models are built upon. It is nonetheless important to understand that the variables in these models do play an essential role in explaining consumer decision-making.

Expected Value/Utility Theory

Originally developed by John von Neumann and Oscar Morgenstern, the Expected Value/Utility Theory posits that a decision-maker makes a decision that he or she deems as maximizing their expected value. This theory is based on the premise that decision-makers are rational economic agents. In the context of destination selection decisions, the basic idea is that a traveler assesses or otherwise estimates the expected value of traveling to each destination from a pool of alternative destination candidates, and chooses the one that provides the highest expected value.

To see how the *expected value* of traveling to a particular destination [EVTD] might be estimated, it is helpful to think of a destination as a basket of attributes (such as cost, location, safety, exoticness, etc.), each of which contributes in either a positive or negative way to the expected value of traveling to the destination. If each attribute makes a separate, independent contribution to the expected value, the expected value of traveling to a particular destination [EVTD] then becomes a simple additive function. That is, EVTD can be calculated by summing the expected values of each of the destination's attributes (how well a destination will perform on each attribute) weighted by their relative importance (how important each attribute is for the traveler). More complicated non-additive models can be developed, but a simple model that adds up the effects of well-chosen attributes often provides a good fit to consumer travel preferences. For example, a simple model that adds up the effects of attributes such as hotel cost, location, and selected features might be helpful to predict choices of targeted travel sectors.

However, visitor decision-making is a very complex process and normative approaches such as these cannot provide a complete decision-making picture. There are several reasons why models based on the expected utility theory, while useful, have inherent limitations. First, as we discussed prior, travelers are not always making rational decisions nor are they always capable of computation-based decision-making. Secondly, travelers are found to make choices that are not necessarily optimal in economic or "rational" terms but rather they make choices that are the most satisfying. For instance, in economic terms, a visitor to Europe for fifteen days may consider visiting as many places and countries as possible. However in the process of traveling from place to place, the visitor may lose significant time on the road, traveling between airports and hotels, packing and unpacking, not to mention the cognitive stress that may come with transitions between languages, different transportation systems, and cultural practices. Less can

be more for some consumers. The normative models, as a result, may not explain why certain decisions are made even when seemingly the choices made run contrary to the utility parameters.

Protection Motivation Theory

This theory explains why consumers may shy away from certain consumptive choices. Consumer decision is a function of choice to protect themselves from being harmed. Bauer (1960) introduced the concepts of risk and uncertainty in his observation that consumer behavior involves risk such that any action taken can produce unanticipated consequences and "some of which at least are likely to be unpleasant." Therefore, decision choice is usually associated with consumer risk assessment.

Consumers go through two cognitive processes when deciding whether or not to engage in a behavior (Floyd, Prentice-Dunn, and Rogers 2000): how risky is the choice (threat appraisal) and how well one can handle the perceived risk (coping appraisal). When consumers believe that the perceived vulnerability to and perceived severity of a risk are high, and their perceived risk-coping ability is low, they are more likely to decide against such a consumptive choice.

In the tourism scenario, such perceived risks can come from multiple fronts. Visiting a travel destination involves significant investment on the part of the consumers in financial and time terms. Financial resources spent on a family vacation, for example, can be significant. One's vacation time resource is also limited, and off-work time spent on leisure travel can be perceived as time well spent if all goes well. If all goes wrong, the loss can be perceived as significant as well. Further, traveling to a destination requires the physical movement of the traveler from a familiar (home) environment to an unfamiliar environment. Travelers are liable for risks associated with a variety of destination natural and human factors, such as natural disasters, terrorist attacks and other crimes, and health risks.

The increasing occurrences of natural and human-induced crises have heightened the importance for the travel industry to safeguard their visitors and their own safety images. Understanding of consumers self-protection tendencies in decision-making can help tourism destinations and businesses to not only systematically monitor visitor risk perceptions, but also develop safety and security mechanisms to protect visitors from harm, as well as develop communication strategies to reduce visitors' worry, fear, and anxiety associated with risky situations, and boost visitors' confidence and trust in a destination's ability to deliver a safe and enjoyable vacation experience.

Is It Safe to Visit?

As a child, did you ever dream of an exciting adventure in the heart of an ancient Egyptian tomb? Were you ever captivated by the stories of powerful pharaohs? Did movies like *The Mummy* or *Indiana Jones* both thrill and fascinate you? Growing up, did you ever dream of visiting Egypt? Egypt in many ways is a dazzling destination with the Pyramids of Giza—the last surviving of the Seven Wonders of the Ancient world, its vast deserts and intriguing Sinai Peninsula, and its famed Nile River.

The U.S. State Department, however, issued an Egypt Travel Warning to United States citizens, asking them to consider the risks of travel to Egypt due to threats from terrorist and violent political opposition groups. In 2016, a number of terrorist groups have committed multiple deadly attacks, targeting public venues and tourist sites and public transportation systems. This situation certainly will undermine travelers' confidence in Egypt's safety and security mechanisms.

Tourism is a very important economic activity for Egypt. In general, Egyptians are very friendly to tourists and will try to provide as much assistance as they can. The Egyptian Government, in the meantime, has also maintained a heavy security presence at major tourist cities, sites, and coastal resorts, and major temples and archaeological sites located in and around the Nile valley cities of Luxor and Aswan. Industry executives remind travelers that there is unrest in every country at one time or another, and thus the best tip they can give is to always be accompanied by a tour guide when touring unfamiliar and potentially dangerous places. The Egyptian Antiquities Ministry guarantees that they are taking every step possible to fully restore the tourist police forces at the many iconic sites.

All these efforts to safeguard travelers, however, may not be enough to persuade travelers to visit Egypt. Safety concerns have been deterring many potential visitors from visiting Egypt: the dream of visiting Pyramids of Giza may have to wait for many.

Think about This

1. Do you think that the global media has blown unrest in Egypt and many other countries out of proportion?
2. As hospitality service providers, one of the most important things we can offer a guest is safety and security. Considering this, would you advise a close friend or family member to visit Egypt so soon after its most recent social and political instability?
3. If you were planning a trip to Egypt for this summer, what kinds of things would you need to consider?

Sources

https://travel.state.gov/content/passports/en/alertswarnings/egypt-travel-warning.html

https://www.tripadvisor.com/Attractions-g294200-Activities-Egypt.html

THEORY OF PLANNED BEHAVIOR

Based on the premise of a rational consumer, the Theory of Planned Behavior (Howard and Sheth 1969) is a cognitive model that suggests three major factors will positively influence traveler decision intention and subsequent purchase behavior: behavior belief, normative belief, and control belief. *Behavior belief* refers to a consumer's attitudes toward a destination option, which include the visitor's beliefs about the likelihood of experiencing a set of attributes at a destination. *Normative belief* refers to the influence of social and subjective norms on the consumer. In other words, consumers take into consideration whether others would endorse such a destination choice. In this sense, whether he or she selects a particular travel destination is a function of not only the influences of social norms, but also how much the consumer intends to conform to such social norms. *Control belief* refers to the traveler's belief about the degree of ease or difficulty in traveling to the destination and how much control one may have in implementing one's travel itinerary and plan. For example, if a person

Your Friends Influence You More Than You Think

Information and suggestions from one's friends and relatives are an important form of word-of-mouth. It can exert significant influences on a traveler's decision-making, because their information in general is to be perceived as having a higher level of reliability and relevancy, when compared to other social information sources. Amy Morin, a psychotherapist and an author, summarized consumer psychology research findings about how one's friends may exert influences on one's life. There are five areas of influences:

1. Self-disciplined friends can improve one's own self-control.
2. Fewer friends increase the likelihood a person will take financial risks.
3. Too many social media connections can increase a person's stress level.
4. Close friends can be a positive force for longevity.
5. Friends influence your consumptive and other choices in life.

Think about This

1. How may one's social circle influence one's travel choices?
2. Does word-of-month (WOM) from one's friends/relatives or e-WOM from online travel communities influence a traveler differently or similarly? Why?
3. What factors may influence how much influence one's social connections may exert on one's travel choices?
4. How can tourism marketers and service providers utilize subjective norms to influence traveler decision-making? Are you able to discuss one specific strategy?

Source

Morin, A. 2014. 5 scientific reasons you should choose your friends carefully. https://www.forbes.com/sites/amymorin/2014/10/17/5-scientific-reasons-you-should-choose-your-friends-carefully/#5cbe2b086181

believes that the Maldives as a destination has the best sands and underwater beauty in the Indian Ocean, and that he or she believes that a trip to this destination would be endorsed enthusiastically by his social circle, and that traveling to and staying there is smooth and safe, this consumer will be more likely to have positive intention to travel to the Maldives. This theory explains why marketing communications oriented at influencing traveler destination choice need to go beyond destination attribute based messages. Peer-related and self-related factors need to be carefully programmed in.

Dual Processes in Decision-Making

According to Nobel Laureate and founder of Behavioral Economics Daniel Kahneman, human decision-making follows a dual-process system: an *effortless system 1* (implicit) and an *effortful system 2* (explicit) (Stanovich and West 2000). The system 1 way of thinking and decision-making possesses the characteristics of being automatic, unconscious reasoning, rapid, associative,

contextualized, and non-verbal, non-logical, and belief-based. This entails consumer cognitive activities such as recognition, perception, and orientation. The system 2 way of decision-making tends to involve conscious reasoning. Such decision-making is controlled, deliberate, logic, rule-based, and sequential. This exhibits behavioral patterns of rule following, comparisons, and weighing of options.

The dual processing system theory recognizes that human rationality is bounded, and that the systems of thought that depend on intuition and emotion, rather than reflection and analysis, are important in understanding consumer decision-making. Further, this dual-process approach acknowledges the importance of judgment heuristics, biases, cues, and situation factors in human decision-making.

A person may employ both automatic and controlled processes in making vacation decisions. What mode is dominant may depend upon the individual's personal disposition, life situation, the individual's experiences, and the nature of the occasion of taking such vacations. For example, researchers have noted that gender may play a role. Females have a higher tendency to rely on *associative* and *contextualized* ways of thinking and decision-making, whereas males may resort more to *rule-based* evaluation and decision-making. Another example is that travelers with low knowledge about a destination or service (e.g., novice visitors) are more likely to process information heuristically and are more influenced by simple cue effects such as expert endorsement or friends' recommendations. This information has been utilized by tourism and hospitality marketers in their effort to gain consumers' trust and engender positive attitudes toward products and services. One such example is Zagat restaurant reviews. Zagat, a restaurant guide, was founded in 1979 and was

regarded as an authority in restaurant reviews prior to the Internet age. Consumers hold a high trust in Zagat reviews and refer to these expert reviews regularly for dining decisions in the United States. Google acquired Zagat in 2011. Google has integrated Zagat into its location-based search services.

THEORY OF CONSUMPTION VALUES

Travelers make decisions based on the value they perceive that the choice will bring them. What may be the various value dimensions associated with a consumptive scenario? Researchers have developed various propositions regarding this. A primary example is the *Theory of*

QUICK TRIP 12.3

Heuristic Cues and Hotel Review Information Trustworthiness

In recent years, with the ready availability of online consumer reviews, consumers have increasingly resorted to online reviews for information and decision support. In fact, according to Forrester Research, more than 80 percent of online consumers consult others' reviews when making purchasing decisions. Online consumer reviews have become a major assistive mechanism for consumer decision support. Travel purchases such as hotel booking and restaurant selection are such products where consumers increasingly resort to online reviews for information.

Meanwhile travelers are increasingly willing to share online their views of and experiences with tourism and hospitality services. With an increasingly large amount of consumer generated information available, one potential challenge is information overload and information trustworthiness on the part of the consumers as these e-WOMs are essentially generated by strangers, albeit fellow travelers. Consumers spend a large amount of time to filter out irrelevant information.

Research on how prospective hotel consumers consult with and process information provided by online reviews has shown that consumers tend to use simplified heuristics to arrive at judgments about the desirability of potential hotel choices. Researchers observe that when a review site provides a reviewer's demographics (e.g., age and gender) alongside a hotel review, prospective hotel customers perceive the review more useful, more trustworthy, and have a higher tendency to select the hotel among similar alternatives.

Think about This

1. How does traveler-generated information assist travel and hospitality consumers?
2. Why do you think providing reviewer demographic information may improve consumers' likelihood to favor a hotel product?
3. What cues do prospective hotel consumers use to arrive at quality judgment?
4. What quantifiable information are provided by tripadvisor.com? Have they effectively simplified cues for traveler decision-making? Can they further improve their review platform design?
5. How do we combat fake or robot-generated reviews?

Source

Su, W. T., Lehto, M. R., Lehto, X. Y., Yi, J. S., Shi, Z., & Liu, X. 2017. The Influence of Reviewer Demographic Information Provision on Trust and Purchase Intent for Users of Online Websites. *Journal of Quality Assurance in Hospitality & Tourism*, 18 (3): 328–353.

Consumption Values developed by Sheth, Newman, and Gross (1991). These scholars suggest that consumer choice is a function of five consumption values: functional value, social value, emotional value, conditional value, and epistemic value. These five values are seen as independent of each other, with each exerting differential influences in given choice situations.

Function value refers to the perceived utility acquired from a product's capacity for functional, utilitarian, or physical performance (e.g., quality perception, price perception). A tourism destination or service provider can provide this value by developing or possessing salient functional, utilitarian, and physical attributes. In this sense, knowledge of how consumers evaluate a business or destination's existing attributes can be helpful in understanding why consumers make their choices for or against a service or product. Therefore, it would be useful for a destination or business to periodically conduct research regarding their target market segments' evaluations of the various functional attributes, and align them with consumer expectations.

Social value of a product or brand is defined as the perceived utility acquired from a consumer's association with one or more social groups. Consumers place higher value on options that allow them to be seen as being associated with certain desirable stereotyped socio-demographic, psychographic, or cultural groups. Travelers can make favorable decisions because of the symbolic meanings that they attach to a destination or product. For instance, when a traveler wants to be viewed as an environmentally responsible person, he or she may have a higher tendency to select destinations they perceive as a green and sustainable destination because of the social value associated with such a choice. Travelers use their travel choices as a means to project their social-image. Tourism products in general possess such symbolic values in excess of their functional value for travelers. In other words, the more a destination or tourism service provider is being perceived as possessing qualities that can help boost one's social image, the more likely the traveler will keep the product in their choice consideration set or make favorable decisions toward the said place or product.

Emotional value refers to the alternative's capacity to evoke positive feelings. Travelers can make a positive decision toward a certain destination or service provider because they perceive them as being capable of delivering desired affects or possessing certain affective traits. For example, a destination may be viewed as being romantic. When a traveler is seeking a sense of romance, this destination can stand out among various alternatives and steer positive decision-making toward this destination.

Epistemic value refers to an alternative's ability to satisfy curiosity, novelty, or desire for knowledge. *Conditional value* refers to an alternative's ability to provide value pertaining to specific circumstances and occasions. For example, some destinations may have seasonal values (e.g., snowbird destinations), or special occasion value (e.g., honeymoon destinations). These conditional associations with places and products can invoke positive associations in traveler's decision-making.

If travelers are value-driven, then tourism destinations and businesses need to understand what travelers value and where they should focus their attention on in order to acquire needed market advantage. The consumptive value model affords an approach for tourism providers to assess how travelers and prospective travelers may value their destinations and businesses differently. This knowledge in return will help them develop better marketing communication messages oriented toward these values. It also allows a destination to strategically develop their offerings to maximize the potential for consumers to make positive decisions and choices.

THE TRAVELER'S BUYING PROCESS

When making a travel purchase, a consumer moves through several stages. The characteristics of each of these steps are examined in this section. The wise marketing manager realizes that different communication strategies are appropriate for different stages of the buying process.

Attention and Awareness

When deciding whether or not to visit a previously unknown destination area, an individual may at first be unaware of its potential as a travel destination. The destination area has to be brought to the awareness or attention of the potential traveler. A prime function in communicating to the consumer is to gain attention. It is easier, less time-consuming, and less costly to sell London as a travel destination than it is to sell Tibet. Part of the reason is that more people know more about and have specific opinions or attitudes about London as a vacation destination than about Tibet. To sell Tibet would require a rather lengthy educational process.

Mass media advertising can be very influential at this point. A slogan or a jingle aimed at arousing curiosity can be successful in gaining the viewer's attention. This is the first step in the buying process. One reason that destinations pursue the Summer or Winter Olympics is that the television and print exposure creates a huge awareness of the destination. From then on, it is up to those at the destination to build on this awareness to move potential visitors through the buying process. As people move from the awareness stage to the familiarity stage, their interest and likelihood to visit increases. However, moving from nonawareness to awareness does not necessarily increase the likelihood of visiting the destination area. This is not surprising. Once aware of a particular destination area, individuals might decide that visiting it will not satisfy needs and wants important to them. They "drop out" of the buying process.

At this point, there is some indication that individuals make an initial judgment as to the extent to which the destination area meets their needs. If it does, it is looked at more closely. At this early stage of the process, consumers' beliefs about a destination's attributes which help to satisfy a potential traveler's specific motives are influential in facilitating a destination to stay in the consumer's destination choice set. Later on in the decision-making process, inhibitors—"attributes which are not congruent with his or her motives" (Um and Crompton 1992)—become more influential.

Knowledge and Comprehension

The task in the next stage of the buying process is to make the customer *goal-directed*. If the potential traveler's attention has been successfully stimulated, she or he seeks out more information on the destination area. The attempt is to become more knowledgeable about what the destination area has to offer, to comprehend what it is all about. The emphasis is on information, and the task of the communicator is to provide sufficient information to direct the potential traveler toward purchase.

As we discussed in the prior section, travelers go through dual information processing when internalizing information. Novice travelers may respond to market information that is presented with heuristic and associative cues. Experienced visitors, however, may prefer detailed or specific information about the destination. Research indicates that communications to first-time travelers need to focus on being persuasive, whereas repeat visitors need to be reminded of the destination as a competitive future alternative.

Advertising is again important at this stage. The choice of media is crucial. Media should be chosen that can convey a great deal of information. Brochures or the web can do this, as can online magazine and newspaper stories. Radio and television advertisement may not effectively provide the large amounts of information needed at this stage. It is important to talk about the destination area in terms of the benefits offered. When a destination presents itself in terms of their benefits to travelers, it will become more relevant to the audience. To the extent that we understand a message, and see it as relevant, we are more inclined to not only pay attention to it but also comprehend it.

Interest and Liking

If the communication so far has been effective, the potential traveler next moves to developing a liking, interest, or attitude about the destination area. The promotional objectives at this stage are to create or reinforce existing positive attitudes or images or to correct negative attitudes or images. A positive attitude will influence the individual's tendency or predisposition to visit that particular destination area. It is also a function of how well we have gained the traveler's attention and provided sufficient information for him to determine whether or not the benefits of the destination area optimally match his needs and wants. Attitudes are difficult to change because new incoming information is often screened to conform to an old attitude. The interest in a particular destination area influences how much effort a consumer will put into the comprehension of a particular message.

Evaluation and Preference

At this stage, the prospective traveler evaluates and compares viable destination options. After evaluating various alternatives, the consumer develops a preference or desire for a destination. The importance of emotive advertising is somewhat less at this stage. The most effective types of messages are *testimonial* and *comparison advertisements*. In a testimonial advertisement, a person, usually a well-known public figure, praises what is being sold. The hope is that if the viewer or reader respects the person in the message, their opinion on the product or service being sold is respected. It is crucial that the spokesperson be believable. It is also important, for maximum impact, that the person chosen to be in the advertisement has some connection with what is being sold. A form of testimonial is the rating found in various guidebooks and online travel magazines. To the extent that the rating system is respected, advertising the rating gains the respect of the readers. The same effect can be

QUICK TRIP 12.4

Marketing Deception: A Tale as Old as Time

Let's say you and your friends are planning a spring break trip to New York. Your friends put you in charge of finding a hotel. You can't afford anything really luxurious but it's important that your rooms be clean and secure. Would you ever book a hotel room without first looking at pictures of it online? In today's world of the Internet and apps you can look at pictures and reviews of hotels in a matter of seconds. Despite the rules of the Federal Trade Commission, descriptions and pictures do not always accurately depict the hotel and its accommodations. Old hotels have been known to post old pictures of the property when it was still in its prime. Sometimes booking guests will not be informed of hotel construction. More often than not, hotels are accused of puffing. This can be defined as "creative wording" in order to make the property sound better than it actually is.

In a *USA Today* article written in May 2011, author Gary Stoller reviews a compelling collection of complaints from frequent travelers. Each of these travelers has had more than one experience in which the online media material significantly oversold the actual quality of the room and hotel. Guests arrive to significant disappointment, leave frustrated, and feel as though they have been taken advantage of. There had been complaints after the Ritz Carlton Coconut Grove put out promotional pictures of one of their beds garnished with a blanket of fresh flowers. Property spokesperson, Michelle Payer, responded to the complaints saying "the general look of the room is what travelers can expect [the hotels may] take creative license and move plants to add beauty to the shots." Although some would say that these added items are deceptive, it can be argued that it's a harmless marketing strategy.

Think about This

1. Do you agree that hotels should be allotted creative license when putting together promotional material?
2. How far is too far?
3. What are the repercussions for "puffing" in online marketing?
4. Should there be a law against inaccurate hotel portrayals?

Source

Stoller, Gary. "Could This Be the Same Hotel We Saw Online?" *USA Today.* 5 May 2011, sec. B: 1B–2B.

---

gained by "testimony" from someone who has already visited the destination area. Leveraging a potential visitor's social media network and incentivizing informal word-of-mouth network to work as social influencers can be effective.

In a comparison advertisement, one destination area or facility is mentioned in a promotional message in comparison with another. The destination areas are compared on particular attributes. For this kind of message to work, it is necessary to select, for the basis of comparison, attributes that the customer thinks are important. It is crucial that the destination area being advertised be stronger on those attributes than the competition.

Intention and Conviction

At this stage in the buying process, the potential travelers are convinced that the benefits of the destination area meet their needs and wants and are almost at the point of purchase. Studies have shown that the intention to purchase precedes the actual purchase.

Purchase and Action

If the potential traveler has reached the conviction stage of the buying process, the barrier to travel is likely to be lack of time or money. It is clear that the motivation is present. The marketing task is to identify the barrier and develop a product to bridge it. If the problem is lack of money, a tour package may be successful. Lodging in smaller, cheaper hotels can be suggested. If the problem is one of time, it may be possible to offer a package that capitalizes on the time available. One of the reasons that fly-cruise packages have been developed is to respond to a market that has the money and the motivation, but not the time. Previously, when ships cruised out of New York much time was lost because two days of bad weather often had to be experienced before the ships

Accommodating the Changing Traveler

Travel-related businesses are increasingly adapting to consumers' tendency of increasing use of online search and purchase, the growing popularity of social media, and fast-evolving digital technologies that empower intelligent consumer decision-making. Businesses can leverage digital innovations to their advantage in direct channel sales, marketing, cross-selling, dynamic pricing, and inventory management (Borgogna et al. 2016). Borgogna and his fellow researchers summarized the following five prevailing themes globally.

1. The increasing use of online channels for search and booking (e.g., airlines, online travel agents [OTAs], and metasearch websites)
2. The use of multiple devices during the research and booking process (e.g., desktops, smartphones, and tablets)
3. The growing popularity of using firsthand experiences shared on social media as supporting input in the travel decision-making process. Partnerships between social media platforms and travel suppliers will become more common as a way to integrate social media into the sales and service channel.
4. The increasing relevance of loyalty programs. Loyalty programs incentivize travelers to stay loyal to businesses and share genuine insights and preferences for travel suppliers.
5. In the corporate market, travel management companies (TMCs) are offering solutions such as applications to blend company policy management reporting requirements with traveler schedule alerts and other functions for ease of use.

Think about This

1. Can you provide examples of practices that integrate social media platforms with purchasing possibilities?
2. Can you give examples of how destinations and travel suppliers can effectively mobilize interested consumers to actual travel purchasers?

Source

Borgogna, A., Stroh, S., Hilz, A., Agarwalla, A., and Jakovijevic, I. 2016. Connecting With The Customer: How Airlines Must Adapt Their Distribution Business Model. https://www.forbes.com/sites/strategyand/2016/11/15/connecting-with-the-customer-how-airlines-must-adapt-their-distribution-business-model/#6b8d05755443

---

reached sunny climates. The solution has been to fly travelers to Florida, sail out of a southern port, and give more sun for the time available.

Another example of how marketers attempt to induce actual purchase is the use of dynamic pricing strategies. With rapid advances in technology, airlines and hotels have developed a new generation of algorithms to understand who the prospective consumer is in terms of his or her online search patterns, timing, past online purchase history, and loyalty status. They then offer differentiating prices at the time of potential online purchase moments. Price customization algorithms and software can change price based on consumer online profile. Given that significant travel purchasing activities are conducted online, this or other similar moment-of-sale strategies can help maximize consumers'

purchasing probability and achieve optimal pricing for the businesses.

Adoption and Advocacy

The final stage of the buying process is the adoption stage. At this point, the traveler has become a repeat purchaser. People return to a destination for several reasons (McKercher and Wong 2004):

- The risk of a bad experience is less.
- They want to meet the same kind of people.
- They feel an emotional attachment to the place.
- They want to explore the destination more widely.

To achieve this end, it is necessary to provide a quality experience to the first-time traveler. It is unlikely that either first-timers or repeat visitors will return to a destination if they are dissatisfied with the experience (Alegre and Cladera 2006). It is further likely that repeat visits are affected more by how well the destination exceeds travelers' expectations than simply meeting expectations; however, advertising also has a role to play. The necessity for some form of communication to the purchaser results because of *cognitive dissonance*. Cognitive dissonance occurs after a choice between two or more alternatives has been made. It is a feeling of anxiety, a feeling that perhaps the choice made was not the best one. The amount of dissonance felt is influenced by the type of decision made. The anxiety is stronger if:

- The rejected alternative is attractive.
- The decision is important.
- The purchaser becomes aware of negative characteristics in the choice chosen.
- The number of alternatives increases.
- The alternatives are perceived as being similar.
- The decision made goes against a strongly held belief.
- The decision is a recent one.

Because vacation travel represents an important decision, it has the potential for creating a great deal of anxiety after the purchase has been made (Figure 12.1). The potential is even greater if the traveler has chosen among a large number of attractive alternate destination areas. The key is to indicate to the traveler as soon as possible after the decision has been made that the decision has been a good one. A note to the purchaser of a package tour or cruise may be sufficient to avoid second thoughts and cancellations. For advertisers, the key is to provide in their advertisements information that purchasers can use to justify to themselves the purchase made, as well as the messages to convince people to repurchase. In today's social media-driven world, engaging travelers post-trip to encourage them to share their travel experiences with their friends and fellow travelers in online travel forums can be effective in cultivating sense of community and thereby a sense of reassurance that a purchase decision was wisely made. This type of traveler engagement will be conducive to managing traveler cognitive dissonance and generating repeat travelers for a destination.

FIGURE 12.1 Cognitive dissonance on travel decisions needs to be managed.

TRAVEL INFORMATION AND DECISION SUPPORT

Travel information plays an essential role for traveler decision-making. Consumers largely depend on information to form interests and opinions, as well as to derive judgments of quality. Although the need for information for travel decision support is apparent, the ways travelers gather information, comprehend information, and utilize information for decision-making is not as well understood. Understanding traveler information behavior is of primary importance to destination marketers.

Information Needs

The value travelers place on travel information has to do with what information needs they have. There are five need domains of travel information (Vogt and Fesenmaier 1998; Choe, Fesenmaier, and Vogt 2017, Figure 12.2). The first is *Functional* value. These needs are goal-oriented. Functional information pertains to product and destination knowledge, uncertainty and risk reduction, utility, efficiency on time spent, and cost/price comparisons. The second need category is *hedonic* need. Visitors seek out information for phenomenological, experiential, sensory, and emotional purposes. The third category of information need is *innovation* need. This need is derived from a traveler's need for novelty seeking, variety seeking, and creativity. The fourth dimension of information need is *aesthetic* need. Travelers seek out information to allow their imagination to roam, and to envision their future trip. The fifth aspect of information need is called *sign* need, which describes interpersonal, social, and symbolic aspects of needs of a traveler including advisory (e.g., information sharing), social (socializing), and symbolic (e.g., demonstrate social status) purposes.

Although traveler information need is multidimensional, these five areas of needs may not be equal in importance. Travelers consider functional information needs the most prominent. There are differences in information needs between the pre-trip information needs (for pre-trip decision-making support) and on-the-go information needs (for on-trip decision-making support). In general, the functional information needs decrease somewhat when at a destination while the importance of hedonic and innovation needs increase.

Traveler Sensitivity to Information

You may have encountered in your Facebook newsfeed paid travel infomercials or traveler-generated contents delivered at a time that Facebook's Dynamic Ads algorithm detects that you have travel interests. Some of them pique your interest and you may click on the provided link to check it out, while others are simply ignored by you. Today's consumers are in fact challenged with information overload with the decentralized and multi-platform-based information dissemination structure afforded by the digital technologies. As a result, understanding of how sensitive consumers are toward information in today's marketplace is useful.

There are a number of factors that will influence one's *sensitivity* to receiving incoming information. Our sensitivity is first a function of how inclined we are to that information. If, for example, we feel strongly inclined toward taking a vacation, we will readily be more receptive to information regarding vacations. If we have a strong preference for a Bahamas vacation, any information about the Bahamas—travel packages, the weather, the political situation—is likely to receive attention. If we have decided against a European vacation and our preference to go there is not strong at a particular time, our sensitivity to information about Europe will be low. Consequently, we will probably largely tune out much of the information pertaining to Europe that comes our way from the trade or other sources. The chance for information to be noticed and processed by consumers will be improved if the information is highly relevant to the consumers' interest and preferences at the time the information is delivered. Today's big data and analytical technology, in fact, has enabled such precise timing and relevancy much more effectively than ever before.

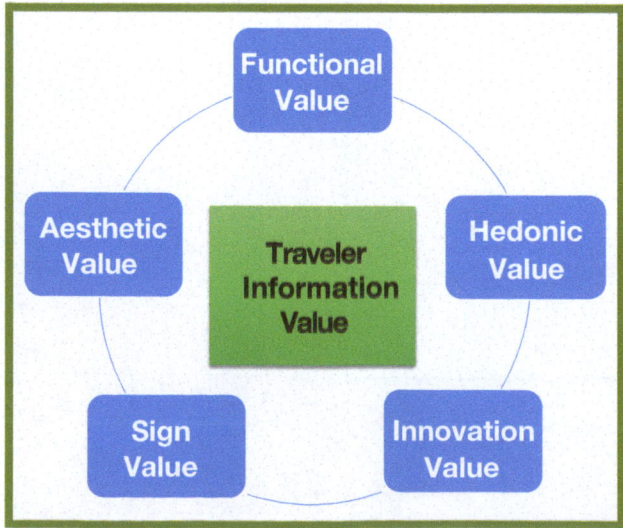

FIGURE 12.2 **Traveler information valuation.** | Adapted from Choe, Fesenmaier, and Vogt 2017.

Our sensitivity to information is also a function of the characteristics of the message itself. If the information received is familiar to us already, it may be too simple and straightforward, or be perceived as boring and thus be ignored or further processed. On the other hand, if the information presented—an advertisement, a travelogue, a personal opinion—is too complicated for us to absorb, the high level of ambiguity may lead us to put up a shield to "defend" ourselves, and the information will not get our attention. This process may be thought of as consumers' effort to control the quantity of information received in today's market environment of information overload. Information presented should be aimed at the capacity of the target audience to absorb it cognitively.

In order to gain visitors' attentions, presenting unique assets of your destination or business with visuals of *aesthetic* qualities that consumers crave (e.g., breathtaking sunsets) may be effective. *Linguistic and communication styles* that fit a particular media platform can improve the chance of a message being processed. Injecting entertainment value such as humor can also attract attention. After all, consumers resonate with values such as uniqueness, aesthetics, and entertainment in addition to practical information such as product availability and price.

Consumer sensitivity to information can also be influenced by *Technical factors* such as the object, product, or service as it actually exists. The various elements of a particular product or service, such as price, quality, service, availability, and distinctiveness can be communicated through the product or service itself. These inputs are termed significative stimuli.

There are several factors that are termed technical. *Size* is an important consideration. To many, size is equated with quality. The larger the company, airplane, or hotel, the better the service is perceived to be. Generally speaking, larger advertisements will receive greater attention. A travel company might use a big advertisement or emphasize the size of its operation to gain more attention and give the impression of quality to the reader. *Color* is an important factor impacting one's sensitivity and interpretation of information. Travelers, for example, may associate the color green with products that are socially responsible and experiences that are peaceful. There are culturally influenced preferences for color as well. Destinations and its service providers need to understand the psychology of color and choose colors carefully in their marketing communications and experience design.

The *intensity* of a stimulus also affects the perception of it. The greater the intensity, the more attention it attracts. Intensity can refer to the brightness of colors,

the use of certain "strong" words, or the importance of a present or past purchase or experience. Stressing the importance of a decision to buy will increase the attention given a message. It can also refer to repeating the stimulus, thereby intensifying the message. The more a message is seen, the greater the chance that it will attract attention. *Moving objects* attract more attention than stationary objects. This accounts for much of the success of advertising on television. Online banner advertising and point-of-purchase displays with moving parts—in a travel agency, for example—can also be used to good effect. The increased popularity of virtual tours over the Internet can have an impact on the visitor. Such virtual tours are shown to result in visitors getting a more vivid image and perceiving the destination as being more attractive.

The *position* of a piece of information can affect whether or not the information will attract attention. In a brochure rack, pamphlets at shoulder height will attract the most attention. When placing advertisements in a newspaper, it is important to consider that the upper part of the page attracts more attention. When placing advertisement in mobile-based social media platforms such as Facebook, the positioning of information needs to coincide with the right timing in the flow of user social activities more so than the size or location factors.

Contrast is another element that affects the attention given a stimulus. If competing messages are bright, colorful, and somewhat gaudy, a very simple, dignified message may be noticed because of the contrast. The final technical factor is that of *isolation*. Advertisers are fond of putting a border called "white space," around their messages to isolate them from other messages on a page. As noted earlier, these elements interact often in contradictory ways. The greatest impact comes when several factors combine to give a more significant effect.

Information Perception Bias

We behave—buy, travel, stay at home, and so on—based in part on our perception of information received. Any information from either the social or commercial environment is molded into an image through our perceptual processes. The resultant image is less a function of the promotional message of a destination than of our individual perception of that message.

The information received, however, is distorted by how that information is perceived because a consumer will internalize the information through his or her own judgment lens. Two people presented with the same travel advertisement may perceive it differently. One person may view the advertisement positively, the other negatively. Feedback from our motives, the alternatives considered, and the decision criteria used will affect our image of information received. If we are strongly motivated to seek a historical, cultural vacation, one which could readily be satisfied by a trip to the province of Quebec, and if it is important (decision criteria) that we avoid crowds, then an advertisement showing throngs of people at an art festival in Quebec will be perceived negatively. Similarly, an advertisement that stresses the magnificent scenery of the province will not be perceived positively because that image runs counter to that which motivates us.

Although information from both the commercial and social environments is distorted, information received from personal sources is less subject to **perceptual bias**. This is because information from the social environment is regarded more favorably by the individual receiving the information. It should be remembered, however, that before a friend or relative gives us information, he or she has already distorted it to meet his or her value system. A recommendation of a wonderful place to visit, stay, or eat will only be given in those terms if it has met with what our friend determines is a wonderful place to visit, stay, or eat. This, of course, depends on whether or not our friend perceives that his or her experience satisfied unmet needs.

There is also liable to be less distortion when information is actively sought. When the visitor is unsure of which vacation will result in a more satisfying experience—when preference for any particular vacation is low—there will be less bias in the way information is perceived.

In addition, there will be greater reliance on the **social environment** for information if the visitor is unsure of the satisfactions from various alternatives and if the purchase is important. To the extent that we are influenced by the social group of which we are a part, our motives will be influenced by the (subjectively weighted) information from our social environment. Similarly, the social environment will affect the alternatives a buyer considers, particularly where experience is lacking.

Also, information received will be fed into the buyer's decisions criteria and will influence those criteria in the direction in which the information is perceived. A visitor, for example, may look for the lowest priced hotel. If information is received that suggests that paying a little more will actually be a better value, and if the visitor perceives this to be true, the decision criterion of "lowest cost" may change.

Traveler Information Behavior Characteristics

Have you sometimes caught yourself watching TV and having your phone at your fingertip texting or posting at the same time? You are not alone. In today's digitally connected world, travel information is becoming omnipresent, and it can take a multitude of shapes and forms. Travel information platforms and channels that travelers utilize are increasingly diverse and seemingly not following a clear and structured pattern, reflecting the more disjoint fashion of traveler decision-making. Increasingly, consumers employ multiple sources and channels for decision support. There are a number of characteristics related to how travelers search and use information:

- **Expansiveness**

Because of the intangible and experiential nature of a travel product, not to mention the distance factor, and the multi-component planning and decision-making modes needed (e.g., transportation, lodging, food, sightseeing), visitors' need for information can be expansive and involving. Travelers' need for and uses of information permeate into the **entire trip spectrum:** including whether to travel, where to travel, what transportation and lodging facilities to use, as well as onsite travel decisions such as where to eat, where to shop, what activities to do, and sites to visit.

According to Expedia research, travelers on average visit thirty-eight sites before booking. The information travelers seek can be as concrete as information about how to pack, what to pack, safety, money exchange, or as abstract as information about how is a place in general or travel philosophy. Figure 12.3 is an illustrative example of a traveler's information use along the travel journey.

- **Continuousness**

Prior to the Internet age, a traveler's information search happened mostly at the pre-trip stage to support the major decisions they had to make for the trip, including destination decisions, accommodation decisions, transportation decisions, onsite attraction, and route decisions. Since most of these decisions were made prior to the trip, so was information search. As a result of the omnipresence of the Internet and wireless connection, social media, smartphone, and other mobile accesses, traveler information search and use has become much more of a continuous process throughout the entirety of

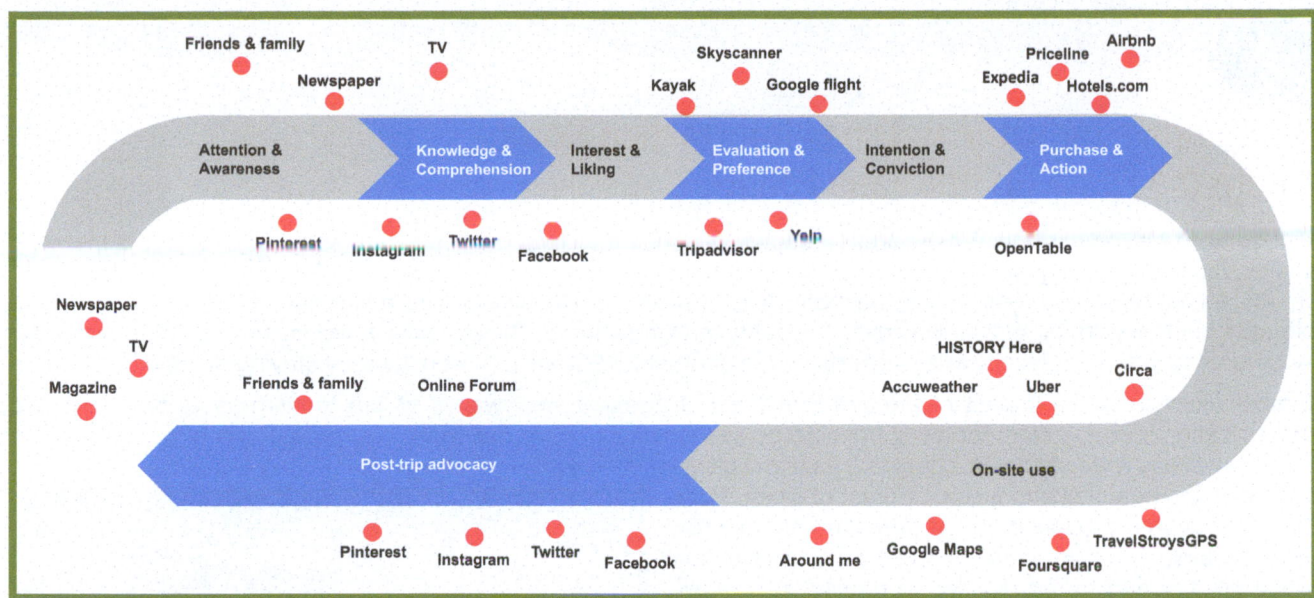

FIGURE 12.3 Traveler information use along the travel journey.

a consumer travel journey instead of the traditional pre-trip decision-making stage. In fact, travel information and visitor information seeking behavior continues after a trip is completed.

- **Multi-dimensional value**

Travelers' search for information for functional purposes of decision-making (availability, choices, price comparisons, peer reviews) but also to satisfy innovation, sign, hedonic, aesthetic needs, as well as sharing and social needs as explained earlier in this chapter. Understanding consumer information value dimensions and use behavior allows marketers to effectively create persuasive communication message content strategies, creative format strategies, and information delivery channel strategies.

- **Multi-channel**

Travelers rely on personal information and prior knowledge. Travelers can obtain their travel information via popular cultural sources such as books, newspapers, and other forms of popular culture literature (such as films and TV shows). Other examples include trade oriented information sources such as tourism organizations, guidebooks, and travel magazines (e.g., *Travel and Leisure, Conde Nast, Lonely Planet, National Geographic*), and traditional travel intermediaries (e.g., travel agency pre-planned itineraries, travel guides).

Thanks to the advancement of digital and mobile technologies, travelers have increasingly utilized online-based, mobile-based, and social media-based information sources and platforms. Personal travel blogs and micro-blogs, online travel communities, and online travel reviews are such examples.

Although use of the Internet to plan and book travel has increased in recent years, there are indications that the traditional travel agency services still play a role for traveler trip planning and purchasing. *Travel + Leisure* magazine reports that millennials, the fastest growing traveler segment, have discovered the value of relying on travel agents, not just to make travel reservations but also to seek trip decision advice such as where to go and where to stay. The 2017–2018 Portrait of American Travelers by MMGY Global (Blount 2017) shows that 33 percent of millennial respondents indicated an intention to use travel agents in the coming two years. When the needs of the traveler are complex, it seems important to people to be able to sit down with a real person. Travelers like that an agent:

- Asks questions to better understand a traveler's needs
- Is willing to help customize itineraries to best fit those needs
- Is able to book complex itineraries that are hard to book online

QUICK TRIP 12.6

The Creative Industry as Travel Information Source: Where the Films Go, the Fans Follow

According to research, popular films and TV shows influence travelers' destination choices. One finding is that fans are flocking to the settings where popular films or TV shows are shot. The movie *Game of Thrones* filmed in Dubrovnik, Croatia, for example, has seen 10 percent more visitor arrivals in 2016, an increase in part due to the town's prominent role as a backdrop in the movie. However, residents in Dubrovnik felt the squeeze when close to 9,300 cruise passengers descended on the city in a single day while another 25,000 visitors were already staying in the city.

Another example is the impact of the film *Star Wars*. It awakens new waves of film tourism as its fans seek out these locations. People from far away travel to go see locations where *Star Wars* was shot. Parts of *Star Wars: The Forces Awakens* were shot at Puzzlewood, a unique place located in the beautiful and historic Forest of Dean. Puzzlewood became a popular tourist attraction as a result, and fans looking for an authentic Luke Skywalker experience are flocking to the location in droves. This small ancient village in West England became almost an overnight sensation for travelers to visit because of *Star Wars*.

Not only have screen tourists spent money in the area on restaurants and hotels, they talk about it in social media which creates further interest from fans all over the world. The tourist volume not only has a locale impact, its impact has spread over the entire Great Britain. Market research shows that screen tourism is one of the major motivators for both international visitors and domestic tourists traveling within the U.K. Thanks to the *Lord of the Rings*, New Zealand has become the most popular tourist destination of film and television fanatics. Below is a list of the world's most popular screen tourism destinations.

© TheLitCreativeServices/Shutterstock.com

FIGURE 12.4 Limestone arch, known as the Azure Window at sunset, in Dwerja, Gozo, Malta: a location that was used as a wedding scene in *Game of Thrones*.

Sample Tourist Destinations Inspired By Film and TV

Rank	Destination	Film
1	New Zealand	Lord of the Rings
2	New York City	Sex and the City
3	Northern Ireland	Game of Thrones
4	Las Vegas	The Hangover
5	West Bay, Dorset	Broadchurch
6	Alnwick Castle, N'thumberland	Harry Potter
7	Paris	Inception
8	Benidorm, Spain	Benidorm
9	Iceland	Game of Thrones
10	Malta	Game of Thrones
11	Skiathos, Greece	Mama Mia
12	Vatican City	Angels and Demons
13	Salzburg	The Sound of Music
14	Ripon, Yorkshire	Downton Abbey
15	Ko Phi Phi Leh, Thailand	The Beach

QUICK TRIP 12.6 CONTINUED

Think about This

1. Why is information from films and TV programs useful in inducing travelers' interests in traveling?
2. When consumers make a decision to visit a place because they see a place in their favorite onscreen film or movie, which one of the dual processes is at work?
3. Using Theory of Consumption Values, can you explain what types of values visitors may place upon visiting film-inspired destinations?
4. How can tourism destinations effectively capitalize on such fanatic sentiments in their marketing activities?
5. What may be the social and economic impacts of film tourism phenomenon in a confined tourism destination such as small historical cities? How best to manage them?

Sources

https://www.buzzfeed.com/annamendoza/middle-earth-wins?utm_term=.xyDEwwBvW#.dcMNqqg6P

https://www.theguardian.com/film/2015/dec/26/uk-tourism-star-wars-fans-feel-force-heroes-footsteps

http://www.puzzlewood.net/

- ### Social, mobile, and location specific

User-generated travel information is prevalent as posting and sharing about trips and leisure activities is one of the most popular online social media activities for consumers. Travelers publish travel-related content via a plethora of platforms and applications. A few such platforms are Instagram, Facebook, Twitter, Wechat, Weibo, Line, and What's up. Some of these applications have worldwide users, while others are more regional-based. As such, travelers' information needs and information behavior has taken on various technology-dictated tendencies and the sources of the information tend to be increasingly coming from social sources. Online user-generated or referred-to information plays a prominent role in traveler decision support.

In some sense, today's travelers are *less "pre-planned"* and more *nimble and spontaneous* in their decision-making and purchases, thanks to smartphones and mobile apps. Because travel planning and decisions have become much more spontaneous, travelers' information search behavior is becoming more dynamic and less structured. Of increasing importance is the use of social media and social networking sites. Social media allow consumers to be providers rather than mere recipients of information. Sites like tripadvisor and I Go You Go allow travelers to post reviews of their vacation experiences.

Travelers play a dual role in information provision. They are *information creators* and *information curators*. They create travel information by posting and blogging about their vacations. They create information by responding to questions and inquiries in virtual travel communities and by commenting online in other public forums (e.g., on travel bloggers sites, online product evaluative sites such as tripadvisor.com, or online newspaper travel sections). On the other hand, they also curate and share travel-related information in their own social spaces. One example would be a person who sees an interesting article about a travel story someone else has written and then shares it in his or her Facebook page with his or her own comments.

Travelers can be powerful *social influencers* for marketers. This increase in review information is moving control of the marketing messages away from companies and into the hands of the consumer. Marketers need to find innovative ways to meet consumers through social media channels and mobile applications. *Location-specific, real-time information* provision through mobile technologies is expected by consumers.

- ### Visual and virtual

We all know that a picture was worth a thousand words in the past. However, the importance of visual information has been magnified by the recent explosion of such information available not only from tourism providers and travel bloggers, but also from consumers themselves via various online channels. For example, Google's research suggests that three out of five travelers' decisions are influenced by watching YouTube videos.

Visual information plays an efficient role in tangibilizing experiential products such as travel. Research also shows that they are more effective in improving travelers' comprehension, recollection, and retention of information. Visual information allows travelers to

QUICK TRIP 12.7

No Apps, No Trips: Useful Travel Apps

There are many travel apps to assist travelers with their trip planning, activity planning, purchasing, or experiencing a trip. Consumers can also simply have apps to get inspired by enjoying places via virtual reality apps. Many of these apps allow travelers to obtain location-specific travel-related information. They greatly assist travelers' information needs. They greatly assist traveler decision-making and enrich traveler onsite destination experiences. Below is a sample list of popular travel apps that travelers can use at various points of their vacation journey.

App Name	What does it do?
GoogleEarth	A free app that has 3D imagery, curated video content, and other features that allow a person to sample places before making visit decisions.
Roadtrippers	A free app with an interactive map of restaurants, attractions, hotels, natural wonders, and "weird stuff" along your route.
Sygic Travel	An app allowing travelers to access attractions in a city and a list of tours one can book on the spot.
Ascape	A free virtual reality app that allows travelers to have teleporting experiences of places. The service has more than one hundred virtual tours of gorgeous destinations around the world including resorts, cities, and experiences.
YouVisit	YouVisit is a free app dedicated specifically to virtual reality tours. The tours include 360° video as well as 360° interactive panoramic photos.
Smart Layover	A free app to allow travelers to book sightseeing tours and last-minute lodging options in over 140 countries.
Four Square	A free app to help tourists locate what people love in a given town.
History HERE	A free app by A&E to assist travelers to locate historic spots in ordinary places.
TravelStorysGPS	A free audio-tour app to use synchronized GPS to inform travelers about their surroundings (e.g., National Parks).
AroundMe	A free app informing tourists about closest gas stations, bars, ATMs, etc.
Wikihood	A free app that compiles information about a given place (important sites, culture, history).

Think about This

1. How do travel apps change consumer trip planning behavior?
2. How do travel apps change the way travelers experience a destination?
3. Would virtual reality apps reduce consumers' motivation to travel to the actual places they have experienced via virtual channels?
4. What about non-app travelers? How may their information behavior differ from app users?

Sources

https://www.gearbrain.com/vr-travel-samsung-gear-vr-google-cardboard-1735875065.html

http://www.huffingtonpost.com/entry/best-travel-websites-and-apps_us_58701134e4b099cdb0fd37d2

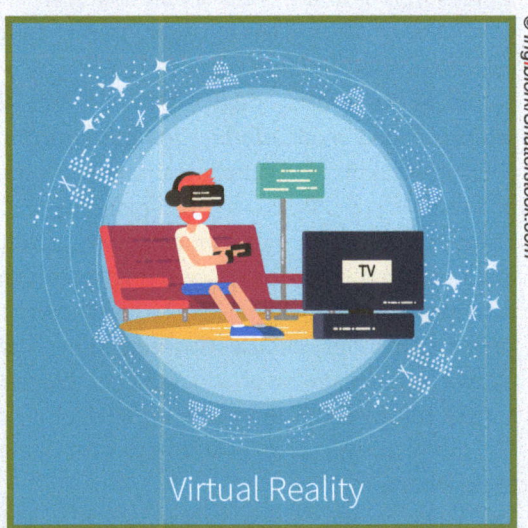

FIGURE 12.5 Illustration of the multiplicity of information platforms.

better engage their imagination and creativity. Providing high quality videos and images is of great importance for destination management organizations and businesses. Creating and curating original visual materials is an important part of destination branding. The millennial market in particular responds well to visual information.

It is worth noticing that virtual reality has increasingly played a role in marketing as consumers gravitate toward vivid visual information. Free Virtual Reality apps like YouVisit VR, Ascape VR, Discovery VR, and Google Street View provide people an immersive travel experience on their smartphones without leaving home. VR travel apps can help travelers to experience a place—or a specific resort, city, museum, hotel, or cruise ship—before they make a decision to visit.

Destination Online Content Strategy: The 3Cs and 4Ps

Where consumers spend their time, marketers follow. Because consumers spend an increasing amount of time on their mobile devices and social media channels, travel service providers have increasingly spent their marketing resources to engage consumers on those platforms through engaging and relevant information content. Given the nature of social media, consumers not only judge information in terms of immediacy, relevancy, credibility, and usefulness but also expect aesthetic, entertainment, and social benefits. Tourism businesses and destinations need to supplement their selling mindset with a focus on *traveler engagement and assistance* through their social media channels.

QUICK TRIP 12.8

I Unlike You, Facebook Style

You and your significant other just broke up. Maybe you're spiteful or heartbroken. Once you've properly notified your best friends you get around to the inevitable status change. You may be surprised to find out that relationship status changes happen quite often between a brand and a follower. ExactTarget research shows that 55 percent of Facebook users have liked a company and then deleted them later when they no longer want to see the company's updated posts.

Facebook pages follow a rather complicated algorithm. If fans of your company are not interacting, hiding, or deleting your posts, fewer of them will appear on fans' walls. In this, not everything you post will be seen by your fans. There are several reasons why consumers will like your brand and this changes their expectations for your Facebook activity. Most fans are motivated to like you in order to get access to special promotions or deals whereas a full 40 percent of Facebook users say that liking a company gives said company no right to market to them. People twenty-four and younger see Facebook as strictly a mode of social media and do not appreciate being marketed to. Furthermore, men are 11 percent less receptive to marketing messages than women. Sixty-three percent of users say that they Unliked a company or brand due to excessive posting. Thirty-eight percent say that they became bored with the company due to the lack of activity or repetitive posts. Nineteen percent say that the company's posts were never relevant to them from the beginning. Finally, 17 percent said that they deleted a company because they became tired of posts which really had no value and mainly consisted of chitchat. These are all things to keep in mind for companies that are promoting their destination through the use of Facebook and other social media sites. The most important thing is to slowly build relationships with consumers through conversational tactics. Ask the consumer what they look forward to at your particular destination. Make them aware of the unique activities and culture that your destination can offer. The most important part of social media is being able to find the middle ground between interaction and promotion. Don't make your Facebook friends want to break up with you. No one ever enjoys that status change.

Think about This

1. What motivates you to like a company or a brand on Facebook?
2. How may Facebook be effectively used for marketing a destination?

Source

http://www.travelmarketreport.com/technology?articleID=5664&LP=1

Information content strategy has become increasingly integral to travel marketing. It is important to recognize that as travelers become not only increasingly active seekers of information, they are also increasingly active providers of information (e.g., trip reviews, blogs, real-time smartphone information sharing, and post-trip travel story posting). Traveler-generated information, both textual and visual, that is uploaded and shared via various social media channels is of astonishingly high volume. Travel experience sharing is a major content domain of online *user-generated content* and information. In fact, it is increasingly recognized that social media is no longer an isolated marketing channel, it has become part of a destination experience itself. Bombarding your followers with advertisements may be a misuse of the social space. While it is important for destinations and tourism business suppliers to create their own content, it is equally important for them to engage in real-time conversations online with consumers and be effective curators of traveler-generated information content.

QUICK TRIP 12.9

Micro Information Moments

According to Think with Google's marketing research, travelers are increasingly turning to mobile devices to get travel itinerary ideas, compare prices, or reserve experiences. Google calls these moments "micro-moments." These micro decision moments are a good example of travelers' departures from traditional sequential and structured decision-making style. Instead, travel-related decision-making has become more spontaneous spurred by micro consumptive moments and influenced by mobile digital technologies.

The big data empowered by digital technologies allow marketers to trace traveler' digital journey—their path-to-purchase patterns—across a multitude of online, mobile, and video channels. Because of this consumer knowledge, tourism service providers and marketers are better able to provide travel brand and product information at these precise decision points. Google classifies these online micro decision points into four moments: dreaming, organizing, booking, and experiencing.

1. **Dreaming moments.** Consumers explore and discover vacation ideas. YouTube and other visual oriented channels are popularly frequented by consumers at this stage.
2. **Organizing moments.** Travelers start to make more concrete plans. Travelers compare destination and activity options. Google search and social information (e.g., personal social groups or online travel social networks) are sought out by travelers.
3. **Booking moments.** Travelers search for more functional information such as route planning, air tickets, and hotel comparisons via online travel channels and offline trade channels. Travelers make their purchases.
4. **Experiencing moments.** These moments are onsite moments. Travelers' searches tend to be related to orientation (maps, routes) and nearby consumptive options (restaurants, shops, activities). Mobile-based Google searches are oftentimes used (e.g., near me searches).

Think about This

1. When is visual information the most impactful?
2. When is trade-generated information impactful?
3. When is traveler-generated information impactful?

Source

https://www.thinkwithgoogle.com/marketing-resources/micro-moments/micro-moments-travel-customer-journey/

QUICK TRIP 12.10

Millennial Traveler Information Use

The millennial generation (born between the years 1980 and 2000) makes up the largest generation to date. They grew up with the rapid advent of digital communication technologies and other high-tech gadgets. It is not an exaggeration to say that they have had their smartphones next to them at all times. This generation is adventurous and values travel and experiences in life.

Millennials' travel information and decision behavior exhibits characteristics that are unlike their predecessor generations and signal what is to come for the upcoming generations. Below is a summary of how millennials utilize travel information, based on research from Topdeck Travel (Lane 2016)—a popular provider for group travel for eighteen- to thirty-year-olds, rezStream Hospitality Solutions, and Hospitaltynet.org.

1. They use Facebook for travel inspiration.
2. They consider travel reviews important.
3. They value friends' recommendations, followed by what's on sale and social media.
4. They check multiple sites before booking their travel to get the best deal possible.
5. They tend to avoid clicking on sponsored or paid content on a website.
6. They are likely to book travel through a smartphone or tablet.
7. They will upgrade their travel experience by purchasing in-flight Wi-Fi.
8. They are spontaneous in experiencing a destination. They use smartphones to search for "things to do" after arriving at a destination.
9. They post their experiences frequently on social media, while traveling as well as upon returning home.
10. Travel apps have become the millennials preferred method of interacting with brands.

Hospitalitynet.org suggests that tourism providers should

- Listen and participate in their social conversations online.
- Ensure that information is mobile friendly and that cross platform compatibility is not an issue.
- Provide better loyalty programs: offer tangible benefits.
- Be authentic. Encourage engagement through hashtag use and other social offerings.
- Be spontaneous.

Think about This

1. What would be ideal destination traits and attributes that are attractive to millennials?
2. How do destinations and businesses serve them effectively?
3. How do you manage potential generational differences in preferences in technology use?
4. Does the use of social media on the go change how millennials experience destinations?
5. How can marketers effectively influence millennials' decision-making process?
6. What kind of messages may appeal to this generation?

Sources

https://www.hospitalitynet.org/news/4075929.html

https://www.rezstream.com/blog/5-ways-millennials-are-using-tech-for-travel

Lane, A. (2016). Are Millennial Travel Trends Shifting in 2016? Forbes: https://www.forbes.com/sites/lealane/2016/01/15/are-millennial-travel-trends-shifting-in-2016-youll-be-surprised/

nSight. 10 Things You Need to Know About Millennial Travelers. www.nsightfortravel.com/10-things-you-need-to-know-about-millennial-travelers/

In a nutshell, when implementing a destination's content strategies, a destination's content activities fall into three areas—the *3Cs:* Create, Curate, and Corral contents.

- *Create* contents: The destination needs to create quality content on its own to engage consumers, the travel trade, and public news media.
- *Curate* contents: The destination needs to curate content created by travelers (e.g., travelers' opinions, ideas, and travel stories and experiences) and frame them for marketing purposes.
- *Corral* contents: The destination needs to channel and corral various voices and contents associated with the destination into a coherent brand story.

When engaging travelers and potential travelers on social media platforms through content engagement, there are four areas (*4 Ps*) that a destination can consider. The 4 Ps are: Planned, Prompt, Personalized, and Participatory.

- *Planned:* A destination's social media activities should have a clear goal and a clear alignment with its marketing goals. Prior to posting on social media, a destination needs to have a clear plan that satisfies the following requirements.
  1. Understand who you are engaging with and what values are they seeking?
  2. Select and provide a rationale for platforms to use.
  3. Develop a content strategy: What types of content should you use?
  4. Understand the big picture: How do the online engagement activities contribute to your bigger goals?
  5. Understand accountability: How do you measure your results?
- *Prompt:* Once engaged in the social media space, a destination needs to be prompt in responses to travelers' enquiries, suggestions, complaints, and compliments.
- *Personalized:* Have personalized messages, incentives, and solutions when addressing travelers.
- *Participatory:* Listening to and participating in the conversations that consumers have about your destination, asking for input/actions, and showing your gratitude.

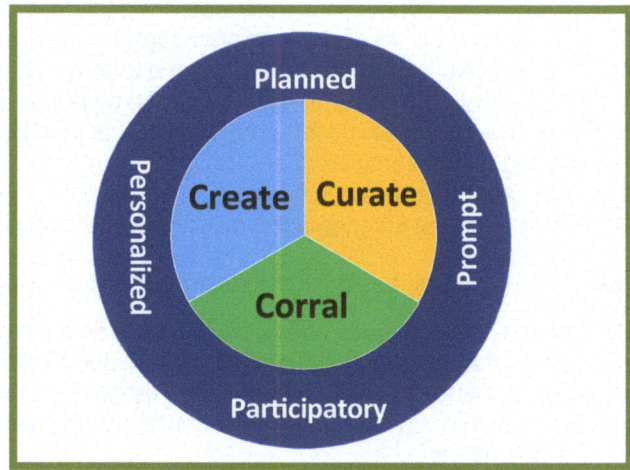

FIGURE 12.6 The 3Cs and 4Ps of Content Strategy.

SUMMARY

Once people are motivated to go on vacation they begin an information search to compare various alternatives. Driven by internal needs and external stimuli, the potential traveler becomes tuned to possible destinations, and destination possibilities are then evaluated as to their viability. Travel to that destination is likely if the traveler likes the destination and develops a preference for it. They seek and receive information from friends and relatives, and travel social influencers, as well as from the commercial environment. Travel decisions involve multiple components and travelers' need for information is expansive. Travelers can employ both automatic and controlled processes in making travel decisions. Information support for both decision processes are needed. Fulfilling traveler micro information moment needs are important. Destination marketers need to formulate effective online content strategies to engage travelers and serve their information needs effectively. Travelers' decision-making and information behavior can vary based on cultural, demographic, and psychographic factors. These variations will be further elaborated upon in the next chapter (Chapter 13).

ACTIVITIES

1. Online social influencers are individuals who are active in creating or curating information in the social media space. Visit a popular travel blogger's website, a popular YouTube video blogger, and a popular online travel forum (e.g., Women who travel) and answer the following questions:
   a. Why is the information contents of the respective site interesting to travelers?
   b. How persuasive are they to travelers?
   c. How do they influence travelers' decision-making?
   d. At what decision stage(s) do they exert the most influence?
   e. Are the three types of social information similar or different in their role as social influencers?
   f. How can the tourism destinations leverage information created by travel bloggers in their marketing activities?

REFERENCES

Alegre, J., and M. Cladera, 2006. Repeat Visitation in Mature Sun and Sand Holiday Destinations. *Journal of Travel Research*, 44 (3), 288–297.

Bauer, R. A. 1960. Consumer behavior as risk taking. In R. S. Hancock (Ed.), *Dynamic marketing for a changing world.* Chicago: American Marketing Association, 389–398.

Blount, A. 2017. 2017–2018 Portrait of American Travelers Study. MMGY GLOBAL, https://www.mmgyglobal.com/news/news-2017%E2%80%932018-portrait-of-american-travelers

Choe Y., D. R. Fesenmaier, and C. Vogt. 2017. Twenty-Five Years Past Vogt: Assessing the Changing Information Needs of American Travellers. In: Schegg R., Stangl B. (Eds) *Information and Communication Technologies in Tourism 2017.* Springer, Cham.

Floyd, D. L., S. Prentice-Dunn, and R. W. Rogers. 2000. "A Meta-Analysis of Research on Protection Motivation Theory." *Journal of Applied Social Psychology* 30 (2), 407–429.

Howard, J., and J. N. Sheth. 1969. *Theory of Buyer Behavior.* New York: John Wiley & Sons, Inc.

McKercher, B., and D. Wong, 2004. Understanding tourism behavior: Examining the combined effects of prior visitation history and destination status. *Journal of Travel Research*, 43 (2), 171–179.

Neumann, J. V. and O. Morgenstern, 1947. Theory of games and economic behavior. Princeton University Press, Princeton, NJ.

Sheth, J.N., B. I. Newman, and B. L. Gross, 1993. Why we buy what we buy: A theory of consumptive values. *Journal of Business Research* 22(2):159–170.

Smallman, C., and Moore. 2010. Process studies of tourists' decision making. *Annals of Tourism Research* 37 (2) 397–422.

Stanovich, K. E., and R. F. West. 2000. "Individual difference in reasoning: implications for the rationality debate?" *Behavioural and Brain Sciences* 23: 645–726. doi:10.1017/s0140525x00003435

Um, S., and J. L. Crompton. 1992. The roles of perceived inhibitors and facilitators in pleasure travel destination decisions. *Journal of Travel Research* 30 (3): 18–25.

Vogt, C. A., and D. R. Fesenmaier. 1998. Expanding the functional information search model. *Annals of Tourism Research* 25 (3), 551–578.

ADDITIONAL READINGS

Borgogna, A., S. Stroh, A. Hilz, A. Agarwalla, and I. Jakovijevic, 2016. Connecting With The Customer: How Airlines Must Adapt Their Distribution Business Model. https://www.forbes.com/sites/strategyand/2016/11/15/connecting-with-the-customer-how-airlines-must-adapt-their-distribution-business-model/#6b8d05755443

Gursoy, D., and K. W. McCleary. 2004. Travelers' prior knowledge and its impact on their information search behavior. *Journal of Hospitality and Tourism Research* 28 (1): 66–94.

https://www.gearbrain.com/vr-travel-samsung-gear-vr-google-cardboard-1735875065.html

https://www.ted.com/talks/daniel_kahneman_the_riddle_of_experience_vs_memory

https://www.thinkwithgoogle.com/consumer-insights/travel-trends-4-mobile-moments-changing-consumer-journey/

https://www.thinkwithgoogle.com/marketing-resources/micro-moments/micro-moments-travel-customer-journey/

http://www.puzzlewood.net/

Hwang, Y.-H. 2010. A theory of unplanned travel decisions: Implications for modeling on-the-go travelers. *Information Technology & Tourism* 12 (3), 283–296.

Jagdish, N., B. Sheth, G. Newman, and L. Gross, 1991. Why we buy what we buy: A theory of consumption values. *Journal of business research*, 22 (2), 159–170.

Keren, G. B. 2012. Framing and communication: The role of frames in theory and in practice. (Netspar Panel Paper; No. 32). Tilburg: NETSPAR.

Lichrou, M., Lisa O'Malley, and Maurice Patterson. 2014. On the marketing implications of place narratives. *Journal of Marketing Management* 30:9–10, pages 832–856.

McCabe, S., C. Li, and Z. Chen, 2016. Time for a radical reappraisal of tourist decision making? Toward a new conceptual model. *Journal of travel research* 55 (1), 3–15.

Morin, A. 2014. *5 Scientific Reasons You Should Choose Your Friends Carefully.* https://www.forbes.com/sites/amymorin/2014/10/17/5-scientific-reasons-you-should-choose-your-friends-carefully/#5cbe2b086181

Pan, S., H. Tsai, and J. Lee, 2011. *Framing New Zealand: Understanding tourism TV commercials, Torism Management,* 32(2011), 596–603.

Ramos, G. M., W. Daamen, and S. Hoogendoorn, 2014. A State-of-the-Art Review: Developments in Utility Theory, Prospect Theory and Regret Theory to Investigate Travellers' Behaviour in Situations Involving Travel Time Uncertainty. *Transport Reviews,* 34 (1).

Sirakaya, E., and Woodside, A. G. 2005. Building and testing theories of decision making by travelers. *Tourism Management*, 26, 815–832.

Su, W. T., M. R. Lehto, X. Y. Lehto, J. S. Yi, Z. Shi, and X. Liu, 2017. The Influence of Reviewer Demographic Information Provision on Trust and Purchase Intent for Users of Online Websites. *Journal of Quality Assurance in Hospitality & Tourism, 18* (3), 328–353.

CHAPTER THIRTEEN

Forces Shaping Tourism
Culture, Time, Sociodemographics, and Psychographics

The World is a book, and those who do not travel read only a page.

SAINT AUGUSTINE

YOUR LEARNING DESTINATION

After examining the cultural, sociodemographic, and psychological factors that shape and influence tourism demand, students will be able to suggest appropriate types of vacation for particular types of travelers and be able to craft effective marketing strategies to travelers based on their background.

WHAT YOU NEED TO KNOW

Having read this chapter, you will be able to:

- Explain the effects of cultural background on travel behavior.
- Explain the effects of time on travel behavior.
- Explain the effects of sociodemographic factors on travel behavior.
- Explain the effects of psychological factors on travel behavior.
- Explain the importance of managing destination image.

BREAKING THE ICE

The Summer Palace is one of the must-see sites in Beijing. A United States couple described their visit as dampened by the huge crowd at the site, the warm and foggy weather, and the sneaky photos others took of them. In the meantime, a Chinese family of four visiting the palace described their visit as wonderful despite the crowd and the subpar weather. What may have

contributed to these divergent opinions regarding the site? As we have discussed in Chapter 11, travel as an experience product is subject to visitors' personal interpretations. Various factors can influence visitor satisfaction. In this chapter, we will discuss how cultural, personal, and interpersonal forces can shape traveler preferences, behavior, and experience satisfaction.

Marketers have long segmented the travel market along cultural factors and socioeconomic criteria such as age, income, gender, and education. It is, therefore, appropriate to understand how and why tourism demand may depend on these criteria. Consumers' psychological characteristics such as lifestyle, attitudes, and perceptions can also shape demand. The role of perception and imagery is discussed in this chapter. Together these demand-shaping factors provide a useful picture of traveler behavioral characteristics, their likes and dislikes. Such knowledge can provide a solid foundation for making destination strategic decisions such as identification of a solid basis for travel market segmentation, selection of target traveler segments, product development, and formulation of marketing communication strategies.

KEY TAKEAWAY POINTS

- Knowledge of the culture of a country or subcultures within that country is important when analyzing travel behavior.
- Traveler social interaction and communication styles can be culturally influenced.

- Travelers' preferences for destination attributes can be culturally influenced.

- Hospitality services provided at a destination can be culturally adapted.

- Availability of time can influence how and how much and when individuals travel.

- A person's demographic background described by factors such as age, gender, family life cycle, income, and education can exert influence on travel preferences and behavior.

- Understanding of consumer perceptual biases is important when formulating marketing communication strategies.

- Destinations need to carefully monitor traveler perceptions of destination attributes.

- Managing and enhancing the projected image of a destination to travelers is an important task performed by destination management organizations.

THE EFFECTS OF CULTURE ON TRAVEL

Culture serves as a barometer of general societal trends. As individuals, we are part of larger social groups by which we are influenced. These groups themselves are part of and influenced by the surrounding cultures. Culture can be defined as a "set of beliefs, values, attitudes, habits, and forms of behavior that are shared by a society and are transmitted from generation to generation" (Bennett and Kassasjin 1982). It is the "collective mental programming of the mind" that distinguishes one group from another (Hofstede 1985). The knowledge of the culture of a country or subcultures within that country is important because

1. **Cultural values influence how people evaluate the world.** Individuals under the influence of a culture tend to examine the world affairs via their shared cultural value lens, therefore forming similar worldviews and perspectives.

2. **Cultural values lead to certain attitudes and perceptions.** The many generally held beliefs and attitudes in a society are reflective of its cultural values.

3. **Cultural values influence behavior.** The degree to which behavior conforms with societal norms determines which goals and behaviors gain social approval or disapproval. To the extent that people are concerned about how others think of them, they will be influenced to behave in ways acceptable to society.

Analyzing a National Culture

The cultures of different countries can vary greatly. In order to successfully attract and satisfy people from a particular country, it is necessary to be aware of these cultural differences. Many theories and models have been developed that are helpful for analyzing and understanding these differences. One popular theory for analyzing cultures has been proposed by Hofstede (1985) and was later further developed by his research team (Hofstede Insights 2017). Hofstede and his team analyzed culturally influenced work values across the globe using data from seventy-six countries. Based on this analysis, they then developed a six-dimensional *National Culture Model* which posits that the value patterns dominant in countries vary along six main dimensions:

1. Individualism versus collectivism
2. Masculinity versus femininity
3. Large versus small power distance
4. Strong versus weak uncertainty avoidance
5. Long-term versus short-term orientation
6. Indulgence versus restraint

Individualism Versus Collectivism. On the first scale—individualism versus collectivism—the issue is the degree to which values reflect the importance of individuals versus the group as a whole. At the individualistic end of the scale, individuals look after their own self-interests and those of their immediate families. At the other end of the scale, people are supposed to look after the interests of their in-group and share similar opinions and beliefs with those of their in-group. People from countries that score high on individualism can have different motives and behaviors than those from countries with high-collectivist scores.

How the individualism versus collectivism tendencies of cultures may influence travel preferences and behavior is what we are concerned with. Research has shown that this factor has a significant influence on traveler behavior in the areas of travel motivation, perception of risk, decision-making style, and evaluation of choices. Below are some specific examples:

- High individualists tend to be more inclined to travel independently than in groups and to be more motivated by the desire to improve themselves. High collectivists tend to prefer to travel in groups, and can be more motivated by the desire for socialization.
- Travelers from collectivist cultures such as Asian, Mediterranean, and Latin American cultures favor higher levels of interpersonal and intercultural contact and interactions when visiting a destination than that of individualistic cultures of Northern Europe and North America.
- Group harmony and high consensus needs of high collectivists may lead to suppression of personal preferences in destination choices in an attempt to comply with group interests.
- Group-oriented activities are relatively more important than individual activities for travelers from more collectivist cultures such as Asia and Greece than travelers from more individualistic cultures such as the United States, Australia, and the United Kingdom.

Masculinity Versus Femininity.

The second dimension is masculinity versus femininity—the degree to which the values held reflect the traditional division between male versus female roles. In many cultures men have traditionally taken on more assertive and dominant roles, while women have taken on more service-oriented and care-taking roles. Members of societies placing more importance on values associated with male roles (what Hofstede might call more masculine societies) tend to place more importance on such things as showing off success, achieving something visible, and making money. Examples of countries or societies falling at this end of the spectrum include Japan, Germany, Austria, Switzerland, some Latin countries, and most Anglo countries.

At the other end of the spectrum, in what Hofstede might call more feminine societies, more importance is placed on such things as people relationships over money, quality of life, and preservation of the environment. Examples of countries or societies showing this tendency include the Nordic countries and some Southeast Asian countries. It has been noted that visitors from more feminine cultures such as Singapore and Thailand attach more importance to socializing and hospitality of hosts than visitors from masculine cultures such as Japan and the United Kingdom (Reisinger 2004). A country's placement on this spectrum would have implications for appropriate marketing appeals. We would expect major decisions, such as where to go for a vacation, more likely to be made by the males in societies that score high on that scale, for example.

Power Distance.

The third dimension is power distance—how society deals with the fact that people are unequal. Some societies let inequalities grow over time into inequalities in power and wealth, while others try to play down inequalities as much as possible. Asian, African, and Latin American countries have large power index scores (indicating inequalities). In the Western society, France, Belgium, Spain, and Italy score rather high while the Nordic and Anglo countries score low on this scale. We might expect messages of a more humanitarian and egalitarian type to appeal to cultures low on this scale.

Uncertainty Avoidance.

The dimension of uncertainty avoidance explains how societies deal with the fact that time runs only one way. We all have to live with the uncertainty of the future. Some societies teach their people to accept and live with this uncertainty. People will take personal risks rather lightly, will not work so hard, and will be relatively tolerant of behaviors and opinions different from their own. These are weak uncertainty avoidance societies. Others try to control the future through such things as formal and informal rules to protect themselves from the uncertainties of human behavior. Some specific examples of how uncertainty avoidance tendencies can influence travel preferences and behavior are:

- People from collectivist cultures tend to have a higher degree of uncertainty avoidance. In behavior, they prefer to travel in groups and have a stronger tendency to avoid uncertain travel situations or destinations.
- Travelers with strong uncertainty avoidance tendencies may resort to a larger number of information sources for trip planning and decision-making compared to those that tolerate high uncertainties.
- The influence of opinion leaders (as experts) would be stronger in strong risk avoidance societies than in weak uncertainty avoidance societies.
- Those in risk-averse cultures tend to prefer packaged tours and vacations.
- Safety is more important for those from high uncertainty avoidance cultures than from low uncertainty avoidance cultures.

Long-Term or Short-Term.

This dimension describes differences in how people from different cultures may prioritize goals of honoring one's collective past versus dealing with challenges of the present. Societies that are long-term-oriented tend to prefer to maintain traditions and norms over societal changes, while the short-term-oriented societies prefer to maintain a more pragmatic or flexible approach toward societal changes. How these different value tendencies influence tourism behavior has yet to be understood by researchers. It may be a reasonable deduction that travelers from societies that are more long-term-oriented may naturally gravitate more toward historical and traditional cultural attractions.

Indulgence Versus Restraint.   This dimension differentiates societies that encourage gratification of basic human drives such as having fun from societies that suppress such needs and implement stricter social norms. This dimension may help explain why different countries value different hospitality service cultures. For example, individuals from a country scoring high on indulgence may expect restaurant and hotel service representatives to visibly demonstrate friendly demeanors such as wearing a smile whereas individuals from a country with higher restraint tendencies may consider such demonstrative body language from their service providers to be unnatural.

Although Hofstede's proposition of national culture provides a useful model for understanding culture differences, it doesn't explain all cultural divergences in the world nor has it been regarded as universally accepted. It is also important to recognize that the cultural characteristics ascribed to a country are in relative terms. An additional note of caution is that when analyzing or attempting to understand the role of cultural factors in tourism, we need to avoid holding a static view of the culture in question. Although culture is accumulated via generations, culture is not static, it is living, and therefore may evolve. People within the same culture may conform to cultural norms and expectations to a varying degree. Certain groups of travelers may deviate significantly from what may be typical travel tendencies of the society they belong to.

Culturally Influenced Travel and Hospitality Practices

Travelers can experience and value a destination product differently due to their inherent cultural traits. It is also important to understand that culture may influence how hospitality services are provided.

Cultural Differences in Social Interaction.   Culture is reflected by the behavioral norms of both the visitors and the hosts. Tourism connects host and guest cultures in a direct way when a traveler sets foot on a destination. *Social interaction,* in general, is in fact a part of a tourism experience. Local residents may disapprove of certain visitor behaviors, and vice versa. For example, the Chinese culture emphasizes the importance of relationships and social harmony. This cultural value can be reflected in their dining behavioral tendencies. Boisterous conversations over the dinner table in commercial spaces are part of the dining culture in China, and business and social relationships are often forged over the dinner table. However, in other cultures, loud conversations over the dinner table may be seen as inappropriate and unacceptable.

Some other examples include personal space perceptions and eye contact. In some cultures, rubbing shoulders with strangers is not seen as inappropriate (as in bumping getting on the subway), but in other cultures, where the need for personal space is much higher, the tolerance of crowding is much lower. Analogously, in certain cultures, direct eye contact with the person you are talking to is a sign of respect and sincerity, whereas in other cultures, avoidance of eye contact is deemed more appropriate. When there are large discrepancies in what is acceptable behavior and what is not between the guest and host cultures, conflicts between and dissatisfaction of both parties can arise.

Cultural Differences in Communication Style.   Culture's effect on society is also shown in the language people use with one another. Language barriers go beyond simply linguistic differences. *Communication styles* can be culturally driven. For example, researchers have found that people in what they call *high context cultures* tend to communicate ideas and opinions in an implicit way whereas people in *low context cultures* tend to exchange information more explicitly through the message itself. China, Japan, Saudi Arabia, and Finland are examples of countries with a high context communication culture. The United States, Australia, Germany, and Switzerland are examples of low context cultures. This distinction is, of course, not absolute or dichotomous.

The explicitness of any particular message communicated can vary on a continuous spectrum ranging from low to high depending on the setting and people involved. Subgroups in the same larger culture also may have different communication styles. For example, in the United States a typical New Yorker will tend to be more explicit in his or her communication style (low context) than a typical Texan (high context).

QUICK TRIP 13.1

National Culture Comparison: Australia Versus China

Hofstede's six-dimensional model of national culture allows us to systematically analyze how values, preferences, and behavioral norms held in different societies tend to differ and how these differences influence traveler decision-making and travel behavior. Hofstede's model provides an index score that ranges from 0 to 100 on each of the six dimensions of cultural tendencies for every country. The values on each index provide practitioners a measure of different cultural traits of a country and can be used to measure cultural distances between different countries. Along these lines, Figure 13.1 compares people from Australia and China on each of the six indexes of Hofstede's model.

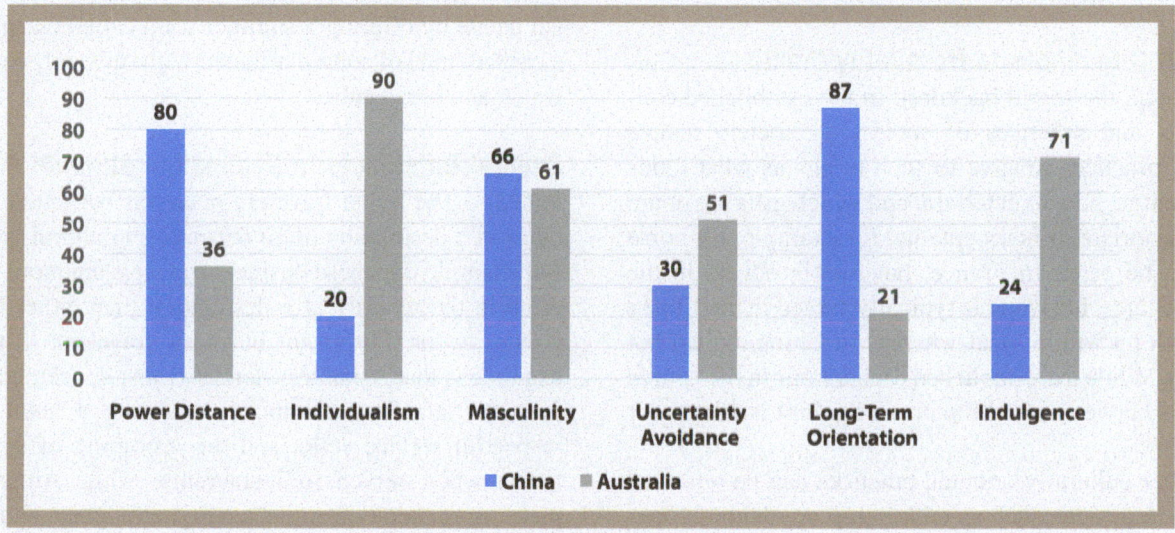

FIGURE 13.1   National Culture Comparison: Australia Versus China.

Think about This

1. Based on information presented in Figure 13.1, how are Australians different from Chinese in their cultural traits and tendencies?
2. Differences in cultural traits can lead to behavioral differences in travel. How may the Australians potentially differ from the Chinese in their travel preferences and behavior?
3. How may tourism and hospitality business providers benefit from this cultural distance information? Are you able to provide a potential application of such information?
4. Why are culturally-oriented service/activity designs important?

Source

https://www.hofstede-insights.com/

In general, people in high context cultures tend to be relational and contemplative, while people in low context cultures tend to be more rule-based and straightforward. You may have seen how destination marketers often elect to communicate a marketing message somewhat differently based on their targeted audiences. McDonald's advertising in high context countries such as Japan and China, for example, are more colorful with more movements and sounds that allow an understanding of a communicated message to be understood in context while similar advertisements in the United States appear to be more straightforward. In Great

Britain, for example, the humor is more subtle than in the United States. Advertisements there use the double meaning to get the point across in a clever way. Such an approach would probably fail in the United States where the punch line has to be very direct to gain attention.

When travelers from a high context culture meet hosts from a low context culture or vice versa, misunderstandings or misinterpretations can occur. It is useful to consider these communication style differences in tourism management. In fact, it is important to consider not only words, but also gestures, expressions, and other body movements in the service contexts.

Cultural Differences in Hospitality Practices.
Culture affects the social backdrop in the established conventions and practices of society. A society adopts various practices relative to such things as what foods can be eaten, how to entertain, and which gifts are or are not appropriate. It is acceptable, for example, for horse meat to be eaten in France, but this is not so in the United States. Ice water is typically served in the United States along with a meal whereas in China, boiled hot water is. While the established dinner hour in the United States is between 6 and 8 p.m., in Spain it is 10 p.m. or later.

Other culturally oriented practices can be observed in service designs such as table setup, method of cooking, or use of spices. In China, in many restaurants, round tables with a lazy Susan are commonly utilized to facilitate the practice of shared dishes and conversations over the dinner table. That practice is not nearly as prevalent in cultures where an individual based dinner course choice and serving size are preferred.

These culturally oriented practices contribute to place uniqueness and diversity, and can become an interesting part of a tourism experience. On the other hand, these differences can become a source of discomfort and dissatisfaction to the visitors. When attracting or servicing visitors from a culture different from our own, it is necessary to know these culturally-influenced established practices. You may notice that hospitality services may adopt different strategies on whether and how much to adapt their services to a local cultural context.

When marketing a destination or hospitality services to overseas markets, marketers tend to adapt to the local taste palette, languages, imageries, word choices,

and cultural norms. One prime example is how McDonald's adapts its menus to its various overseas markets. It has adapted the menu to include foods that are popular in specific countries. For example, McDonald's in Japan serve items such as Teriyaki burgers, shrimp nuggets, shrimp burgers (EBI Filet-O), and green tea flavored milk shakes. This is an effort by McDonald's to adapt its products to the food culture in Japan. McDonald's offers McCurry Pan, a mix of curried vegetables in India. McDonald's breakfast menu in Australia offers Vegemite spread, while for some European countries, it offers Nutella. In Spain, McDonald's has catered to the Spanish palate by offering a summer soup called Gazpacho, a chilled bowl of soup marinated with olive oil, vinegar, water, and bread cubes.

Cultural Differences in Destination Attribute Preferences.
The value travelers place on particular attributes of a destination often depends on cultural factors. For example, Japanese business travelers are more interested in the security at a destination than either North American or European business travelers. Another example is that Asian travelers are most concerned with personal attention/customization during a hotel stay, respectful service style, and the grooming of server's hands when served in restaurants; while Americans place more value on room quality, efficiency, and time saving in a hotel stay, and eye contact and individual treatment in a restaurant setting (Kim, Wen, and Doh 2010).

In Kim et al.'s (2010) restaurant study, Chinese customers judged how crowded a restaurant is by such spatial features as the amount and arrangement of the facilities, while Americans were more sensitive to the number of people in a given space. Because of the risk aversion tendency of people from collectivist cultures noted, Chinese visitors may prefer crowded restaurants, as to them this indicates that the restaurant provides good food quality (as evidenced by the crowds), and therefore is a safe dining choice.

It is also important to determine appropriate providers of travel products in the minds of consumers: Do people tend to purchase vacations directly from suppliers, or are retail travel agents used? When do they start planning a vacation? What alternatives, acceptable to the consumer, are available for distributing the product?

Culturally-Oriented Hotel Amenity and Service Design

If you are to stay at a hotel, what kinds of services do you expect? While your expectations can vary by what types of hotel you are staying at (e.g., luxurious amenities would be expected for high-end hotels), cultural backgrounds of guests can also influence their preferences, and thus hotel practices. In fact, an increasing number of hotel companies are taking guests' cultural background into consideration. Culturally tailored services and amenities can be found in many hotels in the United States.

One particular market that has received increasing attention from the hotel industry is the Chinese tourist market. According to a *Skift* report (2016), Chinese tourists are projected to be the largest overseas tourist market to the United States by 2020. Hotels are re-designing their offerings to cater to Chinese travelers' preferences and habits.

For example, in response to this trend, the Sheraton Boston in the Back Bay neighborhood has updated its in-room amenities to include slippers, instant noodles, an electric kettle, and green tea—items that are welcomed by Chinese guests. Addition of Chinese breakfast foods such as congee is becoming a common practice in many hotels, including the A.C. Hotel in Chicago Downtown. Caesars in Las Vegas took a more aggressive initiative in order to accommodate their Chinese guests. They now offer a hotel room booking and payment system on WeChat, the most widely utilized Chinese social media mobile application.

Think about This

1. How does culture play an important role in shaping traveler needs and wants?
2. For hotels, why is it important for them to tailor their offerings based on guests' cultural backgrounds?
3. What may be other areas that hotels can work on to better accommodate guests from different cultural backgrounds?
4. Is It possible for hospitality and tourism service providers to over-adapt and reduce the novelty value that many travelers may seek when they travel abroad?

Sources

Marcelo, Philip. "More U.S. cities aim to make Chinese travelers feel at home." *Journal Sentinel,* 31 March 2017.

Peltier, Dan. "China Will Be the Largest Overseas Visitor Market for the U.S. by 2020." *Skift,* 17 May 2016.

THE EFFECT OF TIME ON TRAVEL

Time, or rather the availability of time, acts as a major inhibiting factor to travel. The amount of available time and the form in which it is available is, in fact, a major shaper of the destinations that can be visited, the modes of travel that can be used, and the activities that can be engaged in at the destination or en route. The desire to travel and the financial ability to travel are insufficient if one does not have the time to travel. All three factors must be present for travel and tourism to take place.

Spending Time

Time is spent in many *maintenance activities*—activities that involve a certain degree of obligation and that are necessary to sustain and maintain life. Included in this definition are such activities as eating, sleeping, maintaining the house, and caring for the lawn. Time can also be spent at work. For many, this involves a degree of obligation greater than the time spent in maintenance activities.

Leisure can be defined, although some people may feel it is a rather simplified definition, as the time

QUICK TRIP 13.3

The United States Culture

Culture is a complex variable given the increasing globalization and mobility of today's society. Take the United States for example, many argue that because of its size and diversity, it is not possible to talk about a national culture. Indeed, a number of groups in the United States have managed to maintain elements of their own geographic, religious, and ethnic identities. In addition, any attempt to describe a United States culture is fraught with potential charges of promoting stereotypes. Some degree of generalization is possible and desirable, however, if we are to better understand the impact of culture on vacation behavior.

Below is a summary of some of the basic traits of the American culture as compared to other countries.

U.S. Values	Some Other Countries' Values
Personal Control over the Environment	Fate
Change	Tradition
Time & Its Control	Human Interaction
Equality	Hierarchy/Rank/Status
Individualism/Privacy	Group's Welfare
Self-Help	Birthright Inheritance
Competition	Cooperation
Future Orientation	Past Orientation
Action/Work Orientation	"Being" Orientation
Informality	Formality
Directness/Openness/Honesty	Indirectness/Ritual/"Face"
Practicality/Efficiency Materialism/	Idealism
Acquisitiveness	Spiritualism/Detachment

Think about This

1. What cultural traits listed above may most directly influence how Americans travel?
2. Have the United States cultural tendencies impacted the country's hospitality business services? Are you able to give an example or two?
3. Would American visitors be subject to travel situations of conflict when they travel to places that are more oriented toward the traits corresponding to "Some Other Countries' values"?

Source

Kohls, L. R. The Washington International Center, Washington, D.C. http://www1.cmc.edu/pages/faculty/alee/extra/American_values.html

---

remaining after work and maintenance activities have been completed. By its very definition, leisure implies that the individual has a level of discretion over how to spend time that is not present in the other two categories. Leisure is often contrasted with the economic activity of work, and it is connected with pleasure and a feeling of freedom with a minimum of obligation. Leisure is also seen as inner-directed rather than other-directed. It is the time for one's self.

We might expect that the distribution of discretional time would change relative to changes in the family life cycle. This relationship is demonstrated in Figure 13.2. In the young and single phase, people are characterized by great physical capacity, disposable time, and few demands on their income. In the family phase, discretionary income and time decrease, and the physical capacity of the family is limited by that of its weakest member. The third phase is characterized by an excess

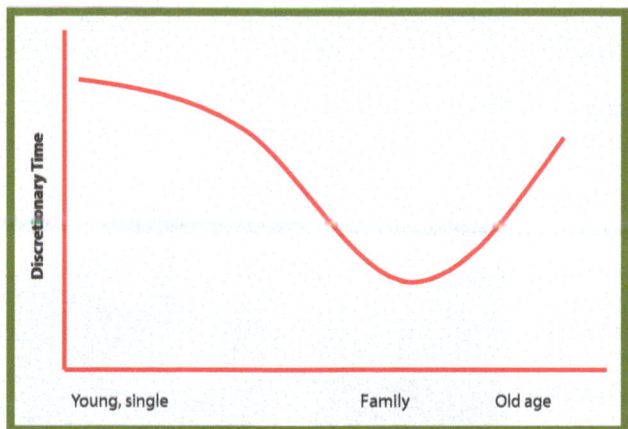

FIGURE 13.2 Time phases in the family life cycle.

of discretionary time and a decrease in physical capacity. We can speculate on the impact this might have on vacation behavior. Young singles would have the time, money, and ability to participate in physically demanding activities. Family activities would be geared to those allowed by the youngest child. Older people would be likely markets during the off-season as well as for last-minute bargains.

Leisure occurs on weekdays, weekends, and on vacations. The importance of this distinction can be illustrated by means of an example. If the workweek were to be reduced by 20 percent, the opportunities for tourism activities would be affected by the way in which the reduction was taken: the workday could be shortened to six-and-a-half hours from eight; the workweek could be shortened from five to four days; one week's paid vacation could be granted in each of three quarters of the year, with one month's vacation in the fourth quarter and with six months' vacation every five years. All three alternatives represent a cut of 20 percent in the workweek, yet the form in which it is taken affects the opportunities to participate in various activities and to visit various destinations.

Time and Money as Resources.   The concepts of work, leisure, and money are intertwined as far as tourism is concerned. Individuals need both leisure and money to travel. Usually this money is earned by working. Thus, it is necessary to work in order to earn money to engage in leisure-time pursuits. The more one works, the more money is earned (and, therefore, available for leisure activities), but the less time one has to spend and enjoy it. Consumers can thus be thought of as having both a time budget and a money budget, and some make rational decisions in allocating one over the other. The auto worker who takes Friday off to lengthen the weekend for a fishing trip chooses time over money. The college professor who chooses not to teach during the summer, but to travel cross-country also chooses time over money. This idea has been expressed as the principle of *resource value inversion*. As consumers' incomes rise, time becomes increasingly precious to them compared to money. Money, after all, can be saved; time cannot. Combined with this is a perception on the part of many that "time is money."

QUICK TRIP 13.4

China's Golden Travel Week

We know that discretional time is essential for leisure travel. Interestingly, a National Holiday policy directed toward increasing discretionary time can significantly influence when and how people travel. In an attempt to stimulate consumer spending and improve citizens' perceived quality of time, the Chinese government in the year 2000 established the "*Golden Week*" policy: *The Chinese Lunar New Year Golden Week* (January or February) and the *National Day Golden Week*" (October 1–8) by law provide two weeks of paid national holidays. Essentially, three days of paid holiday are mandated and the surrounding weekends are re-arranged so that all Chinese workers have two seven-continuous-days of holiday each year.

This policy has led to an unprecedented growth and concentration of leisure and travel activities by Chinese citizens during these time periods. According to a *New York Times* report (2017), China's daily retail sales grew by over 10 percent during the eight-day National Day Golden Week in 2017. This Golden Week break is now a peak season for Chinese people to travel to distant and not-too-distant destinations. Statistics from the China National Administration showed that 705 million trips were made during the 2017 National Day Golden Week, up 11 percent from 2016.

QUICK TRIP 13.4 CONTINUED

China's tourism industry had revenue of 583.6 billion yuan during this week, up 13.9 percent from the same week in 2016. According to the Chinese online travel services company Ctrip, as cited by *Forbes*, the top overseas destinations in 2017 during the Golden Week in October were Thailand, Japan, Singapore, the United States, and Vietnam.

Despite its economic impact, this concentrated travel phenomenon is not without controversies. These golden weeks are deemed to have disrupted people's five-day weekly schedules. It also has created an extreme crowding situation in many tourist attraction sites in China, and placed a high level of stress on highways, railways, and airways.

Think about This

1. What may be the impact of China's Golden Travel Week on traveler experience satisfaction?
2. What strategies would you suggest to tourism and hospitality businesses to help them cope with such a highly concentrated travel flow?
3. What may be attractive travel offerings to Chinese travelers who are cash rich and time poor?

Sources

https://en.wikipedia.org/wiki/Golden_Week_%28China%29

https://www.forbes.com/sites/deborahweinswig/2017/10/03/china-national-day-golden-week-where-will-chinese-tourists-travel-over-the-holiday-this-year/#7caa5abd447f

https://www.nytimes.com/reuters/2017/10/09/business/09reuters-china-tourism.html

FIGURE 13.3 Beijing, China—Crowd of tourists visit BaDaLing Great Wall in autumn.

THE EFFECT OF SOCIODEMOGRAPHICS ON TOURISM DEMAND

Age

Age is strongly related to tourism demand in two very important ways. That is, age is related to both (1) the amount of leisure time available for travel and (2) the type and extent of activities followed. The amount of leisure time available changes curvilinearly, with the younger and older age groups having proportionately more leisure time. Yet the amount of available time is, by itself, insufficient to explain age as a factor in tourism behavior. It is safe to conclude that the rates of participation in the overwhelming majority of leisure activities declines with age. There is a greater decline for active recreational activities than for the more passive forms of recreation. Preferred activities among the elderly are the more passive ones such as visiting friends and relatives, sightseeing, fishing, and playing golf. Yet for many retirees, although the number of activities participated in may drop upon retirement, the amount of time spent on each remaining one in terms of participation often increases.

In general, leisure time decreases with age until children leave the nest, when the amount of leisure time increases. This increase continues with retirement. Though participation in physical activities declines with age (together with a corresponding rise in participation in the gentler forms of recreation), interest levels in activities previously participated in remain high. Opportunities may exist for tapping these interests by developing less physically rigorous and more or socially enriching options to satisfy such expressions of interest.

A skier, for example, may be unable to ski for reasons of age, but may be interested in other related activities such as watching skiers or sharing experiences.

Generational Influence

When analyzing the impact of age on travel and tourism, it is often helpful to study generational cohorts. A *generational cohort* is composed of individuals who were born around the same time and share distinctive social and historical life events during their formative years (Twenge et al. 2010). Each generation is influenced by forces such as critical social, economic occurrences, popular culture and media trends, and technological trends. These broad forces create shared values and shape common consumptive preferences and patterns. These common forces and experiences influence a generational cohort's travel preferences and behavior in ways that go well beyond the effect of simply age alone. There are several major consumer cohorts commonly studied and targeted by providers of visitor travel products.

Baby Boomers, born 1946 to 1964, are defined by individuality, self-fulfillment, and optimism as a result of being coddled in their early years and coming of age in the excesses of the 1960s. This traveler cohort is transitioning into retirement with money and time to spend on travel, and they do. This is a very demanding travel segment that often seeks out less traditional vacation destinations. They are less price sensitive if they deem that they are getting a good product or value. They value health and wellness and personal gratification. Their destination activity choices reflect their belief that "70 is the new 50" and they choose to do things that fit into their lifestyle not age.

Generation Xers, born between 1965 and 1977, are defined as "savvy" because of their exposure to uncertain economic times. They embrace multiculturalism and global thinking. They make less traditional choices in life and in leisure. They believe in self-reliance and balance in family, life, and work. This generation tends to be strongly motivated to relax and unwind when it comes to vacation-taking.

Millennials (or Generation Y)—consists of those born between 1977 and 1995 (sources vary on the exact dates). The millennials were born into a technological and electronic society. They are open-minded and

FIGURE 13.4 Happy senior couple taking selfie on ship of a Mediterranean cruise travel tour.

goal-oriented. They value civic duty, achievement, diversity, and have greater need for peer acceptance and social connections. Millennials are the most populous generation in the United States. They enjoy travel and seek unique rather than cookie-cutter travel experiences.

Generation Z (Centennials)—consists of those born after 1996. The generation Z are "Digital Natives" because they were born into a world of social networks, digital platforms, and mobile computing. They spend a significant portion of their socializing on social media. They are found to be more risk-averse, and have a great sense of social responsibility. They are found to be less brand loyal than previous generations.

Income

Income is an important factor in shaping the demand for travel. It can be argued that the importance of other demographic factors is secondary to that of income (Mohsin and Ryan 2004). A large study of United States vacationers found that income is the leading influence on out-of-town vacations (Peterson and Lambert 2003).

In fact income, together with other demographic characteristics, explains a large portion of differences in vacation participation. Not only does travel itself entail a certain cost, but the traveler must pay for services rendered at the destination as well as have money to engage in various activities during the trip. In addition, expenditures may be required in the form of specialized equipment to engage in various recreational activities while at the destination or en route.

It is difficult, however, to determine the relative importance of income per se, because this variable is inter-related with other socioeconomic variables. Generally speaking, higher income is associated with higher education, with certain jobs, and with certain age groups. Total family income has risen steadily as more wives have entered the labor force. The fact that family income has risen will have an effect upon tourism demand. Yet the fact that more families have two spouses in the labor force will also affect the shape of tourism demand. Different types of vacations and recreational activities may be demanded because of the time pressures involved in having two working spouses. The difficulty arises in determining the effect of these two interrelated variables on the demand for new tourism and recreation products.

It is important to recognize that the income spent on travel is spent at the expense of something else. Travel expenditures are in competition with other expenditures, some of which are discretionary. An individual's *personal disposable income* is the amount of income left after paying taxes. After various necessary personal outlays to maintain basic living needs have been spent, an individual has discretion to do with the remainder whatever is desired. A mink coat may be purchased, money may be saved, or a trip may be taken to Hawaii. It is important to look at income in this way to realize that the trip to Hawaii is in competition not only with a trip to the Bahamas, but also with various other recreational activities and other uses of that discretionary income. As the level of personal income increases, so does the amount of *discretionary income*.

Gender

There are more similarities than differences between the sexes in terms of leisure participation rates. Overall, participation rates in leisure activities do not differ between men and women, although many women engage in slightly fewer activities than do men. As might be expected, nonworking women have slightly higher participation rates than do employed women, except for such things as going out to dinner and either taking part in active sports or watching sports.

Men and women can differ in their destination preferences. For example, when it comes to city destinations, women are found to be more partial to culture rich destinations whereas men are found to be drawn to more traditional metropolitan cities. There is a clear difference between the sexes in terms of preferred activities. Women are more involved in cultural and social activities, and men lead in outdoor recreation and playing and watching sports.

The traditional responsibilities of females relating to domestic work and child care have led to them viewing leisure activities in a way that are task-oriented rather than time-oriented, social rather than physical, and relational as opposed to self-interested. Women travelers are more motivated by rest/relaxation and social reasons compared to men. Women travelers tend to place more emphasis on the emotional and social benefits of travel and destination activities. One example is skiing. Women value the social aspect of an activity rather than its physical benefits more so than men. Women are found to be more likely than men to ski if friends and/or family members are involved. The activity is viewed as recreational rather than competitive.

Significant differences between men and women in souvenir purchases—including merchandise choice and selection factors—have been demonstrated (Combrink

Gender Differences in a Delightful Hotel Experience

Sheraton Grande WalkerHill in Seoul, South Korea, offers a special package for a special room: "Forever Barbie Package" in a Barbie suite room. Everything is pink in this room. The room features Barbie dolls and houses and customers can put on the Barbie dresses in the wardrobe. Millennium Seoul Hilton collaborated with the cosmetic brand Paris Hilton to offer "Paris Hilton X Mango Buffett" that includes nail art service using Paris Hilton nail polish. These examples illustrate that hotel offerings can be tailored to a specific gender, female guests in this case. One of the possible reasons why hotels develop products that mainly target a specific gender could be that there are gender differences in what hotel guests are delighted about. Hotels strive to delight guests as delight is based on guests' satisfaction and a pleasurable experience. Female guests are found to be more likely to be delighted by intangible service offerings including employee friendliness and professionalism. On the other hand, male guests tend to be delighted when individual needs are satisfied such as efficiency and timeliness of service.

Think about This

1. Why do you think the "Forever Barbie Package" or the "Paris Hilton X Mango Buffett" would especially appeal to female guests?
2. What other demographic factors could influence hotel guest delight? How?
3. What may be some delightful offerings for male hotel guests? Are you able to give examples where product/service designs consider gender differences?

Sources

https://www.walkerhill.com/en/Package/1261?tag=barbie

Torres, E., X. Fu, and X. Y. Lehto. 2014. Examining key drivers of customer delight in a hotel experience: A cross-cultural perspective. *International Journal of Hospitality Management* 36 (1): 255–262.

and Swanson 2000). For example, women are more likely to select crafts, postcards, and artistic and authentic clothing than are men. Equally, they are more likely to select merchandise on the basis of appealing colors and design than are men.

Education

The strong correlation between education and income has been well-established. Independent of income, however, the level of education that an individual has tends to influence the type of leisure and travel pursuits chosen. The amount of education obtained will most likely determine the nature of both work and leisure-time activities. By widening one's horizons of interest and enjoyment, education influences the type of activities undertaken. Education itself can serve as the primary reason for travel.

Researchers have found that participation in outdoor recreation tends to increase as the amount of education increases. There is also some evidence to suggest that the more educated prefer those activities that require the development of interpretive and expressive skills. Such activities include attending plays, concerts, and art museums; playing tennis and golf; skiing; reading books; attending adult education classes; and undergoing a wilderness experience.

In general, it appears that the more education people have, the broader their horizons and the more options they will consider. The more-educated travelers also tend to be more sophisticated in their tastes. They may not, however, be bigger spenders. A study of visitors to Hawaii found that visitors with less education spent more per day while on vacation in Hawaii.

LIFE CYCLE EFFECT

Individuals evolve through a certain life cycle. The characteristics of the family at the various stages of its life cycle offer certain opportunities or exert various pressures that affect travel purchase behavior. Although it has been suggested that this traditional life cycle has become outdated because of changing demographics such as the growing number of "dinks" (double income, no kids) and an increase in single parent families, the US Travel Association (USTA) has consumer research that shows that travel behavior varies depending on life stages. USTA indicates that the three core life stage groups—singles, couples, and parents—are defined by combining the demographic variables of children, household composition, and marital status.

Studies have also examined the impact of marriage on vacation behavior. They indicate that single people take part in a much wider variety of activities outside the home than do married people. Married life brings about certain changes in leisure habits. Activities that were previously done alone or with friends are participated in less for reasons intrinsic to the activity itself and more for reasons related to the role of being a spouse.

Presence of Children.   The narrowing of the types of activities participated in is intensified by the presence of children. When a married couple has children, there is a shift from activities primarily for intrinsic satisfaction to activities that are role-related, such as family activities. Before children come on the scene, the spouse is the chief leisure companion. This companionship is diluted by the presence of children.

The presence of children seems to be crucial. Travel is curtailed, more leisure is spent at home, and few new leisure interests are acquired. In at least one case, that of camping, the onset of parenthood has varied effects. Although the addition of young children in a camping family may produce a curtailment of camping activities, the shift to the empty-nest stage produces either an increase or a decrease in the activity. For those couples who enjoy camping, the situation of children leaving the nest may actually increase their participation. For others who saw camping primarily as a family activity, the departure of children from the home may result in less camping.

Most research indicates that family vacation decisions are made jointly by husbands and wives. However, research has also suggested that, when there are children in the home, the wife exerts more influence over the decision-making process and is more likely to seek information on the possible destination choices than when the couple is childless. According to research conducted by HomeAway (2015), one of the world's leading online vacation rental companies, children have a growing influence on a family's vacation planning decisions such as where to go on vacation and what to do once onsite a vacation destination.

Basic attitudes and behavior patterns of family life established in the early years of the family life cycle affect the future activities of both husbands and wives throughout the marriage. Activities undertaken in the early stages of the life span tend to be repeated throughout life. In addition, the types of vacations taken with parents as a child and during early adulthood serve as a model for future vacations.

For the young child, leisure pursuits are restricted by the dictates of parents and the limitations of money. As children enter school, leisure activities outside the home increase. As children grow older, their leisure habits and attitudes are more heavily influenced by their peers. Because of the high rate of social interaction among young people, leisure fads are easily spread. There is also at this stage an attempt to duplicate the behavior and attitudes of older age groups. Particularly important in this respect are college students, who tend to be leaders, often being the first to try new products and services.

As children leave the home, more time and money tends to be available for leisure. Some studies indicate that, in the United States, travel patterns change significantly after age sixty. Up until that time, auto travel is the favored mode of transportation. After that point, travel by bus, plane, or boat is preferred. This can be explained by an increase in available time and money and, perhaps, a reduction in physical abilities. Empty nesters usually want to spend more time in fewer places.

Barriers to Leisure Enjoyment.   Family life stages can also be associated with barriers to travel and leisure enjoyment. In particular, three general barriers to travel related to family life stages have been identified (Hsu and Kang 2009; Nyaupane and Andereck 2008):

- *Intrapersonal,* such as negative individual attitude toward participation
- *Interpersonal,* such as lack of agreement on what to do among family members
- *Structural,* such as a lack of time, money, children being too young.

The literature identifies time and costs as the most constraining factors. Cost is a more constraining factor for the youngest and the oldest, while time is a less

FIGURE 13.5 **Have children will travel: a family hiking in forest.**

important constraining factor for these youngest and oldest age groups than for those who are middle-aged. Understanding these barriers is a crucial step toward knowing what to say, do, and offer to lower those barriers. Research shows that barriers develop and change over the family life cycle. For example, barriers to leisure participation follow an inverted U-shaped pattern when expressed over the life cycle of the family (see Figure 13.6). During the childrearing period, family obligations increase significantly for women and, to a similar but lesser degree, for men. This fact and the fact that neither parent feels there is enough free time represent the barriers felt; they increase until children leave the home, and then their effect drops off sharply.

Identifying barriers predominant at various life cycle stages will enable products, packages, and messages to be targeted to reflect an understanding of these barriers and potential objections of the many market segments. Care must be taken, however, in the use of correlation or regression techniques for projecting or

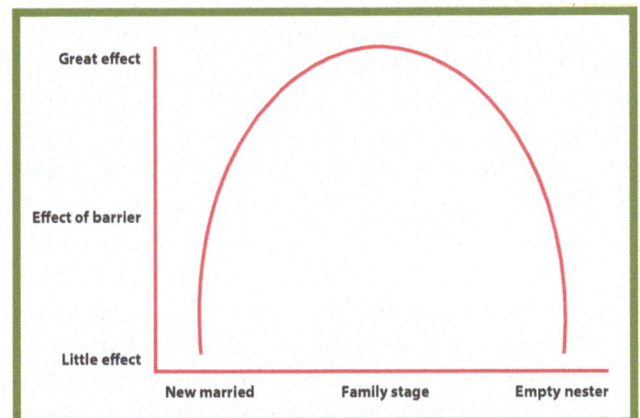

FIGURE 13.6 **Barriers to leisure enjoyment at different family stages (Inverted U-Shaped pattern).**

forecasting leisure activities because of the nonlinear pattern of many of these barriers. The family life cycle stage also provides at best only a partial explanation of leisure behavior.

TRAVELER PSYCHOGRAPHIC CHARACTERISTICS

In addition to cultural, social, and demographic influences, consumer psychographic characteristics can exert influences on their travel choices and behavior. These psychographic factors can include personality, beliefs and attitude, and perception. This section will elaborate upon their influences on travel behavior.

Personality can be thought of as consisting of a variety of traits. Individuals who participate in recreational and visitor activities can be classified in terms of their *personality traits* in an attempt to determine whether such participants exhibit markedly different personality traits than do nonparticipants. The purpose of such analysis is to determine whether or not personality can be used as a variable for segmenting the market. If it is found that certain personality traits are dominant in winter vacations, marketers will know better the kind of visitor to appeal to and will gain valuable information as to what to say to appeal to this potential vacationer. To date, the research evidence is inconclusive as to whether personality is a significant variable in explaining purchase behavior. Although several studies indicate a strong relationship between personality and consumer behavior, and a few indicate no relationship, the great majority indicate that any existing correlation is weak.

Often a person is described as having a certain type of personality. Personality types consist of characteristics that, when taken together, form a certain kind of person. One way of classifying people is to the extent that they are perceived as being *introverted* or *extroverted*. Introverts look into themselves and tend to be shy and reserved. Extroverts are other-oriented, looking outside the self and tending to be objective rather than subjective in outlook. Participants in vigorous physical activity in general tend to be extroverts. The relationship between personality and participation in recreational activities is of interest. As we have seen, recreational activities can serve as a major reason or motivation for vacation travel. If a relationship between certain activities and certain personality traits can be established, an appropriate marketing strategy can be developed.

Psychographics has developed as a way of describing consumer behavior in terms of a distinctive way of living in order to determine whether or not people with distinctive lifestyles have distinctive travel behaviors. *Psychographics* is the development of psychological profiles of consumers and psychologically based measures of distinctive modes of living or lifestyles. It has been shown that demographics are inadequate predictors of nature-based vacation behaviors (Murdy, Yiannakis, and Gibson 2003), and many argue that psychographics is a more useful tool in predicting vacation behavior. However, the psychographic dimensions are unlikely to displace demographic variables, especially income, in segmenting markets.

- **Travel personality**

Dr. Stanley Plog was the pioneer researcher who developed a travel personality system that depicts traveler segments based on their personality, life attitudes, and exhibited travel preferences. A key variable is one's tendency of venturesomeness (Plog 2002). This travel personality system provides an understanding of travelers based on their venturesomeness in travel, ranging from *psychocentrics* (people who are the least venturesome) to *allocentrics* (people who are the most venturesome). The various travel personalities influence traveler destination and activity choices.

Dr. Plog and his industry practice partner Bahir Browsh in fact developed a system which allows travelers to discover their travel personality by taking a travel personality quiz, and then recommends suitable travel destinations for the travelers based on their travel personality profile (www.besttripchoices.com). This travel personality profile includes six travel personality types: venturers, pioneers, voyagers, journeyers, sightseers, and traditionals. The venturers exhibit the most venturesomeness whereas the traditionals exhibit the least. This system can help destinations to create better marketing messages to appeal to travel segments based on their level of venturesomeness, and to better position their experience offerings toward a particular travel personality segment.

TRAVELER PERCEPTIONS AND DESTINATION IMAGE

The decision to travel to a particular destination is linked to our perception of that destination. This implies that an examination of the perception process may help us understand if and how we can influence an individual's perception of a destination in order to increase the likelihood of that individual visiting the destination. The key word is "perceive," for we buy based not so much on what information is actually presented to us, but on how we perceive that information. Thus, the perceptions an individual has of a destination plays an important role in determining whether or not a travel purchase will be made. Perception is reality for most people. Irrespective of the reality of the situation people will buy, or not; travel, or not, based on their perception of the situation.

Traveler perceptions shape their *image of a destination,* which represents a mental picture that he or she conjures up. An *image* is "the set of meanings by which an object is known and through which people describe, remember and relate to it" (Chon 1990). For an individual who has not visited a place previously, the travel decision must be made on the perceived image of that destination. After a visit occurs, personal experience modifies that image. However, that first visit is made on the basis of whether or not the destination—or, at least, one's image of the destination—is likely to meet needs and wants that are important to the individual. In fact perceptions are the most important factor in several important decisions made by visitors: the choice of a destination, what is purchased while on vacation, and the decision to return.

Perceptual Biases

Marketer-generated information (e.g., advertisement) or non-marketer-generated information (e.g., a book, a movie, prior experiences) can influence and shape one's image of a destination. It is important to understand that. However, the information and impressions that do get through to a consumer can be distorted by a number of forces. First there is a tendency on our part to *stabilize our perception* even after the original basis for the perception has changed. A traveler may continue to stay at an old favorite hotel where the level of service has declined because their perception remains in the past. An image, whether positive or negative, may continue long after the factors causing that original image have been changed. This illustrates the difficulty involved in changing an image. Linked with this very closely is that, second, as a creature of habit, a traveler will perceive in a certain *habitual way* until forced to think differently. Stress here is placed on the need for marketers to break through the traveler's "habit barrier" by means of various stimuli.

A third shaping force is related to the extent to which individuals have a tendency to be *confident* or *cautious.* The confident individual takes in a complex situation more quickly, can more readily see positive elements in a situation, and can assimilate more detail. Decisions are made faster by confident persons, but this may come at a cost because the slower decisions of cautious people may be based on more accurate perceptions. This factor points to the need to communicate

different messages to different segments of an intended market.

Further, consumers have a *limited span of attention.* This refers to the number of stimuli that can be taken in at the same time. Experiments have shown this number to be approximately eight. This infers that messages should not consist of too many elements for fear that an important element may be missed or that the message may be disregarded because it is too confusing. The tendency to react to a given stimuli in a certain way is referred to as an *individual's mental set.* This suggests a learned response. It may be possible, for example, to suggest in a campaign, "Whenever you think of hotels, think of Hilton." If the campaign has the desired effect, an individual will think of Hilton (the response) whenever she or he thinks of hotels (the stimulus). Parts of this mental set are the *expectations* we bring to a situation.

People tend to perceive what they expect to perceive. There is a tendency to round out a particular image in our minds by adding pieces that we do not have *based on what we expect to be there.* For example, a highway traveler may see a sign for a motel that advertises an indoor pool. The traveler may expect that if a motel has an indoor pool, it will also have a certain high quality of service in other facilities. This is known as bringing closure to a situation. Another part of our state of readiness is the degree of *familiarity* we have with incoming stimuli. To the extent that we are familiar with the stimulus we will have some idea of how to respond to it.

This effect of past experience manifests itself in several ways. First, if we have visited Germany, then information about Germany will be perceived by us, in part, based on our experience there. If we experienced negatives, we will perceive new information about Germany negatively because it evokes memories of a negative experience. The reverse is also true. In addition, if we perceive new information to be *similar* to an experience with which we are familiar, we will tend to act on that new information in a way similar to our behavior in our previous experience. For example, assume we perceive Austria and Germany to be similar as vacation destinations, yet we have visited only Germany and were pleased with the experience. Information received about Austria will be perceived positively in light of our German experience. This, of course, can work to encourage or discourage purchase behavior.

If we know positive feelings exist for a product or service, we may wish to stress the connection when advertising a new product from the same company. A major selling point in a chain operation is the uniformity of quality standards. The message is that if you stayed at one Holiday Inn and were pleased, you will be pleased when you stay at another Holiday Inn. This can also work in reverse. An unpleasant experience at one chain operation will be generalized into a perception about the entire chain. There are times when an advertiser will have to work hard against this tendency. Some visitors will have a tendency to perceive all "sun 'n fun" destinations as being similar. The task for any one such destination is to show that it is different from the others.

A further complicated factor is that stimuli in close proximity to each other tend to be perceived as being similar. Despite the fact that islands in the Caribbean have unique identities because of different historical and cultural influences, the fact that they are relatively close together means they will be perceived as being similar. Again, the marketing task is to differentiate one from another. Another related part of this perceptual process relates to *context*. A stimulus will be perceived relative to the context in which it is viewed. A resort will be judged, in part, by the perceptions of the media in which the resort is advertised. Advertising in a magazine viewed as exclusive will bring a certain perception of exclusivity to the resort.

Destination Image Components

Destination image is the mental picture that an individual forms of a tourism destination. Destination image influences traveler decision-making in a substantial way and therefore has commanded extensive market research

QUICK TRIP 13.6

Perception of Distance

The subject of distance in general, and perceptions of it in particular, are very important in relation to the study of tourism. Perception of distance influences three crucial tourism decisions: whether to go or stay, where to go, and which route to take. The distance to be traveled may act as a barrier, depending on how it is perceived. The perception of a particular distance is not a constant. For example, the homeward-bound journey seems shorter than the outward-bound journey along the same route; short distances tend to be overestimated to a greater degree than long distances.

On the other hand, by its very nature, the fact people travel to experience differences implies covering some distance. In fact, much of tourist travel revolves around differences. People may travel to a different climate, from snow to sun; to see different scenery, from plains to mountains; or to experience a different culture, from modern to traditional.

Although all of the answers are not known, it does seem that distance can be viewed either positively or negatively in terms of its effect on travel. Certainly the greater the distance the greater the financial cost. As such, distance is a limiting factor. It may also be that great distances represent a psychological barrier because of the tediousness involved in traveling in or the fear of being far from home.

At the same time, a destination may increase in attractiveness because of the distance that must be traveled to get there. In some sense, distance makes the heart fonder because it can promise something unique or exotic to the travelers. It has also been demonstrated that, for some tourists, beyond a certain distance the friction of distance becomes reversed—the farther they go, the farther they want to go. Especially on unplanned trips there may be a tendency to view closer-to-home destinations and attractions as stepping-stones to stopping points farther away than as competition for the farther destination.

Think about This

1. Why is understanding of traveler distance perception important?
2. Are you able to provide examples of strategies employed by destinations to market distance as exotic or uniquely attractive values to travelers?
3. Distance may lead to travelers' sense of uncertainty and insecurity. What can destinations do to manage travelers' psychology of fear?

by destination management organizations. As we learned from Chapter 8, creating and enhancing destination image is one of their primary goals. The intangible nature of the travel product—what a traveler purchases is an experience—and the inability to sample the destination before the travel decision is made make effective destination positioning and image projection all the more crucial in drawing travelers. The starting point of creating a destination image is the understanding of travelers and prospective travelers' current image of a destination. In this context, what is in a destination image held by travelers and how they form this image are what tourism marketers have painstakingly tried to understand.

A destination image—the mental picture of a destination—can be understood along three spectrums of characteristics (Echtner and Ritchie 1993, Figure 13.7):

- Attribute based—Holistic
- Functional—Psychological
- Common—Unique

To better understand what the authors mean by the attribute-holistic spectrum, think of what someone might say when asked to describe their impression of a place. In some cases, he or she may describe the place in terms of information regarding specific attributes, such as its climate and the friendliness of the people. At the other extreme he or she may describe their overall sense of the place, such as a general feeling about the destination or its general atmosphere. One study on Australia

identified the following attributes (Ryan and Cave 2005): Friendly, Sunny, Scenic, Good beaches, Interesting wildlife. The holistic imagery included: Adventure, Laid back, Rugged.

On the functional-psychological spectrum, there are characteristics that are directly measurable (e.g., "low prices") and those that are less tangible (e.g., "generally safe"). Functional and psychological characteristics may be individual attributes or overall impressions. On the common-unique continuum, visitor's imagery of destinations can range from those based on common functional and psychological characteristics of a place to those based on more distinctive or unique features. It is argued that, only by considering all of the spectrums of perceptions can consumers' complete image of a destination be understood and image projection approaches be developed. This is important because "if a destination is found difficult to categorize or is not easily differentiated from other similar destinations, then its likelihood of being considered in the travel decision process is reduced" (Echtner and Ritchie 1993).

Affective Image. Although most tourism image studies have focused on the cognitive or belief aspect of image, image also has an affective component dealing with feelings. Travelers' affective evaluation of a destination in general is related to their cognitive evaluations. In affective terms, Destinations could, for example, be examined on the basis of ratings on the following continuums: "Arousing–Sleepy," "Exciting–Gloomy," "Pleasant–Unpleasant," and "Relaxing–Distressing."

One such example is a study of travelers' affective images of five city-state pairs of destinations (Chicago and Illinois, Los Angeles-California, Dallas-Texas, Boston-Massachusetts, Las Vegas-Nevada) in the United States by Lehto, Lee, and Ismail (2014). This research shows that travelers have very different affective images of particular places (Figure 13.8). For example, California is perceived as exciting whereas Los Angeles is perceived as somewhat distressing. These particular ratings are based on a small sample of United States travelers, so the results in Figure 13.8 for particular locations need to be interpreted with caution. However, given an adequate sample of travelers, this approach can quickly yield results that have important implications for destinations. For example, if a destination is perceived as exciting, what destination attributes and activities can be further developed to sustain and enhance such an image? If a destination is being perceived as boring or distressing, what contributes to such a negative imagery? What can destinations do to change such negative images?

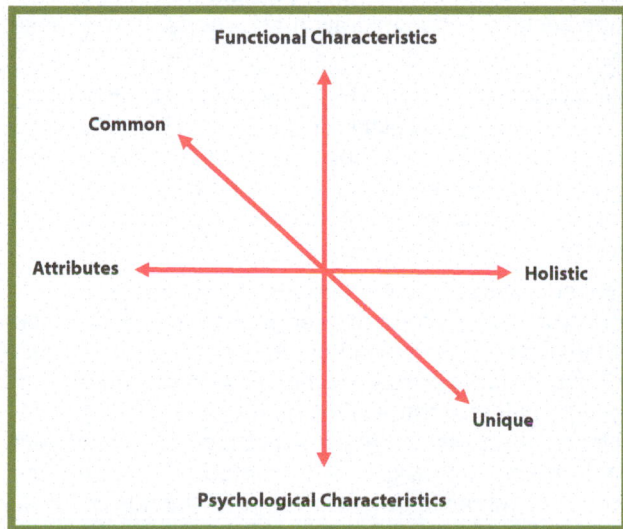

FIGURE 13.7 The Components of Destination Image. | Source: Echtner, C. M., and J. R. B. Ritchie. 1993. The measurement of destination image. *Journal of Travel Research* 31 (4): 4.

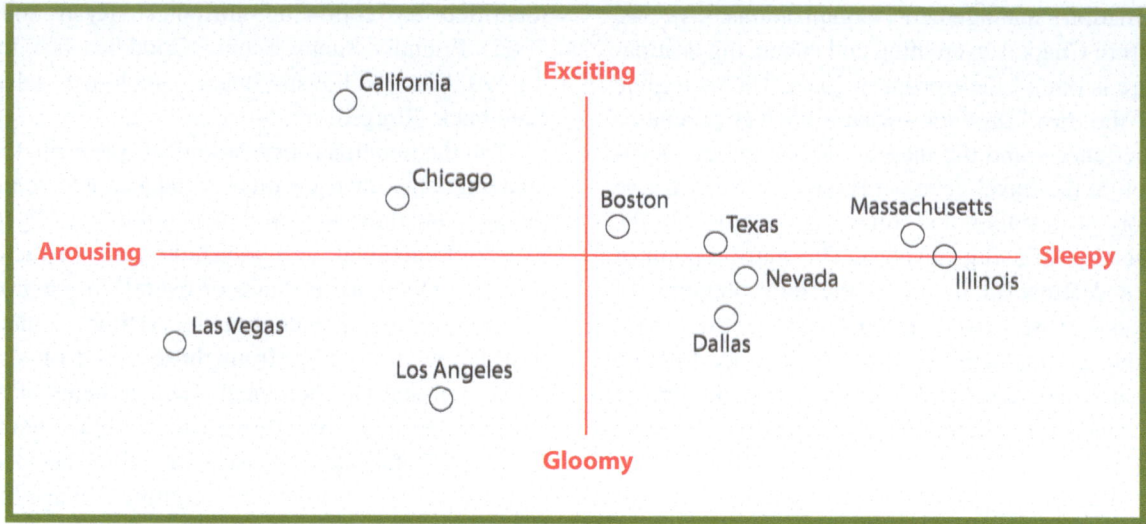

FIGURE 13.8 Destinations on a two-dimensional scale.

Anxiety and Worry in the Age of Permanxiety

Destination safety and security is a destination attribute that is extremely important to travelers. In today's global world, however, negative geopolitical events such as the series of terrorist attacks that took place in London and Paris have become all too frequent occurrences. The impact of these negative events, magnified by today's omnipresent Internet connectivity, has created great anxiety and worry among travelers. A *Skift* report coined the term *Permanxiety* to describe this emerging travel worry culture.

Although terrorist attacks and mass shootings would only drive away travelers temporarily, other factors that worry travelers could have a more permanent impact on whether they would travel or where they would travel to. Certain activities that travelers have to engage in, such as going through security and immigration at airports, could cause traveler anxiety.

Travelers can also be worried about traveling to a destination that is culturally foreign. They may have feelings of worry and anxiety about travel due to their personal conditions such as having a physical disability. Under-represented groups such as LGBT travelers could also fear traveling due to discrimination that they could possibly experience. Media reports from newspaper and social media are further heightening traveler worries. For instance, a story about travelers being discriminated against or not treated well by their Airbnb host might go viral on social media. Such news could add anxiety to travelers planning to use Airbnb services.

What can the hospitality and tourism industry do to mitigate travel anxieties? Some airports, for instance, provide therapy dogs to calm anxious passengers. High-end hotels encourage their customers to engage in wellness-related activities such as meditation retreats and yoga. Hotels can also train their employees how to serve their customers in a way that relieves traveler worries and stress. The key point is that the employees need to understand what could make their customers uneasy and develop a sense of empathy with their customers. Airbnb, for instance, is providing programs via online education and community meetings to train their hosts and make sure they understand their guests' need for safety and security. There are mobile apps that travel companies have created to help alleviate traveler anxiety. One such example is an app called "companion" that connects travelers with their friends or family members. Essentially the latter becomes the virtual travel companion for a traveler. To help address the concern that traveling in an unfamiliar place could worry travelers, this app allows their friends or family members to be able to track their journey via GPS.

Think about This

1. What are other possible factors that could make travelers worry about traveling?
2. What may be things a destination can do to help visitors in need of assistance in unforeseen circumstances such as terrorist attacks? What would such a help system be like?
3. What can other types of businesses in hospitality and tourism industry (e.g., event sites and restaurants) do to alleviate travelers' worries?

Source

Skift. 2017. Travel in an age of Permanxiety. *Skift Magazine,* Issue 07. https://skift.com/2017/10/03/travel-in-an-age-of-permanxiety

QUICK TRIP 13.8

Be Remembered

An effective slogan can go a long way in positioning a unique image in the minds of consumers. Take some time out of your reading for a short exercise. What companies pop into your mind when you read the following taglines?

"Are you in good hands?"	"100% Juice for 100 kids"	"It give you wings"
"What's in your wallet?"	"Snap, Crackle, Pop."	"East Fresh"
"The Happiest place on earth"	"I'm lovin' it"	"Think outside the bun"
	"Just Do It"	"Travel Brilliantly"

Taglines such as these have reached into secluded corners of the world and have been permanently etched into our minds. Marcia Yudkin is a tagline and slogan aficionado. Her interview can be read in an article by Marilee Crocker entitled "Terrific Taglines: Is yours a brand booster or a flop" (2011). In this article, Marcia explains the significance of taglines when it comes to brand differentiation. "It's a short group of words," Marcia says, "that position you and help you stand for something and stand out." A tagline can be used to assure consumers of your devotion to quality products and/or services. As a mechanism which assists the public in recognizing your brand, it gives you the ability to convey a lot of information in very few words.

Taglines provide you with the ability to position yourself within your market according to how you hope to be perceived. For instance, you may want to be seen as the best deal or the company that offers the best customer service. When trying to come up with a slogan/tagline for your company it is important to consider whether or not your target audience would buy a t-shirt or bumper sticker with your slogan/tagline printed on it. If the answer is no, you may want to rethink your tagline. Always test your tagline beforehand, and remember that what is funny to you may not come across as funny to your audience.

Answers: Allstate, Capital One, Disneyland, Juicy Juice, Kellogg's Rice Krispies, McDonald's, Nike, RedBull, Subway, Taco Bell, and Marriott

Think about This

1. If you were commissioned to come up with a tagline for your university what would it be?
2. Who is your target audience? Why would this matter?
3. What feelings are you attempting to evoke from your audience?
4. Does the slogan shine a positive light on the university?
5. Would a community member, an international student, or a potential freshman need to have any background knowledge in order to understand your slogan? Why would this matter?

Source

Crocker, M. (2011). Terrific Taglines: Is Yours a Brand Booster or a Flop? http://www.travelmarketreport.com/retail?articleID=5693&LP=1

Destination Image and Self-Image

Consumers have a tendency to buy things that have attributes consistent with their own image. An individual's total image is made up of several parts. First, the ***real self*** is the objective person—what the individual is deep down. In reality, few of us know ourselves this well. Yet this true self governs our purchase and travel behavior, even if we are unaware of what it is that moves us in a particular way. Second, there is the ***ideal self***. The ideal self is what we would like to be. This aspect of the individual is easier to discover for two reasons that are important to marketers: consumers are more willing to discuss what they aspire to than what they believe really motivates them, and by simple observation of purchase behavior much can be learned about what a consumer is striving for. Last, the ***self-image*** is how consumers perceive themselves. Consumers often make purchases that they feel will maintain or improve their self-image, as they perceive it. Consumers attempt to preserve their self-image in several ways. They:

- Buy products consistent with their self-image
- Avoid products inconsistent with their self-image
- Trade up to products that relate favorably to group norms of behavior
- Avoid products that show a radical departure from accepted group norms

Visitors have favorable attitudes to destinations and products that they perceive to be consistent with their own self-image. It has, in fact, been demonstrated that pre-visit travel interest and purchase likelihood are positively correlated to self-congruity (where there is a low discrepancy between the self-image of an individual and his or her image of the destination) and ideal-self congruity (where there is a low discrepancy between the ideal self-image and the image of the product or destination) (Goh and Litvin 2000).

These three aspects of the self—the real, ideal, and self-image—are concerned with the individual. There are two other aspects of the self that are concerned with external facts. The ***apparent self***—in essence a combination of the real self, ideal self, and self-image—represents how the consumer is seen by outsiders. The impressions that outsiders have of an individual will determine whether or not any commonality of interests or desires is perceived and whether or not any friendships will develop. This affects purchases because we tend to copy the purchases of those we admire. Thus, the picture of myself that I give to others—made up of my real and ideal selves and my self-image—will tell others if they and I seem to be the same type of person. Your buying patterns for a vacation, for example, may influence others who know you to purchase that type of vacation. The ***reference group self*** is how we believe others see us. What is believed, however, is more important than what is real, for behavior is predicted on what we ***believe*** others want us to do.

Managing Destination Image Attributes

It is generally felt that we perceive products and services as consisting of a bundle of benefits or attributes. A vacation package consists of a variety of parts—for example, in a ski vacation, excellent snow conditions, few lift lines, entertainment, saunas, continental cuisine, and so on. The decision to purchase the package will be based on two factors. First, the skier, for example, must believe that the attributes of the package will help satisfy his or her felt needs. Second, the satisfaction of those felt needs must be important to the skier. The former contributes more to determining an individual's attitude toward a product or service. The implication is that if we wish to sell a particular vacation, we should sell that vacation as consisting of a number of benefits that will contribute toward the satisfaction of the buyer's needs.

An individual may be seeking to satisfy several needs at the same time. Our package, therefore, should contain many elements that will aim at satisfying different needs. The provision of American-type meals and English-speaking guides may satisfy primary physiological and safety needs during a trip to Europe, whereas the inclusion of side trips to certain "name" resorts may help in satisfying the need for status.

It is important for a destination to take control of the image it wishes to portray. For example, it has been shown that the image of India that is shown in the Western press is, in many ways, different from that depicted by the Indian government (Bandyopadhyay and Morais 2004). Although the United States media portrayed experiences in India as "bewildering" and "uncertain," the Indian government emphasized the country's "extreme natural and cultural contrasts." In another example, the United States media focused on the charm of India's small villages and folkways whereas the Indian government's promotions ignored such images. Additionally, the American media promoted a royal image of luxury with a focus on "Maharaja palaces" and eco-lodges embedded in historical and natural environments. The Indian government, on the other hand, emphasized India's modern hotels as well as the

Western-style amenities that had recently been added to its old hotels. This has very real marketing implications.

Destination Attribute Assessment.

Effective marketing strategies can be determined only after determining the extent to which potential visitors perceive that a destination contains those attributes that they consider important. This involves a three-step process:

1. What do you, the potential visitor, consider important?
2. Do you *perceive* that we (the destination) have what you consider important?
3. Do we (the destination) *actually* have this?

Data on the first two items can come from quantitative data or from open-ended comments using impressions of critical incidents recorded by visitors (Pritchard and Havitz 2006). Destinations can conduct ***Importance-Performance*** analysis following the three-step process. An illustrative model for this process is contained in Figure 13.9. This process is illustrated through an examination of a study of Ireland's image by French visitors (O'Leary and Deegan 2005). A literature search identified a comprehensive list of attributes that could be used to measure destination image. In a survey of potential visitors from France, individuals were asked what three words or expressions came to mind when they thought of Ireland. Prior to their visit, travelers from France were asked to rate the relative importance of these attributes on a scale of 1 through 5, with 5 being the most important. After their visit, travelers were asked to evaluate the performance of the destination on these same attributes again using a scale of 1 through 5, where 5 indicates "very good."

The discrepancies between importance and performance ratings regarding attributes of a destination will inform a destination about what is important to the traveler, and how a destination is doing in the minds of travelers. The "Do we actually have this" step will allow a destination to understand its tourism resources in relation to what travelers perceive as important. Together, these three questions will allow a destination to chart out a destination image and positioning strategy and positively influence traveler decision-making.

This process can be displayed visually in a perceptual map. A ***perceptual map*** shows the collective perceptions of a segment of the market for a particular destination on factors considered important to them. A perceptual map of Ireland is shown in Figure 13.9. The

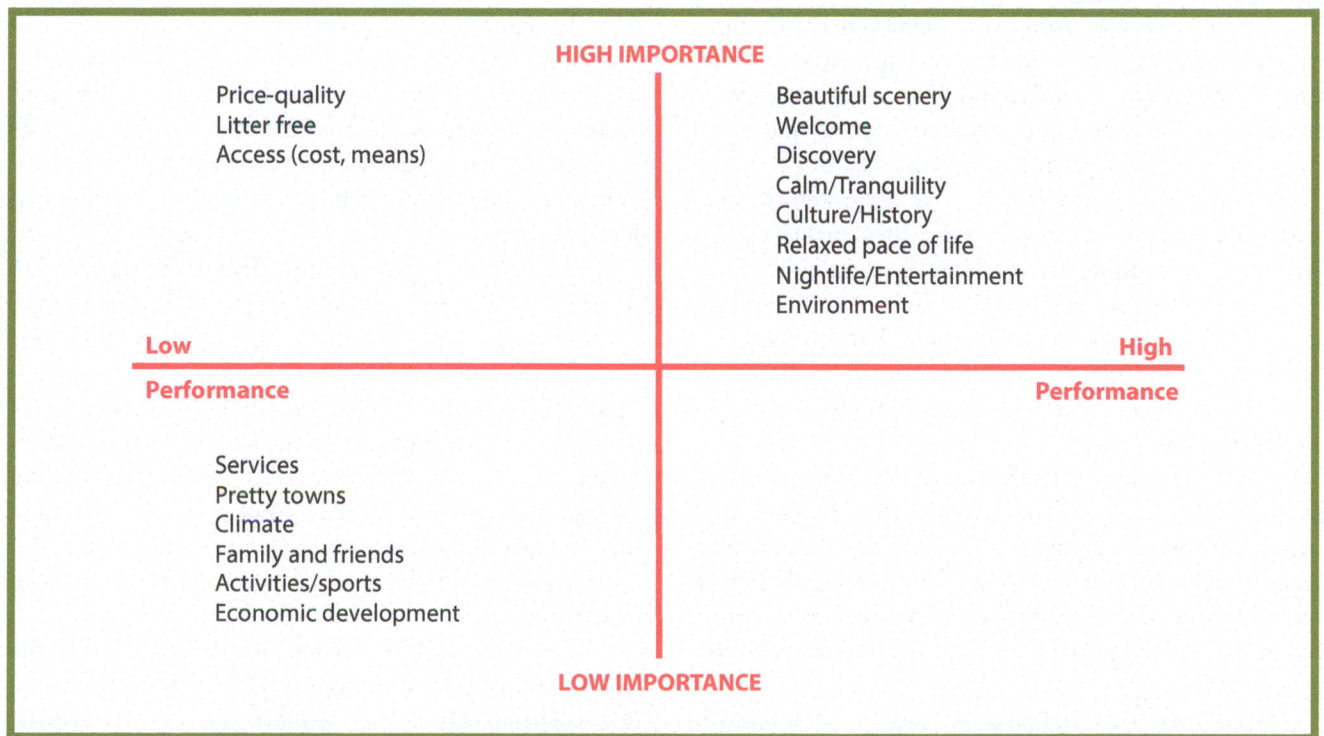

FIGURE 13.9 List of Attributes Developed for French Tourists. | Source: O'Leary, S., and J. Deegan. 2005. Ireland's image as a tourism destination in France: Attribute importance and performance.

importance of vacation attributes has been placed on the horizontal axis and the perception of Ireland for these same attributes has been placed on the vertical axis.

Items in the top left quadrant consist of those attributes that are important to this segment of the market and on which Ireland is perceived as doing a poor job of providing. Ireland is not seen as providing good quality for the money, is not litter-free, and is perceived as being costly. These are items where performance must be improved. However, these items must survive a *reality check*. It may be, for example, that low cost travel options are available but visitors are not aware of them. In this case, where the image is negative on cost but, in actuality, low cost packages are available then the image must be changed. On the other hand, if the country is not litter-free, then the product must be improved.

The product change may, on the other hand, be perceptual. There is a segment of skiers who place high priority on short lift lines. If a ski area is perceived as having long lift lines, it will be necessary to change the product if, in fact, the lines are long. How can a lift line be shortened? A real change would be to open up more hill capacity. This, however, is expensive. A perceived change would be to make the wait *appear* shorter. Some Michigan ski areas provide entertainers or musicians to provide a diversion for those in line to make the time spent in line seem short.

Ireland is seen as strong on certain attributes deemed important to French visitors: beautiful scenery, welcome, discovery, calm/tranquility, culture/history, relaxed pace of life, nightlife/entertainment, and environment. The temptation is to charge full steam ahead with these items as the mainstay of a marketing campaign. Here again, there is the need for a reality check. Are these perceptions truly reflective of Ireland? If the image is positive yet the reality is otherwise, the product needs to be improved. If, on the other hand, these attributes truly are reflective of the destination, they can form the basis for a marketing campaign directed to this segment of the market.

There are certain attributes where Ireland is perceived as doing a poor job: services, pretty towns, climate, family and friends, activities/sports, economic development. However, these are items that score low in importance to visitors from France. As such, they should be given a low priority in terms of improving the product.

Finally, there are items ranked as low in importance and high in performance. It would be foolish to spend time and money to improve things already considered high in performance when they are items not considered important to the visitor. Through the use of perceptual mapping, destinations can determine how or if they should change their tourism product and advertising.

The destination attribute assessment process explained above can lay a foundation for a destination to gain an understanding of place attributes and attractiveness that is instrumental in positively influencing visitor decisions. It can also provide guiding parameters for destination development. For example, a destination can

- *develop a pool of attributes* based on its analysis of its existing tourism resources;
- develop an understanding of how well it *performs* in these attribute areas based on market research;
- develop an understanding of what attributes are deemed as *important* by the target market travelers (via market research);
- *benchmark* its attributes against its competitive set of destinations;
- develop effective marketing communication strategies;
- identify areas of improvement in destination development.

Use of Framing in Marketing of Destination Image. Framing is a communication technique that is frequently utilized in marketing to steer consumers toward a favorable image of a destination. Framing of information refers to the idea that the same information can be described and presented in different ways or "frames." *Framing* can be understood as casting a border, a surrounding on thematically related attributes to *induce a state of mind* from consumers. These frames will interact with information receivers' cognitive system's internal representation and their corresponding behavior.

Destination marketers have been utilizing framing in their marketing communications for many years. Effective advertising usually contains a focused message and a context that help to accentuate the focus, and thus affect how the audience would understand or evaluate it. Tourism marketers commonly use framing techniques such as repeating (frequency) and/or highlighting (duration) certain keywords, concepts, symbols, and images with the intent to promote a desired image of a destination and generate a positive endorsement from consumers.

The importance of framing is well recognized, but some aspects of how to best frame a tourism destination are still being debated. Tourism destinations are traditionally framed as products with a set of attributes to be marketed. When framed as a place product, a destination is defined as "an amalgam of all products, services and experiences provided locally (attractions, accessibility, amenities, available packages, activities, ancillary services)" (Buhalis 2000). An alternative view, however, posits that tourism destination should not be framed as a product, but rather a "place narrative." When it is being framed as such, place becomes a set of meanings constructed by local and cultural narratives. In this later frame, the leading entities in tourism destination shift to local communities instead of being defined by tourism demand. This has important implications in terms of locus of control in tourism planning and marketing of visitor experience. A local community-endorsed destination image may be more authentic to the eyes of the visitors and may, therefore, be more powerful and convincing.

QUICK TRIP 13.9

Framing in Action: 100% Pure New Zealand Campaign

100% Pure New Zealand campaign is one of the longest running and most successful destination marketing campaigns in the world. Since its launch in 1999 to its international markets, this campaign has garnered multiple accolades, and has helped New Zealand achieve remarkable increases in international visitor arrivals in recent years. The campaign signals the first time that New Zealand utilized a single message in all of its markets around the world: which is "The youngest country on earth (New Zealand) has the purest and most unspoiled landscapes."

This focused message was in full display in its first worldwide TV commercial. Natural images such as rolling farm land and spectacularly steep mountains in fact make up of 90 percent of the video images (Figure 13.10). This campaign is an excellent example of how the use of framing can help shape consumer's perceptions and attitudes

FIGURE 13.10 Fiordland National Park, New Zealand.

about a place product. The campaign has reshaped New Zealand from a perceived sleepy, far-away place to one with pristine green wonderland for travelers young and young at heart.

Since the first 100% Pure campaign, New Zealand has launched a campaign series that have all been connected back to the 100% Pure theme: "100% pure relaxation," "100% pure welcome," "100% pure adrenalin," "100% pure you," and "100% Middle-earth." "100% Middle-earth" in fact was named best destination marketing campaign at the 2012 World Travel Awards (TourismZealand 2016). All of these marketing campaigns center on the carefully crafted destination image of 100% Pure New Zealand.

Think about This

1. Watch the 100% Pure New Zealand video. Discuss why this campaign has been so successful.
2. How does Tourism New Zealand frame the campaign? What visual images are the most impactful in influencing travelers' perception of the kind of destination New Zealand is?
3. Research further Tourism Zealand's official website, and explain how Tourism Zealand has used synchronized framing in its marketing activities on TV and print commercials, online channels, social media channels, international public relation, media engagement, and the travel trade.
4. How do the movies Lord of the Rings and The Hobbit help with New Zealand's 100% Pure image?

Sources

Campelo, A., R. Aitken, and J. Gnoth. 2011. Visual rhetoric and ethics in marketing of destinations. Journal of Travel Research 50 (1), 3–14.

http://media.newzealand.com/en/

http://www.newzealand.com/us/

http://www.tourismnewzealand.com/about/what-we-do/campaign-and-activity/

Morgan, N., A. Pritchard, R. Piggott. 2002. New Zealand, 100% Pure. The creation of a powerful niche destination brand. Journal of brand management 9 (4): 335–354.

SUMMARY

The vacation choices that people make are influenced by, and often constrained by, various factors external to them. The culture of which they are a part and the significant events that helped shape their values all act to determine, in part, when, where, and how they will vacation. The time available also determines if, when, and where people will travel. Developments such as increased leisure time, provision of paid vacations, as well as advances in technology, have enabled people to take a vacation and have influenced how far they can go with the amount of free time they have. Demographic and psychological factors also shape the vacation decision and preferences. Attempts to explain vacation behavior using demographic factors alone can be incomplete. Knowledge of cultural, sociodemographic, and psychological characteristics of travelers can be useful in crafting destination marketing strategies. Managing and marketing a favorable destination image are important tasks for destination professionals.

ACTIVITIES

1. Explain why Las Vegas' tag line of "what happens in Vegas, stays in Vegas" is so appealing to many travelers.
2. Develop a marketing campaign for a tourism attraction targeted toward a specific group with a commercial, slogan, and pamphlet that appeals to someone in another country. Then contrast this marketing campaign to what you would propose for a United States citizen in the same demographic target area.
3. Have you ever gone to a website that requires you to choose your country before entering? Go to a website such as www.Gucci.com, www.coca-cola.com, and www.Nike.com, and compare and contrast the differences between the different sites. Explain why these sites have chosen to alter each aspect for the different countries or languages.

REFERENCES

Bandyopadhyay, R., and D. B. Morais. 2004. Representative dissonance: Differences in the way India is portrayed to the USA tourist market. 35th Annual Conference Proceedings of the Travel and Tourism Research Association. CD-ROM, unpaged.

Barrett, Deborah. 2006. *Leadership Communication.* New York, NY: McGraw-Hill.

Bennett, P. D., and H. J. Kassasjin. 1982. *Consumer Behavior.* Englewood Cliffs, NJ: Prentice-Hall, Inc.

Buhalis, D. 2000. "Marketing the competitive destination of the future." *Tourism Management* 21 (1), 97–116.

Chon, K. 1990. The role of destination image in tourism: A review and discussion. *The Tourist Review* 45 (2): 2–9.

Combrink, T., and K. K. Swanson. 2000. Souvenir choice and gender: An evaluation of domestic souvenir choice attributes of tourists in the Four Corners region of the Southwest. 2000 Travel and Tourism Research Association Annual Conference Proceedings, 378–383.

Echtner, C. M., and J. R. B. Ritchie. 1993. "The measurement of destination image." *Journal of Travel Research* 31 (4): 3–13.

Goh, H. K., and S. W. Litvin. 2000. Destination Preference and Self-Congruity. 31st Annual Conference Proceedings of the Travel and Tourism Research Association, 197–203.

Hofstede, G. 1985. The cultural perspective. In *People and Organizations Interacting,* A. Brakel (Ed.). New York: John Wiley & Sons, Inc.

Hofstede Insights. 2017. Geert Hofstede Cultural Dimensions. http://www.geert-hofstede.com/

Home Away. 2015. https://www.homeaway.com/info/media-center/press-releases/2015/new-survey-reveals-the-strong-influence-of-kids-on-family-travel

Hsu, C. H. C., and S. K. Kang. 2009. "Chinese urban mature travelers' motivation and constraints by decision autonomy." *Journal of Travel & Tourism Marketing* 26: 703–721.

https://www.besttripchoices.com

Kim, D-Y, L. Wen, and K. Doh. 2010. "Does cultural difference affect customer's response in a crowded restaurant environment? A comparison of American versus Chinese customers." *Journal of Hospitality & Tourism Research* 34 (1): 103–123.

Lehto, X. Y., G. J. Lee, and J. Ismail. 2014. "Affective image congruence between destinations and their slogans." *International Journal of Tourism Research* 16 (3), 250–260.

Mohsin, A., and C. Ryan. 2004. "Determinants of destination choice: the role of socio-demographic variables." *Tourism Recreation Research* 29 (3): 27–33.

Murdy, J., A. Yiannakis, and H. Gibson. 2003. The confounding effects of demographic variables on predicting nature-based tourist roles across the adult life course. *Targeted Research: The Gateway to Accountability.* 34th Annual Proceedings of the Travel and Tourism Research Association. CD-ROM, unpaged.

Nyaupane, G. P., and K. L. Andereck. 2008. "Understanding travel constraints: application and extension of a leisure constraints model." *Journal of Travel Research* 46: 433–439.

O'Leary, S., and J. Deegan. 2005. "Ireland's image as a tourism destination in France: Attribute importance and performance." *Journal of Travel Research* 43: 247–256.

Peterson, M., and S. L. Lambert. 2003. "A Demographic Perspective on U.S. Consumers' Out-of-Town Vacationing and Commercial Lodging Usage while on Vacation." *Journal of Travel Research* 42(2), 116–124.

Plog, S. 2002. "The power of psychographics and the concept of venturesomeness." *Journal of Travel Research* 40: 244–251.

Pritchard, M. P., and M. E. Havitz. 2006. "Destination appraisal: An analysis of critical incidents." *Annals of Tourism Research* 33 (1): 25–46.

Reisinger, Y. 2004. The influence of tourist national culture on the importance of destination attributes. *Measuring the Tourism Experience.* 35th Annual Conference Proceedings of the Travel and Tourism Research Association. CD-ROM, unpaged.

Ryan, C., and J. Cave. 2005. "Structuring destination image: A qualitative approach." *Journal of Travel Research* 44 (2), 143–150.

Skift. 2017. "Travel in an age of Permanxiety." *Skift Magazine,* Issue 07. https://skift.com/2017/10/03/travel-in-an-age-of-permanxiety

Twenge, J. M., S. M. Campbell, B. J. Hoffman, and C. E. Lance. 2010. "Generational Differences in Work Values: Leisure and Extrinsic Values Increasing, Social and Intrinsic Values Decreasing." *Journal of Management* 36 (5), 1117–1142.

ADDITIONAL READINGS

Fodness, D. 1992. "The impact of family life cycle on the vacation decision-making process." *Journal of Travel Research 31 (2): 8–13.*

Foss, Stephen, and Karen Littlejohn. 2011. *Theories of human communication* (10th ed.). Long Grove, IL: Waveland Press.

Gerald, S. E. 1996. "Framing in advertising and the moderating effect of consumer education." *Journal of Advertising Research* (September/October), 49–64.

http://blog.virtuoso.com/uncategorized/the-truth-about-how-different-generations-travel/

http://media.newzealand.com/en/

http://money.howstuffworks.com/10-items-from-mcdonalds-international-menu8.htm

https://www.communicaid.com/cross-cultural-training/blog/indulgence-vs-restraint-6th-dimension/

https://www.nytimes.com/reuters/2017/10/09/business/09reuters-china-tourism.html

Pan, S., H. Tsai, and J. Lee. 2011. "Framing New Zealand: Understanding tourism TV commercials." *Tourism Management* 32 (2011): 596–603.

Pennington-Gray, L. A., and D. L. Kerstetter. 2001. "What do university-educated women want from their pleasure travel experience?" *Journal of Travel Research* 40: 49–56.

Sakia, M., J. Brown, and J. Mak. 2000. "Population aging and Japanese international travel in the 21st century." *Journal of Travel Research 38 (3): 212–220.*

Sirgy, M. J., and C. Su. 2000. "Destination Image, Self-Congruity, and Travel Behavior: Toward an Integrative Model." *Journal of Travel Research* 38 (4), 340–352.

Witt, P. A., and T. L. Goodale. 1981. "The relationship between barriers to leisure enjoyment and family stages." *Leisure Sciences* 4 (1): 29–49.

Zemke, R., C. Raines, and B. Filipczak. 2000. *Generations at Work.* New York: AMACOM.

CHAPTER FOURTEEN

Traveler Segments

Understanding Travel Purposes

. . . [T]he explorer seeks the undiscovered, the traveler that which has been discovered by the mind working in history, the tourist that which has been discovered by entrepreneurship and prepared for him by the arts of publicity.

PAUL FUSSELL

YOUR LEARNING DESTINATION

Readers will be able to demonstrate their knowledge of visitors by suggesting appropriate vacations, packages, services, and messages to the major segments of the market.

WHAT YOU NEED TO KNOW

Having read this chapter, you will be able to:

- Describe the characteristics of the business traveler segments.
- Identify the characteristics of the leisure traveler segments.
- Suggest appropriate services and vacation experiences for individual segments of the travel market.
- Recommend appropriate messages to engage individual segments of the travel market.

BREAKING THE ICE

As a child, have you traveled with one or both of your parents who were on a business trip? Think about this scenario: If a person travels to Orlando for business for a week, his family may fly there on a Friday to join him for a family theme park fun weekend and fly back together on Sunday. Many children may have had similar experiences growing up, especially if they have two busy working parents whose work requires travel to different places. In fact, appending a family vacation to a business trip is a strategy for business travelers who seek opportunities to spend quality time with their family and share life experiences with their children. How to best serve the needs of both the business traveler and his or her traveling family in this case is what tourism service providers are concerned with.

Chapters 10–13 have examined how an individual—any individual—makes a travel decision, consumes a destination product, and exhibits certain behavioral characteristics as a result of personal, interpersonal, and social cultural dispositions. In order to describe the larger picture of travel flows, it is necessary to understand not only individual but also travel segment characteristics.

KEY TAKEAWAY POINTS

- Business travelers are a lucrative market segment for the global hospitality industry.

- Business travelers are higher spenders than leisure travelers.

- Business travelers appreciate flexibility, predictability, and productivity when they are on the road.

- Business travelers value travel reward programs provided by hotels, car rental companies, and airlines and place high importance on a program that provides maximum earning potential with the easiest redemption terms.

- Combining business with leisure has become a common practice for business travelers.

- Meetings and events are powerful economic engines for many destinations.

- A significant percentage of travelers classify themselves as adventure travelers.

- Adventure travel offerings range from soft adventure to hard adventure.

- Medical tourism is a niche travel market that has witnessed continuous growth.

- There are a number of ways to describe leisure traveler segments. Commonly utilized approaches include demographics, activity settings, geolocations, companionship, travel frequency, activity interests, and benefits sought.

THE BUSINESS TRAVEL MARKET

The global business travel market is a trillion dollar market segment. The regions that have witnessed the most business travel growth in recent years are South Asia, the Middle East, and Southeast Asia. The largest exiting business travel markets in the world are the United States, China, UK, Germany, and Japan. In most developed countries, business travel is the "bread-and-butter" market for tourism for much of the year. This is certainly the case for the United States, Canada, China, and many Western European countries. For example, within the European Union, business travel accounts for almost half of all air passenger trips. Business travel in Asia Pacific, led by China, has outpaced the rest of the world. The growth rate of this segment is largely driven by infrastructure investments exports and service development, according to Global Business Travel Association (2017).

Just as it is inadequate to use the "jumbo jet" approach to analyzing pleasure/personal travel markets, it is equally inappropriate to view the business travel market as an amorphous mass that cannot be further segmented. In fact, this major travel market has many component segments, and the number of segments appears to grow from year to year. The business-related travel market segments can be broadly categorized as follows:

- Regular business travel
- Business travel related to meetings, conventions, and congresses
- Incentive travel

The third category of incentive travel is really a "hybrid" segment (also known as "bleisure" because it is a type of pleasure travel that has been financed for business purposes. Thus, the persons on incentive trips are pleasure travelers and the purchasers are businesses.

Business travelers are more important to travel suppliers than their total numbers would indicate. They use airlines, rental cars, hotels, and travel agents to a greater extent than pleasure travelers. Business travelers, for example, account for over 40 percent of all airline trips and hotel stays, and account for almost two-thirds of rental car revenues. In the United States, direct spending on business travel by U.S. and international travelers totaled $307.2 billion in 2016. This encompassed meetings, events, and incentive programs. United States residents made 457.4 million person-trips for business purposes. Person-trip is measured as "one person on a trip away from home overnight in paid accommodations or on a day or overnight trip to places 50 miles or more away from home" (U.S. Travel Association 2017).

Characteristics of Business Travelers

While leisure travel is usually conducted using one's discretionary time, business travel is dictated by a person's business demands and schedule. Business travel tends to have several distinguishing characteristics.

- Business travelers are less price sensitive than leisure travelers. Business travel is a nondiscretionary expenditure. The business traveler must travel to specific places to do business. As a result, business travel is more stable and less price sensitive than vacation travel.

- Business trips are taken consistently throughout the year, whereas pleasure trips tend to be concentrated in the summer months or public holiday seasons.
- Business travelers tend to be higher spenders on average per day than leisure travelers.
- Business travelers appreciate flexibility, predictability, and productivity when they are on the road.
- Business travelers have higher concerns with work-life balance due to their frequent need for time away from home. They increasingly prefer to have the option to add leisure to business trips. The option to bring family along on business trips helps improve work-life balance.
- There is an increasing tendency for business travelers to use sharing economy accommodation options such as Airbnb services or ridesharing services.
- Business travelers are more likely to be millennials, Generation Xers, and Baby Boomers.
- Business travelers are more technologically savvy. Almost all members of this group travel with personal computers and have a high-speed Internet connection.
- Traditionally, business travelers book through their corporate booking tools or using a corporate travel agent but an increasing percentage of business travelers choose to use their own smartphones to plan and book their own trips rather than using their companies' travel tools. Convenience and better prices drive this trend, indicating that the traveler is now at the center of managed travel programs.

- There are unique challenging aspects of business travel. A Skift research (2017a) notes twelve such areas, including time spent in transit, layovers, changing a flight or train reservation, a subpar work environment while traveling, preparing expense reports, working away from the office, changing a hotel reservation, meals, pre-travel information gathering, travel debriefing with travel department, flight/train booking experiences, and lodging booking experiences.

The Trip Profile of Business Travelers. Business travelers mostly travel for five specific reasons (Skift 2017b):

- To attend a conference/convention/exhibition/business event.
- To attend a meeting with people from another company for business planning or customer service.
- For professional development or training.
- For meetings with co-workers who work in a different location.
- For the purpose of selling/pitching new products or services.

When individuals travel for business, where do they go? Unlike leisure travel, business travel doesn't follow a free choice pattern. Business obligations dictate where they travel to. The majority of business travel occurs within the boundary of a country. International travel is largely driven by international trade and other global business patterns. The top destinations for international business travelers include United Kingdom, Canada, China, Australia, Germany, France, Japan, Singapore, India, and Mexico (Figure 14.1).

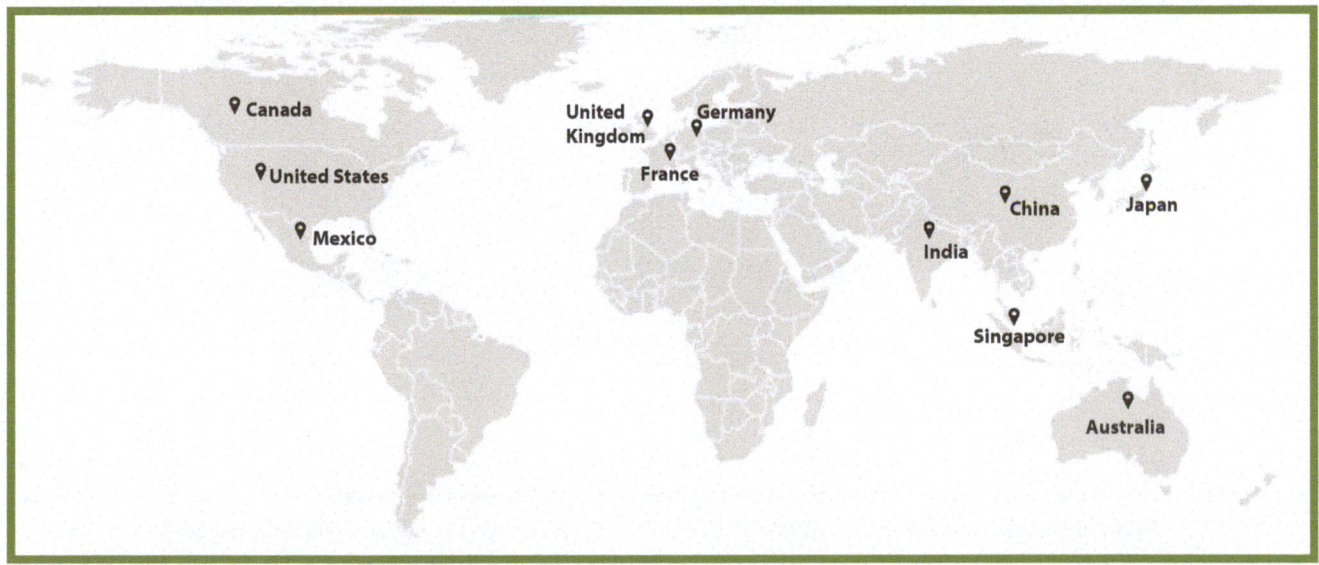

FIGURE 14.1 **Top business travel destinations in the world** | Source: UNWTO Compendium of Tourism Statistics, 2016.

In the United States, most of the business travel destinations are metropolitan cities. Some of the top destinations include New York City, Chicago, San Francisco-Oakland-San Jose area, Los Angeles, Dallas, Phoenix, Washington DC, Seattle-Tacoma, and Houston (Hensel 2017). On average, American business travelers took 6.8 trips in 2016. When broken down by age, millennials took the highest number of business trips (7.4 trips), compared to 6.4 for Generation Xers, and 6.3 for the baby boomers. When American business travelers travel, some general trends are: (1) they often use their own car (35 percent of the time), (2) travel by air (28 percent of the time), and (3) use a rental car (13 percent of the time) or a taxi (11 percent of the time). Their trip length tends to be short: 26 percent of the business trips are day trips, and on average, more than 60 percent of the business travelers stay four nights or fewer away from home (Sheivachman 2016). However, these patterns can vary between countries.

Service Preferences of Business Travelers

Business travelers tend to have behavioral tendencies and hospitality services preferences that are different from those of general leisure travelers. Compared to the pleasure traveler, the business traveler is more time sensitive; service quality is more important than price; and she or he is more experienced and demanding.

In selecting an airline, a hotel, or other services, business travelers place higher emphasis on **location**, **convenience**, and **perks**. For air travel, for instance, business travelers are primarily concerned with the convenience of the airline schedule, and on-time departure record. Reasonable rates, on the other hand, are the most important factor when choosing a car rental company. This is followed in importance by the convenience of the location and the condition of the cars. Location is the number one factor in selecting a hotel, followed by clean, comfortable rooms and room rates. They like frequent-traveler programs, in-room Internet access, and hotel fitness centers.

An increasing number of people combine business and pleasure by adding a few days of pleasure to the beginning or end of a regular business trip or attendance at a business-related convention or meeting. Over half of these vacation person trips were taken over a weekend or long weekend. Travel promoters at travel destinations should realize that business travelers provide a three-part opportunity. First, the business traveler visits to carry out his or her work-related activities. Second, the

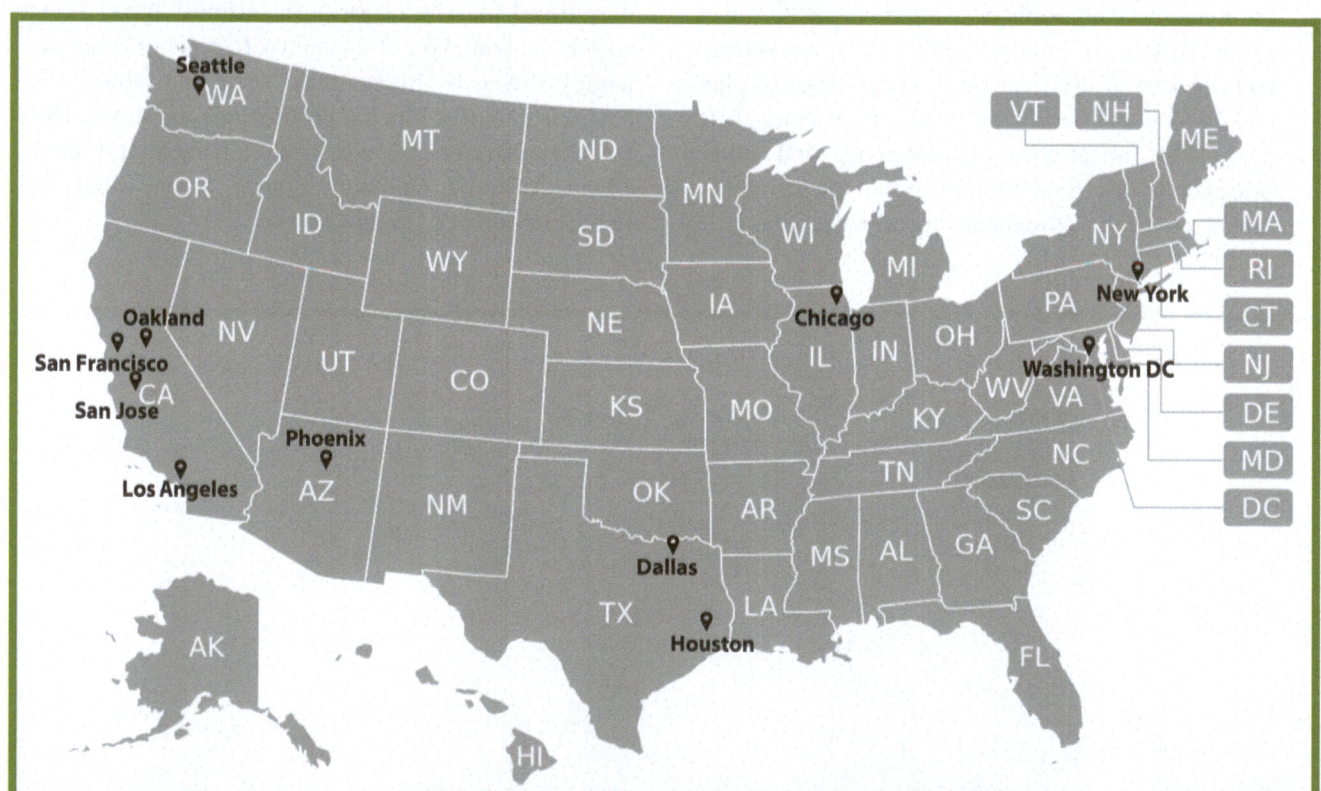

FIGURE 14.2 Popular business travel destinations in the U.S. | Source: https://www.inc.com/anna-hensel/10-us-cities-business-travelers-visit-the-most-infographic.html

traveler and his or her spouse may be convinced to combine business with a leisure trip. Third, she or he may be attracted to return to the destination in the future on a pleasure or business trip.

Frequent Traveler Programs.

A significant percentage of all business travelers belong to some type of a reward program such as a hotel or car loyalty program or an airline frequent flier program. These various reward programs provide a great incentive for business travelers to remain loyal to travel and hospitality service providers.

Because the majority of business travelers use their perks for leisure travel, they place high importance on a program that provides maximum earning potential with the easiest redemption terms. For example, a popular reward program that is geared toward business travelers is the National Car Rental Emerald Club. This program rewards business travelers based on the number of rentals they make. Travelers in this program can enjoy such privileges as exclusive member only discounts and offers, bypassing the check-in counter, and selecting or upgrading their vehicles from the "Emerald Aisle." Higher tier members can enjoy additional complementary services such as guaranteed car availability within a day's notice and car delivery services.

In the hotel sector, many reward programs are structured to attract frequent patrons such as business travelers. A good example of a hotel reward program is the Marriot Rewards program. This program offers ample opportunities for its members to accrue points and redeem them easily. Marriott Rewards has four membership tiers: member, Silver, Gold Elite, and Platinum Elite, depending on the number of nights purchased. While member privileges range from free in-room Wi-Fi (all members), guaranteed room type and free breakfasts (Gold Elite), to an on-arrival gift of bonus points and a food and drink amenity (Platinum). Marriott members can earn and use their points at a variety of its hotel properties and brands. They also earn points through social media shares and follows or by using their car rental partner Hertz's services, which also offers a Hertz Gold Plus Rewards program. Another program that is popular among business travelers is the Hilton HHonors program. Hilton offers one of the largest selection of business travel properties. The HHonors program allows travelers to accrue both HHonors points and miles in their favorite airline program.

To a majority of business travelers, the frequent flier programs they belong to is a major factor in their selection choices of an airline. Belonging to a frequent flyer program means that credit is collected for mileage flown on that particular airline. After a specified number of miles have been flown, the traveler can qualify for upgrades to first class and free trips. In recent years, airlines have reduced the attractiveness of their awards, making it necessary to fly greater distances in order to obtain a particular reward. Increasingly, reward programs tie the amount of money spent rather than how much one travels with rewards. As a result, rewards are maximized when used alongside program-sponsored credit cards. There are many such partnerships between credit card companies and airlines, hotels or car rental companies.

One example is the American Airlines AAdvantage program. In addition to the free trips or upgrades that a traveler can redeem based on certain amount of miles accumulated, this program has other member-based offerings including priority check-in and complimentary same-day reservations of standby flights, preferred seating for its Gold members, three checked bags, same-day flight changes, and alcoholic beverages and snacks in the Main Cabin. Outside of North America, similar reward programs are provided to attract frequent business travelers. British Airways Executive Club (Oneworld), Lufthansa Miles and More (Star Alliance), Singapore Airlines KrisFlyer (Star Alliance), Cathay Pacific Asia Miles (Oneworld), and Emirates Skywards all offer advantageous rewards for its frequent fliers.

Business Traveler Sub-Segments

Although we have been talking about the business traveler, there are actually several segments to this market, each with distinct characteristics. Business travelers can be divided into segments as follows:

- Frequent business travelers
- Luxury or business executive travelers
- Women business travelers
- International business travelers
- Occupation specific travelers

Frequent Business Travelers.

Frequent business travelers (those making more than ten business trips a year) make up less than 20 percent of all business travelers, yet take more than half of all business trips. The business executive travel market is an often targeted segment of frequent travelers that many airlines and hotels make specific efforts to cater to. Airlines have been offering first-class seat service and first-class passenger lounges in airport terminals to these travelers for many years.

QUICK TRIP 14.1

Managed Travel: Travel and Expenses Management for Business Travelers

While business trips have traditionally been arranged by a travel agency or a company travel arranger, the trend is changing: more than 70 percent of the companies in the United States currently do not require their employees to go through a centralized system in arranging and booking business trips. This is in line with the rise of tech-savvy employees that are comfortable using web and smartphone apps. Without having to consult a travel agency, they are able to identify best hotel rates and other travel options on their own.

Usage of information technology is not limited to trip planning. Companies use travel software programs to manage employee travel expenses and reimbursement. These programs allow business travelers to manage their travel expenses both on-site and upon returning. For instance, business travelers are able to take pictures of receipts (e.g., for business lunch meeting) and generate travel expense reports real-time through expense management applications. Keeping receipts, staying on track with expenses, and submitting expense reports was a burden for business travelers in the past that technology is now helping business travelers manage on their trips.

Today's expense management systems are not limited to supporting expense management alone. One example is Concur. Although Concur is known as an expense management system, it can serve as a comprehensive business travel manager that can manage the business travelers' travel process from the beginning to the end. Concur has a reservation system that allows travelers to book everything from hotels to flights. Although their offerings tend to be more expensive and are limited in the range of options compared to online travel services such as Expedia, their reservation system is advanced to an extent where travelers can identify hotels within a certain area and compare different hotel options. Once all the reservations are made on the Concur system, traveler's itinerary and receipts are automatically transferred to their expense report. Therefore, in finalizing the expense report, there is little for the traveler to do. At the management level, Concur allows companies to easily enforce spending policies and centralize business travel expenditures and make better business decisions.

Think about This

1. What are some advantages and disadvantages in using the Concur-managed travel program or similar programs for business travelers and their companies?
2. What other functions can expense management systems such as Concur implement to facilitate business travelers' trip management?

Sources

http://www.cimaglobal.com/Documents/Thought_leadership_docs/white-paper-hub/2016-04-12-Travel-and-Expense-Management.pdf
https://www.concur.com

More recent innovations include special check-in arrangements, bigger seats, and sleeper seats. Many hotel chains have begun to allocate whole floors or wings of their buildings for those business travelers seeking greater luxury in their accommodations. The rooms or suites are more spacious and contain more personal giveaways; the hotels provide their guests with complimentary drinks and express check-in, check-out service. Normally the airlines and hotel companies add a surcharge to their regular prices for the extra comforts and convenience provided to executive travelers.

International Business Travelers. The "typical" international business traveler is a married man over the age of forty-five. This "typical" traveler takes close to twenty trips a year and states that home and family are priorities over work. This person will travel with a laptop computer but prefers watching videos and making phone calls in the air. The ideal in-flight companion is an empty seat. This person is tempted to give up a seat on an overbooked flight although an upgrade on the next flight is also of interest. Executive airline lounges are favored for the opportunity to sit in peace and quiet, use the phone, and get a free drink. The typical international business traveler prefers to make air arrangements by going to a travel agent, looking at a printed flight guide, and having a secretary take care of things. Airlines are chosen on the basis of convenient schedules, on-time performance, and modern planes. Frequent flyer membership also plays a role. United States travelers are likely to belong to five or more such programs. They belong so they can jump ahead of others on an airline's waiting list. Flight upgrades are also important. The traveler prefers to use mileage awards for personal and leisure travel rather than to save the company money on business travel.

Female Business Travelers. The stereotypical business traveler has traditionally been assumed to be a suit and tie wearing, graying male. This is no longer the case. Female business travelers have become increasingly visible. In 1970, women accounted for only 1 percent of all business travelers. This figure has grown substantially since then. Female travelers make up a large share of the business travel market today, representing roughly 40 percent of all business travelers.

Almost half of the women who travel, travel for business (WeConnect International 2017).

Typically, the female business traveler:

- Is married, over the age of 40.
- Is high-tech and highly connected in online and offline social networks.
- Eats at a restaurant away from the hotel when traveling with colleagues and in a hotel restaurant when traveling alone.
- Sees the top benefits from travel as being with new people, experiencing new destinations, and having time for self.
- Tries to incorporate some leisure time into a business trip.
- Values responsive service, a hotel located near business, and affordable rates.
- Is looking for convenience, such as express check-in and check-out and late check-out.
- Has great focus on travel safety and security.

Female business travelers can be further grouped into three segments based on the amount of travel done. The occasional business traveler, taking two to four

FIGURE 14.3 A delayed flight for a business traveler.

business trips a year, makes up 48 percent of the segment; the periodic business traveler, with five to ten business trips a year, comprises 28 percent of all female business travelers; the constant business traveler, with eleven-plus business trips a year, makes up 24 percent of the market. The constant female business traveler, when compared to the occasional female business traveler, is more likely to:

- Add a weekend to a trip
- Add a vacation day to a trip
- Value late check-out
- View business travel as a way to meet new people and network
- Experience a new destination
- Consider that business travel makes their job more interesting
- Value responsive service

When hotels first sought to attract this segment of the market, several mistakes were made. Early attempts to provide "women's floors" and pink wallpaper were viewed by many women as patronizing. They were concerned about such things as security, however. This has resulted in such things as a "club floor"—open to both genders—and accessed by a special key. More hotels are building suites so that women can hold meetings in their rooms without having a bed in view. Room service hours have been expanded as many women dislike eating alone in public. Lighting in hallways and parking lots is getting brighter.

A Multi-Segmentation Typology of Business Travelers.
In addition to focusing on these five single variable based segments of the business travelers discussed above, the tourism and hospitality industry has recently attempted to understand finer segments of travelers

QUICK TRIP 14.2

The Bleisure Travelers

When business travel becomes a necessary lifestyle, mixing work with leisure has become a strategy for better work–life balance for such individuals. Bleisure travelers are individuals who extend a work trip for leisure. In partnership with the Hilton Hotels, the Global Business Travel Association (GBTA) Foundation recently conducted a research on these travelers (2017). The study shows that over one-third of North American business travelers extend business trips for the purpose of leisure time. In fact, almost half of the millennial business travelers do so. Bleisure travelers are a diverse group in the United States and Canada. Some interesting findings include:

- On average they take seven work-related trips and work at companies with 950 employees.
- The highest percentage of these travelers hold middle management positions (42 percent), followed by senior leadership/C-level positions (31 percent).
- Almost 60 percent of these travelers have children at home.
- Forty-four percent of them travel with someone else for the leisure portion of their trip.
- They typically extend their trip for about two nights and tend to usually stay at the same hotel where their work takes them. This is especially true for Gen-X and Baby Boomer travelers and for high-frequency travelers.
- The two most common reasons for taking Bleisure trips are to visit the destination where their work takes them or to visit a new destination convenient to the work location. Bleisure travelers see this as a less expensive way of travel and a good way to spend time away from work and home.

Think about This

1. Research a hotel company of your own. Do they have special offerings for Bleisure travelers?
2. Given the significance of the Bleisure travel market, what can hotels do to better serve them?
3. What can the destinations do to serve these travelers?
4. What does this mean for managed travel programs?

Source

https://www.gbta.org/foundation/pressreleases/Pages/rls_060817.aspx

based on the multi-segmentation method, an approach that segments a market using a combination of variables pertaining to travelers' travel behavioral tendencies, travel arrangement characteristics, work content, demographics, and psychographics. Illustrating this approach, research by CONCUR on the state of business travel (2016) segmented business travelers into six types, corresponding to four types of business travelers and two types of business travel managers/assistants:

- **Savvy Travelers:** Business travel for this group is a necessary part of their jobs. Their age range is between thirty-five to fifty-four. They spend on average US$30,000 for fifteen to thirty trips each year. What they value the most is efficiency of travel, home comfort, familiar vendors, and the ability to stay connected with family. Delays and other trip-related disruptions, safety concerns, and not being able to use loyalty programs are their major concerns.
- **Jet-Setters:** Jet-setters are commercial trade lawyers or persons in a senior leadership position, with an age range of thirty-five to forty-five. They travel to meet with clients or speak at conferences. These travelers spend on average US$45,000 for fifteen to thirty-five trips made annually. They travel frequently and tend to have a generous company travel policy. Jet-setters tend to travel in first class and stay at five-star hotels. They value high-end accommodations and amenities (to impress clients), and the ability to stay connected with family. Their main concerns for business travel are related to situations that prevent them from staying heathy and restful and connected.
- **High-Tech Newbie:** These travelers travel three to seven times a year and spend an average of around US$10,000 a year. These travelers are younger (ages twenty-two to forty-four) and tend to research and reserve their business trips on their own. They also have a tendency to extend their trip to the weekend for leisure purpose and value affordable boutique hotels with local scenes.
- **Approving Manager:** This is the corporate travel manager that processes and manages employee's business travel. They value employees making smart booking decisions (within budget) and maintaining work productivity on the road.
- **Travel Arranger:** These are the longtime executive assistants who plan travel for their bosses and manage expenses. They value connections with their travelers (location and schedule) and worry about

not being able to make reservations based on travelers' preferences.
- **Cautious Planner:** These travelers regard travel as an annoyance. When they have to travel for business, they value safety, familiarity, and low price. Their travel concerns include safety and getting home quickly.

Factors Impacting the Future of Business Travel

There are at least four well-recognized factors that can have a major influence on the future of business travel:

1. Economy
2. Regulation/business travel policies
3. Globalization
4. Technology

As a general rule, the rate of growth of the economy determines the level of business travel and the extent to which that level changes. Business travel activity tends to match the growth of the economy when overall economic performance is weak, but business travel moves ahead of the rate of growth of the economy during times of economic stability and expansion. The United States market follows this pattern more strongly than does the European market. The strong signs for business travel are strong trade, investment, and output growth, whereas the weak signs are high interest rates and unemployment levels.

The second factor affecting the future of business travel is regulation. Its impact is felt in three areas: (1) deregulation of travel and (2) government policy regarding the treatment of business travel expenses for tax purposes, and (3) corporate policies. For example, in 1978, deregulation came to the United States air industry. Airlines were free to set rates based on market demand without being subject to government approval beforehand. As a result, many new airlines came into being and many went out of business. Increased competition kept fares between many major cities low.

Changes in government policy regarding the treatment of business travel expenses for tax purposes is another important issue because business travel is a business expense. For example, one fairly recent change in the United States tax law, limited the tax deductibility of business meals to 50 percent of the cost of the meal. Interestingly, this has not seemed to limit travel, but has changed the way clients are entertained. For example, by bringing a speaker into a meeting, the entire cost of the meal can be deducted. Various attempts have been made to limit the tax deductibility of meetings abroad. Any attempt to do this would have an impact on the amount and type of travel undertaken.

Corporate business travel policies are another important element influencing business travel needs and preferences. Travel remains the third largest controllable expense at United States corporations. More and more companies are concerned about the high cost of travel and are putting more time and effort into controlling their corporate travel costs. Most companies have a formal written travel policy. The most common restrictions on business travelers are travel per diems, restrictions on the type of airfare class, and requirements that travel be approved by upper management. American Express estimates that United States companies lose $15 billion a year to deviations from corporate policy. To combat the problem, a number of companies are experimenting with systems that allow corporate travelers to make their travel plans on their personal computers, but only within the parameters of corporate policy. Almost 80 percent of companies require employees to take the "lowest logical" airfare. There is also a movement away from upscale accommodations and toward more moderate or economy class accommodations. More than 60 percent require employees to stay at hotels in which the company or travel agency has corporate or negotiated rates. Rental car use is also regulated. Over three-quarters of companies impose a size limit on cars rented by employees. Companies—even those serious about managing travel costs—often overlook meal expenses because many corporate cultures consider business meals a perk for travelers who have to spend many days on the road.

The use of technology to replace business travel is another interesting trend with implications toward future travel. Recent research indicates that this trend seems to have leveled off in the United States with just under one-third of travelers reporting the use of teleconferencing, webcasting, or videoconferencing to replace at least one business trip.

QUICK TRIP 14.3

Will Technology Reduce Business Travel?

Digital technology advancements such as video conferencing seem to be a good substitute for business travel. Some examples of such web conferencing software products are Highfive, RingCentral Meetings, Samepage, Blackboard collaborate, and webinato. They offer features such as electronic hand-raising, shared whiteboard, application sharing, presentation streaming, and on-demand webcasting. Video conferencing allows businesses to communicate face-to-face virtually, reducing the amount of money and time spent on travel.

Despite this trend, business travel is still an important growing travel segment. For instance, the number of United States business travelers increased by 1.2 percent in 2016 compared to the previous year. There also is growing recognition of the advantages of a face-to-face meeting compared to videoconferencing. One issue is that video conferencing does not allow individuals to emotionally connect with others. In some cases, individuals need to be in the other company's environment to get to know their culture better and to impress their clients. For instance, a lot of the employees at Accenture, a consulting company, still make frequent business trips because building relationships with their client in person over breakfasts and dinners is very important. In line with this, culturally-important actions such as handshakes cannot be done through video conferencing. Further, there are concerns about security and privacy of video conferencing.

Think about This

1.   Identify other technologies that may impact business trips.
2.   If the number of business trips are significantly reduced by technological advancements, what will be the impact on the tourism industry (e.g., hotel sales)? What strategies should the hospitality and tourism service providers follow to stimulate business travel demand to combat this impact?

Sources

https://skift.com/2017/07/17/u-s-business-travelers-more-like-to-drive-than-fly-to-meetings/

https://www.linkedin.com/pulse/videoconferencing-does-replace-business-travel-dean-bubley

https://www.vyopta.com/blog/business-collaboration/video-conferencing-vs-travel/

MICE Travel Market

A significant percentage of business travelers travel for the purpose of attending corporate or association meetings, conferences, conventions, congresses, or trade expositions and events. This market has been generally termed as the **MICE market**. The term MICE is an acronym for Meetings, Incentives, Conferences, and Exhibitions. Some call this market **the meetings and event market**. Meetings and events are seen as powerful economic engines for many destinations. Meetings represent 25 percent of air travel revenue and over one-third of hotel revenue, even more at business hotels. Success in this market also brings non-financial rewards such as destination overall image enhancement, improvements of city center landscapes, urban regeneration, and increased civic pride. Meeting attendees can also be attracted to return to a destination as vacationers.

When marketing a venue for a conference or meeting, it is important to recognize that **MICE organizers** and the **MICE attendees** have differing perspectives. Generally, meeting organizers consider four aspects when selecting meetings venues: *the quality of meetings facilities, cost, accessibility, and the image of potential locations*. The relative influence of these attributes can vary according to the nature of meetings. The attendees usually consider various professional benefits including education, networking, career enhancement, leadership enhancement, exposure to new research and product, business opportunities, association involvement, and market investigation, among others.

Conventions and meetings are of various sizes, ranging from small business meetings of a few delegates to large conventions of, for instance, associations attracting in excess of 20,000 delegates or more. They can be one-time events such as the Olympic games, or occur on a reoccurring basis.

The MICE industry is specialized in planning, booking, facilitating conferences, exhibitions, and other events. They provide a full range of travel and conference services. **MICE Services** can come from a wide range of entities from corporate meeting planners, to meetings and convention departments of hotels, conference and exhibition centers, cruise lines, destination management organizations (e.g., CVBs) and associations, professional associations, tour operations and transportation companies, food and beverage service providers, and logistic firms.

Figure 14.4 provides a multi-level view of the various business providers servicing the MICE travelers. Destination management organizations usually lead the charge for promoting their destinations as ideal locations for events and conventions. These organizations can take on the form of a government entity or public private–private partnership. The range of locations within which meetings take place is broad. Some typical venue examples are hotels, universities, sports venues, and convention and exhibition facilities.

Although there are dedicated organizations and venues for meetings, it is important to understand that there are other aspects of a destination that are integral for meeting attendees to have a satisfactory experience. The local destination components such as transportation, attractions, restaurants, hotels, shops, and markets will all provide services needed by meetings and conventions visitors. Although not for all, many such visitors will mix business with leisure and take in the sights and sounds of the destination itself. These, what we call **Bleisure travelers**, tend to stay for additional days of leisure time or bring their family and children with them on the trip.

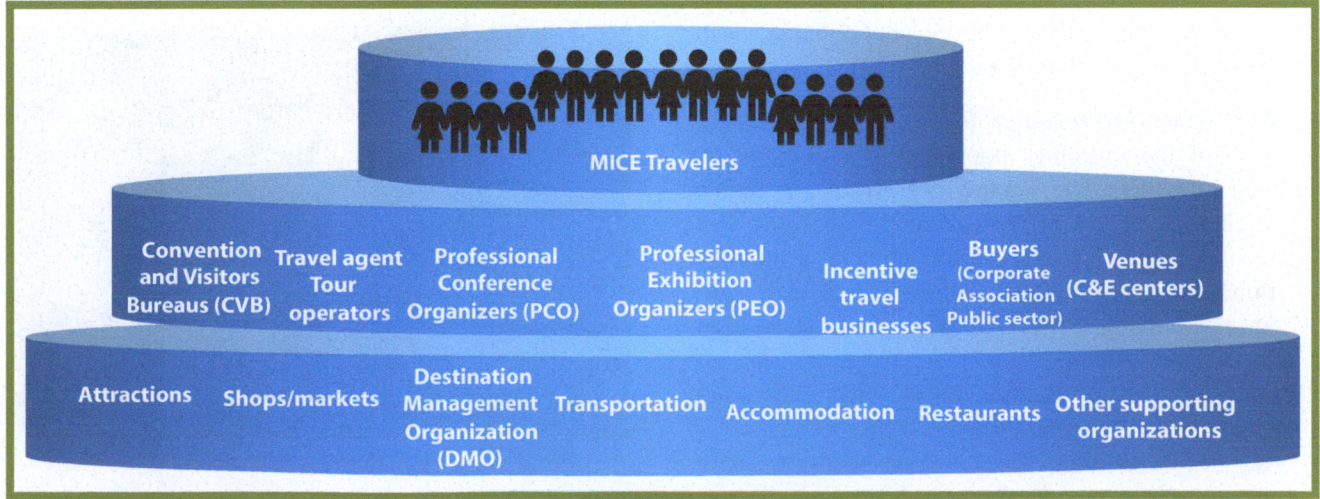

FIGURE 14.4 MICE tourism service providers.

U.S.	EMEA (Europe, Middle East, and Africa)	APEC (Asia Pacific Regions)
Orlando, FL	London, England	Singapore
Las Vegas, NV	Barcelona, Spain	Sydney, Australia
Chicago, IL	Berlin, Germany	Bangkok, Thailand
Atlanta, GA	Amsterdam, Netherlands	Kuala Lumpur, Malaysia
San Diego, CA	Paris, France	Hong Kong
Washington, DC	Madrid, Spain	Shanghai, China
Nashville, TN	Frankfurt, Germany	Melbourne, Australia
Dallas, TX	Rome, Italy	Tokyo, Japan
New York, NY	Munich, Germany	Mumbai, India
Phoenix, AZ	Prague, Czech Republic	Seoul, South Korea

FIGURE 14.5 Top Global Meeting Destinations. | Source: http://www.cvent.com/en/company/cvent-reveals-2017-list-of-top-meeting-destinations-in-us-emea-apac.shtml.

Meetings and Event Destinations. Many countries and cities promote their destinations as ideal locations for meetings and events. Numerous organizations also publish rankings of meetings and event destinations. An example ranking of Top Ten destinations in different regions of the world is given in Figure 14.5. The latter ranking was developed by Cvent, a cloud-based enterprise event management company that sourced more than $11 billion in meetings and events globally in 2016. Destination providers often use these rankings to promote their destinations and benchmark themselves against their competition.

Immersive Event Experiences for Participants. Emergent digital technologies and innovations have been drastically reshaping consumer's event experiences, and are playing an increasingly important role in helping event organizers to deliver immersive experiences at events. Some examples of recent popular "event tech must-haves," according to Kriva (2017), include:

- *Live streaming through drones.* This is an extension of the currently popular live streaming via social media live features or exclusive online streaming websites. The use of drones to do live streaming can capture event content in a multiple dimensional fashion and deliver it to off-site audiences, allowing viewers to experience an event in an immersive fashion.
- *Virtual reality.* Virtual reality technology has entered into the event industry. It has been used for site and venue inspections, interactive sessions with prospective event consumers and corporate clients.

- *Augmented reality.* Digitally enhanced experiences have great potential for event participants. Companies are using the latest technologies to create augmented reality features for events and exhibitions that engage and enhance the visitor experience. Augmented reality technology allows creation of a different live view of a real-world environment and engaging attendees with gamifications.
- *Big data.* Big data management tools allow event professionals to collect and manage tremendous amounts of attendee data, understand attendee's preferences and demands, and create substantially personalized experiences and impactful attendee centric event experiences.
- *Hologram technology.* Holographic 3D can generate the same visual information as a real environment. Hologram technology enables meeting and

FIGURE 14.6 A businessman with holographic interface.

QUICK TRIP 14.4

Mega-Events: The William and Kate Effect

Some events, such as hosting the Olympics, attract large numbers of people to a destination. These mega-events are typically rare occurrences for the host cities and countries. The benefit of such events can be both tangible (shorter term) and intangible (longer term). The shorter term aspects are reflected in the increase in tourism arrivals and expenditures at these locations both during and after such an event. Hosting a mega-event such as the Olympics or the FIFA World Cup can also send a signal of goodwill and policy change and have repercussions in global media attention. Examples of longer term benefits can be improvement of a country or city's overall image and international trade flows. Mega-event hosts usually conduct a cost-benefit analysis to understand whether and how much the benefit outweighs the investment of hosting a mega-event.

The royal wedding of Prince William and Catherine Middleton that took place on 29th April 2011 in London, United Kingdom, was a global event that attracted many visitors from both United Kingdom and other countries. About 600,000 visitors, both domestic and international, descended on London on the wedding day. This was a welcomed boost in tourism from the royal wedding. It provided an opportune time for Britain to soak up the spotlight due to the extensive media coverage. In response, VisitBritain launched a £125 million global marketing campaign called "Visit Britain, You're Invited." Capitalizing on the media frenzy and consumer attention, following the royal wedding, the marketing program targeted the independent and youth traveler market from Germany and the United States. VisitBritain partnered with hostelworld.com in launching this marketing program.

There is, however, a downside to hosting mega-events. One is that a mega-event may potentially create traveler displacement (i.e., regular tourists may alter their travel plans by going to a different location or at a different time), resulting in potential tourism loss. Business travelers, however, do not have a lot of freedom to change their plans. In the case of the British royal wedding, the hustle and bustle associated with the mega-event created a great deal of hassle to business travelers. There were fewer plane seats available. They had to pay much higher prices for hotel rooms. Ground transportation was slow and congested. The morale of the story is that business travelers keep a large part of *our* business afloat and, yet, when there is a media-worthy global event, then business travelers take the back seat.

Think about This

1. What can hoteliers do to provide consistent service to business travelers in light of a global event?
2. Global events drive tourism demand. How do destinations manage uneven travel flow?
3. How can destinations sustain tourist interests after a mega-event such as a royal wedding or a global sports event?
4. Are the costs for infrastructure, stadia, security, and marketing worth the gains from tourism?
5. Are there potential social impacts of mega-events?

Sources

Fourie, J., and M. Santana-Gallego. 2010. The impact of mega-events on tourist arrivals. https://econrsa.org/papers/w_papers/wp171.pdf

http://www.travelweekly.com/Europe-Travel/London-enjoying-modest-boost-from-royal-wedding/?a=europe

event organizers to incorporate 3D holographic displays of images in events and exhibitions. Hotels and convention centers utilize this technology to create high-impact events and high-performance meetings. The visual effect is created through a holographic projection system. It can, for instance, be used to project products or people (speakers, guests) and create captivating high-impact experiences with the attendees.

Incentive Travel.   Incentive travel is a management tool that uses an exceptional travel experience to motivate and/or recognize participants for increased levels of performance in support of organizational goals. The United States is responsible for just over half of world demand. Europe is responsible for an additional 40 percent and Japan and Australia account for the rest. As standards of living have increased, traditional incentives such as cash and merchandise have proven less effective in motivating employees to work harder or to sell more. Travel is touted as doing a better job of satisfying people's needs for achievement, recognition, and rewards than cash or merchandise.

Although incentives have traditionally been targeted toward sales people, an increasing number of programs are being developed for non-salespeople. Programs are either organized within the company sponsoring the trip or by an outside incentive travel house. It is argued by many that programs are more successful when organized in-house because the organizers have a better understanding of the characteristics of the workforce and can do a better job of targeting rewards to motivate them.

QUICK TRIP 14.5

Singapore as a MICE Destination

Singapore has reinvented itself as a conventions destination through strategically orchestrated product development and marketing campaigns. It has been ranked as one of Asia's top convention cities by the International Congress and Convention Association (ICCA). Singapore has attracted very significant organizations to select Singapore as their business incentive travel, and convention event destination choice due to multiple reasons:

- Reputation: the country is a winner of multiple awards for the top business destinations
- Accessibility: its state-of-the-art Changi Airport services more than 100 airlines, flying to 300 cities worldwide, with 4 billion people, within a seven-hour flight radius
- A network of well-trained industry practitioners
- A destination that is known for its state-of-the-art venues and technologies
- A destination known for its political stability and famously low crime rate

In addition to these favorable attributes, strong leadership from Singapore Exhibition & Convention Bureau (SECB) is another factor. SECB is a leading government agency that champions Singapore as the best business event and incentive travel destination. Working with the country's tourism players, it plays the role of an experienced architect in support of the MICE industry practitioners to provide seamless and efficiently run events. SECB is instrumental in promoting Singapore as a premier Business and MICE destination.

One example is that SECB worked with tourism practitioners in Singapore to develop a special incentive travel program called "In Singapore Incentives & Rewards" (INSPIRE). The INSPIRE program assembles itineraries and experiences that showcase the best of Singapore's dining, entertainment, and other attractions suited for their various international incentive travel markets. For example, an INSPIRE Europe & North America program was also launched in April 2016. This is a pilot Western edition of the rewards program, featuring tailored experiences (such as cocktails created by rising Singapore mixologists, and events hosted on rooftop bars or historical venues). INSPIRE also provides thematic business, attractive group airfares, and launched the Great China Market program in April 2017. The latter program offers curated itineraries specifically designed for Chinese incentive travelers. This includes discounted rates and customized experiences at selected hotels and shopping vouchers from popular shopping malls and the Singapore Changi Airport.

Think about Th\is

1. Why should government entities be involved in MICE marketing? What are the advantages of such an organizational structure for a destination to develop into a premier MICE destination?
2. How can MICE industry practitioners benefit from such a government entity?
3. What makes Singapore attractive to international business event organizers?
4. What makes Singapore attractive to incentive travel groups?
5. What may be some of the limitations of such a city-state in developing its MICE market?

Sources

http://www.visitsingapore.com/mice/en/about-us/about-secb/

http://www.visitsingapore.com/mice/en/why-singapore/top-10-reasons/

The people who "buy" destinations for incentive trips are influenced by:

- *Budget.* However, incentive trip planners look for high quality rather than low prices.
- *Time of year.* Employee participation on incentive trips tends to take place in that particular industry's slow season.
- *Participant background.* The level of sophistication and previous travel experiences of the likely participants are important.

- *Incentive history of the users and the competition.* Previously used destinations are less likely to produce spirited competition than are new destinations.
- *Accessibility.*
- *Facilities.* These can include hotel rooms, meeting rooms, restaurants, and local transport.
- *Activities.* Recreation and sports facilities are often attractive.

QUICK TRIP 14.6

Meetings and Conventions Going Green

MCI, an independently owned global meeting planning business headquartered in Geneva, Switzerland, employs 1,900 professionals across 690 cities and 31 countries. MCI sees sustainability as a business imperative, a moral responsibility, an economic opportunity and a driver of innovation for meeting practices.

- **People:** It promotes and manages a healthy and safe working environment for employees, partners, and clients. Its Group Health & Safety director/engineer works with forty health and safety coordinators on training and protocols, plans for advanced crisis management in the event of an emergency, and risk management.
- **Planet:** MCI has reduced the intensity of carbon emissions by having various mechanisms in place to reduce internal carbon footprint. One such example is 32 percent of its reporting offices run on renewable energy with a goal to reach 100 percent by 2020. The company has a Sustainability Champion in each office who leads the charge of creating an annual Sustainability Plan focusing initiatives that lead to improving sustainability performance within the office and on client projects. To benchmark performances between offices, MCI has created a balanced scorecard approach tracking sustainable actions and their outcomes.
- **Profit:** It promotes sustainability in working with its clients. It works with high-profile clients such as SAP, Barcelona Tourism, Danish Maritime Forum and Pacifica Yokohama, Singapore Exhibition & Convention Bureau, and the Las Vegas Sands Corp on improving corporations to create scalable sustainability technology and solutions. MCI also shares their sustainability vision and knowledge with a wide audience at professional conferences, with the goal to contribute to education and initiatives that further best practices across the industry and globe.

Think about This

1. Why is the practice of sustainability in meetings and conventions important?
2. What is MCI's mission? How does MCI translate its mission into sustainable strategies and practices?
3. How does MCI translate sustainable and responsible principles into sustainable and profitable business opportunities?
4. Do further research on MCI's sustainable practices and strategies. What are three take-away business strategies you discovered?

Sources

http://mcisustainability.com

www.meetings-conventions.com

THE LEISURE TRAVEL MARKET

The leisure traveler market serves as an economic engine for many destinations. Over the past decade, the volume of leisure travel has been increasing. In the United States, direct spending on leisure travel by domestic and international travelers totaled $683 billion in 2016. In the United States, domestic travel is defined in terms of "trips." A trip is defined as travel of more than fifty miles away from home. Leisure trips account for almost three-quarters of all U.S. domestic travel. In 2016, there were 1.7 billion person-trips (one person taking one trip) for leisure purposes.

The vast majority of trips in the United States are taken by auto. Trips by plane are less than 10 percent of the total number of trips taken. Overnight trips account for half of all person-trips. Trips of one or two nights are more common than longer stay trips. Thirty percent of all trips are taken in summer with about 25 percent in winter and slightly less in spring and fall. Almost 60 percent of all trips are taken within the traveler's own state while an additional almost 20 percent are taken within the traveler's census region. Nearly half of all general vacation travel is during the summer.

There are a number of ways to describe the segments that comprise the leisure travel market. Some of the most commonly utilized approaches include:

- *Demographics* (e.g., senior travelers, youth travelers, female travelers, affluent travelers, budget travelers)
- *Activity settings* (e.g., resort vacationers, theme park visitors, outdoor vacationers, urban travelers, rural visitors)
- *Geolocation preference* (e.g., international travelers, domestic travelers)
- *Companionship* (e.g., family travelers, solo travelers, group travelers, pet tourism, girlfriend getaways, mancations)
- *Travel frequency* (e.g., first-time travelers, repeat travelers)
- *Activity interests* (e.g., cultural heritage travelers, golf travelers, culinary travelers, medical travelers,

QUICK TRIP 14.7

The Traveling Men

Men's vacations are fast becoming more than just a fishing trip. A "male" vacation nowadays allows guys the time and opportunity to stretch, explore, and express themselves in new ways. Here are some incarnations of the new traveling man:

- **Metro Man.** He seeks fine dining, spa visits, etiquette and wine lessons, and consultations with a personal shopper. This results in a self-improvement vacation that blends relaxation with interesting new experiences.
- **Adventure Man.** A fellow with a hefty bank account, Adventure Man looks for trips like helicopter skiing, yachting, and chartered safaris in Africa. He doesn't mind bringing the kids along—in fact, he finds it a more rewarding vacation with them there.
- **Corporate Man.** He could also be called Junket Man. Mixing business with pleasure, Corporate Man makes the most of each destination. Marketers try to draw him in with ads like the Floridian ad showcasing a business suit-clad man holding swim fins and a sign saying "Bring your other suit."
- **Speed Man.** He is affluent, and he loves to race. He vacations at places like the Skip Barber Racing School to satisfy his need for speed, as does piloting lessons. For him, racing school may simply be a $1,000-per-week vacation, or it could be the beginning of a $30,000-per-year "hobby."

Think about This

1. How do men and women travel differently?
2. What may be their differences in travel motivation?
3. What may be their differences in activity preferences?
4. Provide an example of a destination that is ideal for a "mancation" and explain why.

eco-travelers, ski travelers, extreme adventure travelers, space visitors, destination weddings, casino gaming visitors, sports travelers)

- *Benefits sought* (wellness travelers, adventure travelers, education sojourners, VFR travelers, sightseeing vacationers)
- *Length* (day-trippers, overnight travelers, weekend getaway travelers)

The size of these travel segments can vary by countries and destinations. Travel marketers can also use more than one category of factors (e.g., senior cruise

visitors) to define and fine-tune their leisure travel segments in ways that help them provide more relevant marketing messages and improve their product offerings.

Adventure Tourism

Adventure travel is a segment with significant growth potential. In fact, about 40 percent of travelers classify themselves as adventure travelers (ATTA 2017). The Adventure Travel Trade Association defines adventure

QUICK TRIP 14.8

Travel on Top: What Do Affluent Travelers Want?

According to an Amadeus report, luxury travel is growing at a faster speed than the overall traveler market. North America and Western Europe account for 64 percent of the global outbound travelers. The Asia Pacific luxury travel market, however, represents the fastest growing luxury travel segment. What do affluent travelers want? Below is a list identified by Amadeus Travel Intelligence:

- They value VIP treatments, such as high level of privacy and security (e.g., fast-track through airport security, private helicopter jets).
- They enjoy a sense of exclusiveness (e.g., unavailable and non-Googleable options).
- They enjoy indulgent and authentic experiences. Luxury is becoming more about enrichment than materialism.
- They prefer a high level of tailored service (e.g., door-to-door services on trip) and high product quality standards.
- They prefer trusted travel guardian services (e.g., travel advice, security of information, convenience, 24/7 support).
- Asia Pacific luxury travelers have unique motivations and needs compared to their European Counterparts.

There are six sub-segments of luxury travelers:

- **Always luxury** (4 percent, ultra rich, luxury being part of everyday life)
- **Special occasion luxury seekers** (20 percent, luxury travel is a treat, seeking "wow factor" experience)
- **Bluxury** (31 percent, business plus luxury travel, typically company leaders)
- **Cash rich, time poor** (24 percent, busy lifestyle, treat luxury travel as a chance to reconnect with self and others, value privacy)
- **Strictly opulent** (18 percent, seek best and most travel experiences, want to be seen to be having indulgences)
- **Independent and affluent** (3 percent, turn to luxury travel as a way to pamper self or try something new)

Think about This

1. How are travel trends of the affluent similar or different to those of the general population?
2. What unique marketing implications does this foretell?
3. Affluent individuals can often set new trends for the rest of the population. What may be the potential "trickle-down" effects that the tourism industry needs to cater to?

Source

http://www.amadeus.com/documents/future-traveller-tribes-2030/luxury-travel/shaping-the-future-of-luxury-travel-report.pdf

tourism as involving three elements: physical activity, cultural exchange, and interaction with the natural environment. Adventure travel offerings range from soft adventure to hard adventure.

Soft adventure refers to activities that require a certain degree of mental and physical fitness but only a minimum level of skill and do not necessarily provide the thrill or risk of hard adventure activities. Soft adventure activities are common on vacations and include activities such as snorkeling, fishing, hiking, cycling, canoeing, horseback riding, safaris, and local tours.

Hard adventure is the traditional form of adventure travel that usually requires a higher level of skills on the part of the visitors. Activities commonly associated with hard adventure travel include white-water activities, skydiving, bungee jumping, caving, climbing, abseiling, snowboarding, skiing, diving, ballooning, and mountain biking, among other activities (Buckley 2006). Ultimately, adventure tourism providers are charged with three missions: protecting the nature environment, protecting visitors from harm and risk, and protecting long-term market share by providing adventure experiences that address these travel needs and wants of travelers.

Characteristics of Adventure Travelers.

A typical adventure traveler is male, single, thirty-six years old, and has a college degree. They read *National Geographic* and tend to post about their trips on social media. Adventure travelers see themselves as kind, intellectual, organized, imitative, efficient, interested in indigenous culture and cultural immersion, seeking new experiences, and health conscious. They have no interests in shopping or participating in competitions. At least fourteen different motivations for adventure travel have been identified (Buckley 2012):

- Seeking thrill
- Overcoming fear
- Maintaining physical and mental self-control
- Using skills to perform
- Overcoming challenges to gain a sense of accomplishment
- Fitness motivated
- Seeking a sense of rush
- Appreciating beauty of nature
- Activity as artistic
- Activity as spiritual
- Seeking shared enjoyment with others
- Enhancing self-image in the eyes of others
- Seeking a change from routine
- Competition against other

Among these motivations, seeking a rush appears to be a key motivation, especially among skilled adventure travelers (Buckley 2012). A *rush* is a psychophysiological state experienced by skilled adventure recreationists manifested as a sensation of thrill and flow. However, the *sense of rush* is differentiated from a *sense of risk*. Adventure travelers do not necessarily seek risk. Researchers have noted a *risk-recreation* paradox. This paradox is shaped by the fact that visitors pay to engage in recreational activities that involve some degree of risk and yet adventure travel outfitters and operators aim to minimize risks such as injury and medical and legal costs associated with their products (Buckley 2006).

Adventure travel can occur in nature, or culture, or with a specific activity, according to The Adventure Travel Trade Association (ATTA 2017). The most favorite activity for adventure travelers is hiking. Other popular activities for this travel segment include saddled-up activities (e.g., skydiving, zip-lining, rafting, hang gliding, bungee jumping), paddleboarding, visiting historical sites, getting to know the locals, camping, road cycling, and skiing/snowboarding.

Adventure Traveler Sub-Segments.

A study published in the *Journal of Travel Research* (Sung 2004) classifies adventure travelers into six groups:

1. *General Enthusiasts.* These are usually men with some college education and no children under the age of twelve. The general enthusiast is the most likely to take adventure trips, preferring hard adventure like sea kayaking or mountain climbing to soft adventure like camping. He is also likely to want to arrange his own trip, and to travel to non-American destinations like the South Pacific.

FIGURE 14.7 An extreme sportsman jumps on a rope from a great height.

QUICK TRIP 14.9

Cycling as an Urban Tourism Experience: Bikers and Super Biking Trails

Although bicycle used to be the dominant mode of transport for quite some time, the contemporary dominance of auto-mobility has almost rendered cycling invisible. Automobiles have replaced and overshadowed the use of bicycles, let alone a cycling infrastructure. However, there has been a resurgence. Biking as a form of special interest tourism has witnessed a resurgence in recent years (Reid 2017) due to the increasing need of consumers to maintain an active and healthy lifestyle, and their increasing sense of social responsibility to reduce their carbon footprint and help build sustainable cities. More people are on bikes and are interested in taking on biking as an activity when they vacation. As a result, destinations have increasingly invested in their cycling infrastructure, to cater to their residents as well as visitor needs.

Copenhagen, the Danish capital, for example, has an infrastructure plan centered around a central cycling infrastructure. Urban cycling is appreciated there as an integrative component of an experiential and livable city, and as a health-conducive regional transport mode that also provides an attractive tourist activity. For some, there is no better way to explore a local place than by bike; for others, biking can be their main motivation to travel to a destination.

Cycling in Copenhagen is a good example of how a city embraced a bicycle strategy to strategically make the city the world's best bicycle city (Jensen, Cashmore, and Elle 2017). Similarly, in Germany, cycling is not only a pleasurable activity, but also an increasingly preferred way to get around locally. Many cities have extensive cycling infrastructure. The country, famous for its speed-limit-free stretches of autobahn, is building car-free autobahns for bikes.

Lonelyplanet.com (2012) introduced their ten best bicycle trips around the world. These places are Isle of Wight, England; West Coast, Tasmania, Australia; Luberon and Mont Ventoux, Provence, France; San Juan Islands, Washington, United States; County Clare, Ireland; La Farola, Cuba; National Highway 1, Vietnam; Otago Peninsula, New Zealand; Cape Breton Island, Canada; and Friuli-Venezia Giulia, Italy.

The Guardian ranked top cycling destinations in Europe based on various cycling themes. They are:

1. **Pleasure cycling, Italy:** This is enjoyment-oriented cycling, allowing cycles to take in museum and wine tasting trips.
2. **Tours in the Alps and Pyrenees, France:** For someone looking for a fully guided and supported bike tour.
3. **Mountain biking, Spain:** For mountain bikers with endless rolling trails and precipitous descents.
4. **Marmotte or Maratona, France and Italy:** One-day road cycling for cyclists looking for a challenge.
5. **Mountain biking—the Trans-Alp, Germany and Italy:** This is officially a race but most riders simply aim to finish the trail of 400 mainly off-road miles in seven daily stages.
6. **Do-it-yourself in France:** This is recommended for bike tourists who look for bike-friendly support systems and lodging options.
7. **Winter cycling in Andalucía, Spain:** Road cycling in the benevolent winter climate of Andalucía.
8. **Leisure cycling tour of Sardinia, Italy.**
9. **Cycle-friendly stay at Vélo Ventoux, France.**
10. **Do-it-yourself in Lanzarote, Canary Islands.**

Think about This

1. Does your city have a cycling infrastructure for its residents?
2. What contributes to the increasing popularity of cycling?
3. What attributes of a destination will help make it onto a cyclist's wish list of places to visit?

Sources

Jensen, J., M. Cashmore, and M. Elle. 2017. "Reinventing the bicycle: how calculative practices shape urban environmental governance." *Environmental Politics* 26 (3), 459–479.

Lonelyplanet.com. 2012. "Saddle up for the world's best cycling routes." https://www.lonelyplanet.com/travel-tips-and-articles/saddle-up-for-the-worlds-best-cycling-routes/40625c8c-8a11-5710-a052-1479d27715f8

Reid, C. 2017. *Bike Boom: The Unexpected Resurgence of Cycling.* Island Press: Washington.

Sorrel, C. 2016. "Germany's 62-Mile Bike Autobahn Connects 10 Cities: Welcome to a future of easy, safe, intercity bike travel." https://www.fastcompany.com/3055053/germanys-62-mile-bike-autobahn-connects-10-cities

Walker, P. 2015. Top 10 cycling holidays in Europe. *The Guardian.* https://www.theguardian.com/travel/2015/jan/08/top-10-cycling-holidays-europe-france-italy-spain

2. *Budget Youngsters.* These travelers are generally young (nineteen to thirty-four) and single, with a fairly low income. They prefer to organize their own trips, although they also like to have partially inclusive trips to get professional expertise. The budget youngster prefers to travel with friends to areas around America, perhaps because travel in-country is cheap.

3. *Soft Moderates.* This is a small group composed mostly of middle-aged women who are highly educated but nevertheless have a low income, because there is only one wage earner in the house. The soft moderate is unlikely to have children under the age of twelve. She prefers soft adventure, like hiking and nature trips, in American destinations. The soft moderate would rather not arrange her own trips, and she desires familiarity, not risk-taking.

4. *Upper High Naturalists.* Members of this group are mostly middle-aged, married, and earn high wages. They usually have a dual-income household, but no children under twelve. They prefer both soft and rugged adventures, like hiking or backpacking, and they like to travel with family members and friends. The upper high naturalist seeks novelty trips and exotic destinations like Africa, where they generally stay more than a week and spend more than $1,000.

5. *Family Vacationers.* Family vacationers have generally completed some college and have two incomes in the household to support their children, at least one of which is under age twelve. Favorite travel destinations for the family vacationer include America and South America. These travelers like to have some help in planning their vacations.

6. *Active Soloists.* This group is composed mostly of well-educated, middle-income earners without children under twelve. The active soloists distinctly prefer high-risk, high-adventure activities like hang gliding, and they prefer to travel alone or in an organized group. Of all the groups, this group seems to rely on visitor infrastructure the most when making travel arrangements.

The regions that adventure travelers most often wish to travel to are North America, New Zealand, Australia, South America, South Pacific, Western Europe, Central America, Central Europe, the Caribbean, and Africa. When travelers are looking for an adventure experience, they tend to look for four things:

- the novel and unique;
- wellness;
- challenge, and
- transformation.

Many destinations and tourism operators have strived to attract adventure travelers. For example, Queensland, New Zealand, markets itself as the "Adventure Capital of the World" and offers a diverse range of adventure travel products. The area is known to offer the "awesome foursome" adventures, which includes white-water rafting the rapids on the Shotover River, jet boating through narrow gorges, a helicopter ride, and the Hackett bungee jump into a 134-meter deep canyon (Williams and Soutar 2009).

Casino Gaming

The global casino gaming market generates billions of dollars in revenues every year and multiple new markets are emerging (Statista, 2017). Global gaming market revenue distribution centers by region include the Asia Pacific (43.3 percent, e.g., Macau), the United States (40.1 percent, e.g., Las Vegas), and EMEA (Europe, Middle East, and Africa [10 percent]. Macau's gaming revenue spiked drastically from 2006 to 2013 but has seen a dramatic pullback since its peak. Las Vegas's revenue stream has been stable whereas the traditional markets such as Atlantic City has seen steady revenue decline. Emergent markets include Singapore and potentially Japan. Online gaming has met with high consumer enthusiasm but is met with legal restrictions.

In 1931 gaming was legalized in Nevada. For forty-five years this was the only legal location for gaming in the United States. Nevada was joined by Atlantic City in the mid-1970s. Since the late 1980s, gambling has grown significantly in the United States. Today the industry makes a total contribution of around 137.5 billion U.S. dollars to the U.S. economy (Statista 2017). There are four categories of casinos—*tribal casinos* (located on Indian reservations), *land-based casinos*, *riverboat casinos*, and *racinos* (horse or greyhound racetracks that have casinos). Key casino gaming vendors include companies such as:

- Caesars Entertainment
- Galaxy Entertainment
- Las Vegas Sands
- MGM Resorts
- SJM Holdings

Much of the gambling activity occurs while Americans are traveling away from home. Overall, gambling travelers are older, are less likely to be married or to have children in their households, and are less educated

QUICK TRIP 14.10

Adventure Travel Experiences

Travelers seek adventure experiences all over the globe. *National Geographic Magazine's* selection of top adventure trips includes destinations that span from North America and South America, to Oceania and Africa:

1. Biking on slick rocks at Moab, Utah
2. Ice-skating in winter at Lake Louise, Banff, Canada
3. White-water rafting and other watersports, southern West Virginia
4. Getting intimate with stingrays in their natural habitat in Grand Cayman, Cayman Islands
5. Zip-lining in the rain forest, Costa Rica
6. Hang gliding in Rio de Janeiro, Brazil
7. Rugged beach adventure on Isle of Bute, Scotland
8. Hiking through a chain of volcanic Aeolian Islands, Italy
9. Witnessing the cycle of wildlife in Kruger National Park, South Africa
10. Doing extreme sports (e.g., bungee jumping) on snowcapped mountains in Queenstown, New Zealand

Think about This

1. What attributes of these ten adventure destinations distinguish them from other adventure destinations?
2. What triggers the psycho-physiological state of rush for a traveler?
3. How may cultural adventurists seek experiences different from nature adventurists?
4. What are some strategies adventure experience providers might follow to manage risks associated with adventure travel?

Source

https://www.nationalgeographic.com/travel/photos-top-10-adventure-trips/

QUICK TRIP 14.11

Changing Legacy

Scotland has long been revered for its magnificent landscape and ideal golf courses. However, thanks to a 2010 study, it was found that the Edinburgh festival tourism is worth more than golf tourism. The country's golf industry brought in £190 m last year while festival tourism accrued £261 m in revenue. The report found that the Edinburgh festivals were worth five times as much as single events such as Glastonbury. They are considered a "cultural phenomenon, celebrated globally and treasured locally" (Rice 2011). It is noted that four million people attend Edinburgh's twelve major festivals each year. The Edinburgh Festivals are themselves a cultural phenomenon and will continue to shape the future economic climate of Scotland. These festivals have made financial impact on Scotland and have given the locals a sense of pride in their city. Surveyed guests in the area said that the festivals increased their children's imagination while encouraging them to take risks and experience all that there is to offer.

Think about This

1. Why have festivals had such a success in this location?
2. Would you suggest for other destinations to branch out into such large-scale festivals? Why or why not?
3. What are the positive and negative effects of festivals on the local public?

Source

Rice, S. 2011. The Edinburgh Festivals Impact Study. http://www.bbc.co.uk/news/uk-scotland-edinburgh-east-fife-13502646

than their nongambling counterparts. Casino visitors actually fall into two groups: those for which gambling is the only activity on the trip and for the remainder gambling is only one of multiple activities. This demonstrates that casino visitors are interested in gambling as a form of entertainment. However, entertainment at a casino means more than gaming. It is more than slot machines. It is fake volcanoes, jousting machines, and dancing water fountains in Las Vegas, for example. More than 84 million people in the United States visited a gaming venue within a period of twelve months prior to spring 2017 (Statista 2017).

There are two types of casino locations:

1. *Transient.* Serving the day-tripper market; people travel to the site by car or bus and use little lodging or off-premises food facilities. Most tribal casinos and many riverboats fall into this category.
2. *Destination casinos.* The premiere example continues to be Las Vegas. Over 40 percent arrive by air whereas slightly less than that number drive to the destination. People stay an average of four days, 90 percent in hotels.

Like their neighbors in the United States, Canadians also enjoy gambling. Over 70 percent of Canadians gamble in a given year. While playing the lottery is the most popular gambling activity, in-province casino gambling ranks fourth, out-of-province casino gambling is listed ninth, and out-of-country casino gambling is tenth. It appears that there are two distinct segments—those who prefer to stay inside the province and others who prefer to visit casinos outside the province.

Cruise Tourism

The global cruise travel market enjoys a continuous growth at a steady pace. Cruise travel is a major leisure market. Representing 95 percent of global cruise capacity, the **Cruise Line International Association** has members of sixty cruise lines, including ocean, river, and specialty cruise lines. CLIA members work with 15,000 travel agencies to distribute cruise vacation products. The Global Economic Impact of Cruise travel was US $117 billion, with 23 million cruisers in 2016 (CLIA 2017). Cruise travelers come from all over the world with the United States, China, Germany, UK, Australia, Canada, Italy, Spain, and Brazil generating the most cruise travel demand.

In response to both increased demand, as well as new customer needs and trends, the cruise industry is building new ships, and adding new facilities, amenities, and port locations. Although the traditional cruise travelers are older, the younger generations including the millennials and Generation-Xers have embraced cruise travel. Most cruise travelers travel with their spouses or partners, followed by children. Younger travelers choose shorter trips. Older travelers cruise for a longer period.

Some of the most important factors influencing cruisers vacation choices are destination, cost, overall experience, property/ship, and amenities. Cruisers place high importance on these cruise ship features and amenities: Suite and balcony cabins, private/exclusive access, programs for children of ages thirteen to seventeen and under thirteen, Internet access, spa and salon services, babysitting services, onboard entertainment—musical and comedy, and Broadway shows, adult-only areas, celebrity chef restaurants, sporting facilities, onboard shopping and duty-free stores, casino and gaming, pool/Jacuzzi, health club and gym, specialty restaurants. According to CLIA (2017), several cruise travel trends are worth noting:

- The cruisers are getting younger.
- Travel agent use has increased.
- River cruise demand has increased.
- Private islands are often on cruise itineraries.
- Nearly half of non-cruisers have expressed interest in taking an ocean cruise.
- Cruisers favor drivable port locations.
- Cruisers welcome feature restaurants and dishes created by famous chefs.
- Demand for expedition cruises is increasing as the adventure travel market grows at record pace.

The most visited vacation destinations for cruisers are:

- Caribbean/Bermuda/Mexico East Coast
- Alaska/Pacific Northwest
- Hawaii
- Europe (Mediterranean), US West Coast/Mexico West Coast, Canada/New England, Europe (Non-Mediterranean)
- Around the world circuits
- Australia/New Zealand/Pacific Islands
- Panama Canal
- Rivers including United States rivers
- Cuba
- South America

Medical Tourism

Medical tourism can be defined as travel outside one's natural healthcare jurisdiction for the enhancement or restoration of an individual's health and wellness

FIGURE 14.8 Alaska cruise tourist taking photo of Glacier Bay.

through medical intervention (Carrera and Bridges 2006). Medical tourism is a niche travel market that has witnessed continuous growth. The reasons behind the growth include the aging world population, increasing costs for critical and elective procedures, lack of local state-of-the-art medical technology and expertise, the availability of information over the Internet, and increasing promotion of medical tourism by governmental agencies and private businesses.

Patients Beyond Borders, a medial tourism guidebook (2017), estimates that there are approximately 14 million cross-border patients worldwide, spending an average of USD 3,800–6,000 per visit. Some of the most popular medical tourism destinations are Costa Rica, India, Israel, Malaysia, Mexico, Singapore, South Korea, Taiwan, Thailand, Turkey, and the United States.

What draws people to travel across borders to these countries to seek medical care? A short answer is that these destinations are perceived as having:

- A good healthcare infrastructure
- A demonstrated commitment to quality assurance, and international accreditation

- The potential cost savings for medical procedures
- A reputation for excellence in care
- A history of healthcare innovation and achievement
- State of the art medical technology
- Quality medical staff

The top specialties that medical travelers seek include:

- Cosmetic surgery
- Dentistry (general, restorative, cosmetic)
- Cardiovascular (angioplasty, CABG, transplants)
- Orthopedics (joint and spine, sports medicine)
- Cancer (often high-acuity or last resort)
- Reproductive (fertility, IVF, women's health)
- Weight loss (LAP-BAND, gastric bypass)
- Scans, tests, health screenings, and second opinions

The Senior Travel Market

By the year 2025 there will be twice as many people in the United States sixty-five and older as there are teens. This segment has been called a number of things:

- Mature market
- Muppie market (mature, upscale, post-professional)
- Senior market
- Maturing market

For the most part, traveler motivations and attitudes, as well as behavior while on vacation have all remained remarkably stable over time. This suggests that, as people age, individuals attempt to maintain past patterns of behavior. Thus, while marketing programs aimed at the older traveler may need to be updated, they probably do not require major surgery. The senior market can be segmented on the basis of motivation. Three sub-segments are suggested:

- The Escape and Learn Group, comprising 46 percent of the sample, consists of travelers who want to visit new places and escape everyday routine.
- The Retirees, comprising 19 percent of the sample, made up of travelers who take trips where they stay in one place for a period of time.
- Active Storytellers, the remaining 35 percent, who want to experience new things, visit museums and historic sights, and meet people and socialize.

The significance of seniors as a market segment in tourism is likely to grow over the next several decades. By the year 2030, there will be 65 million older adults in the United States. Many older people have the time, money, and desire to travel. They hold a large share of the country's discretionary income because their children are grown and they no longer have house payments. Because they are time-flexible, they can fill the times of low occupancy felt by many businesses and tourism destinations.

Simply put, seniors will be increasingly important for two reasons. First, there will be more of them and they have the time, money, and desire to travel. Second, their lifestyles are different from those of previous generations. They are increasingly independent about how they choose to live and enjoy their lives. Two demographic items are of particular importance. There will be a high proportion of singles in this population and a higher proportion of women than men. This change over time is related to the fact that women live longer than men, marry men older than themselves, and more widowers remarry than do widows.

Research shows that primary motivators of senior travelers include:

- Needing to change routines
- Seeing new things
- Visiting friends and relatives

- Meeting new people and experiencing new cultures
- Expanding knowledge
- Creating memories

At the same time, these senior travelers expressed concern about such things as:

- *The single supplement penalty.* The cost of a single room was often more than half the cost of a double room. Although some tour operators offer assistance in finding a roommate, the process is not easy and potential roommates are not always compatible.
- *Health/mobility constraints.* Although 60 percent of those age sixty-five or older reported no activity limitations, they considered health as a problem interfering with travel as it prevents them from enjoying the trip or engaging in some activities.
- *The fear of falling ill.* The prospect of having a doctor or nurse close by helps alleviate concern.
- *Uncertainty about political conditions.* Many seniors chose not to travel internationally when there was a question regarding the country's economic or political situation.
- *Quality and quantity of information.* Some seniors had a problem in getting information about upcoming events or trips. More aggressive promotion is needed to reach this group.
- *The pace of itineraries.* People indicated they needed more time to get ready when they were part of a tour. Scheduling was also a problem—packing too many things into a short period of time.
- *Language.* Language was seen as a major barrier to traveling internationally. Tour guides were seen as important in helping overcome this concern.
- *Packing and unpacking.* A more leisurely trip was preferred over tours that go to a new city every day.
- *Meals.* Lack of variety was cited as a problem. Most evening meals consisted of chicken dinners and a greater choice at breakfast was also desired.
- *Concerns related to transportation.* More help was desired for when getting on and off buses. Communication is really important.

Family Travelers

Family vacations are regarded as an opportunity to spend quality time together. Over one-third of all leisure trips are family trips. Americans prioritize traveling as a family. Most families take one to two family vacations a year. Family travelers are a major consumer base for travel businesses such as cruises, resorts, theme parks, and

QUICK TRIP 14.12

Can Cultural Dissimilarity Always Be a Cultural Tourism Resource?

Cultural distance or dissimilarity is a measure of how similar or different the culture of the traveler is from the culture of the host. Cultural dissimilarity can be a factor that strongly motivates some tourists to visit. The term cultural tourists refers to such tourists, as they are curious about a new culture and want to learn more about it by visiting there. But cultural distance can play the role of an inhibitor for tourists too, as cultural dissimilarity can evoke a sense of insecurity and risk when it comes to selecting an international destination. Researchers have found that travelers unwilling to travel to dissimilar cultures, often express concerns about crime, health, political instability, terrorism, foreign foods, cultural barriers, and a destination's political, social, and religious dogma. Tourists can also be anxious about language barriers, behavioral norms, or potential personal safety.

Although novelty and foreignness are integral components of an international tourist experience, travelers are not ready to subject themselves entirely to such foreign elements in an alien environment. In a recent study, Bi and Lehto (2017) found that the impact of cultural dissimilarity on destination choices made by Chinese outbound travelers was not linear. The effect of cultural distance on international destination choices instead followed an inverted U-curve relationship in which there was an optimal point of cultural dissimilarity (Figure 14.9). Countries located near the optimal similarity point were more attractive destinations culture-wise than countries rated at either extreme of similarity (i.e., too similar or too dissimilar).

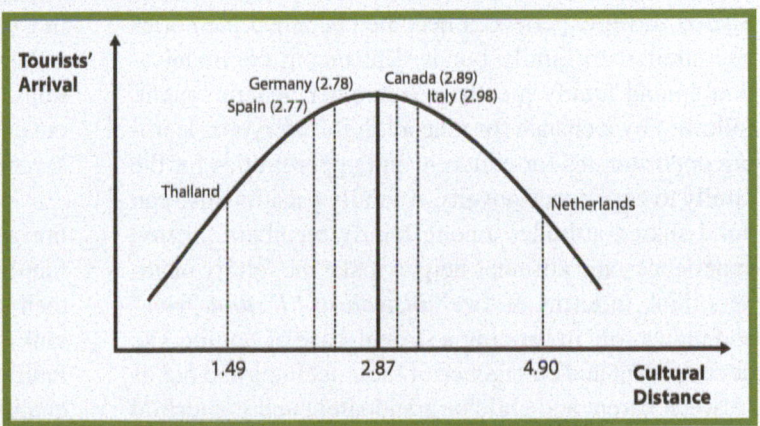

FIGURE 14.9 Cultural dissimilarity and international destination choices. I Adapted from Bi and Lehto (2017).

In the case of Chinese tourists, a cultural distance of 2.88 was optimal. Countries located nearby this point include Canada (2.89), Germany (2.28), Spain (2.77), and Italy (2.98) (Figure 14.9). These countries' cultural resources can be interpreted as having the right level of novelty value for visitors from China. Other factors that need to be considered alongside the cultural dissimilarity include income, geographic distance, and currency exchange rate.

The important point is that the cultural novelty effect gradually increased up to the optimal point, and then became a factor adversely influencing travelers' choices. This shows that tourists are motivated to explore a foreign culture, but only within a safe distance. Therefore, cultural distance needs to be carefully considered for destinations intending to attract international visitors. As a general rule of thumb based on the findings of this research, it would be appropriate for destinations seeking to attract tourists from countries with higher than optimal cultural distance scores to deliver a marketing message that incorporate some elements of cultural similarity and vice versa. For example, to attract Chinese tourists, Thailand (with a low score of 1.49) should emphasize some cultural differences while the Netherlands (with a high score of 4.9) should reinforce some cultural similarities.

Think about This

1. How may the knowledge of an inverted U-shape relationship between cultural dissimilarity and travel intention be utilized in destination marketing practices?
2. When a country is located beyond the optimal cultural distance point, what strategies might these destinations use to endear their visitors and reduce their perceived cultural foreignness and the resulting sense of insecurity?
3. When countries are culturally similar, what strategies might increase the cultural attractiveness of the destination?

Source

Bi, J., and X. Lehto. 2017. "Impact of cultural distance on international destination choices: The case of Chinese outbound travelers." *International Journal of Tourism Research* 2017, 1–10. https://doi.org/10.1002/jtr.2152

various types of all-inclusive vacations. In the United States, the most popular family vacation remains the old-school road trip. Other popular trips include visits to national parks, theme parks, history driven trips (such as visiting the capital city of a country), trips to international destinations, going on guided tours, and ocean cruises. In addition to traveling with immediate family members, family travelers enjoy traveling with friends (other families), and extended families (multi-generation travel).

Recent studies have identified several beneficial elements of family travel (Fu, Lehto, and Park 2014). An opportunity for family bonding is the most valued. Shared travel experiences become cherished memories and strengthen family bonds. Enhancing communication among family members is another benefit sought, followed by a chance for relaxation for everyone, learning opportunities for children, and opportunities for the family to experience novelty. A family vacation also can build shared attitudes among family members. Shared experiences and attitudes help to make the family members think in terms of *"we" instead of "I" and "you"* and play a role in forming a strong sense of family. The development and emergence of these feelings and bonds between parent and child or grandparent and grandchild may well become one of the most effective bases for continuing relationships after the dependency bond has been dissolved or weakened.

What types of vacation experiences do contemporary families look for? They look for family vacations that allow meaningful outdoor/nature experiences for their children and themselves to combat an increasingly static, digital-oriented family lifestyle. According to the American College of Pediatricians (2016), American children spend much less time playing outside than in the past. They now spend an increasing amount of hours on entertainment media, including phones, computers, televisions, and other digital devices. Research has also shown that children who experience nature before the age of eleven tend to grow up caring about nature. They also look for family vacations that allow opportunities for the family to learn about new cultures. Parents value the learning and educational opportunities afforded to their children by international destinations.

Over 90 percent of all adults agree that the interests of their kids are important when planning vacations. The impact of children on the household travel plans is noted in Chapter 13. There is also agreement that children are influential in the selection of destinations, accommodations, and vacation packages. Interestingly, about eight out of every ten children across key age categories (six to seventeen) say they really like taking family vacations.

Destinations, resorts, cruise lines, and other vacation experience providers have attempted to serve the family travel market with travel experiences that cater to their needs. The US News and World Report (2017) ranks best vacation destinations based on input from family travelers and expert opinions on three areas of quality of a destination: distinction, seasonality, and affordability. Figure 14.10 is a list of the top 10 family vacation destinations for the United States, Canada, and Europe.

Visiting Friends and Relatives (VFR)

When people travel to visit friends and relatives, the nature of their trip can vary in many ways. Households visiting friends or relatives tend to spend less money on

US	Canada	Europe
Orlando-Walt Disney World	Vancouver	London
Anaheim-Disneyland	Whistler	Amsterdam
Branson	Niagara Falls	Barcelona
San Diego	Toronto	Florence
Grand Canyon	Quebec City	Prague
Yellowstone	Ottawa	Dublin
Ocean City	Calgary	Stockholm
Washington, DC	Banff	Innsbruck
Maui	Kelowna	Madrid
Honolulu-Oahu	Montreal	Rome

FIGURE 14.10 Top ten family vacation destinations in the US, Canada, and Europe. | *Source: US News and World, report. https://travel.usnews.com/rankings/best-family-vacations/*

a trip compared to those traveling for other reasons. Almost three out of every four person-trips include staying in someone else's home. Winter is the most popular time to visit friends or relatives, probably due to the end-of-year holidays. Surprisingly, two in five trips in this segment involve only one traveler from the household. This figure is much higher than any other leisure travel segment.

The *visiting friends and relatives* (VFR) segment is often assumed to be a homogeneous market. However, in some cases, VFR is just one of several activities engaged in by visitors. It is suggested that the VFR market is better understood if it is segmented on the basis of the following variables (Moscardo et al. 2000):

- Difference between VFR as a travel activity and as a trip type or motive
- Domestic versus international VFR
- Short-haul versus long-haul VFR trips
- Staying with friends or relatives versus staying in commercial accommodation
- Focus of visit (visiting friends, visiting relatives, visiting both friends and relatives)

Although some discount the economic contribution of the VFR market, thinking they spend little because they stay and eat with friends and relatives, this segment contributes to a destination in several ways (Lehto, Morrison, and O'Leary 2001):

- They act as a moderator, compensating for seasonal variations
- International VFRs have longer than average length of stays
- They are a very effective word-of-mouth channel

Travelers with a Disability

It used to be extremely difficult to be a wheelchair-bound traveler. Now, disabled travelers of all types are having an easier time of it, due to the Americans with Disabilities Act of 1990 and the Air Carrier Access Act of 1986. Nevertheless, there are still hurdles in the way of the millions of blind, deaf, and wheelchair-dependent travelers that roam the world each year.

Luckily, with the right resources, these hurdles don't present a major problem. Tony Schrader, a fifty-four-year-old lawyer from Austin, Texas, has been a paraplegic for most of his life. He's an avid traveler who has been with his wife to St. Petersburg, Cozumel, and London, among a host of other places. How did he surmount the marble staircases inside the State Hermitage Museum while he was in Russia? Simple—two volunteers carried him up, at the request of his private guide. What about the sandy beaches in Cozumel, Mexico? A local van with a power lift was waiting at the shore to meet the small boat that carried Schrader from the cruise ship. In London, the narrow streets were not a problem; black cabs equipped with ramps ferried him around the city.

This market is likely to grow larger, studies suggest, especially as the Baby Boomer generation ages, and technological advances make the lives of disabled people more mobile and convenient. The Society for Accessible Travel and Hospitality in New York (2017) estimates that nearly 75 percent of the 54 million disabled Americans have the financial and physical ability to make a trip. However, only about 11 million travel at least once a year.

Group Tours

Package travel has become a significant factor in the expansion of mass tourism markets to both domestic and international destinations in the past sixty years. Some argue that package travel has been declining because of changing visitor preferences toward more individualized and independent travel experiences, whereas others counter that package travel has a considerable economic impact in the United States through job creation and income generation. Package travel is a popular travel product in Asia, especially when it comes to visits to international destinations.

Minority Travel Patterns

The United States is racially and ethnically diverse. The three largest minority groups in the United States—African Americans, Hispanics, and Asian Americans—will make up 35 percent of the population in the United States by 2020. Most Americans, regardless of ethnicity, share similar travel habits. Most vacationers use cars. A typical trip includes two people, an overnight stay, and the primary activity is shopping.

African Americans are the second largest racial group in the United States, and are slightly more likely than the other groups to travel on business, especially to seminars and conventions. They are also more likely to add on vacation travel to business trips. They are more prone to taking group tours and less likely to use recreational vehicles (RVs). The most popular destinations for African Americans are Texas, Georgia, and other Southern states. Washington, DC, and Maryland are also popular in addition to trips to the Caribbean.

Hispanics are more likely to travel with children than are other groups. They also take longer trips and are more likely to take a plane trip and stay at a hotel or motel. Hispanics have a major presence in New Mexico, Hawaii, California, and Texas, and represent the largest minority group (close to 18 percent) in the United States. When considering vacations, Hispanics are likely to want to explore their adopted country before venturing internationally. The only exception to this would be the desire to visit the country they were born in. California, Nevada, Florida, Arizona, Texas, and New Mexico are popular destinations in the United States whereas the Caribbean, Mexico, and South America are favored international destinations.

Asian Americans are the highest income, best educated, and fastest growing racial group in the United States (Pew Research Center 2013). They use planes and rental cars more than average, and are the biggest spenders of the three ethnic groups. California, Nevada, Hawaii, and the Far East are popular among this traveler segment. Asian Americans' main activities include entertainment/amusement parks, family/reunion, and nature/outdoor. Their trip duration on average is 4.2 days, somewhat higher than the average American traveler.

QUICK TRIP 14.13

An Ideal American Vacation Trip

A recent study identified the characteristics of the Ideal Vacation Trip. The ideal trip involves rest and relaxation; spending time with one's spouse, partner, or family; exploration and discovery; and luxury, adventure, and socialization. The most important elements are rest and relaxation and spending time with significant others.

Eight specific groups of motivational factors were identified.

1. **Experiential.** Enthusiastic travelers interested in long, ideally international, trips that give them the freedom to have new, different experiences.
2. **Family focused.** Travelers who want to travel with family members to family-friendly destinations that offer numerous activities.
3. **Casual travelers.** Young, mostly male travelers, who seek rest and relaxation.
4. **Trail blazers.** Older, outdoor enthusiasts who want adventure, to connect with nature, and are less interested in creature comforts.
5. **Reconnectors.** Mainly females who want rest and relaxation and time with their spouse/significant other in romantic, low-key settings such as beaches, cruise ships, and dining out.
6. **Affluentials.** A younger segment looking for relaxation, adventure, and luxury with their significant other in international luxury or upscale resort destinations.
7. **Back to basics.** Frugal travelers looking for rest and relaxation from inexpensive vacations through package deals.
8. **Quintessential travelers.** Highly motivated, passionate travelers interested in all types of destinations (especially international spots) and activities and who like to get involved in the research and planning part of the trip.

Think about This

1. How would these eight travel groups differ in their preferences of destinations? Are you able to suggest one ideal destination and one ideal vacation activity for each group?
2. Would an ideal vacation trip in your country be similar or different? Why?

SUMMARY

Although it is unwise to generalize, careful study of the major segments of the tourism markets is key to getting the big picture of why people travel and how people travel. Understanding of the profiles of these segments suggests many ways of appealing to the various markets. The two major categories of travel purpose are business travel and leisure travel. The patterns and needs of people in both categories are the topic of this chapter. Business travel is the "bread-and-butter" market for many tourism-related businesses. Business travel is broken down into general business; business travel related to meetings, conventions, and congresses; and incentive travel, which is somewhat of a hybrid as the people on the trip are traveling for pleasure although the purchasers of the trip are businesses. The characteristics of those in these market segments are explored in detail. The leisure and personal travel market is comprised of multiple segments. Some notable segments discussed in this chapter include family travelers, senior travelers, adventure travelers, cruise travelers, casino gaming travelers, medical travelers, VFR travelers, and group travelers.

ACTIVITIES

1. Develop a package suitable for students seeking a spring break experience. Then develop one for families looking for a holiday getaway. Why are the elements of the packages suitable for the two market segments?
2. Devise a suitable way to present these packages to the two market segments. Justify your answer.
3. Online, find a travel destination advertisement. Notice the market segment this ad is targeting. How is it attracting a certain type of visitor? Why, in your opinion, is the ad effective? How might it be improved?

REFERENCES

American College of Pediatricians. 2016. The Impact of Media Use and Screen Time on Children, Adolescents, and Families. https://www.acpeds.org/the-college-speaks/position-statements/parenting-issues/the-impact-of-media-use-and-screen-time-on-children-adolescents-and-families

ATTA. 2017. Adventure Travel Trade Association. https://www.adventuretravel.biz/

Buckley, R. 2006. Adventure Tourism. CABI International: Cambridge, MA.

Buckley, R. 2012. "Rush as a key motivation in skilled adventure tourism: Resolving the risk recreation paradox." Tourism Management 33 (4): 961–970.

Carrera, P. M., and F. P. Bridges. 2006. "Globalization and healthcare. Understanding health care and medical tourism." Expert Review of Pharmacoeconomics and Outcomes Research 6, 447–454. doi10.1586/14737167.6.4.447

CLIA. 2017. Cruise Industry Outlook.

CONCUR. 2016. Meet the faces of today's business traveler. https://www.concur.com/newsroom/article/meet-the-faces-of-todays-business-traveler

Fu, X., X. Lehto, and O. Park. 2014. What does vacation do to our family? Contrasting the perspectives of parents and children. Journal of Travel and Tourism Marketing 31 (4): 461–475.

Global Business Travel Association. 2017. https://www.gbta.org/PressReleases/Pages/rls_072814.aspx

Hensel, A. 2017. The 10 U.S. Cities Business Travelers Visit the Most. https://www.inc.com/john-boitnott/6-frequent-traveler-programs-every-business-traveler-should-join.html

Kriva, M. 2017. 5 Event Tech Must-Haves for Immersive Experiences. http://live.mci-group.com/2017/09/5-event-technology-must-haves/

Lehto, X., A. M. Morrison, and J. T. O'Leary. 2001. "Does the visiting friends and relatives' typology make a difference?" Journal of Travel Research 40: 201–212.

Moscardo, G., P. Pearce, A. Morrison, D. Green, and J. T. O'Leary. 2000. "Developing a typology for understanding visiting friends and relatives." Journal of Travel Research 38 (3): 251–259.

Patients Beyond Borders. 2017. https://patientsbeyondborders.com/

Pew Research Center. 2013. The rise of Asian Americans. http://www.pewsocialtrends.org/2012/06/19/the-rise-of-asian-americans/

Sheivachman, A. 2016. Most Frequent Business Travelers. https://skift.com/2016/10/27/millennials-are-now-the-most-frequent-business-travelers/

Skift. 2017a. https://skift.com/2017/10/10/global-business-travelers-agree-on-the-biggest-hassle-time-spent-in-transit/

Skift. 2017b. https://skift.com/2017/04/27/emerging-markets-will-drive-business-travel-growth-over-next-decade/

Sung, H. H. 2004. "Classification of Adventure Travelers: Behavior, Decision Making, and Target Markets." *Journal of Travel Research* 42 (4), 343–356.

The Society for Accessible Travel and Hospitality. 2017. www.sath.org

The Statistics Portal. https://www.statista.com/

U.S. News & World Report. 2017. Best Affordable Family Vacation. https://travel.usnews.com/rankings/best-affordable-family-vacations/

U.S. Travel Association. 2017. https://www.ustravel.org/research/travel-facts-and-figures

WEConnect International. https://weconnectinternational.org/en/

Williams, P., and G. Soutar. 2009. "Value, satisfaction and behavioral intentions in an adventure tourism context." *Annals of Tourism Research* 36 (3): 413–438.

ADDITIONAL READINGS

Benavides, J. 2014. A summary of African-American Travel Interests and Behaviors. Tourism Center, University of Minnesota Extension.

Benavides, J. 2015. A summary of Asian-American Travel Interests and Behaviors. Tourism Center, University of Minnesota Extension.

CLIA. 2016. CLIA Annual Report. https://www.cruising.org

http://investmentwatchblog.com/will-the-casino-industry-continue-to-flourish-in-2017/

http://www.travelchannel.com/interests/travel-tips/articles/best-rewards-programs-for-business-travelers

https://www.adventuretravelnews.com/the-evolution-of-the-adventure-traveler-study-charts-changes-2006-2016#.WcK5CgkfXKg.linkedin

https://www.cruising.org/docs/default-source/research/clia-2017-state-of-the-industry.pdf?sfvrsn=4

https://www.smartmeetings.com/news/96817/best-loyalty-programs-for-business-travelers

https://www.tripit.com/blog/2015/10/the-best-travel-rewards-programs-for-business-travelers.html

IWB. 2017. Will the Casino Industry Continue to Flourish in 2017?

Lehto, X. Y., S. J. Choi, Y. C Lin, and S. M. MacDermid. 2009. "Vacation and family functioning." *Annals of Tourism Research* 36 (3): 459–479.

Parfitt, D. 2016. "6 Family Travel Trends to Watch in 2017." *US News.* https://travel.usnews.com/features/6-family-travel-trends-to-watch-in-2017

Petrak, N. 2011. Emerging trends: Family travel, smart technology, and traveler preferences. http://www.adventure-travelnews.com/emerging-trends-family-travel-smart-technologies-and-traveler-preferences

Sakia, M., J. Brown, and J. Mak. 2000. Population aging and Japanese international travel in the 21st century. *Journal of Travel Research* 38 (3): 212–220.

Sirgy, M. J., and C. Su. 2000. "Destination Image, Self-Congruity, and Travel Behavior: Toward an Integrative Model." *Journal of Travel Research* 38 (4), 340–352.

Witt, P. A., and T. L. Goodale. 1981. "The relationship between barriers to leisure enjoyment and family stages." *Leisure Sciences* 4 (1): 29–49.

Zemke, R., C. Raines, and B. Filipczak. 2000. *Generations at Work.* New York: AMACOM.

PART FOUR

Travel

Travel Flows, Distribution, and Transportation

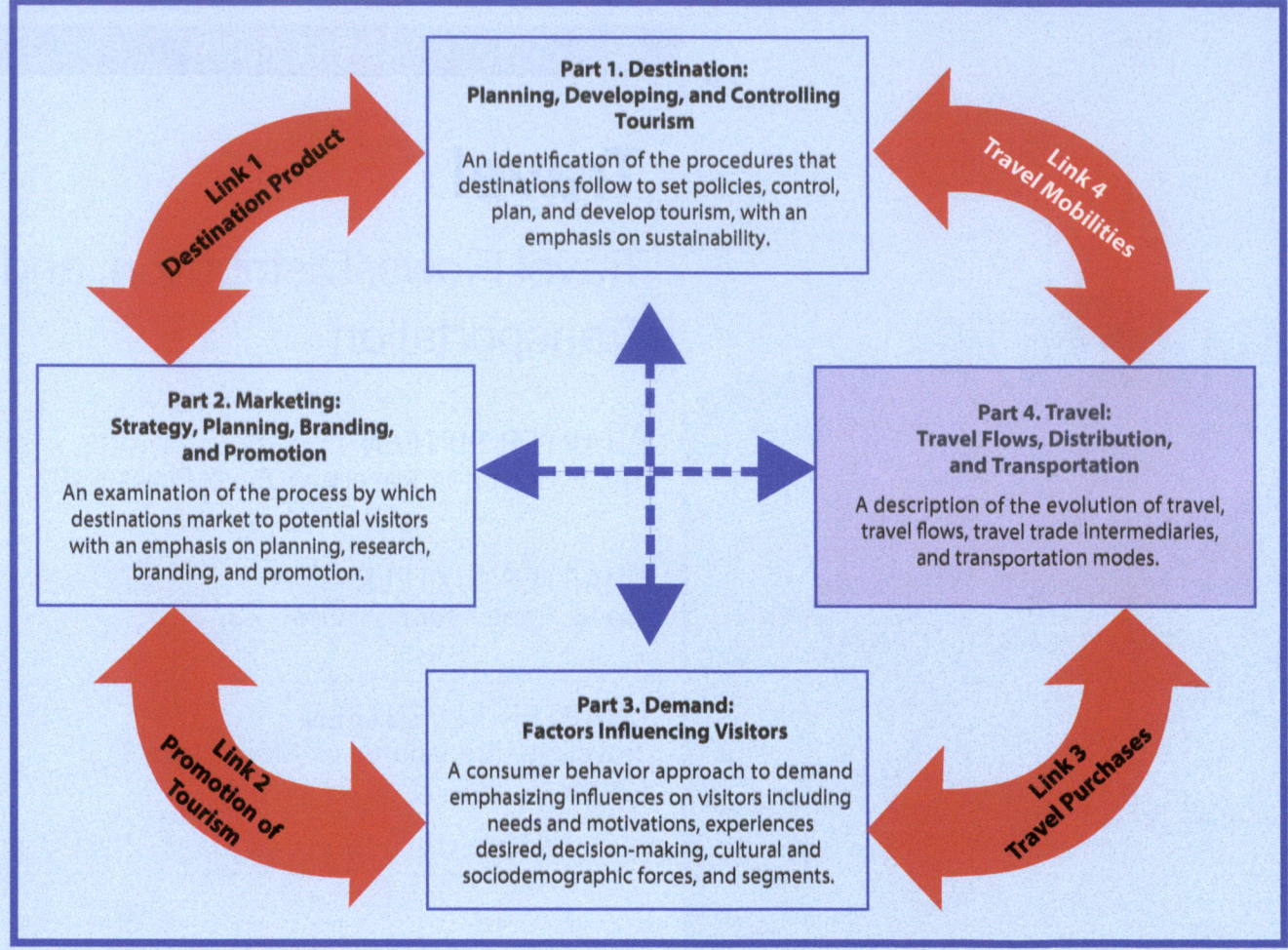

A description of the evolution of travel, travel flows, travel trade intermediaries, and transportation modes.

When the decision has been made to book a travel trip, a set of decisions are taken on whom to travel with and where, when, how to plan and book, and how to get to the destination. The evolution of travel is explained. Flows of travelers among destinations are described. Online and offline *travel distribution channels* and *modes of transportation* are reviewed.

LINK 4: TRAVEL MOBILITIES

The linkage between Parts 4 and 1 (Travel and Destination) is called the *travel mobilities*. It is the combination of who is traveling (travel market segments) and where, when, and how they are traveling. Again, a change in either Travel or Destination may cause a response in the other part of the system.

CHAPTER FIFTEEN

The Evolution of Travel and Travel Flows

Charting the History and Locations of Tourism

Travel is fatal to prejudice, bigotry, and narrow-mindedness, and many of our people need it sorely on these accounts. Broad, wholesome, charitable views of men and things cannot be acquired by vegetating in one little corner of the earth all one's lifetime.

MARK TWAIN

YOUR LEARNING DESTINATION

You will be able to describe the historical evolution of travel and profile the major global flows of tourism.

WHAT YOU NEED TO KNOW

Having read this chapter, you will be able to:

- Describe the historical evolution of travel.
- Quantify the global flows of travel.
- Review the regions and countries with the most international arrivals and receipts.
- Pinpoint the largest outbound travel markets in terms of arrivals and expenditures by region and country.
- Comment on the relative importance of inbound, outbound, and domestic travel.
- Explain forecasts for travel flows in the future.
- Elaborate on some major economic, societal, political, and environmental trends affecting travel flows.

BREAKING THE ICE

Reading the news every day can be a little depressing, especially when you hear about natural disasters and random acts of terrorism affecting tourism. Despite these continual challenges, people keep traveling around the globe. The appetites for travel always seem to be growing, as people want to escape their everyday lives for new environments. The globalization of business and events is another factor stimulating greater flows of visitors.

Think about yourself for a minute. What destinations are on your "bucket list"? Why do you want to go to these places? How will you book these trips and with whom? What transportation modes will you use to get to your favorite destinations? Now multiply this by 7.6 billion people in the world, rising to 9.8 billion by 2050 (United Nations 2017), and you get the picture of how great the potential for travel will be in the future.

KEY TAKEAWAY POINTS

- Despite some setbacks, travel flows in the world are growing steadily.

- Inbound international visitor arrivals will reach 1.8 billion by 2030, according to UNWTO (2011).

- The share of international visitor arrivals in the Asia and Pacific region will increase to 30 percent by 2030.

- The outbound market from the Peoples Republic of China is the largest in terms of volume of travelers and expenditures.

- Emerging economy destinations are gaining market share of international tourism.

- Most of the tourism flows in the world are intra-regional.

- For many advanced economy countries, domestic tourism is larger and more important economically than international tourism.

THE EVOLUTION OF TRAVEL

For tourism to occur, there must be people who have the ability (both regarding time and money), the mobility, and the motivation to travel. Although the era of mass tourism is a relatively recent one, an individual's propensity and ability to take trips has been advanced by numerous developments throughout time. The following materials give you a brief overview of the evolution of travel from ancient to modern times.

- **Ancient Egypt, Greece, and Rome**

In preindustrial times, much of the motivation for travel was to encourage trade. As empires grew, the conditions necessary for travel began to develop. Ancient Egyptians went for both business and pleasure. Travel was essential between the central government and the territories. Hospitality centers were built to accommodate travelers on official business along major routes and in the cities. The ancient Egyptians also traveled for pleasure and to attend public festivals held several times a year. Travel was also for curiosity and sightseeing—people visited the tombs and temples of the pharaohs.

Assyria comprised the area now known as Iraq. As the empire expanded from the Mediterranean in the west to the Persian Gulf in the east, mobility was made easier to facilitate moving the military. Roads were improved, markers were established to indicate distances, and posts and wells developed for safety and nourishment. Today, forts, walls, castles, and battlefields represent significant tourism attractions. The United States interstate highway system was built initially to facilitate transportation in the event of a national emergency.

Although previous civilizations had set the stage for the development of travel, the Greeks and, later, the Romans brought it all together. In Greek times water was the most convenient means of moving commercial goods. This transport mode combined with the fact that cities grew up along the coast to ensure that travel was primarily by sea. Travel for official business was less important as Greece divided into independent city-states. Pleasure travel existed in three areas: for religious festivals, for sporting events (most notably the Olympic Games, Figure 15.1), and to visit cities, especially Athens.

Two developments propelled travel further. First, a system of currency exchange emerged. Previously, travelers paid their way by carrying various goods and selling them at their destinations. The money of Greek city-states was now accepted as international currency, eliminating the need to travel with a cargo of goods. Second, the Greek language spread throughout the Mediterranean area, making it easier to communicate as one traveled.

Travel flourished in Roman times for several reasons. The control of the vast empire stimulated trade and led to the growth of a large middle class with the money to travel. Roman coins were all the traveler had to carry to finance the trip; the means of transportation—roads and waterways—were excellent; communication was relatively easy, as Greek and Latin were the principal languages; and the legal system protected from foreign courts, thereby ensuring the safety of the traveler.

The sporting games started by the Greeks morphed into gladiators' fights to the death. Interest in sightseeing

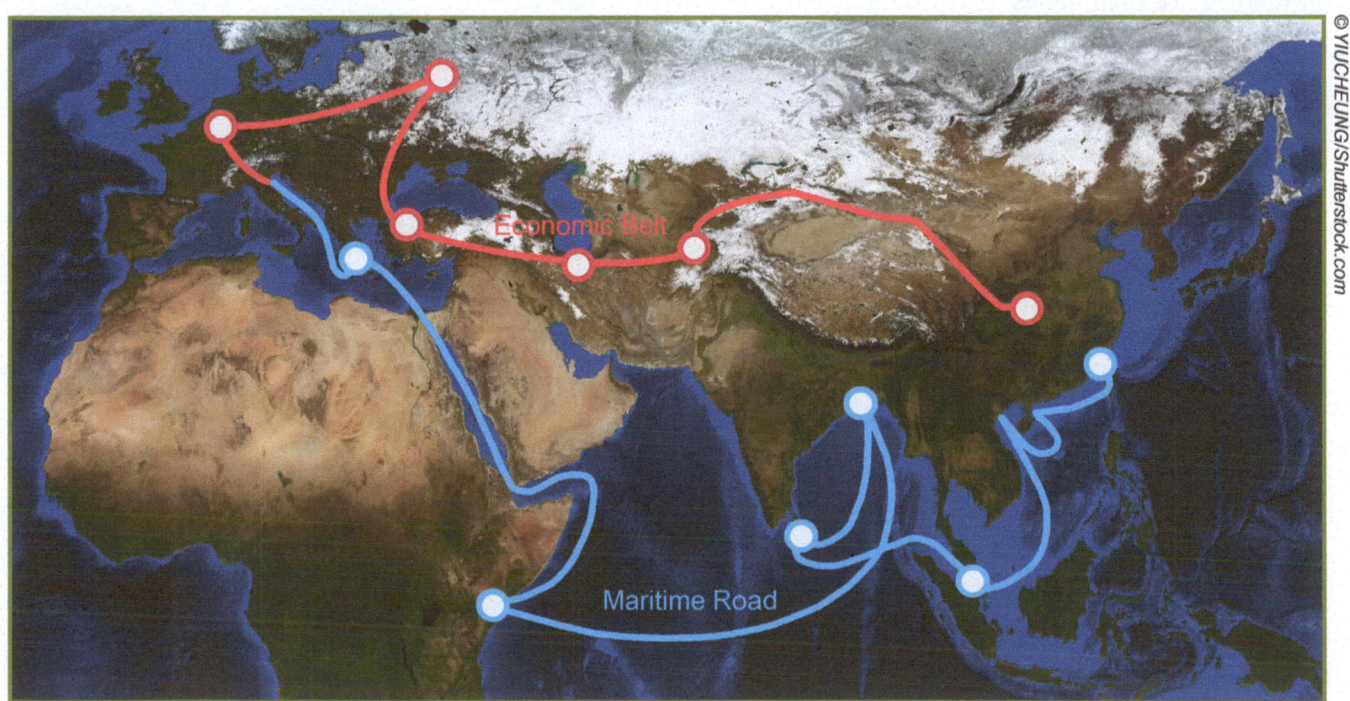

FIGURE 15.1 Olympia in Greece attracted visitors to the early Olympic Games.

grew, particularly in Greece, which had become a part of greater Rome and was the place to see. Touring to Egypt, site of the Sphinx and the pyramids, and to Asia Minor, scene of the Trojan War, expanded. Aristotle visited Asia Minor before establishing his school for students. A final development was that of second homes and vacations associated with them. Villas spread south to Naples, near the sea, the mountains, or mineral spas.

The Silk Routes

It is important to recognize the early travel within Asia and especially that originating from China. Now known as "One Belt and One Road" as coined by President Xi Jinping, the land and maritime silk roads may be among the first sources of business travel (Figure 15.2). The Silk Road began in the second century BC and was used until the fourteenth century AD. It was started in the

FIGURE 15.2 The routes of "One Belt and One Road" originating in China.

The Silk Road Heritage Corridors and UNWTO Silk Road Programme

Acclaimed as the "greatest route in the history of mankind," the ancient Silk Road formed the first bridge between the East and the West and was an important vehicle for trade between the ancient empires of China, Central and Western Asia, the Indian sub-continent, and Rome (UNESCO 2017).

UNESCO's Silk Road Heritage Corridors Project was launched in 2013 to provide policy guidance to destinations and develop a common sustainable tourism strategy for visitor management, site presentation, and promotion. The priorities set for tourism are as follows:

- Provide quality visitor experiences
- Deliver holistic planning
- Identify nodes (large cities), the segments of routes connecting them, and the corridors
- Collaborate on transnational approaches
- Share skills, expertise, and knowledge
- Develop appropriate standards and protocols
- Implement monitoring systems at local, national, and transnational levels
- Provide high quality, consistent, and informative heritage communication and interpretation
- Invest in Intangible Cultural Heritage
- Embrace technology and innovation

UNWTO has established the UNWTO Silk Road Programme (UNWTO 2017). The thirty-three UNWTO Member States participating in the UNWTO Silk Road Programme include Albania, Armenia, Azerbaijan, Bangladesh, Bulgaria, China, Croatia, DPR Korea, Rep. Korea, Egypt, Georgia, Greece, Iran, Iraq, Israel, Italy, Indonesia, Japan, Kazakhstan, Kyrgyzstan, Mongolia, Pakistan, Romania, Russian Federation, Saudi Arabia, San Marino, Spain, Syria, Tajikistan, Turkey, Turkmenistan, Ukraine, and Uzbekistan.

Each year UNWTO develops a Silk Road Action Plan. The three focus areas of the UNWTO's Silk Road Action Plan 2016/2017 are marketing and promotion, destination management and capacity building, and travel facilitation.

China was the historic source of the Silk Road and it is no surprise that it is one of the major proponents of the Silk Road tourism efforts (Figure 15.2). The China National Tourism Administration (CNTA) designated 2015 and 2016 as its Years of Silk Road Tourism.

Applications have been made to UNESCO to include certain areas of the Silk Road on the World Heritage List (WHL).

Think about This

1. With so many countries involved in these projects for the Silk Road, what are some of the coordination problems and issues that may happen?
2. How will inclusion on the World Heritage List help tourism along the Silk Road?
3. What are the benefits for travelers in multi-destination trips, such as visiting several countries along the Silk Road?
4. What can be done to offer visitors authentic cultural and heritage experiences along the Silk Road?

Sources

CNTO Toronto. 2016. Beautiful China 2016—Year of Silk Road Tourism. https://www.youtube.com/watch?v=QYkY1fDbsRE

ICOMOS International Conservation Center. 2017. Silk Roads. http://www.iicc.org.cn/Column.aspx?ColId=42

Nomani, C. S. Experience the Silk Road Plan 2017—UNWTO. https://vimeo.com/183071000

TripAdvisor. 2016. TripAdvisor Travel Trends for the Silk Road 2016. http://cf.cdn.unwto.org/sites/all/files/pdf/travel_trends_guide_ta_final.pdf

UNESCO. 2017. Developing a Sustainable Tourism Strategy for the Silk Roads Heritage Corridor. http://whc.unesco.org/en/activities/826/

UNWTO. 2016. Silk Road Action Plan 2016/2017. Madrid, Spain: UNWTO.

UNWTO. 2017. UNWTO Silk Road Programme. http://silkroad.unwto.org/

Western Han dynasty and originated from the city of Chang'an (now Xi'an in Shaanxi Province). The Silk Road terminated in the UK. The Maritime Silk Road began from Quanzhou in Fujian Province. Together, these two are often called the Silk Routes.

Many products were traded on the Silk Routes, including silk, tea, salt, sugar, spices, and porcelain. Apart from the business transacted, the Silk Routes were a conduit for art, religion, philosophy, language, and science. Use of the Silk Routes overlapped with the Roman Empire.

The Silk Road: Greatest Route in the History of Mankind

"Acclaimed as the 'greatest route in the history of mankind,' the ancient Silk Road formed the first bridge between the East and the West and was an important vehicle for trade between the ancient empires of China, Central and Western Asia, the Indian sub-continent, and Rome. The Silk Road was more than just trade routes, it symbolised the multiple benefits arising from cultural exchange. As a result, countless historic and cultural sites remain along the network of famous routes."

Source: UNESCO. 2017.

As you found out in Chapter 6, trails are a form of tourism development by function and the overland Silk Road is now gaining popularity as a travel route for visitors. The UNWTO has a Silk Road Programme and is promoting cooperation among many countries along the route (UNWTO 2017a).

- **The Middle Ages**

As the Roman Empire collapsed in the fifth century, roads fell into disuse and barbarians made it unsafe to travel. Whereas a Roman courier could cover up to one hundred miles a day, the average daily rate of a journey during the Middle Ages was twenty miles. It was not until the twelfth century that the roads became secure again. This advance was due to the large numbers of travelers going on pilgrimages. Pilgrims traveled to pay homage to a site or as atonement for sin. In other cases, pilgrims journeyed to fulfill a promise made when they were sick.

The next important factor in the history of travel was the Renaissance in the fourteenth century (Figure 15.3). As society transformed from a rural to an urban base, wealth grew, and more people had the money to move around. Pilgrimages were still significant, although journeys to Jerusalem declined due to the growth of Protestantism in Europe. The arrival of

© Kuznetsov Alexey/Shutterstock.com

FIGURE 15.3 The Uffizi Gallery in Florence, the birthplace of the Renaissance.

Renaissance works from Italy provided an impetus to travel for learning. Stable monarchies helped ensure travelers' safety.

• Age of Discovery or Exploration

The beginning of the sixteenth century saw a new age of curiosity and exploration, which culminated in the popularity of the *Grand Tour*. The Grand Tour was initially a sixteenth-century Elizabethan concept, brought about by the need to develop a class of professional statesmen and ambassadors. Young men traveled with ambassadors over Europe to complete their education. The practice continued to develop in the seventeenth and eighteenth centuries until it became fashionable. No gentleman's education was complete until he had spent from one to three years traveling around Europe with a tutor.

The Grand Tour began in France, where the young man studied French, dancing, fencing, riding, and drawing. Before Paris could corrupt the morals or ruin the finances, the student headed for Italy to study sculpture, music appreciation, and art. The return was by way of Germany, Switzerland, and the Low Countries (Holland, Belgium, and Luxembourg). The Grand Tour reached its peak of popularity in the 1750s and 1760s but came to a sudden end by the French Revolution and the Napoleonic Wars.

• Industrial Revolutions

According to the experts, there have been several industrial revolutions. The Industrial Revolution started first in the UK in the late 1700s and then spread to other parts of Western Europe and the United States. It reached its peak during the 1800s and lasted until the early 1900s. This period produced a class of wealthy people who had the time to travel and touring became popular.

In the late eighteenth century and early nineteenth century, two major factors affected the development of tourism. Increased industrialization accounted for both. First, the industrial revolution accelerated the movement from rural to urban areas. This economic change resulted in many people in relatively small areas. The desire or motivation to escape, even for a brief period, was there. Associated with this was the development of steam engines in the form of trains and steamships. This transportation advance allowed the means of mobility to escape. Because of the proximity of the coast to the major urban areas, it was only natural that train lines extended in these directions. However, most visitors to the seaside were day-trippers. It was well into the second half of the eighteenth century before the working classes in Britain had regular holidays and sufficient income to use their leisure time to travel.

The development of spas was largely due to the members of the medical professions. During the seventeenth century, they began to recommend the medicinal properties of mineral waters. The idea originated, however, with the Greeks. Spas on the continent of Europe were developed 200 to 300 years before their growth in England. Development occurred because of three factors: the approval of the medical profession, court patronage, and local entrepreneurship to take advantage of the first two.

Usage by court helped establish spas as the place to be. Today we talk about "mass follows class." It is the idea that people they consider prominent sway the masses in their choices of vacation destinations. Today film, music, and sports stars have taken over the role of influencers. For example, the popular TV series, *Outlander*, is helping to increase tourism in Scotland where it was filmed (Pooran 2017).

The number of people who could afford to "take the waters" was rather small. By the end of the seventeenth century, the influence of the medical profession had declined, and spas were more for entertainment instead of health. Their popularity continued, however, into the nineteenth century. It is possible today to drink from the mineral waters at Bath in England. Hot Springs in Arkansas (Figure 15.4) and Glenwood Springs in Colorado still attract many visitors. Additionally, many Eastern European towns proclaim the beneficial effects of mud packs and hydrotherapy.

The medical profession, the British court, and Napoleon all helped popularize the seaside resort. The original motive for sea bathing was for reasons of health. Dr. Richard Russell argued that sea water was useful against such things as cirrhosis, dropsy, gout, gonorrhea, and scurvy and insisted that people drink a pint of it. It is worthy to note that the good Dr. Russell was a physician in Brighton, a resort near London and on the water (Figure 15.5). The patronage of the Prince Regent, who later became George IV, assured Brighton's fame. Similarly, Princess Charlotte and Queen Victoria respectively frequented Southend and Cowes.

The French Revolution (1789–1799) and the Napoleonic Wars (1800–1815) stimulated the growth of the seaside resort. These events put an end to the Grand Tour; those who would have taken the Grand Tour could not travel to the continent. The now fashionable seaside resorts were the alternative. Toward the end of the nineteenth century, the seaside resorts in Europe became the palaces for the working classes due to the introduction of paid holidays and better wages.

FIGURE 15.4 Hot Springs National Park Historic Landmark District bathhouse, Hot Springs, Arkansas, United States.

FIGURE 15.5 The beach and pier at Brighton on the south coast of England.

The Return of the Deck Chairs. Revival of UK Seaside Resorts

"Multi-coloured beach huts, cheeky postcards, whoops of glee from the children on the beach, and the tang of sharp, sweet vinegar on hot, salty chips wrapped in paper. Seaside resorts in England deliver every treat to our senses. English seaside resorts have a special place in our hearts, as they are where childhood memories are made. The seaside resorts in England represent escape and pure pleasure for grown-ups and kids alike. Surely no one can resist the lure of the pier, with its bright lights and music and irresistible waft of fresh doughnuts in the air." (VisitEngland 2017)

In Victorian times, British seaside resorts were booming as more people had paid holidays and could reach the coast quite easily by train (Figure 15.5). They were spread around the shores of Great Britain and Northern Ireland, with most being situated in England near large cities and major industrial areas. Millions of Britons flocked each year to the sea-side, up until around the 1950s. Some of the most popular seaside resorts were Blackpool, Brighton, Bournemouth, Cowes, Hastings, Margate, Rothesay, St. Ives, Southend, Southport, and Whitby.

The development of air travel and the introduction of package tours to Southern European beach resorts caused a sharp downturn in fortunes of British seaside resorts in the 1960s and 1970s. Many believed that these seaside resorts had seen their heyday and they would never enjoy much tourism again. In many cases, this prediction has been proven wrong as Britain's seaside resorts are experiencing a comeback in the mid-2010s.

Several factors seem to be contributing to the revival of these seaside getaway places. The greater tendency to take short-break holidays is a trend that favors close-to-home destinations rather than foreign shores. Also, there is more familiarity with the offer and a greater sense of safety and security to be on the UK's beaches. Another factor is the reinvestment in seaside resorts and governmental policies to support their reinvention. The restoration of Hastings Pier in East Sussex which reopened in 2016, for example, is symbolic of the resurgence of the British seaside. The refurbishment of the Dreamland amusement park in Margate, Kent, is another example. The UK Government has introduced a policy to boost the economic development of coastal and seaside areas through the Coast Communities Fund (2017). Since 2012, the Fund has produced the following results:

"The government has already provided £170 million for 278 projects around the country since the Coastal Communities Fund was launched in 2012. This has resulted in 2 million more people visiting the coast and spending an additional £171 million."

In September 2017, the Government announced another £40 million in funding for coastal area projects in England.

Holiday camp companies, such as Butlin's and Pontins, were often located near popular seaside towns and they too are experiencing a fresh start in the 2010s. The Butlin's camp in Skegness, Lincolnshire, celebrated its eightieth anniversary in 2016.

So, the deck chairs are coming back to the UK's beaches and the seaside resorts have not died off. A great British tradition is being restored after many years of decline and "liking to be beside the seaside" is in vogue again.

Think about This

1. What are the important lessons to be learned for other destinations in the revival of British seaside resorts?
2. Is it likely in the future that more people will choose to travel to places closer to home, and why or why not?
3. How important do you feel is the search for nostalgia in the revival of British seaside resorts?
4. Seaside resorts were always places that were popular for family holidays. How can seaside resorts again become a favorite place for family trips?

Sources

BBC. 2016. Skegness Butlin's celebrates its 80th year. http://www.bbc.com/news/av/uk-england-37634958/skegness-butlin-s-celebrates-80th-year

Brett, D. 2016. Style revival: Britain's booming seaside towns. https://www.theguardian.com/travel/2016/may/14/once-more-on-to-the-beach-how-britains-seaside-towns-bounced-back

Butlin's. 2017. The Butlin's Story. https://www.butlins.com/get-to-know-us/our-beliefs-and-colourful-story/index.aspx

Chapman, A. 2015. Pier pressure: Best practice in the rehabilitation of British seaside piers. Bournemouth University. http://eprints.bournemouth.ac.uk/22241/1/Pier%20Pressure%20Anya%20Chapman%20PAPER%20FINAL.pdf

Dreamland Margate. 2017. About us. https://www.dreamland.co.uk/about-dreamland

Hastings Pier Charity. 2017. Hastings Pier. http://hastingspier.org.uk/

Mr. Alsop History. 2014. Victorian Britain—Seaside Holidays. https://www.youtube.com/watch?v=rwoU_Rk4m-o

Pontins. 2017. Pontins UK Family Holiday Parks. https://www.pontins.com/holiday-parks/

Ross, P. 2016. Once more on to the beach: how Britain's seaside towns bounced back. *The Guardian,* May 14. https://www.theguardian.com/travel/2016/may/14/once-more-on-to-the-beach-how-britains-seaside-towns-bounced-back

UK Government. 2017. Economic development in coastal and seaside areas. https://www.gov.uk/government/policies/economic-development-in-coastal-and-seaside-areas

VisitEngland. 2017. Seaside resorts in England. https://www.visitengland.com/things-to-do/seaside-resorts

The term *holiday* comes from holy days for religious observances. Ancient Rome featured public holidays for great feasting. As Europe became Christian, certain saints' days and religious festivals became holy days when people fasted and prayed and refrained from work. After the Industrial Revolution, the religious holidays gradually became secularized, and the week's holiday emerged. The vacation was negotiated between employer and workers and was again due to the economic and social changes brought about by the Industrial Revolution. It made sense to take the holidays during the warmer summer months. For the employer, it was advantageous to close the entire factory down for one week rather than face the problems of operating with small groups of people absent over a longer period. Still today certain weeks are associated with the specific holidays of specific cities or towns.

- **The railway era**

Before World War I, the principal mode of domestic transportation was the railway. This situation meant that development concentrated at certain points (Figure 15.6). Regional development occurred with specific resorts growing to serve specific urban areas. The development

FIGURE 15.6 The historic Banff Springs Hotel, opened in 1888, in Alberta, Canada.

of the railway opened countries to travelers. Rail passenger transportation started first in the UK. The rail trip arranged by Thomas Cook in 1841 from Leicester to Loughborough is celebrated as the beginning of travel agencies. By the 1870s in the United States, the completion of the Erie Railroad spurred the development of Niagara Falls as a honeymoon paradise. The vast river network of the United States' interior allowed the development of steamboat excursions, particularly gambling and amusement trips, between New Orleans and St. Louis. The transcontinental Canadian Pacific Railway was completed in 1886, allowing travel from Montréal to British Columbia. The famous Ghan railway journey between Adelaide and Darwin started later in 1929.

History of Banff Springs Hotel

The hotel was developed as part of the CPR's (Canadian Pacific Railway) network of hotels, which built landmark hotels in young cities across Canada to encourage the use of its transcontinental lines. The Banff Springs Hotel is in the lineage of hotels such as the Chateau Lake Louise in Alberta, Le Chateau Frontenac in Québec City, and the Empress Hotel in Victoria, British Columbia.

Source: The Canadian Encyclopedia. 2017. http://www.thecanadianencyclopedia.ca/en/article/banff-springs-hotel/

Tourism in North America developed for the same reasons as in Europe. At first, travel was limited by the need for transportation. The first development of note was that of resorts. With the encouragement of physicians, resorts like Saratoga in New York became fashionable by the early 1800s. Harrison Hot Springs in British Columbia began as a small resort after the opening of the Canadian Pacific Railway. The ocean also became attractive for health reasons initially, although amusements soon sprang up as well.

The world's first national park, Yellowstone, was established in 1872, and this innovation was another catalyst from more travel (National Geographic Society 2017). One source estimates that there are now 6,555 national parks in the world (Bioexpedition 2013). In 1929, there were three million recreational visits to U.S. National Parks, compared with 331 million in 2016 (U.S. National Park Service 2017). Canada's first National Park was established in Banff, Alberta, in 1886 (Parks Canada 2017), and Australia's first park, Royal National Park in New South Wales, was proclaimed in 1879 (Australian Government, 2015). Kruger National Parks was established in South Africa in 1898. In the

UK, the first ten national parks were designated in the 1950s (National Parks UK 2017).

Mass production of the automobile, beginning around the 1920s, allowed the dispersion of destinations and eventually diminished the predominance of railway travel. The between-wars period was also one of rapid development of aviation. This era was one of rapid economic expansion during the *Roaring Twenties* followed by the miserable times of the *Great Depression*. This was a time when the middle classes started to develop and the annual holiday became the norm. People started going to the beaches for their vacations and this was the early days of mass tourism.

- **Post World War II**

Travel increased rapidly after World War II for several reasons. Mass tourism as we know it today is mainly a post-World War II phenomenon (von Lüpke-Schwarz 2013). The introduction of the passenger jet reduced travel time from the United States to Europe from five sailing days or twenty-four flying hours to eight hours; and surplus propeller airplanes were made available to charter operators to transport travelers, not troops, as airlines rushed to purchase new jet aircraft.

The growing popularity of "package holidays" was a catalyst for much more travel in Europe from 1945 onward (Mason 2016). This was a north–south flow from the colder countries to the warmer beach areas of Southern Europe and the Mediterranean. In 1970 the main direction of inclusive air charter flights was north–south, with traffic being centered in Spain and, to a lesser degree, Italy. Spain was linked to the eight major European markets, the most important being the UK. In fact, the UK–Spain route was the most important in terms of volume, accounting for over one-quarter of total traffic within Europe between countries that had at least 1 percent of the market.

Movements became more complex in the 1970s as new destinations opened. The UK–Spain route, although still important, saw its market share drop to 20 percent. Links between the UK and France and the UK and the Netherlands fell below 1 percent, as did those between Scandinavia and Italy. Greece not only emerged as a new destination, but as the second most important after Spain. Of its four markets—UK, France, then West Germany, and Sweden—the UK was the most important. During this time, major flows also developed between the UK and two new destinations: Malta and Portugal.

The north–south movement intensified as new southern destinations were developed and Norway emerged as a growing originating country. The reasons for these changing flows can be explained by developments in the countries of origin, in the destinations, and in the linkages themselves. Population growth in the countries of origin is one reason for the growth. More people with more discretionary income produced a larger potential market. Complementarity is another reason. The north–south traffic is strong because of the movement from colder, northern countries to warmer, southern areas around the Mediterranean coast. The distances involved and the fact that certain markets, particularly the UK, are insular explain the rise in importance of *inclusive tour charters*. The long coastline of Spain and the short distances involved between airport and hotel, together with the proximity of other tourism features, led to an ease of packaging. The availability of surplus military aircraft also helped spur the development of package tours. The Berlin Airlift of 1947 and 1948 showed the advantage of having a pool of operators able to move large quantities of items on short notice. The movement of large numbers of people was seen as an appropriate use of their skills in peacetime.

Yet why did the UK develop a strong inclusive tour charter package (ITC) movement when France, for example, did not? To answer this question, it is necessary to examine the characteristics of the countries more closely. First, France has an attractive coastline of its own. Second, it is relatively close to and has overland links with other Mediterranean countries. Third, the French are very individualistic. Fourth, there have been several industry practices that induced the potential for ITCs. These included such things as high commissions by travel agents and restrictive practices by government authorities and parent airlines. The net result was that, in 1980, the proportion of French visitors taking an organized tour was 5 percent, whereas 50 percent of all British holidays abroad involved inclusive tours.

The 1950s and 1960s were also associated with the family "road trips" on vacation in the United States, Canada, and elsewhere (Kearns 2015). Roadside motels developed and the first theme park, Disneyland in Anaheim, California, was opened in 1955. This was a great time for getting out and seeing the country together.

A Short History of the Great Australian Road Trip. The Family Road Trip

Most people over 50 can recall memorable road trips undertaken with their parents. Come holiday time, mum and dad would load up the car with kids, dogs and cooking, fishing and camping gear, hook up the boat or caravan, if they were lucky enough to own one, and head off on a great adventure.

Source: Lube Mobile. 2013. https://www.lubemobile.com.au/blog/short-history-great-australian-road-trip/

The impacts of the Baby Boomer generation on travel were becoming significant. Those born from 1946 to 1964 started to influence tourism around the mid-1960s. The Baby Boomers were the predominant age group when the first Boeing 747 "jumbo jet" carried passengers in 1970 and they witnessed the dawning of the "information age" and the "digital revolution." They were the first to benefit from the commercialization of the World Wide Web starting around 1996. The Baby Boomers were also in prominence when sustainable development as a concept began, mainly through the Brundtland report of 1987.

- **The Information Age, Web 1.0, and Web 2.0**

The 1970s heralded the information age as personal computers (PCs) came on the market. Although these were the clunky desktop variety of PCs at first, they forever changed how people gathered and used information about travel (Bearne 2016).

The arrival of social networking in the early 2000s was another watershed for travel and tourism, allowing visitors to create and share online content about trips. Faustino (2017) highlights how technology has changed travel in the following ways:

- Made travel more affordable
- Made travel eco-friendly
- Made travel planning a breeze
- Changed the way we find things to do
- Made it easier to capture moments
- Made it easier to stay connected while traveling
- Changed our packing style
- Made travel more time efficient
- Made it possible to keep family in the loop

The "digital revolution" has advanced travel in many positive directions; however, its devices are causing many serious challenges in society. "Smartphone addiction" seems to be on the increase, as people shun human contact in favor of their gadgets (Designtechnica Corporation 2017).

Space tourism began in 2001 when Dennis Tito spent time on the International Space Station in orbit. There are several companies vying to become popular with aspiring space visitors (Figure 15.7) including Virgin Galactic, SpaceX, Bigelow Aerospace, and XCOR Aerospace. With famous entrepreneurs like Sir Richard Branson and Elon Musk involved, these ventures are receiving much media attention. A 14 percent compound average growth rate in the global space tourism market is predicted from 2017 to 2021 (Technavio 2017).

© Lazy Llama/Shutterstock.com

FIGURE 15.7 A space business tourist exploring a new destination?

QUICK TRIP 15.3

The Digital Dilemma

The "digital revolution" as some call it has brought many benefits and conveniences to people worldwide. It has certainly made travel easier and, in many ways, more interesting. Travel destinations can be explored on smartphones, information combed, and bookings made. Digital devices have "unchained" business people from their desks and allowed real-time communications through many online channels.

There can be little doubting that many people just love their phones. However, there is mounting evidence that using smartphones is addictive and that it can harm a person's mental and physical health. An article in *The Wall Street Journal* suggests that smartphone use lowers one's intellect (Carr 2017). Chang (2017) identifies the following eight dangers of excessive phone use:

- Injuries and accidents
- Posture-related disorders
- Screen fatigue
- Reduced attention span
- Sleeping problems
- Disconnection with friends and family
- Identity theft
- Damage to the spine and neck

So, digital devices have their good and bad sides for people, and we can call this a "digital dilemma." Undoubtedly, this device overuse is becoming a greater social and medical problem, as well as raising many human resource management issues in workplaces. Taking a somewhat more focused view, however, in what ways does the "digital dilemma" impact on travel and travel flows?

In answering this question, one interesting opportunity that has arisen for destinations and tourism operators is the "detox" offer. Here, for a price, visitors or guests give up their smartphones and other digital devices for a day, weekend, or longer. For example, the Westin Paris Vendôme offers detoxers the following invitation:

"In these times of hyper-connectivity, The Westin Paris-Vendôme proposes an extraordinary offer. As soon as you arrive, you will be invited to deposit your mobile phones, tablets, laptops and other devices in a safe at the front-office. Then, the hotel has prepared plenty of nice surprises to indulge yourself, clear your mind, relax, in other words: revitalize yourself!"

The Mandarin Oriental Hotel in Manhattan, New York, offers a *Digital Wellness Escape* for $255–345 with spa treatments "Concentrating on the head, eyes, neck, shoulders, hands and feet, this restorative treatment aims to ease the stress and strain resulting from the frequent use of digital devices."

In addition to hotels and spas, some tour operators are also offering digital detox vacations and holidays. For example, Intrepid Travel (2017) is offering a nine-day *Vietnam Active Family Holiday—Digital Detox* with this call to action:

"Log off, shut down and disconnect from tech on this nine-day adventure through Vietnam. Forget the perfect filter or condensing your journey into 140 characters—this is your time to reconnect with the world around you."

Unplugged Weekends is another company offering short-break retreats that focus on living without one's digital devices. They were featured on a BBC documentary in 2014 about digital detoxing.

In summary, while many tourism marketers are encouraging people to make greater use of digital devices when traveling, others are inviting visitors to enjoy travel without their cherished tools.

Think about This

1. Why do you believe people take digital detox breaks like those described above?
2. Would you take a digital detox holiday or vacation? Why or why not?
3. Is digital detoxing a short-term trend or is it destined to become a permanent aspect of society? What are the reasons behind your opinions on this question?
4. How can destinations and tourism businesses take full advantage of this counter-technology trend?

Sources

BBC. 2014. Unplugging from technology—Digital detox: Unplugged Weekend documentary. https://www.youtube.com/watch?v=Em0tjS2G-qI

Carr, N. 2017. How smartphones hijack our minds. *The Wall Street Journal,* October 7. https://www.wsj.com/articles/how-smartphones-hijack-our-minds-1507307811

Chang, A. 2017. The eight dangers of excessive cellphone use. https://www.littlethings.com/dangers-of-using-smartphones/

Firshein, S. 2017. The fastest digital detox is in the middle of the city. https://www.bloomberg.com/news/articles/2017-05-04/the-best-digital-detox-programs-in-big-cities

Intrepid Travel. 2017. Vietnam Active Family Holiday—Digital Detox. https://www.intrepidtravel.com/us/vietnam/vietnam-active-family-holiday-digital-detox-107349

Mandarin Oriental. 2017. Digital Wellness Escape. https://www.mandarinoriental.com/new-york/manhattan/luxury-spa/treatments-menu

Unplugged Weekend. Get Unplugged LTD. 2017. https://www.unpluggedweekend.com/

Wakefield, J. 2016. Net overload 'sparks digital detox for millions of Britons.' BBC, August 4. http://www.bbc.com/news/technology-36964081

Westin Paris Vendôme. 2017. Digital Detox Offer, rates from €448. http://www.thewestinparis.com/digital-detox

The remarkable rise of inbound tourism within the Asia-Pacific region is a major trend in world travel from 1990 onward. In 1990, around 12.9 percent of international visitor arrivals were in Asia and the Pacific; in 2016, the figure was 25 percent (UNWTO 2017d). The Asia-Pacific is also becoming a more significant source of outbound travelers to other regions of the world (Figure 15.8). This "new Silk Route" is particularly being traveled by the outbound market from Mainland China. Some are suggesting that the outbound travel flow from Mainland China will double in the next five years, breaking the 200 million level (Matthew 2017; Renub Research 2017).

India Is the Fastest Growing Outbound Market

With over 62 million passport holders who are potential travellers, India has emerged as the second fastest growing outbound market after China in terms of visitor numbers. In terms of percentage growth, India is the fastest.

Source: BITB New Delhi. 2016.

Tourism Has Almost Uninterrupted Growth

Tourism has boasted virtually uninterrupted growth over time, despite occasional shocks, demonstrating the sector's strength and resilience. International tourist arrivals have increased from 25 million globally in 1950 to 278 million in 1980, 674 million in 2000, and 1,235 million in 2016.

Source: UNWTO. 2017. UNWTO Tourism Highlights 2017 Edition, p. 2.

Now you know about the evolution of travel, it is time to move on to discussing travel flows in the regions and countries of the world.

TRAVEL FLOWS

Tourism is greater in size and scope than it ever has been. Major setbacks occurred after 9/11 and during the global financial crisis in 2007–2009. However, despite natural disasters, economic downturns, political

FIGURE 15.8 Travel to, from, and within the Asia-Pacific region is booming.

difficulties, and acts of terrorism, tourism has proven to be very resilient. The impact of these events caused temporary shifts in travel flows among destinations, but did not halt the worldwide growth of tourism.

Tourism's Capacity to Rebound

"The last six decades have seen extraordinary growth for tourism. In spite of the multiple changes and shocks—from man-made crises, to natural disasters and economic crises, from which the world is still recovering—tourism, although vulnerable, has always bounced back, proving its resilience and capacity to rebound."

Source: Taleb Rifai, UNWTO Secretary-General. 2011. Tourism Towards 2030, p. 5.

As you already know, there are three different flows of visitors within all countries. Inbound travel flows represent the foreign visitors to a country. Outbound travel flows are the residents of the country leaving to visit other countries. Domestic travel flows are the trips taken by residents within their own countries. Large countries with strong economies, such as the United States and China, have significant domestic travel. Inbound tourism tends to be of greater relative importance to smaller, developing countries.

Travel Brings People Closer Together

"Travel and tourism is a remarkable sector, it brings people from different backgrounds, culture and beliefs closer together, driving peace. In addition to the significant socioeconomic benefits to a country's welfare and local livelihoods."

Source: Gloria Guevara, President & CEO, WTTC. 2017.

You should be familiar with the worldwide and regional flows of tourism. The content that follows reviews global travel flows and the tourism within five regions (Europe, Asia and the Pacific, Americas, Africa, and the Middle East).

Global Travel Flows

As you learned in Chapter 1, tourism is one of the world's largest economic sectors (WTTC 2017). To put that in perspective, if tourism were a country, it would have the third largest GDP in the world, behind the United States and China, but ahead of Japan (World Economic Forum 2017). International visitor arrivals in 2016 reached 1.235 billion, the highest level ever (UNWTO 2017d). The average annual growth rate in arrivals from 2005 to 2016 was 3.9 percent.

It is interesting to compare the worldwide market share of the various regions from 1990 to 2030 (Figure 15.9). Asia and the Pacific is rapidly gaining market share at the expense of Europe and the Americas, and will have 30 percent of international visitor arrivals by 2030. Africa and the Middle East are growing in relative importance; however, their market shares in global terms remain relatively small.

Figure 15.10 shows the inbound tourism receipts for the world's five regions. Here, you can see that Europe is also in the lead, but Asia and the Pacific already have a 30 percent share of total receipts.

Figure 15.11 shows the leading country destinations in terms of international visitor arrivals. France was the leading destination in 2016, followed by the United States and Spain. Mainland China has been steadily climbing the ranks of the countries with the most international arrivals.

The regional origin shares of visitors are also changing and the trend in outbound travel is like that just described for inbound travel. Travelers from the Asia-Pacific region are gaining market share the most rapidly, and Europe and the Americas are losing market share (Figure 15.12).

UNWTO Regional Destinations (Inbound)	1990	2016	2030 Forecast
Europe	60.1%	49.8%	41.0%
Asia and Pacific	12.9%	25.0%	30.0%
Americas	21.4%	16.2%	14.0%
Africa	3.4%	4.7%	7.0%
Middle East	2.2%	4.3%	8.0%
World	100.0%	100.0%	100.0%

FIGURE 15.9 Regional shares of international tourist arrivals, 1990–2030. | Sources: UNWTO, 2011, 2017d.

UNWTO Regional Destinations (Inbound)	2016 Receipts USD	Percentages
Europe	$447.3	36.7%
Asia and Pacific	366.7	30.1%
Americas	313.2	25.7%
Middle East	57.6	4.7%
Africa	34.8	2.8%
World	$1,219.6	100.0%

FIGURE 15.10 Regional shares of international tourist receipts, 2016. | Source: UNWTO, 2017d.

UNWTO Country Destinations (Inbound)	2016 Arrivals	2016 Receipts USD Billion
France	82.6	$42.5
United States	75.6	$205.9
Spain	75.6	$60.3
China	59.3	$44.4
Italy	52.4	$40.2
UK	35.8	$39.6
Germany	35.6	$37.4
Mexico	35.0	n.a.
Thailand	32.6	n.a.
Turkey	n.a.	n.a.

FIGURE 15.11 Countries with the most international tourist arrivals, 2016. | Source: UNWTO, 2017d.

UNWTO Regional Origins (Outbound)	1990	2016	2030 Forecast
Europe	57.8%	48.3%	46.0%
Asia and Pacific	13.5%	25.6%	29.9%
Americas	22.8%	17.0%	14.6%
Africa	2.3%	3.2%	5.0%
Middle East	1.9%	2.8%	4.5%
Origin unspecified	1.7%	3.1%	–
World	100.0%	100.0%	100.0%
Same region	80.4%	76.6%	77.6%
Other region	17.9%	20.2%	22.4%

FIGURE 15.12 International tourist arrivals by region of origin, 1990–2016. | Sources: UNWTO, 2011, 2017c, 2017d.

Highest-Spending Outbound Markets	2016 USD Billion
China	261.1
United States	121.5
Germany	81.1
UK	63.6
France	40.9
Canada	29.1
South Korea	26.6
Australia	25.3
Italy	24.7
Hong Kong	24.1

FIGURE 15.13 World's top tourism spenders, 2016. | Source: UNWTO, 2017b.

The Chinese are now the highest-spending outbound market in the world, having overtaken international travelers from the United States. Germany and the UK are in the third and fourth places (Figure 15.13).

You will know that even within the world's regions, there are great differences among countries in their geography, economies, cultures, and other factors. You should also realize that most of the international travel flows are intra-regional, meaning that they are from people going to countries within their own regions. Look at Figure 15.12 and you will see that 76.6 percent of the international visitor arrivals in the world in 2016 were intra-regional, and only 24.4 percent were inter-regional (from region to region).

As you already know, people travel for different purposes. UNWTO reports that in 2016 just over half (53 percent) of all international visitor arrivals were for leisure, recreation, and holidays. The business and professional purpose had a 13 percent share. VFR, health, religion, and other purposes were 27 percent and not specified were 7 percent (UNWTO 2017d). You should realize that these trip-purpose shares are for international travel, and that the proportions for domestic travel within specific countries may be significantly different.

Another interesting aspect of travel flows are the relative shares between countries with advanced economies and those with emerging economies. As you know from reading about the historic evolution of travel, the focus was mainly in two regions, Europe and North America, where now most countries have advanced economies. However, UNWTO expects that the growth in international travel will be at a higher rate (+4.4 percent per year) in emerging economy destinations than in advanced economy destinations (+2.2 percent) from 2010 to 2030. The market share of emerging economy destinations increased from 30 percent to 45 percent from 1980 to 2016, and is expected to continue to grow to 57 percent by 2030 (UNWTO 2011, 2017d).

QUICK TRIP 15.4

The New Golden Hordes? Chinese Travelers on Their National Holidays

In the 1970s, Turner and Ash wrote a book called *The Golden Hordes* that had a focus on mass tourism and the "pleasure periphery." The latter refers mainly to sun and sand resort destinations in Southern Europe and the Mediterranean. Gordon Taylor in reviewing this book made the following observation:

"Additional growth in these traditional markets (North America and Western Europe), plus the recent emergence of Japan as a travel generating nation and the great potential demand of nations like India and China, will mean more people traveling and an intensification of the problems of today."

How prophetic Taylor was in his forecasting of the coming surge in outbound (from) and domestic travel (within) China. More than forty years after his book review, many observers are struggling to describe the huge flows of Chinese travelers. Are these the new Golden Hordes of world tourism? Are they the first example of hyper-mass travel flows?

QUICK TRIP 15.4 CONTINUED

Here is one example of tourism on a scale never before imagined—an estimated 710 million Chinese traveled during the National Day Golden Week holiday on October 1–8, 2017. That is like every resident of the United States taking two round-trips within one week. Some of the results of China's Golden Week policy of its Central Government is significant overcrowding at popular tourism attractions in China, and huge pressure on transportation, especially railways.

The Chinese Government and people are proud of these statistics, and the positive economic impacts they create within the Mainland. That's quite a different perspective from Turner and Ash, who painted their Golden Hordes as a sinister lot that damaged the cultures and environments of tourism destinations. Furthermore, many countries in the world are rolling out the red carpet for the burgeoning outbound flows of Chinese travelers. Turner and Ash took a negative view of the hedonistic behaviors of their Golden Hordes; but today destinations welcome the mega-shopping of Chinese visitors.

Then, which perspective is correct? Is it the rather snobbish view of the European working classes migrating to the beaches each year? Or should we place greater value on the Chinese viewing travel as a sign of economic progress and an important right for their citizens? Or maybe this is just a case of another continent and different time periods? The authors choose to take no sides here on these questions, but rather prefer to have you think about and debate the surrounding issues.

Books like that of Turner and Ash (1975) and Young's *Tourism: Blessing or Blight* (1973), however, are important in warning us about becoming too preoccupied by the magnitude of the flows of travelers. We ought to remember that "quantity" does not always mean "quality." There is a fascination in tourism with "top 10 lists" many of which rank by absolute numbers of visitors. "Badges of honor" are symbolically awarded to destinations that have the greatest volumes of visitors. The "overtourism" backlash in many European cities should remind us counting is not enough in judging success in tourism.

Think about This

1. What are the advantages of and potential problems caused by governmentally-designated holiday periods, such as with the two annual Golden Weeks in China?
2. Some tourism experts imply that "mass destroys class" in terms of destinations and attractions. Do you think this is valid, and why or why not?
3. Do tourism organizations and businesses place too much emphasis on counting visitors? Should they not put a higher priority on the quality of visitor experiences and enjoyment? Explain your opinions on these two questions.
4. China openly celebrates its fabulous growth rates in tourism; while many Europeans bemoan the crowding and urban pressures caused by visitors. Why is there such a wide gap in these perspectives, and which has the greatest validity?

Sources

Crabtree, J. 2017. China's holiday week boosts London as tourists cash in on weak pound. CNBC, October 5. https://www.cnbc.com/2017/10/05/china-golden-week-holiday-boosts-london-as-tourists-cash-in-on-brexit-hit-weak-pound.html

Liang, M. C. 2017. China Focus: "Golden Week" tourism boom boosts economy. *Xinhua,* October 4. http://www.ecns.cn/m/travel/2017/10-04/276029.shtml

Taylor, G. D. 1976. The Golden Hordes: International Tourism and the Pleasure Periphery. Book Review. *Journal of Travel Research* 15 (1): 40–41.

Turner, L., and J. Ash. 1975. *The Golden Hordes: International Tourism and the Pleasure Periphery.* London: Constable and Company.

Weinswig, D. 2017. China National Day Golden Week: Where Will Chinese Tourists Travel Over the Holiday This Year? *Forbes,* October 3. https://www.forbes.com/sites/deborahweinswig/2017/10/03/china-national-day-golden-week-where-will-chinese-tourists-travel-over-the-holiday-this-year/#701686c3447f

Young, G. 1973. *Tourism: Blessing or Blight?* London: Penguin Books Ltd.

QUICK TRIP 15.5

The Fastest-Growing Destinations in the World

What are the fastest-growing destinations in the world, in your opinion? The chances are good that you will think of places such as Bali, the Maldives, Thailand, and other tropical resort areas. However, the following table based on UNWTO data provides a rather surprising set of growth destinations. Four of the ten are places where there have been recent security and terrorism incidents (Egypt, Israel, Palestine, and Tunisia). Two are places with small volumes of international visitor arrivals (Mongolia and Northern Mariana Islands). Then, two others tend to be overshadowed by other countries in their region (the Americas); they are Nicaragua and Uruguay. That leaves Iceland and Vietnam; places that some years ago were not considered as highly desirable tourism destinations.

Destinations	Region	Percent Growth 2015–2016	International Visitors 2016
Palestinian territories	Middle East	57.8%	400,000
Egypt	Middle East	51.0%	5,260,000
Northern Mariana Islands	Asia-Pacific	37.3%	531,000
Iceland	Europe	34.9%	1,790,000
Tunisia	Africa	32.5%	5,700,000
Vietnam	Asia-Pacific	31.2%	10,000,000
Uruguay	Americas	30.2%	3,000,000
Nicaragua	Americas	28.4%	1,500,000
Mongolia	Asia-Pacific	28.3%	404,000
Israel	Europe	25.1%	2,900,000

Source: UNWTO. 2017.

Other statistics provided by the World Economic Forum (WEF) and the World Travel & Tourism Council (WTTC) suggest different "line-ups" of emerging or growth destinations, and these use measures other than international tourist arrivals. On WEF's ranked list of travel and tourism competitiveness, Egypt is 74th among 136 countries; and the others are Iceland (#25), Tunisia (#87), Vietnam (#67), Uruguay (#77), Nicaragua (#92), Mongolia (#102), and Israel (#61). WTTC estimates growth rates in travel and tourism's contribution to national GDPs for one year and for long-term. For WTTC's 2017 (one-year) growth forecast, Egypt ranked 166th among 185 countries; the other ranks were Iceland (#8), Tunisia (#160), Vietnam (#17), Uruguay (no data), Nicaragua (#100), Mongolia (#88), and Israel (#63).

You need to remember that these three data sources use different measurements to rank country destinations. However, there seem to be some large discrepancies between the data in the table, and the other two sets of results.

Think about This

1. Why do you think these three sources of data on destinations have such different results and implications?
2. Do you think it is adequate to measure relative destination growth by international tourist arrivals from one year to the next? Why or why not?
3. Iceland and Vietnam are two countries, from this analysis, that may have the most merit in being labeled as "growth destinations." To what factors, do you attribute these two countries' recent tourism successes?
4. Are the percentage increases in arrivals shown in the table potentially misleading? Why or why not?

QUICK TRIP 15.5 CONTINUED

Sources

Haines, G. 2017. 10 surprising destinations where tourism is booming in 2017. *The Telegraph*. http://www.telegraph.co.uk/travel/news/surprising-countries-where-tourism-is-booming-in-2017/

Street, F. 2017. World's fastest-growing tourist destinations for 2017. CNN Travel. http://edition.cnn.com/travel/article/worlds-fastest-growing-tourist-destinations-2017/index.html

UNWTO. 2017. UNWTO Tourism Highlights 2017. Madrid, Spain: UNWTO.

World Economic Forum. 2017. The Travel & Tourism Competitiveness Report 2017. Geneva, Switzerland: WEF.

World Travel & Tourism Council. 2017. Country Reports. London: WTTC.

The statistics provided by UNWTO are limited to international travel and are mainly focused on inbound flows to destinations. They do not provide data at a sub-country level and have no information on domestic travel. Other data sources provide information on outbound travel and flows at sub-national levels (Euromonitor International 2016). For example, Mastercard (2017) does an annual analysis of the leading destination cities in the world. Figure 15.14 shows the top ten cities for 2016 ranked by overnight international visitors. Bangkok (Figure 15.16), London, and Paris had the most overnight international visitors in 2016.

Another aspect of worldwide travel flows not captured in the UNWTO are figures for the MICE (meeting, incentive, convention, exhibition) markets, which are of great economic significance to many destinations. The International Congress and Convention Association (ICCA) found that 12,227 international association meetings were held in the world in 2016 (ICCA 2017). Figure 15.15 shows the top ten countries for these meetings in 2016, with the United States holding a strong first position.

ICCA also reports that the top five cities for international association meetings in 2016 were all in Europe (Paris, Vienna, Barcelona, Berlin, and London).

Travel flows in the five regions of the world are now reviewed in order of the magnitude of global inbound and outbound tourism market shares. As you already know, the market shares of international travel flows are shifting, particularly because of the growth of tourism in Asia.

Cities	Overnight International Visitors (millions)
Bangkok	19.41
London	19.06
Paris	15.45
Dubai	14.87
Singapore	13.11
New York	12.70
Seoul	12.39
Kuala Lumpur	11.28
Tokyo	11.15
Istanbul	9.16

FIGURE 15.14 Mastercard Destination Cities Index. 2017.

Countries	International Association Conferences
United States	934
Germany	689
UK	582
France	545
Spain	533
Italy	468
PR China	410
Japan	410
Netherlands	368
Canada	287
Portugal	287

FIGURE 15.15 Countries with the most international association meetings in 2016 | Source: ICCA 2017.

Europe

Europe is the leading region of the world in magnitude of travel flows, with almost half of all international visitor arrivals in 2016 at 615.2 million. Southern and Mediterranean Europe received the highest volume of these arrivals at 228.5 million. France (82.6 million), Spain (75.6 million), Italy (52.4 million), UK (35.8 million), Germany (35.6 million), Austria (28.1 million), Greece (24.8 million), and Russia (24.6 million) received the most international visitor arrivals. Turkey would normally be among these top countries, but it had a sharp decline in international tourism in 2016.

A high proportion of the flows of international tourism in Europe is intra-regional, with Europeans traveling to other European countries (European Commission 2017). According to Eurostat (2017), 86 percent of the outbound international trips by Europeans in 2015 were to other places in Europe.

VisitBritain (2017) estimates that Germany has the greatest outbound travel flow among European countries at 100.5 million in 2016. Other European nations with significant outbound travel in 2016 were France (49.3 million), Italy (31.4 million), Netherlands (30.6 million), Spain (23.5 million), Belgium (23 million), and Russia (18.9 million).

UK residents made 70.8 million outbound visits in 2016 (Office for National Statistics 2017). Some 79.6 percent of these visits were to European countries, 5.8 percent were to North America, and 14.6 percent were to other countries.

Asia and the Pacific

There were 308.4 million international visitor arrivals to the Asia and the Pacific region in 2016, an increase of 8.6 percent over 2015. The sub-regional shares were North-East Asia at 50 percent; South-East Asia with 36.7 percent; South Asia at 8.2 percent; and Oceania with 5.1 percent. You already know that the Asia-Pacific region is increasing its share of the world's inbound and outbound international tourism.

Mainland China received the most international visitor arrivals among Asian countries at 59.3 million in 2016, followed by Thailand (32.6 million), and Malaysia (26.8 million). China's two SARs also had significant volumes of arrivals, with Hong Kong at 26.6 million

FIGURE 15.16 Bangkok and Thailand are popular destinations within Asia.

and Macao with 15.7 million international arrivals. Other Asian countries with significant international visitor arrivals were Japan (24 million), South Korea (17.2 million), India (14.6 million), Singapore (12.9 million), Vietnam (10 million), and Indonesia (10 million). Australia had 8.3 million international arrivals and New Zealand had 3.4 million in 2016 (UNWTO 2017d).

Both China and India have huge domestic travel markets. India had 1.65 billion domestic visitor visits in 2016 (Ministry of Tourism, Government of India 2017), while China had 4.44 billion domestic travel trips in 2016 (State Council 2017). The outbound markets from China and India are also large and expanding. There were 135 million outbound travelers from China in 2016 (UNWTO 2017b). The Indian outbound market is smaller than China's, estimated at 21.9 million in 2016, but it is rapidly expanding (Ministry of Tourism, Government of India 2017).

Japan is another Asian country with significant outbound travel flows. In 2016, 17.1 million Japanese departed from Japan (JTB Tourism Research & Consulting Company 2017). The most popular destinations for Japanese were the United States, China, South Korea, Taiwan, Thailand, and Hong Kong. There is also a significant domestic travel market in Japan, with approximately 317 million Japanese people taking overnight domestic trips in 2015 (Japan Tourism Agency 2016).

South Korea had 22.4 million outbound trips in 2016. The most popular outbound country destinations of South Koreans are China (Figure 15.17), Japan, United States, Thailand, and the Philippines. South Koreans made 227 million domestic travel trips in 2014, and 98.5 million of these were overnight trips (OECD 2016).

Hong Kong and Singapore each generate significant flows of outbound travel. According to VisitBritain (2017), Hong Kong had 35.9 million and Singapore had 21.1 million outbound visits in 2016.

Australians took 93.7 million domestic overnight trips in 2016–2017 (July to June). Ten million Australians traveled overseas then with the most favored destinations being New Zealand, Indonesia, and the USA (Tourism Research Australia 2017). New Zealand residents took 2.62 million overseas trips in 2016 and that was a record level for outbound tourism (Stats NZ 2017).

With the fourth largest population in the world after China, India, and the United States, Indonesia is another Asian country that is experiencing significant growth in

© Sofiaworld/Shutterstock.com

FIGURE 15.17 The only way for South Koreans to see their sacred mountain, Paektu (Changbaishan), is by going to China.

domestic, outbound, and inbound travel flows. The largest archipelago on the globe, and the home of Bali, Indonesia, is often overshadowed in tourism by its ASEAN cousins, particularly Thailand and Malaysia.

Travel among the ten countries of ASEAN is increasing as a greater emphasis is being placed on economic and trade integration, including tourism (ASEAN 2017).

Americas

North America, consisting of the United States, Canada, and Mexico together represented about two-thirds (65.5 percent) of total international visitor arrivals to the Americas in 2016. The total of 130.6 million arrivals to North America comprised of 75.6 million to the USA, 35 million to Mexico, and 20 million to Canada. Arrivals to the USA fell in 2016, but increased in Canada and Mexico (UNWTO 2017d).

Tourism is a very important economic sector to the Caribbean nations, which welcomed 25.2 million international visitor arrivals in 2016. The Dominican Republic (6 million), Cuba (4 million) (Figure 15.18), Puerto Rico (3.7 million), and Jamaica (2.2 million) had the greatest volumes of arrivals (UNWTO 2017d).

Central America received 10.7 million international visitor arrivals in 2016, with Costa Rica (2.9 million) and Panama (2 million) being the countries with the most arrivals (UNWTO 2017d).

The South American countries had 32.8 million international visitor arrivals in 2016, up 6.6 percent over 2015. The countries with the most arrivals were Brazil (6.6 million), Chile (5.6 million), Argentina (5.6 million), Peru (3.7 million), and Colombia (3.3 million) (UNWTO 2017d).

Domestic travel flows within North American countries are much more significant than inbound international travel, especially for the United States. The U.S. Travel Association (USTA) estimates that 2.2 billion person-trips were taken in the United States in 2016 (USTA 2017). Statistics Canada indicates that Canadians took 321.7 million person-trips in 2016, and 35.8 percent of this travel was for overnight trips (Statistics Canada 2017). In Mexico, approximately 83 million domestic overnight trips were taken in 2015 (Tourism Review News 2016).

United States residents took 72.6 million international trips in 2016 (U.S. Department of Commerce 2017). Many of these trips (56.1 percent) were to Mexico and Canada, and 43.9 percent were to other destinations. After Mexico and Canada, the most important region for trips was Europe, with a 17.3 percent share of all trips. Canadians had 34.1 million outbound trips in 2016, with the United States, Mexico, France, and the UK being their favorite destinations. Mexicans took 22.3 million outbound trips in 2016 (VisitBritain 2017).

Argentina (10.7 million) and Brazil (8.2 million) have significant volumes of outbound travel (VisitBritain 2017). However, their most favored destinations are different; Argentinians prefer traveling to Chile in the Americas and Spain in Europe, Brazilians favor the United States in the Americas and France in Europe. Brazil also has a large and important domestic travel market (BRIC Group 2017).

FIGURE 15.18 Tourism flows to Cuba are expected to increase.

Africa

International visitor arrivals to Africa expanded by 8.3% in 2016 to a total of 57.8 million. About two-thirds (67.8 percent) of these arrivals were in sub-Saharan Africa, with that sub-region experiencing 10.7 percent growth over 2015. North Africa suffered from terrorism and other security incidents in 2016, but was recovering in 2017 (UNWTO 2017d). Morocco in North Africa (Figure 15.19), followed by South Africa in sub-Saharan Africa had the most international visitor arrivals in 2016, at 10.3 and 10 million respectively. South Africa's arrivals were up 12.8 percent in 2016 over 2015 (UNWTO 2017d).

A majority (72.8 percent in 2016) of South Africa's international visitors are from SADC countries (Southern African Development Community), especially Zimbabwe, Lesotho, Mozambique, Swaziland, and Botswana. Some 25.2 percent were from overseas, with the greatest flows of overseas visitors to South Africa in 2016 being from the UK, United States, Germany, France, the Netherlands, and China (Statistics South Africa 2017b). For Morocco, 49 percent of its arrivals in 2016 were foreigners and 51 percent were Moroccans living abroad (MREs). Its major sources of foreign visitors were France, Spain, UK, Belgium, Maghreb countries (Algeria, Libya, and Tunisia), Germany, Italy, and the Netherlands (Morocco Ministry of Tourism 2017).

Domestic tourism is significant within Africa and especially in South Africa. South Africans took 39.4 million domestic day-trips and 43 million domestic overnight trips in 2016 (Statistics South Africa 2017a). Other African countries are attempting to greatly expand domestic travel flows, including Nigeria, which has the largest population among African nations (New Telegraph 2017). Outbound tourism from Africa is growing and again South Africa is a major market with approximately 5.5 million outbound resident travelers in 2016 (Statistics South Africa 2017b).

Middle East

The Middle East had a decline of around 4 percent to 53.6 million international visitor arrivals in 2016. Ongoing military conflicts, acts of terrorism, and refugee issues are causing havoc with tourism in some Middle Eastern countries, especially Egypt, Syria, and Lebanon. However, more stable destinations including Saudi Arabia and the United Arab Emirates (UAE) are experiencing increased international visitor arrivals, with 18 million and 14.9 million respectively in 2016 (UNWTO 2017d). The instability perceived in Egypt resulted in a drop from 14 million international visitor arrivals in 2010 to 5.3 million in 2016.

FIGURE 15.19 Kasbah Ait Ben Haddou, Atlas Mountains, Morocco.

FIGURE 15.20 Kaaba Masjid Al Haram in Mecca, Saudi Arabia.

UNWTO Top 10 Country Destinations by Arrivals	Foreign Visitor Spending	Domestic Visitor Spending
Thailand	79.2%	20.8%
Spain	54.5%	45.5%
Turkey	50.0%	50.0%
France	27.4%	72.6%
Italy	26.6%	73.4%
United States	20.6%	79.4%
China	18.0%	82.0%
UK	16.9%	83.1%
Mexico	16.1%	83.9%
Germany	12.7%	87.3%

FIGURE 15.21 Shares of foreign vs. domestic visitor spending by destination country. | Source: World Travel & Tourism Council. 2017. Country Reports.

Saudi Arabia receives a significant proportion of its international tourism from Muslims on pilgrimages, especially for *Umrah* and *Hajj* (Figure 15.20). One source estimates that there were eight million pilgrims on *Umrah* in 2016 (Smith 2016). Saudi Arabia receives most of its international visitors for Gulf Cooperation Council nations (Kuwait, UAE, Bahrain, Qatar, and Oman), and from Middle Eastern and South Asian countries. Dubai in the UAE is becoming a much more attractive international destination. Its major sources of visitors are from India, Saudi Arabia, UK, Oman, Pakistan, United States, and China (Dubai Corporation of Tourism & Commerce Marketing 2017).

Saudi Arabia has a significant domestic and outbound tourism markets, at 49.9 and 19.1 million trips respectively in 2016 (Saudi Commission for Tourism & Natural Heritage 2017).

Now you know about the travel flows for the world's regions and countries; however, before leaving this discussion you need to understand more about the relative importance of international and domestic travel. It seems that international tourism gets greater attention, but as Figure 15.21 shows it is sometimes not as important as its domestic cousin. For some emerging economy countries such as Thailand, the spending of international visitors is crucial to their development. Foreign visitor spending is also important to Spain and Turkey, with a 54.5 percent and 50 percent share respectively. However, for the remaining seven countries, domestic visitor spending is much greater than international spending.

Another reality for you to know is about the magnitude of cross-border travel flows in published international tourism statistics. For example, in North America, Canada, Mexico, and the United States get the greatest flows of international visitors from their neighbors. The same is true of the flows among Mainland China, Hong Kong, and Macao.

So, you have had a good "status report" on the travel flows in the world's regions and countries, the focus changes to the predictions of future travel flows and some of the major trends that will influence these movements of people.

TRAVEL FORECASTS AND TRENDS

There are many forecasts of future travel flows and trends, and generally they are very positive (Airbus S.A.S. 2017; Amadeus/Frost & Sullivan 2015; Boeing 2017). For example, IATA predicts 7.2 billion air passengers by 2035, almost double the 3.8 billion in 2016 (International Air Transport Association 2016). The World Travel and Tourism Council (WTTC 2017) estimates that tourism will have a global value of $11.5 trillion by 2027, and the UNWTO forecasts that there will be 1.8 billion international visitor arrivals by 2030 (UNWTO 2011). This UNWTO projection is based on an average annual growth rate of 3.3 percent in international visitor arrivals from 2010 to 2030.

Experience in the last two decades shows that future growth in tourism flows may continue, but there will be "ups and downs" on the way due to factors beyond the control of destinations and tourism businesses. For example, the global economic crisis in 2007–2009 had a deep, negative impact on international tourism. However, global tourism arrivals have grown at above-average rates each year since 2009, demonstrating its robustness. Political influences are also causing temporary disruptions in flows among certain countries. For example, inbound tourism from China to South Korea fell in 2017 after the Chinese Government imposed a travel ban on Chinese tour operators (BBC 2017). The Trump administration in the United States in 2017 was also introducing travel restrictions on certain countries including Chad, Iran, Libya, North Korea, Somalia, Syria, Venezuela, and Yemen (CNN 2017). The fallout from the Brexit vote in 2015 in the UK is expected to influence the travel flows among the UK and European countries (Noakes 2017).

Despite the confidence of the forecasters, an atmosphere of some uncertainty has descended on tourism due to a combination of several external factors. As you know from Chapter 1, tourism is an open system and therefore it is highly susceptible to being influenced by factors beyond the control of those within the tourism sector. Environmentally, climate change is a major threat to the future of tourism and tourism's contribution to global warming must be reduced. The solutions to that global challenge are in our own hands as the Intergovernmental Panel on Climate Change (IPCC) found that scientists are 95 percent certain that humans are the "dominant cause" of global warming since the 1950s (BBC 2013).

Concerns over conflicts, actual and potential, and security and safety, were also casting a large shadow over tourism at the time of writing this new edition. Additionally, the increasing targeting of travelers by terrorists was becoming an issue of much greater concern. Europe has been hit hard with terrorism, but there is instability in many other parts of the world including the Middle East, Western and Eastern Africa, North East Asia, South Asia, and the Southern Philippines. The horrible massacre of innocent people in Las Vegas shows that even advanced economy countries cannot escape these tragic events.

Many people are speculating about the future trends in travel flows and which factors will be influential. Most of these conversations revolve around eight factors: technology, economy, experiences, sharing, society and culture, environmental changes, health and wellness, and safety and security.

The "trendsters" include major players in tourism including American Express, which surveyed about 1,000 consumers in each of China, Mexico, UK, and the United States in 2015. Their survey results produced five important conclusions (American Express Travel 2015):

- Leisure travel is an investment worth making.
- The future of travel will be high-tech and high-touch.
- Future travelers will place a high value on experiences.
- Travel will have to reflect people's distinct needs and passions.
- The human touch is irreplaceable.

From Chapter 11, you know about the increasing importance of experiences when traveling. You also understand that Web 1.0 and 2.0 have changed forever how people search for, book, and share information on their travels. The previous chapters have highlighted for you the generational changes in travel markets, especially from the baby boomers to the millennials. Probably, it is good that you know that for every trend there can be a counter-trend. For example, the American Express survey emphasizes the continuing importance of the "human touch." While there is a trend for people to be using digital devices more; the counter-trend is the growing demand for "digital detox" travel experiences with more of a human (rather than technological) touch. Research is increasingly showing that the use of smartphones is becoming like an addiction (Carr 2017).

There is much research and debate on how the millennials will affect travel flows and patterns in the future. A study by Airbnb (2016) points out that the millennials are the largest generation in history and they will be the predominant group of travelers within the next ten years. TrekkSoft (2016) suggest that the tourism sector should also look out for trips planned and taken together by millennials and baby boomers, as signaled by the trend toward multigenerational travel.

In looking to the future of travel flows, a good question to ask is "Does history repeat itself?" The answer is positive on several fronts. For example, there is now huge interest in spas for health and wellness reasons, repeating a period earlier in the evolution of travel. Drive tourism is booming in Mainland China, as it did almost fifty years ago in North America, Europe, and Australasia. British seaside resorts are rebounding and becoming a viable option for many short break holidays of UK residents. Classic railway journeys are enjoying a revival, especially as a luxury product. Going on pilgrimages also seems to remain a constant in travel as people seek to satisfy their spiritual beliefs and needs. The sharing economy is producing a new set of players that offer authentic experiences staying and dining in local people's homes; however, B&Bs and guest houses were an earlier version of these sorts of offers. So, while there will be new frontiers to be explored such as space travel, it can also be said that history does tend to repeat itself in tourism.

QUICK TRIP 15.6

It's My Bleisure. How to Confuse the Number-Counters

Bleisure is not a word to be found in any dictionary yet, but despite this it is a hot trend in tourism. It can be defined as a combination of business and leisure travel. Whereas tourism statisticians prefer to put visitors in neat boxes, the growing numbers of bleisure travelers are bound to confound the number-counters by blurring the boundaries between market segments.

The following are some of the likely reasons for the popularity of bleisure trips:

- Time poverty
- A concept liked by millennials
- Someone else is paying for the trip (or most of it)
- People may not return to the same destinations
- Family can be brought along
- See more of the world and gain greater knowledge
- Have more and different cultural experiences

Two research studies have been completed on bleisure travel and are listed in the sources. The research by Bridge-Street Global Hospitality (2014) found that 60 percent of respondents had taken bleisure trips and another 20 percent intended to. The remaining 20 percent cited a lack of time to fit in bleisure travel. Some 46 percent add pleasure travel days on every or most trips. The major reason for having bleisure trips is to get cultural experiences and new knowledge. More than half (54 percent) of bleisure trips are taken with family members or significant others.

The Carlson Wagonlit Travel study (CWT Solutions Group 2016) discovered that 46 percent of pleasure travel days are taken at the end of business trips, 34 percent at the trip starts and 20 percent during business trips. It also finds that younger and female business travelers are more likely to engage in bleisure travel. Frequent business travelers are less likely. The propensity to take bleisure trips increases with the distance traveled.

The bleisure idea seems to fit well with the trend for people to want authentic experiences of the cities and other places they visit, even when on business trips. These trips also seem quite compatible with using sharing economy providers such as Airbnb, Uber, and VizEat that allow closer connections with local people and communities.

Bleisure may be more of a new name for a concept rather than a new development in travel. In fact, it has been happening for several decades. You also need to know that it has a "dark side" with income tax, insurance, and human resource management issues.

Think about This

1. How do you feel the bleisure trend will affect travel flows in your country?
2. How should destinations take fullest advantage of the tendency to take bleisure trips?
3. The research indicates that millennial and other younger travelers are more likely to engage in bleisure. Why do you think this is so?
4. Should companies encourage their employees to take bleisure trips? Why or why not?

Sources

BridgeStreet Global Hospitality. The Bleisure Report 2014. Reston, Virginia: BridgeStreet Worldwide. https://skift.com/wp-content/uploads/2014/10/BGH-Bleisure-Report-2014.pdf

CNN Business Traveller. 2016. The fine line between business and pleasure travel. *Travel News Digest.* https://www.youtube.com/watch?v=MEt4-Tq5oe8

CWT Solutions Group. 2016. A quantitative look at the bleisure phenomenon. https://www.carlsonwagonlit.com/content/dam/cwt/pdf/insights/20160712-solutions-group-white-paper-bleisure.pdf

Jainchill, J. 2016. Business travel: "Bleisure" is now more than a buzzword. *Travel Weekly,* August 29. http://www.travelweekly.com/ConsumerSurvey2016/Bleisure-is-now-more-than-a-buzzword

Mandich, M. 2016. New report: What influences the bleisure traveler? *Expedia Media Solutions.* https://blog.advertising.expedia.com/influencing-bleisure-travelers

Veselinovic, M. 2016. Bleisure travelers: A new tribe injects fun into business trips. *CNN Travel,* April 19. http://edition.cnn.com/travel/article/bleisure-travel/index.html

SUMMARY

Travel has evolved continuously since ancient times up until the present where commercial travel into space is becoming a reality. International visitor arrivals have broken the one billion level. Europe predominates in terms of inbound and outbound travel flows, but its market share is being eroded by Asian countries.

The performance of flows of international travel are impressive; however, in many cases domestic travel is larger and more important economically to countries. The future projections for international travel flows for the next ten to fifteen years are very optimistic; however, based on recent experience, it is unlikely that tourism growth will be uninterrupted. You also need to remember that numbers are just numbers, but that the faces and expectations of future travelers are likely to be quite different from the present and the past. A new generation of travelers is in the ascendancy and more visitors from Asia are expected in the future.

There is often a preoccupation with international travel flows in global tourism. However, for many countries domestic tourism remains the "bread and butter" of the tourism sector. When external forces turn negative, domestic tourism becomes even more important for many destinations and should not be neglected.

ACTIVITIES

1. To where have you traveled in the past, both within your own country and abroad?
2. What are the destinations you would most like to visit in the future and why?
3. Are you likely to visit the most popular countries and cities identified in this chapter? Why or why not?
4. Is the safety and security of travel a major concern to you? Which destinations do you feel are safe? Unsafe? Why do you have these perceptions?
5. What are the benefits of traveling within your own country rather than going abroad?
6. How do you feel international travel will benefit you personally?

REFERENCES

Airbnb. 2016. Airbnb and the Rise of Millennial Travel. https://www.airbnbcitizen.com/wp-content/uploads/2016/08/MillennialReport.pdf

Airbus S.A.S. 2017. Global Market Forecast. Growing Horizons 2017/2036. Blagnac Cedex: France.

Amadeus/Frost & Sullivan. 2015. Future Traveller Tribes 2030: Building a More Rewarding Journey. http://www.amadeus.com/web/amadeus/en_1A-corporate/Amadeus-Home/Travel-trends/Travel-community-trends/Future-Traveller-Tribes-2030/1319623906608-Page-AMAD_SolutionDetailPpal

American Express Travel. 2015. Future Travel Trends, July 9.

Association of Southeast Asian Nations. 2017. ASEAN Member States. http://asean.org/asean/asean-member-states/

Australian Government. 2015. National parks. http://www.australia.gov.au/about-australia/australian-story/national-parks

BBC. 2013. A brief history of climate change. http://www.bbc.com/news/science-environment-15874560

BBC. 2017. South Korea tourism hit by China tourism ban. July 11. http://www.bbc.com/news/business-40565119

Bearne, S. 2016. How technology has transformed the travel industry. *The Guardian*, February 29. https://www.theguardian.com/media-network/2016/feb/29/technology-internet-transformed-travel-industry-airbnb

Bioexpedition. 2013. National Parks. Basicplanet. http://www.basicplanet.com/national-parks/

BITB New Delhi. 2016. Tourism Updates. http://www.bitb.org/update6.php

Boeing. 2017. Current Market Outlook 2017–2036. Boeing Commercial Airplanes: Seattle, Washington.

BRIC Group. 2017. The importance of domestic tourism in Brazil. http://bric-investment.com/news/importance-domestic-tourism-brazil/

Carr, N. 2017. How smartphones hijack our minds. *Wall Street Journal*, October 7. https://www.wsj.com/articles/how-smartphones-hijack-our-minds-1507307811

CNN. 2017. Trump administration announces new travel restrictions. September 25. http://edition.cnn.com/2017/09/24/politics/trump-travel-restrictions/index.html

Designtechnica Corporation. 2017. The history of social networking. https://www.digitaltrends.com/features/the-history-of-social-networking/

Dubai Corporation of Tourism & Commerce Marketing. 2017. Dubai Tourism 2016: Performance Report. https://www.visitdubai.com/en/tourism-performance-report-old

Euromonitor International. 2016. Top 100 City Destinations Ranking. Euromonitor International: London, UK.

European Commission. 2017. Eurostat statistics explained. Tourism trips of Europeans. http://ec.europa.eu/eurostat/statistics-explained/index.php/Tourism_trips_of_Europeans

Eurostat. 2017. Share of world destinations for outbound trips of EU residents, EU-28, 2015. http://ec.europa.eu/eurostat/statistics-explained/index.php/Tourism_statistics_-_top_destinations

Faustino, A. 2017. How technology changed the way we travel. Adventure in You. https://www.adventureinyou.com/travel-tips/how-technology-changed-travel/

International Air Transport Association. 2016. IATA forecasts passenger demand to double over 20 years. http://www.iata.org/pressroom/pr/Pages/2016-10-18-02.aspx

International Congress and Convention Association. 2017. The International Association Meetings Market 2016. ICCA Statistics Report—Public Abstract. Amsterdam: ICCA.

Japan Tourism Agency. 2016. White Paper on Tourism in Japan. http://www.mlit.go.jp/kankocho/en/siryou/whitepaper.html

JTB Tourism Research & Consulting Company. 2017. Japanese outbound tourist statistics. https://www.tourism.jp/en/tourism-database/stats/outbound/

Kearns, L. 2015. 5 reasons America became obsessed with Hawaii in the 1960s. *Huffington Post*, March 18. http://www.huffingtonpost.com/2015/03/18/america-obsessed-hawaii-1960s_n_6837068.html

Mason, E. 2016. The package holiday revolution. History Extra, July 16. http://www.historyextra.com/article/feature/package-holiday-revolution-history

Mastercard. 2017. Mastercard Destination Cities Index 2017. https://newsroom.mastercard.com/documents/mastercard-global-destination-cities-index-2017-report/

Matthew, O. 2017. Chinese outbound tourists—new 2017 report. CLSA. https://www.clsa.com/idea/chinese-tourists-expand-their-horizons/

Ministry of Tourism, Government of India. 2017. Domestic tourism in India booming with significant growth in domestic tourist visits. http://pib.nic.in/newsite/PrintRelease.aspx?relid=158781

Ministry of Tourism, Government of India. 2017. India tourism statistics at a glance 2017. http://tourism.gov.in/market-research-and-statistics

Morocco Ministry of Tourism. 2017. http://www.tourisme.gov.ma/fr/tourisme-en-chiffres/arrivees-des-touristes

National Geographic Society. 2017. Travel. U.S. National Parks—in the beginning. http://www.nationalgeographic.com/travel/national-parks/early-history/

National Parks UK. 2017. History of the National Parks. http://www.nationalparks.gov.uk/students/whatisanationalpark/history

New Telegraph. 2017. Nigeria Travel Week to promote domestic tourism. September 30. https://newtelegraphonline.com/2017/09/nigeria-travel-week-promote-domestic-tourism/

Noakes, G. 2017. Seven ways Brexit will influence the travel industry. TTG Media, April 5. https://www.ttgmedia.com/news/news/seven-ways-brexit-will-impact-the-travel-industry--9767

OECD. 2016. OECD Tourism Trends and Policies 2016. Paris: OECD Publishing.

Office for National Statistics (UK). 2017. UK residents visits abroad. https://www.ons.gov.uk/peoplepopulationandcommunity/leisureandtourism/datasets/ukresidentsvisitsabroad

Parks Canada. 2017. Parks Canada Attendance 2016–17. https://www.pc.gc.ca/en/docs/pc/attend

Pooran, N. 2017. Outlander effect leads to a tourism boom for Scotland. STV. https://stv.tv/news/scotland/1388922-tv-drama-outlander-leads-to-tourist-boom-for-scotland/

Renub Research. 2017. China outbound Tourism Market, Outbound Tourist Visits, Tourist Market Spending & Forecast. http://www.renub.com/china-outbound-tourism-market-outbound-tourists-visits-tourists-market-spending-and-forecast-1085-p.php

Saudi Commission for Tourism & Natural Heritage. 2017. Tourism Demand. http://www.mas.gov.sa/en/Dashboard/Pages/default.aspx

Smith, S. 2016. Saudi Arabia hopes for religious tourism boost. BBC News, May 25. http://www.bbc.com/news/world-middle-east-36250851

State Council, Peoples Republic of China. 2017. China tourism revenue grows fast in 2016. http://english.gov.cn/archive/statistics/2017/01/09/content_281475537285546.htm

Statistics Canada. 2017. Travel Survey of Residents of Canada, 2016 (final). http://www.statcan.gc.ca/daily-quotidien/170725/dq170725e-cansim-eng.htm

Statistics South Africa. 2017a. Media release: Domestic tourism survey 2016. http://www.statssa.gov.za/?p=10409

Statistics South Africa. 2017b. Tourism, 2016. http://www.statssa.gov.za/?page_id=1854&PPN=Report-03-51-02&SCH=7037

Stats NZ. 2017. 3.5 million visitor arrivals to NZ in 2016. http://www.stats.govt.nz/browse_for_stats/population/Migration/IntTravelAndMigration_MRDec16.aspx

Technavio. 2017. Global Space Tourism Market 2017–2021. https://www.technavio.com/report/global-media-and-entertainment-services-global-space-tourism-market

Tourism Research Australia. 2017. Travel by Australians. Year ending June 2017. Canberra: Austrade.

Tourism Review News. 2016. Tourism in Mexico to focus on domestic travelers. https://www.tourism-review.com/tourism-in-mexico-expects-100-million-travelers-news4994

TrekkSoft. 2016. Travel Trend Report 2017. Interlaken, Switzerland: Trekksoft AG.

UNESCO. 2017. Developing a Sustainable Tourism Strategy for the Silk Roads Heritage Corridor. http://whc.unesco.org/en/activities/826/

United Nations. 2017. World population projected to reach 9.8 billion in 2050, and 11.2 billion in 2100. https://www.un.org/development/desa/en/news/population/world-population-prospects-2017.html

UNWTO. 2011. Towards 2030 Global Overview. Madrid: Spain.

UNWTO. 2017a. UNWTO Silk Road Programme. http://silkroad.unwto.org/

UNWTO. 2017b. UNWTO World Tourism Barometer, Volume 15, March. UNWTO: Madrid, Spain.

UNWTO. 2017c. UNWTO World Tourism Barometer, Volume 15, June. UNWTO: Madrid, Spain.

UNWTO. 2017d. UNWTO Tourism Highlights 2017 Edition. UNWTO: Madrid, Spain.

U.S. Department of Commerce, International Trade Administration, National Travel and Tourism Office (NTTO). 2017. U.S. citizen travel to international regions. http://tinet.ita.doc.gov/view/m-2016-O-001/index.html

U.S. National Park Service. 2017. About us. History. https://www.nps.gov/aboutus/history.htm

U.S. National Park Service. 2017. Social Science. Annual Visitation Highlights. https://www.nps.gov/subjects/socialscience/annual-visitation-highlights.htm

U.S. Travel Association. 2017. Domestic Travel Fact Sheet. https://www.ustravel.org/system/files/media_root/document/Research_Fact-Sheet_Domestic-Travel.pdf

VisitBritain. 2017. Germany. https://www.visitbritain.org/markets/germany

von Lüpke-Schwarz, M. 2013. A brief history of travel: from elite hobby to mass tourism. Deutsche Welle. http://www.dw.com/en/a-brief-history-of-travel-from-elite-hobby-to-mass-tourism/a-16996047

World Economic Forum. 2017. The world's 10 biggest economies in 2017. https://www.weforum.org/agenda/2017/03/worlds-biggest-economies-in-2017/

World Travel & Tourism Council. 2017. Travel & Tourism Economic Impact 2017 World. https://www.wttc.org/research/economic-research/

CHAPTER SIXTEEN

Travel Trade Intermediaries
Marketing Channels and Distribution in the Tourism System

Thank you Travel Agents for Taking Us Places, Helping Us Choose, Expert Travel Advice, No Hassles, Giving Options, Vacations, and Life Changing Journeys.

A special thanksgiving "Thank you" to travel agents from
NATIONAL ASSOCIATION OF CAREER TRAVEL AGENTS (NACTA) nacta.com

YOUR LEARNING DESTINATION

You will be able to explain the role of companies that enable the sale of tourism products. You'll learn about the role these companies play in the tourism distribution system—ensuring that people can learn about and buy products in an easy and efficient way.

WHAT YOU NEED TO KNOW

Having read this chapter, you will be able to:

- ✔ Describe the tourism distribution system.
- ✔ Explain the role of tourism distribution in tourism marketing.
- ✔ Define direct, indirect, and multi-channel distribution and explain distribution mix strategies.
- ✔ Identify and describe the major types of travel intermediaries.
- ✔ Explain the functions of tourism intermediaries.
- ✔ Explain the role of media in disseminating tourism information.

BREAKING THE ICE

Perhaps you've heard that the role of travel agents has disappeared and that the Internet means that all travel is booked direct these days. If so, think again. Sure, the Internet has changed the tourism system—but many travel agencies have learned to adapt to the new conditions in the system. As you have seen, the tourism system is big and there are many different types of companies that support travelers on their journeys. In fact, some of the biggest companies in the tourism system are tourism intermediaries, companies that bring products together with consumers. Each of these companies has found a unique way to add value—and get paid for it.

Between Consumers and Destinations—Other Companies in the Tourism System

While the organizations that contribute to the destination experience are important to tourism, they are not the only companies in the tourism system. Between the destination and the "on-site"' tourism organizations, there are a variety of companies that contribute to the functioning of the tourism system. Some of these companies help specific segments of the market to plan and buy their travel; others provide important information about the destination and its products. These companies are called travel intermediaries. A travel intermediary is a link between travelers and tourism products. In this chapter we'll explore some of these different types of travel intermediaries and their roles in the tourism system.

KEY TAKEAWAY POINTS

- The function of distribution in tourism is unique. One element that makes it different from other product marketing—travelers move to the product, the travel product doesn't come to the consumer.

- There are a wide variety of companies working to connect tourism product with consumers. These companies are called travel intermediaries. Companies will choose intermediaries that best fit their strategic needs. Many companies use a variety of intermediaries—this is called a multi-channel approach.

- Travel intermediaries form a distribution network that connects consumers with products. Each company in the distribution network must create value in order to remain viable. Intermediaries create value in a variety of ways. For instance, value can be created by aggregating different products, by curating products in meaningful ways, or by adding unique services.

- Different tourism markets have different distribution networks or channels. The distribution network for leisure travel—OTAs, Travel agents, wholesalers and others, differ from distribution networks in the meetings and convention market or the business travel.

- Travel intermediaries—like other parts of the tourism system—are being impacted by technology. Travel intermediaries must respond to changes in the tourism system if they are to continue to thrive.

TOURISM INTERMEDIARIES—A MARKETING PERSPECTIVE

Before we look at some of the sectors of the industry and specific types of companies, it is helpful to spend some time thinking about the role of these companies in the tourism system. From a marketing perspective, the process of getting a product from the producer to the consumer is identified in the traditional 4 Ps as *Place*. In traditional consumer product marketing, the place, P, represents the process of getting a physical product from the place it is produced to the place it is consumed. Of course, tourism works differently from physical products, and the place it is produced is the place it is consumed. In the tourism system, consumers come to the product.

"Distribution" in the Tourism System Is Unique

Tourism intermediaries help *distribute* tourism products. The purpose of distribution is to establish a link between supply and demand, between visitors and tourism destinations and organizations. Travel intermediaries—like travel agents or professional conference organizers—are components of the *distribution system,* which makes tourism services and products available to visitors.

Tourism distribution is different from the distribution in some other industries. There is no physical distribution because tourism services are intangible. Tourism services cannot be physically packaged and shipped to visitors, and they cannot be stored in inventory. So, the distribution is not a physical product—FedEx will not deliver a white box with your cruise ship cabin in it. Even so, other things are moving through the tourism system. *Payments* are moving from one system member to another, *ownership* of the promised service may move from one member of the system to another, and *information* is moving throughout the system.

Distribution's Role in the Marketing Mix

The choices companies make about distribution impact all aspects of their marketing mix. As you may remember from Chapter 7, the tourism distribution system or *distribution mix* is a component of the marketing mix; it is referred to as "place" in the traditional 4 Ps of marketing. Distribution mix decisions must be consistent with the overall marketing mix. The goal of the marketing mix is to reach target markets and achieve the objectives of the company for these markets. The distribution mix affects other marketing mix components and is itself affected by these other components. For example, cruise lines rely on retail travel agencies for about two-thirds of their bookings. Therefore, the cruise lines' pricing structures must be designed to allow for attractive commission rates for agencies.

An important set of promotional decisions will be about the resources allocated to push or pull strategies in the distribution network. *Push strategies* will focus on supporting intermediaries in a way that "pushes" the product through the distribution network to consumers. These may include sales training of travel agents, familiarizations, and brochure support. *Pull strategies* are directed at consumers. Even pull strategies require attention to intermediaries. You can imagine your frustration if you had an advertising campaign that increased interest in your product, but people went to travel agents who couldn't sell your product.

Promotional approaches need to be adapted to suit the choice of travel trade intermediaries. Because retail travel agencies have no inventory, there is no incentive for them to promote specific destinations. The promotional burden rests with destination management organizations (DMOs), transportation companies, and other suppliers of tourism services. In contrast, tour operators carry an inventory of airline seats, hotel rooms, and other tourism services. They have a prior investment (in terms of *blocked space*) with airlines and suppliers in the tour destination areas and are often willing to share the costs of promoting the destination to sell their tours. For the airlines and suppliers of services, the promotional burden is shared through partnerships with tour operators. These partnerships may include joint advertising, joint sponsorship of agent familiarization tours, and other sales promotion activities.

The pricing approaches of tourism suppliers and carriers are influenced by the decision either to distribute directly to the traveler or indirectly through a travel intermediary. When tour operators buy in bulk—such as guaranteeing one hundred rooms per night for three months—they expect and receive lower room rates.

Distribution Channels, Marketing Channels, and Tourism Marketing Systems

As we have discussed, the tourism system is a complex collection of organizations that contribute to the delivery of tourism. In the bigger tourism system are organizations that form subsystems that perform specific functions. So, when a number of organizations in the system work together on a specific task or function, they create subsystems (or smaller systems within the larger system). There are a number of marketing-related tourism subsystems. For example, a tourism *marketing communication system* is a set of companies that interact to facilitate the communication of tourism information. Within the marketing communication system, there are specific *marketing communication channels* that perform specific functions.

When a set of tourism system organizations work together to get a tourism product to market, we may call them a *distribution network* or a *distribution channel*. A company may use a number of distribution channels to get its product to market. The combined set of distribution channels may be called a *distribution system*.

You may remember we discussed supply chains in Chapter 9. It is important to realize that supply chains and distribution networks are closely related concepts. For some companies in the tourism system, individual tourism products are components of larger product offerings. For instance, when Abercrombie and Kent, a luxury wholesaler, offers its clients a package to London, the hotels and local tours are part of their supply chain. From the hotel's perspective, Abercrombie and Kent is part of their distribution chain; from Abercrombie and Kent's perspective, the hotel is part of the supply chain.

The Importance of Creating Value

The tourism distribution system is *complex* and *dynamic*. It's complex because there are many, many organizations involved. It's dynamic because it is changing and adapting all the time. So how can it be so complex and why is it always changing? There are many organizations because each member of the distribution network has found a way to create *value* in the channel. Simply speaking, if an organization can't create some value or benefit that someone in the distribution channel is willing to pay for, it won't be around for too long. Hotels pay OTAs because OTAs provide access to consumers; corporations pay incentive houses because they bring products together in a unique way that can be used in motivation programs. So why is it always changing? Because the marketplace is dynamic. Technology, changing product needs, and the buying behavior of new markets all impact how business is done. For instance, there was a time before ticketless boarding on airlines when travel agents provided the carriers with a broad geographic reach—into every local neighborhood—and someone to write tickets for their passengers. For that service, airlines paid a commission on every ticket purchased. However, as technology reduced the need for these physical tickets, the value of the travel agent changed—at least from the airline's perspective. Airlines reduced and capped the amount they paid for the ticketing because they no longer saw as much value in the service. For travel agents—many of whom were heavily reliant on the income gained as ticket writers for airlines—the change was dramatic and required a complete change in their business model. Some travel agencies disappeared, while others found new ways to add value and found other organizations willing to pay for their services.

Value Creation through Aggregation and Disaggregation

One of the important roles of tourism intermediaries is aggregation, or bringing products together. Aggregation creates value for the customer by allowing them to buy everything at one place. Think about your local grocery store—not only is it close by, but everything you need is in one place. Travel agents and OTAs provide value to the consumer by aggregating products. In fact, with specialist knowledge of the consumer, you may be able to provide specially chosen products for a select consumer, thus creating greater value for the client by reducing the time and effort needed to find products. Travel wholesalers, specializing in a specific market, create tourism and other travel products specifically designed for their target market. Intrepid Travel, a wholesaler, aggregates adventure tourism products, curates them into packages designed for their target market, and offers them to its clients.

DIRECT, INDIRECT, AND MULTICHANNEL DISTRIBUTION CHANNELS

Tourism distribution is either direct or indirect. *Direct distribution* occurs when a carrier, supplier, or DMO sells directly to the traveler; *indirect distribution* occurs when the sale is made through one or more travel trade intermediaries.

There is no doubt that the Internet has made it easier for many companies to increase their direct business with consumers. Today, most tourism companies have some ability to take bookings through their website. Major hotel companies work hard to encourage direct bookings via their own hotel website as opposed to selling their rooms through OTAs or agents.

Every tourism channel includes a product and a consumer. It is not uncommon for tourism products to have three or more intermediaries. For example, a person in Italy buying an Australian resort package may be working with a local travel agent, who is working with a tour wholesaler, who is working with an inbound tour operator, who is working with the resort and other local suppliers.

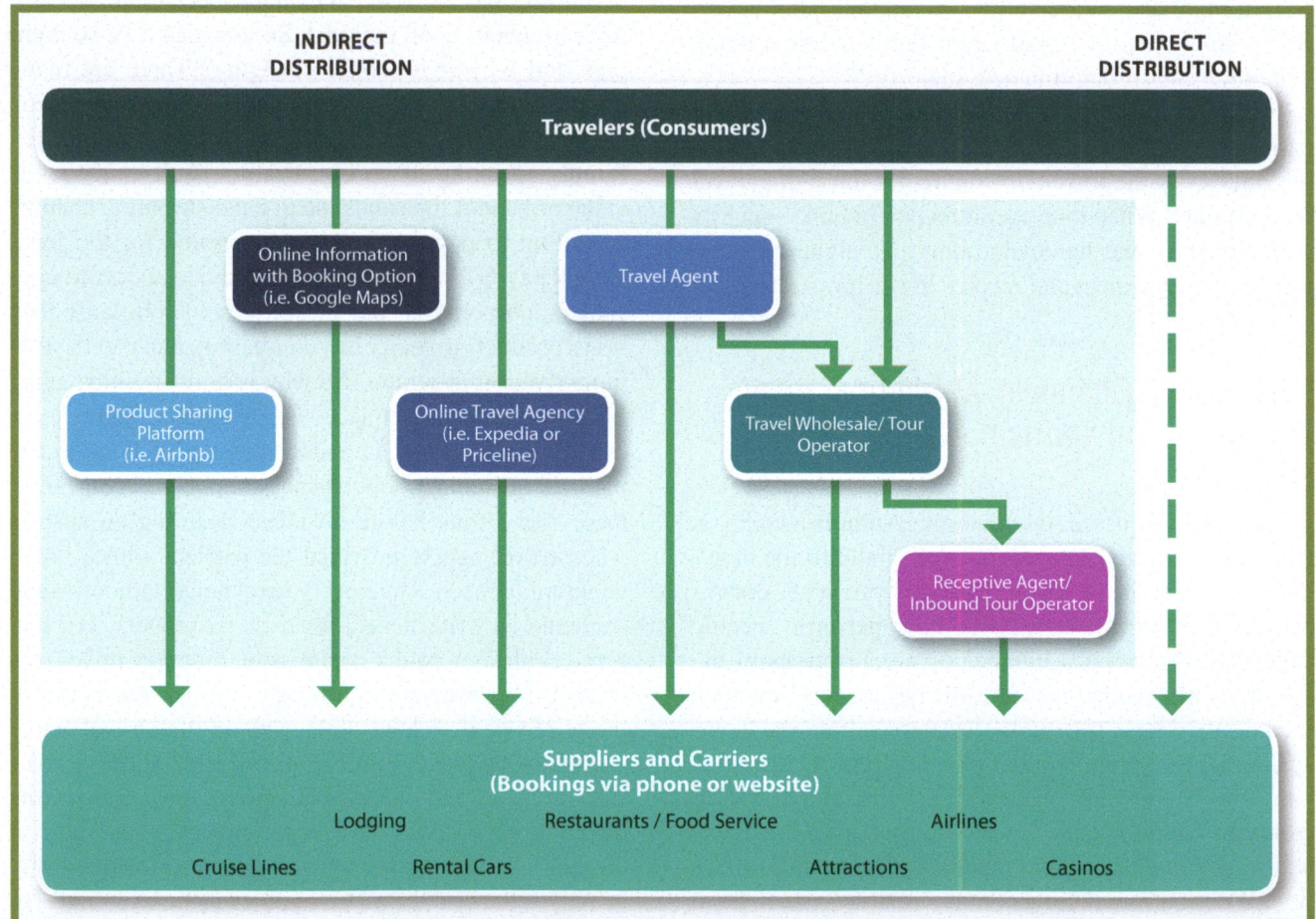

FIGURE 16.1 Travel agents provide personalized service and specialty knowledge. | Source: Morrison, A. M. 2009. *Hospitality and Travel Marketing*. 4th ed

QUICK TRIP 16.1

Demystifying the Digital Marketplace for Hoteliers

With increasing power of the Internet for direct bookings and the importance of the growing OTAs, no part of the tourism industry has struggled more than the hotel sector to adapt to the changing distribution landscape. Hoteliers must manage their distribution strategy carefully to ensure they achieve their reach to potential customers while ensuring they meet revenue goals. In 2016 the American Hotel and Lodging Association, in conjunction with Kalibri Labs, released a special report on "Demystifying the Digital Marketplace: Spotlight on the Hospitality Industry." (Estis Green and Lomano 2016). The diagram below shows the complexity of the many channels available to hoteliers.

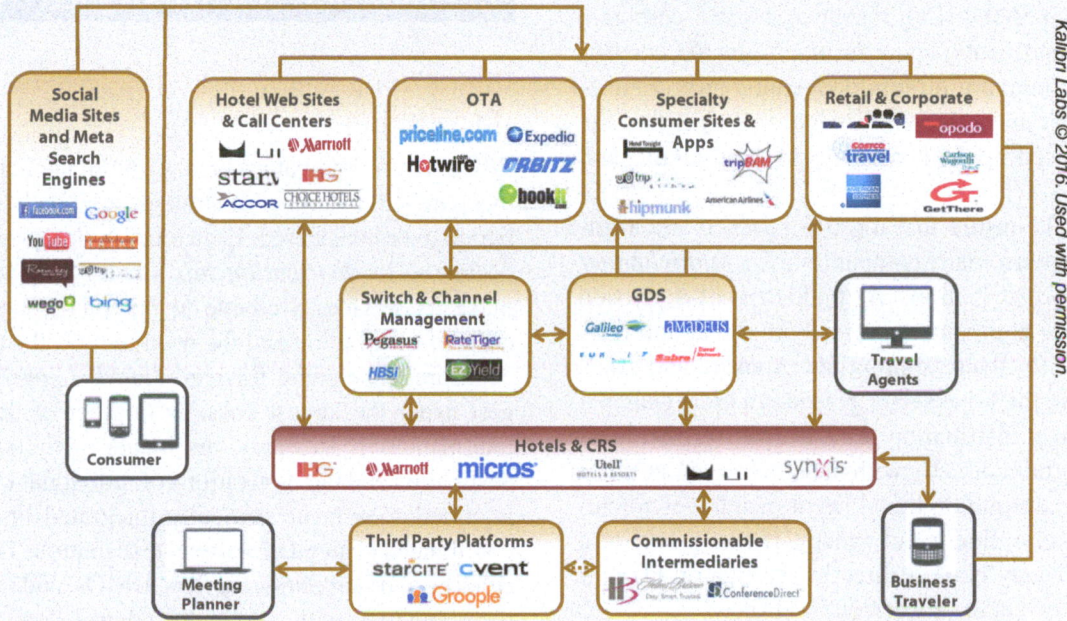

One of the highlights of the report was:

It's All about Optimal Channel Mix

Every single booking, no matter the source, comes with a price tag. A hotel will never get all of its bookings from a single channel and so hotels must work to identify and manage to an optimal channel mix. At the hotel level, managing costs is not simply about negotiating a better deal with a channel vendor such as an OTA. It's about understanding (1) the profile of demand in a hotel's market and (2) the costs associated with getting that demand and then (3) proactively managing to a channel mix deemed optimal because it yields the highest net revenue and profit contribution (Estis Green and Lomano 2016, 2).

Think about This

1. What does it mean when it says "every booking comes with a price tag"? What are the costs of distribution when bookings come direct?
2. The report states that the amount the hotel companies are paying for commission is growing at twice the rate of revenue. What value do the intermediaries provide to the hotel companies to justify that cost?
3. Based on your understanding of the chapter, what strategies do hotels take in managing their distribution network?

Source

Estis Green, C., and M. V. Lomano. 2016. Demystifying the Digital Marketplace: Spotlight on the Hospitality Industry. Washington, DC: HSMAI Foundation.

Tourism intermediaries are companies that have found a way to add value to the process of getting the product to the customer. The value each type of intermediary provides may be different. The value may be created by a wide variety of factors including access to markets, specific knowledge of either the product or the market, or access to technology, to name a few. Intermediaries may specialize in a sector of the market—like leisure travel, corporate travel, or parts of the meeting industry. For instance, in the leisure travel market, there are the travel agent and travel wholesalers. In the incentive travel market, there may be Destination Management Companies (DMCs), incentive houses, corporate incentive departments, and consumers. In the convention market, there are professional conference organizers. With their specialist knowledge, they will find the challenges faced by the companies in these sectors and solve them.

In order to ensure that tourism products are available to consumers, many companies use a *multichannel* approach to distribution. A multichannel approach means that the company manages both direct and indirect channels to ensure appropriate exposure and availability. Again, the hotel sector provides a great example of multichannel distribution. As a leisure traveler, I can book a hotel room directly with the hotel by phone or on their website, through a travel agent or a travel wholesaler, or via an online travel agency. If I am going to a convention, I may book it directly, through an OTA or travel agent, or via the conference website.

Who Pays for the Middleman?

There are several business models used in the tourism industry. A common approach is the agency approach in which sellers receive a commission for each sale. In this case, the product manager needs to ensure that they set their price at a level that allows commission to be paid to the intermediaries. When there is more than one intermediary—for instance a travel agent and a travel wholesaler—there will need to be enough commission for both. Another approach is the merchant approach in which the product manager sells the product at "net" price and allows the middleman to set the margin and so determine the price the consumer pays.

Business to Consumer or Business to Business

It is worth noting that within the distribution network, the final consumer of the travel is not always the purchaser of the travel. While individual travelers may make all the decisions, in some markets it is an association or corporate buyer that determines some of the products being purchased. For example, if an association chose to hold their conference in Las Vegas, attendees—while able to choose whether or not to attend the conference—were not involved in the site selection. For business meetings, the choice of location and hotel for a strategic planning retreat may be made by an in-house meeting planner.

DISTRIBUTION MIX STRATEGIES

Intensive, Exclusive, and Selective Distribution

While many companies use a multichannel strategy, there are still a number of strategic approaches to distribution to be considered. Each tourism organization must decide on its *distribution mix strategy*, or how it will make its services available to potential travelers. The costs of distribution and the need to have the maximum exposure to potential travelers (*market coverage*) suggest using the largest possible number of travel trade intermediaries. However, the image of the services or destination and the motivations of individual travel trade intermediaries favor vertically integrated or vertically coordinated strategies, or direct distribution. These strategies provide suppliers, carriers, DMOs, and travel trade intermediaries with maximum control over sales and reservations. The three broad strategy options available are intensive, exclusive, or selective distribution. An *intensive distribution* strategy means maximizing the exposure of travel services by distributing through all available travel trade intermediaries (high market coverage). *Exclusive distribution* occurs when a carrier, supplier, tour wholesaler or operator, or DMO restricts the number of retail outlets for its services and attempts to have travel agents sell only its services, not those of its competitors. This may be accomplished through franchising or ownership of retail outlets (i.e., through a vertically integrated or vertically coordinated approach). *Selective distribution* is a strategy somewhere between intensive and exclusive distribution (Morrison 2010).

Factors Affecting Distribution Mix Strategy Decisions

For the tourism marketer, the task is to select and design a distribution mix strategy that is not only the most effective in communicating with potential travelers and in accepting reservations, but that is also affordable. The following factors are evaluated in making distribution mix strategy decisions.

Market Coverage. If a tour operator, supplier, carrier, or DMO decides not to use the retail travel agency network, an alternative distribution network has to be developed. In travel trade terms, this is called *bypassing* the retail travel agency network. This may be a lucrative strategy because the costs of travel agency commissions are eliminated. The use of electronic distribution through the Internet and mobile phones is facilitating this strategy of dealing directly with travelers.

Costs. The costs of establishing retail or other direct distribution channels (e.g., a reservations service) are mainly fixed or overhead expenses. Salaries must be paid and offices maintained irrespective of the sales volume generated. Although a part of the compensation of sales representatives may be in the form of commissions, not many people are willing to work on a commission-only basis. In contrast, when working through travel trade intermediaries, only variable costs are incurred. In fact, many travel agency commission payments are made after sales have been completed. Fixed costs are reduced to a minimum.

Positioning and Image. The choice of distribution channel must be consistent with the positioning and image of the supplier, carrier, DMO, or tour wholesaler or operator. An expensive, high-quality tour, destination, or service should be marketed to an upscale demographic market segment through quality intermediaries who cater to upscale travelers.

Motivation of Travel Trade Intermediaries. Each organization within the tourism distribution system has a unique set of objectives and needs. These objectives and needs are not always compatible and can create conflicts and stresses in the tourism distribution system. Travelers want a variety of services and products from which they can select the most satisfying travel experiences. Retail travel agencies want to offer travelers a large inventory of destinations and travel services, but they need to sell a mix of travel services that produce the maximum commissions and service fees. Tour wholesalers and operators want high volume and high profit margins but are concerned about developing tours that motivate retail travel agencies to sell them, while representing a minimum level of risk. Suppliers, carriers, and DMOs want to minimize distribution costs while getting the maximum exposure for their services. They want to generate high traffic volumes and encourage repeat business. The more integration within the channel, the more customer-contact employees are motivated to sell particular services or destinations at the expense of others.

When direct ownership is not feasible or legally permitted, suppliers, carriers, tour wholesalers and operators, and DMOs use a variety of motivation tactics with retail travel agencies. They offer higher commission rates (*overrides*) for higher volumes of booking. These higher rates of commission may be provided through *preferred supplier* or *vendor* relationships between the two parties. Familiarization tours or training seminars are arranged to increase product knowledge. A variety of sales support services may be provided to travel agents, including toll-free telephone "help desks," websites, and in-store merchandising displays.

Characteristics of the Tourism Destination or Service. Not all tourism destinations and services are the same. Some tourism services, including domestic airline tickets, are purchased frequently and are often subject to discounting. They may be distributed through large numbers of retail outlets and in a variety of different ways. Other tourism services and destinations, such as long-haul tours and cruises, can be highly priced, are purchased infrequently, and are usually not subjected to any discounting. Travelers perceive these services to be distinctive, complex, and expensive. The expertise of the travel agent and personal selling by the agent is required to secure bookings. In this case, the tourism destination or organization should be more selective in its choice of retail travel agency outlets.

Economic Concentration. The amount of channel power depends upon the degree of economic concentration among a particular category of tourism organizations. The fewer tour wholesalers or operators serving a particular destination, the greater the power of these companies in dealing with the destination's suppliers and carriers. This is especially true of smaller, long-haul tourism destinations that do not provide the volumes of visitors to be attractive to many tour companies. Examples of these destinations include Sri Lanka and Bhutan, two countries that are highly dependent on relatively few tour operators.

Germany is a country in which travel is exclusively distributed through vertically integrated channels; there is high economic concentration in the travel trade. These channels exert considerable power over destinations that are highly dependent on German visitors. Japan and

South Korea are two other countries in which there is a concentration of power among relatively few travel companies.

There has been a trend to move away from distributing through as many retail travel agencies as possible (intensive distribution) to being more selective in choosing retailers (selective distribution). Carriers, suppliers, and DMOs want the maximum sales volumes. For tour wholesalers and operators, volume is even more critical to profitability. This suggests a strategy of using a maximum number of retail travel agencies. However, many tourism destinations and organizations have found that, while it is more risky to deal with a smaller number of travel agencies, the costs of servicing all agencies are prohibitive. Additionally, a small percentage of travel agencies often produce the majority of the business. A strategy of concentrating on agencies that produce the most sales results in a more efficient distribution system.

INTEGRATION AND CLASSIFICATION OF CHANNELS

Vertical Integration

Every transportation carrier, supplier, DMO, and travel intermediary within the tourism distribution system wants potential travelers to have the maximum amounts of exposure and access to their information to encourage inquiries, bookings, reservations, and payments. The more direct control an organization has over the distribution of its services (through vertical integration), the greater is the assurance that information will be available and that reservations and payments can be made easily and conveniently. *Vertical integration* refers to the ownership by one organization of all or part of a tourism distribution channel.

Horizontal Integration

Tourism companies may also expand their power in a distribution channel through horizontal integration. *Horizontal integration* refers to the ownership of similar businesses by one organization in the tourism distribution channel. This happens often in tourism and usually involves a larger company taking over a smaller organization in the same business.

Classification of Channels

Distribution channels can be classified by three types of degree of control: (1) consensus channels; (2) vertically integrated channels commanded by suppliers, carriers, tour operators, retail travel agents, or other intermediaries; and (3) vertically coordinated channels led by suppliers, carriers, tour operators, retail travel agents, or other intermediaries.

Consensus Channels. In a consensus channel, no single type of tourism organization exercises control over the entire distribution system. The many participants work together because they see it is in their mutual interest to do so. Distribution channels in North America, the United Kingdom, and Australia tend to be of the consensus type.

Vertically Integrated Channels. Vertically integrated channels are those in which the supplier and retail distribution functions are owned or controlled by a single organization. Because tour operators have historically emerged from the retail travel agency field, vertically integrated channels controlled by retail travel agents are commonly found in the United Kingdom, Germany, and North America.

A tour operator may exert control over the entire channel activity through retail travel agency ownership and organization of the channel. This system is found in Germany, where tour operators control not only their own chain of retail travel agency outlets, which deal exclusively with the products of one operator, but also their own system of general retail and direct mail distribution. Touristik Union International, one of the largest German tour operators, controls a network of travel agencies and a large number of resorts and hotels.

Vertically Coordinated Channels. A vertically coordinated channel led by tour operators is one in which the tour operator's power of control over the channel comes from contractual or financial commitments with retail travel agents. *Franchising* is an obvious example of such a system. In Germany, franchising is a large part of travel distribution. Retail travel agency franchising is also rapidly increasing in popularity in Australia, the United Kingdom, the United States, and Canada. The franchisor of a particular company agrees to retail only through certain retail outlets (its franchisees) and to promote no other methods of distribution. The retail franchisee benefits from the much larger pool of marketing resources of the franchiser and the "name recognition" it shares with the many other franchised agencies under the same umbrella. Carlson Wagonlit Travel is a good example of this in North America, while TravelWorld is a major franchised travel agency in Australia.

TRAVEL INTERMEDIARIES

Travel intermediaries include some of the largest companies in the tourism system. Online Travel Agencies (OTAs), travel agencies, and tour wholesalers targeting leisure travelers represent some of the biggest businesses in the industry. Intermediaries focusing on the management of travel expenses and travel experiences are also on the lists of the largest travel companies in many markets. In the following section, we will examine some of the types of intermediaries and their roles in the tourism system.

TRAVEL INTERMEDIARIES: TRAVEL AGENCIES

Online Travel Agencies

Some of the largest companies in the travel system are online travel companies. In 2016, Expedia had sales of $72.4 billion and employed 20,000 people. Its rival, Priceline Group, sold $68.1 billion in travel products (Chipkin 2017).

Major OTAs like Priceline and Expedia include a number of popular brands. They also use a variety of business models. The most common is the *merchant model*, where hotels sell rooms to OTAs at "wholesale" rates and the OTAs "mark-up" the rates when they sell it to consumers; the agency model is a commission-based model. The OTAs list the hotels but don't buy anything upfront (Schmidt 2015). *Metasearch* companies use technology to search across OTAs and identify the best prices available across the Internet. The *Opaque* business model hides the name of the hotel until the purchase is complete. In this way, hotels can deeply discount rooms without lowering the image of their brand by advertising cheap rooms.

While Priceline and Expedia are the largest OTAs, there are a number of other OTAs emerging as important actors in the tourism system. For example, C-Trip, an OTA that began in China, is expanding to new markets.

Travel Agents: Leisure

Functions of Retail Travel Agencies. In essence, retail travel agencies are the department stores of tourism. Around the world, they provide thousands of "travel shops" for suppliers, carriers, DMOs, and the other travel trade intermediaries. A customer can buy all types of travel services at an agency, including tickets for planes and railways, hotels and resorts, packages and tours, car rentals, and travel insurance. The main functions of retail travel agencies are as follows.

FIGURE 16.2 Shanghai is a popular tour destination.

QUICK TRIP 16.2

Cruise Lines and Retail Travel Agencies: A Profitable Relationship

Traditional retail travel agencies have had to weather a stormy relationship with airlines for decades and more recently have had to deal with the growing popularity of OTAs. However, travel agencies have maintained a good relationship with cruise lines based on mutual benefit. Here are some key facts about the use of travel agencies from Cruise Lines International Association (CLIA):

People taking cruises express high satisfaction levels with retail travel agencies.

- Cruise vacationers typically use the services of a travel agent more than non-cruise vacationers (68 percent versus 45 percent). (This may, in fact, be an understatement because some consumers may not realize that their online bookings are actually through travel agencies with online booking capabilities.)
- Ninety-three percent of cruisers express satisfaction with their travel agent, including nearly 60 percent expressing very/extreme satisfaction.
- Travel agents remain the distribution channel offering the best service, according to respondents.
- Sixty-six percent of consumers say professional designations encourage them to use an agent.

Travel agencies who join CLIA receive the designation as a CLIA-affiliated travel agency. CLIA says the following about these travel agencies:

Nearly 14,000 travel agencies across the United States and Canada are affiliated with CLIA. These travel agencies join CLIA for sales and cruise product and business training, for information on current cruise vacation trends, and to be kept informed by CLIA's 26 member cruise lines on cruise news and special offers. By being a CLIA affiliate, these travel agencies have chosen to sell cruise vacations, and by doing so, they are especially qualified in helping you choose the perfect cruise and getting you the best vacation value.

CLIA works hard to build their relationship with the travel agency community. They provide many types of educational courses and professional development professional opportunities including four levels of certification—certified, accredited, master, and elite cruise counselor—online learning opportunities and live training events. Members also become eligible for additional commissions and travel perks and discounts. CLIA conducts a quarterly survey of travel agents cruise trends that it shares widely. All this is working. Since 2010 the number of cruise specialist travel agents has more than doubled, from 12,000 to more than 25,000 in 2016. It seems to be a mutually beneficial relationship—CLIA anticipates that sales through travel agents will continue to grow and eight in ten CLIA certified agents expect their business to increase.

Think about This

1. Why do you think many consumers prefer to use retail travel agencies when planning and booking cruises?
2. Why do you think that cruise lines have chosen to embrace travel agencies while other sectors of the tourism sectors have been less supportive?

Sources

Cruise Lines International Association. 2011. 2011 Cruise Market Profile Study. Used with permission of Cruise Lines International Association.

Cruise Lines International Association. 2011. www.cruising.org/.

Distribution and Sales Network. Travel agencies bring together the sellers and buyers of travel; in this role, they can be called "travel brokers." They act as the official "agents" of travel *principals*—the organizations that actually provide the travel services. Travel agencies provide an enormous distribution network for suppliers, carriers, DMOs, and other travel intermediaries.

The United States has the largest concentration of travel agencies. According to the Airlines Reporting Corporation, there were 15,671 full-service travel agencies in the United States in March of 2010. While the industry is dominated by the large online agencies, many travel agencies are small, and many travel agents work as independent contractors associated with larger agencies. The greatest growth in the number of travel agencies appears to be in the Asia-Pacific region.

In return for their services, suppliers, some carriers, and other travel trade intermediaries pay travel agencies *commissions*, which are normally based on a certain percentage of the total value of the reservation. In most countries, travel agency commission rates are in the 5 to 10 percent range. Special arrangements between individual carriers and suppliers, known as *preferred supplier* or *vendor relationships*, allow the travel agencies to earn extra points of commission (*overrides*). During the 1990s and into the 2000s, most agencies have been charging their customers *service fees* in an effort to improve profitability in the face of disappearing airline commissions from North American airlines.

Reservations and Ticketing. The placement of reservations and the distribution of tickets (mainly for airlines) are traditional roles of retail travel agencies. Reservations and ticketing used to be very time-consuming and labor-intensive, but advances in computer and telecommunications technology have sped up these processes. *Computerized reservation systems* (CRSs), which were first introduced in the early 1970s, have provided travel agencies with instant access to an ever-expanding inventory of the services of the airlines, suppliers, and other travel trade intermediaries. While CRSs began to develop within individual countries, they soon became global in their coverage. Almost all travel agencies today are equipped with CRSs. In 2017, the three major *global distribution systems* (GDSs) were Amadeus, Sabre, and Travelport (which includes GDS brands Apollo, Galileo, and Worldspan). GDSs provide aggregated information for both "brick and mortar" travel agents and OTAs and can be considered the invisible engines behind much of the growth in the industry.

One of the early functions of travel agents was writing tickets for travel reservations, and as air travel grew, ticketing for flights became an important activity for most travel agents. Today, ticketing is a small part of agents' work. Reliance on paper tickets reduced in the 1980s with the introduction of *electronic* or *e-ticketing*, which allows travelers to show up at airline check-ins without a paper ticket. By 2008, paper tickets became a thing of the past, as the International Air Transport Association announced 100 percent implementation of e-ticketing worldwide. Although many of these reservations were being made by travel agencies, travelers were increasingly able to use electronic tickets through their own personal computers. Reliance on printed materials continues to decline as paper boarding passes are replaced by boarding passes on smartphone apps.

Professionalism and Travel Agencies

Throughout the world, travel agency associations are working hard to increase the professionalism of individual travel agents:

- The Association of British Travel Agents has introduced the *Accredited Travel Professional* program that recognizes individual agents' professional qualifications and experience.

- The Travel Institute (formerly the Institute of Certified Travel Agents) in the United States has offered the *Certified Travel Counselor* program since the early 1970s. It now also offers the *Certified Travel Associate* and *Certified Travel Industry Executive* professional designations.

- The Canadian Institute of Travel Counsellors is the Travel Institute's equivalent in Canada and offers the *Certified Travel Counsellor* and *Certified Travel Manager* programs.

- The Australian Federation of Travel Agents has established the *Australian Travel Professionals Program*, which offers six categories of certification for travel agents and tour professionals, including the Certified Travel Counselor.

Information Provision and Travel Counseling. The most traditional role of the retail travel agency is that of serving as a "travel expert." More recently, travel agents have begun describing their services in more personal ways to highlight the direct connection they have with their clients. It is now common for travel agents to call

QUICK TRIP 16.3

Taking the Oath for Travel Agencies: The American Society of Travel Agents Code of Ethics

ASTA is one of the oldest and largest travel agency associations in the world. Although ASTA's headquarters are in Alexandria, Virginia, it has thousands of members worldwide. In fact, the association is represented in more than 120 countries. ASTA has developed a Code of Ethics that spell out the responsibilities of its members:

Responsibilities of Travel Agent, Premium, International Travel Agency Company, and International Travel Agent Associate Members:

1. **Accuracy.** ASTA members will be factual and accurate when providing information about their services and the services of any firm they represent. They will not use deceptive practices.
2. **Disclosure.** ASTA members will provide in writing, upon written request, complete details about the cost, restrictions, and other terms and conditions, of any travel service sold, including cancellation and service fee policies. Full details of the time, place, duration, and nature of any sales or promotional presentation the consumer will be required to attend in connection with his/her travel arrangements shall be disclosed in writing before any payment is accepted.
3. **Responsiveness.** ASTA members will promptly respond substantively to their clients' complaints.
4. **Refunds.** ASTA members will remit any undisputed funds under their control within the specified time limit. Reasons for delay in providing funds will be given to the claimant promptly.
5. **Cooperation.** ASTA members will cooperate with any inquiry conducted by ASTA to resolve any dispute involving consumers.
6. **Confidentiality.** ASTA members will treat every client transaction confidentially and not disclose any information without permission of the client, unless required by law.
7. **Affiliation.** ASTA members will not falsely represent a person's affiliation with their firm.
8. **Conflict of Interest.** ASTA members will not allow any preferred relationship with a supplier to interfere with the interests of their clients.
9. **Compliance.** ASTA members shall not have been convicted of a violation of any federal, state, and local laws and regulations affecting consumers. Pleas of nolo contendere, consent judgments, judicial or administrative decrees, or orders, and assurances of voluntary compliance and similar agreements with federal or state authorities shall be deemed convictions for purposes of these provisions.

The ASTA Code of Ethics describes the responsibilities of travel agencies.

Responsibilities of All Members

1. **Notice.** ASTA members operating tours will promptly advise the agent or client who reserved the space of any change in itinerary, services, features, or price.
2. **Delivery.** ASTA members operating tours will provide all components as stated in their brochure or written confirmation, or provide alternate services of equal or greater value, or provide appropriate compensation.
3. **Credentials.** An ASTA member shall not, in exchange for money or otherwise, provide travel agent credentials to any person as to whom there is no reasonable expectation that the person will engage in a bona fide effort to sell or manage the sale of travel services to the general public on behalf of the member through the period of validity of such credentials. This principle applies to the ASTA member and all affiliated or commonly controlled enterprises.

Think about This

1. What are the benefits for individual travel agencies in adhering to the ASTA Code of Ethics?
2. What benefits does this Code of Ethics provide for consumers in using ASTA member travel agencies?
3. What types of practices does this Code of Ethics promote, and which types of behaviors does it try to eliminate?
4. It is interesting to note that an ASTA Logo Violators List is published by ASTA giving the names of companies that are using the association's logo without its permission. Why is this important in upholding the good name of ASTA and its Code of Ethics?

Sources

American Society of Travel Agents. 2013. www.asta.org/

TravelSense/ASTA. 2011. www.travelsense.org/consumer/logoviolators.cfm

themselves "curators of personal travel experiences" and "travel concierges." Travel agencies are a major source of travel information for individual and group travelers. Travel agents are knowledgeable professionals whose advice and counseling is crucial to many travelers. Travelers expect agents to possess a wide knowledge of travel services and companies, along with an in-depth command of world geography.

Travel Management and Business Travel Agencies

Business travel is an important component of the tourism system. Businesses spend more than $230 billion each year on travel, and Travel and Entertainment (T&E) can be a significant expense for companies (Macke 2015). As you may know from booking your own travel, prices can vary dramatically on many items; for example, flights can be hundreds of dollars different depending on what search parameters you use. Managing these costs is important and a very specialized task that requires specialists. These specialists may be found within companies or working for specialist intermediaries.

Functions of Corporate Travel Departments.
The major function of a corporate travel department is to coordinate and control all of the travel by employees and associates of the organization. The typical roles of the corporate travel department include the following.

Negotiation with Carriers and Suppliers.
A primary role of the corporate travel department is to negotiate for the most competitive prices with airlines, hotels, and car

rental companies. The central coordination of travel has given many corporations greater purchasing and negotiating power when dealing with carriers and suppliers. From a fiscal standpoint, it is in the corporation's best interest for the corporate travel department to negotiate the lowest possible travel prices.

Development of Corporate Travel Policy.
Another important role is the creation of a corporate travel policy outlining the conditions, practices, and processes that must be followed when employees are traveling out of town.

Travel policies should be written and communicated to all employees. The written guidelines cover reservation and ticketing procedures, preferred airlines and travel suppliers, per diems (maximum expenses reimbursed per day), allowable travel expenses, and expense reporting procedures.

Monitoring of Travel Expenses and Travel Policy Compliance.
The corporate travel department is often responsible for setting an annual budget for travel for the company. The control of this budget during the year is exercised by monitoring employee expense reporting and, in particular, ensuring *compliance* with the written corporate travel policies. Since the early 1980s, these departments have helped their organizations gain more control over the use of the growing number of frequent travel reward programs provided by airline, hotel, and car rental firms.

Reservations and Ticketing.
Some corporate travel departments act as in-house travel agencies and take care of the reservations and ticketing for employees. It is

more common, however, for the reservations and ticketing function to be *outsourced* to retail travel agencies. In many countries, the importance of corporate travel accounts to retail travel agencies has greatly increased in the past thirty-five years. The streamlining of corporate travel has brought the independent agency more business and has provided the basis for the establishment of large corporate Travel Management Companies (TMCs) exclusively serving corporations (often called *outplants*). There are also *inplants*, which are travel agency offices located within the physical premises of corporate clients. Another route followed by some corporations is to themselves become travel agencies, operating their own in-house, fully accredited agencies.

Meeting and Incentive Planning. Some corporate travel departments are involved in the organization of corporate meetings and incentive travel trips. In most cases, these tasks are outsourced to other companies that specialize in the organization of meetings and incentive travel. It's also possible that the corporation may employ a full- or part-time meeting planner who may work in a unit outside of the corporate travel department.

Monitoring Travel Agency Performance. Most corporations work with one or more retail travel agencies. The corporate travel department monitors the performance of these travel agencies both in financial terms and in employee satisfaction with agency service levels.

As with leisure travel agencies, efforts are growing to increase the professionalism and professional recognition of corporate travel managers. Associations of corporate travel executives have been created. In North America, the two major associations representing corporate travel managers are the Global Business Transportation Association (GBTA) and the Association of Corporate Travel Executives (ACTE Global). The GBTA has more than 1,000 professional travel manager members and several thousand supplier, carrier, and DMO members. The GBTA describes itself as "the world's premier business travel and meetings organization." It also operates the Certified Corporate Travel Executive program. ACTE Global has a total of 6,000 members spread all around the world. The organization says that it "is a not-for-profit association established to provide executive-level global education and peer-to-peer networking opportunities. Membership spans all of business travel, from corporate buyers to agencies to suppliers, and accords all sectors equal membership."

Travel Agencies—Corporate

The importance of managing business travel has led to the development of travel agencies that specialize in managing travel for business. In the United States, corporate travel agencies are among the largest travel agencies. In fact, after the two big OTAs, remaining companies in the top five of Travel Weekly's Power List (Chipkin 2017)—American Express Global Business Travel ($31.1 billion revenue), BCD travel ($24.6 billion revenue), and Carlson Wagonlit Travel ($22.4 billion revenue)—are all corporate travel agencies.

Corporate travel agencies provide value by enabling many of the functions outlined in the corporate travel departments. By specializing in these issues, corporate travel companies have developed detailed reporting and analysis that assist companies in managing travel costs.

Travel Wholesalers and Tour Operators

Functions of Tour Wholesalers and Tour Operators. The main function of a tour wholesaler is to combine both transportation and ground services into tours to be sold through retail travel agencies to individual or group travelers. This role is performed by independent tour wholesaling companies. The term *wholesaling* implies that these companies do not sell directly to the public.

Many tour wholesalers tailor their tour offerings by target market, destination, mode of transportation, or type of activity or special interest. Some wholesalers cater to specific segments of the market (such as national or ethnic groups), while others "mass market" by promoting popular "sun and sand" destinations. Still other wholesalers specialize in developing tours to specific destinations or regions of the world (e.g., AAT Kings Tours, African Travel, Australian Pacific Touring, China Travel Service, Latour Latin America, and Pacific Delight Tours). Some wholesalers specialize in one type of transportation. The majority of tours marketed by independent tour wholesalers involve air travel.

Tour and package development is also done by other types of organizations. Retail travel agents prepare individual (*FITs*) and group tours (*group inclusive tours*) that they sell to travelers. Airlines and railway companies have wholesaling divisions that put together tours. Companies specializing in incentive travel, cruise lines, travel clubs, educational institutions, and nonprofit organizations (e.g., unions, religious groups, associations, and government and quasi-government agencies) also assemble tours and packages.

A single tour program consists of four parts:

1. Tour planning and preparation
2. Tour marketing
3. Tour administration
4. Tour evaluation

Tour Planning and Preparation. The planning of a tour must begin with some market research. The purpose of this research should be to indicate to the wholesaler which tours will sell and which tour ingredients are essential to attract tour patrons. Both secondary (previously published information) and primary (information collected for the first time) research should be used. Secondary research sources might include the reports of tour operator associations and research organizations, published statistics on arrivals to visitor destinations, directories of tour programs, competitors' brochures, and the wholesaler's own past operating results that show which tours have sold well and have been profitable. Primary research steps might include surveying retail travel agents and past and potential tour patrons.

When planning and developing tours for new destinations, tour wholesalers may participate in *familiarization tours*, sponsored by DMOs, carriers, or suppliers. These trips help the tour wholesaler to determine tour potential, evaluate ground services, and solicit potential government and private sector partnerships for promoting the tour program. At this point, detailed tour specifications are prepared, such as departure dates, tour length, and modes of transportation and ground services to be used. These activities often take place twelve to eighteen months before the first tour departure date.

The actual *tour program* is usually confirmed from twelve to fifteen months prior to the first tour departure. Ground services are negotiated, supplier agreements are signed, and transportation commitments are made. When these steps are completed, the tour program can be finalized. The tour price is calculated by taking the negotiated costs for ground services and adding a markup that, when the expected number of tour patrons is considered, is sufficient to cover fixed costs and the tour wholesaler's profit.

The tour wholesaler's markup is expressed either as a percentage of ground service costs or as a dollar figure. The markup has to be realistic yet also reflect the time and effort involved in organizing the tour. Airfare is added to total ground services costs and markup to arrive at the selling price for the retail travel agent. The final selling price is calculated by adding a retail travel agent commission.

The methods of handling reservations and payments are made and brochure production begins. Brochure production is expensive, and part of the production costs may be paid by the airline involved in the tour or one or more of the ground service suppliers. Appropriate commission rates and volume incentives are also negotiated with retail travel agents. At this point, there are typically ten months left before the first tour departs.

Tour Marketing. The marketing of a tour is the aspect most crucial to its success. The characteristics of the tour marketing program depend upon the size of the wholesaler and the market segments being targeted. All marketing programs involve Internet marketing, brochure distribution, advertising, personal selling, and other sales promotions (e.g., promotional evenings).

Brochures are often large and expensive to produce in high-quality color. While the brochures may be distributed to all travel agencies, it is more efficient to use a selective distribution process. Emphasis should be given to agencies who have provided tour patrons to the wholesaler in the past and especially those who have generated the greatest volumes of past tour patrons. Brochures may also be provided to agencies whose customers fit the profile of the target market for the tour program. Online distribution of brochures in PDF is now commonplace, and this is helping to reduce printing and distribution costs, while also extending the reach of the brochures.

Travel trade advertising may be used to promote a specific tour program or the tour wholesaler's overall services. Advertisements placed in travel trade journals, such as *Travel Weekly*, are normally factual, describing the tours and giving travel agencies booking information. Toll-free telephone numbers, e-mail addresses, and website addresses are included to encourage travel agencies to request tour brochures and other sales materials. In addition, tour wholesalers and operators employ sales representatives who concentrate on selling tours to travel agencies regarded as the best prospects.

Consumer advertising tends to be less about facts and more emotional. Colorful and eye-catching images are used to attract attention and create interest in the tours. Advertisements may be placed in consumer travel magazines and usually recommend travelers to book through travel agencies. Advertising is also done through direct mail using the tour wholesaler's list of past tour patrons and mailing lists of potential patrons. Again, consumer advertisements tend to be of the direct-response variety, urging potential travelers to request a brochure by a toll-free telephone number, fax number, or through e-mail and websites.

QUICK TRIP 16.4

The Advantages of Tours and Packages According to the U.S. Tour Operators Association (USTOA)

The USTOA represents many major tour operator companies with its offices in New York City. The following is a statement prepared by USTOA about the advantages of tours and packages:

> Some people think tours and vacation packages are overly regimented or lack adventure or sophistication. The fact is they encompass a tremendous spectrum of tastes, interests and travel styles—from a multicountry tour to a wine-tasting tour of a particular region to an adventure combining cruising and land-touring. In short, tours and vacation packages are as varied and individual as the millions of Americans who purchase them each year for travel in the United States and throughout the world.

Tours give travelers peace of mind.

- **Savings:** a key benefit to tour and vacation packages. Due to contracting in bulk for accommodations, transportation, tours, meals, and other services, substantial savings are achieved and passed along to the traveler.
- **Volume Purchasing:** often allows for accommodations, airline space, and other arrangements that would otherwise not be obtainable.
- **Peace of Mind:** purchasing a tour package in advance provides certainty of the cost. In addition, the trip has been planned by professionals who are prepared to assist if an unforeseen problem occurs.

USTOA also explains that there are five main groups of vacation travel alternatives: escorted tours, group travel, package travel, independent travel, and charter travel. Some of these involve traveling with a group, while package and independent travel do not.

Think about This

1. Tours appeal to certain types of people, but not to others. Do you agree or disagree with this statement and why?
2. Many tours are sold through traditional retail travel agencies. What are the advantages of using retail travel agencies when planning and booking a tour?
3. Tour guides play a hugely important role in escorted tours. Why do professional tour guides increase customer satisfaction and enjoyment?
4. Independent travel is growing quite rapidly, as is packaged travel. Do you think this trend will continue and that group travel will not grow as quickly? What are your reasons?

Source

U. S. Tour Operators Association. 2017. How to Select a Tour/Vacation.

Marketing begins nine to twelve months prior to departure and continues until a few days beforehand. Reservations, deposits, and payments are requested from one to two months in advance of the departure. If insufficient advance bookings are made, tours may be consolidated or promotion increased.

Tour Administration. The administration of a tour begins six months prior to departure. Detailed schedules or worksheets describing the tour program are prepared and a reservation system sufficient to detail the documentation and payment status of each tour patron is set up. Liaison procedures are established between the reservation system and the ground service suppliers at each destination.

Reservations are usually received by telephone, or via computer from retail travel agencies. They are confirmed, recorded, and filed. Deposits and payments are processed, and documentation is sent to the travel agency for distribution to travelers. Upon completion of the tour, the suppliers are paid. The tour operation part of the tour may be handled by the tour wholesaler or by ground service operators (e.g., inbound tour operators or motor coach companies) or other destination management companies based in the tour destinations.

Tour Evaluation. When the tour is over, the tour wholesaler may evaluate its success through a variety of means. First, it is most important to get each tour patron's opinions on the success of the tour and their satisfaction levels. The tour wholesaler might do this by having each patron complete a questionnaire or comment card at the end of the tour or soon after its completion. Second, the wholesaler might contact all the suppliers involved in the tour to get their reactions. Finally, the tour wholesaler needs to complete an internal evaluation to determine the return on investment for each tour.

Operating Cycle. The tour wholesaling and operations business tends to be seasonal. At any given time, the wholesaler's staff may be preparing the following year's program while marketing and operating the existing year's offering. To reduce seasonality, tour wholesalers may operate tour programs to several destinations that have different seasonal patterns of demand (e.g., winter sports destinations in winter and sun and sand destinations in summer).

Design of Individualized Tour Itineraries. Another traditional role of the retail travel agency has been the design of individualized tour itineraries for their customers. The preparation of *FITs* used to be a mainstay source of business for many travel agencies before the issuing of airline tickets and the booking of prepackaged group tours became more predominant. In this role, the travel agency handles all the air travel and land arrangements for an individual customer in the traveler's destination of choice.

Travel Intermediaries in the Meetings Sector

The meetings industry is sometimes used as an umbrella term to include meetings, events, tradeshows, conventions, and incentive travel. Each of these types of meeting has its own specialists and its own distribution network. In the coming section we will look at some of these specialist intermediaries.

Systems Thinking in Tourism

The meetings market is a system that overlaps the tourism system. If a tourist is defined as someone who travels more than fifty miles and stays overnight, then some meetings create tourists while others don't. Some businesses may organize a meeting that doesn't need an overnight stay or require travel. Even so, many businesses and organizations create meetings that do require travel. Research conducted for the Convention Industry Council—now known as the Event Industry Council, undertook research that found that approximately $130 billion of the $280 billion meetings market overlaps the tourism industry (PWC 2011).

Travel Intermediaries: Incentive Travel Sector

Incentive travel is a special type of business travel. It is provided by a business to a stakeholder—either an employee or an external company—that achieves a specific goal. Incentive travel is a tool to achieve business objectives. While travel incentives can be used to motivate any action, the majority of incentives are designed to stimulate sales. The use of travel as a motivational tool includes a range of tourism services. Incentive travel can include individual travel arrangements or group travel. It can also include domestic or international travel. Companies specializing in solving business challenges using travel as a motivator emerged as a specialty sector of the travel industry. The specialist nature of the sector has allowed a few types of intermediaries to emerge and add value in the incentive travel supply chain.

Incentive Travel Companies work with corporate clients to develop travel programs that achieve corporate objectives. Incentive travel companies combine understanding of effective motivation and engagement strategies with understanding of the travel and event industries.

Destination Management Companies (DMCs) are "professional service companies possessing extensive local knowledge, expertise and resources, specializing in the design and implementation of events, activities, tours and program logistics" (ADMEI 2017).

QUICK TRIP 16.5

TUI and Sustainable Supply Chain Management

The TUI group is one of the largest travel companies is the tourism system. It operates a portfolio of tour operators, travel agencies, online travel portals, over 150 aircraft, over 300 hotels, and 16 cruise liners. TUI employs over 67,000 people and in 2015/16 had revenue of over Euro 17.2 billion. It carries 20 million passengers to over 180 regions. Despite the size and scope, TUI is committed to sustainable tourism.

In their 2016 sustainability report TUI outlined how sustainability initiatives supported their business model.

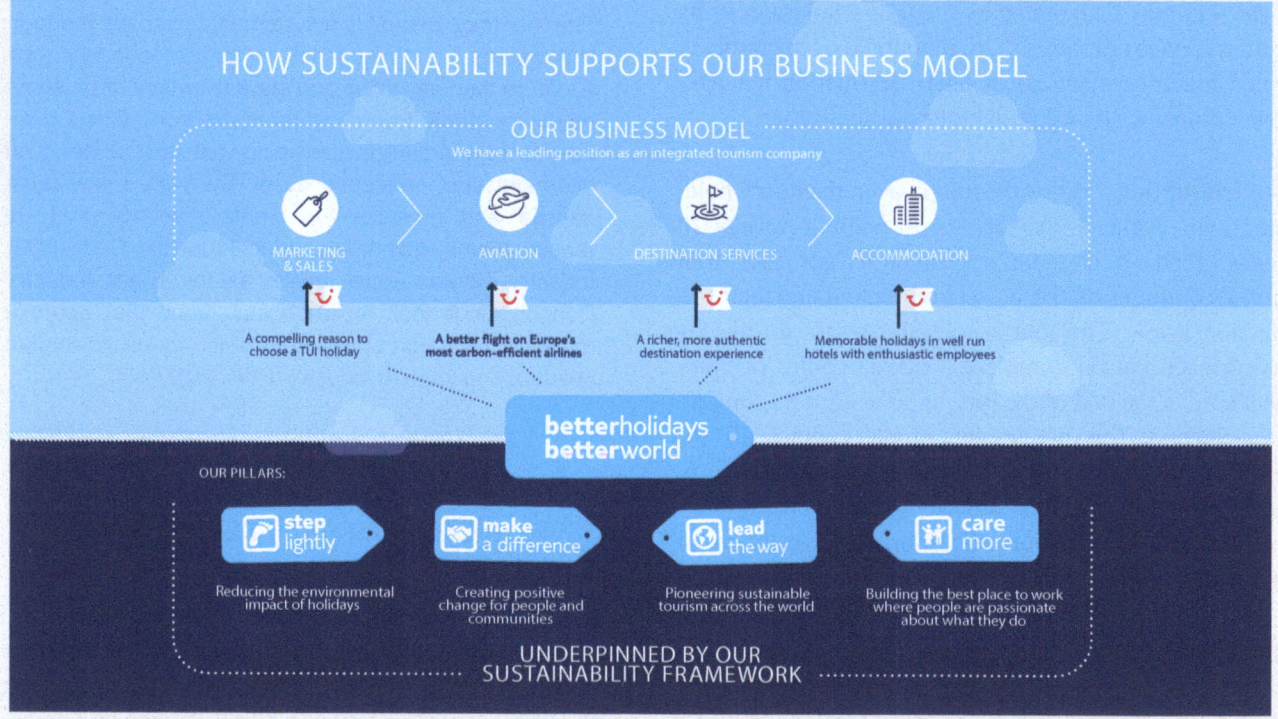

The results of these programs are impressive (see illustration on following page).

The connection between sustainability and the consumer experience is critical. As Jane Ashton, Director of Sustainable Development in the TUI Group says

> Having worked hard over the years to develop more sustainable holiday offerings, our aspiration moving forward is to bring the product advantages of sustainability more to life for our customers, driving greater awareness and appreciation of how sustainability enhances the authenticity and enjoyment of their experience, whilst improving the benefits for host communities.

Travel Intermediaries: Meetings, Conventions, and Events

The meetings, event, and convention sector of the tourism system requires a specialist set of skills and has its own distribution network. Professional Conference Organizers and Meeting planners tend to work for associations or corporations, either directly or through specialist companies serving the market.

Professional Conference Organizers (PCOs) are specialists in creating conferences that meet an organization's objectives. The majority of conventions are initiated by associations. For many associations, conferences are critical to the vibrancy and financial health of organizations. Meeting Planners tend to specialize in business meetings and events.

Think about This

1. TUI Group is committed to sustainability. What challenges do you think TUI Managers may have implementing sustainability policies in a large company like TUI?
2. How could TUI group use its influence to encourage sustainable practices by its clients? What about by its suppliers?
3. How might TUI Groups initiates align with the United Nations SDGs? Consider your answer and then check out the Better Holidays Better World 2016 Report to see how the TUI Group uses the SDGs.

Source

Better Holidays Better World 2016 Report by TUI Group. Copyright © 2017 by TUI Group. Reprinted by permission.

Functions of Convention-Meeting Planners. Organizing a conference or meeting can be considered a project—often a large, complex project—and so meeting and event planners can be considered experts in project management. The major functions of convention-meeting planners are to develop, coordinate, implement, and evaluate conventions and meetings of various sizes and types. There are three distinct stages to this function.

Convention-Meeting Planning. Convention-meeting planners prepare and administer budgets for each event. They coordinate the selection of sites, hotels, meeting and exhibit space, and other suppliers. They also develop bid packages or *requests for proposals* and conduct *site inspections*. They negotiate with hotels, airlines, audiovisual suppliers, meeting facility managers, and other suppliers to get the best deals for their groups. Planners may set up committees to help with the design of speaker, sponsorship, entertainment, and guest programs. Convention-meeting planners design promotions and communicate this information to company employees or association members. For conventions, exhibitions, conferences, and SMERF (social, military, educational, religious, fraternal) markets, this role involves promotions to build attendance to acceptable levels.

Meeting Execution and Onsite Coordination. The convention-meeting planner plays a crucial role during

> ### Meetings Associations
>
> There are several associations of professional convention-meeting planners around the world. In North America, the largest and most important organizations include Meeting Professionals International and the Professional Convention Management Association. An umbrella association of all event and meeting industry-related associations, The Event Industry Council, formerly known as the Convention Industry Council, operates the Certified Meeting Professional® program, while Meeting Professionals International offers the Certification in Meeting Management designation. The major organization based in Europe is the International Congress and Convention Association, located in Amsterdam.

the staging of each event as the liaison between the sponsoring association or company and the service providers at the destination. This person is key in ensuring that the event runs as it was planned and that unexpected problems are corrected.

Convention-Meeting Evaluation. As with incentive travel, the convention-meeting planner must carefully evaluate the success of each event after its completion. A cost-benefit analysis is prepared and may include a comparison of costs with the revenues created through registration and other participant services.

FIGURE 16.3 Meeting and event planners organize tradeshows and other events for associations and businesses to view.

Travel Intermediaries: The Sharing Economy

In recent years, the growth of new technologies has enabled many people who were previously not part of the tourism system to offer new services. Airbnb is a great example of such a company. Originally established in 2008 by Brian Chesky and Joe Gebbia as a way to allow travelers to connect with people willing to share a room in a town or city (e.g., San Francisco) in which all the hotel rooms were booked out; today Airbnb operates in 191 countries and offers over 4,000,000 accommodation listings.

While often compared to hotel companies, Airbnb is a very different type of company. Airbnb is primarily a technology-based sharing platform. Its business model is based on a commission that is paid as a result of the transaction between the guest and the host. They are using their platform to extend their product offerings to tours provided by hosts and other services.

While Airbnb is one of the largest of this new type of intermediary, the type of technology that supports them has enabled a wide range of new companies to enter the tourism system.

Travel Intermediaries: Tourism Media

One of the functions of intermediaries, in addition to facilitating sales, is to distribute information. While many of the tourism intermediaries we have already examined provide information to their channel members or consumers, tourism media companies specialize in information dissemination. Travel is an appealing topic to consumers and so there are a variety of outlets for consumer-focused tourism stories and content. Consumer-focused media include television programming, blogs, newspapers, travel magazines, and guidebooks. In addition, most countires have specialty media providing information to the travel trade.

Consumer Travel Media. Travel has become an important part of many people's lifestyles, and learning about travel is a source of entertainment and recreation for many people. The consumer travel media plays an important role in disseminating information, often considered trusted sources of information. It is also an important mechanism for building awareness for tourism products and destinations. Consumer-focused travel content can be found along a range of approaches. Programs or magazines dedicated to travel and (armchair)

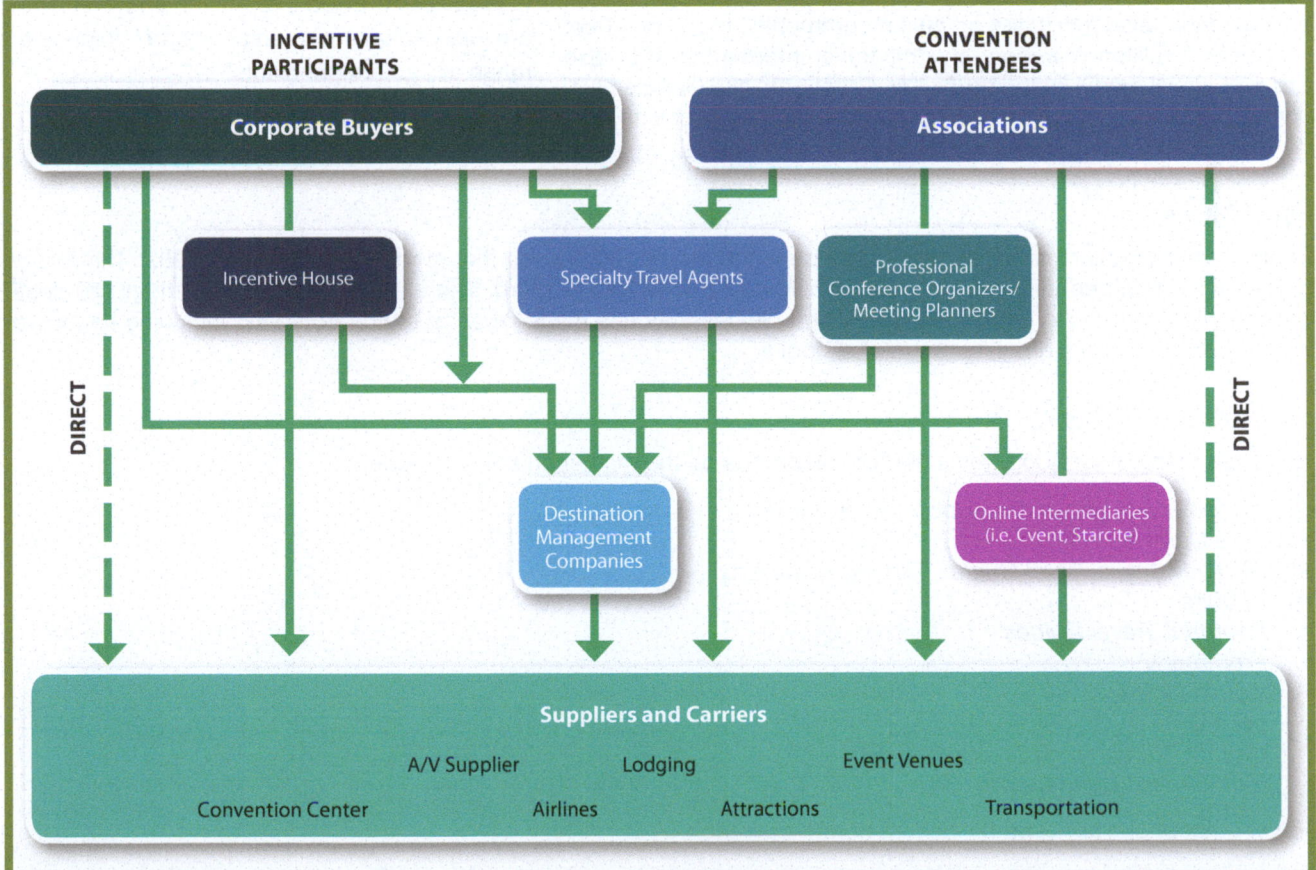

FIGURE 16.4 The Tourism Distribution System: Incentive Travel and Conventions

The Power of Travel Guidebooks

Popular travel guides like *Lonely Planet* and the *Rough Guides* are often taken by visitors on their trips and referred to often. They are also very influential in pre-trip planning as an information source, ranking just after the Internet in order of importance. The main appeals of travel guidebooks are the detailed contents on specific destinations and their impartiality. Are travel guidebooks also a form of tourism promotion? The answer is both "yes" and "no." So let's explore this conundrum in more detail.

Lonely Planet

Lonely Planet is perhaps the best-known travel guidebook on a worldwide basis. It was founded by Tony and Maureen Wheeler in the early 1970s. Today it is a global media company owned by NC2 Media and operates around the world. *Lonely Planet* now publishes over 500 books for 195 countries, and you will see them in the hands of many tourists around the globe. But *Lonely Planet* does more than just produce books. Using the company's understanding of traveler's needs it provides information over a wide range of mediums. It has a magazine, produces several television shows, and dispenses much information through its digital platforms. More than 17 million people visit Lonely Planet.com each month and more than 10 million *Lonely Planet* apps have been downloaded. *Lonely Planet's Flipboard* channel has over 3.2 million flips per month. *Lonely Planet* also facilitates an online community, the Thorn Tree, with over 1 million members sharing travel information. It is also active in social media including Twitter, Facebook, and Google Plus. *Lonely Planet* also has an online partnership with booking.com allowing people using their website to book immediately.

Guidebooks provide information on travel. They are information intermediaries and influence a range of tourism behaviors.

Rough Guides

Another very popular brand of travel guidebooks is the *Rough Guides* that started publishing in 1982. The *Rough Guides* were founded in England by Mark Ellingham and Martin Dunford. There are guides for more than 120 destinations worldwide. Like *Lonely Planet, Rough Guides* now has many types of digital contents, including its award-winning website and a growing range of e-books.

Other Travel Guidebooks

There are many other good travel guidebook brands on the market and they include:

* *Avalon Travel Publishing (Moon Travel Guides)*
* *Blue Guides*
* *DK Eyewitness Travel Guides* (Dorling Kindersley)
* *Fodor's*
* *Footprint Travel Guides*
* *Frommer's*
* *Insight Guides*
* *Let's Go*
* *National Geographic Traveler*
* *Rick Steves' Guidebooks*

Travel guidebooks are used by visitors during their trips.

Think about This

1. Travel guidebooks have a powerful influence on where tourists go and how they spend their money. What are the main appeals of travel guidebooks to tourists in print and digital formats?
2. The publishers of the main travel guidebooks always stress the impartiality of their contents. Are there any steps that a tourism destination or company can take to get positive coverage in travel guidebooks?
3. Tablets, like iPads and smartphones, are becoming a more popular way to view travel guidebooks. Do you think that digital versions of travel guidebooks will eventually replace printed book copies? Why or why not?
4. How can a tourism destination or company promote positive contents written about it in major travel guidebooks?

Sources

Lonelyplanet.com

roughguides.com

---

travelers are common, as are "short format" articles or segments in magazines or television shows.

Increasingly, media companies use a variety of platforms to share their content—with print media available online and online media available in print—but some of the key information intermediaries are outlined as follows.

Travel Programming. In some countries, travel shows are among the most popular shows on television. They provide practical tips on travel and showcase new destinations. Travel-related programming is also a staple of cable television. In recent years, some of the biggest celebrities have come from programming that highlights the experience available while traveling.

Newspapers and Travel Magazines. Travel sections have been an important component of newspapers, particularly weekend editions of newspapers, for some time. These sections often include longer form articles and shorter tips and reviews. Although newspaper

FIGURE 16.5 Travel agents provide personalized service and specialty knowledge.

circulations are declining, online reading of newspapers is increasing. A story featuring your travel product in the *New York Times* travel section is a highly valued publicity. Magazines that target affluent readers with travel-related content have graced coffee tables for years. These magazines feature luxury resorts, new experiences, and dining options.

Guidebooks. Guidebooks provide practical information for travelers ready to go. Most include some information on the culture of the destination as well as specific reviews of tourism products. Frommer's and Fodor's travel guides grew in popularity as travel boomed in the 1960s, and today guidebook companies like Lonely Planet and Rough Guides, as well as books specializing in specific interests, are available throughout the world. The influence of these guidebooks on the development of many destinations has been substantial.

Travel Blogs. Travel blogs are increasingly important to the dissemination of travel-related information as blogging grows in popularity and individual bloggers gain influence.

In addition to consumer media, the travel system is served by a variety of media focused on communicating with other travel industry intermediaries.

Travel Trade Publications. In many markets, the retail travel trade is served by travel industry magazines. The meetings market in many markets also has trade publications focusing on the specific needs of meeting, incentive, or convention planners. While consumer magazines tend to be inspirational and aspirational, trade publications tend to be focused on specific details of offers, new product details, and industry trends. Travel trade e-newsletters function in a similar manner, often providing daily information to travel agents or meeting planners.

QUICK TRIP 16.7

New Intermediaries in the Sharing Economy

The growth of the sharing economy has been an important trend in recent years and nowhere has the impact been bigger than in the tourism system. New technology has created platforms that allow people with spare capacity—rooms, couches, drivers—to connect with people that need these services. Among the largest of the sharing economy companies are Airbnb, which allows people to share rooms and Uber, a ride-sharing company.

These new types of intermediaries, based on technology-enabled sharing platforms, have been very popular with both buyers and sellers. But the new product categories are disruptive to established providers of competitive products, such as hotels and taxi companies. Destination communities, and their legal systems, are also working through how to deal with these new businesses in the tourism system.

The growth of these platforms has been impressive. For example, Airbnb, founded in 2008, is a global platform—with rooms listed in 191 countries. In 2016, Airbnb had more than 2 million rooms available for rent. By comparison, in that same year, Marriott, the largest hotel company after its merger with Starwood, had 1,112,613 rooms available (Chafkin 2016). In the years since 2016 Airbnb has continued its meteoric growth—in 2018 it reported 4 million room listings and noted that it had served over 260 million guests (2018).

No matter how disruptive these new technologies and the products they have enabled may be, it seems they have become important parts of the tourism system.

Airbnb has become an important travel intermediary for a new product category—shared accommodation.

Think about This

1. Compare a sharing economy product with its non-sharing economy competitor (You may compare Uber with a Taxi or Airbnb with a hotel room). What are positives and negatives of the sharing economy product versus the traditional product.
2. Does Airbnb compete directly with hotel companies? Give a reason for your answer.
3. Airbnb is facing a number of issues as it establishes itself in the marketplace. Some of the questions facing the company include: should Airbnb rooms be taxed like hotel rooms? What level of safety requirements should be required in an Airbnb property? Do Airbnb rooms in a community raise the cost of rent for local residents? Choose one of these issues, or another that you have heard about, and research it. In your opinion how should Airbnb respond?

The tourism system is adjusting to new sharing economy entrants. Airports are providing places for Uber and Lyft pickups.

Source

"Airbnb Newsroom: Fast Facts." 2018. https://press.atairbnb.com/fast-facts/

Chafkin, M. 2016. "Airbnb Opens Up the World." *Fast Company*.

SUMMARY

The tourism system has a complex distribution network with many different types of companies working to connect consumers with tourism experiences. Tourism providers must develop distribution strategies that enable their companies to meet their marketing goals and work in collaboration with distribution channel members. As changes come to the tourism system, intermediaries must adapt to changing circumstances. For example, the business model for travel agents has changed as the needs of suppliers and consumers have changed. Success for travel agents, and all members of distribution networks, is providing value that justifies the costs associated with the provision of the service. Many companies specialize in specific tasks or functions in the system to provide the greatest value to their channel partners. For example, PCOs are experts in conference organizations, and travel management companies have specialist knowledge of managing the travel costs of businesses.

ACTIVITIES

1. Select a major tour operator or wholesaler company in your country. Collect the brochures and other printed materials of the company. From these materials, what are the company's specialties in terms of destinations and market segments?
2. What types of tour arrangements does the company offer (e.g., escorted tours, FITs)?
3. Would you or your family be likely to travel with this tour operator? Why or why not?
4. What tours and packages does the company promote on its website?
5. Can the tours and packages be bought online? If not, how can they be booked?
6. What customer guarantees or promises does the company offer online?

REFERENCES

ADMEI. 2017. Media/News. http://www.adme.org/aws/ADME/pt/sp/news

Chipkin, H. 2017. Travel Weekly's 2017 Power List. http://www.travelweekly.com/PowerList2017

Macke, D. 2015. *The Business Traveler—US,* July 2015. mintel.com

Morrison, A. 2010. *Hospitality and Tourism Marketing* (4th ed.). Clifton Park, NY: Delmar.

PWC. 2011. Economic Significance of Meetings to the U.S. Economy.

Schmidt, A. 2015. What Business Model Does Expedia Follow? http://marketrealist.com/2015/09/business-model-expedia-follow/

CHAPTER SEVENTEEN

Traveling—Transportation Modes and Carriers

Mobility and Travel Alternatives

I travel not to go anywhere, but to go. I travel for travel's sake. The great affair is to move.

ROBERT LOUIS STEVENSON

YOUR LEARNING DESTINATION

You will learn what factors in choosing forms—or modes—of transport. You'll also learn about the major forms of transportation in the tourism system. We look at how sometimes transportation can be the journey but sometimes it is the destination.

WHAT YOU NEED TO KNOW

Having read this chapter, you will be able to:

- ✔ Describe the factors that contribute to choices of types of travel.
- ✔ Identify the key ways people travel in the tourism system.
- ✔ Describe ways that travel can be an important tourism experience.
- ✔ Identify ways travel can be more sustainable.

BREAKING THE ICE

In the classic *Around the World in Eighty Days,* Jules Verne proposes an almost unimaginable idea—that you could travel around the world, from London to London, in just eighty days! Today, Phineas Fogg could do his trip in less than a day and you could be on the other side of the world tomorrow if you wanted. Of course, while Phineas Fogg found love on the trip, he didn't stop to enjoy the travel experience. In many cases today, travel is the destination. Luxury trains, customized tours, and ocean and river cruises are just some of the amazing tourism experiences that take place while you are moving.

KEY TAKEAWAY POINTS

- Travel has never been easier and travels have more options than ever before.
- The type of travel you choose may be influenced by its functional utility, aesthetic or emotional appeals, social factors, situational factors, and curiosity.
- Travel may be purely functional—a means to get from A to B—or traveling itself can be the tourism experience the consumer is seeking.
- Airlines are an important means of travel and aviation is expected to continue to grow significantly in the coming years.
- Trains are enjoying a new phase in their story—with many countries developing high-speed rail systems. The experience of traveling by rail also appeals to some travelers and slower but luxurious rail experiences are available around the world.

- Drive tourism is the foundation of many tourism industries, particularly in the developed world. Changes to automobiles in the coming years will impact drive tourism.

- Cruise travel continues to grow, with river cruising growth outpacing ocean cruising. As cruise ships grow in size, the number of variety of experiences available onboard continues to expand.

- Touring is adapting to changing tastes of travelers. Tour operators are providing greater flexibility and customization in their product offerings.

- In the coming years, space tourism will be available to more people . . . maybe.

GETTING AROUND: MOBILITY IN THE MODERN WORLD

There is no doubt that it is easier to travel today than ever before. The "tyranny" of distance has been significantly reduced. It took months to cross the North American continent before the arrival of the train. The transcontinental train reduced that to about four days, and today you can buy a flight that takes about six hours.

Of course, it is not just that travel is faster and easier than ever before. Over the last fifty years, most countries have encouraged visitors and reduced legal barriers to entry. The requirement for visas and other permission to enter have reduced or become more streamlined—particularly for leisure travelers.

• Choosing Travel Options

You travel for a variety of reasons. Sometimes it's to get from A to B; we just need to decide the most efficient way to reach our destination. Other times, the journey itself is the experience we seek.

Why do people select one transportation mode over another for business and pleasure/personal trips? Many theories have been put forward on mode selection decision processes. It is suggested that mode selection is influenced by four variables: characteristics of the mode, destination features, characteristics of those taking the trip, and characteristics of the trip itself (Kelly, Haider, and Williams 2007). In terms of the mode, people are influenced by such things as travel time, cost, frequency, convenience, flexibility, comfort, and safety of the various options available.

Factors at the destination also influence choice. These include whether development at the destination is dispersed or compact. The former would lead to people taking a car, whereas the latter would incline people toward taking public transportation. The presence or lack of transportation infrastructure is also a factor. The

presence of inner city vehicle charges (like those in London), constraints on parking, and the availability of walking and biking trails all have an impact. Parking fees and the availability of public transportation also are part of the decision.

Socioeconomic variables—how much money people can afford to spend, how able they are to walk—as well as situational factors, motivation for travel, and personal values and attitudes factor into the equation. Some people are strongly committed to the idea of public transportation while others are not. A business traveler is unlikely to have the same value perceptions as a pleasure traveler. Speed or time and departure and arrival times may be important to the business traveler, whereas cost/price may be the pleasure traveler's first criterion.

Finally, the characteristics of the trip come into play. These include the size and composition of the travel party, how long the stay is, how accessible the accommodations are, what activities will be undertaken during the vacation, and whether or not several destinations will be visited. People who intend to take part in activities that require a great deal of equipment are more likely to use private transportation. Traveling to a destination using public transportation may, in fact, constrain people in their choice of activity.

One useful classification of selection variables and values has been put forth by Sheth (1975). Sheth's explanation of the transportation mode decision-making process is illustrated in Figure 17.1. He suggests that travelers choose a travel mode based on the actual performance compared to the desired performance on five dimensions, namely the functional, aesthetic/emotional, social/organizational, situational, and curiosity utilities of the alternative modes. The *functional utility* of a mode is simply its likely performance for a specific purpose. Departure and arrival times, safety records, the directness of routes, and the absence of stops or

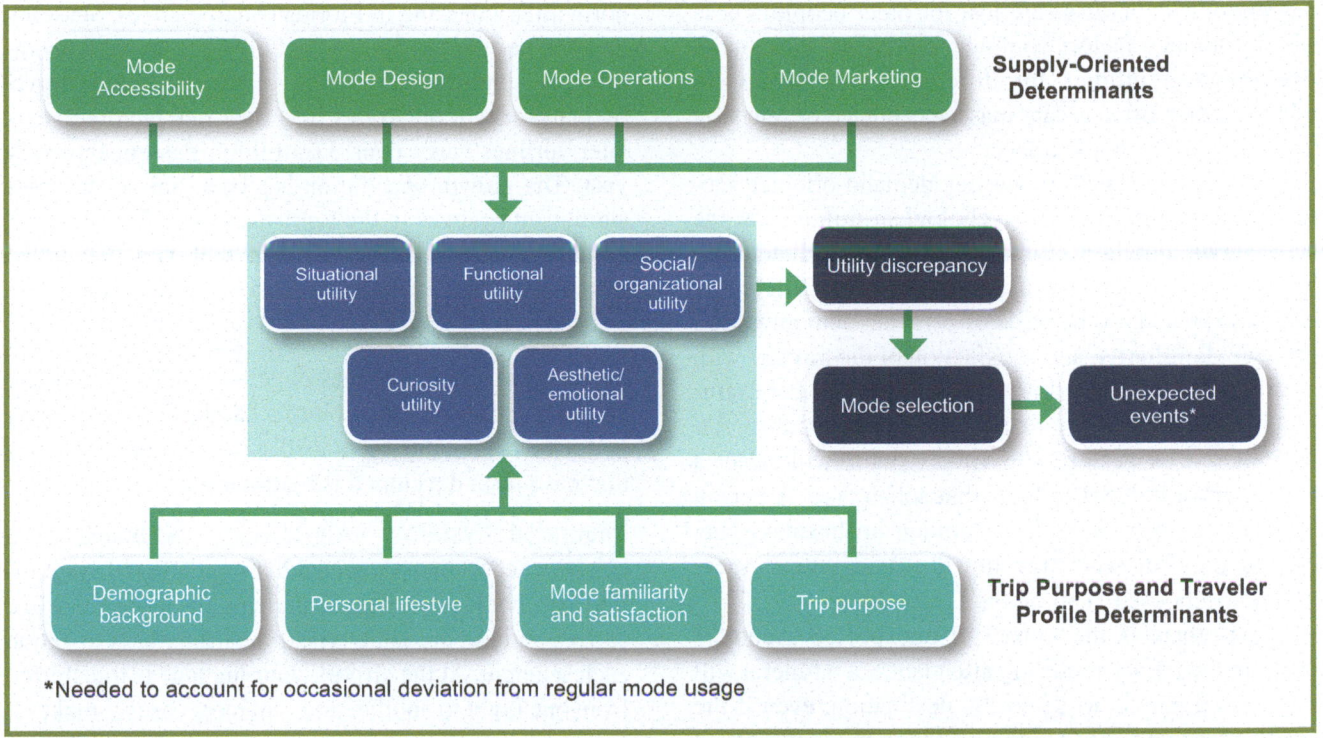

FIGURE 17.1 Travel mode selection model. | *Source:* Sheth, J. N. 1975. A Psychological Model of Travel Mode Selection. In *Advances in Consumer Research, vol. 3.* Proceedings of the Association for Consumer Research, Sixth Annual Conference. 426.

transfers are examples of functional considerations. The functional utility is the net outcome of the positive and negative evaluations the user makes of a particular mode.

Aesthetic or *emotional* reasons relate to such things as fear and social concerns that affect fundamental values of the individual. Often, users associate strong emotional feelings derived from early experiences with a mode of travel. Associations are also developed by early childhood socialization processes. These values often manifest themselves in terms of such things as style, interior and exterior decoration, comfort, luxury, and safety.

Social or *organizational utilities* refer to the stereotypes attributed to various transportation modes. For example, motor coach tours and cruises have been stereotyped as being a mode of transportation and vacation type for persons of retirement age. This may dissuade younger people from taking motor coach tours and cruises.

Situational utilities refer to the locational convenience of the mode and its terminal facilities to the traveler—the *total* set of activities associated with a trip. This might relate to the time in getting to and from the airport as a disincentive to fly. It is similar to the

functional utilities except that the stress is on the activities that are antecedent and subsequent to the actual travel itself.

Curiosity utility concerns the traveler's tendency to try something because it is new and different. This feeling is usually short-lived.

The model presumes that the individual has desired expectations on these five utilities. It also presumes the discrepancy between the image or perception of the utility and the actual experience determines the extent to which that mode of travel is acceptable or not.

Certain supply-oriented and trip-purpose/traveler profile factors influence the traveler's utility assessments. The availability of the mode—the number and convenience of flights, for example—influences the perception of functional and situational utilities. Mode design, including the variety of products or services offered to customers, affects the image of functional, curiosity, and aesthetic/emotional utilities. The way the mode is operated—on-time departures, quality of services, careful handling of the traveler's luggage—influence perceptions of functional and situational utilities. For example, advertisements for cruises that show young people onboard having a great time may dispel perceptions that cruises are just for older people. These supply-oriented factors combine to generate differential psychological utilities for different travel modes. In addition, they often create mass acceptance or rejection of a mode in the marketplace.

In a similar fashion, various demand-oriented factors produce differential psychological utilities for the same mode among a cross-section of users, leading to acceptance by some and rejection by others. Differences can be expected on the basis of personal demographics, lifestyle, familiarity, and satisfaction of the traveler with a particular mode, and the purpose of the trip. For example, income level will influence the mode of transportation chosen. A person who values status will select a way of traveling that reflects that self-image. A person traveling from New York to London on business may choose to fly but, when traveling the same route on vacation, may choose to sail on the Queen Mary.

Last, there is the impact of unexpected events. A death in the family requiring attendance at a funeral will influence a person to fly to the destination, even if the cost is perceived as too high or if the individual is afraid of flying.

GETTING THERE: PLANES, TRAINS, AND AUTOMOBILES

Our ability to get from one place to another has grown by quantum leaps in the last 200 years. In 1807, the first fare-paying, passenger railway, the Swansea and Mumbles Railway, began operation in Wales. The original Mumbles train was powered by a horse, but soon trains were being powered by steam locomotives. The growth of rail changed travel forever. The twentieth century saw the growth of the automobile and air travel. The tyranny of distance was being overcome. These changes in transportation changed the tourism system in innumerable ways. Today, many of the elements of the tourism system—from the grand hotels built by Canadian Pacific along its route in Canada to hotels on every interchange on the United States highway system—have been influenced by planes, trains, or automobiles.

PLANES AND THE PASSENGER AVIATION SYSTEM

In 1914 the first scheduled commercial flight took off from St. Petersburg and landed in Tampa Bay, Florida. The St. Petersburg-Tampa Airboat Line served about 1,200 passengers in the four months it operated and eventually went out of business as its market returned

north after wintering in Florida (Sharpe 2012). Seasonal demand has always been a challenge for tourism operations. Despite this humble beginning, passenger travel by plane caught on. Today, just over one hundred years later, airlines carry over 3.69 billion passengers every year. The growth of aviation has been one of the most significant changes in the tourism system. The complex system of airline services mean that you can travel almost anywhere in the world and be there tomorrow.

• Airline Operations

For many of us, the process of getting to the airport and boarding a flight can be a bit of a hassle. Even so, taking just a few moments to consider the complex systems that have been developed is worthwhile.

Integrated Systems. Air travel is facilitated by a complex set of interconnected but standardized systems. You can book your flights, perhaps on more than one carrier, and use the same type of boarding pass to get on each segment. At the airport, your luggage is transferred from one flight to another and—in most cases—makes it to the destination at the same time as you.

Hubs and Spokes. There is an old joke that even when you go to heaven you'll probably go through Dallas/Fort Worth. So why do so many flights require passengers to go via another airport? As airlines expanded their reach from local regions to transcontinental and international destinations, it was clear that direct flights were not the best way to operate. Hub airports are an efficient way to connect people with destinations. They also allow airlines to serve more destinations.

This hub and spoke approach is evident in both domestic and international air routes. Chicago, Dallas/Fort Worth, and Atlanta are all hubs in the United States. London's Heathrow is the hub between flights originating in Europe and those originating across the Atlantic. Gulf state airports—Dubai and Abu Dhabi, of instance—and Asian airports like Hong Kong are important international hubs.

How does it work? Imagine a small network with nine destinations (see Figure 17.2). In order to create a direct connection between each destination, you would need to have twenty-eight routes. But, by adding a hub at the middle of that network, the number of flights reduces from twenty-eight to just eight (HeathrowAirport 2014).

Airline Alliances

While air travel requires a high level of cooperation between all carriers, the growth of global airline alliances has been an important phenomenon. Airline

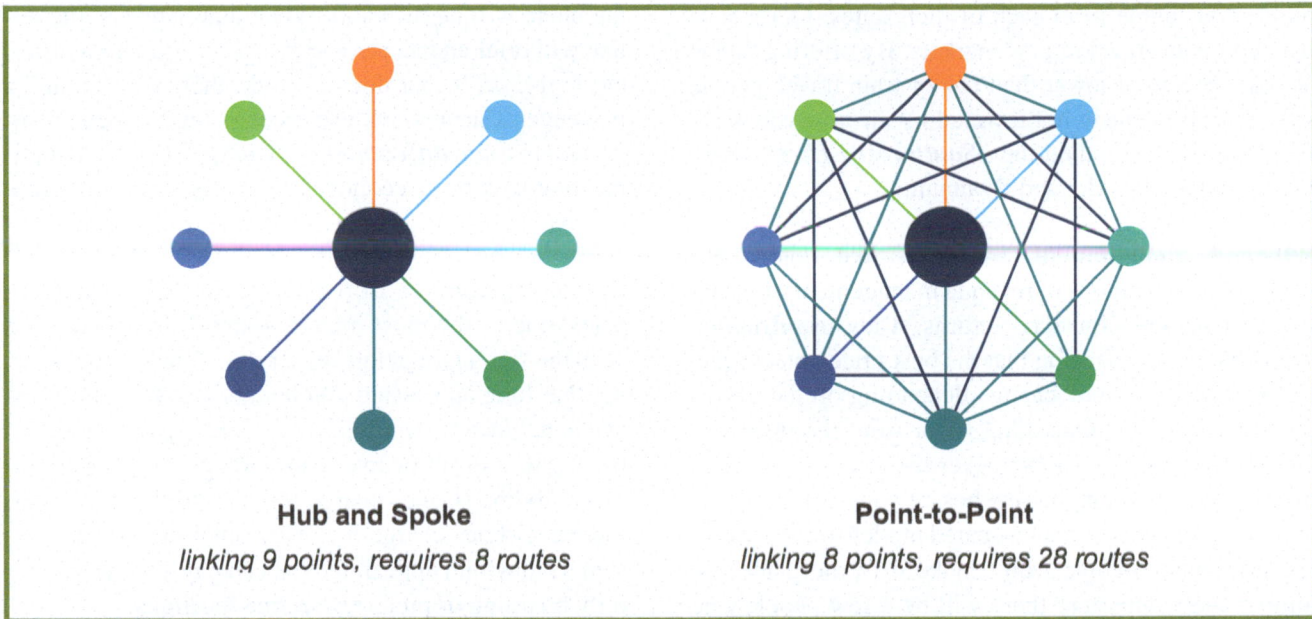

Hub and Spoke

linking 9 points, requires 8 routes

Point-to-Point

linking 8 points, requires 28 routes

FIGURE 17.2 Hub and Spoke systems versus Point-to-Point. | Source: Heathrow Airport your heathrow.com/what-makes-a-hub-airport/

networks are most valuable when they reach the widest set of destinations. So how do you extend the number of destinations if there are places your carrier just can't reach? Join an alliance with a carrier that can and "share" the flight. This type of code-sharing, in which two carriers share the same flight, was one of the drivers of airline alliances. If you have ever booked a flight on one carrier and arrived at the airport and found that the flight was operated by another carrier, you were probably on a code-share flight. For example, Air Canada (AC) is a member of Star Alliance, as are United Airlines (UA) and Air New Zealand (NZ). You could book a trip from Toronto to Auckland—with AC flight numbers for each segment—and travel on planes operated by Air Canada, United, and Air New Zealand before your trip was done.

Starting in the late 1990s, many airlines joined alliances. The three biggest alliances are Star Alliance, Oneworld, and SkyTeam. In addition to code-sharing, many alliances work to achieve greater marketing and operational integration.

Airline Profitability

Despite the growth in passengers, over much of its history the airline industry has struggled to be profitable. In recent years airlines have done better through a series of actions that include adopting new business models, revenue management, and charging for de-aggregated services and value-added services. The strategies are outlined below.

Flag Carriers

Many countries have a carrier that is owned, is partially owned, or was once owned by the government. Even after airlines are privatized they may be considered a flag carrier. It's pretty easy to see that Air Canada, Air New Zealand, and British Airways are all examples of flag carriers. One flag carrier that is less obvious is Australia's Qantas, an acronym of Queensland and Northern Territory Air Service. The United States does not have a flag carrier.

New Business Models. In recent years, airlines have adopted a variety of new business models designed to either increase operational efficiency or attract new customers.

While *Legacy Carriers*—Delta, United, and American—still provide a full range of services, some carriers have chosen different approaches. *Low Cost Carriers* (LCC): The growth of low-cost business models has been one of the most important additions to the aviation system. Low Cost Carriers (LCCs) tend to focus on short-haul routes, although there is a growing number of LCCs serving international routes. LCCs follow a model of low costs of operation and marketing, ensuring that their aircraft carry as many people as possible and that the planes are used with as little downtime as possible. Some LCCs use secondary airports to keep costs low, while others use primary airports but maximize the number of flights from each of their gates. LCCs have opened up air travel to new markets. By offering flights at costs as low or lower than bus or train travel, people who have previously not traveled by air now choose to fly. This effect is called the *"Southwest Effect."* Other LCCs include EasyJet and Ryannair.

Revenue Management. Airlines, like hotels, use sophisticated methods of revenue management to ensure the best possible financial returns. They use *dynamic pricing* models, meaning that the best price you can pay for a given flight may change depending on the day of the week you buy. One thing is for sure: the price you pay for your seat is almost never the same as the price paid by the person in the seat beside you.

Airlines also use sophisticated models for determining how many people won't make it to the plane. On almost every departure there will be a few people who have something come up and who can't make it to the flight before it leaves. Airlines develop models to determine how many seats they can sell in anticipation of the people who won't make it. The airline actually sells more seats than it has on any given flight. This is called *overselling*. Most of the time this works because of the sophistication of the modeling, but every now and then the plane will be oversold. When that happens, the airline will offer an incentive to passengers to take a different flight, or, if that doesn't work, they will "bump" a passenger. Carriers are also recognizing the benefits of providing more *differentiated seating*. They are experimenting with basic economy, economy, preferred economy, economy plus, business class, and first-class seats.

De-Aggregation of Services. In the last couple of years, one of the most important trends in aviation has been the "de-aggregation" of services. There was a time, not that long ago, when you bought a ticket on a flight and it included transportation of your luggage, a meal on the flight, a drink or two, and perhaps some entertainment. Today, airlines charge for each of these services. Indeed, airlines charge for many other things that consumers may find appealing. You can pay a fee to get priority boarding or preferred seating locations.

Sustainability and Aviation

One of the challenges of the aviation industry is its contribution to sustainability, particularly environmental sustainability. According to the International Air

FIGURE 17.3 Aviation creates global connectivity in the tourism system.

QUICK TRIP 17.1

The Future of Aviation

The International Air Transport Association (IATA) projects that demand for passenger flights will double in the coming twenty years and expects 7.2 billion passengers in 2035. A lot of that growth will come from the developing world. If growth projections are correct, China will be the largest air travel market by 2024; India, with one of the fastest projected growth forecasts, will be the third largest market by 2025; and Indonesia will be a top-five market by the middle of the 2020s (IATA 2016).

Boeing and Airbus are the two largest airline manufacturers. Their products, aircraft, are very high cost capital purchases for the airlines that buy them, and the product development time for aircraft is long. For instance, Airbus' A380 took over ten years to develop. These companies must look strategically to the future and both companies provide market forecasts for the coming twenty years. What do the airlines predict for the period to 2035?

Air traffic will double in the next twenty years.

- There will be demand for over 32,000 new aircraft in the coming twenty years. That will double the number of passenger aircraft currently in the air.
- Asia/Pacific will drive the demand. This region accounts for almost 40 percent of the new planes.
- The greatest growth will be in smaller, single aisle planes. Airbus projects a market of almost 23,000 new single aisle planes, with 8,100 new twin aisle planes and 1,600 very large aircraft (Airbus 2015).
- Airbus notes that air traffic growth is driven by three factors: economics; demographic changes in air travelers including population growth, urbanization, and the growth of the middle class in developing countries like China and India; and greater connectivity between people and regions.
- It is expected that air travel will double in the coming fifteen years (Boeing 2015).

Think about This

1. What changes will the tourism system need to make to accommodate this growth?
2. Assuming the projections are accurate, what potential pitfalls do you see in these projections and how can they be overcome?
3. Aviation is the biggest contributor to greenhouse gases in the tourism system. How might the airline manufacturers respond to issues of climate change?

Sources

Airbus. 2015. Global Market Forecast: Flying by the Numbers 2015–2034. Airbus.

Boeing. 2015. Current Market Outlook 2015-2034. Seattle, WA: Boeing.

IATA. 2016. "IATA Forecasts Passenger Demand to Double Over 20 years." International Air Transport Association (IATA) accessed 10/21/2017. http://www.iata.org/pressroom/pr/Pages/2016-10-18-02.aspx

Transport Association, the aviation sector considers its greatest sustainability challenge is reducing greenhouse gas (GHG) emissions. The aviation sector is the largest contributor to GHG and climate change in the tourism system. The industry has set ambition targets to mitigate CO2 emissions. It is seeking to improve fuel efficiency, cap emissions at 2020, and reduce emissions by 50 percent by 2050. The airline industry has worked hard to reduce GHGs and has made incremental improvements in energy efficiency. Unfortunately, those gains in reducing carbon per passenger mile traveled have been overwhelmed by the increase in the number of passenger miles flown. The industry is pursuing alternative fuels and committing to carbon offsetting to achieve its goals.

Systems Thinking and Aviation— Preparing for the Arrival of the A380

The Airbus A380 ushered in a new generation of double-deck, wide-body jets. The A380 accommodates up to 550 people in a standard three class configuration. In preparation for the new generation of aircraft, airports around the world needed to undertake major redevelopment of terminals and systems (Gopwani 2005). San Francisco spent $2.1 billion on new terminals and other items to accommodate the generation vehicles. London Heathrow plans to spend $800 million for enhancements that include double-decker passenger ramps and enlarged baggage conveyors. New customs facilities are also required at many terminals to process the larger number of passengers (Phillips 2005).

TRAINS AND PASSENGER RAIL SYSTEMS

Trains provide an important form of transportation for many parts of the tourism system. The mode of land-based transportation trains are among the most cost-effective and environmentally friendly travel options.

Rail Operations

Some call the early years of the twentieth century the golden age of passenger rail. Certainly, in this period before the rise of car and air travel, the impact of train travel was at its greatest. Nevertheless, in many parts of the world, passenger rail transportation is enjoying a renaissance.

Perhaps more than other modes of transportation, the story of rail varies by country and region. Trains opened up the North American continent from its Atlantic to Pacific coasts, and they were the major stimulant in the nineteenth and early twentieth centuries to vacations within the United States, Canada, and Europe. They also provided critical links from major centers in Asia.

The first transcontinental route in the United States was completed in 1869. In the 1800s, it took ten days (240 hours) and $40 ($800 in 2011) to travel by train from New York to San Francisco. In 2011, it took seventy-three hours at a cost of $310. In 1929, the first year for which comprehensive train statistics are available, approximately 780.5 million paying passengers took the train. The heyday of the train in most of the major developed countries lasted approximately one hundred years, from the 1830s to the 1930s. In the 1920s and 1930s, the automobile began to gain more popularity as a passenger mode, mainly drawing away traffic from the train. Rail passenger traffic in the United States began to decline in the 1920s during what some people have called the "age of abundant energy." In the late 1950s, the number of route miles served by trains in the United States was surpassed by the number served by airlines. By 1963, the number of passengers carried intercity by airlines passed the number carried by trains. It was not until the mid-1970s to the early 1980s, which could be referred to as the "age of uncertain energy," that the slide in the popularity of the train as a passenger transportation mode seemed to be halted.

The demise of the railway as a passenger travel mode was so alarming that in 1958 the U.S. Interstate Commerce Commission (ICC) ordered a detailed study of the situation. The results of this study became known as the Hosmer Report, and it predicted the eventual disappearance of the train as a passenger travel mode in the United States. The recommendations of the Hosmer Report were never officially accepted, and it was not until 1970 that the federal government took some concrete action to improve the failing rail passenger travel business. In October 1970, the Rail Passenger Service Act became law. The act created the National Railroad Passenger Corporation, now commonly known as Amtrak. Amtrak began its operations in May 1971, and it was intended to be a profit-making corporation. In fiscal year (FY) 2016, Amtrak had 21,300 route miles across forty-six states and, in that year, carried 31.3 million passengers. Approximately 70 percent of the miles traveled by Amtrak trains are on rails owned by other railroads for which freight takes precedence over passengers. Due to wear and tear on those tracks, train speeds are low and on-time performance is poor. In FY2016, Amtrak had revenues of $3.24 billion and total expenses of $4.26 billion for a year-end loss of over $1 billion (Amtrak 2016).

QUICK TRIP 17.2

High-Speed Rail in the United States and Canada

Why doesn't the United States or Canada have the same high-speed rail services as China and Europe? Amtrak's Acela Express runs the Northeast Corridor from Washington, DC, to Boston reaching maximum speed of up to 150 mph, mainly in the stretch between Boston and New York, but other high-speed rail projects have failed to materialize.

Glenn Luk, an investment fund manager and self-confessed high-speed rail fan, identifies six important reasons why high-speed rail hasn't developed in the United States (Luk 2017).

They are:

Acela is Amtrak's high-speed rail along the Northeast Corridor.

- Lack of population density and so relatively small feeder markets.
- The United State's unique model of urban and suburban development. Many communities are spread out and not designed for train transportation.
- The strength of property rights. Many new train tracks would need to go through existing communities and—people's homes. Buying that land is expensive.
- Car culture and America's lingering obsession with the automobile.
- The lasting power of network effects. In addition to having a relatively low density of population, the United States cities are often distant from each other making developing networks of high-speed trains difficult.
- An existing rail network geared to long-haul commercial freight travel.

While these observations were made about the United States, many of the same issues are true in Canada and Australia.

Despite these challenges, several high-speed rail initiatives are in development. For example, there is a public initiative with the California High Speed Rail Authority planning to link Anaheim and San Francisco by 2029, and a private initiative, XpressWest to connect Las Vegas to Southern California. In Canada, there are plans to develop high-speed rail between Toronto and Windsor as early as 2025 (Fitzpatrick 2017).

Think about This

1. What are the advantages of high-speed rail travel to air travel? Compile a list of pros and cons.
2. Should government invest in high-speed rail? Development of this type of infrastructure is considered the role of the government. Compare the two projects in California and contrast their differing approaches to funding.
3. What impact on the tourism system will these projects have?

Sources

Fitzpatrick, M. 2017. "High-speed rail in Ontario, finally? Not so fast." CBCNews. http://www.cbc.ca/news/canada/high-speed-rail-in-ontario-finally-not-so-fast-1.4123920

Luk, G. 2017. "Why doesn't the United States have high-speed bullet trains like Europe and Asia?" *Forbes*.

Via Rail Canada, Canada's equivalent of Amtrak, is an independent crown corporation that was created in 1978. Both Amtrak and Via Rail have the sole national responsibility for marketing and providing intercity passenger rail transportation. Since their inception, both organizations have been successful in increasing passenger volumes that had been falling continuously beforehand. They have done so primarily by improving the equipment and services they offer, as well as by more effectively promoting the benefits of traveling by train. Recent promotions by Via Rail and Amtrak have emphasized the rest and relaxation benefits of taking the train. They have also begun to point out that the downtown-to-downtown routing of trains actually saves passengers' time.

• The Rise of High-Speed Rail

European and Asian governments have actively supported high-speed rail in large part because of high gas prices and dense populations. In 1964 the Japanese bullet train reached speeds of 130 mph. In 2007 the TGV in France recorded a record 357 mph, while in 2010 China's Beijing-Shanghai train hit 302 mph. In contrast, the Acela service between New York and Washington, DC, has a top speed of 150 mph, but old tracks often keep speeds at half that. By 2025, Japan plans a maglev (magnetic levitation) line between Tokyo and Nagoya with top speeds of 310 mph.

These trains travel faster than the automobile, and they actually cut down on the time that passengers would take to drive between the major cities. France's TGV and Japan's Shinkansen (Bullet Train) have an average speed of 186 mph, whereas German and Italian trains travel at speeds of 155 mph. In 2009, a marketing alliance of seven high-speed train operators was formed with an online reservation system for booking international train fares. Known as Railteam, the alliance consists of Eurostar; France's SNCF; Germany's Deutsche Bahn; and operators from Austria, Belgium, Switzerland, and the Netherlands. People are able to travel to more than one hundred destinations on one ticket. This development is significant as it will make it easier for trains to compete with air travel. It is estimated that at point-to-point journeys of under four-and-a-half hours, trains achieve a 50 percent market share when competing with air.

European and Asian governments have been active supporters of high-speed rail travel. It makes more sense in these countries compared to the United States because of high gas prices and dense populations, as previously mentioned. However, even in these countries, a number

© candybox images/Shutterstock.com

FIGURE 17.4 Relax and enjoy the space on a train.

of high-speed plans have been postponed because of the cost.

China, on the other hand, has added more than 22,000 kilometers, or 13,670 miles, of high-speed rail—and it plans to add even half as much again in the next couple of years. Not only does China have the most high-speed rail, but it has the fastest. The operating speed of the new "Fuxing" or "Rejuvenation" is 217 mph (Neuman 2017).

AUTOMOBILES AND THE HIGHWAY SYSTEM

The incredible freedom of being able to get in a car and explore has been one of the most important changes in the tourism system. As the influence of cars and road transportation has increased, people have enjoyed mobility that could have only been imagined by generations past.

Traveling by automobile is now the single most predominant travel mode in North America. Most travel surveys have shown that automobile trips account for over 85 percent of the pleasure and personal and business trips taken by Canadians and 75 percent of intercity passenger miles in the United States. The nuclear family unit traveling by private automobile has been the major source of pleasure and personal travel demand, as well as the marketing target for a majority of visitor-oriented businesses in the United States and Canada. It is not difficult to see why, considering the statistics that have been discussed earlier.

Just as they have done with trains, many experts have tried to explain why the automobile is selected over other modes of transportation. One such report found the major attractive attributes of the automobile to be as follows:

- Control of the route and the stops en route.
- Control of departure times.
- Ability to carry baggage and equipment easily.
- Low out-of-pocket expense of traveling with three or more persons.
- Freedom to use the automobile once the destination is reached.

Other surveys have shown that many people perceive the automobile to be a relatively safe mode of transportation, and others indicate that people like driving as a recreational experience.

The type and structure of drive tourism is determined by a number of factors (Prideaux and Carson 2011):

- Distance between the generating region and the destination. As the distance increases, there is a tendency to move from private automobile travel to mass public transport. Low-cost airfares, combined with the ability to rent a car at the destination, have led to a movement away from long-distance drive tourism to the fly-drive vacation.
- Quality of the road network between origin and destination.
- National levels of car ownership. As gross domestic product (GDP) increases, so does the percentage of the population that can afford to buy an automobile.
- Structure of the journey between origin and destination. Some visitors want to get to the destination as quickly as possible while others prefer to drive leisurely, stopping to visit various attractions en route.

FIGURE 17.5 The freedom of the road is a strong appeal for car travel.

© Deam Drobot/Shutterstock.com

- Visitor driving skills. Having to drive on the "other" side of the road or drive long distances on highways (leading to fatigue) may reduce the inclination to drive while on vacation. Accident rates in general are higher for visitors than for residents.
- Quality of the driving infrastructure. The better the quality, the greater the inclination to drive.
- Modes of transportation available at the destination. If the destination is a large city, public transport is likely to be an attractive option due to difficulties of parking, congestion, and so forth. On the other hand, the lack of mass transit in much of the United States makes driving more attractive.

Systems Thinking in Tourism

The tourism system is dynamic, which means that it changes and adapts as components of the system change. When trains were "king," cities along the tracks built their tourism around stops on the railway line. The grand central stations were testimony to the importance of the train to the economic—and tourism—life of these cities. So too were the grand hotels that were built along the rail lines. The grand hotels of the Canadian Pacific hotel built in the 1890s and early twentieth century are great examples of the system responding to the opportunities presented the transportation modes.

When cars became dominant, people could travel beyond the cities on the rail tracks, and new locations attracted visitors. The automobile brought about a more random pattern of travel movements, opened up new destinations, and spurred the development of elaborate networks of new automobile-oriented facilities and services along highways and roads. The tourist court, motel, and the motor hotel were three of the new facility types that developed in the United States and Canada after World War II. In fact, the whole development pattern in North America was fashioned directly and indirectly to accommodate the private automobile. The spirit of this time is captured in the many stories of folks "Getting their kicks on Route 66."

But the system kept changing. As anyone who has seen the classic animated movie *Cars* knows, in the United States, as the interstate freeway system grew, small towns bypassed by "the interstate" lost tourism business. Today, many hotels are located just off of exits on the interstate, away from many communities' business districts.

Of course, the system continues to change as new technologies arrive. It will be exciting to see what the next twenty years has in store—and how the tourism industry will respond.

TAKING "HOME" WITH YOU WHEN YOU GO

The recreational vehicle, or RV, is an extension of Northern Americans' love affair with the automobile. The President's Commission on Americans Outdoors found that 43 percent of American adults consider driving for pleasure a main recreational pastime. RVs offer the opportunity to combine driving and camping. They have grown tremendously in popularity in recent years; there has been an increased interest in touring the country in rented recreational vehicles.

Since World War II, interest in camping has grown rapidly in North America and elsewhere. The United States has more than 14,000 public and private parks and commercial campgrounds containing about a million campsites. Canada has been said to have 250,000 campsites and Mexico 10,000 campsites. The increasing popularity of the RV led directly to a number of new camping phenomena during the 1990s, including the franchised, condominium, and timesharing condominium campgrounds. In a condominium campground, the RV owner buys the site and pays a monthly fee for the maintenance of the common areas. In a timeshare operation, the use of the site for one week or more each year is purchased.

RENTAL CARS AND CAR SHARE

The car rental industry provides travelers, both leisure and business, with access to a car—even when they don't have their own car with them. Car rental is a global sector and represents a significant part of the tourism industry. In the United States, it is estimated that the industry will be worth $34.2 billion by 2020 (Rogers 2015). Of that figure, almost half is for leisure car rental and just over 26 percent is for business car rental. In recent years, the car rental industry has faced interesting challenges. Rental car operations began at airports, where people arrived from out of town and needed local transportation, but in recent years, rental car facilities have extended into communities. Enterprise, a rental car company that started out as an "in the neighborhood"-based alternative to airport-based rental car companies, is now the market leader with 35 percent of the market (Lifschutz 2017). The industry has been characterized by continuing *industry consolidation* as the three largest car rental companies—Enterprise, Hertz, and Avis—acquire smaller competitors. Today, these three companies—and the brands they operate—control 95 percent of the market.

Systems Thinking in Tourism

The tourism system relies on infrastructure to function. Airlines require air traffic controllers to ensure that the 9,700 planes in the air at any given time stay safe. Similarly, we need safe roads and bridges to ensure road travel remains attractive. For this reason, U.S. Travel, the industry association for the travel industry in the United States, advocates to congress for budget allocations to improve infrastructure.

New technologies and consumer trends are changing this part of the tourism system. Car-sharing is a fast-growing trend as consumers become more familiar with the concept. Avis acquired Zipcar, the car-share leader, as a means to revitalize its business. Avis is actively working with a Google subsidiary, Waymo, and Hertz is working with Apple on *self-driving* cars.

Other changes in the rental car business have included significant shifts in car fleets toward smaller and more fuel-efficient models. Many renters seek *hybrid* and other green options when renting a car. Despite the increased interest in green options, there is also a strong trend in the sector toward luxury rentals. *Fly-drive packages* offering rental cars with flights have made significant gains in popularity as more travelers have begun to substitute air travel for travel by the private automobile.

Of course, the United States isn't the only country where people like driving. In China, demand for rental cars has increased by over 19 percent each year between 2012 and 2017. This is projected to continue to grow at over 12.5 percent for the next five years, reaching a value of $18.2 billion in 2022.

BUSES AND MOTOR COACHES

Motor coaches account for 604 million passenger trips and 61.8 billion passenger miles in the United States and Canada, according to the American Bus Association. The motor coach industry is characterized by many companies—over 3,300 in the United States and almost 300 in Canada. These motor coaches are used not only for scheduled services, commuter services, and airport shuttle services, but also for sightseeing tours and trips.

Point-to-point travel by bus typically represents a low-cost travel option for consumers. In the United States, Greyhound and Megabus are among the largest, but there are other regional bus carriers like Adirondack

Trailways, RedCoach, and Peterpan. Although the largest companies operate nationally, the corridor along the major cities of the east coast of the U.S. are some of the most heavily serviced. In some destinations, including multiple countries across Europe, it is possible to buy "hop-on, hop-off" bus passes. For instance, Busabout offers bus "loops" that travel through multiple countries to popular visitor cities—Paris, Bruges, Prague, Vienna, and Munich, to name a few—allowing people to travel cost-effectively from one location to another. Although relatively low priced, there is a growing trend for greater amenities and customer support on buses, and it is now common for bus companies to provide mobile apps, free online Wi-Fi, and bus-tracker services (Antolin and Schwieterman 2017).

New business models are being adopted by city-to-city bus companies. For example, Flixbus is expanding across Europe by providing local bus companies with marketing services including marketing, pricing, quality control, and customer management. Their business model allows the network to grow quickly, but it means that there is variation in the service delivery, which is provided by a variety of smaller bus companies. This service is not unlike "Uber for small bus companies." The business model has been very successful, and Flixbus is expanding rapidly.

AT THE DESTINATION

While travel to the destination is important, travel around the destination is just as important to the travel experience.

Iconic Local Travel. In many destinations, the travel around the destination can be an important part of the tourism experience. A yellow taxi in New York is for many an authentic part of their trip to the Big Apple. Indeed, many cities have iconic local transportation experiences. A ferry from Circular Quay in Sydney, a cable car in San Francisco, a trolley in New Orleans, double-decker buses in London—perhaps slightly modified for tours—or a boat down the Seine in Paris are all important tourism assets for these destinations and great ways to get around.

Passes and Packages. Many destinations will also package their local transportation to make it easier for visitors and locals to see the sights. Bus passes, bus and train passes, and even bus, train, and ferry passes are available in many cities. In some cities, these passes may be available with entry to museums and other attractions. Of course, city tours are an important part of the local tourism system.

© holbox/Shutterstock.com

FIGURE 17.6 Iconic cable car in San Francisco.

Greater Energy Efficiency and Lower Green House Gas Emissions. Changes in local travel are having significant impacts on the visitor experience. Many cities and municipalities are experimenting with new models of local transportation. Many of these new methods of transportation are more energy efficient—with lower Green House Gas emissions. Buses that run on Liquid Petroleum Gas (LPG) and monorails or other types of people movers are becoming more common in cities around the world.

Sharing Economy. The sharing economy is changing transportations cities in many ways. Bike-share programs are being adopted in cities across the world, from Sydney to Shanghai to Chicago. These programs allow people to rent a bike, travel from one site to another, and leave it there for the next renter. Car-share programs like Zipcar are becoming viable alternatives to rental cars.

Slow Tourism

Slow tourism grew from the Slow Food movement. Where Slow Food promotes local food and traditional cooking, as opposed to fast food like McDonalds, slow tourism encourages visitors to slow down to a pace that is more sustainable and responsible and discover destinations. The proponents of slow tourism encourage use of bicycles and public transportation at the destination.

WHEN TRAVEL IS THE DESTINATION

Sometimes transportation is less about getting from place to place and more about the travel experience itself. In these cases, the journey is truly the destination. Travelers can be motivated by the mode of travel more than the destination itself. Cruise ships are destinations in their own right, providing shopping, entertainment, and food and beverage that rival the very best land-based destinations. In some cases, the places the cruise ships stop are secondary to the ship-based experience.

Cruising

Much has changed since the days when cruise ships were used primarily for transportation. The steamship era had its beginnings in the 1840s when Sir Samuel Cunard pioneered the first transatlantic scheduled liner trips at that time. Cruising began as one way to use surplus tonnage, but it soon became an important service for a new breed of international travelers. In 1957,

transatlantic ship traffic reached a new post–World War II high as some 1,036,000 passengers were transported on ocean liners. Although travel by ship remained strong for several years thereafter, by 1958 the aircraft had eclipsed it in terms of volumes of transatlantic passengers. Just as the automobile led to the demise of the train, the introduction of intercontinental commercial airline service precipitated the rapid decline in the use of ships as a scheduled passenger transportation mode. Transatlantic scheduled passenger ship traffic declined rapidly. Passenger departures from New York fell from approximately 500,000 in 1960 to 50,000 in 1975. The decline in scheduled liner passenger transport volumes has been so great that it has almost completely disappeared in this modern-day era.

Although point-to-point travel on cruise ships declined dramatically, eventually a new type of cruise product was introduced to the tourism system. This new product focused on cruising as a vacation experience, and this has been one of the fastest-growing segments of the travel industry in the last thirty years. It is estimated that almost 26 million travelers cruised in 2017. The cruise sector of the tourism system continues to grow. In 2017, the Cruise Line Industry Association (CLIA), reported cruise lines were already committed to building an additional ninety-seven new vessels, with capacity for a quarter million people by 2026 (CLIA 2016).

- **Ocean Cruising**

Caribbean. The Caribbean was the new generation of cruise destinations. It is fairly close to its North American market. The islands of the Caribbean were developed by different Western nations, thus providing contrasts in style. Additional attractions include the fact that English is the predominant language and that the U.S. dollar is accepted nearly everywhere. The Caribbean is not a year-round cruising area due to the hurricane season from June to November. In recent years, the Bahamas has become an increasingly important destination for cruising. In 2017, cruise ships began to offer itineraries that include Cuba. The Panama Canal is important for positioning cruises between the Caribbean and Alaska during the switch from the winter to the summer season.

Alaska and the Arctic. Alaska offers scenery, wildlife, and a mild summer climate. Recent concern for the environment has resulted in a limited number of large cruise ships. The short season runs from only May to September and puts increased pressure on port facilities. Growth of this market is constrained by the ability of the infrastructure to cope.

QUICK TRIP 17.3

One of a Kind

As thousands of people turn sixty-five on a daily basis many are dreading the idea of a retirement home. Their minds are still young and they yearn to experience all that they can. Although retirement homes may not be exciting destinations, they are extremely convenient. These complexes tend to function as miniature societies where everything one would need is just down the hallway. There are barbers, grocery stores, restaurants, workout facilities, lounge areas, maybe a movie theatre. Still, the element of adventure is missing. As you can see, adventure and convenience don't usually go hand in hand. But, if you're someone who desires both, retiring on a cruise ship may be just for you. Residents dock the ship to unpack only once and they are surrounded by friends and countless convenient amenities. Then when the ship docks at an exciting new destination they are free to explore before returning to their floating metropolis. As for the prices, retiring to a cruise ship is far more cost efficient than maintaining a captain and crew on your privately owned yacht. Retiring to a cruise ship demands a unique retiree who is after the thrill of day-to-day living and won't let age get in the way of adventures to be had.

Think about This

1.   Would you ever consider retiring on a cruise ship? Why or why not?
2.   How would a retirement cruise ship differ in amenities from any other cruise ship?
3.   Would you ever consider working on a cruise ship of any sort? Why or why not?

Source

http://www.topretirements.com/blog/adventurous-retirement-2/retirement-on-a-cruise-ship-combines-adventure-with-convenience.html/

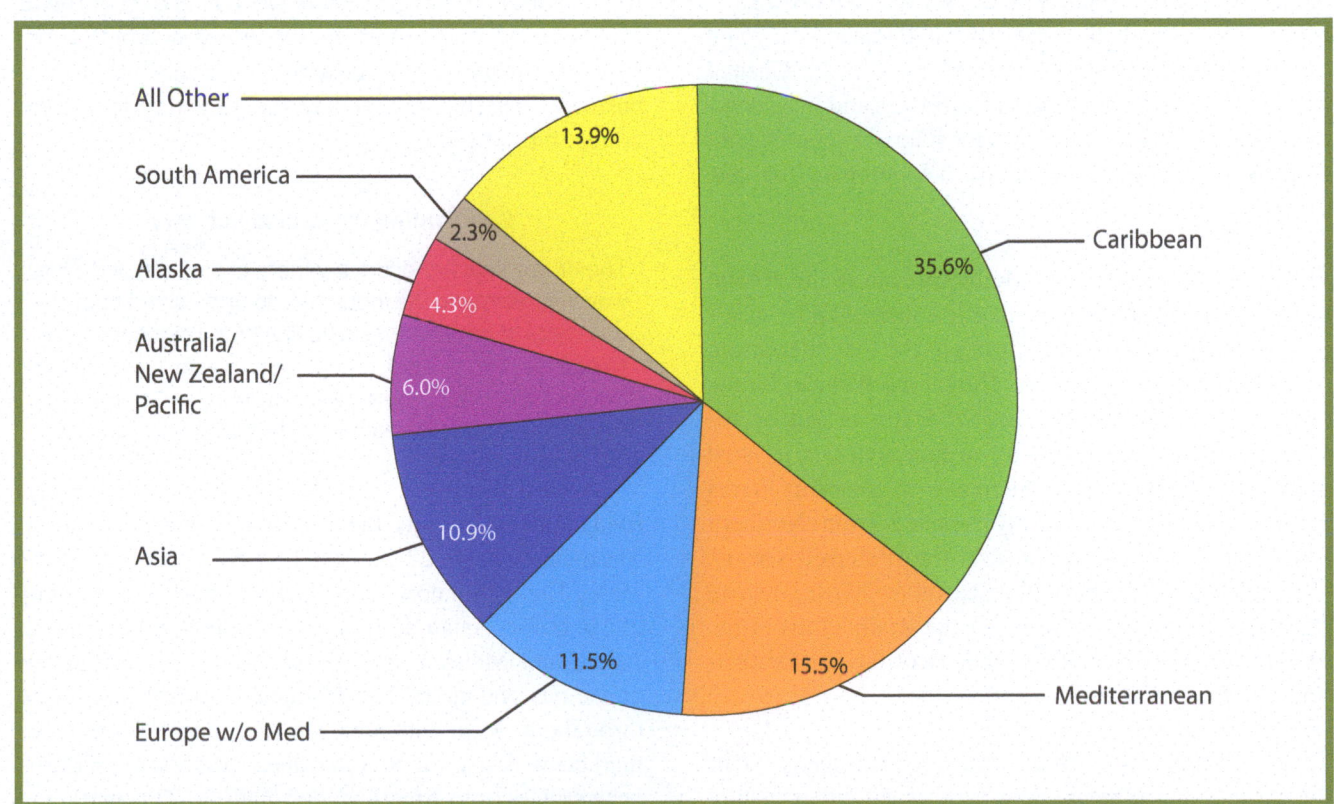

FIGURE 17.7   2017 Cruise Capacity Share by Region.

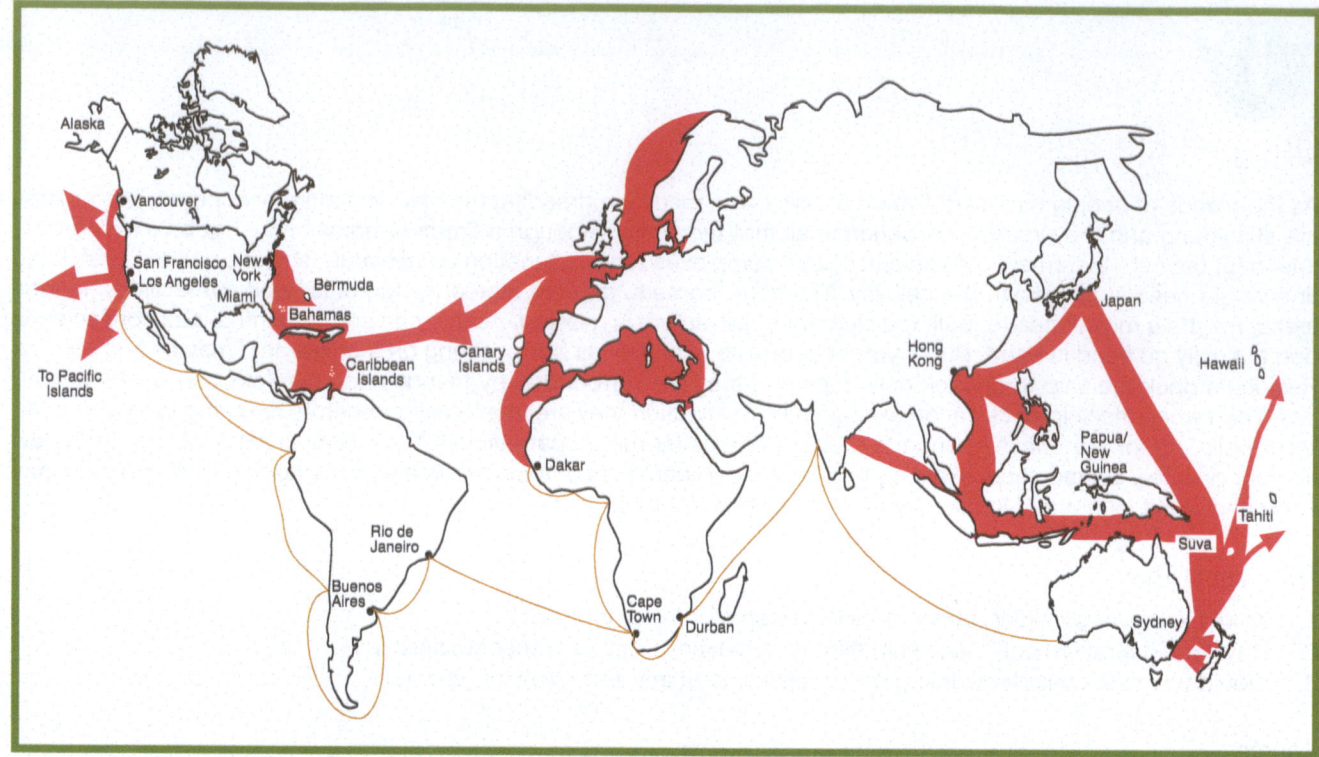

FIGURE 17.8 Major Cruise Routes in the World | Source: Christopher, J. *The Business of Tourism*, 2nd ed. London: Pitman Publishers.

In 2016, the Crystal Serenity set sail from Alaska to New York through the "Northwest Passage"—a route that had long been sought by sailors. Climate Change has opened this remote region to cruisers and local communities in Canada's Northern most territories—Yukon, Northwest, and Nunavit—must now prepare for new cruise operations.

The Mediterranean. The Mediterranean is the second most important cruising destination measured by available capacity. Itineraries through the Mediterranean may feature destinations like Barcelona, Venice, Rome, or the Greek Islands. The United States is well represented in terms of passengers to this area due to large numbers of United States citizens with ancestors in this region. The region is easily reached from Northern European ports, and summer is the preferred season, although there is no particular season for Mediterranean cruising. An important issue for the destinations of the Mediterranean is managing capacity of the port destinations for the cruise ships.

Europe (without the Mediterranean). Europe is one of the earliest cruise areas. Destinations are either mature holiday destinations in their own right, or major cities where cruises are a welcome but marginal addition. The year-round cruising accounts for about 1 percent of the world market, but 21 percent of the UK market. Growth is anticipated and the area has the infrastructure to cope. Cruise companies know the area well, it gets good repeat business, and the region has the facilities to handle cruise ships.

Segmenting the Cruise Industry

The cruise industry offers a variety of cruise types. One way to understand the industry is to understand the various types of vessels available. The broad categories are: Contemporary, Luxury, and River cruise lines. Within these categories there are several subcategories. Cruises can also be segmented by market and activity.

Asia. Asia represents the fastest-growing destination. The market grew 23 percent between 2016 and 2017 alone. The region now accounts for almost 11 percent of cruise traffic. Asian destinations in China, South Korea, Japan, and Malaysia are seeing strong growth. Asian cruise passengers are highly likely to travel on cruises throughout Asia, although some cruisers from these markets will visit the Mediterranean and travel on European cruises or to American destinations. This market is dominated by Chinese travelers (68 percent), but includes cruisers from Japan, Singapore, and other Asian markets (CLIA 2017).

QUICK TRIP 17.4

The Largest Cruise Ships

The Symphony of the Seas will be the world's largest cruise ship when it sets sail in April 2018. It is 1,188 feet long and 215 feet wide. It can accommodate 5,500 guests and 2,100 crew members. It has sixteen guest decks and seven neighborhoods. There are pools, spas, restaurants, conference rooms, entertainment venues, casinos, and plenty of shopping opportunities (Goldstein 2017). The Symphony of the Seas, operated by Royal Caribbean International lines, is the latest in a new generation of mega-cruise ships accommodating over 5,000 passengers, called Quantum Ultra class vessels. Symphony of the Seas will join her sister ships, Oasis of the Seas and Allure of the Seas. Spectrum of the Seas, which is designed for Asian ports, is under construction and will join the fleet in 2019 (2017).

As the tourism system prepares for the arrival of the new generation of mega-cruise ships a number of concerns are being raised including the concerns that many ports cannot accommodate the large vessels, local infrastructure is insufficient to get people on and off the vessel in time and the appeal of the cruise facilities themselves may make destinations and their attractions irrelevant. Additionally, some of these vessels are planning to serve destinations that already receive many cruise visitors. Symphony of the Seas will visit Barcelona—a destination that is already struggling with over-tourism.

Think about This

1. Does this product appeal to you? Why or why not?
2. What changes do you believe this will have to the tourism system organizations supporting the cruise industry where these vessels travel?
3. What benefits do tourism destinations receive from cruise visitors? What are the costs of cruise visitors? (Think about the triple bottom line when answering this question.)
4. Do cruise ships have any responsibility to respond to criticisms of over-tourism in the destinations they visit?

Sources

2017 "Keel laid for another giant Royal Caribbean ship, Spectrum of the Seas." *USA Today.*

Goldstein, M. 2017. "Royal Caribbean Drops More Details on World's Largest Cruise Ship." *Forbes.* Oct .16, 2017.

© Solarsys/Shutterstock.com

Allure of the Seas is one of the world's largest cruise ships. It can accommodate over 5,000 guests and 2,100 crew.

• River Cruising

In recent years, river cruising has been one of the fastest-growing segments of the cruise market. By 2015 there were 184 river cruise ships operating in the world. In 2017, thirteen new river cruise ships will come online. The fastest growth in river cruises has occurred on the Danube, but growth has occurred across Asia and the United States as well. In fact, a luxury 185-guest riverboat—the "America"—began cruising on the Mississippi in 2016.

Cruising Trends

What are the trends facing the cruise industry in the final years as we approach the 2020s? CLIA, the Cruise Line Industry Association, identifies the following eight trends (CLIA 2016):

1. New generation takes to the water
2. Travel agent use will increase
3. River cruiser demand will increase
4. More private islands on cruise itineraries
5. Newer cruisers will take to the sea
6. Drivable port locations are in favor
7. Celebrity chefs will lure cruise passengers
8. Demand for expedition cruises will increase

River cruises tend to be smaller scale and more intimate than ocean cruise ships. One of the important growth factors of this part of the cruise industry has been the growing amenities and quality of the customer experience. Features like balconies, which allow you to sit on the ship and watch the castles of Europe as you float by, are proving to be very popular. River cruises tend to attract more affluent, well-traveled adults who are seeking luxury experiences.

• Rail Experiences

Across the world, there are a number of rail experiences that transcend the utility of transportation. Short-duration train excursions through scenic surroundings have proven to be major attractions to pleasure travelers in recent years. For example, two major excursions of this type in Canada are the Algoma Central Railway in Ontario and the Royal Hudson Steam Train in British Columbia. The Strasburg Railroad in Pennsylvania is one example in the United States.

In other places, longer train trips provide a stage for unique or luxury experiences. The experience of riding aboard the Orient Express, made famous by mystery writer Agatha Christie, was reintroduced in 1983 after a complete restoration of the train. The Eastern and Oriental Express operates through South East Asia, offering

FIGURE 17.9 River cruising is the fastest growing segment of the cruise market.

© Ieoks/Shutterstock.com

FIGURE 17.10 The Deccan Odyssey provides luxurious train travel in India.

unique luxury to travelers, and the Deccan Odyssey is a Palace on Wheels in India. In Australia, the Ghan travels through the very center of the country from Darwin to Adelaide.

- **Tours**

While buses can provide point-to-point travel, motor coach tours can be a complete travel experience. In order to be effective in the marketplace, tour operators are moving to itineraries that go beyond sightseeing and embrace experiential tourism, which is discussed in Chapter 9. Today, the best tour operators provide insightful guides and incorporate experiences that allow guests to experience a destination—through tasting local specialties or trying new experiences—and enjoy shared memories.

People go on tours for practical and emotional reasons. The practical benefits are convenience, expertise, safety, and price. Tours are *convenient* in that the vacation can be spent concentrating on the experience rather than on making the arrangements. Having someone else doing the driving is important in terms of dealing with city traffic, driving in unfamiliar areas, and spending

TABLE 17.1 Reasons Why Clients Choose a Motor Coach Tour

Reason	Under 50	50+
Make new friends	91%	72%
More convenient	91	67
Safe	83	61
Learn more	86	51
Less expensive	74	54

time reading maps rather than enjoying the scenery. Tours offer the convenience of being picked up and delivered to hotels, sights, and entertainment. Accommodation and event tickets are guaranteed, which is particularly important for high-season events or times. Finally, the idea of the baggage being taken care of is appreciated.

People who take tours feel that *they can see and do more* than if they were traveling alone. There is the feeling that the operator has the expertise to select the best places to see. Because of this, participants can actually see more because they do not have to spend time evaluating all of the options. Also, there is *safety in numbers*. This is particularly true for older or female travelers and for urban or unfamiliar destinations.

The *fixed price* of a tour is an important feature. The most important part, however, is not the absolute price, but rather the fact that the costs are known beforehand. There is little to no danger of being halfway through one's vacation and running out of money because of poor budgeting. The tour is prepaid; the only other costs are some meals, sightseeing, and shopping.

People also take tours for emotional reasons, such as companionship, an opportunity to learn, shared activities, and security. Tours offer the opportunity to *meet new people and make new friends*. Many see it as an opportunity to get an overview of a destination—to discover and learn. Group travel is seen as a way of participating in activities with others who have the same interests. This can include physical activity tours such as skiing or water sports, as well as theater, garden, or historic homes tours. In all of this, there is the opportunity to be further educated in a particular area.

The security angle comes from the feeling of being an insider even in an unfamiliar place. This is an emotional appeal compared to the physical feeling of safety, as explored previously.

The operators of tour programs must overcome some negative images of tours. The negative images that people have about tours fall into four categories: perceptions of the bus, the tour experience, the group concept, and the types of people who take tours. For a number of people, tours are associated rather negatively with buses. The term *motor coach* is used by the industry to designate touring buses. Particularly in Europe, most coaches are extremely comfortable with videos, attendants who serve drinks, and reclining seats. However, despite the fact that such equipment is available in the United States (albeit on a lesser scale), the image brought to mind is too often the school or commuter bus. The bus is seen as too slow, too confining, and too uncomfortable. It is viewed as a cheap and old-fashioned way to travel. Travelers also have a negative image of bus terminals and view this as an undesirable place to start a vacation. Additionally, some people—particularly men—dislike the idea of giving up control to the coach driver. They complain about not being able to control the lights, the fans, or where and when to stop.

For people who do not take tours, the experience itself is perceived negatively. Touring, to many, is equated with regimentation, inflexibility, and passivity. The tour is seen as a shallow, boring, and impersonal experience. There are also those who think that rather than receiving the advantages of group power, being part of a group involves getting second-class treatment from hotels and restaurants. Yet another barrier to be overcome in selling tours is the group aspect. There is a fear of not relating well to other members of the group. To many people, a vacation involves having personal space and freedom. Being part of a group limits both of these. Last, many have a negative perception of the kinds of people who take tours. People who travel as part of a group are seen by many, stereotypically, as infirm, older, inexperienced travelers. This translates into a personality profile of tour-goers as passive and lacking in self-confidence.

Tour operators are working to overcome these negatives. In addition to embracing more experiential travel components, tour operators are working to address other changes. For instance, some tour operators are using different modes of transportation, including river cruises. Others are combining flights with coach travel to ensure that travelers get the most from their time. This is a particularly important strategy in destinations like Canada, the United States, and Australia, where distances between feature destinations can be long. Hub and spoke concepts can be used to bring people to a destination where they can relax on their own. Shorter mini-trips can be packaged with more free time, and tours themed around recreational activities can be developed to appeal to the younger, more active crowd. Some operators are even avoiding the word "tour" using terms like "adventure holiday," "expedition," "discovery trip," or "excursion."

QUICK TRIP 17.5

Space—The New Frontier for Tourism

Virgin Galactic chairman Sir Richard Branson announced in late 2017 that his company would be sending people to space by early 2018. Virgin Galactic describes itself as the first spaceflight company and its purpose is to become the spaceline for Earth; democratizing access to space for the benefit of life on Earth. A seat with Virgin Galactic to space, and membership in the Future Astronaut community, costs $250,000 (Caughill 2017).

But Virgin Galactic isn't the only company preparing to send visitors to space. SpaceX, a company founded by Elon Musk, is planning to take two tourists to the moon by the end of 2018 (Chang 2017). Blue Origin, the company founded by Jeff Bezos, is also planning on taking tourists to space by 2019 (Wattles 2017).

© Steve Mann/Shutterstock.com

When the travelers flying Virgin Galactic, SpaceX, or Blue Origin spacecraft make the trip to space they will join a very small number of people who can say they are "space tourists." Dennis Tito, the first space tourist, and six other people traveled on Russian Soyuz rockets to the International Space station in the first decade of the twenty-first century, before the program was terminated.

As the market for space tourism grows, the tourism system will change to accommodate the new market. Spaceport America, located in New Mexico, has Virgin Galactic and

A new generation of space tourists may be traveling in the next few years.

SpaceX as tenants and may be one of the first of a new type of tourism infrastructure. Intermediaries will also respond to the challenge of selling space flight. If it all seems far-fetched it is interesting to remember that Virgin Galactic has already chosen one hundred agents to train as "Accredited Space Agents" (Totten 2014).

Think about This

1. If you had the resources, would you travel to space? Why or why not?
2. While this is undoubtedly an expensive tourism experience, does this trip represent good value for money?
3. Consider how the tourism system may change as space tourism becomes more popular.
4. As we prepare for the tourism system to expand into space, do we need to consider environmental and social or heritage issues? Do sustainable tourism principles apply to space destinations?

Sources

Caughill, P. 2017. "Richard Branson Reveals Virgin Galactic's Latest Launch Plans." NBC. https://www.nbcnews.com/mach/science/richard-branson-reveals-virgin-galactic-s-latest-launch-plans-ncna812746

Chang, K. 2017. "SpaceX Plans to Send 2 Tourists Around the Moon in 2018." *New York Times.* https://www.nytimes.com/2017/02/27/science/spacex-moon-tourists.html

Totten, S. 2014. "Traveling to Space? There's an agent for that." *Marketplace.* https://www.marketplace.org/2014/05/02/world/traveling-space-theres-agent

Wattles, J. 2017. "Blue Origin CEO: We're taking tourists to space within 18 months." CNN. http://money.cnn.com/2017/10/05/technology/future/blue-origin-launch-human-space-tourism/index.html

SUMMARY

The world is smaller than ever and travelers have the ability to travel more easily than ever. While car travel is dominant, the jet age allows people to travel across the country and across the world in greater numbers than at any time in history. Old forms of travel are finding new life in the tourism system in new forms—like high-speed rail—and with new functions—cruise ships as floating resorts. New technologies are creating new forms of transportation—from ridesharing to driverless cars to space travel—and it is clear the tourism system will continue to change as it embraces these new opportunities.

ACTIVITIES

1. In small groups or as a class, discuss different ways students have traveled. Have individuals' modes of travel changed since increasing fuel costs? Discuss how students believe their travel choices will be affected over the next few years.
2. Think of a place in the United States you would like visit. Then online, compare flight, train, and bus travel to the area in terms of time, cost, convenience, and comfort. Which would you choose and why?
3. Discuss some of the changes anticipated for automobiles in the coming years. Already on the horizon are more electric vehicles, and more autonomous or driverless cars. How do you think these changes will impact drive tourism?
4. How much would you pay to travel to the moon? Consider the market for space travel and possible products that may be offered to future travelers.

ACRONYMS

CLIA (Cruise Lines International Asociation)   LCC (Low Cost Carrier)
GDP (Gross Domestic Product)   LPG (Liquid Petroluem Gas)
GHG (Green House Gas)   RV (Recreational Vehicle)

REFERENCES

Amtrak. 2016. Management's Discussion and Analysis of Financial Condition and Results of Operations and Consolidated Financial Statements with Report of Independent Auditors. Washington DC: National Railroad Passenger Corporation and Subsidiaries (Amtrak)

Antolin, B, and J Schwieterman. 2017. Running Express: 2017 Outlook for the Intercity Bus Industry in the United States Chicago Chaddick Institute for Metropolitan Development at DePaul University.

CLIA. 2016. 2017 Cruise Industry Outlook. Washington, DC: Cruise Lines International Association.

CLIA. 2017. State of Asia Cruise Industry and Research Findings Washington, DC: Cruise Lines Industry Association.

Gopwani, J. 2005. "Airports around the World Prepare for Arrival of Airbus A380." *AviationPros.* http://www.aviation-pros.com/news/10435115/airports-around-the-world-prepare-for-arrival-of-airbus-a380

HeathrowAirport. 2014. "What Makes a Hub Airport." Heathrow Airport. http://your.heathrow.com/what-makes-a-hub-airport/

Kelly, J., W. Haider, and P. W. Williams. 2007. "A Behaviorial Assessment of Tourism Transportation Options for Reducing Energy Consumption and Greenhouse Gases." *Journal of Travel Research* 45:297–309.

Lifschutz, M. 2017. Car Rental in The US. In IBISWorld Industry Report. Ibisworld.com IBISWorld

Neuman, S. 2017 "New Bullet Trains to Put China Out Front On High-Speed Rail." http://www.npr.org/sections/thetwo-way/2017/08/22/545279475/new-bullet-trains-to-put-china-out-front-on-high-speed-rail

Phillips, D. 2005. "Airports Bracing for Airbus A380." *New York Times.* March 5, 2005.

Prideaux, B., and D.B. Carson. 2011. *Drive Tourism: Trends and Emerging Markets* New York: Routledge.

Rogers, L 2015. Car Rentals—US—June 2015 Mintel.com.

Sharpe, T. 2012. "World's First Commercial Airline | The Greatest Moments in Flight." *Space.com.* https://www.space.com/16657-worlds-first-commercial-airline-the-greatest-moments-in-flight.html.

Sheth, J. L. 1975. "A Psychological Model of Travel Mode Selection." Advances in Consumer Research—Sixth Annual Conference.

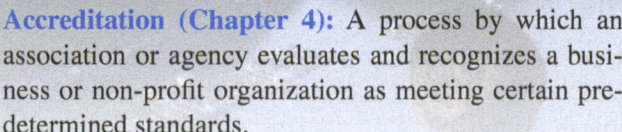

Accreditation (Chapter 4): A process by which an association or agency evaluates and recognizes a business or non-profit organization as meeting certain pre-determined standards.

Activity breadth (Chapter 11): The number of available destination activity schemes or categories.

Activity depth (Chapter 11): The number of available destination activities within each broad scheme or category.

Adventure tourism (Chapter 14): A form of travel that involves the seeking of a sense of adventure in physical activity, cultural exchange, and interaction with the natural environment.

Affective image (Chapter 13): A destination image component dealing with feelings.

Agency model (Chapter 16): Sellers receive a commission for each sale of a travel product.

Alderfer's ERG theory (Chapter 10): A theory which conceptualizes Maslow's Need Hierarchy into three categories—that of existence, relatedness, and growth.

All-inclusive package (Chapter 16): This is a vacation package that includes a complete range of tourism services included in the price. Items normally included are air fares, ground transfers and baggage handling, accommodation, meals, local sightseeing, recreational activities, and entertainment.

Alternative tourism (Chapter 6): This term refers to various forms of low-impact or "soft" tourism. These forms of tourism provide an alternative to mass and resort tourism which may have a high impact on the environment and local peoples.

Attractions (Chapter 1): The places and things that draw visitors to the destination. Some attractions are built, others are based on nature, culture, and history and heritage. Distinctive resorts and hotels, transporta-

tion routes and equipment, and cuisine also function as visitor attractions.

Augmented reality (Chapter 7): Technology that adds, or augments, computer generated information on the user's view of the world.

Authenticity (Chapter 11): A sense of the genuine, the real, the original, and the uniqueness of a destination.

Autonomous car (Chapter 17): Autonomous cars or self-driving cars are capable of sensing the environment and driving without human input.

Balance of payments (Chapter 2): A type of economic accounting system; this is the difference between what a country exports (sells) to other countries and what it imports (buys) from other countries. When a country exports more than it imports, it has a positive balance of payments or trade. A negative balance of payments is where a country imports more than it exports.

Big data (Chapter 7): Big data refers to the large amounts of data companies collect on consumers through tracking online behavior including online purchases and search behaviors. Analysis of this data enables marketers to target products and services to individual consumers.

Bilateral agreement (Chapter 4): An agreement between two countries, often in trade or transportation. Bilateral air agreements are an example; these agreements mainly address the questions of which airlines can fly between the two countries and to which airports they can fly.

Bleisure (Chapter 14, 15): A trip in which visitors combine business and leisure.

Brand (Chapter 7): Brand refers to a logo, sign, symbol, or design to identify a product. A brand is also the set of associations that consumers have of a product or service.

Brand equity (Chapter 7): The value of a brand.

Brand identity (Chapter 7): A set of factors or characteristics for which brand strategists want the product or service to be known.

Brand strategist (Chapter 7): Marketers working to implement brand strategies.

Built facilities (Chapter 1): Constructed facilities that support attractions and events, including hotels, resorts and other lodging, food and beverages, shopping, convention and exhibition centers, and other. They can also function as attractions and event venues.

Business travel market (Chapter 14): Travel where the primary motivation is to conduct business. This includes regular business or corporate travel, incentive travel, and travel related to meetings, conventions, congresses, trade shows, and exhibitions.

Carriers (Chapter 16, 17): These are companies that provide transportation for visitors and include airlines, railroad companies, bus operators, ferry services, and other transportation providers.

Carrying capacity (Chapter 2): A measurement that indicates the ability of an environment or natural resource to accommodate a certain type of use. There is also the concept of social carrying capacity, which refers to a society's capacity to cope with a certain type of activity.

Certification (Chapter 4): A process by which people are tested and evaluated to determine mastery of a specific skills or a field of knowledge.

Climate change (Chapter 15): Climate change is a change in Earth's overall climate. This could be a change in Earth's average temperature, for example. Or it could be a change in Earth's typical precipitation patterns (NASA).

Co-creation (Chapter 9): Co-creation or co-production recognizes that some tourism products and services are created by both the service provider and the consumer.

Code sharing (Chapter 4): One common feature of a strategic alliance between two airline companies. This arrangement allows one airline to use its own two-character code to advertise a flight as its own, when the flight is actually being operated by its partner airline.

Cognitive dissonance (Chapter 12): A feeling of anxiety or doubt that people experience after they have made purchases. This anxiety revolves around whether they have selected the best tourism destination area or other travel service.

Collateral, printed (Chapter 8): Printed materials produced by tourism organizations including visitor guides, calendars of festivals and events, and maps.

Collectivism (Chapter 13): One dimension of the National Culture Model which suggests that people are supposed to look after the interests of their in-group and share similar opinions and beliefs with those of their in-group.

Commission (Chapter 16): An amount of money, normally expressed as a percentage of the fare, rate or price, paid to a retail travel agency by suppliers, carriers, and other intermediaries such as tour operators.

Commodification (Chapter 2): The process where cultural activities, like rituals and festivals, are modified for sale to visitors.

Community based tourism (CBT) (Chapter 2): Tourism organized by a community, often in rural locations. Community based tourism typically takes into account the social, environmental and economic benefits of tourism to the host community.

Computer reservation systems (CRS) (Chapter 9, 16): A computer system operated by an airline, hotel chain, rental car, or other travel company which allows retail travel agencies to check the availability and prices, and make reservations for their clients. Some systems also provide access for individual travelers.

Consolidator, travel (Chapter 16): A special form of travel agent. These are private firms that buy unsold airline seats, cruise berths, and other types of travel options in bulk and sell these at a discount to retail travel agencies and individual travelers. The "consolidator" term comes from the combination of these firms' bookings to qualify for group or discounted prices.

Convention-meeting planners (Chapter 9, 16): Employees of corporations, associations, government agencies, and other nonprofit groups who plan and coordinate meetings, conventions, conferences, exhibitions, or trade shows.

Conversion study (Chapter 8): A research technique used to determine the percentage of people who request travel information materials that actually visit the destination or use the service after being sent the materials.

Coordination (Chapter 3): Getting people to work together harmoniously and to avoid overlapping in tasks and responsibilities. This role is often fulfilled by government agencies or destination management organizations (DMOs).

Corporate social responsibility or CSR (Chapter 2): Corporate social responsibility occurs when companies go beyond their legal requirements to address social or environmental issues.

Corporate travel department (Chapter 14, 16): Special departments created by corporations, government agencies, and nonprofit organizations to coordinate and control all of the travel by employees and associates of the organization. These departments establish organization-wide travel policies and negotiate the best prices on travel.

Cost-benefit analysis (Chapter 2, 6): An economic analysis technique used to determine which economic sector produces the most benefit in terms of foreign exchange, employment, taxes, or income generated relative to the costs of development.

Cultural identity (Chapter 2): The identity belonging to a group that shares a similar cultural heritage.

Cultural assets (Chapter 2): Tangible (heritage buildings, artifacts, etc.) and intangible (dances, stories, folklore) assets of a specific culture.

Culture (Chapter 13): A set of beliefs, values, attitudes, habits, and forms of behavior shared by a society and passed from generation to generation (Bennett and Kassasjian 1982).

Customer relationship management (Chapter 8): Customer relationship management (CRM) is a marketing technique designed to maximize the customer relationship. CRM is also associated with database marketing.

Database marketing (Chapter 8): A process increasingly being used in tourism to encourage repeat usage. Computer technology allows the manipulation of relational databases on past and potential visitors, and is facilitating this process.

Demonstration effect (Chapter 2): An economic phenomenon that occurs when local residents, exposed to goods imported for visitor use, begin to demand those goods for themselves. This automatically increases the demand for imports.

Destination (Chapter 1): A destination is a geographic area that attracts visitors. Destinations range in size from an individual community to a group of several countries, where there is a concerted effort to develop and market tourism.

Destination attribute assessment (Chapter 13): A three-step process for marketers to evaluate the attributes of a destination: What does the potential visitor consider important? Does the potential visitor perceive that a destination has what they consider important? Does the destination actually have it?

Destination image (Chapter 13): The mental picture that an individual forms of a tourism destination.

Destination management company (DMC) (Chapter 16): Also known as inbound tour operators, receptive tour operators or receptive services operators. These are companies who provide sightseeing, guiding, and transportation services within specific destination areas. Other types of DMCs specialize in catering to meeting and incentive travel groups.

Destination management (marketing) organization (DMO) (Chapter 8): Government and nongovernmental organizations with the responsibility of marketing specific tourism destinations to the travel trade and individual travelers. These organizations operate at all geographic levels from multi-country regions (e.g., European Travel Commission) to individual communities (e.g., convention and visitors bureaus).

Destination product (Chapter 1): The destination product is a combination of interdependent components, consisting of infrastructure, transportation, built facilities, attractions and events, and service quality and friendliness.

Destination push and pull proposition (Chapter 10): A proposition suggesting a two-tiered scheme of motivational factors: the "push" and the "pull."

Destination restorative qualities (Chapter 10): A delineation of attributes and characteristics of a destination that are restorative to visitors. The model identifies six different restorative aspects of a destination including compatibility, extent, mental away-ness, physical away-ness, orientation, and fascination. A destination or setting needs to consider each of these six aspects to optimally serve visitor needs for recuperation and rejuvenation.

Development control (Chapter 3): Introducing and enforcing development controls to ensure that the environment and cultural heritage are not harmed and that all other procedures and codes have been followed.

Development stimulation (Chapter 3): Identifying tourism project development opportunities, seeking investors and developers for these projects, and providing financial and fiscal incentives.

Differentiated seating (Chapter 17): Airlines are experimenting with additional classes of seats including basic economy, economy plus, and economy preferred as a means of maximizing revenue.

Direct distribution (Chapter 16): Direct distribution is when the product sells directly to the consumer.

Direct employment (Chapter 2): Employment in jobs directly related to tourism like lodging, attractions, or transportation.

Direct marketing (Chapter 8): Marketing directed to the consumer, often through personalized communication.

Distribution mix (Chapter 16): The combination of direct and indirect (through travel trade intermediaries) distribution that a tourism organization selects to use to market its services or destination area.

Domestic tourism (Chapter 1): Visits by residents within their own country.

Drive tourism (Chapter 17): Vacations where the auto is the mode of transportation.

Dual processes in decision-making (Chapter 12): A theory which proposes that human decision-making follows a dual-process system: an effortless system 1 (implicit) and an effortful system 2 (explicit). This dual processing system theory recognizes that human rationality is bounded, and that the systems of thought that depend on intuition and emotion, rather than reflection and analysis, are important in understanding consumer decision-making.

Dynamic pricing (Chapter 17): Dynamic pricing is a pricing strategy in which businesses set flexible prices based on current market demand. Dynamic pricing is standard practice in the airline industry.

Economic feasibility study (Chapter 6): A study to determine the economic feasibility of a tourism development project opportunity. A project is economically feasible if it provides a rate of return acceptable to the investors in the project.

Economic Impact Models (Chapter 2): Models that measure the economic impacts—direct, indirect, and induced—of tourism expenditures.

Ecotourism (Chapter 2; 6): Environmentally responsible travel to natural areas, in order to enjoy and appreciate nature (and accompanying cultural features, both past and present) that promote conservation, have a low visitor impact and provide for beneficially active socio-economic involvement of local peoples.

Emerging economies (Chapter 15): Countries which are experiencing rapid economic growth.

Enclave tourism (Chapter 2): Tourism where all the needs of the visitors are supplied by the provider, often a resort or cruise. Enclave tourism may limit the economic contribution of tourism to local communities.

Environmental impact analysis (Chapter 6): A process of evaluating the likely environmental impacts of a proposed project or development, taking into account inter-related socio-economic, cultural and human-health impacts, both beneficial and adverse (UNEP—Convention on Biological Diversity 2017).

Environmental scanning (Chapter 7): A technique used to identify and analyze the impact of external environmental forces on a tourism organization's marketing. These external forces include legislation and regulation, political situations, social and cultural characteristics, economic conditions, technology, transportation, and competition.

Escorted tour (Chapter 9): A type of organized tour that includes the services of a tour director or manager who accompanies an individual or group throughout the tour.

Events (Chapter 1): Gatherings of groups of people for short period of times for entertainment, celebration, family, and business reasons or purposes.

Exclusive distribution (Chapter 16): Exclusive distribution occurs when a product restricts the retail outlets and attempts to have the travel agents sell only their product in the product category.

Expected value/utility theory (Chapter 12): A theory that outlines how the decision-maker reaches a decision that he or she deems as maximizing its expected value.

Experience (Chapter 1, 9, 11): A travel experience is a term to describe the interaction of the visitor with the destination and service providers. Experience often involves visitor participation in the delivery of the tourism product or service.

Experience cueing (Chapter 11): A strategy for tourism and leisure service providers to facilitate visitor experience through visual, aural and other sensory cues/clues to optimally engage their sensory reservoir.

Experience theming (Chapter 11): The practice of designing an experience that has identifiable characteristics such as distinguishable features, specific materials, and recognizable spatial configurations.

Experiential travel (Chapter 9): Experiential travel that allows visitors to actively participate in their travel, as opposed to passively sightseeing.

Familiarization tour or trip (Chapter 8): Also known as a "fam," these trips are organized for selected tour operators or wholesalers, retail travel agents, or travel writers. Having experienced the destination or travel service first-hand, the intermediaries are in a much better position to sell it. Familiarization tours may involve the inspection of facilities, visits to tourism attractions, and contacts with the local travel trade (e.g., inbound tour operators). Fams may be conducted in small groups or on an individual basis.

Family life cycle (Chapter 7): Family life cycle is a composite of marital status, age, and the numbers and ages of children in the home.

Five Ps (5 Ps) of tourism destination planning (Chapter 5): A framework for tourism destination planning consisting of policy, principals, participants, process, and plan.

Flag carrier (Chapter 17): Airline operated, partially operated, or once operated by the government of a country.

Flow (Chapter 11): A state of mental *concentration* or complete absorption with the activity at hand and the situation.

Focus group (Chapter 8): A marketing research technique involving a small group of people, typically eight to twelve persons. A moderator is used to lead the group to reach a consensus on one or more questions or issues.

Fully independent tour (FIT) (Chapter 16): A service provided by retail travel agencies and some tour operators in which all the air travel and land arrangements are made for an individual customer in the traveler's destination of choice.

Framing (Chapter 13): A communication technique that is frequently utilized in marketing in which the same information can be described and presented in different ways to steer consumers toward a favorable image of a destination.

Frequent flier program (FFP) (Chapter 8): Recognition programs that were first introduced in the early 1980s to reward frequent travelers and to build loyalty among these travelers with the airline. Frequent flier miles are the "currency" of these programs.

Frequent guest program (FGP) (Chapter 8): Guest recognition programs that were first introduced in the early 1980s to reward frequent travelers and to build loyalty among these travelers with the hotel chain. These programs reward guests with room upgrades, free stays, merchandise, or frequent flyer miles.

Frequent traveler program (Chapter 14): A reward program such as a hotel or car loyalty program or an airline frequent flier program which allows travelers to enjoy such privileges as exclusive member only discounts, offers, and other benefits.

Front and back regions (Chapter 11): A classification of visitor spaces. The front regions signify spaces that are, to a varying degree, set up for visitors. The back regions refer to spaces that represent, to a varying degree, what is native or local to the destination that visitors visit.

Fulfillment (Chapter 8): The process used by tourism organizations to send printed collateral materials to people who request them.

Generational cohort (Chapter 13): A cohort of individuals who were born around the same time and share distinctive social and historical life events during their formative years These broad forces create shared values and shape common consumptive preferences and patterns.

Generation Xers (Chapter 13): Individuals born between 1965 and 1977. They are defined as "savvy" travelers because of their exposure to uncertain economic times. They embrace multiculturalism and global thinking.

Generation Z (Centennials) (Chapter 13): Individuals born after 1996. The generation Z are "Digital Natives" because they were born into a world of social networks, digital platforms, and mobile computing.

Greenhouse gases (Chapter 2, 17): Greenhouse gases (GHG) are gases that contribute to climate change. They include carbon dioxide, methane, and ozone.

Group inclusive tour (GIT) (Chapter 16): An all-inclusive package with a specified minimum size (number of travelers) involving one or more groups traveling on scheduled or chartered air service (Morrison 2010).

Global distribution systems (GDS) (Chapter 16): Computerized reservation systems that are global in their coverage. Four of the major systems are Amadeus, Galileo, Sabre, and Worldspan.

Ground or land tour arrangements (Chapter 16): Travel arrangements made for group or individual travelers at a destination. These include items such as airport transfers, lodging, meals, entertainment, sightseeing, and ground transportation by coach or other means.

Guests (Chapter 1): The people who choose to visit a destination.

Hard adventure travel (Chapter 14): The traditional form of adventure travel that usually requires a higher level of skills on the part of the traveler.

High speed trains (Chapter 17); Rail transportation that operates significantly faster than traditional rail services, typically over 124 mph (200km/hr.)

Horizontal integration (Chapter 16): The acquisition and ownership of similar businesses by one organization in the tourism distribution channel.

Hosts (Chapter 1): Hosting is welcoming and serving visitors within destinations, and involves both tourism service staff and local residents.

Hub and spoke (Chapter 17): Hub and spoke networks are a means of connecting many destinations. By using a hub, the number of trips required to connect multiple destinations is reduced considerably.

Import substitution (Chapter 2): An economic strategy aimed at minimizing the leakage from a destination area's economy caused by imported goods and services.

Inbound tourism (Chapter 1): Visits to a country by non-residents of that country.

Inbound tour operator (Chapter 16): Tour operators who provide the ground or land tour arrangements within specific destinations for group and individual travelers. They are also called receptive tour or receptive services operators.

Incentive travel (Chapter 14): Travel that is financed by a business to its employees as a reward for excellence of work performance.

Incentive travel planning company (Chapter 16): A specialized tour wholesaler who primarily serves corporate clients and arranges trips that are given to certain of their client's employees or dealers as a reward for outstanding sales or work performance.

Indirect distribution (Chapter 16): When the sale of a product occurs through one or more travel intermediaries.

Indirect employment (Chapter 2): Employment in industries that support tourism like construction or agriculture.

Individualism (Chapter 13): One dimension of the National Culture Model which proposes that individuals look after their own self-interests and those of their immediate families.

Information needs (Chapter 12): The five domains of values that travelers place on travel information including functional, hedonic, innovation, sign, and aesthetic values.

Information perception bias (Chapter 12): The proposition a consumer will internalize the information through his or her own judgment lens. A marketing message can be distorted by a consumer in that process.

Infrastructure (Chapter 1): Consists mainly of underground and surface preparation and construction that provide the systems needed by a destination to serve tourism businesses and visitors, and meet the needs of residents.

Inplants (Chapter 16): A travel agency staff member is located in the offices of a corporate client.

Input-output analysis (Chapter 2): An economic analysis technique which examines the interactions among different economic sectors. It is used to determine the impacts of tourism on the other economic sectors of a destination area.

Intangible (Chapter 9): Unable to be touched. Many tourism experiences are intangible.

Integrated marketing communication (Chapter 8): The process of ensuring consistent marketing messaging across promotional techniques.

Intellectual property (cultural) (Chapter 2): Local knowledge of customs, remedies, and other heritage.

Intensive distribution (Chapter 16): Maximizing the exposure of travel services by distributing through all available intermediaries.

Interlining (Chapter 4): Travel by an air passenger on two or more airlines on a trip. More broadly, interlining refers to cooperative agreements between two or more airlines.

Internal tourism (Chapter 1): Visits by residents and non-residents within a country (domestic + inbound international).

Internal Marketing (Chapter 9): Marketing focused at internal audiences. In a company internal marketing is directed to management and staff.

International tourism (Chapter 1): The combination of inbound and outbound tourism for a specific country. Also, often used to describe the totality of outbound tourism in the world.

Internet (Chapter 8): A worldwide network of connected computer networks. Also known as "cyberspace" or the "information superhighway," one of the most popular Internet functions is the World Wide Web.

Invisible export (Chapter 2): Because of the intangible nature of tourism services, it is said to be an invisible export when foreigners visit another country and spend money there. Tourism is not a physical good that must be shipped out to other countries.

Kaizen (Chapter 9): Kaizen or continuous improvement is a management commitment to improving product quality through a deliberate process of continuous improvement.

Leakage (Chapter 2): An economic term that refers to the monetary value of goods and services that must be imported to service the needs of tourism.

Legacy carriers (Chapter 17): Legacy carriers are airlines that operated before route liberalization (US) and typically provide higher quality services than low cost carriers including first and business class seating, frequent flyer programs, and other amenities.

Legislation (Chapter 4): The laws enacted by governments in a destination that affect tourism.

Leisure time (Chapter 1): The time people have discretion over. During leisure time people can do what they want.

Leisure travel market (Chapter 14): Travel where the primary motivation is to take a vacation or holiday, or to travel for some other personal (nonbusiness) reason.

Localness (Chapter 11): Unique locale-specific features of a destination.

Low cost carriers (LCCs) (Chapter 17): Low cost carriers are airlines that operate on a low-cost business model, often focusing on short haul routes, secondary airports, and limited additional services for consumers.

Marketing (Chapter 7): Marketing is a management process that creates value for consumers by satisfying their needs and wants and in creating that value achieves organizational goals.

Marketing mix (Chapter 7): The combination of factors that tourism marketing managers use to attract visitors. These factors include product, price, place, promotion, packaging, programming, partnership, and people.

Marketing orientation (Chapter 7): The organization's marketing efforts are focused on the wants and needs of the visitor.

Marketing plan (Chapter 7): A written document that describes the actions that a tourism organization will undertake to achieve its marketing goals and objectives.

Market segmentation (Chapter 7): The division of the tourism market into groups which share common characteristics.

Market study (Chapter 6): One component of an economic feasibility study which analyzes the project's market potential.

Masculinity versus femininity (Chapter 13): One dimension of the National Culture Model which explains that the degree to which the values held reflect the traditional division between male versus female roles.

Maslow's hierarchy of needs (Chapter 10): A theory of motivation denoting that human beings possess five ordered innate needs with self-actualization at the top and survival at the bottom of a hierarchy.

Max-Neef's need classification scheme (Chapter 10): A theory which classifies fundamental human needs into nine non-hierarchical dimensions: subsistence, protection, affection, understanding, participation, leisure, creation, identity, and freedom.

Medical tourism (Chapter 14): Travel outside one's natural healthcare jurisdiction for the enhancement or restoration of an individual's health through medical intervention.

Meeting planner (Chapter 16): A professional responsible for the project management of meetings for corporations, associations, and other organizations.

Merchant model (Chapter 16): Intermediary buys the product at a "net" rate and adds a margin that determines what the consumer pays.

Metasearch (Chapter 16): Travel intermediaries that use technology to search across OTAs and identify the best prices for travel on the internet.

MICE markets (Chapter 14, 16): An acronym for the meetings, incentives, conventions, and exhibition markets.

Millennials (or Generation Y) (Chapter 13): Individuals born between 1977 and 1995. The Millennials were born into a technological and electronic society. They are open-minded and goal-oriented.

Multi-segmentation of business travelers (Chapter 14): An approach that segments the business travel market using a combination of variables pertaining to travelers' behavioral tendencies, travel arrangement characteristics, work content, demographics, and psychographics.

Multiplier effect (Chapter 2): An economic term that describes the indirect and induced effects of income and employment generated by tourism. Income multipliers measure the amount of local income generated per unit of visitor expenditure (Wanhill 1994).

Multilateral agreement (Chapter 4): An agreement between several countries, often in trade or transportation. The General Agreement on Tariffs and Trade (GATT) is one example.

National Culture Model (Chapter 13): A model which posits that the value patterns dominant in countries vary along six main dimensions: Individualism versus collectivism; Masculinity versus femininity; Large versus small power distance; Strong versus weak uncertainty avoidance; Long-term versus short-term orientation; and Indulgence versus restraint.

National tourism: (Chapter 1): Visits by the residents of a country to other countries plus visits by residents within their own country (domestic + outbound international).

Native species (Chapter 11): The indigenous flora and fauna contributing to the creation of regional boundaries and inherent uniqueness.

Online travel agencies (OTAs) (Chapter 16): Online databases and reservations services that allow travelers to make travel reservations in their own homes or offices via computer modems and the World Wide Web. Examples include Travelocity, Preview Travel, and Expedia.

Opaque business model (Chapter 16): An online travel sales model in which the brand name of the product is hidden until purchase is complete.

Open Skies agreement (Chapter 17): In 2008 an "Open Skies" agreement was signed between the United States and eleven European Union (EU) countries that allows airlines to fly between any of the affected countries. This is regarded as the first step in negotiations intended to open up the U.S. domestic market.

Outbound tourism (Chapter 1): Visits by the residents of a country to other countries.

Override commission (Chapter 16): A higher commission, normally in return for higher sales levels or other marketing support.

Overselling (Chapter 17): Selling more than the available capacity of a tourism product on the expectation that some of the sales will not materialize. Airlines model seat utilization and oversell seats on a plane.

Overtourism (Chapter 5): Over-capacity situations such as overcrowding in destinations that are accompanied by resident complaints and resentment of tourism.

Packaging (Chapter 7, 9): The assembly of travel packages that combine the services and products of several tourism organizations into a single-price offering.

Partnerships (Chapter 7, 9) Partnership is one of the eight Ps of tourism marketing and can range from loose collaborations to legally binding partnership arrangements.

Perceptual map (Chapter 13): A map which represents the collective perceptions of a segment of the market for a particular destination on factors considered important to them.

Performance indicators (Chapter 8): Performance indicators, sometimes known as Key Performance Indicators or KPIs, provide information on progress toward a specific goal.

Perishability (Chapter 9): A thing that goes bad, or is lost, quickly. Many tourism products are perishable in that if they are not used within a given time they are lost. For example, the opportunity to sell a hotel room for tonight is lost if the room is unsold by today.

Permission marketing (Chapter 8): Marketing to consumers that have indicated they are interested in receiving messages from the marketer.

Policy statement (Chapter 3): A statement of the guidelines, goals, and initiatives for tourism in a destination.

Portfolio management (Chapter 9): Managing several products and services to reduce risk and optimize returns.

Positioning (Chapter 7): A marketing process used by tourism organizations to create a perception or image in the targeted visitor's mind.

Power distance (Chapter 13): One dimension of the National Culture Model which denotes how society deals with the fact that people are unequal.

Preferred supplier or vendor (Chapter 16): A marketing arrangement in which a seller commits to providing preferential support for a product, normally in response to additional sales and marketing support.

Primary research (Chapter 8): Also known as original research, this is information collected for the first time by an organization or individual.

Principals, travel (Chapter 8): A term in travel used to refer to suppliers and carriers who use retail travel companies as their agents.

Product (Chapter 9): A bundle of attributes (features, functions, benefits, and uses) capable of exchange or use (AMA).

Product life cycle (PLC) (Chapter 9): The observation that products move through a lifecycle that includes introduction, growth, maturity, and decline.

Production orientation (Chapter 7): Production orientation is when an organizations marketing efforts are guided by focus on services or products.

Professional conference organizer (PCO) (Chapter 16): Professional conference organizer are specialists in creating conferences.

Programming (Chapter 9): One of the 8 Ps of tourism marketing, programming includes special activities, events, and other activities to increase customer spending or enhance a tourism experience.

Promotions (Chapter 8): Tourism marketers communicate with consumers through a wide range of promotions. Promotions can be used to inform, persuade, or remind consumers about the product or service.

Pull strategies (Chapter 16): Pull strategies are directed at consumers are and are intended to "pull" the product through the distribution network or supply chain.

Push strategies (Chapter 16): Push strategies focus on supporting intermediaries in a way that pushes the product through the distribution network towards consumers.

Receptive tour operator (Chapter 16): Tour operators who provide the ground or land tour arrangements within specific destinations for group and individual travelers. They are also called inbound tour operators.

Recreation (Chapter 1): The activities in which people participate in their leisure time.

Regulations (Chapter 4): Rules introduced and enforced by government agencies that usually are derived from legislation.

Relationship marketing (Chapter 8): Marketing activities in which a tourism organization engages to build and enhance long-term relationships with individual visitors and other organizations.

Representative firms (Chapter 8): Companies that represent a tourism destination area or tourism organization in a foreign country, and which provide public relations and other promotional services.

Retail travel agency (Chapter 16): In essence, they are the department stores of tourism. They provide thousands of "travel shops" for suppliers, carriers, destination management organizations, and the other travel trade intermediaries, and receive commissions for their services. A customer can buy all types of travel services at an agency including tickets for planes and railways, hotels and resorts, packages and tours, car rentals, and travel insurance.

Revenue management (Chapter 17): Sophisticated methods employed by tourism operators, including hotels and airlines, to ensure highest possible financial returns.

Sales orientation (Chapter 7): An organization with a sales orientation is focused on selling product or services. These organizations tend to be focused on the needs of the seller, not the consumer.

Seasonality (Chapter 2): Seasonality is the degree to which tourism demand is impacted by seasons.

Sense of place (Chapter 11): The association or connection that a visitor develops with a particular destination.

Service quality and friendliness (Chapter 1): Represent the human factor in the destination product. All those involved in "hosting" visitors are involved, and include both tourism service staff and local communities. It is the way that visitor services are delivered by service providers, as well as the general feeling of friendliness and warmth radiated by the resident population of the destination.

Servicescape (Chapter 11): The domains which represent physical surroundings of the service provider including ambience, space, signs, and symbols used for the setting, and humanics.

Sharing economy (Chapter 10, 16, 17): The sharing economy, also known as collaborative consumption, is where an owner of a resource rents it, normally using a technology platform. Airbnb and Uber are sharing economy companies.

Situation or SWOT analysis (Chapter 7): A marketing technique used to analyze the strengths, weaknesses, opportunities, and threats of a tourism destination or tourism organization.

Slow tourism (Chapter 17): Slow tourism encourages visitors to slow down to a pace that is more sustainable. It encourages visitors to use public transport and bicycles when possible.

SMERF markets (Chapter 9): An acronym commonly used in tourism for meetings and other events held by social, military, educational, religious, or fraternal groups.

Social enterprise (Chapter 2): Businesses established to achieve social objectives.

Social entrepreneur (Chapter 2): An entrepreneur who initiates a business to solve social or environmental challenges.

Societal marketing orientation (Chapter 7): An organization with a societal marketing focus is focused on both the needs of the consumer and the community.

Soft adventure travel (Chapter 14): Travel activities that require a certain degree of mental and physical fitness but only a minimum level of skill.

Staged authenticity (Chapter 2): Modifying or staging of cultural elements or activities to create the impression of authenticity for a visitor audience.

Stakeholder (Chapter 7): People or organizations with an interest or concern in the operation of a tourism business, destination, or organization.

Strategic alliances (Chapter 7): These are long-term agreements between companies or countries to invest in joint marketing programs. Strategic alliances have been especially popular among airline companies.

Strategic planning (Chapter 5): A long-range planning process used in overall tourism planning where the timeframe is three or more years into the future.

Superstructure (Chapter 6): Generally considered to imply building construction for tourism development.

Suppliers (Chapter 16): Tourism organizations that provide facilities and services within and between tourism destinations. These include hotels, restaurants, attractions, car rental firms, casinos and other gaming operations, and cruise lines.

Supply chain (Chapter 2, 16): System of organizations, people, resources required to create a product and deliver it to a consumer.

Sustainable tourism development (Chapter 2, 6): Sustainable tourism development is described by the United Nations World Tourism Organization as tourism that takes account of its current and future economic, social and environmental impacts, addressing the needs of visitors, the industry, the environment and host communities (UNWTO).

System (Chapter 1): A set of interrelated elements and components that work together toward common goals or objectives. Von Bertalanffy defines a system as "a set of elements standing in interrelation among themselves and with the environments."

Ten As (10 As) (Chapter 1): Attributes of successful destinations that include attractiveness, activities, access, appearance, assurance, appreciation, awareness, availability, action, and accountability.

The 3Cs and 4Ps of content strategy (Chapter 12): A model of destination content strategy. It posits that a destination's content activities fall into three areas—the 3Cs: Create, Curate, and Corral contents. The approach towards the 3Cs needs to be Planned, Prompt, Personalized, and Participatory—The 4 Ps.

The component view of tourism experience (Chapter 11): A view which holds that a tourism experience contains multiple value domains for a consumer.

The process view of tourism experience (Chapter 11): A view which suggests that a tourism experience as a consumptive event encompasses multiple time-based stages.

Theory of consumption values (Chapter 12): A theory which suggests consumer choice is a function of five consumption values: functional, social, emotional, conditional, and epistemic values. These five values are seen as independent of each other, with each exerting differential influences in given choice situations.

Theory of planned behavior (Chapter 12): A cognitive model that suggests three major factors positively influence traveler decision intention and subsequent purchase behavior: behavior, normative, and control beliefs.

Timesharing (Chapter 4): Also known as vacation or interval ownership, this is a procedure where the ownership of a hotel or resort is split among multiple owners according to time intervals such as weeks.

Tourism (Chapter 1): Tourism is a social, cultural, and economic phenomenon which entails the movement of people to countries or places outside their usual environment for personal or business/professional purposes. These people are called visitors (which may be either visitors or excursionists; residents or non-residents) and tourism has to do with their activities, some of which imply tourism expenditure (UNWTO).

Tourism destination planning (Chapter 5): A systematic, step-by-step, and participative process to plan the future directions for tourism in a destination.

Tourism destination system (Chapter 1): A conceptual model showing the relationships and interdependency between the destination product and tourism impacts, tourism policy, tourism organizations, legislation and regulations, destination planning, sustainable tourism development, and destination marketing.

Tourism experience (Chapter 9, 11): A concept describing an individual's engagement with, participation in, and sense-making of events and activities pertaining to a tourism destination.

Tourism experiencescape (Chapter 11): A model that describes the eight experiential specificities and qualities which help tourism providers to optimally situate the visitor to fully enjoy a trip. They are aesthetics, entertainment, education, escapism, serendipity, localness, personalization, and communitas.

Tourism policy (Chapter 3): The basic statement on tourism in a destination expressed as policy guidelines, goals, and initiatives. Tourism policy gives guidance for all those directly and indirectly involved in tourism by creating a roadmap for the future.

Tourism policy-setting (Chapter 3): A systematic process used to develop a tourism policy for a destination.

Tourism product (Chapter 6): A term that is roughly synonymous with the destination product, meaning all the facilities and services offered for the visitors to a destination.

Tourism satellite accounts (TSAs) (Chapter 2): A standardized framework for measuring the economic impact of tourism. An economic accounting system for complex service sectors such as tourism. For tourism, this means adding up the impacts of tourism that have traditionally been allocated to other economic sectors

Tourism system (Chapter 1): A systematic approach to the study of tourism consisting of four main elements (destination, marketing, demand, and travel) and four major links (destination product, promotion of tourism, travel purchase, and travel mobilities). The tourism system approach emphasizes the interdependency in tourism—that it consists of several interrelated elements working together to achieve common purposes.

Visitor aesthetic judgment (Chapter 11): A concept explaining how a place is taken in aesthetically by a visitor and how a destination's aesthetic qualities are being judged.

Tour operator (Chapter 16): Tour operators assemble the numerous components of travel into packaged vacations or tours and offer these for sale through retail travel agents. Tour operators are tour wholesalers, but also operate all or part of their tours by providing tour escorts or managers, and ground/land tour arrangements.

Tour wholesaler (Chapter 16): Tour wholesalers assemble the numerous components of travel into packaged vacations or tours and offer these for sale through retail travel agents. They do not provide tour operating services.

Transportation (Chapter 1, 17): The systems required to connect places within and outside of the destination. These include air, road, railway, water, and other modes of transport.

Travel (Chapter 1, 15, 16, 17): Refers to the act of moving outside of one's usual environment for business or pleasure, but not for commuting or traveling to or from school.

Travel and tourism sector (Chapter 1): A term used by some organizations, including the World Travel & Tourism Council, to describe tourism and those involved in this economic sector.

Travel benefit (Chapter 10): Positive personal outcomes brought upon consumers as a result of travel, or one's general beliefs about such positive outcomes.

Travel career ladder (Chapter 10): A concept developed by Philip Pearce which suggests that people's needs, travel decisions, and decision-making processes are not static; they change over a person's lifetime based on their actual travel experiences.

Travel decision-making (Chapter 12): A concept delineating an individual making a travel decision that he or she deems as maximizing their expected value.

Travel gain durability (Chapter 10): The degree of endurance or durability of the impact travel has on a traveler.

Travel management system (Chapter 14): Software applications that an organization uses to manage its employees' business travel reservations, expenses, and reimbursements.

Travel motivation (Chapter 10): Consumers' psychological impetuses for using travel to satisfy fundamental human needs.

Travel motivation POST scheme (Chapter 10): A model explaining the psychological drives that propel the development of travel motives, the nature of these motives, the psychological potencies of these motives, and action-oriented goals that people derive from these motives.

Travel need (Chapter 10): Manifest human need, expressible in terms of fundamental needs such as Maslow's self-actualization, intellectual and aesthetic needs, or Alderfer's growth needs.

Travel personality system (Chapter 13): A system that depicts traveler segments based on their personality, life attitudes, and exhibited travel preferences. This travel system provides an understanding of travelers based on their venturesomeness in travel, ranging from psychocentrics to allocentrics.

Travel trade intermediaries (Chapter 16): A term used to collectively refer to all the travel distribution channels including retail travel agencies, tour wholesalers and operators, corporate travel departments, incentive travel planning companies, and convention/meeting planners.

Travel want (Chapter 10): Consumers' tangible articulations of their travel needs and motivations.

Traveler's buying process (Chapter 12): A model suggesting that when making a travel purchase, a consumer moves through several stages including attention and awareness, knowledge and comprehension, interest and liking, evaluation and preference, intention and conviction, purchase and action, and adoption and advocacy.

Traveler sensitivity to information (Chapter 12): A concept positing one's sensitivity toward receiving incoming information. One's sensitivity is a function of how inclined one is to a piece of information and the characteristics of the message itself.

Triple bottom line (Chapter 2, 6): An approach that considers the positives and negatives of an activity along three dimensions: Economic, Social/Cultural, Environment. These dimensions are sometimes simplified to people, planet, profit.

Uncertainty avoidance (Chapter 13): One dimension of National Culture Model which explains that societies deal with the fact that there is uncertainty involved in decisions made.

User experience (Chapter 9): The experience of the person using a product or service. Also called customer experience.

Vertical integration (Chapter 16): The acquisition and ownership by one organization of all or part of a tourism distribution channel.

VFR (Chapter 14): An acronym used for people who are visiting their friends or relatives in a destination area.

Virtual reality (Chapter 7): A computer-generated simulation of a realistic experience.

Visioning (Chapter 5): A process used in long-term or strategic planning in which the desired future situation for the destination area or tourism organization is determined.

Visitors (Chapter 1): The people who go to destinations for leisure, business, VFR, or personal purposes. Also, they referred to as tourists, travelers, or guests.

Word of mouth (Chapter 8): Recommendations given about tourism destinations or services by people to their friends, relatives, or business colleagues.

Workforce migration (Chapter 2): Migration by a workforce to a new location. This may happen when tourism attracts workers from surrounding communities.

World Heritage List (Chapter 1, 4): A list of natural and cultural sites (maintained by UNESCO) whose outstanding values should be preserved for all humanity and to ensure their protection through a closer cooperation among nations (UNESCO World Heritage Centre 2017).

World Wide Web (WWW) (Chapter 8): An Internet function which provides a worldwide collection of sites containing text, graphics, sound, and video that are created in hypertext and can be accessed through the use of Universal Resource Locators (URLs).